PERSPECTIVES ON THE USE OF NONAVERSIVE AND AVERSIVE INTERVENTIONS FOR PERSONS WITH DEVELOPMENTAL DISABILITIES

Alan C. Repp
Nirbhay N. Singh
Editors

SYCAMORE
PUBLISHING COMPANY

Library of Congress Cataloging-in-Publication Data

Perspectives on the use of nonaversive and aversive interventions
for persons with developmental disabilities/Alan C. Repp, Nirbhay N.
Singh, editors.
p. cm.
Includes index.
ISBN 0-0625233-1-3
1. Learning disabilities--Treatment. 2. Learning disabled
children--Rehabilitation. I. Repp, Alan C. II. Singh, Nirbhay N.
RC394.L37P47 1990
616.85'889--dc20 90-10012
CIP

Sycamore Publishing Company
P.O. Box 133
Sycamore, IL 60178
(815) 756-5388

Sycamore Publishing Company is dedicated to publishing effective approaches to educating persons with diverse abilities.

Dedicated to

B.F. Skinner

for his vision of human nature

CONTENTS

CONTRIBUTORS ix
PREFACE xiii

PART I : INTRODUCTION

CHAPTER 1 **Nonaversive and Aversive Interventions: Introduction** 3
Nirbhay N. Singh, John W. Lloyd and Kathy A. Kendall
CHAPTER 2 **Nonaversive and Aversive Interventions: Overview** 17
Alan C. Repp

PART II : MYTHS, ETHICS, AND SCIENCE

CHAPTER 3 **Myths About Punishment** 33
Anne M. Donnellan and Gary W. LaVigna
CHAPTER 4 **Myths that (Mis)Guide Our Profession** 59
Saul Axelrod
CHAPTER 5 **Recent Developments in Nonaversive Treatment: A Review of Rationale, Methods, and Recommendations** 73
James K. Luiselli
CHAPTER 6 **Moral and Scientific Aspects of the Punishment Controversy** 87
Linda J. Hayes and Christopher McCurry
CHAPTER 7 **A Conceptual Framework for Judging the Humaneness and Effectiveness of Behavioral Treatment** 103
Stephen R. Schroeder, Andrew Oldenquist, and Johannes Rojahn
CHAPTER 8 **The Role of Reinforcement in Reducing Inappropriate Behavior: Some Myths and Misconceptions** 119
Ahmos Rolider and Ron Van Houten
CHAPTER 9 **Re-Framing the Debate: Finding Middle Ground and Defining the Role of Social Validity** 129
Mark Wolery and David L. Gast
CHAPTER 10 **One Educator's Perspective on the Use of Punishment or Aversives: Advocating for Supportive and Protective Systems** 145
Sharon Freagon
CHAPTER 11 **Transmission of Behavior Management Technologies from Researchers to Practitioners: A Need for Professional Self-Evaluation** 157
Doug Guess

PART III: TREATMENTS: DATA AND DISCUSSION

CHAPTER 12	**Client Characteristics and Treatment Selection: Legitimate Influences and Misleading Inferences** *Timothy J. H. Paisey, Robert B. Whitney, and Pamela M. Hislop*	175
CHAPTER 13	**Flash Bonding or Cold Fusion? A Case Analysis of Gentle Teaching** *F. J. Barrera and George M. Teodoro*	199
CHAPTER 14	**Effects of Gentle Teaching and Alternative Treatment on Self-Injury** *Linzi J. Jones, Nirbhay N. Singh, and Kathy A. Kendall*	215
CHAPTER 15	**Responsibility and Quality of Life** *Jay Birnbrauer*	231
CHAPTER 16	**Gentle Teaching and the Practice of Human Interdependence: A Preliminary Group Study of 15 Persons with Severe Behavioral Disorders and Their Caregivers** *John J. McGee and Liliana Gonzalez*	237
CHAPTER 17	**Serious Self-Injury: The Ethics of Treatment and Research** *Earl C. Butterfield*	255
CHAPTER 18	**Balancing Freedom from Harm and Right to Treatment for Persons with Developmental Disabilities** *Maurice A. Feldman*	261
CHAPTER 19	**Preventing Serious Behavior Problems Through Skill Development and Early Interventions** *Glen Dunlap, Lynn Foster Johnson, and Frank R. Robbins*	273
CHAPTER 20	**When and When Not to Consider the Use of Aversive Interventions in the Behavioral Treatment of Autistic Children** *Tristram Smith*	287

Part IV : FUNCTIONAL ANALYSIS

CHAPTER 21	**The Experimental (Functional) Analysis of Behavior Disorders: Methodology, Applications, and Limitations** *Brian A. Iwata, Timothy R. Vollmer, and Jennifer R. Zarcone*	301
CHAPTER 22	**A Taxonomic Approach to the Nonaversive Treatment of Maladaptive Behavior of Persons with Developmental Disabilities** *Alan C. Repp and Kathryn G. Karsh*	331
CHAPTER 23	**Use of Functional Analysis and Acceptability Measures to Assess and Treat Severe Behavior Problems: An Outpatient Clinic Model** *David Wacker, Mark Steege, John Northup, Thomas Reimers, Wendy Berg, and Gary Sasso*	349

CHAPTER 24 **The Wrong Issue: Aversive vs. Nonaversive Treatment The Right Issue: Functional vs. Nonfunctional Treatment** 361
Edward G. Carr, Sarah Robinson, and Laura Wray Palumbo

CHAPTER 25 **Diagnosing Severe Behavior Problems** 381
David A.M. Pyles and Jon S. Bailey

CHAPTER 26 **The Eclipse of Aversive Technology: A Triadic Approach to Assessment and Treatment** 403
Carl Schrader and Robert Gaylord-Ross

PART V : BASIC AND APPLIED RESEARCH: REVIEWS AND COMMENTARY

CHAPTER 27 **Modifying the Behavior of Behavior Modifiers: Arguments for Counter-Control Against Aversive Procedures** 421
Dick Sobsey

CHAPTER 28 **The Controversy Over Aversives: Basic Operant Research and the Side Effects of Punishment** 435
Thomas R. Linscheid and Patricia Meinhold

CHAPTER 29 **Laboratory to Application: An Experimental Analysis of Severe-Problem Behavior** 451
W. Frank Epling and W. David Pierce

CHAPTER 30 **On the Empirical Basis for Using Aversive and Nonaversive Therapy** 465
David A. Coe and Johnny L. Matson

PART VI: TREATMENT PROVIDERS

CHAPTER 31 **Least Restrictive Use of Reductive Procedures: Guidelines and Competencies** 479
Gina Green

CHAPTER 32 **"Damn It Burris, I'm Not a Product of *Walden Two*," or Who's Controlling the Controllers** *495*
John R. Lutzker

CHAPTER 33 **Treatment Acceptability: Consumer, Therapist, and Society** 503
Shirley O'Brien and Kathryn G. Karsh

AUTHOR INDEX 517

SUBJECT INDEX 529

CONTRIBUTORS

Saul Axelrod, Ph.D.
Special Education Program
Temple University
Philadelphia, PA 19122

Jon S. Bailey, Ph.D.
Department of Psychology
Florida State University
Tallahassee, FL 32310

F. J. Barrera, Ph.D.
Applied Behaviour Analysis Program
Southwestern Regional Centre, MCSS
R. R. #1
Blenheim, Ontario Canada NOP 1AO

Wendy Berg, M.A.
Pediatrics
The University of Iowa
251 University Hospital School
Iowa City, IA 52242

Jay S. Birnbrauer, Ph.D.
Department of Psychology
Murdoch University
Murdoch, Western Australia 6150

Earl C. Butterfield, Ph.D.
Educational Psychology
University of Washington
DQ-12
Seattle, WA 98195

Edward G. Carr, Ph.D.
Department of Psychology
State University of New York
Stony Brook, NY 11794-2500

David A. Coe, M.A.
Department of Psychology
Louisiana State University
Baton Rouge, LA 70803

Anne M. Donnellan, Ph.D.
University of Wisconsin-Madison
Rehabilitation Psychology and
Special Education
Room 405, 432 N. Murray Street
Madison, WI 53706

Glen Dunlap, Ph.D.
Department of Child and
Family Studies
Florida Mental Health Institute
University of South Florida
13301 Bruce B. Downs Boulevard
Tampa, FL 33612

W. Frank Epling, Ph.D.
Department of Psychology
University of Alberta
Center for Experimental Sociology
1-48 Tory Building
Edmonton, Alberta Canada T6G 2H4

Maurice A. Feldman, Ph.D.
Surrey Place Centre and
Department of Psychiatry
University of Toronto and
Department of Special Education
Ontario Institute for Studies in Education
2 Surrey Place
Toronto, Ontario Canada M5S 2C2

Sharon Freagon, Ph.D.
Department of Educational Psychology,
Counseling and Special Education
Northern Illinois University
DeKalb, IL 60115

David L. Gast, Ph.D.
Department of Special Education
University of Georgia
521 Adenhold Hall
Athens, GA 30602

Robert Gaylord-Ross, Ph.D.
Department of Special Education
San Francisco State University
1600 Holloway Avenue
San Francisco, CA 94132

Liliana Gonzalez, B.A.
Creighton University
Center on Gentle Teaching
2205 South 10 Street
Omaha, NE 68108

Gina Green, Ph.D.
Behavior Analysis Department
E.K. Shriver Center for Mental
Retardation, Inc.
200 Trapelo Road
Waltham, MA 02254

Doug Guess, Ed.D.
Department of Special Education
University of Kansas
Dole Building
Lawrence, KS 66045

Linda J. Hayes, Ph.D.
Psychology Department
University of Nevada-Reno
Reno, NV 89557-0062

Pamela M. Hislop, B.A.
State of Connecticut
Department of Mental Retardation
Region 5
Meriden Center, Undercliff Road
Meriden, CT 06450

Brian A. Iwata, Ph.D.
Department of Psychology
University of Florida
Gainesville, FL 32601

Lynn Foster Johnson, M.A.
Department of Child and
Family Studies
Florida Mental Health Institute
University of South Florida
13301 Bruce B. Downs Boulevard
Tampa, FL 33612

Linzi J. Jones, M.A.
Department of Psychology
University of Otago
P.O. Box 56
Dunedin, Otago, New Zealand

Kathryn G. Karsh, Ed.D.
Educational Research and
Services Center
425 Fisk Avenue
DeKalb, IL 60115

Kathy A. Kendall, B.S.
Commonwealth Institute for Child
and Family Studies
P.O. Box 1-L
Richmond, VA 23201

Gary LaVigna, Ph.D.
Institute for Applied Behavior Analysis
5777 W. Century Blvd., Suite 590
Los Angeles, CA 90045

Thomas R. Linscheid, Ph.D.
Department of Pediatrics and Psychology
Ohio State University Hospital
and Children's Hospital
700 Children's Drive
Columbus, OH 43205

John W. Lloyd, Ph.D.
Curriculum, Instruction
and Special Education
University of Virginia
Curry School of Education
Charlottesville, VA 22903

Jame K. Luiselli, Ed.D.
Psychological and Educational
Resource Associates
6 Walden Street
Concord, MA 01742

John R. Lutzker, Ph.D.
Department of Psychology
University of Judaism
15600 Mulholland Drive
Los Angeles, CA 90077

Johnny L. Matson, Ph.D.
Department of Psychology
Louisiana State University
Baton Rouge, LA 70803

Christopher McCurry, M.A.
Psychology Department
University of Nevada-Reno
Reno, NV 89557-0062

John J. McGee, Ph.D.
Department of Psychiatry
and Behavioral Sciences
Creighton University
2205 South 10 Street
Omaha, NE 68108

Patricia Meinhold, Ph.D.
Department of Pediatrics
Ohio State University
and Children's Hospital
700 Children's Drive
Columbus, OH 43205

John Northup
School Psychology
The University of Iowa
251 University Hospital School
Iowa City, IA 52242

Shirley O'Brien, Ph.D.
Educational Research and
Services Center
425 Fisk Avenue
DeKalb, IL 60115

Andrew G. Oldenquist, Ph.D.
Department of Philosophy
The Ohio State University
230 N. Oval Mall
Columbus, OH 43210

Timothy J. H. Paisey, Ph.D.
State of Connecticut
Department of Mental Retardation
Region 5
20 Brookside Avenue
New Haven, CT 06515

Laura Wray Palumbo, M.A.
Department of Psychology
State University of New York
Stony Brook, NY 11794-2500

W. David Pierce, Ph.D.
Department of Sociology
University of Alberta
Center for Experimental Sociology
1-48 Tory Building
Edmonton, Alberta Canada T6G 2H4

David A. M. Pyles, M.S.
Department of Psychology
Florida State University
Tallahassee, FL 32310

Thomas Reimers, Ph.D.
Pediatrics
The University of Iowa
251 University Hospital School
Iowa City, IA 52242

Alan C. Repp, Ph.D.
Department of Educational Psychology,
Counseling and Special Education
Northern Illinois University
DeKalb, IL 60115

Frank R. Robbins, Ph.D.
Department of Child
and Family Studies
Florida Mental Health Institute
University of South Florida
13301 Bruce B. Downs Boulevard
Tampa, FL 33612

Sarah Robinson, M.A.
Department of Psychology
State University of New York
Stony Brook, NY 11794-2500

Johannes Rojahn, Ph.D.
Department of Psychology and Psychiatry
The Nisonger Center for MR/DD
The Ohio State University
1581 Dodd Drive
Columbus, OH 43210-1296

Ahmos E. Rolider, Ph.D.
McMaster University
Hamilton, Ontario Canada L8N 3Z5

Gary Sasso, Ph.D.
Department of Special Education
The University of Iowa
251 University Hospital School
Iowa City, IA 52242

Carl Schrader, Ph.D.
Behavioral Counseling &
Research Center
454 Las Gallinas
San Rafael, CA 94903
and Spectrum Center
1150 Virginia
Berkeley, CA 94702

Stephen R. Schroeder, Ph.D.
Director of Bureau of Child Research
1052 Dole Human Development Center
University of Kansas
Lawrence, KS 66045

Nirbhay N. Singh, Ph.D.
Department of Psychiatry
Medical College of Virginia
P.O. Box 489
Richmond, VA 23298

Tristram Smith, Ph.D.
Department of Psychology
University of California, Los Angeles
405 Hilgard Avenue
Los Angeles, CA 90024-1563

Dick Sobsey, Ed.D.
Department of Educational Psychology
Severe Disabilities Program
University of Alberta
6-102 Education North
Edmonton, Alberta T6G 2G5

Mark Steege, Ph.D.
School Psychology
University of Southern Maine
400 Bailey Hall
Gorham, ME 04038

George M. Teodoro, B.A.
Applied Behaviour Analysis Program
Southwestern Regional Centre, MCSS
R.R. #1
Blenheim, Ontario Canada N0P 1A0

Ron VanHouten, Ph.D.
Mt. Saint Vincent University
Halifax, Nova Scotia Canada B2X 2V5

Timothy R. Vollmer
Department of Psychology
University of Florida
Gainesville, FL 32601

David Wacker, Ph.D.
Pediatrics
The University of Iowa
251 University Hospital School
Iowa City, IA 52242

Robert B. Whitney, B.A.
State of Connecticut
Department of Mental Retardation
Region 5
455 Wintergreen Avenue
New Haven, CT 06515

Mark Wolery, Ph.D.
Department of Special Education
University of Kentucky
Lexington, KY 40506-0001

Jennifer R. Zarcone
Department of Psychology
University of Florida
Gainesville, FL 326011

PREFACE

When we conceived this book, we were interested in presenting a forum through which respected behaviorists could discuss this issue in a rational manner without attacking each other on a personal level. At conferences and elsewhere, we have seen the issue dissolve into one in which individuals literally deride each other's competence, and that, to say the least, is unfortunate. While regrettable in a personal sense, it is deplorable in other ways. First, it averts the issue which is really how we can best help persons with developmental disabilities. Second, in a similar view, it is anti-scientific, and most of us believe that only a better understanding of the science of human behavior will help us learn how to deal more effectively with these problem behaviors, whether we personally choose to use aversives or nonaversives.

The point has been well made by Donnellan and LaVigna in their chapter: "Perhaps the most damaging result of this kind of reaction to controversy is that, again like religious adherents, we begin to associate only with other adherents or to read or publish only that which supports our myths. Behaviors of some individuals on both sides of the debate on aversives demonstrate this point. For example, some researchers who do fine work in developing nonaversive behavioral interventions refused to contribute papers to this book when invited to do so." Donnellan and LaVigna conclude by reminding us of the magnitude of the job before us and urge that our energies be directed toward that job. We agree completely with their point. Our hope is that this book will stimulate our community to think about this issue in a collegial manner. Our sole objective is to learn more about how to help persons with developmental disabilities; it is not to engage in counterproductive personal attacks over this issue. We believe that the authors of these chapters have helped us address this objective.

We wish to thank the many people whose efforts have made this book possible. Above all, we thank our contributors for sharing their knowledge and expertise with us. We were unusually fortunate in having as our contributors some of the very best researchers and clinicians in the field. We could not have produced this book without the dedication of our secretaries, Maureen Sullivan, Amy Hewett, and Patti Fremeau, who dealt with all the correspondence and helped prepare portions of the manuscript. We are particularly grateful to Joan Mueller Cochrane who managed the production of this book, to Peggy Smith who was responsible for the copy-editing, and to Bob Cohen and Frances Dyson for administrative support. We also acknowledge the Educational Research and Services Center and the Commonwealth Institute for Child and Family Studies for support that facilitated the completion of this book. Finally, our deepest appreciation is due to our respective families who gave us love, understanding, and noncontingent reinforcement during the preparation of this book.

Alan C. Repp
Nirbhay N. Singh

PART I

CHAPTER

1

NONAVERSIVE AND AVERSIVE INTERVENTIONS: ISSUES

Nirbhay N. Singh
Medical College of Virginia

John W. Lloyd
University of Virginia

Kathy A. Kendall
Commonwealth Institute for Child and Family Studies

We must not cease from exploration and the end of all our exploring will be to arrive where we began and to know the place for the first time. *T. S. Eliot*

Some individuals do things that are so unusual and that arouse such feelings of distress in us that we are willing to use extraordinary means to help them no longer do those things. The actions that provoke us are many:

- These individuals may hit, bite, or pinch themselves; they may poke their fingers an inch into their own eye sockets; they may nibble nearly continuously at their own lips until the flesh of the lips is gone.

- They may not follow directions; they may brush all of the materials off from a table in front of them when a teacher approaches; they may cry and hide under a table for hours.

- They may physically attack others, children or adults, with a fury that elicits the label of "banshee"; they may throw heavy objects such as televisions across rooms regardless of whom the objects hit.

People charged with helping individuals who have serious behavior problems have different tolerances for these behaviors. However, most people have little reservation about the need to decrease frequent, intense self-injurious behavior such as head banging; they will agree that something must be done and that whatever is done should be effective and the effects should be immediate.

Teachers, psychologists, nurses, and other mental health professionals have discovered and refined myriad procedures for controlling or eliminating serious behavior problems. A partial list might include these:

- If the individual engages in serious maladaptive behavior to escape or avoid engaging in tasks deemed to be important for the individual, then teachers can attenuate the demands of the task.

- Teaching compliance to the task demands can be used to remove the function of the maladaptive behavior.

- The aversiveness of the task can be reduced so that the individual will have less reason to engage in maladaptive behavior.

- If the individual has uncontrolled violent, explosive outbursts and no clear antecedents or consequences are apparent, then psychotropic medication (e.g., lithium carbonate, propranolol) may be considered a likely treatment.

- Some form of contingent aversive stimulation, together with a positive reinforcement program, may be used to control the behavior if it is life-threatening to the individual.

- If the individual uses maladaptive behavior as a means of communication, then communication training may be the treatment of choice.

Just as reasonable people may consider it more important to decrease some behaviors than others, they also may differ about what it is that should be done to decrease behaviors. They may disagree, for example, about whether it is appropriate to use a procedure that requires caregivers to withhold a basic need, such as food, so that it can be used to reinforce appropriate behavior, or to inflict pain on the individual in an effort to reduce a greater, self-inflicted pain.

This book presents a thorough discussion of whether it is appropriate to use certain interventions. Many of the leading authorities on the habilitation and education of individuals who display serious behavior problems present their views in later chapters. The arguments that are advanced in the following chapters are many and complex. Some are built on research and evidence, others are grounded in philosophy and ethics, and still others are based on personal feelings. All of them refer to a variety of procedures that have technical names and meanings.

PROCEDURES UNDER QUESTION

The underlying disagreement that arises in discussions of procedures for treating serious behavior problems, such as those described previously, is whether some of those procedures should ever be used. When a person often behaves maladaptively (e.g., injures himself or herself), caregivers seek means of decreasing the frequency, intensity, or duration of the behavior. That is, we want to have the person perform the behavior less often (or not at all), less fervently, or for shorter periods of time.

Some of the procedures used to accomplish this have been called *punishment* techniques. The word punishment and other terms used in this book have technical meanings, and a knowledge of these meanings is important in understanding the following discussion. Table 1 presents a list of some of the most commonly used terms in this text, their definition, and examples of their application in this context. Readers who are unfamiliar

Table 1: Definitions and Examples of Some Procedures Commonly Used to Influence Maladaptive Behavior

PROCEDURE	DEFINITION	EXAMPLE
Reinforcement[1]	The delivery of a consequence which increases the chances of the behavior recurring.	After every minute when Amy has kept her hands at her sides, the teacher stands near her, talks pleasantly to her, and gives her a token that she may use to "buy" special treats.
Punishment	The delivery of a consequence which decreases the chances of the behavior recurring. (Often these consequences are called **aversives**.)	When Amy pokes her finger into her eye socket, the teacher says "No," and holds smelling salts under Amy's nose.
Extinction	The discontinuation of an environmental event that has served as a reinforcer for a behavior.[2] Extinction decreases the chances of the behavior recurring.	When Amy pokes her finger into her eye socket, the teacher turns away and stops talking.[3]
Response Cost	The removal of a reinforcer contingent upon the behavior occurring. This decreases the chances of the behavior recurring.	When Amy pokes her finger into her eye socket, the teacher takes away the tokens that Amy has accumulated.
Time Out	The imposition of a brief time period when reinforcement is not available.	When Amy pokes her finger into her eye socket, the teacher stops awarding her tokens for three minutes.
Overcorrection	The institution of a more appropriate response and repeated practice of it contingent upon the behavior occurring. This decreases the chances of the behavior recurring.	When Amy pokes her finger into her eye socket, the teacher pulls Amy's hand away from her face, tells her to keep her hands down, and requires her to practice flexing and relaxing her hands repeatedly.
Visual or Facial Screening	The blocking of an individual's field of vision contingent upon the performance of a behavior. This decreases the chances of the behavior recurring.	When Amy pokes her finger into her eye socket, the teacher removes the poking finger and covers Amy's eyes with her hand (visual screening) or a terry-cloth bib (facial screening) for five seconds.
Restraint	The physical restriction of parts of the body involved in a behavior in order to make performance of the behavior impossible.	When Amy has been poking her finger into her eye frequently, the staff may decide to restrain her by wrapping a soft cloth around her wrists and running it behind her back. This "soft-tie" makes it impossible for Amy to raise her hands as high as her face.

[1]Reinforcement may be either positive or negative. In both cases, reinforcement increases behavior. Negative reinforcement is not the same as punishment.

[2]Technically, extinction also may include the discontinuation of a negative reinforcement contingency. The definition and example given here do not reflect this.

[3]This example assumes that eye-gouging is maintained by social attention. The details of extinction procedures vary, depending upon what feature of the environment maintains the behavior (see Kazdin, 1984).

with the ideas and terms presented in Table 1 should review a basic text on behavior modification (e.g., Alberto & Troutman, 1990; Kazdin, 1984; Rusch, Rose, & Greenwood, 1988; Wolery, Bailey, & Sugai, 1988).

The idea of *contingency* is a concept that undergirds all of the procedures described in Table 1. This central idea refers to the linked nature of two events. As the examples show, the idea of contingency is easily expressed as an "if...then" relationship. If behavior X occurs, then consequence Y occurs. Many, but not all, intervention procedures are based on building a contingent relationship between certain behaviors and other environmental consequences.

There are many other important concepts and terms that will be defined and discussed in this text. For example, later chapters include illustrations of procedures such as *functional analysis* and of comprehensive approaches to treatment such as *Gentle Teaching*. Readers who develop a working knowledge of these concepts will have a solid basis for developing improved treatment programs, as well as the knowledge to consider the issues intelligently.

QUESTIONS, ISSUES, AND CONCERNS

The debate regarding the use of aversive procedures has raged for almost a decade without being resolved either philosophically or empirically. Those who appear to have the greatest involvement, individuals who engage in serious behavior problems, are often in no position to let their views be known. Their parents and advocates are strongly divided on the use of aversive procedures. As attested by the contributors of this book, both researchers and clinicians are also divided in their views.

What, then, are the issues, concerns, and questions that divide so many rational people? What started off as a simple question of whether to use aversive procedures in any therapeutic intervention for serious behavior problems has grown, by now, into a large set of philosophical, ethical, legal, and empirical questions. These include:

- What procedures do we use to assist individuals to control their severe behavior problems?
- Are aversive procedures coercive? Do they topographically resemble torture?
- Given the present state of our knowledge, can we make an informed judgment about the use of alternative treatment procedures, regardless of whether they are aversive?
- Do we have the knowledge that will enable us to provide the best and most effective treatment for the target behavior(s) of all individuals?
- Do we have good scientific evidence to show that either procedure, aversive or nonaversive, is more effective than the other?
- Are all procedures, aversive or nonaversive, always effective? Under what conditions are the various behavioral procedures effective in controlling serious problem behaviors? Are they effective with escape-motivated behavior? Self-stimulatory behavior? Attention-seeking behaviors?
- Is it moral to deny an individual with developmental disabilities access to effective intervention? Does the proscription of aversive procedures restrict the rights of individuals to effective treatment?
- Does a functional analysis of the problem behavior invariably indicate that the most effective treatment of choice will be nonaversive?
- Can the use of an aversive procedure ethically or morally be justified if treatment results in less physical damage, greater happiness, longer life, or less pain to the individual when compared to a less-effective but nonaversive treatment?
- Are aversive procedures associated with undesirable side effects, such as the emergence of new problem responses, agitation, resistance, treat-

ment-elicited aggression, and social avoidance?

- Should punishment procedures be used as a last resort after all else has failed? Should nonaversive procedures be used before any punishment procedures?

- Are we ethically bound to use treatment procedures that minimize, as rapidly as possible, physical damage and psychological harm?

- Should an individual receive the most effective treatment as soon as possible, without being exposed to less intrusive treatments that are not likely to be effective, in an effort to reduce prolonged suffering?

- Is the use of aversive procedures, on a coerced or nonvoluntary basis, ever morally justified?

- What do we do when caregivers charged with the treatment of an individual are given unlimited resources and, even using these resources (e.g., bringing in the best experts on nonaversive intervention), are not successful in altering the individual's life-threatening behavior?

- Are there alternatives to the use of aversive interventions?

- What is the potential for misusing aversive and nonaversive procedures?

- Should we advocate a complete ban on the use of any procedure that can be considered to be aversive to an individual? Are these procedures unnatural processes such that we do not use them with persons who are not handicapped? Do we use punishment in everyday life?

- Is punishment a common process in child development?

- Is it possible to have an aversive-free society?

- If we agree that it is desirable to use nonaversive procedures, can we accomplish our socially valid objectives and those of society in general without employing aversive procedures?

- Do we advocate the use of aversive procedures with some individuals because we value them less as human beings as a consequence of their disabilities? Or do we value them more highly and want them to be able to participate in life to the limits of their potential?

- Is aversive treatment dehumanizing to the individual who engages in severe behavior problems? Is it dehumanizing to the caregiver or parent who has to implement the aversive treatment? Is it dehumanizing to let the individual suffer self-inflicted pain because nonaversive interventions may not be fully effective?

- Are Local Human Rights Committees able to make the best judgment with regard to the rights of the individual? What are the criteria for such judgments--philosophical, ethical, legal, or empirical? Do philosophical, legal, or ethical considerations take precedence over empirical knowledge?

RESPONSES

As would be expected, responses to these questions, issues, and concerns have taken a variety of forms. Advocacy and professional associations have issued position statements, often at variance with one another. These organizations include: The Association for Behavior Analysis Task Force on the Right to Effective Behavioral Treatment which issued its statement in May, 1989, an abbreviated version of which is presented in Appendix A. Statements by other organizations, including American Association on Mental Retardation (Appendix B), The Association for Persons with Severe Handicaps (Appendix C), Division 33 of the American Psychological Association (Appendix D), and Council for Children with Behavioral Disorders (Appendix E), are included at the end of this chapter.

These position statements and the views of leading professionals in the field have been a source of great controversy; this issue tends to polarize the views of both professionals and lay people (e.g., Berkowitz, 1987; Durand, 1989; Gardner, 1989; Jacobson, 1988; McFalk, 1989; Reynolds, 1987; Schroeder & Schroeder, 1989; Spreat & Lanzi, 1989). In a sense, this is exactly what is needed to encourage us to make further advances in our ability to assist individuals with severe behavior problems; it encourages us to develop and refine diverse but empirically validated approaches. This controversy can be seen as a challenge for us to resolve this issue by being able to provide treatments that are effective, rapid, and socially acceptable.

PERSPECTIVES

As will become apparent to the reader, the authors of the various chapters in this book differ about the acceptability of using aversive procedures to improve the lives of individuals with serious behavior problems. However, as should also be apparent, the authors of the chapters do not differ in their commitment to improving the lives of these individuals. Everyone represented here shares a humane concern for the betterment of the condition of individuals with markedly different behaviors that are distressing to most people.

In general, we assume that advocates of a position that differs from our own believe that their recommendations are in the interests of the individuals that they serve. To assume otherwise is to suggest that some of our colleagues operate from a position of indifference or even contempt for the welfare of others. Who would reasonably accuse one of the authors of these chapters of planning to do ill to people in her or his charge? However, although we are all concerned with the well-being of these individuals, we are far from reaching a consensus as to the treatment modality that would best achieve this. Indeed, this was apparent at the National Institutes of Health Consensus Conference on Destructive Behavior; the final statements from the conference failed to satisfy advocates of nonaversive treatment (Weiss, 1990).

The appropriateness of different treatments for changing behaviors has been raised previously. The present arguments against using aversive procedures are, in fact, echoes of concerns that were evident at least 200 years ago when, for example, Jean Colombier (1736-1789) argued that "The bad treatment and particularly the beating should be considered crimes deserving of exemplary punishment" (quoted in Zilboorg & Henry, 1941, p. 316).

In the next chapter, Alan Repp provides a synopsis of all the contributions. This is followed by individual chapters presenting the various authorities' contributions to the discussion. The contributors to this book provide a broad spectrum of views, procedures, guidelines, and data, all pertaining to the issue of interventions concerned with reducing maladaptive behaviors. This text should serve as a resource for thoughtful discussion of the issues and a basis for further research so that more innovative and effective ways of helping people with severe behavior problems can be developed and implemented.

REFERENCES

Alberto, P. A., & Troutman, A. C. (1990). *Applied behavior analysis for teachers* (3rd ed.). Columbus, OH: Merrill.

Berkowitz, A. J. (1987). The AAMD position statement on aversive therapy. *Mental Retardation, 25*, 118.

Durand, V. M. (1989). Least restrictive alternative or rapid suppression? *Psychology in Mental Retardation and Developmental Disabilities, 14*, 7-9.

Gardner, W. I. (1989). But in the meantime: A client perspective of the debate over the use of aversive/intrusive therapy procedures. *The Behavior Therapist, 12*, 179-181.

Jacobson, J. W. (1988). Aversive conditioning: The jury is out. *Psychology in Mental Retardation and Developmental Disabilities, 13*, 5-7.

Kazdin, A. E. (1984). *Behavior modification in applied settings* (3rd ed.). Homewood, IL: Dorsey.

McFalk, J. (1989). Towards a more positive approach. *Psychology in Mental Retardation and Developmental Disabilities, 14*, 5-6.

Reynolds, W. B. (September, 1987). *Invited address at the Community Services for Autistic Adults and Children's Annual Symposium for the Advancement of Non-Aversive Behavioral Technology*. Rockville, MD.

Rusch, F. R., Rose, T., & Greenwood, C. R. (1988). *Introduction to behavior analysis in special education*. Englewood Cliffs, NJ: Prentice-Hall.

Schroeder, S. R., & Schroeder, C. S. (1989). The role of the AAMR in the aversives controversy. *Mental Retardation, 27*, iii-v.

Spreat, S., & Lanzi, F. (1989). Role of human rights committees in the review of restrictive/aversive behavior modification procedures: A national survey. *Mental Retardation, 27*, 375-382.

Weiss, R. (1990). Consensus eludes conference on destructive behavior. *Journal of NIH Research, 1*(4), 56-57.

Wolery, M., Bailey, D. B., Jr., & Sugai, G. M. (1988). *Effective teaching: Principles and procedures of applied behavior analysis with exceptional students*. Needham, MA: Allyn and Bacon.

Zilboorg, G., & Henry, G. W. (1941). *A history of medical psychology*. New York: W. W. Norton.

APPENDIX A

The Association for Behavior Analysis: Position Statement on Clients' Rights to Effective Behavioral Treatment, May, 1989.

Formal methods of behavior change, derived from the field of behavior analysis and referred to here as Behavioral Treatment, provide an effective means for establishing new patterns of adaptive behavior and alleviating a number of debilitating behavioral disorders. As uses of behavioral treatment become more widespread, particularly in clinical, educational, and other settings that serve dependent populations, it is necessary to take steps to ensure that clients' rights are protected, that treatment is based on scientific findings, that service is provided in a manner consistent with the highest standards of excellence and that individuals who are in need of service will not be denied access to the most effective treatment available.

The Association for Behavior Analysis issues the following position statement on clients' rights to effective behavioral treatment as a set of guiding principles to protect individuals from harm as a result of either the lack or the inappropriate use of behavioral treatment.

The Association for Behavior Analysis, through a majority vote of its members, declares that individuals who receive behavioral treatment have a right to:

1. A therapeutic physical and social environment. Characteristics of such an environment include but are not limited to: an acceptable standard of living, opportunities for stimulation and training, therapeutic social interaction, and freedom from undue physical or social restriction.
2. Services whose overriding goal is personal welfare. The client participates, either directly or through authorized proxy, in the development and implementation of treatment programs. In cases where withholding or implementing treatment involves potential risk and the client does not have the capacity to provide consent, individual welfare is protected through two mechanisms: Peer Review Committees, imposing professional standards, determine the clinical propriety of treatment programs; Human Rights Committees, imposing community standards, determine the acceptability of treatment programs and the degree to which they may compromise an individual's rights.
3. Treatment by a competent behavior analyst. The behavior analyst's training reflects appropriate academic preparation, including knowledge of behavioral principles, methods of assessment and treatment, research methodology, and professional ethics, as well as practical experience. In cases where a problem or treatment is complex or may pose risk, direct involvement by a doctoral-level behavior analyst is necessary.
4. Programs that teach functional skills. Improvement in functioning requires the acquisition of adaptive behaviors that will increase independence, as well as the elimination of behaviors that are dangerous or that in some other way serve as barriers to independence.
5. Behavioral assessment and ongoing evaluation. Pretreatment assessment, including both interviews and measures of behavior, attempts to identify factors relevant to behavioral maintenance and treatment. The continued use of objective behavioral measurement documents response to treatment.
6. The most effective treatment procedures available. An individual is entitled to effective and scientifically validated treatment; in turn, the behavior analyst has an obligation to use only those procedures demonstrated by research to be effective. Decisions on the use of potentially restrictive treatment are based on consideration of its absolute and relative level of restrictiveness, the amount of time required to produce a clinically significant outcome, and the consequences that would result from delayed intervention.

This statement is an abbreviated version of a report by the Association for Behavior Analysis Task Force on the Right to Effective Behavioral Treatment. Reprinted with permission of the Association for Behavior Analysis.

APPENDIX B

American Association on Mental Retardation: Position Statement on Aversive Therapy.

Some persons who have mental retardation or developmental disabilities continue to be subjected to inhumane forms of aversive procedures as a means of behavior modification. The American Association on Mental Retardation (AAMR) condemns such practices and urges their immediate elimination. The aversive procedures to be eliminated have some or all of the following characteristics:

1. Obvious signs of physical pain experienced by the individual;
2. Potential or actual physical side effects, including tissue damage, physical illness, severe stress, and/ordeath; and
3. Dehumanization of the individual, through means such as social degradation, social isolation, verbal abuse, techniques inappropriate for the individual's age, and treatment out of proportion to the target behavior. Such dehumanization is equally unacceptable whether or not an individual has a disability

This statement is intended to articulate important values and principles and to challenge the field of developmental disabilities to promote research activities leading to identification, testing,implementation, and dissemination of nonaversive alternatives to address severe behavioral disorders. Specific regulations regarding research, clinical practice, or individuals in making professional judgements are the province of regulatory agencies, funders, and certifying bodies.

Eliminating inhumane aversive procedures is a reflection of a growing concern for reducing actions by professionals and others that compromise the lives of persons with mental retardation or other developmental disabilities and their families. Relationships between providers and consumers should foster empowerment of the consumer, enhance choice, and integration of persons with mental retardation or other developmental disabilities into community settings.

The AAMR urges continuing research into humane methods of behavior management and support of existing programs and environments that successfully habilitate individuals with complex behaviors.

---

[1] Initially passed by the Legislative and Social Issues (LASI) Committee and adopted by the AAMR Board of Directors, December, 1986. Revised by an *ad hoc* Task Force on Aversive Procedures and adopted by the Board of Directors, January 20, 1990.

APPENDIX C

The Association for Persons with Severe Handicaps: Resolution on the Cessation of Intrusive Interventions.

WHEREAS, In order to realize the goals and objectives of The Association for Persons with Severe Handicaps, including the right of each person who has severe handicaps to grow, develop, and enjoy life in integrated and normalized community environments, the following resolution is adopted:

WHEREAS, Educational and other habilitative services must employ instructional and management strategies which are consistent with the right of each individual with severe handicaps to an effective treatment which does not compromise the equally important right to freedom from harm. This requires educational and habilitative procedures free from chemical restraint, aversive stimuli, environmental deprivation or exclusion from services;

THEREFORE, TASH calls for the cessation of the use of any treatment option which exhibits some or all of the following characteristics: (1) obvious signs of physical pain experienced by the individual; (2) potential or actual side effects such as tissue damage, physical illness, severe physical or emotionalstress, and/or death that would properly require the involvement of medical personnel; (3) dehumanization of persons with severe handicaps because the procedures are normally unacceptable for persons who do not have handicaps in community environment; (4) extreme ambivalence and discomfort by family, staff, and/or caregivers regarding the necessity of such extreme strategies or their own involvement in such interventions; and (5) obvious repulsion and/or stress felt by peers who do not have handicaps and community members who cannot reconcile extreme procedures with acceptable standard practice;

IT IS FURTHER RESOLVED, THAT The Association for Persons with Severe Handicaps' resources and expertise be dedicated to the development, implementation, evaluation, dissemination, and advocacy of educational and management practices which are appropriate for use in integrated environments and which are consistent with the commitment to a high quality of life for individuals with severe handicaps.

APPENDIX D

Division 33 (Mental Retardation and Developmental Disabilities) of American Psychological Association: Guidelines on Effective Behavioral Treatment for Persons with Mental Retardation and Developmental Disabilities.

Whereas concerns have been voiced by many persons about the use of behavioral procedures, principally those that are restrictive,

And whereas Division 33 shares concerns that persons with disabilities should receive the highest quality treatment services available,

And whereas the members of Division 33 include applied behavior analysts continually engaged in research and practice with persons with disabilities, the Division has adopted the following guidelines as policy:

This policy pertains to the development, implementation, and monitoring of applied behavior analytic procedures with persons with mental retardation and other developmental disabilities. The following is a statement of foundations and principles.

Foundations

Applied behavior analytic services encompass all applications of operational procedures and techniques derived from manipulations of controlling stimuli or manipulations of motivational conditions, positive reinforcement, negative reinforcement, positive punishment, and negative punishment principles as defined within the body of research-based knowledge known as operant learning theory.

Applied behavior analytic services are provided in accordance with the American Psychological Associations' most current edition of the Standards for Providers of Psychological Services and, as additionally applicable, the most current relevant Specialty Guidelines.

No provisions of these principles shall be interpreted as limiting applied research or publication of research findings using behavior analytic procedures that have been approved by a relevant human subjects review board and that meet ethical standards for research with human subjects as described in other APA policies and publications.

Principles

The composition and application of applied behavior analytic procedures provided by a practitioner or service unit shall be responsive to the needs of the persons and of the settings served.

The needs of the persons served shall take precedence over the organizational needs or ideological position of the settings in which services are delivered.

The protection of legal and civil rights of persons served, as determined in prevailing statutes, standards, and policies applicable in the particular service setting, shall be of primary concern.

Applied behavior analytic treatment procedures will be employed for the purposes of increasing the self-control of persons, and for the purpose of assisting them in achieving enhanced participation in life activities and their fullest human potential.

When the client does not evidence pathological behavior (deemed undesirable by referral agents and clients or duly appointed guardians according to law), but does evidence substantial adaptive deficits, there is an assumed need for the psychologist to participate in the development and implementation of positive programming services designed to increase self-care, social, and other skill performances.

Highly restrictive procedures (which may entail interventions often referred to as aversive) shall not be instituted without the combined use of procedures that reinforce incompatible, alternate, or other behavior. Highly restrictive procedures shall not be employed until there has been sufficient determination that the use of less restrictive procedures was or would be ineffective or harm would come to the client because of gradual change in the client's particular problematic behavior.

Highly restrictive or aversive procedures are applied only in instances in which there is an immediate physical danger to self or others, or there may be permanent sensory or other physical impairment, or the client may be prevented from receiving necessary medical, surgical, or emergency medical services, or the frequency or intensity of the problematic behavior prevents adequate participation in normal activities appropriate for the individual's circumstances and personal goals.

Highly restrictive procedures shall be discontinued when the individual's response to less restrictive procedures indicates that treatment benefits can be maintained through these less restrictive procedures. Evaluation of the individual's response to less restrictive procedures shall be ongoing and documented. Multiple high restriction procedures shall only be employed in instances in which more limited applications of restrictive components have been ineffective, and reinforcing contingencies are instituted for incompatible, alternate, or other behavior. Procedures selected for application and implementation of an intervention shall meet the following criteria, all of which must be satisfied:

1. Determination on the basis of the professional and scientific literature of the probability that a specific technique will be appropriate for this particular behavior and individual.

   Peer-reviewed intervention studies shall constitute the primary source of information for the rendering of the determination of the appropriateness of a treatment technique. It is recognized that all behavioral treatments must be tailored to the individual and the natural environment; hence, alterations in procedures from those in published reports of studies will be necessary. Nevertheless, there are several factors that may enhance the salience of particular studies to the design of interventions for specific individuals.

   These factors include (a) presentation of objective information to account for all components of the intervention as applied; (b) demonstration of experimental control of the target behavior, (c) similarities in age of target individuals, and in related learning histories, (d) ability to determine whether the disability characteristics of target subjects are similar to those of the potential client (e.g., presence of multiple handicapping conditions, specific neurological factors, medical contraindications), and (e) ability to apply the intervention approximately as designed due to the inability to obtain the necessary ancillary personnel and/or agreement of qualified personnel or consultants to develop or implement a comparable but individualized, intervention.

2. Determination on the basis of behavioral assessment of the probability that a specific technique will be appropriate for this particular behavior and individual.

   Behavior assessment may encompass baseline data gathering, functional analysis, application of attention or activity control conditions, activity re-scheduling, assessment of pre-existing reinforcing values of various classes of stimulation and activity, review of previous accounts of attempts at treatment, and other procedures that are currently demonstrated to be accurate procedures to assess behavior.

3. Determination on the basis of peer and human rights review procedures and guardian approval of the appropriateness of the specific techniques for the particular behavior and individual.

   Participation of the client will be secured in accordance with the Standards for Providers of Psychological Services.

   Procedures for which approval shall be sought shall be those which have met criteria of 1 and 2 above, and constitute the least restrictive procedure considered likely to be effective.

4. Determination on the basis of continued monitoring of whether the intervention should be continued, modified, discontinued, or supplanted by a different intervention.

   Such determinations shall be rendered on a periodic basis as determined appropriate by the practitioner or required by programmatic policies or consent obtained or agreements during the course of due process.

5. Determination of the success of a treatment procedure shall be rendered with regard to an array of criteria.

   Criteria against which the success of a treatment procedure shall be assessed include (a) degree and rapidity of behavioral change, (b) generalization, (c) maintenance, (d) the character and magnitude of side effects, positive or negative (if any), (e) consumer (client, family, or advocate) satisfaction and life-style outcomes, and (f) local public acceptability of treatment and maintenance procedures and degree of behavior change.

   No provisions of these principles should be interpreted as proscribing the use of any applied behavior analytic procedure which is indicated as appropriate according to the foregoing criteria. The responsibility for the design, implementation, and evaluation of an applied behavior analytic procedure is solely that of the supervising practitioner, subject to the initial and subsequent approval of the legal guardian and duly constituted review boards.

Reprinted with permission from *Psychology in Mental Retardation and Developmental Disabilities*, 1989, *14*(2), 3-4.

APPENDIX E

Council for Children with Behavioral Disorders: Policy Statement on the Use of Behavior Reduction Procedures

---

The Council for Children with Behavioral Disorders (CCBD) serves the interests of children and youth who are considered handicapped because of their behavior. A major concern of this organization is insuring that these youngsters receive appropriate and effective services. The past two decades have seen increasing use of behavioral treatment services for dealing with children's inappropriate, problematic, and/or oppositional behavior in various settings. These services are based on strategies derived from behavioral, social learning, and applied behavior analysis research. Research clearly indicates that they are effective in improving children's academic and social functioning; in facilitating their behavioral self-control; and in enhancing their access to living a free, successful, normal, and happy life. However, because these procedures frequently are used to control behavior, they also have considerable potential of misapplication and abuse.

The most controversial behavioral procedures are those used to decrease children's inappropriate or problematic behavior. The CCBD Executive Committee has reviewed the literature on these strategies in a paper entitled, *Use of Behavior Reductive Strategies with Children with Behavioral Disorders*. This paper concluded that, although progress has been made toward developing less aversive, intrusive and restrictive behavior reduction alternatives, this technology has not advanced to the point where it is clearly effective in all situations with all types of children and with all types of problem behaviors.

CCBD advocates the continued development of more positive behavior reduction alternatives; and where feasible, these should be used. However, it is often difficult for practitioners to decide which, when, where, and how behavior reduction strategies should be administered. Ultimately, such decisions must be decided on a case-by-case basis by qualified professionals. The following recommendations, derived from the literature review, are intended to guide professionals in the appropriate use of behavior reduction procedures:

Behavioral services should be provided in conjunction with appropriate and effective planning.

The needs of the child should determine the particular service he or she receives. The services to be provided should be based upon prior assessment and baseline information, and should have precedence in the research literature; the procedures selected should have been demonstrated as effective under similar conditions, with children with similar characteristics (e.g., age, type of disability, intelligence, learning history, repertoires), and with similar target behavior(s). Selection of the particular intervention procedures also should be based on the likelihood of success in consideration of previous interventions attempted, available resources, and training and experience of the practitioner(s) involved in the delivery of services.

Behavioral services should be provided by competent professionals.

Professionals providing services to behaviorally disordered children should be fully academically trained in a social services profession and have specific courses related to behavioral interventions. They should have intensive and direct experience with behaviorally disordered children under the supervision of an experienced and qualified mentor. Further, they should be fully licensed in the state in which they are providing services. Finally, they should periodically update their skills through professional seminars and/or academic coursework.

Behavioral procedures selected should be the most effective but least restrictive and intrusive available.

The most effective treatment is one which employs the most powerful but safest, least aversive, intrusive, and restrictive procedures available. In selecting and implementing the most effective treatment option(s), professionals should:

a. identify behaviors to be strengthened, reduced, and/or eliminated by employing a thorough functional analysis of the youngster's behavior and the relative frequency with which these occur in various ecological settings and contexts.

b. identify related variables that may be facilitating or maintaining appropriate and inappropriate behavior.

c. identify the potential contributions of social models and social expectancies in terms of their maintenance of appropriate and inappropriate behaviors.

d. in cases where behavior is to be reduced, select competing or alternative behaviors to be strengthened which may serve as a replacement for an inappropriate behavior.

e. document the history of prior interventions and their effects and use this information to select the least aversive, intrusive, or restrictive intervention to attain treatment goals specified in the individual education plan (IEP).

In cases where more aversive, intrusive, or restrictive procedures are being considered to reduce or eliminate a particular problem behavior, professionals should:

a. consider their use procedures only after a program based on more positive alternatives and analysis and modification of setting variables (e.g., teacher behavior, space, curriculum, methods of communication, interpersonal interactions) have been attempted and documented as ineffective in reducing the problem behavior.

b. consider their use only with behaviors that pose immediate danger to a youngster or others and which might result in serious bodily harm, significant destruction of property, or with behaviors that pose a risk of severe and sustained restriction of the individual's opportunity to participate in educational, social, or vocational activities identified in his or her IEP.

c. refer a plan to use more aversive, intrusive, or restrictive procedures to a human rights committee composed of personnel who have an appropriate understanding of the procedures and their social, behavioral, and ecological implications in an intervention program.

d. select procedures that have been empirically documented in theprofesionalandscienificlitera ture as effective for reducing the particular problem behavior displayed by individuals with characteristics and skills similar to that of the youngster whose behavior will be reduced.

e. in the absence of empirical documentation, select interventions producing the least dangerous potential outcomes including side effects.

f. implement the procedures only if they have been approved by a human rights committee *and* the youngster's parent or guardian, and if they may be safely and faithfully conducted by qualifiedpersonnel in the treatment setting.

g. monitor and document the effects of the intervention plan and subject these data to frequent andongoing review by the human rights committee and the youngster's parent or guardian; subject acontinuing program to a peer review committee consisting of qualified professionals who are unconnected with the institution, school, or agency providing the services.

h. continue the use of these procedures only as long as necessary to meet the treatment objectives stipulated in the individual's IEP.

i. use these procedures only in a program which concomitantly develops the youngster's competing and alternative behaviors and which provides a long-range strategy for maintaining these behaviors and for transferring these to non-treatment settings.

It is further recognized that it is the responsibility of professionals to allow a child to participate as fully as possible in the planning of his or her educational and treatment program. Professionals also are obliged to explain to a child's parents or guardians the specific procedures and rationale of an intervention program. Finally, professionals are responsible for keeping a child's parent or guardians fully and frequently informed regarding their child's progress in the program and for involving them in planning significant changes that must be made to the program.

Reprinted with permission from the Council for Children with Behavioral Disorders.

CHAPTER

2

NONAVERSIVE AND AVERSIVE INTERVENTIONS: OVERVIEW

Alan C. Repp
Educational Research and Services Center
and
Northern Illinois University

"Not to rescue a person from an unhappy organization of his behavior is to punish him, in that it leaves him in a state of recurrent punishment" (Baer, 1970, p. 246).

Baer, as he so often does, has put the issue to us. Leaving a person in an unhappy state is unacceptable ethically; our task, then, is to act, to rescue. But how we rescue is, of course, the center of this issue. Do we rescue with aversives, with nonaversives, or with a combination of the two?

The purpose of this book is to answer that question, and we are pleased that 61 authors have contributed 32 chapters addressing that question. In this chapter, we will present brief summaries of all the contributions, and we have done so in the five major sections of the book: (a) myths, ethics, and science; (b) interventions: treatments and discussions; (c) functional analyses; (d) basic and applied research: reviews and commentary; and (e) interventionists.

MYTHS, ETHICS, AND SCIENCE

Donnellan and LaVigna address Baer's question directly, writing that the necessity of punishment is a myth. They reason that maladaptive behavior is frequently learned behavior, learned through positive or negative reinforcement. As such, the individual is capable of learning to behave in a different way. The problem becomes centered, of course, not on the individual but rather on us. Are we skilled enough to arrange environments to promote adaptive behavior and decelerate maladaptive behavior? That becomes the question, and as such, shifts the focus. Donnellan and LaVigna argue, as we have elsewhere (O'Brien & Repp, in press; Repp, 1983), that nonaversive procedures are often used without consideration of basic factors (e.g., reinforcer selection, schedules of reinforcement, competing reinforcers). They also argue that by using punishment as a last resort (as in the principle of Least Restrictive Alternative), we have given it a certain status, the status of being more effective than reinforcement in reducing behavior; and that attributed status, they believe, is a myth and a crucial mistake.

Axelrod also discusses myths, but has drawn a different conclusion. He has rephrased the question operationally and functionally: "Is a combination of positive reinforcement and punishment more effective than positive reinforcement alone?"

Axelrod thinks so. Further, he believes that denying a person effective procedures that will remove this "unhappy organization" is unethical (see also Van Houten, Axelrod, Bailey, Favell, Foxx, Iwata, & Lovaas, 1988), the denial often causing the loss of social, educational, and vocational opportunities. In a clever analogy, he regards disallowing effective punishment procedures to be like disallowing surgery when a new medication proves effective. Keep the surgery, but change the conditions under which it can be used.

Luiselli reprises one of the concerns of LaVigna and Donnellan, arguing that we are biased in our belief that aversive programming is the most effective alternative. Indeed, he believes that this bias provides a critical challenge to us, a challenge to develop nonaversive strategies that are effective and efficient. Luiselli suggests we perform functional assessments that identify the controlling relationship between the problem behavior and its controlling variables. Several alternative assessments are discussed, including analogue assessments (Iwata et al., 1982), indirect instruments (Durand & Crimmins, 1988), and the scatter plot (Touchette, MacDonald, & Langer, 1985). From this assessment, the treatment focus can be directed toward functional equivalence, a procedure that teaches responses that serve the same function as the problem behavior. Other alternatives are offered, such as compliance training and stimulus control procedures. The challenge, then, is for us to research these procedures further and to develop new alternatives.

Hayes and McCurry also address the moral issue noting that controversy exists when scientific information is lacking and we turn to traditions such as moralism. In an incisive chapter, they suggest that the moral issue is based on cultural rather than scientific behaviors and as such presents a conundrum. The problem is that cultural behaviors are artificial in that they have no basis in biological and other such circumstances. As such, they are arbitrary; i.e., there is not, indeed there cannot be, fixed standards of truth. We believe that the use of aversives is right or wrong because of the attributions or values of our social or professional groups. Indeed, this behavior is one in which Guess strongly believes groups should engage. In this view, what is right is not right *per se* (i.e., because of natural functions or laws); rather, it is right because our group believes it is right. Therefore, "right" is defined by our culture.

The scientific issue, on the other hand, is based on scientific rather than cultural behaviors. The basic question is: Does it work? In this discussion, Hayes and McCurry provide us a brief and fascinating review of two behavioral literatures. They note that most of the work supporting aversives is based on laboratory work with rats, and that some professionals argue that principles from this work are easily translatable to human behavior. Because there is little research on the effective use of aversives with humans, they discuss this point of translation in terms of two other areas of study -- schedules of reinforcement and stimulus equivalence. In both cases, they note that the results with humans and infrahumans are not the same. The authors conclude that the moral argument is unresolvable as it is based on cultural rather than scientific behavior. Similarly, the scientific argument is presently unresolvable as it is based on the presumption that we have sufficient research on the use of aversives and nonaversives and, unfortunately, this presumption is false.

The moral or ethical issue is continued by Schroeder, Oldenquist, and Rojahn who suggest that a central point is the following one: "We must ask whether the client appears even more dehumanized without a particular therapy than with it." With this sentence, the authors have put forward the position of those who advocate the use of aversives. They provide an interesting discussion of both ethical and scientific principles involved in judging the humaneness of behavioral treatments. They note the difficulty of making judgments when dignity appears to conflict with the value of maximal contentment of our clients. Further, the authors disagree with those who say that using punishment with persons with handicaps puts them in a status similar to that of a prisoner. They argue that there is, instead, a clear difference between coercive and restrictive measures toward criminals and the treatment of persons with disabilities.

Schroeder et al. suggest that the moral way of deciding whether the use of punishment is acceptable is to reverse roles, to ask whether we would accept the treatment if we were in the same condition (i.e., developmentally disabled and with a severe behavior problem). They go on to warn that there certainly are grounds on which to criticize aversive therapies (e.g., indignity, depersonalization, long-term effectiveness). In addition to a discussion of ethical principles, they discuss scientific principles on which to judge the effectiveness of behavioral treatments. Like Coe and Matson, they point to weaknesses in many of the literature reviews. Unlike the former, however, they argue against group research studies. Instead, they argue for intra-subject designs that allow evaluation of time, sequence, and generalization effects. In conclusion, they urge us to merge ethical and scientific principles in our consideration of this issue. To ignore one is as great an error as to ignore the other.

Several authors have discussed myths related to research on the efficacy of punishment procedures. Van Houten and Rolider discuss what they consider another myth, the labelling of our procedures. In doing so, they have taken an interesting approach to the issue of whether or not to use aversives. Instead of arguing one way or another, they argue that the three most common differential reinforcement procedures (DRO, DRI, DRL) are really punishment procedures. The apparent implication related to this controversy is that since virtually everybody is using punishment anyway, ...

The authors reason that since reinforcement is reduced in DRO and DRI when a particular response is emitted, the amount of reinforcement is reduced following a response, and we have what amounts to a negative punishment paradigm (Repp, 1983). The authors promise that their analysis will provide new ways to consider these procedures and, hence, ways to improve their efficacy. Some of their suggestions are (a) when a response occurs, to make the postponement of reinforcement longer than the regular response-reinforcer interval in DRO; (b) to add discriminative stimuli to indicate the procedure is in effect; and (c) to make the magnitude of reinforcement significant.

Wolery and Gast suggest that we take a reasoned approach to this controversy. They reject the black-or-white, all-or-none, dichotomous approach to the issue of using aversives. They believe that we should view the definitions of aversives, of problem behaviors, and of treatment effectiveness from the perspective of a continuum. When we do not and choose the dichotomous approach instead, we artificially establish two groups, one which will and one which never will use aversives. In a brief but interesting comment on academe, they note that such an approach builds vitas, reputations, and careers; it does not, however, build the best lives for our clients.

Not restricting their criticism to these topics, Wolery and Gast provide an interesting discussion of social validity, a construct used by many of those conducting research in this area. They note that both sides of the issue use social validity to support their decision, thus weakening the construct. They suggest that social validity can exist only if three conditions are met: (a) The goals are socially significant. (b) The procedures are socially appropriate. (c) The effects are socially important. Because some advocates on either side of the issue do not use all three criteria, the authors believe that the problem exists. Social validity is relative: It is subject to the zeitgeist, it changes across raters, and it is subject to measurement problems. The authors note these problems, as well as ways that we can address them.

Freagon has taken a strong stance on the issue, arguing that the question of whether to use aversives is an irrelevant one. To her, the use of severe punishment or aversives is immoral and is, indeed, abusive. She argues that practices like those at BRI would not be allowed with persons who do not have disabilities, and that they are allowed because we value those with disabilities less than those without. She believes that the correct alternative is an approach that maintains families, integrates persons in the community, and safeguards their rights. A heavy emphasis on programs for preschool children is seen as a way to lessen the probability that these children will ever incur aversives. Although she comes from a different perspective, her emphasis on early intervention and parental support has the same objective as that presented by Dunlap, Johnson, and Robbins.

Guess also provides an interesting perspective on the issue of aversives while addressing it from the position of a social scientist. He argues that our research agenda has been very limited, too circumspective and narrow. As a result, we have developed a pyramidal training model in which a relatively small group of teacher trainers who accepted the aversive research of years past has unduly convinced students that the safe use of aversives was justified; these students in turn carried the argument to very large numbers of service providers, students, administrators, and so forth. Guess argues that induction into a profession is a result of both training and indoctrination. In our case, academicians have trained their students to use aversives while providing a doctrinaire that the academicians' acceptance of aversives is objective rather than subjective. To Guess, the data simply do not support the objective acceptance of aversives. He goes on to make several recommendations regarding our research agenda, including methodological suggestions (e.g., in design and data collection), cautions about not overstating the success of nonaversives, and calls for much broader, integrative, cross-disciplinary research.

TREATMENTS: DATA AND DISCUSSIONS

Failure to effect successful treatment probably happens to most of us; the appearance of failures in the literature, however, is rare. In that sense, the chapters by Barrera and Teodoro and by Paisey, Whitney and Hislop are refreshing. In the humanistic sense, however, they are disappointing as they remind us that we sometimes fail to help our clients despite our best efforts. In some respect, the challenge of cases like these may be what brings many of us to this field. Simply put, can we figure out how to help this individual? When we see the care brought forth by these authors in their treatment programs, we appreciate their skills. Paisey, Whitney, and Hislop, for example, provide a wide-ranging discussion of the use of aversives and offer many provocative conclusions drawn from theory and data. In their carefully reasoned paper, they analyze the logic behind rejecting aversives in favor of the sole use of nonaversives.

In the methodological area, they discuss several of the points brought forth by those who reject the use of aversives. The first is that criticisms of the methodology of punishment studies tend to be about dated research, and are not applicable to the experimental control shown in current studies. Additionally, where weaknesses now exist, they tend to be distributed across studies of both aversive and nonaversive procedures.The authors also challenge the assumption that conducting a functional analysis is sufficient to ensure the success of nonaversive procedures. They provide seven case studies demonstrating extraordinary professional and administrative commitment to functional analyses and nonaversive procedures. Sadly, many of these cases did not result in complete success. Their conclusion is that instead of leading to the sole use of nonaversives, a functional analysis leads one to reject alternative explanations of (and treatment procedures for) the behavior. Indeed, they reason that if a functional analysis suggests that behavior is internally motivated, nonaversives seldom will be effective because the maintaining reinforcers cannot be overridden by the new procedure.

The authors also discuss the selective use of both nonaversive and aversive procedures. They criticize the external validity of the communication theory of maladaptive behavior, noting an interaction between subject selection, subject characteristics, and treatment success. They also argue that aversive procedures are used selectively, not randomly as some have said. Their data show that aversives are primarily used with behaviors that put persons at risk (e.g., head banging), a use they presume to occur because nonaversives have failed to solve the problem. They also criticize the assumption that aversives are more often used with persons with severe handicaps because they lack sufficient representation. Instead, with data, they argue that this disproportionate use of aversives occurs because high risk behaviors are more often found with persons with severe handicaps.

Paisey et al. end with what amounts to a challenge to all of us doing research in this field. They conclude that the success of nonaversive procedures is to some extent motivation-restricted; i.e., these procedures have been far more successful with persons who are escape-motivated than with those who are motivated by self-stimulation or attention. In addition, from their and others' data, they reason that nonaversives are much more likely to fail with a behavior that is endogenously reinforced, maintained by multiple contingencies, or that is one among a set of maladaptive behaviors. The challenge, then, is to learn whether nonaversive procedures can be developed for the general audience of persons with these severe behavior problems, a challenge the authors have very well put before the field.

Barrera and Teodoro constantly question their own use of a procedure (Gentle Teaching) and made commendable efforts at improving their technology. Their failure, while focused on Gentle Teaching, really addresses a larger issue: Why do any nonaversive or aversive procedures fail? Is the failure, as they initially suspected, with their implementation of the procedure or, as they later suspected, with the treatment itself? Another possibility, of course, can be found in their concluding comments. They suggest that the power of Gentle Teaching relies on the power of the reinforcers employed, and that a careful pre-baseline assessment of potential reinforcers is fundamental. No one can argue with this suggestion, and, fortunately, we have a technology for this assessment (e.g., Green, Reid, White, Halford, Brittain, & Gardner, 1988; Mason, McGee, Farmer-Dougan, & Risley, 1989; Pace, Ivancic, Edwards, Iwata, & Page, 1985; Wacker, Berg, Wiggins, Muldoon, & Cavanaugh, 1985).

A second chapter also criticizes Gentle Teaching. The authors (Jones, Singh, & Kendall) argue that, in general, replication of McGee's results with this procedure might be difficult because they believe the methods have not been operationally defined. Data on two subjects are presented and show little difference between visual screening and Gentle Teaching in reducing headbanging and mouthing. In addition, oral hygiene was more effective than either procedure for the subject for whom it was used. Jones et al. follow the concerns of Barrera and Teodoro with bonding, which is a central component of Gentle Teaching. They found virtually no bonding under the Gentle Teaching condition but some bonding under a punishment condition, a finding which McGee (1985) suggests should not occur.

McGee's chapter provides a nice counterpoint to these two chapters. In it, he articulates his philosophy and methods, while providing data on 15 subjects showing the effects of Gentle Teaching. No procedure, from reinforcement to electric shock, is universally effective, and failure to replicate McGee's findings should be taken in that context. While the focus has been on specific components of Gentle Teaching, the contribution of the procedure may be far greater in the general than in the specific. By that, I mean that McGee has emphasized the role of the caregiver more than any of the rest of us have. Yes, we look at attention, escape, and so forth, but McGee is asking us to look at far more complex social interactions than those. His code, for example, consists of tens of behaviors of the caregiver and the client (see Table 2). In constructing such a code, he has presented a challenge to us to refine our research techniques (e.g., our ability to develop very complex recording schemata) in order to learn which of these variables are prepotent. After all, one of the criticisms of this procedure is that it only packages behavioral procedures that others have found effective. If this is true, then it cannot perforce be all wrong. Perhaps the reaction to Gentle Teaching has been more to the claims by some of its proponents of universal effectiveness than to its components. More research by independent experimenters, of course, will answer that question.

Birnbrauer challenges us to change our roles, to become educators of those involved with these problems. To him, as with Axelrod, aversives are natural contingencies found in the lives of us all, and the issue becomes one of learning how to use punishment correctly and how to create conditions in which clients will maximize their access to reinforcement. He argues for what would be an ecobehavioral approach (see Schroeder, 1990) in which the effects of maladaptive behavior on the individual as well as on all others in the environment are assessed. Birnbrauer has applied such an analysis to the behavior of staff as well as to the completely benign environments some advocate. The results of such an analysis are instructive, suggesting that the issue is far more complex than we might expect.

Birnbrauer, Barrera and Teodoro, and others have highlighted our need to know more about interventions and analyses. To learn more, of course, we need to do more research (of the type, for example, that Carr does). Butterfield directs himself to the central question in this pursuit of knowledge: Can we ethically meet the considerations of both the researchers and the clinicians? With an enlightening style, he shapes our thinking and develops a rule for conducting research and for implementing aversive interventions: "The treatment that minimizes physical damage and psychological harm is the clinically ethical choice." Further, "the use of efficacious treatments that nevertheless cause some physical damage or psychological harm is clinically ethical if they result in less damage or harm than any other efficacious treatment and less than no treatment at all." In an analogy using his research with heart patients, Butterfield provides an interesting discussion. While experts took sides on which were the best treatment procedures, none of the experts advocated correctly. Is that our predicament? Do we know enough to preclude the use of aversives? Some, like Axelrod, would say no. Others, like Donnellan and LaVigna, would say yes.

Feldman discusses both groups, those for and those against the use of aversives, and, although coming to a different conclusion, iterates some of the issues discussed by Donnellan and LaVigna. To him, the question is what to do for someone, for example, with self-injury for whom nonaversives have either failed or will take longer to affect than will aversives. While Donnellan and LaVigna would argue that a multi-element approach should be used, Feldman would counter that not all people would be helped sufficiently to ignore the use of aversives. His conclusion is one that others have reached: A morally and scientifically sound technology for treatment must come from research, particularly that which addresses the complex interaction of setting variables, client characteristics, and interventions. One of the positive outcomes of this issue, Feldman notes, is the development of research on the use of nonaversives, particularly research that improves our technology rather than research that only becomes another demonstration of the effectiveness of a particular procedure.

Dunlap, Johnson, and Robbins have capitalized on one of the points we know; i.e., that at least some of these serious maladaptive behaviors serve a function. They argue that many behavior problems can be prevented by early intervention programs that focus on skill development. Central to their thesis is the belief that many behavior problems serve communicative functions, and that they occur because individuals have not been taught adaptive, alternative behaviors that serve the same function. The authors suggest that this approach is more productive than the ones that concentrate either solely on suppressing behavior or on manipulating stimulus-correlated conditions. While the authors admit that there is no direct empirical support for their contention that early intervention can prevent severe behavior problems, they do present a logical argument for their position. Additionally, they present compelling data from a project based upon the suggestions made in their chapter.

Dunlap et al. present an interesting thesis and challenge, both to themselves and others in the field. Their involvement, then, is not so much with the question of whether we should use aversives to address severe behavior problems. Instead, it is an effort to design programs based upon teaching functional skills, working with parents, and utilizing the scientific basis provided by child development, instructional technology, and applied behavior analysis.

Smith contends that the primary arguments against aversives (aversives have negative side effects, and effective nonaversive alternatives always can be found) are fallacious. He warns, however, that aversives should only be used as a last resort, by staff skilled at teaching complex behaviors, and with procedural safeguards. He discusses aversives and makes an interesting point. Although many agree that aversives should be defined functionally, in practice they are often defined on the basis of their effects on those who administer them. He goes on to note that many autistic children find acts functionally aversive that retarded children do not, and find painful stimuli ineffective that others find functionally aversive. Smith believes, however, that the use of aversives should be dependent on the extent to which it will promote normalization, and, further, that the use should involve parents from the level of informed consent to treatment when possible.

FUNCTIONAL ANALYSES

Several chapters address the issue of functional analysis, in particular whether such an analysis can lead to more effective treatment procedures. Iwata, Vollmer, and Zarcone note that efforts to treat maladaptive behavior by topography, as well as efforts to find the most effective treatment for a particular behavior, are misguided as they ignore the possibility that two people may engage in the same behavior for different reasons. They discuss descriptive and functional analyses and note problems with indirect assessments such as the MAS (Durand & Crimmins, 1988), direct assessments which do not provide environmental correlates of behavior (e.g., the Scatter Plot of Touchette, MacDonald, & Langer, 1985), and direct, naturalistic assessments which can seldom identify reinforcers that are on thin reinforcement schedules. The authors argue instead for a functional analysis through direct, controlled observation, a procedure generally referred to as analogue assessment (Iwata, Dorsey, Slifer, Bauman, & Richman, 1982). They go on to provide valuable examples of functional analyses of behavior maintained by positive reinforcement, negative reinforcement, and automatic reinforcement, and they argue after a convincing analysis of the literature that we cannot be satisfied with a system limited to selecting "least restrictive" alternatives. We must, at least in addition, seek alternatives most likely to be effective given the function of behavior.

The chapter by Repp and Karsh supports the contentions of Iwata et al., as these authors also stress the need to choose treatments based on the function of behavior. They offer a model based on a taxonomy that allows a functional analysis during a baseline assessment, a treatment choice based on that assessment, and an experimental procedure for validating the taxonomy for those interested in the research aspects. The emphasis here is on selecting treatments based upon hypotheses of the controlling conditions. An effort is made to differentiate environmentally dependent from environmentally independent behaviors, and to identify through the taxonomy the environmentally dependent behaviors that are controlled by positive reinforcement, negative reinforcement, or self-stimulation.

Wacker, Steege, Northrup, Reimers, Berg, and Sasso discuss the procedures they use in an outpatient clinic at the University of Iowa, and present us with an excellent model, the basis of which is a functional analysis. The authors cleverly address the time constraints of an outpatient clinic by scheduling brief analogue conditions that represent possible maintaining conditions for the presenting problem. Care is taken to address the acceptability of treatment to parents and other consumers. This is an especially good approach to a primary problem of outpatient programs that have difficulty maintaining the program once the patient leaves the clinic. The authors discuss the interaction between acceptability and treatment integrity as well as factors that affect treatment effectiveness. Some of the suggestions include (a) appropriate functional analyses; (b) generalizability of treatment across settings, people, and time; and (c) functional equivalence training.

As we and others have argued (O'Brien & Repp, in press; Repp, Felce, and Barton, 1988; Repp, Singh, Olinger, & Olson, 1990), treatment efficacy can be substantially improved if treatment is tied to the conditions maintaining problem behaviors. In lucid style, Carr, Robinson, and Palumbo address this point. To them, the real question is not whether to use aversives; instead, the real question is whether to use functional procedures (i.e., procedures based on a functional analysis). While we would probably all answer yes to this question, we should understand that these authors have extended considerably our understanding of functional analyses and have noted that our assessment strategy is still in an embryonic state.

Carr et al. suggest, as have others, that we analyze settings to determine the conditions maintaining behavior. In addition, however, they suggest that we determine the reinforcing contingencies as well. From this information, a treatment paradigm could be selected that allows appropriate behavior to access the *same* reinforcers at least as efficiently as the problem behavior has. We should note that this approach is extremely different from the traditional functional analyses of antecedents or settings. In this case, the analysis is more of the function of the behavior (i.e., what change does it produce in the environment) than it is of conditions (i.e., what effect does a particular antecedent have on a behavior). The technology for extending this approach is difficult, although suggestions have been made. For example, Barrera and Teodoro presented data on the time lag between SIB and rewards. This type of analysis conducted during a baseline assessment may identify the reinforcing contingencies which the client can be taught to access through adaptive behaviors. A broader analysis has also been suggested in our computer-based programs that provide contingency analyses of both antecedent and subsequent events (Repp & Deitz,1990; Repp, Harman, Felce, Van Acker, & Karsh, 1989; Repp, Karsh, Van Acker, Felce, & Harman, 1989).

Many of the authors have been calling for better functional analyses and a more complete system for choosing our interventions. Schrader and Gaylord-Ross address this issue and provide the Triadic Model comprised of (a) an assessment of the effects of setting events and antecedents on the target behavior, (b) an assessment of the effects of the consequences of the target behavior, and (c) an assessment of the skills of the client. From this information, they have been able to analyze the function of the maladaptive behavior and build skill behaviors that might perform the same function for the individual. This is an interesting approach, and, loosely speaking, a more holistic approach than the functional analysis methodology advocated by others. It can be an approach that prevents the emergence of the other maladaptive behaviors (cf. Dunlap, Johnson, & Robbins).

Pyles and Bailey also argue for a functional analysis, and differentiate between behavior analysis and behavior modification. In so doing, they make an interesting distinction between Active Behavior Management (which relies on the manipulation of subsequent events) and Passive Behavior Management (which relies on the manipulation of antecedent events). The authors suggest that the latter is a more appropriate procedure as it bases treatment on the results of a functional analysis. In their decision-making model, which in part is a criticism of the least restrictive model, the authors provide steps for determining the maintaining causes of behavior. From this information, the authors believe they are more likely to develop successful nonaversive treatment procedures.

BASIC AND APPLIED RESEARCH: REVIEWS AND COMMENTARY

Perhaps to the surprise of some, Skinner has agreed that an aversive could be used under certain conditions. The conditions, to Sobsey, however, are extremely restrictive, and he finds in his literature review that they have not been met. His analysis finds aversives to have short-lived effects, to be subject to harmful misuse, and to obscure the real function of the problem behavior. In addition, he criticizes the research involving aversives for the following reasons: (a) Basic research findings are cited as support for applied use when applied research cannot attain the same degree of experimental control. (b) Designs cannot account for regression effects of the high-rate problem behaviors. (c) Studies comparing aversives and nonaversives are biased in favor of aversives.

Sobsey provides several interesting analyses of this research. Because (at least in recent years) aversives are used almost only after nonaversives have failed, one cannot assess sequence effects. We do not know, for example, whether nonaversives would have been just as effective had they been used after aversives. Second, research that uses physical restraint as a procedure misrepresents the data. Sobsey reasons that behaviors like SIB occur in bouts. If during the intervention phase a person is restrained for a minute following the first SIB, then the expected string of responses cannot possibly occur for that minute. An adequate comparison cannot then be made between a treatment phase with restraint and a baseline phase without restraint. Sobsey suggests that a fairer analysis of the effects of any restraint procedure would be made by eliminating data from baseline and other conditions that occurred within the restraint duration (e.g., one minute) from the first occurrence in each episode. Sobsey concludes by arguing that if aversives are ever used, the rights of the client must be better protected, and a court order should be required before implementation.

Hayes and McCurry noted the problem of those who argue from a moral perspective, a problem has also been addressed by Linscheid and Meinhold. These authors also argue that evidence of the effects of aversive stimuli may have been misrepresented. The former argued against those who say that the positive effects of punishment can be directly translated from laboratory studies with infrahumans. In this way, Hayes and McCurry lessened the position of those who argue for the use of aversives.

Linscheid and Meinhold examine the literature on negative side effects of punishment in laboratory studies and argue that these findings cannot be directly translated to applied settings. In this way, they lessen the position of those who argue against the use of aversives. The authors, for example, note that the antiaversive group argues that the punishment literature shows that aversive stimulation results in elicited aggression. The applied literature, however, shows that negative side effects occur at a low rate (while positive side effects occur at a much higher rate). In their review of the laboratory research, they note that several factors affect punishment-induced aggression, such as proximity to another subject and cage size, interaction of intensity of aversive stimulation and the species serving as subjects, and opportunity for escape. They go on to note that in laboratory experiments, both positive reinforcement and extinction can lead to aggression. Since these two procedures are in all nonaversive programs, and since they can be induced by particular schedules of reinforcement, we must carefully choose the schedule of reinforcement in DRI and DRA programs. The authors also suggest that interventions are more likely to be successful in altering rates of behavior when they involve interval rather than ratio schedules. Interestingly, DRI and DRA almost never involve interval schedules with these problem behaviors (O'Brien & Repp, in press). These authors suggest that those who both support the nonaversive approach and use the laboratory research to argue against the use of aversives may have a dilemma. A further problem for this group may be the authors' conclusion that the conditions under which aggression is studied in the laboratory are generally not present in applied settings.

Linscheid and Meinhold also suggest that a simple interpretation of the communication theory (i.e., teaching the person to substitute a response that will lead to the same consequence that the maladaptive behavior does) somewhat ignores the literature of response allocation. This literature is reviewed in part by Epling and Pierce who provide a provocative means of predicting rates of problem behavior through consideration of the matching law (Herrnstein, 1961). The basic idea here is that the rate or duration of behavior is positively related to its rate of reinforcement and inversely related to the rate of reinforcement for other behaviors in the repertoire. Although not discussed by others in this context, the matching law is the behavioral or scientific reason we say that adaptive alternatives must be taught and reinforced if a maladaptive behavior is to be reduced. Similarly, it explains the need to assess potential reinforcers before using them in treatment (Repp et al., 1988) and to maximize reinforcement of the alternative behaviors being taught.

While Linscheid and Meinhold and Pierce and Epling review studies in basic research, Coe and Matson use reviews of applied research to make suggestions that are quite basic to that research body. They suggest that the issue of whether or not to use aversives is not properly addressed by the moral argument against aversives; the decision, instead, should be based upon a number of research findings, such as magnitude, speed, durability, and generality of effect; side effects; clinical significance; labor intensiveness; and controlling variables. Further, they point to the weakness of trying to compare the effects of various treatments across studies when these treatments are used on behaviors that may be differentially difficult to modify. As a result, they suggest that we move to large-scale group studies in which effectiveness is more systematically studied.

From their review of literature, the authors go on to criticize those who argue for the sole use of nonaversives. They believe this argument ignores the methodological weaknesses of the supporting literature, as well as the effectiveness of various aversive procedures. They conclude by warning that the use of less effective procedures is unethical, and that by restricting ourselves to these procedures, we are making persons with developmental disabilities "...suffer for ideological whims."

TREATMENT PROVIDERS

Green is also concerned with the choice of treatment procedures, and she focuses on rules associated with least restrictive alternatives. To her, these rules have been misguided for several reasons, two of which are that little attention has been paid to procedures that appear benign and to the skills necessary to program them. She raises many interesting points and focuses on proactive behaviors of the treatment providers. That is, instead of writing what we should not do, Green has written a careful task analysis of what we should do to provide better interventions. This is an excellent framework not only for increasing the probability that clients will receive proper treatment, but also for training programs independent of specific challenging behaviors. We would all do well to follow these guidelines in our training program not just as guidelines, but as the behaviors to teach our students. Lutzker's chapter continues the concern with the behavior of those using behavioral procedures. He presents multiple arguments against the use of aversives with developmentally disabled persons and presents an alternative to the use of aversives: an ecobehavioral analysis of contingencies maintaining the problem behavior. Lutzker criticizes organizations like the Association for Behavior Analysis and Association for the Advancement of Behavior Therapy for not having developed policies on this issue, a position supported by Guess who argued that all organizations should make known their position on this issue. He further criticizes presumptions that we have sufficient research on aversives and that we have sufficient safeguards on those using aversive procedures through human rights committees. Since these concerns have not been met, Lutzker believes we should turn to ecobehavioral analyses which will lead to broader-based nonaversive treatment procedures.

The book concludes with the chapter by O'Brien and Karsh. In it, they discuss treatment and acceptability in terms of consumers, therapists, and society. Treatment acceptability is, in general, a social phenomenon, which is not to say that we are unable to manipulate it. It does, however, return us to the point made by Hayes and McCurry. There can be a considerable difference between culturally based and scientifically based behaviors. What we believe, we believe. We have long histories of reinforcement (and punishment?) for these beliefs, and whether new information changes those beliefs (either way in this issue) is person-specific.

CONCLUDING REMARKS

In the beginning of this chapter, I quoted Baer and suggested that rescuing persons from an unhappy state leads to the following question: Do we rescue with aversives, with nonaversives, or with a combination of the two. As you read this book, you may resolve this issue for yourself, perhaps in a way that changes your present opinion.

Reading these chapters many times, I have found that the issue for myself is now broader. The questions have become: Why do I believe what I believe? Why do I act as I act? Am I as effective a therapist as I can be? What can make me more effective? Why do I choose the treatments I choose? The authors of these chapters have broadened my perspective and have caused me to examine and change many of my entering beliefs. They have been informative and challenging. Hopefully, you, too, will be informed and challenged; if you are, we will have met our objective for this book.

REFERENCES

Baer, D. M., (1970). A case for the selective reinforcement of punishment. In C. Neuringer & J.L. Michaels (Eds.), *Behavior modification in clinical psychology*. New York: Appleton-Century-Crofts.

Durand, V. M., & Crimmins, D. B. (1988). Identifying the variables maintaining self-injurious behavior. *Journal of Autism and Developmental Disorders, 18*, 99-117.

Green, C. W., Reid, D. H., White, L. K., Halford, R. C., Brittain, D. P., & Gardner, S. M. (1988). Identifying reinforcers for persons with profound handicaps: Staff opinion versus systematic assessment of preferences. *Journal of Applied Behavior Analysis, 21*, 32-43.

Herrnstein, R. J. (1961). Relative and absolute strength of response as a function of frequency of reinforcement. *Journal of the Experimental Analysis of Behavior, 4*, 267-272.

Iwata, B. A., Dorsey, M. F., Slifer, K. J., Bauman, K. E., & Richman, G. S. (1982). Toward a functional analysis of self-injury. *Analysis and Intervention in Developmental Disabilities, 2*, 1-20.

Mason, S. A., McGee, G. G., Farmer-Dougan, V., & Risley, T. R. (1989). A practical strategy for ongoing reinforcer assessment. *Journal of Applied Behavior Analysis, 22*, 171-179.

McGee, J. J. (1985). Examples of the use of gentle teaching. *Mental Handicap in New Zealand, 9*, 11-20.

O'Brien, S., & Repp, A. C. (in press). A review of 30 years of research on the use of differential reinforcement to reduce inappropriate responding. *Behavior Modification*.

Pace, G. M., Ivancic, M. T., Edwards, G. L., Iwata, B. A., & Page, T. J. (1985). Assessment of stimulus preference and reinforcer value with profoundly retarded individuals. *Journal of Applied Behavior Analysis, 18*, 249-255.

Repp, A. C. (1983). *Teaching the mentally retarded*. Englewood Cliffs, NJ: Prentice-Hall.

Repp, A. C., & Deitz, D. E. D. (1990). An ecobehavioral taxonomy for stereotypic responding. In S. Schroeder (Ed.), *Ecobehavioral analysis and developmental disabilities: The twenty-first century* (pp. 122-140). New York: Springer-Verlag.

Repp, A. C., Felce, D., & Barton, L. E. (1988). Basing the treatment of stereotypic and self-injurious behaviors on hypotheses of their causes. *Journal of Applied Behavior Analysis, 21*, 281-290.

Repp, A. C., Harman, M. L., Felce, D., Van Acker, R., & Karsh, K. G. (1989). Conducting behavioral assessments on computer-collected data. Behavioral Assessment, 11, 249-268.

Repp, A. C., Karsh, K. G., Van Acker, R., Felce, D., & Harman, M. (1989). A computer-based system for collecting and analyzing observational data. *Journal of Special Education Technology, 9*, 207-217.

Repp, A. C., Singh, N. N., Olinger, E., & Olson, D. R. (1990). The use of functional analyses to test causes of self-injurious behaviour: Rationale, current status, and future directions. *Journal of Mental Deficiency Research, 34*, 95-105.

Schroeder, S. (Ed.) 1990). *Ecobehavioral analysis and developmental disabilities: The twenty-first century*. New York: Springer-Verlag.

Touchette, P. E., MacDonald, R. F., & Langer, S. N. (1985). A scatter plot for identifying stimulus control of problem behavior. *Journal of Applied Behavior Analysis, 18*, 343-351.

Van Houten, R., Axelrod, S., Bailey, J. S., Favell, J. E., Foxx, R. M., Iwata, B., & Lovaas, O. I. (1988). The right to effective behavioral treatment. *Journal of Applied Behavior Analysis, 21*, 381-384.

Wacker, D. P., Berg, W. K., Wiggins, B., Muldoon, M., & Cavanaugh, J. (1985). Evaluation of reinforcer preferences for profoundly handicapped students. *Journal of Applied Behavior Analysis, 18*, 173-178.

PART II

CHAPTER

3

MYTHS ABOUT PUNISHMENT

Anne M. Donnellan, Ph.D.
University of Wisconsin-Madison

Gary W. LaVigna, Ph.D.
Institute for Applied Behavior Analysis - Los Angeles

The great enemy of the truth is very often not the lie - deliberate, contrived and dishonest - but the myth - persistent, persuasive and unrealistic. John F. Kennedy

The results of behavioral research over the last 25 years reveal that what are often taken as truths regarding punishment are, in reality, myths which are beginning to crumble in the light of new understanding (LaVigna, Donnellan, & Willis, in preparation). Positive alternatives are rendering the traditional use of punishment obsolete and unnecessary (e.g., Sidman, 1989), and many are calling for the cessation of the use of aversive interventions at least with dependent populations [e.g., The Association for Persons with Severe Handicaps (TASH); Autism Society of America (ASA); Association for Retarded Citizens-USA, (ARC-USA), etc.]. The mythology around punishment persists, however, and contributes to the controversy on the topic and confuses many well-meaning professionals and non-professionals alike. This paper will refer to a number of reviews of the literature that support a positive approach to behavior management. We will concentrate on some of the critical issues and the underlying myths that contribute to the shrinking but nonetheless continuing support for the use of a technology heavily reliant on punishment (Cataldo, 1989; Van Houten et al., 1988). Finally, we will make the case that myths can be expected in any endeavor as complex as the study of behavioral phenomena in applied settings; and, moreover, that the impact of mythology on our work has such serious consequences for individuals who are dependent/disabled that serious consideration should be given to the study of our own behavior as both subject and object of the science of behavior (Krasner & Houts, 1984).

The word punishment, of course, may have different meanings. Webster's Third New International Dictionary defines it as "the act of punishing: the infliction of a punisher; retributive suffering, pain or loss." For the lay person, such retribution may be the defining quality of punishment. In contrast, for the applied behavior analyst, punishment is defined as a consequence that reduces the probability that the punished behavior will occur in the future. In this latter case, the defining quality of punishment is its effect on future occurrence. A punishing (i.e., decreasing) effect on future behavior can be accomplished through either the contingent presentation or through the contingent removal of a stimulus or event. It is with reference to this technical definition that the myths of punishment are being illuminated in the penetrating light of empirical study.

Presently, the controversy around the use of punishment with dependent populations is complicated by the inclusion of the term "aversive." Aversives, from the infinitive "to avert" (Webster's: to turn away in order to escape), in technical jargon refer to stimuli, actions, or events that an individual ordinarily would act to avoid. Accordingly, punishment by either presentation or by removal is considered to be aversive. Of course, for the layperson as well as the professional, words such as "aversives," "punisher," "punishment," "retribution," "penalty", etc., often get misused and are easily misunderstood. Moreover, some stimuli typically considered aversive can be reinforcing for certain individuals under specific conditions. Bondage is one example. In the professional literature concerned with developmental disabilities, restraint has been demonstrated, under some circumstances, to be a reinforcer rather than a punisher (Favell, McGimsey, & Jones, 1978). Aversives and punishment are obviously not equivalent terms (See Hutchinson, 1977). For the purposes of this paper, however, the word punishment or punishment/aversives will refer to the variety of behavior reduction procedures encompassed by both forms of punishment (e.g., Cataldo, 1989).

A review of some of the myths regarding these behavior reduction procedures reflects some of the current patterns of thinking and of practice with dependent populations. Webster's defines myth as: "a belief given uncritical acceptance by the members of a group especially in support of existing or traditional practices or institutions."

MYTHS

Myth #1: Punishment is necessary.

The first and most basic myth of concern here is that "misbehavior" needs to be punished so that it won't happen again, i.e., *punishment is necessary to control undesirable behavior.* This is likely the oldest of the myths in *applied* behavior analysis and apparently has no equivalent in the literature from the operant animal laboratories (e.g., Hutchinson, 1977). An oft quoted (e.g., Iwata, 1988) and early example of the myth is illustrated in an article by the eminent behavioral psychologist, Donald Baer. In his 1970 commentary calling for the selective and cautious use and study of punishment, Baer (1970) describes a hypothetical (but familiar) situation to address the complex moral issues raised by using/not using punishment. We excerpt it at length here:

> It will be even more of a shame if objections to such research on punishment are intrinsically confused in their own moral stance. Suppose, for example, that I show you a child, institutionalized as a retardate [sic], who has over the years developed a very successful attention-compelling behavior - self-destruction. Suppose that in this case, the child pulls persistently at his ear and has finally come to a point where, unrestrained, he will in fact literally rip it from his head. He has, let us say, half succeeded in this venture already. As a result, he wears a straitjacket throughout the hours of his existence, and he is so heavily tranquilized that he lies in a semi-stupor gazing vacantly at the ceiling. *I suggest that he was taught his performance* (emphasis added). He was reinforced for ear-tugging rather than for other, more desirable behaviors, because his caretakers were busy and could

> ignore more acceptable behavior more easily than self-destructive behavior. Successively in their busy lives, they became used to his current self-destructive behavior, so that only when it was more self-destructive than usual would they consider that they must do something. Thereby, they reinforced intense self-destruction rather than mild self-destruction. Had they designed a shaping program to instruct the child in his own destruction, they could hardly have proceeded better. (p. 244-245)

What Baer has described is clearly a shaping procedure, effective in this hypothetical case, although not by design. He then describes a moral trap which he sees resulting when behavior therapists appear with shock apparatus in hand:

> They note the existence of self-destroyers in our institution, and wonder if they might not end that horror with some carefully applied aversive faradic controls. Some of us will be very interested until we discover that they mean electric shock. If we refuse *because* they mean electric shock, then I suggest that we have fallen thoroughly into the moral trap. In our professional wisdom, we have assigned people to institutional life, allowed them to be taught their own self-destruction, and confined them to a small hell in consequence. Can we now refuse that they endure a small number of painful episodes over a short span of sessions, hopefully designed to let them live the rest of their lives awake and untied?...
> *Not to rescue a person from an unhappy organization of his behavior is to punish him, in that it leaves him in a state of recurrent punishment.* (p. 245-246)

Baer goes on to caution us about the dangers of reliance on punishment and, as he says, he is certainly not "... recommending it as a way of life or a way of psychotherapy" (p.248). Nonetheless, we respectfully submit that Baer, in this early work, and others who follow a similar logic to this day (e.g., Van Houten, et al., 1988; Cataldo, 1989; Iwata, 1988), are struggling to avoid a moral trap when they are actually in a conceptual trap. We are not suggesting that all behavior is learned, nor is Baer. In this case, however, having presented us with a picture of behavior learned via a haphazard but nonetheless effective shaping procedure, Baer proceeds to conclude that we must get rid of the learned behavior. Certainly we would agree. He suggests, however, that the behavior be reduced via an aversive procedure such as shock.

The question then becomes: Why should one come to such a conclusion based on the facts presented? In fact, a valid conclusion might be that having shaped up an overt, observable and measurable behavior, we could reverse this process and shape out the behavior. Certainly there are no data to suggest the contrary in either the animal or human literature. In fact, any operant psychology student ever confronted with a Barnaby box learned the importance of shaping out behaviors.

In our book *Alternatives to Punishment* (LaVigna & Donnellan, 1986), we speculate that the tendency to assume that punishment is necessary is a myth supported by a number of factors, including: a) a predisposition to punish (i.e., aggress against) that which offends (i.e., punishes) us; b) our social learning experiences in childhood; and c) our professional training. That is, there are any number of studies demonstrating punishment elicited aggression. Moreover, many of us raised in our culture were punished as children (spare the rod). Finally, as Guess, elsewhere in the volume, and others have suggested, the preponderance of aversive procedures in the behavior reduction literature alone (see reviews in Cataldo, 1989; Clark, 1987; Lennox, Miltenberger, Spengler, & Erfanian, 1988), and the widespread dissemination of these procedures, have made their own contribution to the belief that punishment is necessary to reduce behavior.

Whatever the cause, we find the position that punishment/aversives are necessary to be one that is conceptually untenable. Why would an operant that is demonstrably changeable by one set of stimulus events (aversive events) not be equally changeable by another set of stimulus events (reinforcing events)? In fact, essentially every behavior that has been modified with punishment/aversive events also has been modified with reinforcing events, as two recent reviews make clear (Carr, Taylor, Carlson, & Robinson, 1989; Cataldo, 1989). Topography of the behavior should not make the difference. We submit that in the operant model as presented in Fig. 1, the relevant variables affecting results have more to do with the contingencies, conditions, and conditioning history affecting the events than with the topography of the behavior or even the nature of the stimuli.

Hutchinson (1977) describes a number of experiments with humans and animals that show the intricacies of these issues. In one set of experiments, for example, previous experience with noncontingent shock caused the contingent presentation of shock to increase the behavior. Similar results have been reported by others

EVENT		**CONDITIONS/ CONTINGENCIES***		**RESULTS**
Reinforcing	+	Functionally analyzed controlled and monitored	=	Behavior change
Aversive	+	Functionally analyzed controlled and monitored	=	Behavior change

*These may not be known or under experimentor's control

Figure 1: Operant Model

(Morse, Mead, & Kelleher, 1967; Stretch, Orloff, & Dalrymple, 1968) and, as Hutchinson reminds us:

> "...have served as the evidential base for a theoretical position that electric shock and other aversive stimuli can serve as positive reinforcer-like events, depending upon the schedule of presentation of such events" (p.429).

Our point is not to question that punishment /aversives can have dramatic effects on behavior, but to offer a reminder that these effects can differ widely, depending on previous history and stimulus-response contingency relationships. Basic texts caution us that, in order to be effective, stimuli must be chosen carefully to address the presenting conditions. A loud tower clock is certainly a stimulus event under the proper conditions - likely aversive if it is too close by, likely reinforcing if it signals the successful end of a difficult task, and very likely neutral if it is thousands of miles away on the River Thames. Our example is perhaps self-evident. Why should it not be as self-evident that a demonstration of behavior change brought about by squirting ice water in a child's face provides considerable evidence that the behavior also could have been reduced by using positive contingencies? Moreover, it should suggest that any previously tried positive attempts were unsuccessful because the reinforcing events were not presented in a manner that was sufficiently reinforcing under the presenting conditions. We describe elsewhere, for example, the importance of setting the proper interval for a DRO schedule to meet individual conditions, decision rules for choosing an "incompatible behavior" in an ALT-R or DRI program by applying the "100% Rule" (see discussion below), and providing feedback to the client which considers the person's cognitive and communicative ability (Donnellan, LaVigna, Negri-Shoultz, & Fassbender, 1988; LaVigna & Donnellan, 1986). Attention to this level of detail often makes the difference between success and failure of a procedure or set of procedures. Certainly Lovaas & Favell (1987) call for attention to this level of detail when using aversive/punishment procedures.

Too often, however, similar cautions are not offered to those attempting positive interventions. In fact, "procedural decay" (see Chapter 11 by Guess) can be found in the literature on nonaversives as well as in practice. Recently, after reviewing the literature on nonaversive technology for an NIH "consensus conference," Carr et al. (1989) suggested the following:

> In DRI, an alternative behavior is chosen that is physically incompatible with the problem behavior. For example, if a young boy is observed to slap himself in the face repeatedly, one may teach him to draw pictures on a piece of paper. As long as both of his hands are in contact with the paper and the crayon is being moved across the surface of the paper, the child receives reinforcement on an intermittent basis. It is obvious from this example that the behavior of drawing pictures is physically incompatible with face-slapping; *therefore, increases in the frequency of drawing will necessarily produce decreases in the frequency of self-injury* (p.6, emphasis added).

The example is good in that it stresses the need to choose a behavior that is truly incompatible with the target behavior. However, the conclusion, a common one, is faulty. The behavior of drawing pictures and that of face slapping cannot be defined as the universe of possibilities and, therefore, an increase of one will not necessarily result in a decrease of the other. If the behaviors are natural opposites or can be defined to meet the 100% rule (Donnellan et al., 1988; LaVigna and Donnellan, 1986), then the conclusion would be correct. For example, increasing in-seat behavior will necessarily, by definition, decrease out-of-seat behavior; increasing the proportion of events we define as "compliance" will necessarily decrease the proportion of "non-compliant" events. Unfortunately, few behaviors can be so defined. Rather, as in the example by Carr et al., the intervention may decrease waving, scratching, tapping, touching, throwing, and many other behaviors in the boy's repertoire, each with its own reinforcement history. That is, the reinforcement may be effective in increasing drawing, but the target behavior may be unaffected. Some would then draw the erroneous conclusion that positive reinforcement did not work. This common error will be even more widespread if the decay continues as it does in the statement of the NIH consensus panel (NIH 1989) which drew the following conclusion from Carr et al.'s example:

> In DRI an alternative behavior is chosen that is physically incompatible with the problem behavior; *increasing the frequency of this incompatible behavior will necessarily produce a decrease in the undesirable behavior.* (p. 12, emphasis added).

There are many other parameters to be considered in using DRI or any other procedure effectively (LaVigna and Donnellan, 1986). Moreover, even the most carefully designed intervention is not guaranteed to bring about the hoped for change. But, if well designed and carefully executed, even if unsuccessful, such a procedure may provide critical information about what other positive strategies to try (Willis, LaVigna, & Donnellan, 1989).

To assume instead that a treatment failure is a function of the ineffectiveness of reinforcement per se (thereby necessitating a punishment procedure) makes little or no sense. "Positive reinforcement cannot not work" (P. Touchette, Personal Communication, Jan. 13, 1986). Yet most of the recent behavior reduction studies based on punishment/aversive procedures state that positive procedures were tried first in accordance with the notion of the least restrictive means (Martin, 1979, 1981) required by law or regulation. Typically, there is no explanation given for the failure; rather, it is simply stated as part of the rationale for using the punishment.

There is no intent here to judge morally the researchers/practitioners who use punishment/aversives because "nothing else worked." No one has a corner on values in this discussion. Our intent here is to question the logic and practice behind such claims because the issues are so important to the lives of thousands of dependent clients. Instead of saying "positive reinforcement doesn't work," we might say instead, paraphrasing Lord Chesterton, "It's not that positive procedures were tried and found wanting but that they have not been sufficiently tried."

Sometimes, as we note in our model in Fig. 1, the relevant conditions for success of a given procedure are unknown to, or not under the control of, the researcher or the practitioner. Perhaps the authors of research articles could be encouraged to state just that and even to speculate on what went wrong in such an event. This approach to scientific reporting likely would be more helpful to the professional community and at least not contribute further to the mythology about the necessity for punishment. Such clarity certainly would be more in line with Sidman's (1989) position on the topic:

> Mistakes, a temporary lack of relevant information, or an occasional emergency may justify punishment as a treatment of last resort, but never as the treatment of choice. To use punishment occasionally as an act of desperation is not the same as advocating the use of punishment as a principle of behavior management (p.7).

A recent case exemplifies the need to demythologize punishment. A state level external review team was asked to approve the use of a shock self-generating device for an adult woman, "Jayne," living in a state institution. Jayne had learned to display dangerous self-injurious behaviors and aggression. The rationale for the request for the shock device was twofold. One, all positive alternatives had been tried unsuccessfully. Two, previous attempts at controlling the behavior with shock also had met with minimal success. In the case of the failure of shock, however, the shock was said not to have worked because of problems of staff consistency, reliability, etc., all problems that would be controlled if they were allowed to use the device. Clearly, staff held a belief that shock always would be an effective intervention if they could get the conditions right. No such review of the failure of positive alternatives was made. As is so often the case, staff had no similar belief system about the power of positive interventions. Rather, they believed that "positive reinforcement doesn't work."

With a little probing and problem solving, it was learned that the only reinforcer available in the institution that had been found to work consistently for Jayne was the opportunity to stay in bed until ten o'clock each morning. This reinforcement option was rejected as too much of a burden for the institutional staff. How much pain and time and effort would have been saved if the professional literature had provided staff with clear and parsimonious explanations for the failure of a given positive procedure where the failure led someone to choose a punitive procedure! Of course advocates argue that Jayne has a right to be in an environment that allows her to sleep late and work afternoons if she so chooses, but that is not at issue here. At least, we now can understand the logic of the position of staff better than their original claim that punishment was necessary because all positive options failed. In fact, staff now are helping to pursue a course aimed at moving Jayne back into the community because they say she "can't make it in the institution." The mythology about institutions that lies behind that comment will have to await another paper.

One of the conditions sustaining the myth about the necessity for punishment/aversives is lack of familiarity with the wide variety of options that have been used successfully to address challenging behaviors. Instead, practitioners are left with the notion that a trial of what one knows (usually DRO or DRI) is sufficient and then one shifts to punishment. We have long noted, with considerable dismay, that staff misinterpret the power of punishment precisely because of the emphasis put on the rights of individuals who will be subject to such punishment (see discussion later in this chapter). For example, in Minnesota, which has had long-standing regulations limiting the use of punishment/aversive procedures, administrators have been required to demonstrate that their staff are qualified to use these procedures (Minnesota Dept. of Human Services Rule 9515.2700-9525.2810). However, there is no similar requirement that staff know about and demonstrate their ability to use positive procedures.

We recently reviewed the life situations and treatment of three Minnesota state hospital clients who had been subjected to many years of aversive interventions. We found numerous notes about inservices on aversives, restraints, etc., and absolutely no indication of inservices on positive alternatives, programming, etc., (Donnellan & Negri-Shoultz, 1986). Thus, staff are left with the impression that positive interventions are not very important or very powerful, or that they are very difficult to implement successfully. Furthermore, because of additional training, they have higher status as one qualified to use the really powerful techniques - the aversives. Typically, there is no equivalent improvement in status for using reinforcement effectively.

Our own review of the literature on nonaversive interventions revealed that there are a dozen or more positive strategies that can be used to effectively eliminate problem behavior without punishment (LaVigna & Donnellan, 1986). These include ecological manipulations, positive programming (LaVigna, Willis and Donnellan, 1989), the differential reinforcement of other behavior (DRO), the differential reinforcement of low rates of responding (DRL), the differential reinforcement of alternative responses (Alt-R) including incompatible responses (DRI), stimulus control, instructional control, shaping, etc., and, perhaps most importantly, the combining of these procedures into comprehensive, individualized and multielement treatment plans (LaVigna and Donnellan, 1988; LaVigna et al., 1989).

However, often we find they are effective even in isolation and even for very severe problems if carefully designed. An example is our recent use of a fairly simple DRO procedure with an 11-year old with autism who broke windows and glass with his forehead. His mother came to us at a TASH meeting in desperation. A week earlier, her boy had broken an entire parking lot full of windshields, headlights and windows and she was faced with several lawsuits as well as an injured child. In problem solving with her, this mom realized that, like Baer's (1970) example of a child pulling his ear off, her son was getting more attention for his problem behavior than any of his other attention-seeking strategies. Always hesitant to do consultations at a distance, we nevertheless made a few suggestions because of the desperate nature of the situation. By problem solving with her, we helped her design a very simple DRO-Progressive schedule with the attention to reinforcement and reinforcement intervals that we have found to be critical in using DRO (see Donnellan et al., 1988; LaVigna &

Donnellan, 1986, for further discussion of DRO-Progressive strategies). His behavior occurred about three times a week or about every other day. Assuming that this rate continued, a reinforcement interval of 50% of the interresponse time (IRT) would at least allow him a 50% chance of reinforcement. Accordingly, his mom paid him off with increasing muliples of pictures of pizza slices each day that he went without breaking glass with his forehead. Day 1 he received one picture of a pizza slice; day 2, two pictures of slices; Day 3, three pictures, and then three pictures each day until he had enough for a large pie at Pizza Hut. If he broke glass, he received no picture and he was "recycled"; i.e., he started the following day at one picture of a slice of pizza. With this simple procedure and some changes in her general level of attention to him, his mother brought the behavior under control and has had no further incidences of window smashing in over 30 months of follow-up.

This experience points to another fallacy about punishment which is as ubiquitous as it is dangerous. It is rather a corollary of Myth #1 (that is, if myths can have corollaries), which suggests that nonaversive strategies only work for minor behavior problems, for really severe behavior problems, punishment is essential. Additionally, the more severe the problem, the more intrusive the intervention will have to be. Myth #1 on the necessity for punishment/aversives and this corollary form a major part of "The Myth Model of Aversive Control" as illustrated in Figure 2.

This mythology may partially account for the findings of Spreat, Lipinski, Dickerson, Nass, and Dorsey, (1989). They used vignettes to assess factors associated with the acceptability of contingent shock and found that the mental retardation professionals rated the procedure more appropriate where the behavior was (a) a serious problem, (b) occurred frequently, and (c) had been unresponsive to less

EVENT		CONDITIONS/ CONTINGENCIES		RESULTS
Reinforcing[1]	+	Randomly arranged for limited time	=	Minor behavior change--perhaps
Aversive[2]	+	Carefully controlled constantly adjusted	=	Behavior change-guaranteed

[1]Only for minor problems
[2]Essential for serious problems

Figure 2: Myth Model of Aversive Control

intrusive methods of therapy. Spreat and his colleagues suggested that their study provided evidence that practitioners do not support the TASH position against aversives that was noted earlier. Another way of understanding these results is that the respondents may have been confused about the need for, and value of, shock and other highly intrusive interventions because of their training which was based on the aversive literature from the early days of applied behavior analysis (Guess, Chapter 11). That is, the mythology concerning the need for aversive intervention in serious cases may have been fueled by the preponderance and proliferation of studies using highly intrusive interventions to produce dramatic suppressive effects on high-rate behaviors, such as self-stimulation and severe injurious behavior. Failures are not typically reported (Cataldo, 1989). Returning to an earlier point, it is interesting to note that animal journals tend to publish studies about effects in whichever direction they go. Applied journals typically do not publish articles showing that a person worsened because of a treatment failure. Perhaps this helps account for the absence of mythology of punishment in the animal literature.

Guess and his colleagues (Guess, Chapter 11; Guess, Helmstetter, Turnbull, & Knowlton, 1987) have suggested that these early studies had at least as much to do with empirically validating the functional relationship between isolated variables as they had with demonstrating any long-term benefit to the subject. Thus, as important as some of these early studies were, we must note that little or no attention was paid to functional analysis or to maintenance or generalization. In their follow-up of the early work on overcorrection, Foxx and Livesay (1984), for example, commented that the suppressive effects typically disappeared as the researchers left the setting. However intermittent and transient their success, the dramatic suppression must have been highly reinforcing to the researchers because such studies proliferated and formed the basis of much of the technology promulgated over the last 25 years in textbooks and workshops (see Guess, Chapter 11). Methodological or clinical weakness of those studies aside, in the aggregate, the sheer numbers fallaciously suggest that punishment/aversive procedures are essential for some very difficult and high-rate behaviors (Cataldo, 1989).

Ironically, the notion of the "least intrusive intervention" also may have contributed to the myth about the need for punishment with difficult problems. Derived from the legal notion of the "least drastic means" test, it addresses the need to strike a balance between the good that the state seeks to affect and the level of intrusiveness that may be justified to bring about the effect (see Martin, 1979, for a review of this issue). As applied to medical intervention and combined with Hippocrates' "first do no harm," this test has been used often to judge the validity of medical interventions in the context of the standards of a given time and place. Many have sought to use a similar model to judge behavioral interventions, and, to a limited extent, it has worked (see LaVigna & Donnellan, 1986). Today, human rights review panels would be unlikely to allow the use of a highly intrusive intervention to produce a minor effect. No longer do we find studies using shock to teach color discrimination, for example, though some kinds of "procedural decay" are still rampant in practice (Guess, Chapter 11). With some exceptions, in the recent literature and debates, shock and other highly intrusive interventions are reserved for situations in which the behavior under discussion is dramatic and dangerous and/or very high rate. This result is misinterpreted to mean that the powerful interventions are necessary for the major problems. Then the fact that review teams require evidence of "failure" of nonaversive or less aversive interventions before aversive interventions are tried seems to give added support to the notion that the power is in the aversives and it may be this notion that Spreat et al.'s (1989) study inadvertently tapped.

Our intention is not to criticize efforts to protect human subjects. We applaud any such effort. In fact, we spent years trying, naively and unsuccessfully, to help states develop regulations for the use of aversive procedures (see LaVigna & Donnellan, 1986). Unfortunately, these well-intentioned efforts have helped produce an unanticipated effect: The idea of a continuum of intrusiveness ("aversiveness") inherent in the "least intrusive means" has come to be equated with a notion of a continuum of effectiveness. There is belief that sounds something like: "...we know procedure X (usually shock) will work but the ethics of the situation require that the behavior must be bad enough to justify X and that we must try other weaker procedures first." (See earlier discussion regarding Baer's hypothetical example.) As a result, once started on the continuum of aversiveness, the tendency is to try more and more aversives, or more reliable equipment to deliver the aversives (Iwata, 1986). Only rarely do researchers or practitioners shift from aversives to nonaversives. Instead, the Myth Model results in a situation such as that which we found in the Minnesota review mentioned earlier (Donnellan & Negri-Shoultz, 1986), as depicted in Fig. 3.

Confronted with a behavior problem, conscientious professionals try a positive approach. If it works, they try it or a similar approach with other clients and problems. Sometimes these positive ap-

Results of Myth Model

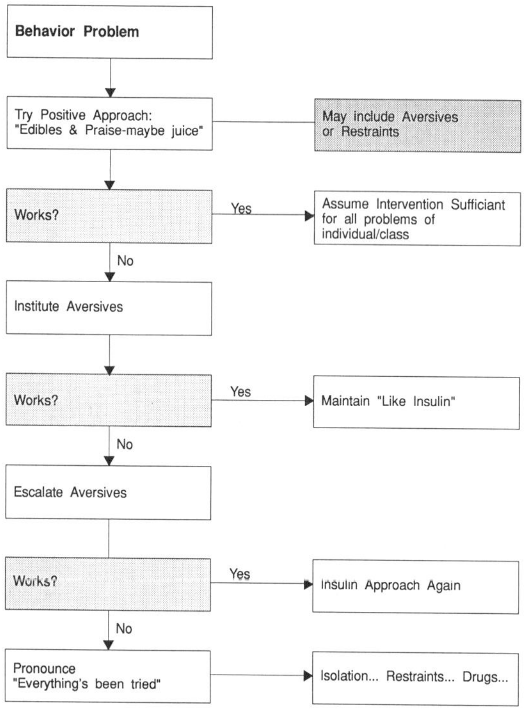

Figure 3: Results of Myth Model

proaches do not work because staff have not been taught adequately to assess individual situations and design the multi-element interventions that may be required (Carr et al., 1989; LaVigna et al., 1989). They often make innocent but important errors. Furthermore, even skilled staff may not have access to, or control over, the relevant variables. When the positive approach fails, they shift to aversives. If these suppress the behavior, they are considered successful even if the effects do not generalize or show durability. For Minnesota client MU, a DRO procedure had been tried and discontinued after four days despite the fact that his behavior had started to show a decrease. It was not rapid enough, apparently. He then was placed on a contingent electric shock program in which someone had to be with him with the shock stick virtually 24 hours per day. At the time of our review, the shock program had been in effect for three years and he was being shocked about 100 times a day. The behavioral scientist consultant and staff agreed that 100 shocks per day was tolerable: "It's like insulin...something he will need for the rest of his life" (Donnellan & Negri-Shoultz, 1986, p.V-MU26). It appears that the "continuum of intrusiveness" can become not only a "continuum of effectiveness," but also a "continuum of need" regardless of whether or not the intrusive procedures have the desired results. In a second case, eight months of shock failed to control the SIB of another client, EB. The consultant said it would take a different piece of shock equipment, one with a higher voltage. Staff refused so they went to the next step on the continuum, restraint and medication. At the time of our review, EB was in essentially 24-hour restraint, with a staff person having to be with him the entire time (see Fig. 3). The third client, LS, is illustrative of what can happen next if practitioners are committed to the notion that the continuum is one of intrusiveness/effectiveness. None of a wide variety of aversives had had any significant effect on her behavior. She was given considerable medication and restraint. Finally, just before our review, a psychiatric consultant had decreed she would benefit from:

> ...a highly structured small living situation (1:1) so she can receive attention and care, including aversive conditioning....If [aversive intervention] should fail, further psychiatric intervention such as ECT and perhaps psychosurgery should be attempted (Donnellan & Negri-Shoultz, 1986, p.V-LS 24-25).

Nowhere in our review of the years of interventions for these three clients were we able to find evidence of serious consideration of nonaversive interventions to be used when aversives failed. Yet, if our field followed the Operant Model (Fig. 1) rather than the Myth Model (Fig. 2), we would have about as many examples of people trying nonaversives after the failure of aversives as the reverse. Instead, these are fairly rare and fairly recent. Some notable recent exceptions include LaVigna, (1988) and Berkman and Meyer (1988). Touchette's 1983 study was an early exception. He investigated the effectiveness of a positive procedure on the self-biting of a severely handicapped adolescent boy. This longstanding problem was so serious that reconstructive surgery was required to replace the veins he had bitten out of his shoulder with his own teeth.

Touchette attempted to identify situations in which this problem behavior did not occur. These were very few, but included periods when no demands were being placed on the boy to engage in any activities and when he had free access to his favorite foods. The problem came under rapid control by scheduling continuous sessions that had these characteristics. By gradually introducing activity requirements and controlled access to food over several months of treatment, the student eventually was able to participate in a normal day without biting himself. His behavior maintained over years of follow-up.

Myth #2: Punishment is more effective.

Touchette's report is doubly important because it challenges a second myth of punishment; i.e., even if positive alternatives are effective, *punishment is more effective in eliminating behavior problems*. Touchette reported that several punishment procedures, including contingent electrical shock, previously had been tried by others without success. In this case, punishment did not work while a positive alternative did.

Beyond the speed and degree of effects on future occurrence, effectiveness is measured in many ways. These include the extent to which the results carry over to situations and settings where treatment is not taking place (generalization). In addition, effectiveness is measured by the extent to which results continue after treatment is terminated (maintenance and durability) and the extent to which there are negative and positive side effects. Finally, social and clinical validity must be considered. Individuals on both sides of the debate on the use of aversives generally agree on the importance of these measures of effectiveness (Favell et al., 1982; LaVigna et al., in preparation), though adequate measures of these outcomes are scarce in the literature (Carr et al., 1989; Clark, 1987; Guess, Chapter 11).

Against these criteria, an unbiased review of the literature could conclude that an empirical case can be made against punishment (Donnellan and LaVigna, 1988; LaVigna, 1987; LaVigna et al., in preparation). The contingent presentation of an aversive stimulus or event may result in the rapid and significant suppression of a response, but not necessarily (e.g., Romanczyk, & Goren, 1975; Jones, Simmons & Frankel, 1974). Further, the lack of durability (Foxx & Livesay, 1984), poor generalization (e.g., Corte, Wolf, & Locke, 1971; Singh, Dawson, & Gregory, 1980), negative side effects (Azrin, Hake, & Hutchinson, 1965; Ulrich & Favell, 1970), and questionable social validity (Elliott, Witt, Galvin, & Peterson, 1984; Kazdin, 1980; Witt & Elliott, 1985) seriously limit the effectiveness of punishment, particularly for purposes of social and community integration (LaVigna et al., in preparation).

There is general agreement in the field that research and treatment should address this full range of outcome requirements and not just speed and degree of effects. This suggests the need for multielement treatment "packages" to produce fully satisfactory results, but where each element can only address a limited subset of the desired outcomes. For example, stimulus control (Touchette, 1983; Touchette, MacDonald, & Langer, 1985) and stimulus satiation (Rast, Johnston,

Drum, & Conrin, 1981) can produce rapid and total control, and may even preclude the occurrence of targeted behavior, while durable and generalized effects with good social and clinical validity can be addressed through ecological manipulations (Rhodes, 1967) and positive programming (LaVigna et al., 1989). By avoiding the inclusion of aversive elements, we believe negative side effects can be minimized and treatment procedures will be acceptable; i.e., socially valid, allowing the generalization of treatment for social and community integration. Such nonaversive, multielement treatment packages are showing promise in solving even the most difficult problems (Donnellan, LaVigna, Zambito, & Thvedt, 1985) and are rendering the use of punishment unnecessary and, in many ways, counterproductive (Berkman & Meyer, 1988; LaVigna, 1988).

Myth #3: Punishment is easier.

With mounting evidence that punishment is not necessary and not so effective as reinforcement, and despite the increasing number of administrative regulations that require training when punishment is to be used, there exists a myth that *punishment is easier* or simpler to use. In the case of EB in Minnesota, for example, the consultant said he was recommending the higher voltage shock machine because there were only 10 people in America who could work with EB without using aversives. If one is only concerned with the retributional use of punishment, which has the retaliatory goal of visiting pain and/or loss on the offending person, then in that sense we agree with Baer's (1970) article in which he went on to warn about the problems of employing punishment:

> One of the delights of moralistic argument, I am discovering, is the ease with which it can be extended in all direction. Let me now warn us against punishment.
>
> Punishment works, I submit. There is too much affirmative, careful demonstration to resist that conclusion. Consequently, punishers should succeed often in eliminating the behavior they mean to eliminate. That may reinforce them, which is to say, their rate of using punishment in the future and in more diverse situations will rise. Contributing to that tendency is the extreme simplicity of punishment technique and technology. Anyone with a hand to swing is equipped with a punishing device. (p. 247).

Of course, punishment is not always simple if the purpose is durable therapy or rehabilitation. Rather, as noted earlier, to "work" as Baer (1970) would want it to, even within a limited framework of effectiveness, punishment must be carried out with exacting precision and consistency. This conclusion is shared by many prominent researchers who have studied punishment as it is applied to the solution of human behavior problems (e.g., Lovaas & Favell, 1987). These methodological requirements are rigorous and demanding in their own right. In addition, however, administrative safeguards, which protect client's rights, and oversight and monitoring, which many believe are necessary to prevent abuse, are mandated now in most educational and clinical settings. When we combine these administrative requirements with rigorous methodological requirements, punishment turns out to be *significantly* more difficult for the practitioner than the increasingly available alternatives (see, for example, Foxx, McMorrow, Bittle, & Bechtel, 1986).

Moreover, while we have argued earlier that the successful use of nonaversive procedures also require precision and care, we have demonstrated that these procedures can be taught to and carried out by naive staff (Donnellan, LaVigna, Schuler, & Woodward, 1982). In one case, we worked with teachers in a setting in which punishment procedures traditionally would be used (Donnellan & LaVigna, 1986). Instead, positive procedures were used exclusively to modify the classroom behavior problems of five adolescent students with autism or a similar handicapping condition. Some of the behavior problems were severe enough to jeopardize the student's home placement. All the target behaviors either were eliminated or reduced to an acceptable level. When the positive procedures were gradually withdrawn or discontinued, the behaviors did not return nor did there appear to be a substitution of other problems.

While punishment may be only easier in the retributional sense or in the short run, this apparent simplicity has likely resulted in the reinforcement of the practitioner/researcher's use of punishment, as Baer predicted almost 20 years ago. The increased use of aversives in more diverse situations (Guess, Chapter 11), in turn, has contributed to the perpetuation of the punishment mythology.

Other Myths:

We have addressed a few myths about punishment; there are many others. Some have turned the continuum of intrusiveness into a continuum of need that is determined not only by the topography of the behavior, but also by the nature of the subject population. Specifically, this myth suggests that individuals with certain developmental disabilities *need* aversives because of their significant impairments. Schroeder, Rojahn, and Oldenquist (1989), for example, dismiss what they call the reciprocity argument, "The Golden Rule" for individuals labelled profoundly retarded because of this need:

> A person with a profound disability can be assumed to object to physical restraint or aversive treatment for destructive and self-injurious behavior; he or she may even think it cruel, if capable of that concept....But suppose we ask, "How would you like it done to you?" The question is easily rejected if you are not disabled and have no need for aversive treatment (e.g., if you are an alcoholic or a criminal, who is rational and hence can respond to very different techniques) (pp.53-54).

This particular myth probably also grows out of the historical overuse of aversive interventions on people with profound disabilities in institutions (Cataldo, 1989; Guess, Chapter 11; Guess et al., 1987). It tends to evaporate when one points out that the most complex schedules of reinforcement and the very principles of operant conditioning were first clearly demonstrated on inra-human subjects who, though not rational, could respond to a wide variety of positive techniques. In the laboratory, we learned: "There are no dumb pigeons, only dumb shapers." Thus, it may not be the subject who *needs* aversives. Moreover, as noted earlier, the literature demonstrates that neither the nature of the disabling condition nor the topography of the behavior appears to be the critical variables in determining which intervention will be successful (Carr et al., 1989).

Another myth is that aversives are rapid while nonaversive procedures are slow. The NIH-supported consensus panel, mentioned earlier, seems to draw on this mythology to support what they call "behavior reduction procedures" - curiously defined to include only aversive procedures:

> Behavior reduction procedures should be selected for their rapid effectiveness only if the exigencies of the clinical situations require transient use of such restrictive interventions and *only* after appropriate review and informed consent are ensured (pp. 25-26).

In fact, Carr et al. (1989), in their paper for the same panel, pointed out that

Guess et al.'s (1987) extensive review showed aversive procedures took an average of 15 hours per subject to suppress aggression and 0.9 hours to suppress self-injury. Of course, under some conditions, aversives can produce rapid effects. Also, of course, under some conditions, so can nonaversives (e.g., Deitz, Repp, & Deitz, 1976; Touchette, 1983) and so can neutral stimuli, (Hutchinson, 1977). Perhaps our efforts would be more fruitful if put toward the identification of conditions that maximize the efficacy of nonaversive interventions rather than continuing the mythology that aversives have some absolute measure of superiority.

WHY DO WE HAVE MYTHS?

There are other myths and correlated misunderstandings. For example, the myth that punishers are necessary to reduce behavior problems in order for the individual to be "ready" for other learning (Cataldo, 1989; Iwata, 1986) has not been addressed here. Still, the reader might be tempted to argue, either from a particular study or experience one or the other of the points that we have raised relative to these myths. We then would bring up further points and the argument could go on indefinitely. Instead, we will explore why myths exist in this field of applied behavior analysis, a field so committed to objectivity and science.

We can begin by agreeing that, though our science has made great contributions to our knowledge, we each can and, in fact, often must extrapolate beyond the limited hard data available to us to try to understand the diverse and complex phenomena with which we deal. Certainly Cataldo (1988) appears to be expressing this notion:

> Not all policy and practice can be based on what we know, because there is much we do not know. However, we must avoid policy and practice that is contrary to what we know, and we should not justify policy and practice on knowledge that does not exist (p. 106).

If we agree in principle, then we can begin to address the quintessential myth that behavioral psychology is atheoretical, a purely objective science unencumbered by value positions or assumptions. Azrin clearly represented this value-free notion when he told a panel discussion on aversives that he did not deal with the ethical and other value issues: "I'm a scientist, I just follow the data" (Azrin, 1987). For discussion purposes, we take the position that this is impossible; that one cannot operate without some theory or value, not theory in the colloquial sense of an unproven notion, of course, but

> "...rules and standards that orient and set boundaries for problems and interpretations made in research. In this sense, theory is a name for practices that prescribe what topics are important and what phenomena will be accepted as data for inquiry into those topics. Theories give shape to what researchers think, talk about and feel "(Popkewitz & St. Maurice, in press, p. 2).

In a similar vein, Krasner and Houts (1984) offered the following definition of values:

> We include under the term values not only the everyday meaning of cherished personal and sociocultural norms but also the shared assumptions that communities of scientists make and use to guide their investigations (p. 840).

Both sets of authors deny the value neutrality of science. But the early behaviorists, disillusioned with the nonscientific approach of most psychological theory, adopted this logical positivistic philosophy which posited an atheoretical, value-free approach to science. We present-day behaviorists grew up in that tradition. According to Krasner and Houts (1984), in such an approach,

> ...classical meta-ethical questions such as what norms and standards are of value were judged unanswerable because what is knowable consists of what is given as "raw data" in observation. Under this analysis, ethics was relegated to the meaningless ...The result of this analysis of science was to sharpen the fact-value distinction, leaving ethics and values to unscientific, speculative philosophers, and bolstering the claim that science and "scientific" philosophy remain value neutral (p. 841).

Historically, our literature offers many examples to support the analysis of Krasner and Houts. Early on, Baer (1970) built his case for the selective use of punishment around the dichotomy:

> I have only a few points to mention here, and they are essentially moralistic rather than scientific points. Moralistic points are typically brief, perhaps because they require no experimental design.
>
> I have suggested that we know what we can demonstrate. I have also suggested that we *think* we know that punishment is inherently a bad technique for accomplishing desirable behavioral changes....If there is a moral point here, it is the one familiar to all scientists and practitioners alike: we had better get what we know in line with what we can demonstrate (p.244).

Baer first makes a clear distinction between the moral and scientific issues. He then goes on to describe the hypothetical situation excerpted earlier and to draw conclusions that curiously ignore the "data" created and demonstrated. He does this while warning us not to let our moral stand affect our scientific judgment lest we fall into a moral trap. In fact, Baer seems to be taking a moral position that says punishment ought to be available to those who need it. He develops a case about shaping self-abuse which he believes has not been (and should not be) demonstrated in the literature; thus, at least as he defines knowledge, he doesn't "know" what to do. Therefore, he must make judgments based on some value (that treatment not be withheld), some unproven assumptions (that shock works), or something other than what he would likely define as complete and hard data. He then extrapolates from the portion of the scientific data that supports his moral judgment and also happens to support the mythology of the necessity of punishment. He ignores the "scientific data" which he created and by which he "demonstrated" that the ear pulling was shaped by attention and "forgets" that there is evidence that it, therefore, might be readily amenable to a new, controlled, alternative shaping procedure.

Obviously, the intent here is not to impugn Baer. On the contrary, the point is that if this kind of interplay of science and values, of fact and mythology, can be displayed by someone with his brilliance and dedication to scientific rigor, in fact, it cannot be escaped. Noted scientist and scientific historian James Gleick (1989) suggests that the very notion that science deals only with facts, based on data, is itself a myth:

> A myth about science suggests that new theories arise when they are necessary to explain new facts. The messy and more interesting reality is that "facts" themselves tend to depend on the theories of the fact finders (p. 41).

We all might reconsider the position that the work we are engaged in is a value-free, atheoretical, pure scientific endeavor. This position, belief or wish, blinds us to the reality and prevents us from using our cognitive judgment in the management of our inescapable value biases.

Unfortunately, the position that values are separate from data in science continues to dominate discussion on the use of aversives with dependent populations. Cataldo's (1989) review of the literature for the NIH consensus conference begins by restating the science-ethics/values dichotomy:

> Frequently with the advancement of knowledge and technology comes debate, disagreement and controversy over how, or if, such advancements should be used...For example,...antiseptic procedures...If viewed in this context, the controversy over the use of some forms of behavioral interventions for destructive behaviors of those with developmental disabilities could be approached in a manner similar to other previous and contemporary ethical dilemmas resulting from advances in science--*namely by the careful review of the existing data by competent scientists followed by the careful formation of policy on applications of that knowledge base with input by other scholars, ethicists, and advocates for the targeted treatment populations, and the like.* This paper contributes to a first step in this process by reviewing much of the existing data on the use of behavioral procedures to decrease destructive behaviors of persons with developmental disabilities (p. 1, emphasis added).

Cataldo suggests that he will be a neutral participant contributing to the discussion only the value-free scientific data. The very language he has chosen is the language of our science (APA Style Manual), a discourse pattern which conveys that scientists are neutral observers:

> "...stylistically objective-sounding, as if an impartial, neutral third person were "merely" pulling together, summarizing and interpreting the results of research from multiple sources (Popkewitz & St. Maurice, in press, p.6).

In fact, Cataldo here is not and, we are arguing, cannot be totally neutral. Values are revealed in the text. For example, the definition of the problem is "...the destructive behaviors of those with developmental disabilities." He has either so defined it or agreed to such a definition. The definition or choice of the problem is of critical importance, as the assumptions of the definition affect both the questions raised and the outcomes (see Gleick, 1989). An easy example is the common definition of a certain social phenomenon as "the problem of high school dropouts" which obscures the questions or answers obtainable if the problem is defined as: "the problem of the inability of high schools to retain their students." In the present instance, Cataldo could have defined the problem to be researched as "reactions of individuals with developmental disabilities to destructive experiences in their lives." In fact, Cataldo reports that most of the punishment studies come out of institutional settings; i.e., life situations that are documented as counterproductive to positive growth and development and likely help create aggression and other problematic behaviors (e.g., Blatt & Kaplan, 1966; Baer, 1970). Cataldo even suggests that the failure of a shock intervention reported in one instance might have been the result of the individual's remaining in the institution and using the behavior to control staff (p. 41). Another value position might have emphasized the limitations of research that ignores such a context or that proceeds without even a rudimentary functional analysis; that may have been trying to suppress an individual's sole means of dealing with an intolerable situation; that paid inadequate attention to the least intrusive means test and to developmental issues (Carr et al., 1989; Donnellan & Kilman,

1986; Guess, Chapter 11); or all of the above.

These issues were ill understood in the past. Thus, such an alternative analysis would be a critique, not a criticism of early researchers - an acknowledgement of the limited value of some of their results for understanding the behavior of individuals in such situations - which, in turn, might guide us to more fruitful research efforts in the future. Moreover, it is an acknowledgment of the biases that our point of view, historically, ethnically, and "fashionably" rooted, plays in our choice of the focus or problems chosen for study, and the inevitable consequences of this choice on the questions asked and the answers obtained. To ignore these issues in 1989 is to disregard the new information available, legitimize the outdated process that developed and disseminated these data, and leave the reader believing that science supports the old myths. To choose to ignore these issues and to ignore the myths is a value-based decision, not a value-free decision.

Similarly, Cataldo (1989) refers to these behavior reduction techniques that are central to the controversy as "advances in science." From other value positions, these would not be considered advances but techniques that are passe and inappropriate for community programming (e.g., LaVigna et al.,1989). In fact, there is very little that is new in the punishment literature except the shock apparatus that Cataldo himself helped develop and which many others consider a step backwards (see Iwata, 1988, for a discussion of this matter).

Our purpose here is not to suggest that Cataldo or anyone else writing on this topic necessarily adopt our values any more than we would suggest that they, or we, abandon the APA style of writing. We are merely pointing out that our science is inevitably value laden. Moreover, any style of discourse influences the way that we (and our audience) understand our data and our thoughts, and the way that we frame a question influences the answer. The APA style adds to the appearance of neutral, durable, and credible knowledge (see Popkewitz & St. Maurice, in press), and tends to negate the influence of our own values and assumptions. Yet, if everything we do is shaded by our experiences, our values, assumptions, and even myths, then the admission of such influence on our behavior will make for a better science.

To explore this issue, Krasner and Houts (1984) studied the value systems of behavioral psychologists. They first reviewed a number of articles which challenge the notion that scientific observation provides "theoretically neutral, objective knowledge," those which point to the "implausibility of objective observation" and those which demonstrated that "theory and assumptions logically precede observation." They concluded:

> Therefore, the fundamental assumption of objectivism is untenable, because it is neither physically nor philosophically possible to obtain knowledge without first choosing some assumptive framework....Though such assumptions are often tacitly held and subtly acquired in the socialization process of becoming a scientist, we believe it is fruitful to think of them as decisions that the scientist makes. As choices among an array of available assumptions, none of which has prior claim to "truth," discipline-specific assumptions function as value systems for the scientist. In this regard the epistemological status of scientific claims may be no less relativistic than the comparable status of value claims in philosophical ethics (p.841).

Krasner and Houts next looked for and found some significant differences in the value systems of behaviorists and other psychologists. For example, behaviorists endorsed a factual, quantitative, empirical and objectivist approach to the study of human behavior, but separated their beliefs about their discipline from other beliefs they held. Krasner and Houts commented:

> If, as our case study suggests, psychology as a science is not value free, then it is incumbent upon us as scientists to continue the systematic investigation of the relationship between our values and our research.... It is both propitious and pragmatic that such a science of scientists should begin with psychologists, scientists whose discipline requires them to be at once subject and object of their own research (p. 848).

As behaviorists, we agree. If we do not scrutinize our own behavior, we are likely to continue to perpetuate the myths that get in the way of our science, our practice and, perhaps most important, our discourse.

Earlier, we defined myths as beliefs given uncritical acceptance by a group. Campbell (1988) suggests further that myths may be the link to that group or society: "If you want to find your own mythology, the key is with what society do you associate" (p.22). Though we are dedicated to scientific inquiry, we, like our ancestors, are faced with more phenomena than we can explain. We develop an explanatory system, canons, rituals and so on to help us deal with the phenomena. We explain those we can, and those which we cannot remain mysteries. We say that mysteries ultimately can be known by following the canons of science and do not acknowledge the possible influence of these mysteries until we can make them predictable. In the meantime, if our experiences do not fit our data, we develop myths around them. If others do not adhere to our myths, if they challenge our relationship to our mysteries, they are outside our society. We describe them as being "non-scientists," of being merely advocates, if, for example, they challenge the validity of data collected in institutional settings with no clinical or social validity - especially if those settings are convenient for our data collection and those data support our myths. When our beliefs are seriously challenged, we draw together the inner circle of our society to present a united position. We close off debate, our arguments resting as much on authority and mythology as what we "know," and present in our specialized language to cover up what we cannot explain or defend. This is done, of course, under the rubric of science, but it looks more like the historical reactions of formalized religions. We dismiss advocates' concerns because their data do not fit our notion of science. If advocates cannot "prove" that good intervention begins with the kind of interesting, varied and supportive environments non-disabled people can access, for example, we dismiss them as unscientific speculation or misread their concerns (e.g., Cataldo, 1989, pp.50-51). In the meantime, we continue to publish data produced in highly aberrant environments in which none of us would want our own loved ones to be placed. We choose not to investigate the influence of these environments on the phenomena that we are studying, and so they remain mysteries. Like the old-time religion, we have a perfect explanatory system: If there is something that we (the believers in what we define as science) can't explain, it's a mystery; if you (the non-believer) can't explain it then it's heresy.

Perhaps the most damaging result of this kind of reaction to controversy is that, again like religious adherents, we begin to associate only with other adherents or to read or publish only that which supports our myths. Behavior of some individuals on both sides of the debate on aversives demonstrates this point. For example, some researchers who do fine work in developing nonaversive behavioral interventions refused to contribute papers to this book when invited to do so. On the other hand, people in leadership positions who believe aversives are necessary have published reports that obscure rather than elucidate the issues. The position paper of the task force on the right to effective treatment of the Association for Behavior Analysis (ABA) is a good example of how a scientific group, challenged on its basic and dearly held beliefs, begins to operate in ways more similar to religious hierarchies than a group dedicated to open scientific inquiry.

The task force report (Van Houten et al., 1988) is written in the neutral APA style as though it were a neutral, objective piece. However, every member of the task force has authored papers supporting the necessity for aversives with dependent populations. There are members of ABA who take dissenting positions and who have made significant contributions to the literature on effective, nonaversive behavior reduction strategies, but their positions are not represented. The task force report was published in at least two prominent scientific journals, a rather unusual action in itself. One of these is the *Journal of Applied Behavior Analysis* (JABA) which did not commission the report. The action editor who accepted it for publication is a co-author of the report, and the article was accepted 12 days after submission, leaving little or no opportunity for independent review or response.

Obviously, the report was intended for a wide audience of behavioral scientists and practitioners outside the disability community, but, curiously, it does little to elucidate the issues for those who might be unfamiliar with the present controversy. Nowhere is it mentioned that the "effective," "restrictive" treatments the report supports are likely aversive, for example, or that there is controversy over the fact that they are intended to be used on individuals with significant disabilities. The words "disabled" and "aversive" are never used, in fact, and so this information can only be gleaned by those readers who know already by the authors' other works; readers who understand their use of terms such as "functional skills," "therapeutic environment," "authorized proxy" or "quicker acting but temporarily more restrictive procedures," by readers who are aware that these authors have each written in support of the use of shock and other highly intrusive interventions on these populations; and by readers who know that these procedures are used almost exclusively on dependent and vulnerable populations. The term "effective treatment" is used throughout, although the procedures that they are defending typically do not meet the criteria for effectiveness that several of these same authors developed in an earlier paper (Favell et al., 1978). And, finally, the authors suggest that the practitioner be limited to those treatments which have been documented as successful in the literature but do not delineate for the readers the historical weaknesses of that literature and do not direct the reader to other works presenting an alternative opinion.

These authors likely intended for the publication of this paper to support deeply held values and beliefs, and there is much to be commended in their work. Despite the objective and scientific sounding language, however, they prepared a report that is unlikely to support objective scientific discourse or inquiry on a critical topic in our field. In fact, it does nothing so well as to support the status quo. It defends segregation and institutional placements, and the use of aversives within those placements, based on a mythology about the need for punishment and a need for such placements (Allen et al., 1989). Read in context, the report of the task force on the right to effective treatment seems less like a scientific paper than an encyclical. It is, in fact, not so different from *Malleus Maleficarum* (Kramer & Spranger, 1486/1971), outlining for the inquisition the procedural safeguards to assure that each accused heretic had an opportunity to respond to less intrusive means. The power to use pain was granted only to inquisitors who could get approval from the pope on the basis that no less intrusive method was effective in rooting out error. The pain to be inflicted was justified by the resulting good for the individual. (See O'Brien, 1990, for a discussion of the use of pain as a tool in professional work.)

Certainly, like the rest of us, Van Houten et al. (1988) are entitled to present their opinions and influence the opinion of others. But, in so doing, it is critical that we all separate out our myths, and that we heed the warning of Baer (1970) and get what we "know" in line with what we can "demonstrate." Then, when we must rely on our beliefs, our values and our myths, we can present them honestly and openly. To continue to ignore the effect of our beliefs on our own behavior puts both our clients and our field at risk.

As a case in point, we return to the review of the treatment of the Minnesota state hospital clients (Donnellan & Negri-Shoultz, 1986) which first brought us to the notion of the myth model of aversive control. As noted, our field has not found ways (or we have not chosen to find ways) to scientifically document the impact of institutional and other "aberrant" life experiences on the "destructive" behavior of the people we study and treat. From our review of the behavioral literature, these issues remain mysteries, as yet unexplained, and their influence has been mostly ignored or tacitly approved.

In such an institutional context, shock was used on two profoundly disabled men (see discussion above). For EB, staff refused to reinstitute shock at the level suggested by the prominent behavioral scientist. They worked instead with a community agency to place the man in a supported apartment after he had spent almost 50 years in an institution, the last few years in around-the-clock restraints. At the time of this writing, we were informed that 19 months after leaving the institution, without punishment but with some positive programs (LaVigna, Willis & Donnellan, 1989), including a communication system, a job, and a different environment, he remains out of restraints and with no SIB.

Client MU remains in the institution. No systematic carefully designed alternative program (beyond the four-day DRO attempt noted earlier) had been tried before the consultant wrote: "It is reasonable to try electric shock at this point because every alternative treatment option has been tried" (Donnellan & Negri-Shoultz, 1986, Section VMU, p. 10). Despite the success of EB's case, an additional three years has passed, for a total of six years, in which MU is still on the same unit and still on a shock program. To protect his "right to privacy," we were not able to obtain information on the present rate of shock. We do know that from their own data, as well as documentation in the literature (Bruel, Fielding, Joyce, Peters, & Weisler, 1982), that this young man historically has adapted to shock. Three years ago, when he was being shocked 100 times/day and the explanation was that "it's like insulin...something he will need the rest of his life." The prominent behavioral scientist, who apparently continues to supervise the shock program, expressed his concern in this manner: "...the literature will say it's not functioning as a punisher, why are you doing that?...What's bothering me is I am getting out of science." We agree. It's not science. It's mythology. And it appears that, as a function of the mythology, this young man has been on shock, restraint, and other punishments/aversives virtually every day for at least two-thirds of his life.

We agree, too, with Krasner and Houts' (1984) assessment about how to address the problem of sorting out the mythology. They suggest both further studies and the self-examination of the assumptions and values of groups of scientists. In particular, they stress the need to relate such assumptions to broader sociocultural and personal values in order to understand how the latter impact the goals of research and the influence of science on social planning and social policy. They add:

> "Only after such extensive research and critical self-examination will it be possible to demythologize the traditional view of science and develop the much needed integration of philosophy, history, sociology and the psychology of science" (p. 848).

It's a big job. From our openly value-laden perspective, we suggest that for the sake of those who may be victimized by our mythology, for the schism it is causing in our field, and for the negative impact it is having on the reputation of behavior analysis in general, we stop arguing about the "right to effective treatment" and get on with that job.

NOTE

The authors would like to acknowledge Beverly Kilman, Tom Nerney, Tom Donnellan, Tom Popkewitz, John O'Brien, Rud Turnbull, Doug Guess, Jayne Miller, and Pat Mirenda for their willingness to share ideas and read various drafts of this paper.

REFERENCES

Allen, W.B., Friedman, M., Berry, M.F., Buckley, E.G., Chan, S.T.S., Destro, R.A., Guess, F.S., & Ramirez, B.C. (1989). *Medical discrimination against children with disabilities*. Washington, DC: U.S. Civil Rights Commission.

Azrin, N. (1987, June). *Panel discussion. Conference on current perspectives on intrusive procedures*. Richmond Hill, Ontario.

Azrin, N.H., Hake, D.F., & Hutchinson, R.R. (1965). Elicitation of aggression by a physical blow. *Journal of the Experimental Analysis of Behavior, 8*, 55-57.

The Association for Retarded Citizens. (1987). Position statement on behavior management. *TASH Newsletter, 13*, 3.

The Association for Persons with Severe Handicaps. (1987). TASH resolution on the cessation of intrusive interventions. *TASH Newsletter, 13*, 3.

Baer, D.M. (1970). A case for the selective reinforcement of punishment. In C. Neuringer & J.L. Michaels (Eds.), *Behavior modification in clinical psychology* (pp.243-249). New York: Appleton Century Crofts.

Berkman, K. A., & Meyer, L. H. (1988). Alternative strategies and multiple outcomes in the remediation of severe self-injury: Going "all out" nonaversively. *Journal of the Association for Persons with Severe Handicaps., 13*, 76-86.

Blatt, B., & Kaplan, F. (1966). *Christmas in purgatory: A photographic essay on mental retardation*. Boston: Allyn & Bacon.

Bruel, H. H., Fielding, L., Joyce, M., Peters, W., & Weisler, N. (1982). Thirty-month demonstration project for treatment of self-injurious behavior in severely retarded individuals. In J. H. Hollis & C. E. Meyers (Eds.), *Life-threatening behavior: Analysis and Intervention* (pp. 191-275). Washington, DC: American Association on Mental Deficiency.

Campbell, J.(1988) *The power of myth*. New York: Doubleday.

Carr, E.G., Taylor, J.C., Carlson, J.I., & Robinson, S. (1989). Reinforcement and stimulus-based treatments for severe be havior problems in developmental disabilities. *Consensus development conference on treatment of destructive behaviors in persons with developmental disabilities report*. Bethesda, MD: National Institutes of Health.

Cataldo, M. (1988). Knowledge based approaches toward assisting the developmentally disabled and other considerations. In *Behavior management and community integration for individuals with developmental disabilities and severe behavior problems*. Washington, DC: Office of Special Education and Rehabilitative Services, U.S. Department of Education.

Cataldo, M.F. (1989). The effects of punishment and other behavior reducing procedures on the destructive behaviors of persons with developmental disabilities. *Consensus development conference on treatment of destructive behaviors in persons with developmental disabilities report*. Bethesda, MD: National Institutes of Health.

Clark, M. (1987). *A review of the literature regarding decelerative procedures*. Unpublished manuscript, University of Wisconsin, Madison, WI.

Corte, H., Wolf, M.M., & Locke, B.J. (1971). A comparison of procedures in the elimination of self-injurious behavior of retarded adolescents. *Journal of Applied Behavior Analysis, 4*, 201-213.

Deitz, S.M., Repp, A.C., & Deitz, D.E.D. (1976). Reducing inappropriate classroom behavior of retarded students through three procedures of differential reinforcement. *Journal of Mental Deficiency Research, 20*, 155-170.

Donnellan, A.M., & Kilman, B.A. (1986). Behavioral approaches to social skill development: Strengths, limitations and alternatives. In I.E. Schopler & G.B. Mesibov (Eds.) *Social Behavior and Autism*. New York: Plenum.

Donnellan, A. M., & LaVigna, G. W. (1986). Non-aversive control of socially stigmatizing behaviors. *The Pointer, 30*, 25-31.

Donnellan, A. M., & LaVigna, G. W. (1988). The empirical case against punishment: A review of the literature (Abstract). In *Autism: Focus on the Family*. Washington, D.C.: Autism Society of America.

Donnellan, A. M., LaVigna, G. W., Negri-Shoultz, N., & Fassbender, L. L. (1988). *Progress without punishment*. New York, NY: Teachers College Press.

Donnellan, A. M., LaVigna, G. W., Schuler, A. L., & Woodward, P. (1982). A strategy for widespread dissemination of inservice training of classroom personnel. *Teacher Education and Special Education, 5*(4), 36-42.

Donnellan, A. M., LaVigna, G. W., Zambito, J., & Thvedt, J. (1985). A time limited intensive intervention program model to support community placement for persons with severe behavior problems. *Journal of the Association for Persons with Severe Handicaps, 10*, 123-131.

Donnellan, A.M., & Negri-Shoultz, N. (1986) *A review and evaluation of interventions implemented by Fairbault State Hospital for selected class members in Welsch v. Levine.* Minneapolis: Office of the Court Master, Welsch v. Levine.

Elliott, S.N., Witt, J.C., Galvin, G.A., & Peterson, R. (1984). Acceptability of positive and reductive behavioral interventions: Factors that influence teachers' decisions. *Journal of School Psychology, 22*, 353-360.

Favell, J. E., Azrin, N. H., Baumeister, A. A., Con, E. G., Dorsey, M. F., Forehand, R., Foxx, R. M., Lovaas, O. I., Rincover, A., Risley, T. R., Romonczyk, R. G., Russo, D. C., Schroeder, S. R., & Solnick, J. V. (1982). The treatment of self-injurious behavior. *Behavior Therapy, 3,* 529-554.

Favell, J. E., McGimsey, J. F., & Jones, M. L. (1978). The use of physical restraint in the treatment of self-injury and as a positive reinforcement. *Journal of Applied Behavior Analysis, 11*, 225-241.

Foxx, R. M., & Livesay, J. (1984). Maintenance of response suppression following overcorrection: A 10-year retrospective examination of eight cases. *Analysis and Intervention In Developmental Disabilities, 4,* 65-80.

Foxx, R. M., McMorrow, M., Bittle, R., & Bechtel, D. (1986). The successful treatment of a dually-diagnosed deaf man's aggression with a program that included contingent electric shock. *Behavior Therapy, 17,* 170-186.

Gleick, J. (October 23, 1989). Review of *Wonderful life: The Burgess Shale and the nature of history. New York Times Book Review*, p. 41.

Guess, D., Helmstetter, E., Turnbull, H. R., & Knowlton, S. (1987). *Use of aversive procedures with persons who are disabled: An historical review and critical analysis, (Monograph #2). Seattle: The Association for Persons with Severe Handicaps.*

Hutchinson, R.R. (1977). By-products of aversive control. In W.K. Honig & J.E.R. Staddon (Eds.) *Handbook of Operant Behavior*. Englewood Cliffs, NJ: Prentice-Hall.

Iwata, B. (1986). *Self-injurious behavior.* Workshop presented to State Department of Mental Health, Augusta Maine, February.

Iwata, B.A. (1988). The development and adoption of controversial default technologies. The Behavior Analyst, 11, 149-159.

Kazdin, A.E. (1980). Acceptability of alternative treatments for deviant child behavior. *Journal of Applied Behavior Analysis, 13*, 259-273.

Kramer, H., & Spranger, J. (1971). *Malleus maleficarum* (M. Summers, Trans.). New York: Dover. (Original work published 1486).

Krasner L. & Houts, A.C. (1984). A Study of the value systems of Behavioral Scientists. *American Psychologist, 39*, 840-850.

LaVigna, G.W. (May, 1987). *The empirical case against punishment.* A paper presented at the Annual Convention of the Association for Behavior Analysis, Nashville, TN.

LaVigna, G.W.(May, 1988). *Analysis and treatment after removal from a "last resort" punishment program.* A symposium presented at the Annual Convention of the Association for Behavior Analysis, Philadelphia, PA.

LaVigna, G. W., & Donnellan, A. M. (1986). *Alternatives to punishment: Solving behavior problems with non-aversive strategies*. New York, NY: Irvington.

LaVigna, G. W., & Donnellan, A. M. (1988). A conceptual format for breaking the barriers to community and social integration (abstract). In *Autism: Focus on the Family*. Washington, D C: Autism Society of America.

LaVigna, G. W., Donnellan, A. M., & Willis, T. J. (in preparation) *Response to "The right to effective behavioral treatment:" The empirical case against punishment.*

LaVigna, G. W., Willis, T. J., & Donnellan, A. M. (1989). The role of positive programming in behavioral treatment. In E. Cipani (Ed.), *Behavioral approaches to the treatment of aberrant behavior*. AAMD Monograph Series. Washington, DC: American Association on Mental Deficiency.

Lennox, D., Miltenberger, R., Spengler, P., & Erfanian, N. (1988). Decelerative treatment practices with persons who have mental retardation: A review of five years of the literature. *American Journal on Mental Retardation, 92*, 492-501.

Lovaas, O. I., & Favell, J. E. (1987). Protection for clients undergoing aversive/restrictive interventions. *Education and Treatment of Children, 10*, 311-325.

Martin, R. (1979). *Legal challenges in regulating behavior change*. Champaign, IL: Research Press.

Martin, R. (1981). Legal issues in preserving client rights. In H. G. Christian & H. Clark (Eds.), *Preservation of client rights*. New York, NY: Free Press.

Morse, W. H., Mead, R. N., & Kelleher, R. T. (1967). Modulation of elicited behavior by a fixed-interval schedule of electric shock presentation. *Science, 157*, 215-217.

National Institutes of Health (NIH) (1989). *Consensus development conference on treatment of destructive behaviors in persons with developmental disabilities report*.(Draft). Bethesda, MD: National Institutes of Health, Office of Medical Applications Research.

O'Brien, J. *(1990). Against pain as a tool in professional work on people with severe disabilities.* Manuscript submitted for publication.

Popkewitz, T.S., & St. Maurice, H.(in press). Social studies education and theory: Science, knowledge and history. In J. Shaver, (Ed.), *The handbook on research in social education*. New York: McMillan.

Rast, J., Johnston, J., Drum, C., & Conrin, J. (1981). The relation of food quantity to rumination behavior. *Journal of Applied Behavior Analysis, 14*, 121-130.

Rhodes, W.C. (1967). The disturbing child: A problem of ecological management. *Exceptional Children, 33* , 449-455.

Romanczyk, R.G., & Goren, E.R. (1975). Severe self-injurious behavior: The problem of clinical control. Journal of Consulting and Clinical Psychology, 43, 730-739.

Schroeder, S.R., Rojahn, J., & Oldenquist, A. (1989). Treatment of destructive behaviors among people with developmental disabilities. *Consensus development conference on treatment of destructive behaviors in persons with developmental disabilities. Bethesda, MD: National Institutes of Health.*

Sidman, M. (1989) *Coercion and its fallout*. Boston: Authors Cooperative, Inc.

Simmons, J.Q., and Frankel, F. (1974). An extinction procedure for eliminating self-destructive behavior in a 9-year-old autistic girl. *Journal of Autism and Childhood Schizophrenia, 4*, 241-250.

Singh, N.N., Dawson, M.J., & Gregory, P.R. (1980). Suppression of chronic hyperventilation using response-contingent aromatic ammonia. *Behavior Therapy, 11*, 561-566.

Spreat, S., Lipinski, D., Dickerson, R., Nass, R., & Dorsey, M. (1989). The acceptability of electric shock programs. *Behavior Modification, 13*, 245-256.

Stretch, R., Orloff, E. R., & Dalrymple, S. D. (1968). Maintenance of responding by fixed-interval schedule of electric shock presentation in squirrel monkeys. *Science, 162*, 583-586.

Touchette, P. E. (1983). *Nonaversive amelioration of SIB by stimulus control transfer*. Paper presented at the Annual Convention of the American Psychological Association, Anaheim, CA.

Touchette, P.E., MacDonald, R.F., & Langer, S.N. (1985). A scatter plot for identifying stimulus control of problem behavior. *Journal of Applied Behavior Analysis, 18,* 343-351.

Ulrich, R.E., & Favell, J.E. (1970). Human aggression. In C. Neuringer & J.L. Michael (Eds.), *Behavior modification in clinical psychology* (pp. 105-132). New York: Appleton-Century-Croft.

Van Houten, R., Axelrod, S., Bailey, J. S., Favell, J. E., Foxx, R. M., Iwata, B. A., & Lovaas, O. I. (1988). The right to effective behavioral treatment. *The Behavior Analyst, 11*, 111-114.

Willis, T. J., LaVigna, G. W., & Donnellan, A. M. (1989). *Behavior assessment guide*. Los Angeles: Institute for Applied Behavior Analysis.

Witt, J. C., & Elliott, S.N. (1985). Acceptability of classroom management strategies. In T.R. Kratochwill (Ed.), *Advances in School Psychology, Vol. 4,* (pp. 251-288). Hillsdale, NJ: Lawrence Erlbaum Associates.

CHAPTER

4

MYTHS THAT (MIS)GUIDE OUR PROFESSION

Saul Axelrod
Temple University

The ultimate lesson of science is humility.

For me, the initial appeal of applied behavior analysis was not the discriminative stimuli, S deltas, or the reinforcers. Rather, the appeal was the notion that human behavior could and should be studied through the use of scientific methods. This approach was in opposition to the subjective and arrogant approaches of schools ranging from psychoanalysis and EST in clinical psychology to "whole-child," and "open-education" philosophies that dominated and failed education. Applied behavior analysis was a humble approach to solving human problems. It asserted that even the most simple claim must be backed with scientific evidence.

Undoubtedly, applied behavior analysis introduced and refined many scientific practices for the study of human behavior. The use of direct and continuous measurement, the application of intrasubject replication designs, and the emphasis on parsimonious explanations created a unique niche for applied behavior analysis.

The fact that the approach was scientific in some respects, however, did not mean that it was scientific in all respects. Thus, early studies required measures of interobserver reliability on the *subjects'* behavior, but did not require such measures on the program *implementer's* behavior. Therefore, a study may have centered on the notion that a teacher's contingent social attention increased students' on-task behavior. Yet, measures were not taken to determine whether, in fact, the teachers did perform the stated operations. In this case, the field adjusted its standards, and now many journal editors require measures of treatment integrity.

Other violations of scientific principles also were evident. An applied behavior analyst might speculate that an outcome would occur simply because the events that preceded it would seem to predict such an outcome. Axelrod (1983, p. 64) stated, for example, that an advantage of peer tutoring programs was that they freed the teacher to work with students in need of assistance. Whether, in fact, this outcome occurs is yet to be shown.

The violations of scientific methodology described above may not produce a great deal of harm to the field; other violations may. Presently, a serious disagreement exists within the behavioral community about which procedures are ethical and effective and which are not.

Specifically, the question centers on the role of punishment and negative reinforcement in the repertoire of corrective procedures. The debate is particularly crucial, given that many of the recipients of the procedures are sufficiently handicapped to preclude conventional channels of communication on their part.

Seemingly, such a debate should not exist within a discipline committed to the scientific method; the data should speak for themselves. Yet, the debate does exist in books such as the present one, in newsletters, in journal articles, and at professional conferences. The data may speak for themselves, but this is irrelevant if professionals fail to attend to them.

The damage caused by such a debate could be immense. Comprising only a small proportion of the fields of psychology and education, applied behaviorists always have had to fight for professional and public acceptance. If behaviorists give other professionals and the public contradictory messages, the field may have difficulty progressing and its proponents will fail to multiply.

On the pages that follow, I will describe a variety of notions that control many of the practices within our field, yet are not scientifically based. In each case, I will present a rebuttal to the myth and will attempt to correct prevailing misunderstandings.

MYTH ONE - AVERSIVE PROCEDURES ARE NON-NORMALIZED AND UNNATURAL PROCESSES AND THEREFORE SHOULD NOT BE USED ON PEOPLE WITH HANDICAPS

If anything, aversive procedures are too normalized and too often are used with nonhandicapped populations. Where do we begin? Religions punish the inobservant with excommunication and damnation. Governments punish lawbreakers with fines, suspensions, and jail sentences. Schools attempt to punish students with detentions and failing grades. Parents punish their children by grounding, spanking, and reprimanding them. The critical point here is not that these practices *should* exist, but that they *do* exist. They *are* normalized practices.

In the conduct of one's daily life, a multitude of behaviors is controlled by negative, rather than positive reinforcement. The consequences for preparing a good meal for one's family are too often the absence of criticism rather than the presence of praise. One consequence of clothing one's self in public is avoiding ridicule and fines. When college professors submit their grades on time, they do not receive a letter from the dean. When they are tardy in this respect, they *do* receive a letter from the dean.

Aversive procedures are used too often with nonhandicapped and handicapped populations, and such practices should be changed. But eliminating all forms of aversive conditioning is impossible. Aversive conditioning is a natural process that is partly responsible for the survival of the human species. People learn to keep their eyes closed in dusty areas because of the punishing consequences of opening their eyes. People avoid walking off cliffs, touching boiling water, and eating bitter chocolate due to punishing, or potentially punishing, consequences.

A related question is whether handicapped populations are exposed to unusual punishment procedures because they are devalued by society's mainstream and are frequently incapable of advocating for themselves. Our field must constantly examine itself in order to avoid such injustices. In investigating the question, however, we should remember that many individuals with handicaps exhibit serious misbehaviors that are seldom seen in nonhandicapped populations, and that some people are so cognitively handicapped that less restrictive procedures are not feasible. Finally, we should not assume that the public is always opposed to the use of punishment procedures. Frentz and Kelley (1986) found, for example, that parents considered a punishment procedure, response cost, more acceptable than positive reinforcement in treating noncompliance.

MYTH TWO - POSITIVE REINFORCEMENT HAS SUPERIOR MODIFICATION CHARACTERISTICS TO PUNISHMENT

There are at least two major issues raised by the present claim. The first is that punishment procedures fail to generalize across settings and time (i.e., they lack the properties of stimulus generalization and maintenance). The claim is that the effect of punishment is experienced only in the original setting and that, once the punishment procedure is removed, the progress disappears. The second criticism is that punishment produces adverse side effects while positive reinforcement does not.

An examination of the behavioral literature does indeed reveal the failure of some punishment procedures to generalize across time. That is, in many cases, when punishment procedures are terminated, progress declines. The same, however, is true for positive reinforcement, traffic lights, and many forms of medication. The remarkable buoyancy of behavior is what permits the reversal and multielement research (Ulman & Sulzer-Azaroff, 1975) designs to be useful. If behaviors were not so responsive to impending consequences, the designs could not be used.

A similar point can be made about stimulus generalization. A punishment procedure applied at home tends not to produce improvement in a school environment in which the procedure is not being applied. The same, however, can be said for positive reinforcement procedures, which also lack magic qualities. Again, we must remember that humans show a singular tendency to respond to imminent contingencies.

The failure of behavioral procedures to produce generalization is not all bad. Sometimes stimulus discrimination is exactly what we want. We want children to behave in a docile manner during religious services and in a more enthusiastic manner on the school playground. In other cases, the failure to achieve generalization is a problem. Our field has recognized this difficulty and efforts have been made to address it (e.g., Stokes & Baer, 1977). The point is not that generalization is never a problem, but that it is a problem for all behavioral procedures, whether they are based on punishment or reinforcement.

The second issue is whether punishment results in undesirable side effects. Undoubtedly, there are many documented examples of such side effects. Azrin and Holz (1966) and Newsom, Favell, and Rincover (1983) point to examples of aggression toward both the persons implementing and not implementing punishment, temper tantrums, crying, and social avoidance of the person implementing punishment. To present a balanced picture of the issue, Newsom et al. (1983, pp. 301-305) also point out that such side effects seldom occur, and that a number of desirable side effects have been noted in using punishment. These include improved social relations (once certain antisocial behaviors disappear), increased attention to task, and increased play behavior. Also, a recent article by Matson and Taras (1989) reviewed 23 relevant journals over the period of 1967 to 1987. The authors found that when aversive procedures were used, positive side effects were reported 11 times more frequently than negative side effects.

We also should note that positive reinforcement procedures are sometimes associated with undesirable side effects. Balsam and Bondy (1983), for example, point to inattention, clinging, excessive dependence, lying, stealing, cheating, conniving, and aggression as problems that sometimes accompany positive reinforcement procedures. As a personal note, I recently attempted to use a consumable reinforcer with a student with a severe handicap. He became so distracted and enraged at the requirement that he work for the reinforcer that the procedure had to be discontinued.

The point here is not to make a case for punishment and against positive reinforcement. Indeed research may prove positive reinforcement superior to punishment. Rather, the point is that neither procedure is all good nor all bad. Also, punishment may be a necessary component for remediation in many cases, and if adverse side effects of punishment do occur, they may be effectively treated.

MYTH THREE - THERE IS NO EVIDENCE THAT PUNISHMENT PROCEDURES WORK BETTER THAN POSITIVE REINFORCEMENT PROCEDURES

Actually, this is true. A variety of experimental problems make examining this question, as well as other questions comparing different procedures, difficult. Problems include identification of the optimal level of each treatment, the user preference for treatment, the population chosen to serve as subjects, and the behavior selected as the dependent variable (Johnston, 1988; Van Houten, 1983).

The real problem with the claim that punishment does not work better than positive reinforcement, however, is that the wrong question is being raised. Behaviorists are not recommending that punishment procedures *alone* be used; rather, that when punishment procedures *are* used, they be used *in conjunction* with positive reinforcement procedures. This point was made in the review by Matson and Taras (1989) which revealed that practically all studies using aversive procedures also had a component that reinforced appropriate behavior. The question then becomes: Is a combination of positive reinforcement and punishment more effective than positive reinforcement alone?

Here the answer is clear. The combination of reinforcement and punishment is superior to reinforcement alone. This effect was demonstrated early in the basic literature by Azrin and Holz (1966). It also has been demonstrated in more contemporary applied literature by Pfifner and O'Leary (1987) who found that a reinforcement system, offering such incentives as praise, public posting, extra recess, and special activities, was initially ineffective in controlling the disruptive behavior of eight children in a remedial summer school program. Later, when reprimands for inappropriate behavior were combined with positive reinforcers, student behavior came under control. These authors also demonstrated that they could fade the reprimands without losing behavioral gains.

Other researchers also have shown that adding a positive reinforcement component to a punishment procedure will enhance the program's effectiveness. Solnick, Rincover, and Peterson (1977) demonstrated, for example, that the more reinforcing the time-in environment was, the more effective the time-out procedure would be. Also, Zegiob, Jenkins, Becker, and Bristow (1976) found that facial screening resulted in a partial suppression of ritualistic hand clapping in a boy with schizophrenia. Later, when the boy was reinforced for appropriate verbal behavior, hand clapping almost disappeared and appropriate verbal behavior increased. Thus, an ideal program for eliminating behaviors of some urgency might be to use a combination of reinforcement and punishment, with the gradual removal of the punishment and even the reinforcement component. Meanwhile, it is difficult to see why a program involving two powerful procedures--positive reinforcement and punishment--would not be more effective than a program with only one of the components (Axelrod, 1987).

MYTH FOUR - PUNISHMENT SHOULD ONLY BE USED AS A LAST RESORT-OR-ONE IS OBLIGATED TO USE POSITIVE REINFORCEMENT PROCEDURES BEFORE ATTEMPTING PUNISHMENT PROCEDURES

Sometimes punishment should be used from the outset; at other times, it should not be used at all. The crucial issue here is: How urgent and important is it that a particular behavior cease? In the case of talking out in class, one could argue that punishment should be used as a program component only after curricular modifications and positive reinforcement components have been exhausted. In the case of walking a crooked line from the classroom to the school yard, one could argue that punishment should never be used (perhaps the teacher could change the requirements.) In the case of attempting to stab a homebound teacher with a knife (a case with which I am personally familiar), one can only ethically demand that the problem be eliminated immediately. Failing to use a combination of reinforcement and punishment in such a case is an unconscionable injustice to both the teacher and the student.

Implicit in the present myth is that there is no harm in failing for a while. In fact, there is harm in failing. In one case, I was asked to recommend a procedure to deal with a young man who frequently pushed out his rectum through internal muscular control. My recommendation was to use contingent electric shock (a procedure I had never recommended before, nor have I since). While permission was pending to implement my recommendation, less intrusive, ineffective procedures were used with this client. He killed himself prior to an opportunity to receive electric shock. Sometimes there is great harm in failing.

A variety of problems can occur when ineffective procedures are implemented. For example, the efforts of parents or staff may extinguish following several, or even one or two, failures. Individuals whose inappropriate behaviors continue may be responsible for long-term or permanent injury to themselves or others. The individuals may also lose important social, educational, and vocational opportunities, as well as becoming exposed to chemical restraints or institutionalization.

If practitioners are not given ethical and effective techniques, they may find other ways of dealing with the problems they encounter. Rusch, Hall, and Griffin (1986) found, for example, that the exhibition of aggressive and self-injurious behaviors significantly differentiated abused from non-abused people with mental retardation. Other research has shown that the above behaviors were the major factors associated with admission and readmission of individuals with mental retardation into large public institutions (Hill & Bruininks, 1984; Lakin, Hill, Hauber, Bruininks, & Heal, 1983).

MYTH FIVE - HUMAN RIGHTS COMMITTEES ARE THE BEST SAFEGUARDS FOR PROTECTING CLIENTS' RIGHTS

In order to deal with seriously disruptive and dangerous behaviors, a variety of restrictive procedures has been applied in a diversity of situations. The restrictive procedures have included 24-hour monitoring, reduced access to reinforcers, and applications of punishment procedures. Questions that immediately arise are: a) How far can we go in order to modify human behavior?, and b) What are some basic human rights of which people should not be deprived?

The two major mechanisms for ensuring program integrity and client protection are the Peer Review Committee (PRC) and the Human Rights Committee (HRC). PRCs consist of experts in applied behavior analysis who make certain that programs are carried out in conformity with behavioral principles and research. *PRCs determine the clinical appropriateness of programs.*

HRCs consist of interested citizens from a wide variety of backgrounds. Thus, the HRC might consist of a construction worker, a parent of a child with autism, a homemaker, a corporate attorney, a clerk, a person with a disability, a nurse, and a retired senior citizen. The role of the HRC is to determine whether proposed programs meet community standards of treatment acceptability and whether clients are receiving the basic human rights of privacy, medical care, education, social interaction, and physical exercise (Van Houten, Axelrod, Bailey, Favell, Foxx, Iwata, & Lovaas, 1988). The italicized words above hint at the major point of this section. *When HRCs engage in clinical review of behavioral programs, they are violating their mandate.*

A recent study by Spreat and Lanzi (in press) comprehensively examined the role HRCs play in the review of restrictive procedures. Their survey indicated that the majority of HRCs dealt with questions of safety, informed consent, public offensivity, and *clinical appropriateness.* They further reported that conflict between a facility and its HRC was common in the area of clinical appropriateness. Such conflict frequently resulted in delayed implementation of programs. The Spreat and Lanzi survey also revealed that only about 33% of HRC members had been trained in applied behavior analysis principles. Thus, it was common for HRCs to make clinical judgments while lacking the skills to do so.

In what way can a well-intentioned but unskilled HRC do harm to a person's program? One common manner is to require that a less intense punisher initially be used and that the intensity of punishment be gradually increased if the less intense level proves ineffective. This is in direct opposition to research indicating that punishment be delivered at full intensity, rather than gradually (Azrin, Holz, & Hake, 1963; Masserman, 1946). The effect of the gradual introduction of a punisher is to require a more intense punisher than would be necessary had the punisher been delivered at a reasonable intensity from the start (Van Houten, 1983). This practice is comparable to requiring physicians to use low dosages of medication when there is evidence that higher dosages are required to effectively treat a medical disorder.

Another common practice for HRCs is to require that a person be released from time-out as soon as she or he becomes calm. Teachers applying the procedure in this manner may find that it helps them to escape the immediate problem, but that it does not produce a future decrease in the disruptive behavior. Due to the immediate negative reinforcement effect of the procedure for the teacher (i.e., it removes the unruly person), time-out may be applied indefinitely although it produces no decrease in the overall rate of the behavior. Proceeding in this manner, a student would be in a more restrictive situation than would be the case had time-out had been applied for a long enough period to eliminate the problem behavior. The benevolent motives of the HRC are hindering, rather than helping, the student. To paraphrase an old expression used by Samuel Johnson, "The path to restrictiveness is paved with good intentions."

Central to the guidelines under which most facilities operate is the theme that the least restrictive alternative should be the method of choice (Spreat & Lipinski, 1986). Van Houten et al. (1988), however, have amended this concept to include the least restrictive *effective* alternative. This modification prevents clients from being repeatedly exposed to ineffective procedures. Ineffective treatment itself is restrictive when it allows an individual to inflict personal injury, or when it interferes with social, vocational, or educational opportunities. Thus, HRCs provide a crucial service to the field when they stay within their bounds. When they exceed their bounds, they become part of the problem, rather than part of the solution.

MYTH SIX - HIERARCHIES OF TREATMENT ALTERNATIVES PROTECT PEOPLE FROM UNNECESSARILY RESTRICTIVEPROCEDURES

In a prevailing effort to prevent people from receiving unnecessarily restrictive treatment, many facilities devise and use a hierarchical list of procedures. At one end of the list are procedures that are considered nonrestrictive or minimally restrictive. At the other end of the list are procedures that are considered maximally restrictive. In a survey of facilities using restrictive procedures, Spreat and Lanzi (in press) found reprimands and extinction to be among the least restrictive procedures; exclusion time-out and overcorrection were in the middle; and seclusion time-out, electric shock, and water mist were at the most restrictive end.

One may wonder, what is the basis for such ratings? Some bases that would seem appropriate would include the side effects of each procedure, the physical danger of the procedures to the offending individual and the program implementer, and the amount of time that the person is removed from ongoing programs. None of these factors seems to prevail in constructing a hierarchy of treatment procedures.

In examining the perceived restrictiveness of extinction (among the least restrictive), overcorrection (in the middle), and electric shock (the most restrictive), people generally ignore side effects. In using extinction, the problem of extinction burst can make the procedure too dangerous to employ. In applying overcorrection procedures, many researchers (e.g., Azrin & Wesolowski, 1975; Lambert, Bruwier, & Cobben, 1975) have found the client's reaction to be so severe that the procedures had to be discontinued or greatly modified. On the other hand, there is little evidence of harmful side effects of electric shock (Carr & Lovaas, 1983, p. 235).

Similarly, when one examines physical danger to the offender and implementer, as well as time away from the program, procedures such as exclusion time-out and overcorrection should come out worse than electric shock and water mist. The hierarchy that prevails in most settings, however, is reversed.

What appears to be most influential in constructing treatment hierarchies is *public offensiveness* . This is an important consideration in any program. Ignoring public sentiment would be harmful to the field and to the individuals whom it serves. How, then, should professionals proceed when public sentiment is in opposition to the optimal treatment protocol? Yielding to or compromising with public opinion could be harmful to the individuals whom behaviorists are serving. The best strategy then would be to *educate* the public as to the rationale for applying a certain procedure. In this regard, behaviorists would be no different from physicians who once had to convince the public that dissecting cadavers was not a medical perversion, but a necessary practice for research and educational purposes.

MYTH SEVEN - THE ASSOCIATION FOR BEHAVIOR ANALYSIS IS PROPUNISHMENT

The debate over whether the use of aversive procedures in selected situations is ethical and necessary is similar to the debate over the ethics of medically performed abortions. The emotion on either side of each argument has one obvious similarity. Another similarity is the use of labels in the debates. The abortion question takes on one meaning when one side calls itself "prolife." The implication is that the other side is "antilife" or "prodeath." It takes on still another meaning if one side calls itself "prochoice," the implication being that the other side is "antichoice."

In the debate over the use of aversive procedures, one side can call itself "antipunishment," implying that its opponents are "propunishment." On the other hand, professionals who see the need to use all available treatment options can call itself "protreatment," implying that the other side is "antitreatment."

The use of labels in this manner may be functional in winning a refereed debate or a political campaign, but it does not resolve the question of whether the use of aversive procedures is necessary. The fact does remain, however, that there is widespread disagreement among professional organizations on this key question.

In 1982, the executive committee of The Association for Persons with Severe Handicaps (TASH) passed a resolution that implicitly rejected the use of many forms of punishment with persons with severe handicaps. Later, a book written by LaVigna & Donnellan, (1986) went further in explicitly rejecting all forms of punishment, as well as extinction.

Some professional organizations took a different position on the question of appropriate treatment. The Executive Committee of the Association for Behavior Analysis (ABA) appointed a task force to specify the treatment rights that each individual should be granted. The report of the task force (which was later endorsed by its members and became official ABA policy) specified a number of individual rights. These include the rights to a therapeutic environment, services with a goal of personal welfare, a competent behavior analyst, a program that teaches functional skills, ongoing evaluation of programs, and effective treatment (Van Houten et al., 1988).

In describing the right to effective treatment, the ABA task force specified that exposing individuals to restrictive procedures should be prohibited unless such procedures were necessary to produce safe and socially significant behavior change. The report also stated that individuals should not be unnecessarily exposed to nonrestrictive but ineffective procedures.

Such a position can hardly be regarded as "propunishment." Rather, it is a protreatment position in its most comprehensive and ethical sense. It prohibits the use of restrictive procedures when unnecessary. It prohibits the excessive application of nonaversive but ineffective procedures. Yet, it also recognizes the importance of behavior change in people's lives and extends treatment options to include the use of restrictive procedures when necessary and when in the person's best interests.

In a related manner, the position of B. F. Skinner, the modern founder of behaviorism, has been brought into the debate. Although the opinion of any one individual should not be decisive on any question, it is difficult to ignore the position of a person with Skinner's prestige. At one point, the Community Services for Autistic Adults and Children was circulating a videotaped interview of Skinner that gave the impression that he was opposed to the use of punishment procedures. Skinner complained that the editing of the tape distorted his views, and he clarified his views with the following statement: "Some autistic children, for example, will seriously injure themselves unless drugged or restrained, and other treatment is then virtually impossible. If brief and harmless stimuli, made precisely contingent on self-destructive behavior, suppress the behavior and leave the children free to develop in other ways, I believe it can be justified" ("Skinner Joins..." 1988).

MYTH EIGHT - NONAVERSIVE PROCEDURES ARE NOW AVAILABLE TO TREAT ALL BEHAVIORAL DISORDERS

Claims that aberrant behavior can be managed without the use of aversive procedures are occurring with greater frequency. Donnellan and LaVigna (1987) claimed, for example, "Our review of the literature and experience with over 500 cases convince us that strategies are presently available to deal with *any* problem without resorting to aversive events." Yet, a book by the same authors (LaVigna & Donnellan, 1986) leaves me unconvinced that such a goal has been reached. Rather than dealing with serious misbehaviors and individuals with major handicaps, the text deals mainly with mild management problems and people who have minimal impairments. Also, the authors frequently made treatment recommendations without citing supportive research and, at times (perhaps, unknowingly), recommended using punishment procedures (Axelrod, 1987).

A much publicized alternative to procedures using a punishment component is known as *Gentle Teaching* (Menolascino & McGee, 1983; McGee, 1985). The approach purportedly rejects the use of punishment procedures and, instead, emphasizes developing a humanistic and liberated relationship between student and teacher (or client and therapist) that results in bonding. The bonding is said to help teachers gain control over inappropriate student behavior.

The assertions concerning the effectiveness of the Gentle Teaching approach are vast. McGee (1985), for example, claims to have successfully treated 650 individuals at a psychiatric institute over a five-year period. The behaviors professedly included self-injury and aggression, and the clients were described as having all levels of mental retardation.

Mudford's (1985) examination of McGee's Gentle Teaching approach reached far different conclusions. Mudford pointed to McGee's failures to: (a) describe applied behavior analysis practices and concepts correctly, (b) deal with individuals with profound impairments, and (c) use research designs to evaluate treatment outcomes. He also indicated that McGee used the same punishment procedures that he had condemned in the work of others! Thus, Mudford (1985) argues for the continuation of mainstreamed behavioral practices.

Also, Jordan, Singh, and Repp (1989) point out that there has been no independent evaluation of McGee's success with Gentle Teaching, and that most of McGee's results are in the form of informal observations of client progress. Rather than using experimental control conditions, Jordan et al. (1989) indicate that McGee employs before-and-after videotaped vignettes. In a direct comparison of visual screening and Gentle Teaching in reducing three cases of stereotyped behavior, visual screening was found to be superior in dealing with the target behavior and resulted in more bonding between the clients and the program implementer than Gentle Teaching (Jordan, et al., 1989)!

Rimland (Blake, 1988) recently conducted a survey of professionals on the necessity to use aversive procedures *in selected cases*. The report cited a review of more than 60 studies by LaGrow and Repp (1984) which found that "aversive procedures as a class were more effective than positive procedures, manipulation of the environment, and sensory extinction." Rimland concluded that if his own son, who has autism, were to engage in self-injurious behavior, he would use aversive procedures, including electric shock, if positive reinforcement procedures proved ineffective.

Recently, TASH made its first annual Award for Distinguished Contributions to Non-Aversive Behavioral Intervention (Setting the Stage, 1988). Also, the federal government has awarded Dr. Robert Horner, University of Oregon, a grant of $5.5 million to explore nonaversive technology for behavior management. I applaud such efforts and hope that more professional organizations and granting agencies will engage in similar practices. As for myself, I recently participated in a study in which the noncompliant and aggressive behaviors of a 40 year-old man were modified without the use of aversive procedures (Neuman, Park-Yu, & Axelrod, 1988).

Regardless of the development of new technologies of nonaversive behavior management, I do not believe that our field should abandon the option of using aversive techniques *in selected cases*. We have not reached the point where we can discard an effective technology. At present, we cannot even be certain of the types of behavior problems that we may encounter. In this regard, we are similar to the medical profession that did not predict the onset of the lethal disease AIDS. If we disallow procedures that might be effective, we are relegating ourselves to a position in which we do not regard behavioral disorders with complete seriousness and with complete commitment. The medical profession does not outlaw surgery when new forms of medication prove effective. Rather, it changes the conditions under which surgery can be used.

I believe this is the same posture our field should take. When we become more sophisticated in this use of nonaversive strategies, we should limit the conditions under which restrictive procedures are used.

MYTH NINE - PEOPLE WHO OPPOSE THE USE OF PUNISHMENT PROCEDURES WITH INDIVIDUALS WITH DISABILITIES NEVER PUNISH PROFESSIONALS WHO DISAGREE WITH THEM

After listening to and reading the comments of those who advocate the use of nonaversive practices in developmental disabilities, one cannot help but wonder whether the advocates have eliminated the use of aversive procedures in all aspects of their own lives. Do they use only positive procedures with their children, with their spouses, with their colleagues, and with professionals who disagree with them?

Obviously, observing the practices of the advocates in their personal lives is difficult. Observing their behavior toward professionals who disagree with them is much easier. In fact, the advocates have used criticism during television shows (e.g., ABC's *Nightline*); they have harassed presenters at professional conferences; they vehemently have denounced SIBIS (an electric shock device designed to reduce self-injury) at a press conference; and they have called for the closure of the Behavior Research Institute in Providence, Rhode Island.

None of the above actions sounds like a positive approach toward behavior change; nor do the words of LaVigna and Donnellan (1986, p.7) who sarcastically state that if one were only interested in eliminating behavior a "flaming arrow through the heart would be sufficient." The same authors are devisive when they state, "Those who are irrevocably wedded to the use of aversive intervention will dismiss our position out of hand" (p. 182).

As mentioned earlier, McGee is aproponent of the Gentle Teaching approach and an opponent of the use of punishment procedures. Yet, in a summary of McGee's tactics, Mudford (1985) stated, "The conclusion is inevitable that (McGee's) ill-researched vitriolic attack on mainstream behavior analysts/therapists...is definitely incorrect and possibly libellous" (p. 268). Iwata (1988) wonders, "Why is it the same people who denounce the use of relatively harmless aversive contingencies to eliminate life-threatening behavior of a retarded individual, not only support aversive cultural practices, but also routinely subject their own children and coworkers to stimuli that are functionally similar to the ones they abhor?" (p. 150).

The advocates also have been consistent supporters of legislation that would punish professionals who disagree with them. For example, a bill that was presented to the Massachusetts Legislature (Senate Bill #607) would revoke or suspend a program's license, approval, certification, and funding if the program violated its position on the use of restrictive procedures. In a similar manner, a bill that was presented to the United States Senate (Senate Bill #1673) would disallow Medicare/Medicaid payments. Neither of these bills, nor ones that were presented to the legislatures of Minnesota and California, have become law to date but, without doubt, their intent is to *punish* the behavior of professionals whose practices they deem inappropriate.

As I observe the actions of the advocates, I must agree that I probably would use punishment procedures also if I wished to change some practices of other professionals. Perhaps that is the lesson in all of this. Sometimes changing human behavior without invoking punishment practices may be impossible.

CONCLUDING COMMENTS

An individual's right to effective and humane treatment is undeniable. Yet, defining the parameters of such a right is a matter of great debate among professionals. Those who reject a procedure on philosophical grounds are obligated to replace it with one that is at least as effective or to show that an individual is better off with the behavior remaining unchanged. In my own opinion, this has not always been done; thus, some people have been denied their right to effective treatment. *"Not to rescue a person from an unhappy organization of his behavior is to punish him, in that it leaves him in a state of recurrent punishment"* (Baer, 1970, p. 246).

My support for the *selective* use of restrictive procedures does not mean that our field does not have important questions to investigate. Some that occur to me are as follows:

1. Are behavior analysis procedures--both restrictive and nonrestrictive--being applied properly?
2. Has success with punishment procedures diminished the search for less restrictive alternatives?
3. Are punishment procedures left in effect too long without efforts made to withdraw them?
4. Are procedures used with people with handicaps that would not be used on people without handicaps?
5. Is the term "punishment" so emotionally charged that an objective evaluation of the process is no longer feasible?

Our chore is always to investigate questions and devise procedures that will improve the quality and diversity of behavioral technology. Our present mandate is to implement the least restrictive but effective techniques, while simultaneously devising alternatives that are equally effective, and less restrictive. This outcome will not be achieved by exploiting the emotions of the public, or through political manipulation, but through further development of the same humane and scientific process that accounts for the immense gains that applied behavior analysts have already made.

REFERENCES

Axelrod, S. (1983). *Behavior modification for the classroom teacher* (2nd ed.). New York: McGraw-Hill.

Axelrod, S. (1987). Doing it without arrows [Review of *Alternatives to punishment: Solving behavior problems with non-aversive strategies*]. *The Behavior Analyst, 10*, 243-251.

Azrin, N. H., & Holz, W. C. (1966). Punishment. In W. K. Honig (Ed.), *Operant behavior: Areas of research and application* (pp. 213-270). New York: Appleton-Century-Crofts.

Azrin, N. H., Holz, W. C., & Hake, D. (1963). Fixed-ratio punishment. *Journal of the Experimental Analysis of Behavior, 6*, 141-148.

Azrin, N. H., & Wesolowski, M. D. (1975). Eliminating habitual vomiting in a retarded adult by positive practice and self-correction. *Journal of Behavior Therapy and Experimental Psychiatry, 6*, 145-148.

Baer, D. M., (1970). A case for the selective reinforcement of punishment. In C. Neuringer & J. L. Michael (Eds.), *Behavior modification in clinical psychology*. New York: Appleton-Century-Crofts.

Balsam, P. D., & Bondy, A. S. (1983). The negative side effects of reward. *Journal of Applied Behavior Analysis, 16*, 283-296.

Blake, A. (1988). Aversives: Are they needed? Are they ethical? *Autism Research Review, 2,* 1-3, 6, 8.

Carr, E. G., & Lovaas, O. I. (1983). Contingent electric shock as a treatment for severe behavior problems. In S. Axelrod & J. Apsche (Eds.), *The effects of punishment on human behavior* (pp. 221-245). New York: Academic Press.

Donnellan, A. M., & LaVigna, G. W. (1987, December). A note of cautious optimism. *DD Directions, 2.*

Frentz, C., & Kelley, M. L. (1986). Parents' acceptance of reductive treatment methods: The influence of problem severity and perception of child behavior. *Behavior Therapy, 17*, 75-81.

Hill, B. K., & Bruininks, R. H. (1984). Maladaptive behavior of mentally retarded individuals in residential facilities. *American Journal of Mental Deficiency, 88*, 380-387.

Iwata, B. A. (1988). The development and adoption of controversial default technologies. *The Behavior Analyst, 11,* 149-157.

Johnston, J. (1988). Strategic and tactical limitations of comparison studies. *The Behavior Analyst, 11,* 1-9.

Jordan, J., Singh, N. N., & Repp, A. C. (1989). An evaluation of gentle teaching and visual screening in the reduction of stereotyping. *Journal of Applied Behavioral Analysis, 22*, 9-22.

LaGrow, S. T., & Repp, A. C. (1984). Stereotypic responding: Review of intervention research. *American Journal of Mental Deficiency, 88,* 595-609.

Lakin, K. C., Hill, B. K., Hauber, F. A., Bruininks, R. H., & Heal, L.W. (1983). New admissions and readmissions to a national sample of public residential facilities. *American Journal of Mental Deficiency, 88*, 13-20.

Lambert, J. L., Bruwier, D., & Cobben, A. (1975). La reducion d'un comportement stereotype chex un enfant arriere mental profond: Comparaison de cinq methodes. *Revue Suisse de Psychologie Pure et Applique, 34,* 1-18.

La Vigna G. W., & Donnellan, A. M. (1986). *Alternatives to punishment: Solving behavior problems with non-aversive strategies.* New York: Irvington.

Masserman, J. H. (1946). *Principles of dynamic psychiatry.* Philadelphia: Saunders.

Matson, J. L., & Taras, M. E. (1989). A 20-year review of punishment procedures and alternative methods to treat problem behaviors in developmentally disabled persons. *Research in Developmental Disabilities, 10*, 85-104.

McGee, J. J. (1985). Examples of the use of gentle teaching. *Mental Handicap in New Zealand, 9*, 11-20.

Menolascino, F. J., & McGee, J. J. (1983). Persons with severe mental retardation and behavioral challenges from disconnectedness to human engagement. *Mental Handicap in New Zealand, 9,* 25-30.

Mudford, O. C. (1985). Treatment selection in behaviour reduction: Gentle teaching versus the least intrusive treatment model. *Australia and New Zealand Journal of Developmental Disabilities, 4*, 265-270.

Neuman, P., Park-Yu, N., & Axelrod, S. (1988). *Decreasing problem behaviors through functional analysis: A low-technology approach.* Paper presented at the meeting of the Association for Behavior Analysis, Philadelphia, PA.

Newsom, C., Favell, J. E., & Rincover, A. (1983). Side effects of punishment. In S. Axelrod & J. Apsche (Eds.), *The effects of punishment on human behavior* (pp. 285-316). New York: Academic Press.

Pfifner, L. J., & O'Leary, S. G. (1987). The efficacy of all-positive management as a function of the prior use of negative consequences. *Journal of Applied Behavior Analysis, 20,* 265-271.

Rusch, R. G., Hall, J. C., & Griffen, H. C. (1986). Abuse-provoking characteristics of institutionalized mentally retarded individuals. *American Journal of Mental Deficiency, 90*, 618-624.

Skinner joins aversives debate (1988, June). *APA Monitor*, pp. 22-23.

Solnick, J., Rincover, A., & Peterson, C. (1977). Some determinants of the reinforcing and punishing effects of timeout. *Journal of Applied Behavior Analysis, 10*, 415-424.

Spreat, S., & Lanzi, F. (in press). The role of human rights committees in the review of the restrictive/aversive behavior modification procedures: Results of a national survey. *Mental Retardation*.

Spreat, S., & Lipinski, D. P. (1986). Survey of state policies regarding the use of restrictive/aversive behavior modification procedures. *Behavioral Residential Treatment, 1*, 137-152.

Stokes, T. F., & Baer, D. M. (1977). An implicit technology of generalization. *Journal of Applied Behavior Analysis, 10,* 349-367.

The Association for Persons with Severe Handicaps (1988). *Setting the stage for non-aversive behavioral intervention*, pp. 1, 6.

Ulman, J. D., & Sulzer-Azaroff, B. (1975). Multielement baseline design in educational research. In E. Ramp & G. Semb (Eds.), *Behavior analysis: Areas of research and application* (pp. 377-391). Englewood Cliffs, NJ: Prentice-Hall.

Van Houten, R. (1983). Punishment: From the animal laboratory to the applied setting. In S. Axelrod & J. Apsche (Eds.), *The effects of punishment on human be-havior* (pp. 13-44). New York: Academic Press.

Van Houten, R., Axelrod, S., Bailey, J. S., Favell, J. E., Foxx, R. M., Iwata, B. A., & Lovaas, O. I. (1988). The right to effective behavioral treatment. *The Behavior Analyst, 11,* 111-114.

Zegiob, L. E., Jenkins, J., Becker, J., & Bristow, A. (1976). Facial screening: Effects on appropriate and inappropriate behaviors. *Journal of Behavior Therapy and Experimental Psychiatry, 7,* 355-357.

CHAPTER

5

RECENT DEVELOPMENTS IN NONAVERSIVE TREATMENT: A REVIEW OF RATIONALE, METHODS, AND RECOMMENDATIONS

James K. Luiselli
Psychological And Educational Resource Associates

During the initial meeting of case consultation for a severely mentally retarded adolescent with ruminative vomiting behavior, the author was confronted by the administrator of the client's service agency. Was I aware, he asked, of the use of contingent lemon juice as a treatment for rumination? I responded that I had knowledge of this strategy and was familiar with the relevant published research. This person then stated that he had read several journal articles on the topic and, since they demonstrated that "lemon juice treatment" was effective, shouldn't it be utilized with the present client? I indicated that there were many potential ill effects associated with this form of intervention and went on to enumerate these concerns (e.g. liquid aspiration, mouth irritations, gastric distress). Furthermore, I added, aversive treatment with noxious stimuli is subject to abuse, particularly in naturalistic settings where it is often difficult to maintain proper supervision and document treatment outcome in an objective manner. The administrator replied that supervision would not be a problem and that he would guarantee that "the program" would not be abused. My next response was to emphasize that a functional analysis of the behavior had not been performed so that we did not actually know what was controlling this client's rumination. Couldn't the results of a functional analysis indicate that lemon juice should be the treatment of choice? he asked. I then went on to review several less intrusive methods that also might be considered, such as food satiation, mealtime pacing, and increased water intake. These techniques could "take too long to work" complained the administrator; we needed a program that would stop rumination quickly--why not use the lemon juice?

As a private clinician and consultant to numerous program settings for persons with disabilities, the author has encountered many situations similar to the preceding illustration. Although treatment acceptability research demonstrates consistently that respondents show a decided preference for differential reinforcement methods over more invasive strategies (Miltenberger, Parrish, Rickert, & Kohr, 1989; Pickering, Morgan, Houts, & Rodrique, 1988; Tarnowski,

Rasanke, Mulick, & Kelly, 1989), the majority of practitioners within "real world" applied settings tend to rely on negative approaches to instruction and behavioral intervention[1]. This orientation is reflected in several ways: (a) a reliance on reprimands or "harsh" verbal directives; (b) withholding or "taking away" of clients' preferred activities; (c) a routine requirement of clients to "make amends" for their undesired behavior; and (d) a tendency towards physical interactions, such as forced prompting, guided compliance, and manual restraint. As in the earlier example, some persons are readily inclined to apply aversive stimuli in the forms of distasteful solutions, unpleasant odors, or water sprays.

The premise of this chapter is that a bias exists toward aversive programming as the most effective means to control serious behavior disorders. In many ways, the major challenge to behavioral clinicians is how to overcome this bias, develop alternative nonaversive strategies, and translate these methods into effective and efficient programs. The author's contention is that many professionals revert to aversive treatment without considering nonaversive alternatives that are less restrictive.

This chapter is a review of recent developments in the design of nonaversive treatment strategies in therapeutic programming for seriously challenging behaviors of persons with developmental disabilities. It begins with a discussion of some of the factors that influence the adoption of aversive procedures and the limitations associated with their use. Next, particular strategies that avoid some or all of these limitations will be presented. The focus will be on methods that are relatively novel, but have received substantive empirical documentation through controlled clinical and experimental research. For each strategy, relevant studies will be described, with an emphasis on the clinical implications of these findings and how they contribute to the formulation of a nonaversive technology of behavior change.

PUNISHMENT, AVERSIVES, AND PROCEDURAL CONCERNS

As highlighted in other chapters in this book, any discussion concerning the debate over aversive versus nonaversive intervention must begin with an accurate definition of the terminology. Conceptual confusion and terminological inconsistencies contribute to much of the controversy surrounding this treatment debate (Matson & DiLorenzo, 1984). The principle upon which this discourse is based is that of punishment. For the purpose of this chapter, the definition of punishment is the one presented by Azrin and Holz (1966) over two decades ago: "Punishment is a reduction of the future probability of a specific response as a result of the immediate delivery of a stimulus for that response" (p. 381). This description, of course, represents a functional definition since there is no *a priori* assumption of what this stimulus should be. Thus, if an adult praised a child, smiled at him, and delivered a pat on the back each time he misbehaved and the frequency of misbehavior decreased following systematic implementation of this consequence, then the procedure qualifies as punishment. For this reason, "punishing stimuli" is perhaps a better descriptive term than "aversive stimuli" within an operant conceptualization since the former label does not imply that the delivered stimulus must induce pain, discomfort, or distress (Matson & DiLorenzo, 1984). However, some procedures can be considered "aversive" by virtue of their intended purpose and

[1]This conclusion is based upon the author's observation of habilitative and therapeutic programming within diverse clinical environments. It is recognized that other professionals may disagree with the statement.

how they are applied. For example, the contingent delivery of stimuli, such as electric shock, hand slapping, hair pulling, lemon juice, Tabasco sauce, or water spray, are intended to provide a punishment effect because they are *unpleasant* to the recipient. As a type of punishment, this approach is defined best as *response-contingent aversive stimulation*. Certain physical interventions such as contingent exercise, forced movement, manual restraint, and overcorrection also exert operant control because their contingent application induces discomfort, fatigue, and the like.

The fact that aversive treatment methods rely on the inducement of pain, discomfort, physical fatigue, or similar unpleasant stimulation to modify behavior is one reason why such intervention is criticized. Many individuals believe that increasing the distress in persons who already are afflicted with handicapping conditions and have a limited capacity to tolerate their surroundings is improper. There are, of course, other related concerns. Any procedure that requires the presentation of a noxious stimulus or forced physical interaction is subject to abuse and potential injury to the recipient and/or implementer. By definition, aversive procedures do not teach alternative behaviors or the skills that are necessary to function more proficiently. Also, it might be added that when practitioners adopt aversive strategies within applied settings, a negative atmosphere is often created, whereby efforts are devoted disproportionately toward response reduction versus skill acquisition. In fact, some have described a depersonalization that extends from the practitioner to the client when aversive and punishment-based interventions are applied (Guess, Helmstetter, Turnbull, & Knowlton, 1987). A final criticism of aversive behavioral intervention is that it is associated with numerous undesirable side effects, such as the emergence of new problem responses, agitation, aggression, resistance, and social avoidance. It should be emphasized that reports on side effects have been primarily anecdotal as opposed to empirically determined. Furthermore, there appears to be a discrepancy between the summarized incidence of negative side effects presented by different investigators (see Guess et al., 1987; Matson & Taras, 1989).

REVIEW OF RECENT DEVELOPMENTS

Functional Assessment and Intervention

The first treatment development actually concerns the area of assessment. Functional assessment refers to the identification of controlling relationships between problem behaviors and various interpersonal, environmental, and organismic variables. The objective of such assessment is to determine how such variables, singularly or in combination, affect the rate, intensity, and maintenance of a behavior disorder. The information gathered from this assessment is then used to formulate an individually tailored treatment program.

Analogue Clinical Assessment

This approach represents an experimentally based strategy for empirical functional analysis. The intent of this methodology is to assess a client's behavior within specific interpersonal conditions that approximate different sources of control. These conditions are predetermined, presented for a standard duration (e.g., 15 minutes), and sequenced randomly. To illustrate, Iwata, Dorsey, Slifer, Bauman and Richman (1982) recorded the self-injurious behavior (SIB) of nine developmentally disabled children within four stimulus conditions: (a) *Social Disapproval* (each SIB was followed by a reprimand such as, "Don't do that!"), (b) *Academic Demand* (task demands were interrupted briefly contingent upon SIB), (c) *Unstructured Play* (each child engaged in isolate or cooperative play, with social attention delivered for non-SIB), and (d) *Alone* (each child was observed without the presence of toys or an attending adult). The results showed that, for six of the nine children, rates of SIB were differentiated by condition. Higher rates in the *Alone* condition suggested that SIB was maintained by sensory stimulation. Increased responding under conditions of *Social Disapproval* meant that the behavior provided an attention- eliciting function. Higher response frequencies in the *Academic Demand* condition indicated that escape or avoidance from the task requirements was the maintaining variable.

The importance of functional behavioral assessment is that it ensures that treatments are not selected arbitrarily, but are matched to relevant causal variables. Thus, Carr and associates (Carr & Newsom, 1985; Carr, Newsom, & Binkoff, 1980) found that the tantrumous and aggressive behaviors of developmentally disabled children occurred at high rates when teacher demands were presented, but rarely were encountered in the absence of demands. Given the escape-motivated function of these behaviors, treatment focused on the introduction of preferred reinforcers into teaching sessions in an effort to attenuate the aversiveness of demand conditions. Frequency of problem behaviors decreased substantially following this manipulation. Similarly, Mace, Browder, and Linn (1987) assessed the stereotypic behavior of a six-year-old mentally retarded boy within a variety of contexts, and determined that responding was most frequent when he was presented with difficult tasks and when stereotypy delayed instructional demands. A successful intervention was established by making tasks less difficult through implementation of a graduated prompt hierarchy and reinforcement for compliance combined with escape extinction (maintaining instruction while stereotypy occurred).

Another recent example of assessment-based treatment selection was described by Repp, Felce, and Barton (1988). In this study, hypotheses concerning the causes of problem behaviors in three special education students were generated, and functionally based treatment programs then were designed and evaluated. The procedures included social extinction for behaviors assumed to be controlled by positive reinforcement, reinforced compliance plus escape extinction for behaviors that were negatively-reinforced, and increased engagement with activities for behaviors judged to be reinforced by sensory stimulation. For each child, the treatment derived from the informal functional analysis proved to be the most effective one in producing behavior reduction.

Alternative Assessment Methods

Some of the concerns in conducting a functional behavior analysis through analogue clinical assessment are that it requires a predetermined sequencing of stimulus conditions, systematic data collection procedures, assignment of external observers, and staff training. These requirements can be too time-intensive or impractical for the busy clinician, and may be beyond the capabilities of most applied settings. It is significant, therefore, that researchers have developed more efficient alternatives to analogue methodologies. One such instrument is the Motivation Assessment Scale (MAS) designed by Durand and Crimmins (1988). It consists of a 16-item questionnaire that samples the contextual determinants of self-injurious behavior by having direct-care providers respond to questions such as, "Does the behavior occur following a command to perform a difficult task?" or "Does the behavior occur repeatedly, over and over, in the same way?" Respondents answer each question along a seven-point Likert-type scale ranging from "never" to "always." As stated by Durand and Crimmins (1988):

> "The 16 questions represent four examples from each of four maintaining variables--sensory consequences, escape, attention, and tangible consequences. A score is obtained for each of the four categories of maintaining variables by adding the scores for each of the category's four questions and computing a mean. High scores on one or more of these categories indicate that these variables may be responsible for the maintenance of the student's self-injury" (p. 102).

In a validity study of the MAS, Durand and Crimmins (1988) found that teachers' ratings on this instrument for eight students with self-injury predicted how the children would respond under conditions of analogue assessments similar to Iwata et al. (1982). Therefore, this and similar methods can be utilized as a means to identify controlling relationships in a clinically efficient manner. Although designed specifically to assess sources of control related to self-injury, this device presumably could be adapted to other aberrant behaviors.

Another practical alternative to analogue assessment is the scatterplot recording format (Touchette, MacDonald, & Langer, 1985). This method entails the construction of a grid with time segments (e.g., hours, half-hours) sequenced vertically and successive days designated horizontally. The intersections of the time segments and days produce a series of cell blocks on the grid. Data are entered by leaving a cell blank to indicate nonoccurrence of behavior and filling in the cell to indicate that the behavior was exhibited. It is also possible to score low- and high-rate behaviors by placing a coded symbol in the cell. Visual inspection of the grid on a daily basis reveals various patterns of responding that may be associated with type of activity, time of day, absence/presence of people, location, and similar environmental conditions. This depiction enables the practitioner to isolate sources of stimulus control and setting events for problem behaviors. In a series of three case studies with developmentally handicapped persons, Touchette et al. (1985) demonstrated how a scatter plot analysis could be used for treatment selection by eliminating those stimuli that controlled problem behaviors and introducing stimuli that were correlated with low rates or an absence of maladaptive responding.

SUMMARY. Treatment programs for clients with severe behavior disorders should be based upon an accurate determination of antecedent, consequence, and setting conditions that control responding. Although the process of conducting a functional analysis has been performed largely through clinical observation, an important recent development has been the formulation of empirically-oriented assessment methods. These approaches include assessment under analogue clinical conditions and utilization of questionnaires and data collection forms by practitioners. Some topics for research in this regard are the comparison of different functional assessment methodologies, the design of cost-efficient recording formats, and the evaluation of social validity.

Functional Equivalence

One of the most significant developments in the conceptualization of behavior disorders is a focus on *functional equivalence*. In keeping with the preceding discussion on assessment, this concept posits that treatment should attempt to teach responses and compensatory skills that serve the same function as the problem behavior(s). A particular emphasis has been placed on the communicative function of seriously challenging behaviors. Donnellan, Mirenda, Mesaros, and Fassbender (1984), for example, list seven motivational sources of behavior disorders and possible communication messages associated with them: (a) *positive reinforcement* in the form of attention ("Pay attention to me.") or access to materials ("I want ----."), (b) *negative reinforcement* ("I don't want this anymore."), (c) *extinction/frustration* ("I need help."), (d) *sensory stimulation* ("I'm bored."), (e) *arousal reduction* ("I'm tense/anxious/overwhelmed."), (f) *respondent conditioning* ("I'm frightened."), and (g) *physiological* ("I'm hurt" or "I don't feel well."). Upon isolating the communication intent of overt, motor behaviors such as self-injury, aggression, and noncompliance, the practitioner then formulates a strategy to teach the client how to impart this message in an alternative form.

As acknowledged by Donnellan et al. (1984), there are several advantages inherent in a functional equivalence orientation towards behavioral intervention. First, this approach attempts to eliminate problem behaviors by expanding a person's repertoire of skills. Such a perspective makes imminent sense when seeking behavioral deceleration in a developmentally disabled population where skill deficits are prominent. As suggested in an earlier section, procedures that emphasize skill acquisition usually are more readily embraced by personnel who are responsible for implementing treatment programs. And finally, since training of alternative behaviors and skills would commonly involve access to naturally occurring reinforcers, a likelihood exists that generalization and maintenance would be facilitated.

An experimentally elegant analysis of *functional communication training* for the treatment of behavior disorders was conducted by Carr and Durand (1985). They studied four children with developmental disabilities (ages 7-14 years) who engaged in behaviors such as aggression, tantrums, self-injury, and noncompliance. The target problems were measured while the children participated in teaching sessions in which they received either an easy or difficult task or were given adult attention during either 33% or 100% of timed intervals. For some children, behaviors were most frequent under the condition in which adult attention was at a maximum level and tasks were difficult. This outcome suggested that responding was escape/avoidance motivated. For others, the condition that was associated with high-rate problem behaviors was when tasks were easy and attention was reduced. The function of these behaviors appeared to be the elicitation of attention.

Having isolated the contextual determinants for each child's behavior, Carr and Durand (1985) then identified a verbal communicative phrase that signalled adult assistance or attention. A phrase was trained to be produced following a teacher's question, "Do you have any questions?" Children who were most problematic during the difficult task condition were taught to say, "I don't understand.", as a means to prompt teacher assistance. For situations in which low levels of attention were correlated with frequent problems, the phrase, "Am I doing good work?", was taught to prompt teacher praise. The results from the communication training interventions were an immediate suppression of problem behaviors for all children. Interestingly, response reduction was not achieved when the children were taught to make a verbal response that was unrelated to the suspected controlling stimuli. Therefore, the specific form of verbal response was not relevant, but rather, its functional equivalency to the problem behavior(s).

The results of Carr and Durand (1985) and subsequent replications (Durand & Carr, 1987; Durand & Crimmins, 1987) are based upon using a *preemptive* verbal strategy as a treatment for aberrant behaviors. A recent study by Steege, Wacker, Berg, Cigrand, Novak, and Cooper

(1988) also evaluated a procedure of differential reinforcement of communication but as applied to developmentally handicapped persons who were *nonverbal*. Two children (ages six and seven) were observed within analogue assessment conditions to identify influences on their self-injurious behaviors functionally. In each case, self-injury was most prevalent during demand situations. Treatment entailed teaching the children to press a microswitch that activated the prerecorded message, "Stop." Brief withdrawal of task demands was instituted following each switch activation. Results showed near-suppression of self-injurious behavior during application of the communication training intervention.

SUMMARY. Functional equivalence is an approach toward behavior deceleration that is based upon identifying the "message" of problem responses and then training an alternative form of communication. Research to date has focused primarily on the establishment of verbal language repertoires, although nonverbal responses (e.g., sign language) also have been targeted and likely could be analyzed in other ways with developmentally disabled persons who do not speak.

Compliance Training and Instructional Control Strategies

Many clients who engage in seriously problematic behaviors also demonstrate difficulties with compliance and generalized instruction-following. The observation that behavior problems and noncompliance are common in the repertoires of persons with developmental disabilities suggests that they may constitute a functional response class. Within a response class, responding may covary directly or inversely as a result of manipulations aimed at a subgroup of behaviors. Wahler (1975), for example, revealed that "clusters" of behavior covaried with regularity over time. As applied to clinical intervention, the phenomenon of covariation forms the basis of compliance training programs. Compliance training assumes that if aberrant behaviors and instruction-following behaviors are inversely related, then the frequency of management problems may be reduced by increasing compliance directly. With this approach, reinforcement contingencies to foster compliant responding are arranged in lieu of prescribing decelerative procedures for each target behavior.

Russo, Cataldo, and Cushing (1981) conducted research with three children (ages 3-5 years) who displayed noncompliance with adult requests and engaged in negative behaviors such as aggression, tantrums, and self-injury. Following baseline assessment, a compliance training procedure was introduced that featured primary and social reinforcement for compliance to requests within a predetermined latency period. For all children, intervention produced an increase in compliance and corollary reduction in problem behaviors. These results provided preliminary evidence for the concept of an inverse response class and the possibility of indirect modification of behavior disorders. Additionally, the authors cited three reasons to encourage research on response covariation in general and compliance training in particular. First, the focus of intervention is one that is positively-oriented. Second, treatment can become more economical and efficient since multiple behavior changes may be established by targeting only one member of the response class. And third, an alternative is available to direct interventions where ethical objections are of concern. For example, the difficulties associated with the physical intervention and aversive stimulation procedures noted earlier would be avoided since operant consequences are not implemented contingent upon a problem behavior but, instead, are arranged as reinforcement for compliance and instruction-following.

In an extension of covariation assessment and compliance training, Parrish, Cataldo, Kolko, Neef, and Egel (1986) evaluated four children (ages 3-5 years) with mild to moderate mental retardation. Frequency of compliant responding to adult-initiated instructions and the rate of aggression, disruption, destruction, and pica target behaviors were recorded. During some phases of the study, the children were exposed to compliance training procedures in which appropriate request-following was reinforced with edibles, touch, and praise while problem behaviors were untreated. In other phases, compliance training was discontinued and procedures such as DRO, social disapproval, and contingent observation were programmed for the target problems. As a function of compliance training, instruction-following increased and individual target behaviors decreased. Similarly, when these behaviors were reduced with the contingency management programs, the rate of compliance improved. The various patterns of covariation observed in this study provides further evidence of the inverse relationships between compliance and behavior disorders and argues favorably for a response class interpretation of treatment.

One limitation of the research conducted by Russo et al. (1981) and Parrish et al. (1986) is that the children were evaluated under analogue conditions, thereby influencing the generality and social validity of the findings. Mace, Kratochwill, and Fiello (1983) described a clinical application of compliance training with a 19-year-old male with severe mental retardation. Tantrums and aggressive behaviors were reduced without direct intervention by providing physical guidance on a prompt-hierarchy sequence and reinforcing compliance. Treatment was implemented along multiple change-agents and within varied settings, and was shown to be durable over an eight-month follow-up period.

Another analysis of instructional behavior within the concept of response class was reported by Singer, Singer, and Horner (1987). The participants in their study were four students (ages 7-10 years) who had moderate to severe mental retardation and histories of noncompliant behavior. An intervention strategy termed "pretask requesting" was evaluated. It involved the presentation of requests that had a high probability of compliance immediately prior to instructions that had a low probability of compliance. The high probability requests included such statements as, "Shake hands," and "Say your name." Three such commands were delivered in rapid succession, preceding a low probability request that involved transitioning from a preferred to a less preferred activity. The pretask manipulation was associated with near-100% compliance with the previous low probability instructions. The authors concluded that, "Pretask requesting is functional due to the pretask responses coming from the same class of responses as the target responses (i.e., compliance with requests)" (p. 289). Although this study did not include a measure of isolated problem behaviors that covaried with compliance, it does describe a simple, preemptive method to increase instruction-following. Also, this approach could be utilized as a means to improve compliance within a covariation model to treat behavior disorders.

Mace, Hock, Lalli, West, Belfiore, Pinter, and Brown (1988) carried out an extensive analysis of the interrelationship between low probability and high probability command sequences for the treatment of noncompliant behaviors. Their results showed that task noncompliance by mentally retarded adults could be decreased by instituting a sequence of high probability commands immediately preceding specific task requests. In addition to improved compliance, some participants evinced reduced compliance latencies and task duration. Simple experimenter attention and a delay in the contiguity between presentation of high and low probability commands were associated with lower rates of compliance. Mace et al. (1988) attributed their results to the "behavioral momentum" that was established through the increased reinforcement accompanying compliance with the high probability commands. By manipulating reinforcement density, a momentum of compliant behavior is produced that may then extend to requests where compliance is unlikely.

SUMMARY. Clinically significant changes in problem behaviors can be attained by manipulating the presentation of instructions and commands. One approach is to target management problems and compliant behavior as inverse members of a functional response class. In this conceptualization, the application of positive reinforcement to increase compliance is intended to produce corresponding decreases in the target problems. Another therapeutic manipulation that may be utilized for the treatment of noncompliance as a primary disorder is to "embed" low probability commands within the context of a high probability command sequence. This approach may be effective because compliant/noncompliant behaviors are of the same response class, stimulus control over instruction-following is achieved, or "behavioral momentum" is established by a manipulation of reinforcement density.

Stimulus Control and Transfer

Many behavior disorders reflect very precise stimulus control. In some situations, problems only occur when particular conditions exist or are encountered. When these conditions are absent, problem behaviors virtually may not occur or else be displayed at a significantly diminished rate. A determination of stimulus control has many implications for treatment planning and implementation. First, if a clinician can isolate the conditions that set the occasion for aberrant behavior, effective modifications should be possible by eliminating these stimuli. Another approach is to identify stimuli that are correlated with the display of appropriate, alternative behaviors and then introduce them into the conditions that provoked undesired responding. Or, one can design environments that set the occasion for the *absence* of problem behaviors and gradually transfer control from those contexts to conditions that previously were problematic.

Pace, Iwata, Edwards, and McCosh (1986) employed a stimulus control and transfer paradigm to treat the self-injurious behaviors of adolescents with profound mental retardation. Both individuals also engaged in "self-restraint" by purposefully restricting their movements; for example, by placing hands into pockets, grasping objects, and sitting on hands. At the start of the study, the clients were maintained in mechanical restraint devices that prevented the occurrence of self-injurious responses. When the devices were removed, self-injury was observed at near-continuous levels. Since an absence of self-injurious behavior was correlated with the wearing of restraint devices, the objective of treatment was to maintain this stimulus control while gradually fading the protective equipment. For one client, fading was accomplished by reducing the length of his arm restraints from 47 cm. to 5 cm. in a series of eight steps. When fading was up to a length of 5 cm., each device was covered with fabric and transferred eventually to tennis wristbands. For the second client, continuous restraint was induced via inflatable air splints. By reducing the air pressure systematically in 5 mm/Hg decrements, the experimenters faded it to a level of 1 mm/Hg while maintaining an absence of self-injury. Therefore, for both of these clients, stimulus control was transferred successfully from full restraint to stimuli that were independent of any restraint function (tennis wristbands, deflated air splints).

In the area of feeding disorders, the author (Luiselli, 1989b; Luiselli & Gleason, 1985) has evaluated stimulus control interventions to treat multihandicapped children who display severe food aversion. These children presented chronic histories of food refusal characterized by agitation, tantrums, resistance, and vomiting during attempts at oral feeding. Some children consumed only one or two food products, such as pureed baby food or yogurt, and rejected all other substances. Other children showed very erratic feeding patterns that were marked by minimal consumption and variable food preferences. Of significance was the fact that all of these children had been exposed previously to force-feeding efforts. Treatment entailed the use of highly preferred sensory stimulation (lights, rocking motion) to "desensitize" the children to feeding interactions with adult trainers. The stimulation first was incorporated as a setting event and then as contingent reinforcement for increased tolerance of feeding demands. In this regard, a graduated hierarchy of food presentation was established so that the children learned initially to accept oral contact with a utensil, insertion of the utensil into their mouths, delivery of a small quantity of preferred food from the utensil, and consumption of increased amounts of the food. Finally, the texture and composition of the preferred foods were altered gradually along a predetermined sequence. Eventually, various features of the training environment were eliminated to a point where the children were eating under naturalistic conditions and without external sensory reinforcement. As a result of intervention, near-100% levels of oral feeding were achieved, the variety of food types was expanded widely, and problems of resistance, agitation, and emesis were eliminated (see Luiselli, 1989a for a more detailed discussion of this treatment approach).

Touchette et al. (1985) presented several case studies that incorporated stimulus change interventions to modify severe behavior disorders. For example, a behavior analysis revealed that the assaultiveness of a 14-year-old developmentally disabled girl was most frequent between 1:00-4:00 p.m. on Monday through Thursday of each week. This time period was when the client attended prevocational and community living classes. Assaultive behavior was least likely to occur during early morning each weekday, lunch, after 4:00 p.m., and on Friday, Saturday, and Sunday. Further analysis indicated that the demands of individualized and group instruction did not set the occasion for assaults. Treatment consisted of developing a new afternoon schedule that approximated staff interactions encountered by the girl on the weekends and evenings. Informal activities, such as listening to stories and applying cosmetics, were substituted for the previous prevocational and community living classes. These activities were changed every 15 minutes and were terminated following signs of inattentiveness. The revised activity schedule resulted in an immediate decrease in assaultive behavior. Over time, the original activities in the girl's schedule (including those that were associated with the problem behavior) were reinstated slowly until full programming was in place. Assaultiveness did not increase during this phase and remained absent at a one-year follow-up.

SUMMARY. Stimulus control manipulations are often overlooked as a therapeutic management strategy. This approach is predicated on discovering and programming conditions that are correlated with diminished frequencies or nonoccurrence of problem behaviors. Once such conditions are established, stimulus fading procedures can be used to introduce situations that previously provoked undesired behaviors. The primary objective of stimulus control and transfer procedures is to maintain consistent levels of appropriate responding and, as such, represent a desirable method of nonaversive intervention.

CONCLUSIONS

Whatever one's position in the aversive versus nonaversive debate, there appears to be consensus on at least one point; namely, the need to design and evaluate alternatives to punishment. This chapter has discussed several recent developments in the formulation of nonaversive alternatives, the rationale for such intervention, and respective research findings. The techniques surveyed in this review, although methodologically distinct, share two common characteristics. On one hand, there is an emphasis on assessment-derived intervention whereby treatment strategies are tailored systematically to functionally controlling variables (see Luiselli & Singh, in press). And second, there is less concentration on consequence-control procedures in favor of antecedent and preemptive approaches. Such treatment seeks to establish response repertoires and arrange conditions that prevent or minimize the occurrence of behavior disorders rather than intervene contingently when problems are displayed. Instead, the manipulation of setting events, response classes, and stimulus control variables are often the focus of intervention.

Although this chapter included descriptions of research studies concerned with nonaversive alternatives, there is an obvious need for further applications of these strategies with diverse clinical disorders and within a variety of applied settings. In fact, one of the reasons for the suggested bias toward aversive programming is that research on nonaversive methods has lagged behind other management approaches. The author's experience is that many clinicians and practitioners are simply unaware of preemptive, stimulus change, and ecological manipulations that can be programmed therapeutically. By expanding research on these and similar methodologies, clinical applications should become more widespread. In addition, future research on nonaversive alternatives should include measures of social validity and consumer satisfaction.

Does the availability of alternative methods mean that punishment procedures, including those that incorporate aversive stimulation, should be prohibited? Probably not. Any responsible and skilled clinician can recount experiences with clients in which problem behaviors persisted despite every effort to apply constructive, positively based, and nonintrusive programs. To reject categorically particular procedures severely limits therapeutic options and the opportunity to improve the quality of life through the judicious, balanced, and ethical application of empirically-validated methods. However, in contemplating this point, the reader is urged to consider comments by Iwata (1988) during his Presidential Address to the Association for Behavior Analysis. In discussing the adoption of aversive contingencies in cases where nonaversive interventions were previously ineffective, he states:

> "But, in the case of aversive contingencies, the previous failure of positive reinforcement usually (and I emphasize usually) is not an inherent one. Instead, aversive contingencies are called into play when *we* have failed to find or establish a positive reinforcer, when *we* have failed to deliver that reinforcer in an effective manner, when *we* have failed to find a suitable response to displace the target, when *we* have failed to examine the stimulus conditions that contribute to the problem, and when *we* have failed to generate

the sources necessary to maintain a successful program" (p. 152).

The message from these comments dovetails with the premise explicated earlier in the chapter; i.e., aversive strategies typically are selected prematurely, without exploring alternative strategies, and with the assumption that they will produce the most potent therapeutic effects. Thus, though clinicians should be armed with a full spectrum of therapy procedures, this author would argue that there is little need to resort to aversives, that such techniques are required rarely, and that they should play a limited role in therapeutic programming for severe behavior disorders.

REFERENCES

Azrin, N.H., & Holz, W.C. (1966). Punishment. In W.K. Honig (Ed.), *Operant behavior: Areas of research and application* (pp. 380-447). New York: Appleton-Century-Crofts.

Carr, E. G., & Durand , V. M. (1985). Reducing behavior problems through functional communication training. *Journal of Applied Behavior Analysis, 18*, 111-126.

Carr, E. G., & Newsom, C. (1985). Demand-related tantrums: Conceptualization and treatment. *Behavior Modification, 9*, 403-426.

Carr, E. G., Newsom, C., & Binkoff, J. A. (1980). Escape as a factor in the aggressive behavior of two retarded children. *Journal of Applied Behavior Analysis, 13*, 101-117.

Donnellan, A. M., Mirenda, P. L., Mesaros, R. A., & Fassbender, L. L. (1984). Analyzing the communicative functions of aberrant behavior. *Journal of the Association for Persons with Severe Handicaps, 3*, 201-212.

Durand, V. M., & Carr, E. G. (1987). Social influences on self-stimulatory behavior: Analysis and treatment application. *Journal of Applied Behavior Analysis, 20*, 119-132.

Durand, V. M., & Crimmins, D. B. (1987). Assessment and treatment of psychotic speech in an autistic child. *Journal of Autism and Developmental Disorders, 17*, 17-28.

Durand, V. M., & Crimmins, D. B. (1988). Identifying the variables maintaining self-injurious behavior. *Journal of Autism and Developmental Disorders, 18*, 99-117.

Guess, D., Helmstetter, E., Turnbull, H. R., & Knowlton, S. (1987). *Use of aversive procedures with persons who are disabled: An historical review and critical analysis.* Seattle, WA: The Association for Persons with Severe Handicaps.

Iwata, B. A., Dorsey, M. F., Slifer, K. J., Bauman, K. E., & Richman, G. S. (1982). Towards a functional analysis of self-injury. *Analysis and Intervention in Developmental Disabilities, 2*, 3-20.

Iwata, B. A. (1988). The development and adoption of controversial default technologies. *The Behavior Analyst, 11*, 149-157.

Luiselli, J. K. (1989a). Behavioral assessment and treatment of pediatric feeding disorders in developmental disabilities. In M. Hersen, R. M. Eisler, & P. M. Miller (Eds.), *Progress in behavior modification.* Vol. 24. Newbury Park, CA: Sage.

Luiselli, J. K. (1989b). *Inducement of oral feeding in multihandicapped children displaying chronic food refusal.* Manuscript submitted for publication.

Luiselli, J. K., & Gleason, D. J. (1985). Combining sensory reinforcement and texture fading procedures to overcome chronic food refusal. *Journal of Behavior Therapy & Experimental Psychiatry, 18*, 149-156.

Luiselli, J. K., & Singh, N. N. (Eds.) (in press). Contemporary issues in assessment-based treatment of childhood disorders. *Behavior Modification*.

Mace, F. C., Browder, D. M., & Linn, Y. (1987). Analysis of demand conditions associated with stereotypy. *Journal of Behavior Therapy & Experimental Psychiatry, 18*, 25-32.

Mace, F. C., Hock, M. L., Lalli, J. S., West, B. J., Belfiore, P., Pinter, E., & Brown, D. K. (1988). Behavioral momentum in the treatment of noncompliance. *Journal of Applied Behavior Analysis, 21*, 123-141.

Mace, F. C., Kratochwill, T. R., & Fiello. R. A. (1983). Positive treatment of aggressive behavior in a mentally retarded adult. *Behavior Therapy, 14*, 689-696.

Matson, J. L., & DiLorenzo, T. (1984). *Punishment and its alternatives*. New York: Springer.

Matson, J. L., & Taras, M. E. (1989). A 20-year review of punishment and alternative methods to treat problem behaviors in developmentally delayed persons. *Research in Developmental Disabilities, 10*, 85-104.

Miltenberger, R. G., Parrish, J. M., Rickert, V., & Kohr, M. (1989). Assessing treatment acceptability with consumers of outpatient child behavior management services. *Child & Family Behavior Therapy, 11*, 35-44.

Pace, G. M., Iwata, B. A., Edwards, G. L., & McCosh, K. C. (1986). Stimulus fading and transfer in treatment of self-restraint and self-injurious behaviors. *Journal of Applied Behavior Analysis, 19*, 381-389.

Parrish, J. M., Cataldo, M. F., Kolko, D. J., Neef, N. A., & Egel, A. L. (1986). Experimental analysis of response covariation among compliant and inappropriate behaviors. *Journal of Applied Behavior Analysis, 19*, 241-254.

Pickering, D., Morgan, S. B., Houts, A. C., & Rodrique, J. R. (1988). Acceptability of treatments for self-abuse: Do risk-benefit information and being a parent make a difference? *Journal of Clinical Child Psychology, 17*, 209-216.

Repp, A. C., Felce, D., & Barton, L. E. (1988). Basing the treatment of stereotypic and self-injurious behaviors on hypotheses of their causes. *Journal of Applied Behavior Analysis, 21*, 281-289.

Russo, D. C., Cataldo, M. F., & Cushing, P. J. (1981). Compliance training and behavioral covariation in the treatment of multiple behavior problems. *Journal of Applied Behavior Analysis, 14*, 209-222.

Singer, G. H. S., Singer, J., & Horner, R. H. (1987). Using pretask requests to increase the probability of compliance for students with severe disabilities. *The Journal of the Association for Persons with Severe Handicaps, 12*, 287-291.

Steege, M. W., Wacker, D. P., Berg, W. K., Cigrand, K., Novak, C. G., & Cooper, L. J. (1988). *The application of differential reinforcement of communication in the treatment of self-injury in individuals with severe multiple handicaps*. Paper presented at Annual Convention, The Association for Behavior Analysis, Philadelphia, PA.

Tarnowski, K. J., Rasanke, L. K., Mulick, J. A., & Kelly, P. A. (1989). Acceptability of behavioral interventions for self-injurious behavior. *American Journal of Mental Retardation, 93*, 575-580.

Touchette, P. E., MacDonald, R. F., & Langer, S. N. (1985). A scatter plot for identifying stimulus control of problem behavior. *Journal of Applied Behavior Analysis, 18*, 343-351.

Wahler, R. G. (1975). Some structural aspects of deviant child behavior. *Journal of Applied Behavior Analysis, 8*, 27-42.

CHAPTER

6

MORAL AND SCIENTIFIC ASPECTS OF THE PUNISHMENT CONTROVERSY

Linda J. Hayes and Christopher McCurry
University of Nevada-Reno

Controversies arise under two sets of circumstances: When the information necessary to support opposing positions is lacking and when opposing positions are based on tradition not information. In principle, therefore, a controversy could arise under any conditions whatsoever since we never have access to "all the information" and we always operate on the basis of tradition. Usually, however, controversies arise when particular kinds of information are lacking--information available by way of scientific investigation--and when positions are based on particular kinds of traditions; namely, moralistic ones. The current controversy over the use of aversive procedures with mentally retarded persons is a good example of this situation. Applied psychology is divided between supporters of the use of aversive procedures as treatment and those who want a prohibition of all aversive procedures. The respective arguments have both scientific and moral undertones. We consider each of these aspects in the pages to follow.

THE MORAL ISSUE

What is right or wrong, and thereby should or should not be done, is a moral argument having its sources and bases not in fact or evidence, as we understand these terms in a scientific context, but rather, in cultural tradition. Both sides of the debate over the use of aversive procedures have employed the rhetoric of morality: Each holds its position to be right, the other's wrong (Sobsey, 1987; Thompson, Gardner, & Baumeister, 1988).

Acts of this sort have a number of distinguishing features, among which is their resistance to change: It is virtually impossible to resolve a moral conflict "from within," as no grounds exist for abandoning one position in favor of another. It is not even possible to *understand* a moral controversy from the standpoint of those involved in it, as this would entail understanding each side from the standpoint of the other, which neither side is able to do. On the contrary, to understand a controversy and to see how it might be resolved, we must approach it "from without." In other words, we must examine this particular moral conflict over the use of aversive procedures with mentally retarded persons as an instance of a larger class of such events, and attempt to describe the features responsible for class membership. In taking this perspective, we adopt the position of analyst as opposed to antagonist.

We proceed now to an examination of the nature, operations, and evolution of actions having their sources and bases in cultural tradition--to an examination of cultural acts.

Cultural Acts

What constitutes a cultural act is a matter of some disagreement among behavior scientists. The disagreement has concerned such issues as the agent of action involved, the operations by which practices are acquired and maintained, and how their strength is to be measured. For example, Glenn (1986), in the anthropological tradition of Harris (1979), takes the position that a cultural act or practice is not individual behavior, but, rather, a set of behaviors conceived as a set because of their relation to a particular long-term consequence. Biglan (1988) isolates a similar subject matter, although he stops short of a classification based solely on the contingencies of reinforcement involved, arguing that other kinds of consequences (e.g., death) are relevant to the strength of cultural practices. S. C. Hayes (1988) argues that, while cultural practices are manifested in the behavior of individuals and are thereby not distinguishable from individual behavior at the time of their occurrence, practices are nonetheless distinguishable from individual performances. According to Hayes, a practice may be distinguished from individual behavior on the basis of its social means of propagation and its inherently social measure of strength.

Practices of an anthropological or sociological sort are not the ones that we are interested in, however. This is not to say that we fail to recognize the legitimacy of a subject matter articulated at this level. It is just that we wish to consider cultural events of a psychological sort. In other words, we are interested in cultural *behaviors*, not practices as defined by these and other social scientists. We believe that a useful distinction between cultural behaviors and those of either an idiosyncratic or species-specific sort may be made and, further, that the variables responsible for the strength of cultural behaviors differ from those responsible for the strength of the other types. Let us proceed, then, to a definition of cultural behavior.

DEFINITION OF CULTURAL BEHAVIOR. Kantor's (1982) conception of cultural behavior is best suited to our purposes. According to him (1982, p. 164), cultural behaviors have two defining characteristics: First, they are correlated with institutional or conventional stimulus functions; and second, they are acquired through a culturization process operating under specific group circumstances.

The first characteristic may be taken to mean that cultural behaviors are actions shared among a group smaller than the entire species. Actions shared by all members of the species are almost certainly coordinated with natural properties of stimuli, as is the case of unconditioned reflexes. Institutional functions, by contrast, do not inhere in the natural properties of stimulus objects. They are attributed to stimuli by persons in a particular group, and correspond to actions shared among members of that group.

The second characteristic, having to do with the means by which cultural actions are acquired, eliminates from this class idiosyncratic actions shared as a result of chance circumstances. Instead, cultural actions are shared among members of a group as an outcome of their group living situation. Most of our behavior by this definition is cultural, including all of our linguistic behavior and at least some aspects of how we dress, eat, work, and care for our children.

CHARACTERISTICS OF CULTURAL BEHAVIOR. *Artificiality.* Responding coordinated with stimulation inhering in attributed as opposed to natural properties of stimuli has certain distinctive features. Among them is an artificiality in the sense that cultural behaviors have no basis in biological, environmental, social, or rational circumstances. This means, essentially, that "what may function as aesthetic reactions may not be aesthetic, rational actions may not be reasonable, economic reactions may not be economically advantageous, industrial processes may not be mechanically sound, hygienic reactions may not be conducive to health," etc. (Kantor, 1982, p.166).

It is possible, of course, that at least some cultural actions were not artificial, or not wholly so, when first originating. Nonetheless, their limited distribution among the human population suggests that their evolution is such as to render them artificial over time. Implied by this circumstance is that the more complex the civilization, the more intensified is the artificiality of the cultural behavior found in it. In this regard, we may cite such examples as attributing powers or potencies to rabbits' feet, horseshoes, and four-leaf clovers.

Arbitrariness. Being artificial, the morphological characteristics of cultural behavior are not constrained by the impact this behavior has on such things as survival, ecological adaptation, economic viability, etc. As such, there are no fixed or accepted standards for their performance apart from the actions themselves (Kantor, 1982). In other words, while cultural actions are arbitrary in form, whatever their form happens to be constitutes the standard.

Rigidity of Form. For the same reason that the morphological characteristics of cultural behaviors are unconstrained, they remain relatively resistant to change (Kantor, 1982, p. 171). In other words, because the effects of cultural acts are unrelated to their formal characteristics, they do not provide a means for the modification of these characteristics. Moreover, the greater the number of people engaging in a particular cultural act, the more rigid its form becomes. This is the case because inevitable idiosyncratic variations in form are readily observed against a standard obvious in the performances of a great many others; and these variations, once noted, may be modified to conform to the standard. (Nonetheless, when cultural behavior is altered or ceases to exist, it is by way of idiosyncratic variations in form that it does so. This is an issue to which we now turn).

THE EVOLUTION OF CULTURAL BEHAVIOR. Cultural behaviors tend to persist when a number of conditions prevail, one of which we have mentioned already; namely, when the group engaging in such acts is large. This circumstance is related to another: the absence of alternatives. When the group behaving in a particular manner is so large that contact with alternative actions is very infrequently made, the behavior tends to persist unchanged. The absence of alternatives is also produced by such conditions as geographical isolation.

Other conditions favoring the perpetuation of cultural behavior have to do with particular characteristics of the acts themselves. The more intimate the act, the more likely it is to persist. For example, acts of belief tend to persist when they concern the believer personally, such as a belief in the transnatural soul. Beliefs of this sort are further fixed by the fact that they concern fundamentally unobservable items. Beliefs concerning observable entities change as observations of those entities suggest changes in what we believe about them.

Cultural behaviors do evolve, however, despite the various conditions favoring their perpetuation. This evolution occurs through variations in the form of individual performances, and is fostered primarily by the social (i.e., economic, political, familial) circumstances of those performers.

EXAMPLES OF CULTURAL BEHAVIOR. As already mentioned, most of our behavior is cultural, and examples are, consequently, everywhere we look. Our linguistic repertoire provides a particularly good illustration of this category, however, because it is completely artificial in the sense discussed above. For instance, there is nothing about the natural properties of a table that gives rise to the response "table," as may be obvious from the fact that this object stimulates other responses in other language communities around the world. Such acts are also relatively resistant to morphological change.

While less obvious, an especially relevant example of cultural action is a class of what we may call evaluative responses. The value of a person, thing, or event may constitute one of its stimulational functions, and actions coordinated with such functions are evaluative. Not all evaluative actions are cultural, though. Stimuli may have value in the accomplishment of particular ends or in the fulfillment of particular purposes. For example, to pound in a tent peg, a rock may have the value of a hammer. In such cases, the value function inheres in the natural properties of the stimulus object: A leaf does not have the value of a hammer. Evaluative actions coordinated with value functions inhering in natural properties of stimuli are not cultural. Alternatively, evaluative actions may be coordinated with value functions *attributed* to objects under group auspices. Under these conditions, the evaluative action is an example of cultural behavior.

Distinguishing between the attributed and natural properties of stimuli is not always a simple matter. Attributed properties may be mistaken for natural ones when the group for which attributed properties obtain is large enough to obscure the artificiality of the coordinated acts. An example would be when the group adopting causal constructions is so large that alternatives do not appear to be available. The tendency under such conditions is to see causality as a property of nature. Nonetheless, the distribution of actions with respect to particular stimuli remains the only adequate means of distinguishing between the natural and attributed properties of the stimuli involved. Hence, when actions vary from place to place or time to time, we may assume that the functions of the stimuli coordinated with those actions are attributed functions and the acts are thereby of a cultural character. Evaluative actions are very often of this sort.

What constitutes good and bad art, for example, is a classic case of evaluative cultural action. By our logic, whatever one's evaluation of a particular work of art might be, it has no basis in biological, environmental, humanistic, or rational circumstances. It is, rather, an arbitrary response shared by the particular group in which one is a member; and what that group finds "good" does not become "bad" by means of persuasion. On the contrary, our artistic preferences are relatively impervious to influences of this sort as is characteristic of cultural actions generally. As long as the group having a particular preference is large enough or salient enough for other reasons to present this preference as a standard of performance, we may expect resistance to change in such evaluative action.

Evaluating the modification of behavior by aversive means as right or wrong, in the absence of any other criterion upon which to make this evaluation, is an action of the cultural sort we have been discussing. As such, the arguments have their sources and bases in cultural traditions, not in biological, environmental, social, or rational circumstances. In other words, *believing it right or wrong to use aversive procedures with retarded persons can be justified only on the grounds that this is what people in your group believe.* Were it otherwise, everyone would believe the same thing, which, obviously, is not the case.

Objections To This Analysis

We may anticipate a certain resistance to our analysis of the moral aspect of the controversy over the use of aversive procedures. It will be claimed at this juncture that the controversy is not as simple as is implied by our analysis. Indeed, the arguments in favor of and opposed to the use of aversive procedures with mentally retarded persons are not usually cast in terms of right or wrong without further embellishment. More typically, the arguments specify conditions that must be met in order for an evaluation of this sort to be made, and these conditions are such as to suggest that the evaluative responses made under their consideration are not entirely cultural in character. In particular, the artificiality of the evaluative response will be denied

DETERRENCE. Those who favor the use of aversive procedures do so on the grounds that it serves a worthy purpose; namely, the elimination of behaviors that are debilitating or life-threatening. In other words, these positions hold that there should be an overall beneficial effect of punishment, either through deterrence or through making the punisher a better person (i.e., one less likely to do wrong again).Strictly speaking, from these positions, the rights of the individual are secondary to the aims of those in a position to punish.

Those who favor the use of aversive procedures tend to defend their position on teleological or deterrent grounds. They argue that, while punishment is an unpleasant business, it serves the worthy purpose of eliminating debilitating or life-threatening behaviors.

Those opposed point to certain troublesome implications of these positions, among which is the tendency to allow the end to justify the means. When this happens, such practices as incapacitation (confinement) and capital punishment could be deemed to be justifiable, since both deter (at least for that one individual) future inappropriate behavior.

RETRIBUTION. Among the classic non-consequentialist theories of punishment is the Retributivist position (Ezorsky, 1972; Hoekema, 1986). This class of argument may be thought of as a *human rights* position. It is based on the idea that there is a moral balance in the universe that becomes upset when an individual suffers at the hands of a wrong-doer. According to this position, the role of punishment is not to improve the person punished, nor is it to deter future wrong-doing. Instead, punishment is used to redress the moral imbalance at hand by making the guilty person suffer. Oddly though, from this point of view, the rights of the individual are considered paramount, even while that individual is being punished: It is essential to the Retributivist position that one is punished only if one is actually guilty and only to the degree that one deserves to be punished (i.e., just enough to even things out).

The Rebributivist position offers a certain other-worldly appeal, but it is not without practical problems; namely, ascertaining guilt and innocence with the precision necessary to deal with cosmic moral balances, and determining with equal precision what punishment fits the particular wrong doing. Moreover, the concept of moral balance is difficult to apply in the context of aversive therapies with mentally retarded persons. How can the application of a painful stimulus to an individual correct the moral imbalance that occurred when the same individual struck his head against a wall?

Despite these problems, the anti-aversive therapy stance has much in common with the Retributivist position. A central concern of the anti-punishment lobby is the issue of human rights. Implied by this concern is the notion that there *is* a moral balance in the world that *can* be thrown out of whack, but only if we *do* use punishment with mentally retarded persons.

LESSONS LEARNED. This admittedly brief contact with moral philosophy reminds us that aversive control has been used and is an integral part of Western culture (Roos, 1974). We have only to consider the behavior of parents toward their children, governments toward their citizens, and religions toward their followers to know that this is true. Threats of spankings, prison, and eternal damnation have been used, and still are being used, to control behavior and to keep our society safe and just. Punishment has been considered a moral imperative (i.e., Spare the rod and spoil the child) and a political reality (i.e., Speak softly but carry a big stick).

The prevalence of aversive practices in our society does not mean that the society as a whole is supportive of this form of social control, however. The history of moral philosophizing also reminds us that debate over the use of such practices has been going on for centuries. It continues today over the use of aversive procedures with mentally retarded persons, among other similar issues. As a society, it would seem, we are ambivalent about aversive control (Ezorsky, 1972).

What now may be considered societal ambivalence toward aversive practices may be revealed later to be a period of transition from a society in which such practices are commonplace to one in which they are absent. In other words, the cultural stimulus functions of mentally retarded persons may be changing. This direction is suggested by changes that already have taken place in our perception of acceptable practices of family interaction, for instance, and, among many others, in the treatment of animals.

The *fact* of societal evolution, while inevitable, is not proof of its value, however, any more than is the fact of biological evolution. Change occurs by chance in both cases; and while some changes persist and some do not, those that persist do not necessarily contribute to the survival of the underlying entity, be it a species or a society. Hence, if we wish to address the question of whether or not the elimination of aversive practices in our society is good or right, we must appeal to something other than the trend in this direction itself. On what grounds *can* we evaluate the elimination of aversive practices in our society? More specifically, on what grounds can we evaluate the elimination of aversive practices with mentally retarded persons? As previously discussed, some have argued that aversive procedures are good because they work, while others have argued that they are bad because they don't work. Both positions imply workability as a value. We do not quarrel with workability as a value. However, we recognize that for workability to function as a criterion upon which changes in cultural behavior or social practices may be evaluated, it must be able to be demonstrated. This demonstration is a responsibility of science, and it is to this aspect of the controversy that we now turn.

THE SCIENTIFIC ISSUE

Almost all of the early work on aversive control was conducted with animal subjects, primarily rats (see Azrin & Holz, 1966, for a review). Animal findings indicate that punishment is effective in suppressing behavior only under certain conditions. These conditions may be summarized as follows: (a) the greater the intensity of the aversive stimulus, the greater the response suppression (Azrin & Holz, 1966); (b) punishment is more effective when the aversive stimulus is introduced at maximum intensity rather than when its intensity is increased gradually (Azrin & Holz, 1966); (c) punishment is most effective when delivered immediately after the targeted response than when it is delayed (Azrin,

1956; Azrin, Holz, & Hake, 1963; Kimble, 1963; Zimmerman & Ferster, 1963); (d) punishment is more effective when it is delivered on a continuous rather than an intermittent schedule (Azrin & Holz, 1966); (e) the effect of punishment can be enhanced by removing the source of reinforcement for the targeted response (Azrin & Holz, 1961; 1966); and (f) punishment is more effective when other behavior is being reinforced while the targeted response is being punished (Azrin & Holz, 1966).

The animal literature also notes certain side effects of punishment, including: (a) the occurrence of disruptive emotional responses upon the presentation of the aversive stimulus (Azrin & Holz, 1966; Skinner, 1953); (b) escape and/or avoidance of the punishment situation (Azrin, Hake, Holz, & Hutchinson, 1965; Azrin, & Holz, 1966); and (c) aggression toward the source of punishment (Azrin, Hutchinson, & Hake, 1963; Hutchinson, 1977).

While some maintain that animal data are "easily transferable to human research and practice" (Matson & DiLorenzo, 1984, p.2), others suggest that interspecies extrapolation be done with caution (see Hayes, 1988, for a discussion). Nonetheless, the animal findings cited above have formed the basis upon which aversive procedures for controlling human behavior have been articulated (Matson & Di Lorenzo, 1984; Griffith, 1986; Thompson et al, 1988). These procedures, along with certain side effects of their use, appear in numerous textbooks on behavior modification (for example see, Kazdin, 1980; Martin & Pear, 1978; Sulzer-Azaroff & Mayer, 1977).

This situation is not peculiar to the case of aversive control. All of the principles of behavior underlying behavior modification procedures were originally discovered in the animal laboratory. The case of aversive control is somewhat different, however, because research on nonaversive procedures with humans has been extensive compared to human research on aversive control. Applications involving aversive control have also been relatively limited, both in number and variety. In Bellack and Hersen's (1977, p. 235) words: "(m)any of the variables that contribute to the maximal efficacy of the punishment stimulus... have been ignored by clinical researchers when carrying out their treatments." This circumstance has not prevented both sides in the current debate from citing data to suggest that their position is the correct one, however. (For an actual debate, see Zabel, 1985).

As suggested earlier, controversies arise when the information necessary to support opposing positions is lacking. It seems reasonable to suppose that the controversy over the use of aversive procedures with mentally retarded persons is a product of insufficient information, at least in part. The very existence of an argument over whether and under what conditions punishment is effective in controlling behavior suggests a dearth of definitive data on this issue and, the need for further research if the scientific issue is to be resolved.

If research and treatment efforts were inseparable, as has been proposed by Haywood (1976), these data might be available now. Without them, however, the scientific status of the two sides in this debate cannot be determined, much less with any precision.

Problems of Generalizing from Animals to Humans

An issue of much greater scope suggests itself as a means of addressing the scientific aspects of the controversy, however. That issue is the workability of generalizations from animal to human situations. In recent years, the assumption that the principles of behavior derived from animal investigations are applicable to human behavior without significant alteration has been challenged by a series of contradictory findings.

Among the first indications of a noncorrespondence between the animal and human cases occurred in the context of schedule performances. Human fixed interval (FI) performance does not show the scallop characteristic of animals performance on this schedule (Leander, Lippman, & Meyer, 1968; Lippman & Meyer, 1967; Weiner, 1964, 1965).

Human schedule performance more like that of animals is able to be induced, however, by requiring the subject to engage in concurrent verbal tasks such as solving math problems or reading aloud (Laties & Weiss, 1963; Lowe, Harzem, & Hughes, 1978). These procedures, it is argued, are effective because they eliminate the counting assumed to be taking place during the scheduled intervals which, in turn, is held to be responsible for the steady, as opposed to scalloping, performances observed of humans on these schedules. Subsequent work by Lowe, Beasty, and Bentall (1983) supported the notion that interference from human verbal action, including counting and other forms of self-instruction, was indeed the reason for the noncorrespondence between human and animal schedule performances. They found human performances identical to those of animal subjects when the human subjects were infants without language.

Verbal behavior in the form of self instruction has been identified as the reason for other differences between human and animal behavior. Catania and his colleagues (Catania, Matthews, & Shimmoff, 1982; Shimmoff, Catania, & Matthews, 1981) have argued that self-instruction produces an insensitivity to changes in contingencies not seen in animal subjects. Similarly, Lowe (1979) and Malott (1989) argue that instructions produce a powerful effect on human behavior because they influence self-instructions. (For a more extensive review of this literature, see Hayes, Zettle, and Rosenfarb, 1989).

Perhaps the most telling example of the difference between animal and human behavior has been seen in the work on stimulus equivalence. When humans are taught a series of conditional discriminations, the stimuli involved in these discriminations become connected with one another in ways that are not directly trained. This phenomenon is typically investigated in a matching sample procedure. For example, suppose a person is taught to choose an unfamiliar object from an array of such objects (the comparisons), given the presence of another unfamiliar object (the sample). For purposes of discussion, we may say the person has learned "given A, choose B", where A and B represent the unfamiliar objects. The person then is taught to choose another unfamiliar object from another array, given the same sample. That is, the person is taught "given A, choose C." With this training, it is likely that when the person is given B or C as samples, A will be selected from among the comparisons without explicit training. This performance is called derived symmetry. The person is also likely to select C, given B as a sample; and to select B, given C as a sample; even though these performances also have not been explicitly trained. This set of events is called stimulus equivalence (Sidman, 1971; Sidman, Cresson, & Wilson-Morris, 1974).

Stimulus equivalence has been demonstrated with normal adults (Hayes, Tilley, & Hayes, 1988; Wulfert & Hayes, 1988), normal and retarded children with expressive speech (Devaney, Hayes, & Nelson, 1986), and retarded adults with some language (Dixon & Spradlin, 1976). It has not been found with animal subjects, including primates, despite several attempts to find it (D'Amato, Salmon, Loukas, & Tomie, 1985; Kendall, 1983; Lipkens, Kop, & Matthjis, 1988; Sidman, Rauzin, Lazar, Cunningham, Tailby, & Carrigan, 1982). In these studies, animal subjects learned the conditional discriminations involved; namely, "given A, choose B", and "given A, choose C", but they did not show the derived relations of symmetry and equivalence. In short, knowing that "X goes with Y" did not entail "Y goes with X" for these subjects.

This difference between human and animal behavior also has been attributed to the human verbal repertoire. In this case, however, linguistic acts are not said to *interfere* with the equivalencing act, as has been argued previously about human schedule performance and insensitivity to contingencies. Rather, the equivalencing act is taken to *be* a linguistic event (Hayes & Hayes, 1989).

The derived symmetrical relation of equivalence illustrates the similarity between these two cases most obviously. When a person learns to call an object by its correct name, it happens that, upon hearing the name, the person also will be able to select the correct object although never having done so before. In short, the relation that "X goes with Y" entails the relation that "Y goes with X" for humans. This entailment is a central characteristic of language; it is a defining feature of equivalence; and it is observed only among humans with some linguistic ability (Devany, Hayes, & Nelson, 1986). From these facts and conditions, one can draw the conclusion that language and equivalence are the same process (Lowe, 1979; Hayes, & Hayes, 1989). Consequently, the reason that animals do not engage in verbal behavior is the same reason that they do not show equivalence.

Taken together, recent evidence suggests that humans and animals behave differently and that the difference is due to the linguistic abilities of humans. It is interesting to note that Skinner (1938) warned of this difference as early as 1938. The question thus arises: What difference does the presence of a linguistic repertoire make, and how does this relate to the use of aversive procedures with mentally retarded persons?

Verbal Repertoires and Aversive Procedures

CHARACTERISTICS OF A VERBAL REPERTOIRE. Before dealing with the issue of aversive control directly, we must consider what a linguistic repertoire enables more generally. In doing so, we refer back to certain characteristics of the cultural behavior class to which linguistic acts belong, among other properties of the linguistic class in particular.

Specificity. Linguistic acts are arbitrary in form, meaning that their forms are not determined by the natural properties of the stimulus events with which they are coordinated. Their forms are conventional. As such, their forms are free to vary to a much greater extent than is the case for behaviors of nonarbitrary form. The result is that an enormous number of response forms exist in any given language community, and the number may be expanded in accordance with however fine grained is the perception of the nonlinguistic world for that community (Parrott, 1984). To exemplify this feature another way, a verbal stimulus comes to "mean" something very specific (i.e., control a specific response). They mean those events that participate in equivalence classes with them, and only those events.

This circumstance prevents intrusions in meaning from other event sources as often happens with stimuli of nonarbitrary form. For example, if a rat were to encounter a distinctive auditory stimulus and immediately thereafter put his nose in the food cup and find food, the distinctive noise might come to control the behavior of putting his nose in the cup. On the other hand, if a human being heard a distinctive noise of the form, "Hi Joe," and immediately thereafter looked to the ground and found a ten-dollar bill, it is very unlikely that "Hi Joe" would evoke looking down on a subsequent occasion. This means, essentially, that a verbal repertoire may override the effects of chance happenings that might otherwise participate in the control of behavior (Hayes & Meyerson, 1986).

The specificity of verbal functions also may override the effect of delays in contingency relations. For example, suppose a person takes a GRE test and six weeks later the results come in the mail. Suppose the results are much better than expected. It is unlikely that whatever the person was doing before reading the results will be made more probable by this consequence. Rather, preparing for tests is likely to be made more probable, despite the six-week delay between this behavior and the relevant consequence (Hayes & Hayes, 1989).

Substitutability. Related to this issue is the expansion of the psychological present made possible by verbal events. It is only by way of verbal events that responding with respect to the past or future is possible. The past is brought to bear in the present by way of a listener's historical contacts with the events being discussed. The not-yet-existing events of the future are verbally constructed on the model of already existing events. Similarly, it is only by way of verbal stimulation that distant, remote, intangible, or nonexistent events can operate. In summary, the response potential of the verbal organism is not restricted by the objective character of the immediate stimulational context as it is for nonverbal organisms. (See Parrott, 1984, and Hayes & Hayes, 1989, for more detailed discussions of these and related issues.)

AVERSIVE PROCEDURES WITH VERBAL ORGANISMS. Before proceeding with our analysis, we wish to make it clear that our analysis applies only to humans with at least some language ability. We have neither reason nor data to suggest that aversive procedures developed on the basis of animal findings are not, or could not be, effective with humans without language. With this limitation acknowledged, we consider the workability of aversive procedures with verbal human beings.

Intensity. Animal research suggests that the greater the intensity of the aversive stimulus, the greater the response suppression. Intensity is not defined in terms of its effect on behavior in this context. Rather, it refers to a property of the aversive stimulus itself, such as its number, magnitude, brightness, density, temperature, etc. As such, we must ask, does the suppressive effect of a stimulus depend on its intensity and further increase proportionally with its intensity for a verbal human being?

Equivalence research suggests that this is not, in fact, the case. This research has shown that a previously neutral stimulus may acquire suppressive effects as a result of its having become a member of an equivalence class involving an already aversive stimulus (Hayes, Brownstein, Devany, Kohlenberg, & Shelby, 1987). This acquisition of aversive properties does not depend on a direct pairing of the neutral stimulus with the already aversive stimulus, nor does its continued strength depend on subsequent pairings of the two as required for nonverbal organisms. Further, once established, equivalence classes tend to persist. Consequently, seemingly innocuous stimuli may continue to have powerful aversive effects long after their original inclusion in an aversive class. Human phobic reactions have been explained by appeal to events of this sort (Hayes, 1988), for example. In short, the morphological characteristics of stimuli are not predictive of their aversiveness for verbal human beings: Being called a "liar" or a "cheat" may have a much greater suppressive effect than a slap for a verbal human.

Immediacy. The animal literature also suggests that punishment will be most effective if delivered immediately following the targeted response. As discussed above, one of the most significant features of a verbal repertoire is its role in overcoming the constraints of the immediate situational context. Consequences do not have to be immediate to have effects on the behavior of verbal humans. This applies to reinforcement as well as to punishment. Delayed punishment may be quite effective.

Durability. The substitutional character of verbal events may also explain certain other differences between animal and human reactions to punishment. The effects of punishment tend to be somewhat transient with animal subjects, punished behaviors recurring upon the cessation of the punishment contingency; while for verbal humans, the effect of punishment does not appear to depend on continuing experience with the punishment contingency. A verbal human may have to be punished for stealing only once in a lifetime. Presumably, this effect may be attributed to the role of verbal behavior in keeping the punishing consequences "psychologically," though not physically, present.

Generalizability. Generalization also may operate differently for verbal humans. In the absence of language, generalization can occur only on the basis of commonalities in physical circumstances. Language provides another means for generalization-like effects. Circumstances that seem similar in physical terms may "mean" very different things to a verbal organism, and generalization may occur across these constructed, as opposed to physical, properties. As such, generalization may not be able to be predicted or controlled in precisely the same manner with verbal humans as has been observed with animals.

Summary. We do not mean to suggest that animal findings are completely useless in the design of aversive procedures for use with verbal humans. After all, verbal humans respond to the physical properties of stimuli as well as their attributed properties. Still, verbal behavior so changes a person's contact with the world that its understanding cannot be achieved by reliance on animal findings.

Moreover, it is likely that at least some of the specific arguments over the workability of aversive procedures with mentally retarded persons have their sources in a failure to consider crucial differences in the organisms studied. Studies of animal behavior and the behavior of humans without language undoubtedly will reveal different findings than those with language-able humans.

CONCLUSIONS

The struggle over treatment for mentally retarded persons is not subsiding. It seems likely that we will continue to ask the courts to determine what is and is not an appropriate treatment or habilitation program. The courts, in turn, will continue to resist explicitly stating what can and cannot be done. Legal authority must to some degree continue to defer to the judgment of the expert and the professional whose decisions are "presumptively valid," and will in some way maintain that "liability may be imposed only when the decision by the professional is such a substantial departure from accepted professional judgment, practice, or standards" (*Youngberg v. Romeo*, 1982, p. 16). The question, of course, is: "What is or what should be accepted professional judgment, practice, or standards?" We have considered the moral, as well as the scientific, issues involved in this controversy and, based on our analysis, make the following suggestions toward its resolution.

Resolving the Moral Aspect of the Controversy

We take the position that those arguing that aversive procedures are bad (or good), independent of any other criterion upon which to make this evaluation, have only the fact that others in their group make the same argument upon which to justify their claim. Arguments of this sort are based on cultural tradition, not consequential circumstances of any kind. As such, no grounds exist for abandoning one position in favor of another.

A resolution for this kind of controversy occurs when one of the traditions represented in the debate dissolves for reasons not specifically related to the issue at hand. There are some indications that our culture is becoming one in which aversive procedures are not tolerated for reasons having nothing to do with their workability. Arguing over whether such a change is good or bad is exactly the same kind of argument.

Resolving the Scientific Aspect of the Controversy

For those arguing that aversive procedures are either good or bad because of some conditions of workability, we take the position that those conditions are not yet known and, until such time as they are, the scientific aspects of this controversy cannot be resolved.

REFERENCES

Azrin, N. H. (1956). Some effects of two intermittent schedules of immediate and non-immediate punishment. *Journal of Psychology, 42*, 3-21.

Azrin, N. H. & Holz, W. C. (1961). Punishment during fixed interval reinforcement. *Journal of the Experimental Analysis of Behavior, 4*, 343-347.

Azrin, N. H., & Holz, W. C. (1966). Punishment. In W. K. Honig (Ed.), *Operant behavior: Areas of research and practice* (pp. 380-447). New York: Appleton-Century-Crofts.

Azrin, N. H., Holz, W. C., & Hake, D. F. (1963). Fixed-ratio punishment. *Journal of the Experimental Analysis of Behavior, 6*, 141-148.

Azrin, N. H., Hake, D. F., Holz, W. C., & Hutchinson, R. R. (1965). Motivational aspects of escape from punishment. *Journal of the Experimental Analysis of Behavior, 8*, 31-44.

Azrin, N. H., Hutchinson, R. R., & Hake, D. F. (1963). Pain-induced fighting in the squirrel monkey. *Journal of the Experimental Analysis of Behavior, 6*, 620.

Bellack, A. S., & Hersen, M. (1977). *Behavior modification: An introductory textbook*. New York: Oxford University Press.

Biglan, A. (1988). Behavior analysis and the larger context. *Behavior Analysis, 23*, 25-32.

Catania, A. C., Matthews, B. A., & Shimmoff, E. (1982). Instructed versus shaped human verbal behavior: Interactions with nonverbal responding. *Journal of the Experimental Analysis of Behavior, 38*, 233-248.

D'Amato, M. R., Salmon, D. P., Loukas, E., & Tomie, A. (1985). Symmetry and transitivity of conditional relations in monkeys (Cebus apella) and pigeons (Columba livia). *Journal of the Experimental Analysis of Behavior, 44*, 35-47.

Devaney, J. M., Hayes, S. C., & Nelson, R. O. (1986). Equivalence class formation in language-able and language disabled children. *Journal of the Experimental Analysis of Behavior, 46*, 243-257.

Dixon, M. H., & Spradlin, J. E. (1976). Establishing stimulus equivalence among retarded adolescents. *Journal of the Experimental Child Psychology, 21*, 144-164.

Ezorsky, G. (1972). *Philosophical perspectives on punishment*. Albany, NY: State University of New York Press.

Glenn, S. (1986). Metacontingencies in Walden Two. *Behavior Analysis and Social Action, 5*, 2-8.

Griffith, R. G. (1986). Administrative considerations and responsibilities: Legal and ethical issues. In R. P. Barrett (Ed.), *Severe behavior disorders in the mentally retarded* (pp. 359-394). New York: Plenum.

Harris, M. (1979). *Cultural materials: The struggle for a science of culture*. New York: Simon & Schuster.

Hayes, L. J., Tilley, K. L., & Hayes, S. C. (1988). Extending equivalence class membership to gustatory stimuli. *Psychological Record, 38*, 473-482.

Hayes, S. C. (1988). Upward and downward continuity: It's time to change our strategic assumptions. *Behavior Analysis, 22,* 91-190.

Hayes, S. C., Brownstein, A. J., Devany, J. M., Kohlenberg, B. S., & Shelby, J. (1987). Stimulus equivalence and the symbolic control of behavior. *Mexican Journal of Behavior Analysis*.

Hayes, S. C., & Hayes, L. J. (1989). The verbal action of the listener as a basis for rule governance. In S. C. Hayes (Ed.), *Rule-governed behavior: Cognition, contingencies and instructional control*. New York: Plenum.

Hayes, S. C., & Meyerson, J. (May, 1986). *Rules, delays, causes and specificity*. Invited address presented to The Association for Behavior Analysis, Milwaukee.

Hayes, S. C., Zettle, R. D., & Rosenfarb, I. (1989). Rule Following. In S. C. Hayes (Ed.), *Rule-governed behavior: Cognition, contingencies and instructional control*. New York: Plenum.

Haywood, H. C. (1976). The ethics of doing research... and of not doing it. *American Journal of Mental Deficiency, 81*, 311-317.

Hoekema, D. A. (1986). *Rights and wrongs: Coercion, punishment, and the state*. Cranbury, NJ: Associated University Press.

Hutchinson, R. R. (1977). By-products of aversive control. In W. K. Honig & J. E. R. Staddon (Eds.), *Handbook of operant behavior*. Englewood Cliffs, NJ: Prentice-Hall.

Kantor, J. R. (1982). *Cultural Psychology*. Chicago: Principia.

Kazdin, A. E. (1980). *Behavior modification in applied settings*. Homewood, IL: Dorsey.

Kendall, S. B. (1983). Tests for mediated transfer in pigeons. *Psychological Record, 33*, 245-256.

Kimble, G. A. (1961). *Hilgard and Marquis' conditioning and learning*. New York: Appleton-Century-Crofts.

Laties, V. G., & Weiss, B. (1963). Effects of concurrent task on fixed- interval responding in humans. *Journal of the Experimental Analysis of Behavior, 6*, 431-436.

Leander, J. D., Lippman, L. G., & Meyer, M. M. (1968). Fixed interval performance as related to subjects' verbalizations of the reinforcement contingency. *Psychological Record, 18*, 469-474.

Lipkens, R., Kop, P. F. M., & Matthjis, W. (1988). A test of symmetry and transitivity in the conditional discrimination performances of pigeons. *Journal of the Experimental Analysis of Behavior, 49*, 395-409.

Lippman, L. G., & Meyer, M. M. (1967). Fixed interval perfromance as related to instructions and to subjects' verbalizations of the contingency. *Psychonomic Science, 8*, 135-136.

Lowe, C. F. (1979). Determinants of human operant behavior. In M. D. Zeiler & P. Harzem (Eds.), *Advances in analysis of behavior: Vol 1. Reinforcement and the organization of behavior* (pp. 159-192). Chichester, England: Wiley.

Lowe, C. F., Beasty, A., & Bentall, R. P., (1983). The role of verbal behavior in human learning. *Journal of the Experimental Analysis of Behavior, 39*, 157-164.

Lowe, C. F., Harzem, P., & Hughes, S. (1978). Determinants of operant behavior in humans: Some differences from animals. *Quarterly Journal of Experimental Psychology, 30*, 373-386.

Malott, R. W. (1989). The achievement of evasive goals: Control by rules describing contingencies that are not direct acting. In S. C. Hayes (Ed.), *Rule-governed behavior: Cognition, contingencies and instructional control*. New York: Plenum.

Martin, G. L., & Pear, J. J. (1978). *Behavior modification: What it is and how to do it.* Englewood Cliffs, NJ: Prentice-Hall.

Matson, J. L., & DiLorenzo, T. M. (Eds.), (1984). *Punishment and its alternatives: A new perspective on behavior modification*. New York: Springer.

Parrott, L. J. (1984). Listening and understanding. *The Behavior Analyst, 7*, 449-516.

Roos, T. L. (1974). Human rights and behavior modification. *Mental Retardation, 12*, 3-6.

Shimmoff, E., Catania, A. C., & Matthews, B. A. (1981). Uninstructed human responding: Sensitivity of low-rate performance to schedule contingencies. *Journal of the Experimental Analysis of Behavior, 36*, 207-220.

Sidman, M. (1971). Reading and auditory-visual equivalences. *Journal of Speech and Hearing Research, 14*, 5-13.

Sidman, M., Cresson, O., & Wilson-Morris, M. (1974). Acquisition of matching-to-sample via mediated transfer. *Journal of the Experimental Analysis of Behavior, 22*, 261-273.

Sidman, M., Rauzin, R., Lazar, R., Cunningham, S., Tailby, W., & Carrigan, P. (1982). A search for symmetry in the conditional discriminations of rhesus monkeys, baboons and children. *Journal of the Experimental Analysis of Behavior, 37*, 23-44.

Skinner, B. F. (1953). *Science and human behavior*. New York: MacMillan.

Skinner, B. F. (1938). *The behavior of organisms*. New York: Appleton- Century-Crofts.

Sobsey, R. (1987). Non-aversive behavior management: The verdict is in. *AAMD News and Notes, 1*(2), p. 2.

Sulzer-Azaroff, B., & Mayer, G. R. (1977). *Applying behavior analysis procedures with children and youth*. New York: Holt, Rinehart & Winston.

Thompson, T., Gardner, W. I., & Baumeister, A. A. (1988). Ethical interventions for persons with retardation, autism, and related developmental disorders. In J. A. Stark, F. J. Menolascino, M. H. Albarelli, & V. C. Gray (Eds.), *Mental retardation and mental health*. New York: Springer-Verlag.

Weiner, H. (1964). Conditioning history and human fixed-interval performance.

Journal of the Experimental Analysis of Behavior, 7, 383-385.

Weiner, H. (1965). Conditioning history and maladaptive human operant behavior. *Psychological Reports, 17*, 935-942.

Wulfert, E., & Hayes, S. C. (1988). Transfer of conditional sequencing through conditional equivalence classes. *Journal of the Experimental Analysis of Behavior, 50*, 125-144.

Youngberg v. Romeo, 102 S. Ct. (1982).

Zabel, R. H. (1985). Aversives in special education programs for behaviorally disordered students: A debate. *Behavior Disorders, 10*, 295-304.

Zimmerman, J., & Ferster, C. B. (1963). Intermittent punishment of S- responding in matching to sample. *Journal of the Experimental Analysis of Behavior, 6*, 349-356.

CHAPTER

7

A CONCEPTUAL FRAMEWORK FOR JUDGING THE HUMANENESS AND EFFECTIVENESS OF BEHAVIORAL TREATMENT

Stephen R. Schroeder
Bureau of Child Research

Andrew Oldenquist and Johannes Rojahn
The Ohio State University

The history of the aversives controversy dates back to the beginning of applied behavior analysis more than 30 years ago (Schroeder, 1990). There have been three eras: (a) the prehistoric era of the 1960's during which applied behavior analysis was entertained as a paradigm not only for difficult-to-treat clinical and educational problems but also for larger societal problems; (b) the civil rights era of the 1970's during which the use of behavior analysis was modified by constraints imposed by considerations of individual constitutional rights and liberties; and (c) the moral philosophy era of the 1980's which has been characterized by terminological confusion, adversarial political activity, negative publicity, strong advocacy, bitter ad hominem rhetoric, and polarization of professionals into factions (Schroeder & Schroeder, 1989).

The lessons from this history are that behavior analysts must be more proactively involved in the aversives debate or else it will threaten the very foundations of all behavior analytic endeavors. Obviously, the debate is over much more than whether a particular treatment or device should be banned or not. It extends to questioning whether behavior analysis as a scientific paradigm should be used in *any* form to deliver clinical services to people, especially those with disabilities who have diminished capacity to consent.

There is a wide spectrum of opinion on these issues, with the scientific paradigm (Mulick & Kedesdy, 1988) on one end of the continuum and ideological paradigms (e.g., Wolfensberger, 1989) on the other end. At stake are the principles by which empirical behavioral research is linked to ethical policies and practices, the rules of evidence by which clinical decisions are made, and, finally, the very survival of the field of behavior analysis. Logic dictates that similar types of lawful functional relationships governing aversive treatments also hold for other types of behavioral treatments, such as positive reinforcement and stimulus-based treatments. Therefore, the same integrated set of guidelines for judging their ethical acceptability and effectiveness should apply to all behavioral intervention procedures.

Turnbull et al. (1986) offered a thought-provoking widely cited model for analyzing the moral aspects of special education and behavioral interventions and applied it to the moral aspects of aversive procedures. They proposed that a decision on whether or not aversive procedures should be used should be based primarily on their efficacy.

> There is yet another way to answer the question of whether we would tolerate aversive intervention as a means to accomplish given ends. It is to base one's decision on the efficacy of aversive procedures. After all, the efficacy test subsumes Judaism (prohibiting intrusive interventions unless direct and sustained results can be achieved thereby), utilitarianism (justifying aversive intervention by whether it advances the greater good of the greater number of people), Aristotelian rationalism (justifying aversive intervention by whether it enhances the rational capacities of people), and causalism (justifying aversive intervention by "no-harm" or "low-harm" criteria). One way of formulating the efficacy/effectiveness standard is this: What is right is what works, for the individual would not want that which does not work.
>
> A combination of these approaches yields interesting results. Under a combined approach, what is right is what we want for ourselves and for others; we want only that which works; and we do not want that which does not work, particularly if the procedure is deliberately painful and imposed on especially vulnerable people. By extension, we do not want to harm others because we ourselves would not want to be harmed; thus, we do not want to harm either the person who administers or the person who receives aversive procedures.
>
> In this formulation of right and wrong, the efficacy of aversive intervention has a major role in determining its rightness, but only as we are willing to apply aversive intervention to ourselves and to others. By this standard, we would conclude that most aversive procedures for most behaviors do not work. Thus they are desirable neither for ourselves nor others. Accordingly they are morally wrong, especially when they are compulsory. Similarly, we also would conclude that aversive procedures for some behaviors do actual harm to the recipient and possibly to the administrator and thus are not what we want for ourselves or others; accordingly they are morally wrong, especially when they are compulsory. (p. 202)

We agree with this approach in many respects, especially with the view that ineffective treatments rarely, if ever, could be justified as humane. We disagree, however, with the blanket view that "most aversive procedures for most behaviors do not work." We offer comprehensive criteria for judging efficacy that have been used in the research literature demonstrating that aversives *do* work for certain behaviors of certain individuals, under certain circumstances, in certain settings (see the recent review by Cataldo, 1989). We also offer a slightly different conceptual framework for judging the humaneness of aversive treatments.

JUDGING THE HUMANENESS OF BEHAVIORAL TREATMENTS

In this section, we will highlight some of the ethical principles that we regard as being at the heart of the matter in the aversives controversy and point out the fallaciousness of some arguments frequently used in the current debate.

Beyond that, a "reciprocity" approach will be proposed as a model for testing the moral acceptability of therapies for persons with mental retardation and developmental disabilities.

Some Principles

Utilitarianism enjoins everyone, including health care professionals, to further the general happiness of humanity. This very general principle does not have much to say about the situation of persons who are developmentally disabled, our focus instead being on the rights and welfare of this particular group. Utilitarian considerations are more obviously relevant to, say, the AIDS policy and allocation of scarce resources. However, on the local level, there can be conflicts between utilitarianism construed as aiming only at treatment effectiveness and the values of dignity and of clients conceived as ends-in-themselves.

Paternalism means treating adults in ways they do not want to be treated, for their own good. It is treating adults as we think children should be treated. In the Western world especially, there is a sense that paternalism conflicts with *autonomy* and is justifiable only under very special conditions (consider the opposition to motorcycle helmet laws).

Americans put a higher value on autonomy and are more individualistic than most other peoples. Yet, most people think restricting the autonomy of persons with developmental disabilities when otherwise they would harm themselves or others is right. This position is in general a sound one. The person who is profoundly developmentally delayed or disabled is often as much like a developmentally younger person (dependence on others for elementary care) as any people with whom health professionals deal; and meeting the fundamental needs of such persons would seem to outweigh the value of autonomy. The principle is the same in the case of aged parents who become incompetent: Sometimes we must choose paternalistically contrary to their wills (over their loud protests) when we decide, for example, that they should no longer live alone.

Dignity is a principle that requires us to treat people in ways that acknowledge their worth and status as human beings, especially people who are at risk for being treated otherwise--prisoners and handicapped, senile, and terminally ill people. Whereas autonomy is dependent on degree of competence, the diminished autonomy of infants and people with severe disability being clear examples, dignity contrastingly is independent of a client's competence. Respect for dignity requires that we take special care that they do not live in ways that are dehumanizing or degrading. It is not an easy concept to define, but the contrast with uncared-for animals partly shapes our idea: Minimally, dignified treatment requires sanitation, cleanliness, comfort, and attempts at respectful communication and consent, all of these at levels that separate human life from that of wild or stray animals. How clients appear to us is relevant to what strikes us as undignified, and the untreated behavior and physical condition of severely disabled persons may look dehumanized and undignified; thus, therapy often involves a behavior that itself appears undignified, and in such a situation, the therapy may also look undignified.

In some situations, the value of dignity and the closely related value of personhood (values that we hold and not necessarily ones that the person who is disabled holds) are likely to clash with the utilitarian value of maximal contentment or happiness. We should be sensitive to the fact that interventions that we think of as dehumanizing or undignified may disturb us for different reasons than they disturb persons with disabilities, and may not distress the latter any more or less than they offend us.

We must ask whether the client appears even more dehumanized without a particular therapy than with it. Therapists also sometimes may be forced to consider whether a small increase in the appearance of dehumanization or indignity is outweighed by a great increase in treatment effectiveness, and also whether in a particular case the appearance of indignity (to the therapists and observers) is "subjective" in the sense that it will wear off as one gets used to it. Obviously, one has to be extremely careful about this, since people can become jaded and inured to genuinely degrading and dehumanizing treatment. One cannot, however, simply assume that this happens, as is sometimes assumed in the literature critical of aversive therapies.

On the other side, morality sometimes requires a sacrifice in the effectiveness of treatment for the sake of dignity and the avoidance of depersonalization. For example, the supporters of "death with dignity" for terminally ill patients take seriously principles that are plainly distinct from the goal of effective treatment. Banning surgical lobotomy as a treatment for inappropriate behavior may be a case where most informed people agree that avoiding depersonalization is a stronger consideration than maximal treatment effectiveness. The matter is not one of "science versus morals," but of the universal human condition in which our norms often conflict with one another, and we must make hard choices about particular cases.

Not everyone feels the same way about the dignity or indignity of different therapies for inappropriate behaviors. Dignity is a difficult concept on which to agree; some people say they would want to be killed if bedridden in posey rest restraints and spoon-fed, while others do not express such ideas. As a therapy for disabled persons, severe drugging perhaps offends the most because it further disables the mind and diminishes human interaction. Physical restraint offends our sensibilities because it can block acceptable, as well as unacceptable, behavior. Aversive interventions offend because they physically resemble a notion of punishment that is based on retribution or mistreatment. However, one cannot rationally judge the morality of these measures by simply pointing out how different they are from acceptable treatment of non-disabled persons, such as criminals or ordinary citizens. Different situations justify different treatments, and a sensitive moral appraisal should involve reflection in terms of hypothetical reciprocity, which we shall discuss shortly.

Rights often depend on our competencies, or our likelihood to harm ourselves or others, and not just on being human. Hence, restriction of freedom of movement is not always a violation of rights (of criminals, for example). Justified paternalism obviously restricts rights. We can express this point by saying we have stewardship over people who would otherwise harm themselves and (innocently) harm others. The matter is one of transferring disabled persons' rights to others who have the responsibility to act in their behalf, and it is not a matter of the loss or abrogation of rights, which is how we characterize the case with criminals.

There is a very clear difference between coercive and restrictive measures toward disabled persons and toward criminals, and the point would hardly need to be made except that some writers have made the comparison. The use of the word "punishment" for some therapies is unfortunate, for it not only suggests that disabled persons are being treated like criminals, but it also invites insidious comparisons of the motives and mental states of therapists with those of punishers of prisoners.

People also have rights not to be treated cruelly. But the conclusion that a therapy, whether pharmacological or aversive, is cruel because it hurts the client or is intentionally painful does not follow. If pain is caused intentionally as a necessary means to a good end, and is not excessive, there is no reason to call it cruel or inhumane. Nor does everything painful do harm. Harm implies mental or physical damage, and the justification of a therapy, painful or not, lies in diminishing harm in the sense of mental and physical damage.

Reciprocity Arguments

Perhaps the most powerful and persuasive means of testing the moral acceptability of therapies for people with disabilities are reciprocity and role reversal arguments. These arguments have their theoretical basis in the Golden Rule and Kantian ethics, and take a number of forms in twentieth century ethical theory.

A person with profound mental retardation can be assumed to object to physical restraint or aversive treatment for destructive and self-injurious behavior; he or she may even think it cruel, if capable of that concept. On utilitarian grounds, one can argue that the objection should be overridden, just as that of a person with diminished intellectual capacity who doesn't want a penicillin shot. But suppose we ask, "How would you like it done to you?" The question is easily rejected if you are not disabled and have no need for aversive treatment (e.g., if you are an alcoholic or a criminal who is capable of rational thinking and hence can respond to very different techniques). Somewhat more biblically, we may ask, "Is what you are about to do unto others something you can accept being done unto you?" To avoid the same rejection of the question, we can reformulate it as, "Would you choose that therapy if you were in the disabled person's shoes?" This question has force and can mean either:

(1) Would you choose it if you were severely disabled and banging your head? (which gets the same answer as asking the disabled head banger, and hence doesn't advance the argument); or

(2) Would you choose it conditionally now, while normal, for yourself were you to become a severely disabled head banger?

Of course, one needs to specify precisely what the behavior and the proposed intervention are before attempting to answer this question. If what one is asked to choose is aversive intervention, we think that the answer most people would give to question (2) would be yes if in addition, aversive intervention was thought to be the only effective option available. One's answer should be the same for a loved one, when imagined in that situation. Someone reasoning hypothetically this way would consider the effects on one's dignity (in an institutional setting), on physical safety, and on everything else relevant, and compare them with the options of pain, restraint, constant interference by attendants, drugging, ignoring the behavior, etc. If asked to choose among a number of therapies, all believed to be effective, different people would likely diverge in choice and would choose dependent on a detailed description of the situation.

We are morally (and logically) obliged to accept, for ourselves, an act that we propose to do to another, given the hypothetical situation in which we are on the receiving end. The next step of the argument is that we cannot morally accept a therapy for others if we would not want it used on ourselves, given the hypothetical situation in which we are the disabled person.

This kind of argument has the merit of sidestepping theoretical questions about morality and religion, ethical relativism, and whether there are objective "moral facts." It just says that we can morally accept a therapy for others only if we can accept it for ourself in a hypothetical role reversal situation. There could still be disagreements: One person, but not another, might think that the indignity of a shocking device would be worse than the greater pain and danger of self-injury. Reasoning about this can be complex since the indignity is something we contemplate from our non-disabled status, whereas, in the hypothetical situation, I am like another person, at least in the sense that I would be aware of the pain but (very likely) not the indignity; does this sort of consideration count in the decision I have to make now? Nonetheless, different people come closer to moral agreement when they not only agree about the facts of the matter (conditionally, at least, if the facts are not known), but also suppose themselves or their loved ones to be the object of the therapy. This role-reversal experiment in thought is an effective way to eliminate self-interest, inadequate empathy, and implications of pet theories that one merely thinks one can accept.

Some Fallacious Arguments

Reciprocity arguments only work when we suppose ourselves on the receiving end of what we propose to do in the same circumstances. The logic behind the argument is that similar cases must be judged similarly, hence the real case and the hypothetical case (with us as participants) must be as close as can be imagined to exact similarity. Thus, asking how we would like to be drugged or shocked, either in general or for drunkenness or reckless driving, is a confused and irrelevant approach, because the dissimilarity of the cases does not permit the deduction that if one case is unacceptable, so is the other. Drugging someone into passivity; using physical restraint, automatic shocking devices, and other aversive therapies; constant intervention by attendants; and indeed any non-consensual, paternalistic intervention, would be affronts to dignity (not to mention being actionable assaults!) if done to people who do not require these measures. Fallacious arguments such as this one are tempting. The recent literature contains many fallacious moral arguments, mostly on the emotionally charged issue of aversive therapies.

There are grounds for morally criticizing aversive therapies, and these deserve our most serious attention. They have to do with indignity and depersonalization, doubts about long-term effectiveness, and viable alternatives. But arguments that are question-begging, and ad hominem in the sense of hinting and speculating that the motives of therapists are like those of Nazis, and the therapies themselves like prison torture, merely cause offense without proving anything.

Neo-Kantian and Utilitarian Arguments

The neo-Kantian/reciprocity approach, in the view of most contemporary ethicists, is sounder than a purely utilitarian one, as the latter is usually criticized for letting us treat people as a means to a good end, if the general good is thereby maximized. Neo-Kantian theories are based on universalized self-interest; i.e., asking whether we can accept a policy when we do not know whether we will be on the "giving" or the "receiving" end [this is John Rawls' (1971) version of it]; or, what amounts to the same thing, asking if we can accept the policy in a hypothetical role-reversal situation [this is Richard Hare's (1963) version of it]. Utilitarianism, on the other hand, has a hard time in making its single principle of maximal general happiness consistent with such elusive, but enduring, concepts as dignity, honor, fairness, and justice.

JUDGING THE EFFECTIVENESS OF BEHAVIOR TREATMENT

Single Subject and Group Methodologies Must Be Sound

Research on intervention with destructive behaviors of people with mental retardation and developmental disabilities does not lend itself well to group research designs. Assembly of a relatively homogeneous group of any size is very difficult. Both inter- and intra-individual variability in the data are high, so statistically reliable effects are small due to huge error terms. Thus, statistically reliable effects often do not match clinically significant effects to many individual members of the group. As a result, the intervention literature is made up almost exclusively of single-subject studies.

Experimental analyses of the behavior of single subjects can be potent research designs (Johnston & Pennypacker, 1980; Sidman, 1960) if they contain internal validity. The main criteria for internal validity in single-subject designs are that (a) data must be recorded reliably, (b) data must be recorded repeatedly, (c) procedures must be described in sufficient detail to permit replication, and (d) the effects of the procedures must be replicated (Birnbrauer, Peterson, & Solnick, 1974).

Most criticisms of single-subject research center on its lack of generality or external validity. The fact is that the generality is *unknown* until the experiment is replicated. Replicability establishes the boundary conditions for generality in single-subject research. Problems of internal and external validity of the research on destructive behavior are directly relevant because these issues have been ignored by many recent reviewers of the literature. The result is that we now have several published reviews on the same material that have come to diametrically opposite conclusions about the data. There is no widely accepted way, such as meta-analysis, to aggregate statistically the results of single-subject experiments, even though this has recently been proposed (White, Rusch, Kazdin, & Hartmann, 1989). The only reasonable way at present seems to be to apply the criteria for internal and external validity in giving weight to different studies to be included in a review. We recommend that these guidelines be followed in evaluating studies.

Measurement Instrumentation Must Be Valid and Reliable

At a recent NIMH workshop (*Psychopharmacology Bulletin*, 1985, *21*[2]), the available psychometric instruments for research on persons with mental and developmental disabilities were reviewed. At present this is a fledgling area that needs to be expanded greatly. There are very few psychometrically valid and reliable instruments available for use at present.

Comparison of Intervention Procedures Must Be Done Carefully

The question of how to compare therapeutic procedures is as old as clinical research itself. With respect to people who are retarded, the question has been an acute one since clinicians often are charged to use the most effective treatment in the least restrictive environment. Obviously, criteria other than scientific research have been used to make such decisions since the technology for deciding the most effective treatment is not agreed upon at present by clinical researchers.

Generally, two comparison strategies have been used: (a) enumeration of positive results of different procedures across different experiments, and (b) intra-subject comparisons of procedures within the same experiment. There are many problems with both of these strategies. Comparisons across studies are weak because of the heterogeneity of the subjects and variations in procedures, samples, and parameters of the independent variables. Most intra-subject comparisons across treatments and behaviors fail because multiple baseline and reversal designs hopelessly confound order effects related to time and presentation sequence. In addition, response covariation and response generalization show that target behaviors and collateral behaviors are often not orthogonal. Therefore, only an intra-subject design where time, sequence, and generalization effects can be controlled, or at least evaluated by counterbalancing or randomizing the treatment sequences, would seem adequate for appropriate comparison of the intervention procedures.

Criteria for Success Must Be Comprehensive

Criteria that have been applied to judge effectiveness of behavior management procedures are: (a) degree and rapidity of suppression, (b) generalization, (c) durability of suppression (maintenance), and (d) covariation; i.e., positive and/or negative side effects resulting from changes in collateral behaviors. The other criteria that have received attention in recent years are consumer satisfaction (Holman, 1977), clinical significance (Risley, 1970), social validity (Wolf, 1978) and community acceptance (Kazdin, 1980).

With respect to *degree and rapidity of suppression*, reviews that have compared results of different procedures across experiments and within the same subjects tend to agree that punishment procedures, together with differential reinforcement of alternative positive behaviors, produce the most immediate and complete suppression. Other management procedures have not been compared satisfactorily enough to suggest any firm conclusions.

On the question of maintenance or *durability of results*, there is too much disagreement to draw a firm conclusion. Few studies have provided follow-up data more than a year beyond treatment. Those that have are not encouraging irrespective of whether the treatment procedures have been positive or aversive (see Favell & Reid, 1988 for a review). It seems reasonable to ask what the guidelines for maintenance should be unless real life-style changes and permanent environmental changes have been affected during follow-up. If an individual is returned to a pathogenic environment which sets the occasion for destructive behavior, it would seem that the appropriate measures should be resistance to relapse or behavioral momentum. Such measures are rarely used in studies of maintenance. Thus, comparisons among studies should be made with caution when estimates of the effectiveness and durability of different interventions are made. Intra-subject comparisons within the same experiment may be more trustworthy.

The literature on applied behavior analysis contains a substantial amount of research on techniques for assuring *generalization of treatment effects*, which Stokes and Baer (1977) have called an "implicit technology of generalization." They argue that generalization traditionally has not been viewed as an operant to be programmed, but a description of a "natural outcome" of any behavior-change process. That intended programming is not the case is reflected in the titles of some of the generalization training strategies that they identified in their review of the research (e.g., "train and hope," "train sufficient exemplars," "train loosely," "use indiscriminate contingencies," "program common stimuli," etc.). These strategies suggest a paradox in applied behavior analysis research; e.g., what Hartmann and Atkinson (1973) have called this "Having your cake and eating it, too." On the one hand, N = 1 research designs (e.g., reversal and multiple baseline designs) depend on a demonstration of strong differential discriminative stimulus control and therefore are dependent upon the lack of stimulus or response generalization. The more generalization, the less powerful is the demonstration of differential stimulus control. They note somewhat sarcastically the possibility that "Mother Nature provides special favors for behavior modifiers; she holds back 'behavioral traps' and other factors promoting generalization until the final treatment condition is concluded, and then releases her hold just before that reassuring follow-up call is placed and that final paragraph is written." This is a particularly critical issue with treatment of inappropriate behavior, where lack of generalization and maintenance has been more the rule than the exception (Schroeder et al., 1982). This reason has led some to involve parents, or other caregivers who are willing to use strong consequences, in avoiding reliance on the medical model of only removing behavioral pathology, committing a major portion of their lives to managing the client, and in utilizing the coping resources available to them (Lovaas et al., 1973). Clearly, a high priority for future research is generalization and maintenance of alternative behavior.

Another consideration is *covariation*. Initially, this issue arose around the use of intrusive punishment, especially electrical stimulation, as a behavior management procedure and its concomitant, possibly negative, physical and conditioned emotional side effects. The latter fears have not been borne out by research. But, "substitution" (Schroeder & MacLean, 1987) has been observed recently in a wide variety of settings and with virtually every procedure whose major focus is deceleration of high rate behaviors. Earlier studies did not report such covariation. Most of the research literature on generalization in this area has used the "train-and-hope" procedure, and has been biased toward publishing exclusively positive instances of generalization (Stokes & Baer, 1977).

Covariation is of two kinds. In one type, transitional changes may occur in the target responses as a function of a change in stimulus conditions or reinforcement contingency; i.e., the contrast effect (Reynolds, 1961). Examples would be rebound effects in follow-up baselines, end-of-session effects, extinction bursts, etc. In a second type, changes in collateral behaviors may occur as a function of changes in the target behaviors and vice versa. As Sajwaj, Twardosz, & Burke (1972) have pointed out, such "side effects" may be of four possible kinds: (a) desirable behaviors may increase, (b) undesirable behaviors may decrease, (c) desirable behaviors may decrease, or (d) undesirable behaviors may increase. The result in any given situation might be a function of (a) the reinforcing or punishing effects of a particular contingent stimulus used, (b) the membership of a given target behavior in a wider response class, or (c) alterations in setting conditions to the extent that other behaviors are now affected by existing reinforcement contingencies. We suggest that future studies be designed to look at the covariation effects of various intervention strategies, both within treatment settings and at other times.

Research on covariation raises some interesting possibilities. Perhaps an inaccessible target behavior can be indirectly altered by manipulating its covariants. Chained behaviors sometimes can be averted by intervening early in the chain, as was shown with ruminative vomiting (Jackson et al., 1975).

Suppression of inappropriate concurrent behaviors often is negatively related to increases in appropriate behavior. But what is the nature of this relationship? For instance, Lovaas, Young, & Newsom (1987) contend that self-stimulatory behavior is so reinforcing for some autistic children who are mentally retarded that they will endure pain for the opportunity to do it. The inappropriate behavior apparently is so compelling that it reduces the time available for allocation to appropriate behaviors. Does this mean that programming of appropriate behaviors cannot proceed until self-stimulation is inhibited (Risley, 1968)? Such results on covariation have given rise to a new behavioral theory-competing behavior analysis (Horner & Billingsley, 1988). The range of applicability of this theory remains to be discovered. A major implication of this approach is the incorporation of recent models, such as ecological analysis and ecobehavioral analysis (Rogers-Warren & Warren, 1977), which study the subject in the complex, natural environment.

Social Criteria

Nonscientific but nonetheless important methods for judging comparative effectiveness of an intervention procedure, other than statistically significant changes in the dependent variable, have been *consumer satisfaction* (Holman, 1977), *clinical significance, social validity*, and *community acceptance*.

Clinical significance (Risley, 1970) and *social validity* (Wolf, 1978) are equally subjective measures used by a number of applied researchers to judge the importance of research. In practice, they amount to judging whether intervention produced a substantial change in rate of a target behavior. Rate is presumed to reflect response strength (Skinner, 1953). However, Herrnstein (1970) and Baum (1973) have argued that either choice or time allocation reflects response strength better than rate in terms of their correlation with manipulation of reinforcement contingencies. There are many low rate behavior problems, whose clinical significance cannot be denied (e.g., suicide, murder, some severe SIB), that require multidimensional measurement because of their nature. Finally, the clinical significance criterion does not recognize the heuristic value of research where new domains and procedures are being delineated. Kazdin (1976) has suggested the use of N=1 statistics for this purpose. We cannot presumably evaluate this issue thoroughly. For the time being, measures of social validity may be important and desirable, but they are mostly in the eye of the beholder, and reliability of consensus among researchers is low. Therefore, this criterion should be used loosely, taking into account bias and rate of false positives by the raters.

Social Validity. Kazdin and Matson (1981) have provided a clear and useful conceptualization of social validation methods for selecting treatments and evaluating the acceptability of their effects on people with mental retardation. They propose two methods: (a) *social comparison; i.e., comparing the performance of the individual to that of the surrounding community in everyday life; and (b) subjective evaluation;, i.e., soliciting opinions and ratings by persons who are in a special position, by virtue of their expertise or relationship to the individual, to assist in evaluating the specific behaviors that are socially important to habilitation.*

Community Acceptance

There are only a few studies assessing acceptability of intervention procedures for destructive behaviors of people with mental retardation (see Morgan, 1989, for a review). These are well-conducted studies that generally agree that the order of acceptability is stimulus control procedures, DRI, DRO, time-out, overcorrection, contingent restraint, mildly aversive stimuli (e.g., water mist), and intensely aversive stimuli (e.g., ammonia, shock, paddling). This order is generally true for parents, teachers, administrators, and direct care staff, but the degree of acceptability in the intermediate range depends greatly on (a) rater characteristics; e.g., education, professional experience with the population, relationship to the individual client observed; (b) intervenor characteristics; e.g., acceptance of the procedure, time and resources to do it, skill in doing it, perceived risks and effects on the client; and (c) client characteristics; e.g., age, sex, residence, time duration, success of past procedures, retardation level, behavior frequency and severity, type of target behavior, side effects, and perceived aversiveness of type of procedure to the client. This area is a potentially fertile one for research and needs expansion before firm conclusions can be drawn about community acceptability. An important paper by Singh and Katz (1985) showed that students' ratings of time-out, overcorrection, and DRI changed favorably after systematic instruction relative to ratings of a control procedure called "humanistic parenting."

CONSUMER SATISFACTION is another subjective criterion sometimes used to assess the client's view of the therapist and treatment outcomes (see McMahon & Forehand, 1983, for a review). As might be anticipated, the few existing studies in this area are with higher functioning clients who can communicate readily. The inclusion of the client in the choice of intervention procedures is an area likely to receive much more attention in the future.

Dealing with Sampling Bias and Cofactors

Since most of the available research is single-subject research, sampling bias and subject-ascertainment bias can be addressed only through replication and restriction of one's generalizations concerning applicability of the results to different populations. The subjects of these interventions are usually atypical by definition, and they defy homogeneous grouping. Subject and treatment selection are usually regulated by internal and external review boards. Therefore, generalizations about the results of these experiments must be made with great caution.

From the epidemiological literature, we know that there are a variety of cofactors (IQ, age, organicity, age of onset, chronicity, communication deficits, etc.); i.e., other variables, which are related to the prevalence of destructive behaviors. One especially important cofactor is the frequent use of psychotropic medication in this population. Yet, these variables are often neglected in behavioral intervention research (Schroeder, Lewis, & Lipton, 1983). This deficit is a serious one which should result in less weight being given to studies in which psychotropic medication is not controlled or otherwise properly assessed.

Social Ecological Setting Factors

The effectiveness of behavior interventions depends greatly on the environmental context in which they are performed. We have written extensively on these issues (Schroeder, in press-b; Schroeder, Rojahn, Mulick, & Schroeder, in press; Schroeder et al., 1982). The appropriate philosophical approach of the service delivery system, the mechanisms for judging risk/benefit ratios of individual cases by internal and external program review, suitable staffing patterns, good staff training, and consistent programming organizational patterns are all essential for effective behavioral interventions.

MERGING VALUES AND TECHNOLOGY

Does ethical knowledge take precedence over scientific knowledge in judging whether to use or not to use aversive behavioral treatments? This is really an academic rather than a practical question. Decisions that are not highly informed from both knowledge bases are at high risk of being wrong. Scientists must proceed with a value system and ethicists must be informed in the relevant science. In practice, ethics and science are inseparable. The merging of values and behavioral technology was elaborated nicely by Horner (1987) in 12 principles. We have adapted these principles (Schroeder, 1988) for the development of behavioral technology in community settings, and we propose them for guidelines in the development of technology for all behavior interventions, be they nonaversive or aversive.

Table 1 PRINCIPLES FOR THE DEVELOPMENT OF COMMUNITY-REFERENCED BEHAVIORAL TECHNOLOGY

[Italics indicate where the text has been modified (Adapted from Horner, 1987)]

1. ETHICAL, BEHAVIORAL PROCEDURES. The standards for ethical support of people with severe disabilities has been developed rapidly over the past 10 years. Behavior intervention procedures should be consistent with the Resolution on Intrusive Interventions (1981) by The Association for Persons with Severe Handicaps, the ethical guidelines established by The Association for the Advancement of Behavior Therapy (Favell et al., 1982), and the Bill of Consumer Rights proposed by the Association for Applied Analysis (Van Houten et al., 1988) *to the extent that they agree.*

The evolving message from these statements of value has many important features. Taken together, however, these value statements reiterate two important criteria for managing severe behavior problems: (a) It is unacceptable to harm people, even when that harm is perceived as being in the person's best interest; and (b) procedures used in response to severe, excess behaviors should be acceptable for use in nondisabled people in typical, age-appropriate, community settings *whenever possible.*

2. EFFECTIVE TECHNOLOGY. The needed technology must be effective in school and community settings. The technology needs to do more than simply reduce problem behaviors. In many cases, the need will be for reducing the rate of occurrence of a response to zero before the socially significant effect is felt.

3. MARRIAGE OF VALUES AND TECHNOLOGY. Values without technology often produce unuseful rhetoric. Technology without values can easily lead to inappropriate applications. *Procedures should* meld high ethical standards with the most advanced behavioral technology available.

4. HIGH METHODOLOGICAL RIGOR. The current debate over how to respond to severe behavior problems consistently returns to the need for data. Unfortunately, there are few research reports or clinical demonstrations that provide adequate methodological sophistication to add credibly to the existing knowledge base. The need is for new dependent variables, careful attention to research design, and stringent measurement procedures.

5. ADDRESS THE MOST SEVERE BEHAVIOR PROBLEMS. The technology targeted should also include the small number of people in both institutional and community settings who pose the most significant behavioral challenges. *If we are to respond to the real needs of the field, we must demonstrate that our technology will be working with individuals of all ages*, with varying learning histories, and with extreme rates and levels of problem behavior. We do not need to develop a technology that is effective only with people who are compliant.

6. COMMUNITY FOCUSED. The focus should be on the development of a technology that can be used in typical school, work, and community settings.

7. COMPREHENSIVE TECHNOLOGY. There are no simple solutions to severe behavior problems. We avoid the trap of searching for a single variable for oversimplified solutions. The effective response to severe behaviors will require a constellation of environmental modifications. This is an important issue because it will force the extension of existing behavioral technology and the expansion of traditional research methodology.

8. PRACTICAL PROCEDURES. We must define the roles and functions of direct line staff. The technology that is developed needs to define what is expected of the classroom teacher, the supported work job coach, the residential staff, and families. A part of the needed technology is to define the systems that these individuals can use to minimize the development of severe problems, and to collaborate in the solutions for severe problems that do arise. To the extent possible, the procedures designed and evaluated by us should be of direct value for teachers, parents, and other direct support individuals.

9. NATIONAL CONSENSUS. The use of the procedures should result in consensus that severe behavior problems can be managed by community-referenced procedures in typical school, work, and living settings. This effort will demand an intense focus on credible research results and collaboration with consumer, provider, research, and policy making groups.

Table 1 (cont.)

10. FOCUS ON STUDENT LIFESTYLE. An effective technology of behavior analysis should do much more than modify a target behavior. The technical expansion that is needed is a recognition of the lifestyle impact that good behavioral programming should produce. In addition to assessing if an undesirable behavior has been reduced, we must ask such questions as: What does the student do? With whom does the student interact? Where does the student go in the community? How much support does he/she need?" These are basic questions related to how the student is living his/her life, and dramatically extend the expectations placed on our technology of applied behavior.

11. INTERDISCIPLINARY COLLABORATION. The challenge presented by severe behavior problems is complex. No one discipline has the full array of answers. Procedures that expand our capacity to respond to severe behavior challenges will need the national experts from multiple disciplines, including psychology, special education, communication disorders, and medicine.

12. CONSUMER INVOLVEMENT. An effective technology for severe behavior management must be developed **with,** rather than for, consumers. To be effective, the procedure should make major efforts to include parents, siblings and advocates, as well as consumer social validation, as an ongoing part of the research and training.

13. SOCIAL ECOLOGICAL ADAPTATION. *Behavioral techniques should reflect the social ecology of a particular community in terms of accessibility, continuity, resource networking, cultural and ethnic specificity, and respect for religious, racial, and social values.*

REFERENCES

Baum, W. M. (1973). The correlation-based law of effect. *Journal of the Experimental Analysis of Behavior, 10*, 137-153.

Birnbrauer, J. S., Peterson, C. R., & Solnick, J. V. (1974). Design and interpretation of studies of single subjects. *American Journal of Mental Deficiency, 79*, 191-203.

Cataldo, M. F. (1989). *The effects of punishment and other behavior reducing procedures on destructive behaviors of persons with developmental disabilities.* Paper prepared for the NICHD Consensus Development Conference on Destructive Behavior, Bethesda, MD.

Favell, J. E., & Reid, D. H. (1988). Generalizing and maintaining improvement in problem behavior. In R. H. Horner, G. Dunlap, & R. L. Koegel (Eds.), *Generalization and maintenance (pp. 171-196)*. Baltimore, MD: Paul H. Brookes.

Favell, J. E., et al. (1982). The treatment of self-injurious behavior. *Behavior Therapy, 13*, 529-554.

Hare, R. (1963). *Freedom and reason.* London: Oxford University Press.

Hartmann, D. P., & Atkinson, C. (1973). Having your cake and eating it too: A note on some apparent contradictions between therapeutic achievements and design requirements in N= 1 studies. *Behavior Therapy, 4*, 589-591.

Herrnstein, R. J. (1970). On the law of effect. *Journal of the Experimental Analysis of Behavior, 13*, 243-266.

Holman, J. (1977). The moral risk and high cost of ecological concern in applied behavior analysis. In A. Rogers-Warren & S. Warren (Eds.), *Ecological perspectives in behavior analysis* (pp. 63-100). Baltimore, MD: University Park Press.

Horner, R. H. (1987). *Community-referenced technologies for nonaversive behavior management*. Grant application to NIDRR; CFDA 84.133B, Washington, DC, unpublished.

Horner, R. H., & Billingsley, F. F. (1988). The effect of competing behavior on the generalization and maintenance of adaptive behavior in applied settings. In R. H. Horner, G. Dunlap, & R. L. Koegel (Eds.), *Generalization and maintenance* (pp. 197-220). Baltimore, MD: Paul H. Brookes.

Jackson, G. M., Johnson, C. R., Ackron, G. S., & Crowley, R. (1975). Food satiation as a procedure to decelerate vomiting. *American Journal of Mental Deficiency, 80*, 223-227.

Johnston, J. M., & Pennypacker, H. S. (1980). *Strategies and tactics of human behavioral research.* Hillsdale, NJ: Erlbaum.

Kazdin, A. E. (1976). Statistical analysis for single-case experimental designs. In M. Hersen & D. Barlow (Eds.), *Single case experimental designs* (pp. 265-316). New York, NY: Pergamon.

Kazdin, A. E. (1980). Acceptability of alternative treatments for deviant child behavior. *Journal of Applied Behavior Analysis, 13*, 259-273.

Kazdin, A. E., & Matson, J. L. (1981). Social validation and mental retardation. *Applied Research in Mental Retardation, 2*, 39-53.

Lovaas, O. I., Koegel, R., Simmons, J. Q., & Long, J. S. (1973). Some generalization and follow-up measures on autistic children in behavior therapy. *Journal of Applied Behavior Analysis, 6*, 131-164.

Lovaas, O. I., Newsom, C., & Hickman, C. (1987). Self-stimulatory behavior and perceptual development. *Journal of Applied Behavior Analysis, 20*, 45-68.

McMahon, R. J., & Forehand, R. L. (1983). Consumer satisfaction in behavioral treatment of children: Types, issues, and recommendations. *Behavior Therapy, 14*, 209-225.

Morgan, R. L. (1989). Judgments of restrictiveness, social acceptability, and usage: Review of research on procedures to decrease behavior. *American Journal on Mental Retardation, 94*, 121-133.

Mulick, J. A., & Kedesdy, J. H. (1988). Self-injurious behavior, its treatment, and normalization. *Mental Retardation, 26*, 223-229.

Rawls, J. (1971). *A theory of justice.* Cambridge, MA: Harvard University Press.

Reynolds, G. S. (1961). Behavioral contrast. *Journal of the Experimental Analysis of Behavior, 4*, 57-71.

Risley, T. R. (1968). The effects and side effects of punishing the autistic behaviors of a deviant child. *Journal of Applied Behavior Analysis, 1*, 21-34.

Risley, T. R. (1970). Behavior modification: An experimental therapeutic endeavor. In L. A. Hamerlynch, P. O. Davidson, & L. E. Acker (Eds.), *Behavior modification and ideal health services (pp. 123-162).* Calgary, Alberta, Canada: University of Calgary Press.

Rogers-Warren, A., & Warren, S. (Eds.), (1977). *Ecological perspectives in behavior analysis.* Baltimore, MD: University Park Press.

Sajwaj, T., Twardosz, S., & Burke, M. (1972). Side effects of extinction procedures in a remedial school. *Journal of Applied Behavior Analysis, 5*, 163-175.

Schroeder, S. R. (1988). *Toward a humane and effective integration of people with developmental disabilities and behavioral disturbances into society in the U.S.* Paper presented at a Symposium on Community

Integration and Behavior Management, Office of Special Education and Rehabilitation Services, Washington, DC.

Schroeder, S. R. (submitted). A history of the aversives controversy (1960-1990).

Schroeder, S. R. (Ed.). (1990). *Ecobehavioral analysis and developmental disabilities: The twenty-first century.* New York, NY: Springer-Verlag.

Schroeder, S. R., & MacLean, W. (1987). If it isn't one thing, it's another: Experimental analysis of covariation in behavior management data of severely disturbed retarded persons. In S. Landesman & P. Vietze (Eds.), *Living environments and mental retardation* (pp. 315-338). Washington, DC: AAMD Monograph .

Schroeder, S., Kanoy, R., Thios, S., Mulick, J., Rojahn, J., Stephens, M., & Hawk,B. (1982). Antecedent conditions affecting management and maintenance of programs for the chronically self-injurious. In J. Hollis & C. E. Meyers (Eds.), *Life-threatening behavior* (pp. 105-159). Washington, DC: AAMD Monograph Series No. 5.

Schroeder, S. R., Lewis, M. H., & Lipton, M. A. (1983). Interactions of pharmacotherapy and behavior therapy among children with learning and behavior disorders. In K. Gadow & I. Bialer (Eds.), *Advances in learning and behavioral disabilities* (Vol. 2, pp. 179-225). Greenwich, CT: JAI.

Schroeder, S., Rojahn, J., Mulick, J., & Schroeder, C. (in press). Analysis of self-injurious behavior: Its development and management. In J. L. Matson & J. R. McCartney (Eds.), *Handbook of behavior modification for the mentally retarded* (2nd ed.). New York, NY: Plenum.

Schroeder, S. R., & Schroeder, C. S. (1989). The role of the AAMR in the aversives controversy. *Mental Retardation, 27*(3), iii-iv.

Sidman, M. (1960). *Tactics of scientific research*. New York, NY: Basic Books.

Singh, N. N., & Katz, R. C. (1985). On the modification of acceptability ratings for alternative child treatments. *Behavior Modification, 9*, 375-386.

Skinner, B. F. (1953). *Science and human behavior*. New York, NY: Macmillan.

Stokes, T. F., & Baer, D. M. (1977). An implicit technology of generalization. *Journal of Applied Behavior Analysis, 10*, 349-367.

The Association for Persons with Severe Handicaps. (1987). Resolution on the cessation of intrusive interventions. *TASH Newsletter, May*(5), 3.

Turnbull, H. R., Guess, D., Backus, L., Barber, P., Fiedler, C., Helmstetter, E., & Summers, J. A. (1986). A model for analyzing the normal aspects of special education and behavioral interventions: The moral aspects of aversive procedures. In P. Dokecki & R. Zaner (Eds.), *Ethics and decision making for persons with severe handicaps: Toward an ethically relevant research agenda* (pp. 167-210). Baltimore, MD: Paul H. Brookes.

Van Houten, R., Axelrod, S., Bailey, J. S., Favell, J. E., Foxx, R. M., Iwata, B. A., & Lovaas, O. I. (1988). The right to effective behavioral treatment. *The Behavior Analyst, 11*, 111-114.

White, D. M., Rusch, F. R., Kazdin, A. E., & Hartmann, D. P. (1989). Applications of meta analysis in individual-subject research. *Behavioral Assessment, 11*, 281-296.

Wolf, M. M. (1978). Social validity: The case for subjective measurement or how applied behavior analysis is finding its heart. *Journal of Applied Behavior Analysis, 11*, 203-214.

Wolfensberger, W. (1989). Self-injurious behavior, behavioristic responses, and social role valorization: A reply to Mulick and Kedesdy. *Mental Retardation, 27*(3), 181-184.

CHAPTER

8

THE ROLE OF REINFORCEMENT IN REDUCING INAPPROPRIATE BEHAVIOR: SOME MYTHS AND MISCONCEPTIONS

Ahmos Rolider
McMaster University

Ron Van Houten
Mount Saint Vincent University

We have long known that punishment is more effective in reducing inappropriate behavior when used in combination with the reinforcement of alternative behavior (Azrin & Holz, 1966). Indeed, it has been recommended and sometimes legally mandated by the least restrictive treatment model that punishment should be employed only after attempts to eliminate the problem through the use of reinforcement procedures alone have failed (Carr & Lovaas, 1983; Sulzer-Azaroff & Mayer, 1977). Three reinforcement procedures frequently employed to reduce inappropriate behavior are differential reinforcement of other behaviors (DRO) (Bostow & Bailey, 1969), differential reinforcement of low rates of responding (DRL) (Deitz & Repp, 1973), and differential reinforcement of incompatible behavior (DRI) (Young & Wincze, 1974). Because of the generally accepted position that these reinforcement procedures always should be employed alone before introducing punishment to decelerate an undesirable behavior, we must have a clear understanding of how these procedures work, as well as the factors that influence their efficacy. Unfortunately, there exists in the literature many misconceptions about how these procedures work and, as a consequence, how they should be employed.

One purpose of this paper is to examine the way each of these procedures has been conceptualized in the past and to propose a more parsimonious explanation of why these procedures work. The second purpose is to examine the impact of this new way of conceptualizing these procedures on how they should be employed. The third purpose is to recommend future research based upon the new analysis of these procedures.

PROCEDURES INVOLVING THE DIFFERENTIAL REINFORCEMENT OF OTHER BEHAVIORS

Differential reinforcement of other behavior refers to a procedure where reinforcement is delivered provided a particular behavior is not engaged in for a specified period of time (Reynolds, 1961). This procedure also has been termed "omission training" since the reinforcer is delivered if the behavior is omitted (Uhl & Garcia, 1969). For this reason, Poling and Ryan (1982) favor Zeiler's (1970, 1976) alternative of renaming DRO, differential reinforcement of not responding.

One problem with conceptualizing DRO as a reinforcement procedure is that it specifies that reinforcement is made contingent upon the absence of a particular behavior rather than the occurrence of a specific response. Making reinforcement contingent upon the absence of behavior does not pass Lindsley's *Dead Man Test* (White, 1986) since a dead person could easily meet the DRO contingency. This fact should lead one to suspect that something is wrong with the way that the DRO procedure is presently conceptualized.

Let's examine what actually takes place when a DRO procedure is put into effect. First, reinforcement is delivered on a regular basis. Second, emission of a specific response produces a reduction in the density of this ongoing baseline of reinforcement. Thus, the amount of reinforcement available is reduced following a behavior. This is how one normally defines a type 2 punishment contingency. That DRO is a punishment procedure is not readily apparent because we normally only look at extreme causes. For instance, the typical example of type 2 punishment involves the termination or removal of some reinforcers contingent upon a behavior. The top frame in Figure 1 illustrates this example. However, if, instead of removing a continuously available reinforcer contingent upon a behavior, one removed a frequently presented reinforcer as in Frame 2, the result is a discriminable reduction in the amount of reinforcement following a response. Clearly, one approximates the first instance as one increases the frequency of reinforcement in the second instance. In the third frame, one has a so-called DRO procedure where the interval between reinforcement is much less than the interval between a response and a reinforcement. Again, the emission of each behavior is associated with an immediate reduction in the density of reinforcement. Next, the final frame illustrates the usual DRO procedure where the interval between reinforcement is the same as the interval between a response and a reinforcement. Hence the reduction in reinforcement density is not so apparent, but nonetheless exists.

This argument is similar to the one made by Herrnstein and Hineline (1966) to explain Sidman's avoidance learning in terms of the negative reinforcement of responding by a reduction in shock density. In Sidman's avoidance learning, there are two intervals: a shock-shock interval and a response-shock interval. Normally, shocks are timed by the shock-shock interval. Whenever the subject responds, the shock-shock interval stops functioning and the response-shock interval begins. All subsequent responses

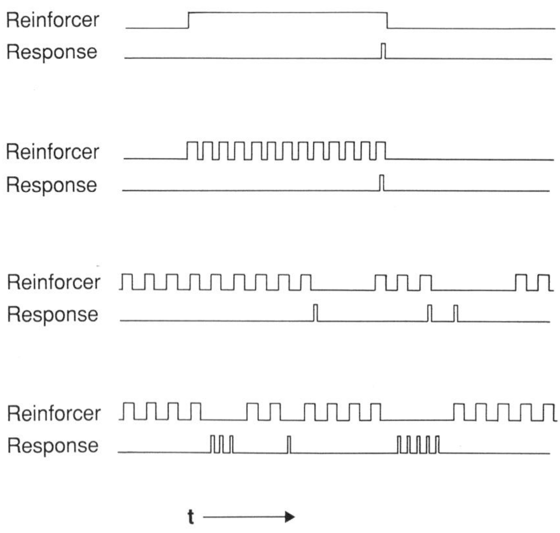

Figure 1: The top frame represents the arrangement of reinforcement and the response in type 2 punishment procedure. The second frame represents the arrangement in a type 2 punishment procedure when the reinforcer is prevented in a pulsed rather than a continuous basis. The third frame represents the arrangement when a response postpones reinforcement for a longer period than the reinforcer-reinforcer interval. The final frame illustrates the arrangement during a standard DRO procedure where the response-reinforcer interval is the same as the reinforcer-reinforcer interval. In all cases, events occur when the line is displaced up.

reset the response-shock interval until the failure of responding causes the response-shock interval to run out. Then a shock is delivered and the shock-shock interval is reinstated. The upper part of the top frame in Figure 2 illustrates the Sidman avoidance procedure where the shock-shock interval equals the response-shock interval. One can see the density of shock is somewhat reduced following the emission of a response. The mirror image of this negative reinforcement procedure is the DRO procedure illustrated in the lower portion of the top frame. Here the density of reinforcement is somewhat reduced following the emission of a response.

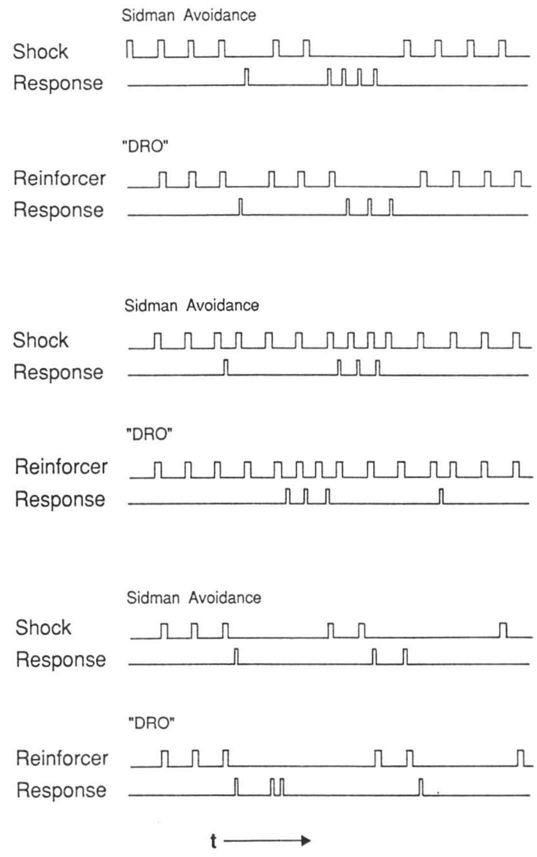

Figure 2: The upper portion of the top frame illustrates the arrangement on a Sidman avoidance learning schedule where the shock-shock interval equals the response shock interval. The lower portion of the procedure illustrates the standard DRO procedure where the response-reinforcer interval equals the reinforcer-reinforcer interval. The upper portion of the middle frame illustrates the arrangement on a Sidman avoidance learning schedule where the response-shock interval is shorter than the shock-shock interval. The lower portion of the middle frame illustrates the arrangement on a DRO schedule where the response-reinforcer interval is shorter than the reinforcer-reinforcer interval. The upper portion of the bottom frame illustrates the arrangement on a Sidman avoidance learning schedule where the response-shock interval is three times longer than the reinforcer-reinforcer interval. The lower portion of the bottom frame shows the arrangement on DRO where the response-reinforcer interval is three times longer than the reinforcer-reinforcer interval. In all cases, events occur when the line is displaced up.

The Sidman avoidance procedure is not called the differential punishment of other behavior, so why call the mirror image of this procedure, which involves reducing reinforcement density following a behavior, the differential reinforcement of other behavior?

The top of the middle frame examines what happens in Sidman's avoidance learning when the shock-shock interval is shorter than the response-shock interval. In this case, some responding leads to an increase in shock density and the subject does not learn to respond. The analogous situation with the so-called DRO procedure involves the response reinforcement interval being shorter than the reinforcer-reinforcer interval. Under these conditions, initial responding should actually increase the density of responding and this procedure therefore should be ineffective. The top portion of the lower frame in Figure 2 portrays the condition where the response-shock interval is longer than the shock-shock interval. This situation provides the clearest reduction in shock density following responding and the fastest learning. The lower portion of the bottom frame illustrates the condition where the response-reinforcer interval is longer than the reinforcer-reinforcer interval. Under this condition, one would obtain the greatest reduction in reinforcer density following responding and therefore the largest punishment effect. Empirically testing whether these outcomes actually occur would strengthen the evidence that DRO is a punishment procedure.

An alternative way of conceptualizing DRO would be that its effects are the result of a reduction in the overall percentage of reinforcement produced by the target behavior resulting from the increased delivery of reinforcement on a DRO schedule (McDowell, 1988). According to equation 3 of the matching law, the rate of responding should be a direct function of the percentage of reinforcement provided by all sources produced by that response (Herrnstein, 1970). Therefore, any procedure that results in an increase in the overall level of reinforcement that is not associated with a particular response should result in a reduction in the rate of that response. It would be possible to determine how much this factor contributes to the efficacy of DRO by first introducing a high background level of reinforcement following a baseline condition. Next, a DRO could be introduced that involves postponing the delivery of these reinforcers each time a target behavior occurs. Any reductions associated with the introduction of a high density of reinforcement should be a function of the matching law. Any reductions associated with the introduction of the DRO schedule, however, cannot be attributed to the action of the matching law since the introduction of the DRO schedule would not be associated with an increase in the overall level of reinforcement delivered.

Foxx and Shapiro (1978) conducted just such an experiment. Following a baseline period, a condition of increased reinforcement was introduced. Next, a DRO schedule was introduced that postponed the delivery of these reinforcers contingent upon disruptive behavior. The results of this experiment indicated that the introduction of the enhanced reinforcement condition had little effect on the percentage of disruptive behavior while the introduction of the DRO procedure produced a substantial reduction in disruptive behavior. These results strongly support the conceptualization of DRO as a type 2 punishment procedure.

One clear advantage of conceptualizing DRO as a punishment procedure is that it fits well with the definition of punishment as a change in the environment which decreases the frequency of a behavior it follows (Van Houten, 1983). It is more parsimonious to have reinforcement increase the frequency of particular behaviors. One possible criticism of this position is that type II punishment involves the actual taking away of something following a response. However, there is little difference between stopping the intermittent stroking of someone's arm (possible contact reinforcement) every several seconds following an unwanted behavior and stopping the continuous stroking of someone's arm following an unwanted behavior.

Since the so-called DRO procedure involves the contingent reduction in reinforcement density, a better name that is consistent with the actual process would be contingent reduction in reinforcement density (CRRD) or contingent reinforcement postponement (CRP).

Applied Implications

The preceding analysis has several applied implications. First, CRP should be more effective in applied situations if the response-reinforcer or postponement interval is longer than the reinforcer-reinforcer interval. For example, a CRP schedule with a two-minute reinforcer-reinforcer interval and a five-minute response-reinforcer interval should produce faster learning than a schedule where both intervals are set at two minutes. This procedure should be more effective because it should be easier for the client to discriminate the reduction in reinforcer density with an inappropriate response.

Another implication of this conceptualization is that the CRP procedure should work best when stimuli are added to make it easier for the client to discriminate a reduction in reinforcement density. One example for the literature is the non-exclusionary time-out procedure reported by Foxx and Shapiro (1978). Children were given edibles and praise every four minutes (the reinforcer-reinforcer interval) provided they were wearing a ribbon. Whenever they engaged in misbehavior, the ribbon was removed for 3 minutes and reinforcers were not delivered. Although Foxx and Shapiro referred to this as a time-out procedure, it clearly illustrates the CRP procedure or what otherwise would be referred to as DRO. Indeed, all time-out procedures are essentially CRP procedures and vice versa (time-out can be defined as a transition from a pre-change condition to a less reinforcing post-change condition; Van Houten, 1983).

With developmentally handicapped individuals, an added stimulus should be employed in order to facilitate learning whenever a CRP procedure is employed. One can draw attention to the relationship by pointing or tapping on the ribbon whenever a reinforcer is delivered, and by taking the ribbon away whenever a response occurs. This can help the client discriminate the contingencies in effect.

Another approach that might work with higher functioning clients would be to use a verbal mediator to establish rule governed behavior. It is important to point out to the client when giving the reinforcer that they did not engage in the punishment response and, hence, will receive the reinforcer; and when they emit the behavior, it is important to point out that they will not receive reinforcement for a while.

Another factor that should influence the magnitude of the CRP procedure is the difference between the density of reinforcement following a response and when a response does not occur -- the greater the difference, the larger the effect produced. One way to maximize the difference is to ensure that the background level of reinforcement is not so high as to render the addition or removal of reinforcers relatively unimportant. Another way to accomplish the same objective would be to utilize as many possible normally available reinforcers as part of the CRP arrangement.

Since many practitioners have used DRO as the positive reinforcement element of their treatment package to reduce inappropriate behaviors, one could question whether the categorization of this procedure as a form of punishment has practical or ethical implications. Since the CRP procedure is an example of type 2 punishment, it is necessary to provide a good background level of reinforcement in order to reduce the level of reinforcement following an inappropriate response; hence, the application of CRP ensures the delivery of some reinforcement. Further, the most important way to increase the effectiveness of the CRP procedure is to enhance the level of reinforcement so that its removal will be a more effective punisher. Enhancing the effectiveness of CRP in this manner is analogous to enhancing the efficacy of time-out by enhancing the amount of reinforcement in the time-in situation (Solnick, Rincover, & Peterson (1977)). Although the proper use of the CRP procedure does assure that the client will receive an adequate level of reinforcement, it does little to ensure that this reinforcement is used effectively to teach the client. For this reason, practitioners should always look at whether clients have the functional behaviors in their repertoire that they require, and if a client does not, the practitioner should take steps to see that they are taught.

PROCEDURES INVOLVING THE DIFFERENTIAL REINFORCEMENT OF LOW RATES OF BEHAVIOR

On a DRL schedule, a response is only reinforced if it is preceded by a minimum time without a response (Ferster & Skinner, 1957). An important point to note here is that in the experimental-literature, DRL refers to a response dependent schedule of reinforcement in which a reinforcer immediately follows a response. What has been called a DRL schedule in the applied literature does not satisfy this important condition of a schedule of reinforcement. For example, Deitz and Repp (1973) provided reinforcement to students if they did not engage in an inappropriate behavior more than a specified number of times during a specific interval of time. This procedure can easily be conceptualized as a type 2 punishment procedure where a scheduled reinforcer is not delivered if the inappropriate response occurs more than the specified number of times during an interval of time. In a true DRL schedule, the reinforcer would be made contingent upon the inappropriate response provided that a minimum period of time without a response occurred. The result of this contingency often would be to produce short bursts of relatively high rates of responding (Harzem, 1969). The ethical justification of a procedure that could lead to frequent short bursts of relatively high frequency inappropriate responding certainly should be questionable. However, it should be noted that this effect has not been reported in the applied literature because the schedule employed in the applied literature is not a true DRL schedule.[1]

Not only is the applied DRL procedure a punishment procedure, but it also can be shown to be a minor variation of the CRP procedure discussed earlier. Instead of a single response being associated with a reduction in reinforcement density, the so-called applied DRL procedure has a series of responses associated with a reduction in reinforcement density. The same considerations discussed in regard to the CRP procedure also apply to the DRL procedure.

[1]Editors' note. See Deitz (1977), and Singh, Dawson, & Manning (1981) who have provided applied examples of laboratory method of programming DRL.

PROCEDURES INVOLVING THE DIFFERENTIAL REINFORCEMENT OF INCOMPATIBLE BEHAVIOR

Another important strategy in the treatment of inappropriate behavior is the reinforcement of incompatible or competing behavior (La Vigna & Donnellan, 1986; Sulzer-Azaroff & Mayer, 1977). Some studies have shown that this procedure can be an effective part of a treatment package (Hall, Lund, & Jackson, 1968; Zimmerman & Zimmerman, 1962). The major disadvantage of this approach is that the competing behavior may return to baseline levels when reinforcement is discontinued and the target behavior will then recover to its original level (Mulick, Leitenberg, & Rawson, 1976; Pacitti & Smith, 1977). Van Houten (1983) has pointed out that reinforcing an alternative behavior without punishing the inappropriate behavior sets up a concurrent schedule of reinforcement that would be expected to maintain both behaviors at rates proportional to the amount of reinforcement associated with each behavior. Therefore, if the amount of reinforcement provided for the competing behavior is more than can be applied on a long-term basis, this approach cannot be expected to succeed in the absence of punishment. A second problem with the competing response approach is that a behavior that completely competes with the inappropriate behavior might be viewed as bizarre or inappropriate if it occurs at too high a frequency. A third problem with the competing response approach is that some inappropriate behaviors, such as some forms of self-stimulation, are so reinforcing to the client that it is difficult or impossible to find reasonable reinforcers that can compete with them.

DIFFERENTIAL REINFORCEMENT OF FUNCTIONAL BEHAVIOR

One very important goal in behavior analysis is to teach a variety of functional behaviors that will make contact with reinforcers normally available in the environment (Stokes & Baer, 1977). In one study, Carr and Durand (1985) were able to demonstrate that teaching functional behavior, such as how to appropriately ask for help with difficult work or how to ask for more attention, was able to reduce substantially or eliminate tantrum behavior which functioned as an escape or attention producing response, respectively. Although reinforcing functional behavior may not always ensure that inappropriate behavior will decline, it is always possible to combine reinforcement of competing behavior with punishment of the inappropriate behavior. Indeed, several studies have shown that decreasing the frequency of inappropriate behavior can produce increases in appropriate functional behavior (Koegel & Covert, 1972; Koegel, Firestone, Kramme, and Dunlap, 1974). Perhaps the best strategy in light of these results is to attempt first to teach functional behaviors if they are absent, using the best reinforcers available, and then introduce punishment for the inappropriate behavior only if reinforcement of functional behavior fails to produce a sufficient change in the undesirable behavior. The advantage of this approach is that it stresses the importance of teaching new behaviors in the treatment of inappropriate behavior. Further, in situations where serious inappropriate behavior requires the use of very intrusive punishment procedures, these procedures should be employed only after effective one-on-one teaching procedures have been introduced to teach important functional skills. Then all reductive techniques will have as one of their goals the establishment of an effective teaching situation.

CONCLUSION

Several of the most frequently employed "reinforcement" strategies have been analyzed and discussed. A close examination of the DRO and DRL procedures indicated that both techniques are functionally punishment procedures involving the reduction of reinforcement density contingent upon the occurrence of an inappropriate behavior. A more appropriate label suggested for both procedures is contingent reinforcement postponement or CRP. One advantage of the CRP procedure is that it requires one first to establish a high background level of reinforcement for the client. However, it should be carefully noted that CRP, under certain conditions, can be a highly intrusive procedure. How intrusive CRP can be depends upon the way in which it is implemented. For example, the combination of a long postponement interval along with the use of powerful normally available reinforcement, in some cases, could be considered intrusive.

The analysis of DRO and DRL as punishment procedure suggests several ways to increase their efficiency. First, one can use a response-reinforcer interval that is longer than the reinforcer-reinforcer interval used to provide background reinforcement. Second, stimuli can be added to enable the client to more readily discriminate which interval is in effect. For example, a badge or ribbon could then be removed whenever the inappropriate behavior occurred to signal the start of the response-reinforcer interval. The badge or ribbon then could be reintroduced at the end of the interval. The removal of a stimulus paired with reinforcement could serve as an effective conditioned punisher. Third, the magnitude of the difference in reinforcer density prevailing in the absence of a response and following a response could be increased. One of the easiest ways to accomplish this would be to employ normally available plus added reinforcers rather than just added reinforcers in the CRP contingency.

The DRI procedure also was discussed and seems to have three limitations. First, incompatible behaviors always may not be the functional behaviors that the client needs. Second, high levels of incompatible behaviors may be "inappropriate." Third, the incompatible behaviors might not be ones that are normally maintained in the natural setting.

The final procedure examined seemed to offer the most promise. The differential reinforcement of functional behavior assures that the behavior taught will be of immediate long-term benefit to the client. This approach is viewed as most valuable because it places primary emphasis on the importance of teaching new behaviors that are most likely to prove functional for the client. This approach should minimize the need to use punishment procedures and should ensure that punishment is not employed inappropriately.

REFERENCES

Azrin, N. H., & Holz, W. C. (1966). Punishment. In W. K. Honig (Ed.) *Operant behavior: Areas of research and application*, New York: Appleton-Century-Crofts.

Bostow, D. E., & Bailey, J. B. (1969). Modification of severe disruptive and aggressive behavior using brief time-out and reinforcement procedures. *Journal of Applied Behavior Analysis, 2*, 31-37.

Carr, E. G., & Durand, V. M. (1985). Reducing behavior through functional communication training. *Journal of Applied Behavior Analysis, 18*, 111-126.

Carr, E. G., & Lovaas, O. I. (1983). Contingent electric shock as a treatment for severe behavior problems. In Axelrod & Apsche (Eds.), *The effects of punishment on human behavior*. New York: Academic Press.

Deitz, S. M., & Repp, A. C. (1973). Decreasing classroom misbehaviors through the use of DRL schedule of reinforcement. *Journal of Applied Behavior Analysis, 6*, 457-463.

Ferster, C. B., & Skinner, B. F. (1957). *Schedules of reinforcement*. New York: Appleton-Century-Crofts.

Foxx, R. M., & Shapiro, S. T. (1978). The time-out ribbon: A non-exclusionary time-out procedure. *Journal of Applied Behavior Analysis, 11*, 125-136.

Hall, R. V., Lund, D., & Jackson, D. (1968). Effects of teacher attention on study behavior. *Journal of Applied Behavior Analysis, 1*, 1-12.

Harzem, P. (1969). Temporal discrimination. In R. M. Gilbert & N. S. Suterhalan (Eds.), *Animal discrimination learning*. London: Academic Press (pp. 299-334).

Herrnstein, R. J. (1970). On the law of effect. *Journal of the Experimental Analysis of Behavior,13*, 243-246.

Herrnstein, R. J., & Hineline, P. N. (1966). Negative reinforcement as shock-frequency reduction. *Journal of the Experimental Analysis of Behavior, 9*, 421-430.

Koegel, R. L., & Covert, A. (1972). The relationship of self-stimulation to learning in autistic children. *Journal of Applied Behavior Analysis, 5*, 381-387.

Koegel, R. L., Firestone, P. B., Kramme, K. W., & Dunlap, G. (1974). Increasing spontaneous play by suppressing self-stimulation in autistic children. *Journal of Applied Behavior Analysis, 7, 521-528.*

LaVigna, G. W., & Donnellan, A. M. (1986). *Alternatives to punishment: Solving behavior problems with non-aversive strategies*. New York: Irvington Publishers, Inc.

McDowell, J. J. (1988). Matching theory in natural human environments. *The Behavior Analyst, 11*, 95-109.

Mulick, J. A., Leitenberg, H., & Rawson, R. A. (1976). Alternative response training, differential reinforcement of other behavior, and extinction in squirrel monkies (Saimiri Sciureus). *Journal of the Experimental Analysis of Behavior, 25*, 311-320.

Pacitti, W. A., & Smith, N. F. (1977). A direct comparison of four methods for eliminating a response. *Learning and Motivation, 8*, 229-237.

Poling, A., & Ryan, C. (1982). Differential reinforcement of other behavior schedules: Therapeutic applications. *Behavior Modification, 6*, 3-21.

Reynolds, G. S. (1961). Behavioral contrast. *Journal of the Experimental Analysis of Behavior, 4*, 57-71.

Solnick, J. V., Rincover, A., & Peterson, C. R. (1977). Some determinants of the reinforcing and punishing effects of time-out. *Journal of Applied Behavior Analysis, 10*, 415-424.

Stokes, T. F., & Baer, D. M. (1977). An implicit technology of generalization. *Journal of Applied Behavior Analysis, 10*, 349-367.

Sulzer-Azaroff, B., & Mayer, G. R. (1977). *Applying behavior analysis procedures with children and youth.* New York: Holt, Rinehart & Winston.

Uhl, C. N., & Garcia, E. E. (1969). Comparison of omission with extinction in response elimination in rats. *Journal of Comparative and Physiological Psychology, 69*, 554-562.

Van Houten, R. (1983). Punishment from the animal laboratory to the applied setting. In S. Axelrod & J. Apsche (Eds.), *The effects of punishment on human behavior.* New York: Academic Press.

White, O. R. (1986). Precision teaching-precision learning. *Exceptional Children, 52*, 522-534.

Young, J. A., & Wincze, J. P. (1974). The effects of the reinforcement of compatible and incompatible alternative behaviors on the self-injurious and related behaviors of a profoundly retarded female adult. *Behavior Therapy, 5*, 614-623.

Zeiler, M. D. (1970). Other behavior: Consequences of reinforcing not responding. *Journal of Psychology, 74*, 149-155.

Zeiler, M. D. (1976). Positive reinforcement and the elimination of reinforced responses. *Journal of the Experimental Analysis of Behavior, 26*, 37-44.

Zimmerman, E. M., & Zimmerman, J. (1962). The alteration of behavior in a special classroom situation. *Journal of the Experimental Analysis of Behavior, 5*, 59-60.

CHAPTER

9

RE-FRAMING THE DEBATE: FINDING MIDDLE GROUND AND DEFINING THE ROLE OF SOCIAL VALIDITY

Mark Wolery
University of Kentucky

David L. Gast
University of Georgia

Frequently, thinking about, discussing, and advocating practices is easier for dichotomous categories than for those that are on a continuum (Baer, 1978). For example, we can more easily argue about instructional strategies that are effective or ineffective in teaching students than argue about procedures that are effective to some degree or are effective in some conditions but not others. However, many, if not most, things in life occur on continua rather than in dichotomous categories; examples are height, weight, work productivity, adaptive functioning, intellectual performance, effectiveness of treatment strategies, and acceptability of procedures. Sensitivity to continua allow us to deal with the broad "middle ground" rather than with only the extremes. For example, temperature occurs at extremes of cold and hot (e.g., 30 degrees below zero and 120 degrees above zero); however, the temperatures of many days occur in a broad range that is neither cold nor hot but that can be more accurately characterized as moderate, warm, or cool. Without recognizing the continuum of daily temperature, we would be forced to declare all days as being either hot or cold, inevitably leading to a debate over what is hot and what is cold.

The debate over the use of aversive procedures often is posed as an argument about dichotomous categories; however, we suggest that the debate is best represented on a continuous rather than a binary scale. This chapter has three purposes: (a) to argue that approaching the debate from positions of the extreme is counterproductive, (b) to examine the role of social validity in the debate, and (c) to re-frame the debate from use/non-use of aversives to the conditions under which any attempts to reduce problem behavior should be conducted.

FRAMING THE DEBATE ON A CONTINUUM

In this section, a case is built for the notion that treatment strategies, including those that incorporate aversive procedures, exist on a continuum. Although much of this case may be familiar to most special educators and behavioral scientists, the rhetoric in the debate indicates that it may need mention. Further, a description of some of the dangers of framing the debate in dichotomous categories rather than on a continuum is presented.

Delineating what is and is not meant by aversive procedures may be helpful. Since aversive procedures by definition include aversive stimuli, the definition of aversive stimuli is critical to the debate on the use of aversive procedures. Two potential definitions of aversive stimuli exist, one being a functional definition and the other a social definition. The functional definition states that a stimulus is aversive if an individual's behavior increases or maintains when the stimulus is withdrawn contingent upon the occurrence of a specific behavior (i.e., negative reinforcement), and/or the occurrence of behavior decreases when the stimulus is presented contingent upon that behavior (Type I punishment). The social definition is based on the physical characteristics of the stimulus, and suggests that particular stimuli are aversive because they appear to inflict pain, cause discomfort, or are viewed as unpleasant. This designation is made separate from a demonstration that a relationship exists between the individual's behavior and the contingent presentation or withdrawal of the stimulus. Much of the debate on the use of aversive procedures appears to adopt the latter view. That is, some stimuli are viewed as aversive because of how they are perceived rather than how they affect behavior. A logical extension of this position is that stimuli perceived to be aversive by some are aversive to all individuals. Such a proposition, however, ignores considerable logical and empirical evidence that the reinforcement and aversive value of stimuli are individually determined. Although the lack of universal aversive or reinforcing stimuli argues for framing the debate on a continuum, it is possible to frame the debate in dichotomous categories using the functional definition of aversive stimuli. That is, stimuli and procedures that have punishing or negative reinforcing relationships with a behavior of an individual are aversive.

However, a closer examination of the effects of stimuli indicates that their reinforcement or aversive value cannot be easily categorized. Most behavior analysts are familiar with the use of a powerful reinforcer that loses its value; i.e., satiation occurs. Most analysts also are familiar with individuals who appear to adapt to the aversiveness of punishment procedures. Thus, the reinforcement or aversive value of stimuli can shift. For an empirical demonstration, the data presented by White, Nielsen, and Johnson (1972) on the duration of timeout suggest that experience with longer durations will cause shorter durations that were previously effective to lose their reductive power. Similarly, the value of one stimulus relative to another may shift with use and time. Consumption of salty food may be a more powerful reinforcer than liquids for an individual at one point, but the relative strength of drink may shift after consumption of the salty food. Similarly, the reinforcing or aversive value of stimuli may vary across individuals. For example, contingent access to food probably will be a more powerful reinforcer for a "hungry" than a well-fed individual. The point is that the reinforcing or punishing value of any given stimulus may vary both across individuals and within the individual based on the time factor. This dynamic value of stimuli clearly argues for conceptualizing stimuli on a continuum rather than on a binary scale.

If one adopts a functional definition of aversive stimuli and a dynamic view of the aversive value of stimuli, then three things follow. First, no stimulus can be labeled as aversive or as reinforcing without assessment. Although many stimuli may be aversive to a large proportion of the population, exceptions are likely. Second, no hierarchy of aversive procedures can be stated universally; that is, the procedures that are aversive to one individual may not be aversive to another, or their relative value may vary from individual to individual. Third, establishing a hierarchy of aversive procedures for a given individual will be subject to revision as time passes and as procedures are used.

The most accurate view of the value of stimuli is the notion that all possible environmental stimuli exist on a continuum where the extremes would be described as a powerful positive reinforcer and a powerful aversive stimulus. The potential reinforcing and aversive values are individually determined, and their effectiveness as reinforcers or punishers is demonstrated only when they are contingently applied to or withdrawn from the individual's behavior. Thus, for each individual, a stimulus at a given point in time may hold reinforcing value, aversive value, or no value. The strength of that stimulus may change over time. Further, whether it is used and the manner in which it is used may influence its strength from one instance to another. No stimulus can be judged automatically or universally as neutral, reinforcing, or aversive.

Although the argument for perceiving the debate on a continuum has been based on the reinforcing or aversive value of stimuli, other relevant factors also argue for framing the debate on a continuum rather than in dichotomous categories. An example is the severity of the problem behavior. An analysis of the severity of the problem behavior must include the extent to which it threatens the individual's life; the potential physical harm the behavior causes to the individual and others; the degree to which the behavior interferes with living and interacting in the community; the degree to which the behavior interferes with learning adaptive, functional skills; and the degree to which caregivers, family members, and society in general perceives the behavior as unacceptable. Each of these factors occur on a continuum. For instance, the effect of behaviors on community living may range from no interference to minimal, moderate, or extreme interference. Thus, behavior cannot be perceived in the dichotomous categories of being a problem or a non-problem. Some behaviors are more problematic than others. Similarly, other factors important in the debate occur on continua. Obvious examples include the skill of the interventionists; the degree to which motivating and maintaining variables are known; the strength of motivating and maintaining variables; the history of the individual with different treatment options; the availability and deliverability of powerful reinforcers; the strength of contextual variables, such as the curriculum; the presence of mediating variables, such as health problems, medication effects, and distal but conditional setting events; and many other variables. In short, many important factors relevant to the debate cannot be conceptualized as dichotomous, either-or issues; they are relative variables that occur on continua.

Several dangers exist when the presence of the continuum is ignored, and also when the debate about the use of various stimuli is posed as occurring in dichotomous categories. First, framing the debate in the context of dichotomous categories may lead researchers and practitioners to ignore the relative strength of the relationships that exist between stimuli and behavior. The use of dichotomous categories; i.e., aversive procedures and nonaversive procedures, may lead to the assumption that the members of each category are of equal value. That is, all nonaversive procedures are equally powerful and all aversive procedures are equally powerful. This may result in three undesirable outcomes: (a) use of procedures in either category that are not effective, (b) use of procedures that have limited effectiveness, or (c) use of procedures that have, for lack of a better word, "excessive" effectiveness.

While effectiveness/ineffectiveness is only one dimension on which instructional and reductive procedures should be selected, it certainly is a critical dimension, particularly for individuals with handicaps. Use of ineffective strategies, except to determine whether they are or are not effective, cannot be justified on grounds of humane treatment. Humane treatment implies that the individual will benefit from participation in that treatment. Little, if any, benefit exists for participating in ineffective treatment. Little disagreement is likely on this point and, hopefully, individuals are rarely exposed, at least for extended periods, to ineffective strategies.

A more likely outcome of viewing the issue in dichotomous categories is the use of inferior or inefficient but effective treatments. For example, if one assumes that aversive procedures can be used and if that person sees the debate in terms of dichotomous categories, then one aversive procedure may be viewed as being as appropriate as another. This, of course, may not be the case because, despite the demonstrated reductive value of two aversive procedures, the efficiency of one may be considerably greater than the efficiency of the other. One aversive procedure may result in "elimination" of the behavior within two or three observational sessions, while the other may result in a general reduction and eventual "elimination" over the course of many sessions. When the debate is framed in terms of a continuum, the researcher and practitioner are obligated to assess the efficiency as well as the effectiveness of procedures. A strong case must be developed by the user of a treatment when another treatment will result in the same outcome more efficiently.

Also, when the continuum is ignored, "excessive" or extreme aversive or nonaversive procedures may be used unnecessarily. For example, compliance with a teacher's requests may be established through differential reinforcement, a nonaversive strategy. However, failure to note the continuum of reinforcing stimuli may result in the presentation of excessive reinforcement (e.g, treats, large tangibles) when contingent access to short periods of free time may be sufficient. On the other hand, contingent loss of previously earned reinforcers for noncompliance may be effective. However, failure to appreciate the continuum may lead to loss of large or highly valued reinforcers for relatively minor offenses.

Second, when the debate is framed as one of dichotomous categories, researchers and practitioners may focus more on means than on ends. By definition, instructional and reduction strategies, procedures, and so forth are means to establish particular ends. The ends, most would agree, are realizing individually determined goals (which vary by age and functioning level), participating in society, and obtaining an acceptable quality of life. A continuum-based conceptualization of procedures allows clients and treatment agents to select from a broad array of strategies that will allow them to work toward the agreed upon ends. The dichotomous conceptualization potentially restricts the means available. The restriction of means leads to arguments over the means, and it causes the outcomes to assume a less important status.

Third, framing the debate in terms of dichotomous categories automatically forces researchers and practitioners into one of two artificial camps: those who will and those who will not use aversive procedures. The identification of each camp then is seen in its extremes: Those who use aversive procedures are automatically seen as never using nonaversive strategies and always using the "most extreme" strategies, and those who use nonaversive procedures are seen as only using nonaversive procedures, some of which have questionable effectiveness and efficiency, as well as being cumbersome to implement. In reality, most analysts would prefer to see a world of humane treatment without the use of aversive procedures. However, many, under the assumption that humane treatment must be both effective and efficient, would be willing to use some procedures that would be judged on their physical characteristics as mildly aversive procedures and, in their functional relationships with behavior, be considered powerfully aversive procedures. The dichotomous approach forces the group that, under some conditions, would use aversive procedures into defending all aversive procedures (i.e., the extremes), and forces the group that advocate nonaversive treatment into the position of never using effective and efficient procedures that may have an aversive component, regardless of how mild it may be. Further, the two camps then argue over the logical and empirical justification for their separate positions. This arguing has several outcomes: (a) Members of each camp increase the number of entries on their vita, (b) members of each camp build reputations and careers, and (c) the middle ground is ignored. Ignoring the middle ground will likely result in retarding the development, testing, and adoption of strategies that are simultaneously acceptable and effective. When the debate is focused on a continuum, the extremes can be ignored (perhaps even prohibited), and the middle ground can receive more intense study. Vita still can be enhanced and reputations and careers developed, but the middle ground will not be lost; rather, it will be explored and charted.

UTILITY OF SOCIAL VALIDITY IN THE DEBATE

Since Wolf's (1978) classic paper on social validity, professionals have responded by supplying information on the importance and acceptance of their programs and investigations with increasing frequency. As Wolf indicated, social validity should be assessed on multiple dimensions:

> 1. The social significance of the goals. Are the specific behavioral goals really what society wants?
> 2. The social appropriateness of the procedures. Do the ends justify the means? That is, do the participants, caregivers, and other consumers consider the treatment procedures acceptable?
> 3. The social importance of the effects. Are consumers satisfied with all the results, including any unpredicted ones? (p. 207).

Social validity has entered the debate over the use of aversive procedures at a number of levels. First, it is recommended as a criterion from which we select our interventions (Evans & Meyer, 1985; Wolery, Bailey, & Sugai, 1988). Second, it is used to build cases that our papers should be published. Third, it has been used to justify the positions that are assumed in the debate. It is this third issue that warrants discussion. Interestingly, both camps of the debate have cited social validity to justify their respective positions. Members of both camps appear to agree on the social importance of reducing the inappropriate or problem behaviors of their clients. They acknowledge that society values individuals who do not engage in aggressive, disruptive, self-injurious, and other maladaptive behaviors. Therefore, there is little debate about the importance or validity of the goals. There is, however, disagreement on the other dimensions of social validity (i.e., the procedures and the effects). Those who advocate nonaversive procedures claim that such strategies are more socially valid than aversive techniques (LaVigna & Donnellan, 1986; Snell, 1987). In many cases, this point is reasonable. Most special educators, behavioral scientists, and parents would agree that nonaversive procedures are more acceptable than aversive procedures. However, those who advocate the reasoned use of aversive procedures also use social validity to support their position. Specifically, they claim that aversive procedures are effective and that the nonaversive procedures alone have a weak data base with severe behavior problems (Axelrod, 1987). Objective reviewers of the issue must agree; the data base supporting aversive procedures is more extensive than that supporting nonaversive procedures. Does this mean that both positions are socially valid? How can both camps claim that their positions have social validity? Does it mean that social validity occurs on a continuum rather than in the dichotomous categories of valid or not valid? If opposing positions claim social validity, is it a meaningful construct? This is not a new question. Wolf (1978) described his early concern about the utility of "social importance" (compare pages 203-206). The question raises serious issues about (a) the characteristics of social validity, and (b) the manner in which social validity is assessed.

If we look to social validity to help resolve the debate on the use of aversive procedures, then we must be intellectually honest and realize that social validity on two of the three dimensions is inadequate; "three of three" is the only acceptable criterion. An investigation cannot be said to be socially valid if only the goals and procedures are measured, and an investigation cannot be judged as socially valid if only the goals and effects are measured. If social validity is to have utility in developing a practice that truly has social importance, then our investigations and programs must be assessed and yield positive findings on all three dimensions of social validity. Further, the amount or degree of validity should be reported. As we have discussed earlier, our research and practice should not focus on the extremes of the debate; rather, emphasis should be placed on the middle ground. Perhaps requiring assessment of all three dimensions of social validity will assist the field in this regard. Specifically, programs designed to reduce inappropriate behavior and promote adaptive functioning must document the social importance of the goals, procedures, and effects. Similarly, perhaps the dimensions should be tied together and evaluated as a unit rather than separately. That is, the goals and procedures should be evaluated in the context of whether the procedures are appropriate for the identified goals, and the procedures and the effects should be evaluated in a similar context. The questions really should be: "Given these goals, is this procedure acceptable?", "Is this procedure acceptable at its demonstrated level of effectiveness?" and "Are these effects important, given the procedures used to establish them?" Support for this recommendation comes from Reimers and Wacker (1988). They found that parents' acceptability of procedures which had been used is correlated with the effectiveness of those procedures. If such criteria were used, then perhaps social validity has a central role to play in resolving the debate and moving the field toward defendable practices and solutions. However, we make this recommendation cautiously for several reasons.

A careful re-reading of Wolf (1978) suggests that much of that seminal paper was devoted to defining social validity and discussing how to measure it. A considerable amount of work remains to be done on both of these tasks. For example, social validity uses a relative rather than absolute standard. As Wolf (1978) suggested in discussing his initial misgivings about the notion of social importance, "The editors most frequently reported that the particular manuscripts that they had been asked to review didn't have much of it. On the other hand, they reported that a few manuscripts had a moderate amount of it. And an occasional one or two had a lot of it" (p. 205). This statement illustrates the relative nature of social validity. If it is a relative, continuum-based notion, and if no clear criteria or standard exists for having or not having social importance, can the construct be of use? At issue is the following question: Do experts, consumers, or other relevant persons reliably agree as to what is an adequate or inadequate amount of social validity? Clearly, a related issue is whether an investigation or program is socially valid if the three dimensions have varying amounts of it. For example, is a program socially valid if the goals have high validity, the procedures moderate validity, and its effects have little validity? Or, on the other hand, is a program valid if the goals have a considerable amount, the procedures a minimal amount, and the effects a considerable amount of validity? This seems to be at the heart of the issue in terms of the debate on the use of aversive procedures. Research on social validity bears on this issue. The social validity of a given procedure varies depending upon the severity of the problem being addressed (Kazdin, 1980a; Tarnowski, Rasnake, Mulick, & Kelly, 1989). Further, the rating of acceptability can be increased by providing judges with more information about the procedures (Singh & Katz, 1985), and the acceptability of procedures may be related to their effectiveness (Reimers & Wacker, 1988). These studies illustrate the fact that social validity is relative.

Another problem is that social validity, being a social phenomenon, is subject to the zeitgeist of the day. An illustration of this problem is seen in the overcorrection literature. After the first reports on the use of overcorrection (e.g., Foxx & Azrin, 1973), there was a great increase in research on and use of overcorrection. Many investigators from different sites published an astounding amount of research. This research and the resulting practice suggest that overcorrection was seen as a socially valid procedure in the mid- to late 1970s. To argue that it no longer is a socially valid procedure acknowledges that social validity may change from time to time. Other examples of how the social acceptability of a practice changes with time include placement of individuals with moderate retardation in residential institutions, reliance on sheltered employment settings, use of behavior management procedures without assessing the controlling variables through a functional analysis, and use of segregated schools. Is a construct that is so closely tied to the prevailing zeitgeist of any utility?

The research on social validity indicates that the acceptability of different interventions can be discriminated by a variety of judges, such as undergraduate psychology students (Kazdin, 1980a; Singh & Katz, 1985), children (Kazdin, 1984, parents (Kazdin, 1984; Norton, Austen, Allen, & Hilton, 1983), teachers (Norton et al., 1983), special educators (Irvin & Lundervold, 1988), and staff members of an in-patient psychiatric program for children (Kazdin, French, & Sherick, 1981). Generally, less restrictive procedures are rated as more acceptable. The question remains, however, whether a group of experts or consumers would rate a given procedure or set of effects differently. That is, would experts from the nonaversive camp rate the acceptability of a procedure differently from experts who, under certain conditions, would use aversive procedures? The current debate suggests that the answer clearly is "yes." If this is the case, then what benefits accrue when social validity is assessed?

This leads directly to the selection criteria used for recruiting judges. Who are the best judges? Traditionally, the judges are assumed to be experts and "consumer(s) or representatives of the relevant community" (Wolf, 1978, p. 209). In part, the answer to the question of who are the best judges is tied to the nature of the problem being studied. If we are investigating a procedure for facilitating the transition of preschoolers to kindergarten classes, then appropriate judges may be kindergarten teachers and administrators of elementary schools. If, however, we are investigating a procedure for facilitating the transition of adolescents from home to community living, then kindergarten teachers and elementary school administrators are inappropriate. However, this example illustrates some of the difficulties. If a program is attempting to establish a group home in a given neighborhood, the parents of the individuals who are to live in the group home may judge the neighborhood as appropriate and rate the goals, procedures, and effects as highly valid. Yet, the residents of that neighborhood may not want the group home in their area. Are we to assume that a lack of social validity exists? Or, are the members of the neighborhood inappropriate judges? Several questions are pertinent: What qualifies an individual or group of individuals to be judges of social validity? How is the relevant community defined? How many judges are necessary? Must multiple groups (e.g., consumers and experts) be used? Are some judges more appropriate evaluators of different dimensions of social validity? What methodologies should be used in selecting judges? Of course many other questions surrounding this issue could be formulated. However, a more cynical view is that the only appropriate judges are those who support the intents, procedures, and outcomes of our research and programs. If this is so, then the utility of the construct of social validity is diminished considerably.

Related concerns deal with how social validity is measured. These concerns are not new, but are, in our view, under-investigated. The level of measurement that is used to document social validity requires further analysis. Kazdin (1977) suggested that social validity of goals, procedures, and effects could be assessed at the subjective and objective levels. Unfortunately but understandably, the field has tended to employ questionnaires, ratings scales, and interviews as primary measurement strategies. Use of more objective measurement strategies are desirable but are less frequently used. The concern is about the reliability and validity of the social validity measures. A second concern about the methodology for assessing social validity is the application of appropriate experimental designs. Frequently, social validity appears to be a supplemental component of a program or study. While this also is understandable, when the authors want to make a strong case that their goals, procedures, or effects are socially valid, the use of rigorous experimental designs is necessary. This recommendation enables investigators to build a strong and believable case for the statements they make about social validity. A usual response to such suggestions is that social validity deals with values rather than empirical issues. A rejoinder to this charge agrees that social validity deals with values, but maintains that identification of societal values is a sticky proposition and one for which the scientific method is most appropriate. While values originate from many sources other than science, the identification of societal values is an empirical task. For example, perhaps rather than asking judges to rate the social validity of procedure "X," we should ask them to make comparative judgments about the procedure and several other strategies. The research question is then moved from the acceptability or unacceptability of procedure "X" to the relative acceptability of procedure "X" in comparison to other procedures. Kazdin and his colleagues (Kazdin, 1980a, 1980b, 1984; Kazdin et al., 1981) have provided us with a model for such research. Similarly, the social validity of the effects could be evaluated in this manner. Traditional group designs are well suited for such questions.

In summary, although social validity is a widely accepted notion, its utility in clarifying the debate and moving research forward has been questioned. This questioning occurs because it uses a relative rather than absolute standard, changes with the passage of time, and is subject to other influences. At a minimum, the social validity of the goals, procedures, and effects must be assessed for each investigation or program rather than simply for one or two of these dimensions. The utility of social validity is probably related to which judges are selected, how it is measured, and whether appropriate experimental designs are employed. These issues deserve more discussion and study.

RE-FRAMING THE CONDITIONS OF ACTIVE TREATMENT FOR PROBLEM BEHAVIORS

Special educators, behavioral psychologists, and their professional organizations have come to recognize that indiscriminate use of aversive procedures is undesirable, inappropriate, and unacceptable. Most acknowledge that on the continuum of interventions, some are more desirable than others and that some are clearly unacceptable. As a result, statements, guidelines, and recommendations concerning punishment procedures have been proposed (Favell et al., 1982; Guess, Helmstetter, Turnbull, & Knowlton, 1987; Horner et al., 1989; Lovaas & Favell, 1987; Repp & Deitz, 1978; The Association for Persons with Severe Handicaps, 1985; Wood & Braaten, 1983; Wood & Lakin, 1978). In nearly all cases, these statements are designed to bring about more reasoned use of aversive procedures or to restrict use of aversive procedures. Some are tied to particular types of behaviors (e.g., Favell et al., 1982) and others address particular types of aversive procedures (Guess et al., 1987).

Recently, authors have attempted to delineate the characteristics of individuals' right to treatment (Favell & Reid, 1988; Van Houten et al., 1988). The recommendations concerning right to treatment are similar in many instances to the guidelines for controlling the use of aversive procedures. However, the right to treatment guidelines also apply to goals that are solely related to acquisition and generalization of new behaviors in addition to treatment designed to address problem behaviors. What has not been presented, however, is a description of conditions under which all behavior reductive procedures, aversive or nonaversive, should be implemented. We have attempted to list and briefly describe below the conditions under that professionals should plan programs that address problem behavior. Our contention is that the conditions under which nonaversive procedures are used are identical to those under which aversive procedures could be employed. These conditions have been described elsewhere in more detail (cf. Wolery et al., 1988, Chapter 18).

Systematic Use Of A Decision Model

A decision model should be employed to ensure that individuals' rights are protected, appropriate planning is completed, best-practice implementation occurs, and appropriate review is obtained. In addition, use of a decision model helps establish the point that the professionals have acted reasonably. Several decision models have been described (cf. Evans & Meyer, 1985; Gaylord-Ross, 1980; Lynch, McGuigan, & Shoemaker, 1983; Wolery et al., 1988).

Assessment Of Motivational Factors Related To The Problem Behavior

In the past few years, considerable attention has been given to identifying the motivational factors that cause and maintain problem behaviors. Means for conceptualizing problem behaviors in terms of their communicative functions (Donnellan, Mirenda, Mesaros, & Fassbender, 1984) and procedures for assessing which motivational factors may be operating (Durand & Crimmins, 1988; Touchette, MacDonald, & Langer, 1985) have been proposed. Likewise, means for conceptualizing how existing relationships may interfere with the maintenance and generalization of treatment gains have been described (Horner & Billingsley, 1988). In short, the technology now appears to exist for identifying motivational factors for many problem behaviors.

Use Of Assessment Data In Planning Interventions

As noted above, motivational factors can be identified for many problem behaviors. When this is done, then that information should be used to plan the treatment program (Evans & Meyer, 1985; Favell et al., 1982; Wolery et al., 1988). Examples exist showing that such assessment information can lead to differential treatments (Durand & Carr, 1985; Iwata, Dorsey, Slifer, Bauman, & Richman, 1982). Clearly, a link must be established between the functional analysis of the problem and its subsequent treatment (Durand, 1987; Repp, Felce, & Barton, 1988).

Deliberate And Concentrated Attempts To Teach And Reinforce Adaptive Behaviors

Programs designed to eliminate or reduce the occurrence of problem behavior should be fashioned, or used concomitantly with other procedures, to establish adaptive responses.

Many, but not all, nonaversive procedures are designed to establish new responses, some of which replace the target problem behavior (Donnellan, LaVigna, Negri-Shoultz, & Fassbender, 1988). However, when any strategy is used to reduce problem behaviors, attempts should be made to establish replacement responses. These attempts must transcend acquisition of an alternative or replacement behavior in the treatment setting, and attempts to ensure maintenance and generalization of the replacement behaviors must be included (Horner & Billingsley, 1988).

Reliable Measurement Of The Target Behaviors And Treatment Implementation

Measurement of target behaviors is a hallmark of applied research and best-practice, and when the goal of the intervention is to treat problem behavior, measurement is a critical component. To be useful, data must be collected reliably and, fortunately, the methods for measuring reliability are well known. Similarly, the implementation of the treatment variable or package should be monitored. Billingsley, White, and Munson (1980) proposed a method for measuring the reliability with which treatments are implemented. In short, it involves an operational description of the procedure(s), development of an observational system based on that description, and use of that system to collect data on the extent to which the planned treatment is implemented. This is particularly important when the goal of treatment is to reduce behavior because it may lead to the identification of (a) incorrect implementation, (b) drift in the implementation, and (c) hypotheses about the reasons for effectiveness or lack of effectiveness.

Periodic Monitoring Of Side Effects Of Intervention

The potential for the occurrence of side effects when punishment procedures have been used is well known, as are the types of side effects. Some side effects will be transient, while others will endure; some may be positive, but others will be negative. Likewise, the potential for side effects may occur with reinforcement procedures (Balsam & Bondy, 1983). When a program is used to reduce the occurrence of problem behaviors, potential side effects should be monitored for two reasons. First, a new program may need to be developed to deal with the side effects; i.e., to ensure that negative side effects do not endure and to ensure that positive side effects are facilitated.

Second, information concerning the occurrence of side effects is needed in making judgments about the continuation or modification of the program.

Attention Given To The Maintenance And Generalization Of Adaptive Outcomes

The efficacy of any intervention designed to treat problem behaviors must be evaluated in terms of whether the desirable outcomes endure and occur in all relevant contexts. Establishing such results requires careful consideration of many variables (cf. Horner & Billingsley, 1988). Any plan designed to reduce the occurrence of a problem behavior should include a detailed description of procedures for ensuring maintenance and generalization of the effects.

Informed Consent From Parents And Administrative Authorities

Obtaining informed consent from families and administrative authorities routinely is recommended for programs using aversive procedures (Evans & Meyer, 1985; Favell et al., 1982). Barton, Brulle, and Repp (1983) suggested that informed consent from families should include the following components: (a) description of the procedure, (b) results of previous attempts to treat the problem, (c) rationale for the proposed procedure, (d) description of measurement procedures, (e) anticipated outcome and duration of the program, (f) qualifications of the persons using the procedure, and (g) written description of results from any human rights committees. The intent of such consent is to ensure that families understand and approve of the proposed procedures. It is an initial measure of whether the proposed procedures have a sufficient amount of social validity to warrant use. In addition, all treatment programs designed to reduce problem behavior should be submitted for review by human rights committees. This also provides an initial, measure of the proposed procedures social validity.

Prior Peer Review Of The Intervention Plan

Prior peer review should go beyond a human rights committee's permission to use a procedure. It should include consultation with experts who have treated similar problems with similar individuals. Peer review allows the intervention team to be sure that the proposed procedure reflects best-practice and has a base in the empirical literature.

Open Implementation Of The Intervention

Open implementation allows interested parties to observe, evaluate, and comment on the implementation of the planned program. Such opportunity sets the stage for suggestions that may improve the program and provides a minimum level of assurance that the interventionist will not be accused falsely of abuse or maltreatment.

Implementation By A Competent Team Of Professionals

Competent professionals should implement, supervise the implementation, and evaluate programs designed to reduce problem behaviors (Wood & Braaten, 1983). This is necessary because problem behaviors and their environmental relationships can be complex, treatment procedures can be difficult to implement reliably and correctly, and the effects can be multiple.

SUMMARY

In this chapter, three major points have been made. First, the debate over the use of aversives should be framed in terms of a continuum rather than in terms of dichotomous categories (i.e., aversives vs. nonaversives). The rationale for this recommendation is that (a) it reflects the realities of the issue more accurately, and (b) failure to recognize the continua that are involved in the debate can lead to undesirable and counterproductive outcomes. In fact, a dichotomous conceptualization is likely to lead to a fruitless continuation of the debate, while conceptualizing the debate in terms of a continuum may lead to the development and use of strategies that are simultaneously more effective and acceptable than those currently being employed.

Second, the role and utility of social validity has been questioned. The use of social validity to justify the positions of both camps, the relative nature of social validity, the fact that it occurs on a continuum, as well as the susceptibility of social validity to the prevailing zeitgeist, suggest that we (a) examine the criteria by which social validity judges are recruited, (b) employ objective measures of social validity, (c) assess the degree or amount of social validity rather than its presence or absence, and (d) use more rigorous experimental designs when evaluating the social validity of our studies. Also, if social validity is to have a role in the debate over the use of aversive procedures, then all three dimensions (goals, procedures, and effects) must be measured, analyzed, and reported.

Third, the conditions should be similar under which any program (aversive, nonaversive, and combinations of the two) designed to treat problem behaviors should be implemented. An initial listing of these conditions has been proposed. The conditions are proposed to shift the debate toward the middle ground, to ensure the most appropriate treatment of problem behaviors, to protect the individual whose behavior is being treated, and, finally, to protect the interventionists who are treating problem behaviors.

NOTE

The authors appreciate the thoughtful comments provided on an earlier draft of this chapter by Melinda J. Ault, Patricia M. Doyle, John W. Schuster, and Vincent Winterling of the Department of Special Education, University of Kentucky.

REFERENCES

The Association for Persons with Severe Handicaps (1985). Resolution on intrusive interventions. *TASH Newsletter, 11* (November) p. 3. Seattle, WA: The Association for Persons with Severe Handicaps.

Axelrod, S. (1987). Doing it without arrows: A review of Lavigna and Donnellan's *Alternatives to punishment: Solving behavior problems with non-aversive strateiges. The Behavior Analyst, 10*, 243-251.

Baer, D. M. (1978). On the relation between basic and applied research: In A. C. Catania and T. A. Brigham (Eds.), *Handbook of applied behaviors analysis: Social and instructional processes* (pp. 11-16). New York: Irvington.

Balsam, P. D., & Bondy, A. S. (1983). The negative side effects of reward. *Journal of Applied Behavior Analysis, 16*, 283-296.

Barton, L. E., Brulle, A. R., & Repp, A. C. (1983). Aversive techniques and the doctrine of the least restrictive alternative. *Exceptional Education Quarterly, 4(3)*, 1-8.

Billingsley, F. F., White, O. R., & Munson, R. (1980). Procedural reliability: A rationale and an example. *Behavioral Assessment, 2*, 229-241.

Donnellan, A. M., LaVigna, G. W., Negri-Shoultz, N., & Fassbender, L. L. (1988). *Progress without punishment: Effective approaches for learners with behavior problems*. New York: Teachers College Press.

Donnellan, A. M., Mirenda, P. L., Mesaros, R. A., & Fassbender, L. L. (1984). Analyzing the communicative functions of aberrant behavior. *Journal of the Association for Persons with Severe Handicaps, 9*, 201-212.

Durand, V. M. (1987). "Look homeward angel:" A call to return to our (functional) roots. *The Behavior Analyst, 10*, 299-302.

Durand, V. M., & Carr, E. G. (1985). Self-injurious behavior: Motivating conditions and guidelines for treatment. *School Psychology Review, 14*, 171-176.

Durand, V. M., & Crimmins, D. B. (1988). Identifying the variables maintaining self-injurious behavior. *Journal of Autism and Developmental Disorders, 18*, 99-117.

Evans, I., & Meyer, L. (1985). An *educative approach to behavior problems: A practical decision model for interventions with severely handicapped learners*. Baltimore: Paul H. Brookes.

Favell, J. E., Azrin, N. H., Baumeister, A. A., Carr, E. G., Dorsey, M. F., Forehand, R., Foxx, R. M., Lovaas, O. I., Rincover, A., Risley, T. R., Romanczyk, R. G., Russo, D. C., Schroeder, S. R., & Solnick, J. V. (1982). The treatment of self-injurious behavior. *Behavior Therapy, 13*, 529-554.

Favell, J. E., & Reid, D. H. (1988). Generalizing and maintaining improvement in problem behavior. In R. H. Horner, G. Dunlap, & R. L. Koegel (Eds.), *Generalization and maintenance: Life-style changes in applied settings* (pp. 171-196). Baltimore, MD: Paul H. Brookes.

Foxx, R. M., & Azrin, N. H. (1973). The elimination of autistic self-stimulatory behavior by overcorrection. *Journal of Applied Behavior Analysis, 6*, 1-14.

Gaylord-Ross, R. (1980). A decision model for the treatment of aberrant behavior in applied settings. In W. Sailor, B. Wilcox, & L. Brown (Eds.), *Methods of instruction for severely handicapped students* (pp. 135-158). Baltimore: Paul H. Brookes.

Guess, D., Helmstetter, E., Turnbull, H. R. III, & Knowlton, S. (1987). Use of aversive procedures with persons who are disabled: A historical review and critical analysis, *TASH Monograph Series, No. 2*. Seattle: The Association for Person with Severe Handicaps.

Horner, R. H., & Billingsley, F. F. (1988). The effect of competing behavior on the generalization and maintenance of adaptive behavior in applied settings. In R. H. Horner, G. Dunlap, & R. L. Koegel (Eds.), *Generalization and maintenance: Life-style changes in applied settings* (pp. 197-220). Baltimore: Paul H. Brookes.

Horner, R. H., Dunlap, G., Koegel, R. L., Carr, E. G., Sailor, W., Anderson, J., Albin, R. W., & O'Neill, R. E. (1989). *Toward a technology of "nonaversive" behavioral support*. Manuscript submitted for publication.

Irvin, L. K., & Lundervold, D. A. (1988). Social validation of decelerative (punishment) procedures by special educators of severely handicapped students. *Research in Developmental Disabilities, 9*, 331-350.

Iwata, B. A., Dorsey, M. F., Slifer, K. J., Bauman, K. E., & Richman, G. S. (1982).

Toward a functional analysis of self-injury. *Analysis and Intervention in Developmental Disabilities, 2*, 3-20.

Kazdin, A. E. (1977). Assessing the clinical or applied importance of behavior change through social validation. *Behavior Modification, 1*, 427-451.

Kazdin, A. E. (1980a). Acceptability of alternative treatments for deviant child behavior. *Journal of Applied Behavior Analysis, 13*, 259-273.

Kazdin, A. E. (1980b). Acceptability of timeout from reinforcement procedures for disruptive child behavior. *Behavior Therapy, 11*, 329-344.

Kazdin, A. E. (1984). Acceptability of aversive procedures and medication as treatment alternatives for deviant child behavior. *Journal of Abnormal Child Psychology, 12*, 289-302.

Kazdin, A. E., French, N. H., & Sherick, R. B. (1981). Acceptability of alternative treatments for children: Evaluations by inpatient children, parents, and staff. *Journal of Consulting and Clinical Psychology, 49*, 900-907.

LaVigna, G. W., & Donnellan, A. (1986). *Alternatives to punishment: Solving behavior problems with non-aversive strategies*. New York: Irvington.

Lovaas. O. I., & Favell, J. E. (1987). Protection of clients undergoing aversive/restrictive interventions. *Education and Treatment of Children, 10*, 311-325.

Lynch, V., McGuigan, C., & Shoemaker, S. (1983). An introduction to systematic instruction. *British Columbia Journal of Special Education, 7*, 1-13.

Norton, G. R., Austen, S., Allen, G. E., & Hilton, J. (1983). Acceptability of time out from reinforcement procedures for disruptive child behavior: A further analysis. *Child and Family Behavior Therapy, 5*, 31-41.

Reimers, T. M., & Wacker, D. P. (1988). Parents' ratings of acceptability of behavioral treatment recommendations made in an outpatient clinic: A preliminary analysis of the influence of treatment effectiveness. *Behavioral Disorders, 14*, 7-15.

Repp, A. C., & Deitz, D. E. D. (1978). Ethical issues in reducing responding of institutionalized mentally retarded persons. *Mental Retardation, 16*, 45-46.

Repp, A. C., Felce, D., & Barton, L. E. (1988). Basing the treatment of stereotypic and self-injurious behaviors on hypotheses of their causes. *Journal of Applied Behavior Analysis, 21*, 281-289.

Singh, N. N., & Katz, R. C. (1985). On the modification of acceptability ratings for alternative child treatments. *Behavior Modification, 9*, 375-386.

Snell, M. E. (1987). In response to Axelrod's review of *Alternatives to Punishment*. *The Behavior Analyst, 10*, 295-297.

Tarnowski, K. J., Rasnake, L. K., Mulick, J. A., & Kelly, P. A. (1989). Acceptability of behavioral interventions for self-injurious behavior. *American Journal on Mental Retardation, 93*, 575-580.

Touchette, P. E., MacDonald, R. F., & Langer, S. N. (1985). A scatter plot for identifying stimulus control of problem behavior. *Journal of Applied Behavior* Analysis, 18, 343-351.

Van Houten, R., Axelrod, S., Bailey, J. S., Favell, J. E., Foxx, R. M., Iwata, B. A., & Lovaas, O. I. (1988). The right to effective behavioral treatment. *The Behavior Analyst, 11*, 111-114.

White, G., Nielsen, G., & Johnson, S. (1972). Timeout duration and the suppression of deviant behavior in children. *Journal of Applied Behavior Analysis, 5*, 11-120.

Wolery, M., Bailey, D. B., & Sugai, G. M. (1988). *Effective teaching: Principles and procedures of applied behavior anlaysis with exceptional children*. Boston: Allyn and Bacon.

Wolf, M. M. (1978). Social validity: The case for subjective measurement or how applied behavior analysis is finding its heart. *Journal of Applied Behavior Analysis, 11*, 203-214.

Wood, F. H., & Braaten, S. (1983). Developing guidelines for the use of punishing interventions in the schools. *Exceptional Education Quarterly, 4(3)*, 68-75.

Wood, F. H., & Lakin, K. C. (Eds.). (1978). *Punishment and aversive stimulation in special education: Legal, theoretical and practical issues in their use with emotionally disturbed children and youth*. Minneapolis, MN: Advanced Training Institute.

CHAPTER

10

ONE EDUCATOR'S PERSPECTIVE ON THE USE OF PUNISHMENT OR AVERSIVES: ADVOCATING FOR SUPPORTIVE AND PROTECTIVE SYSTEMS

Sharon Freagon
Northern Illinois University

Professionals and parents continue to debate the merits of specific technologies and practices using positive programming or aversives to reduce or eliminate challenging behavior that injures self or others. Others provide a moderate view espousing no conclusive evidence one way or another. This author's position is that we must implement and provide each and every child with disabilities the same rights; the same family and community structures that promote happiness, growth, learning, achievement, and the same protection from harm that are afforded children not identified as having disabilities. Until then, discussions and debates about the use of punishment or aversives are irrelevant, immoral and unethical. Some will say this position is naive, presumptuous, and judgmental. Throughout this chapter, a case will be made that we as a society have a reverse order of priority in treatment of persons with disabilities. We have applied technology before applying regard and value.

THE USE OF SEVERE PUNISHMENT OR AVERSIVES IN PRACTICE

In 1982, the Office for Children (OFC) for the Commonwealth of Massachusetts issued group home licenses for the Behavior Research Institute, Inc. (BRI), a private, not-for-profit, charitable agency, approving the following hierarchy of punishments or aversives for use with individuals served by BRI:

1. Ignore
2. Firm "No"
3. Token fines
4. Water spray
5. Vapor spray
6. Taste aversives
7. Contingent physical exercise
8. Time-out helmet
9. Ammonia
10. Hand squeeze
11. Spank
12. Muscle squeeze
13. Pinch
14. Brief cool shower
15. Time-out helmet with safety

tube and optional automatic vapor spray

When conducting a licensing study from September, 1984, through April 1, 1985, the OFC found that BRI was actually using the following hierarchy:

1. Ignore
2. Firm "No"
3. Token fines
4. Water squirt to the face or back of neck
5. a. Vapor Spray I to the back of neck (compressed air mixed with water vapor lasting approximately 3 seconds)
b. Air Spray (same as Vapor Spray I without the water)
6. a. White Noise Visual Screen (a football helmet with an opaque screen to occlude vision and a masking or other unpleasant repetitive noise)
b. Taste Aversive (vinegar, vanilla extract, lemon juice, jalapeno pepper spray, or other taste aversives applied to lip or tongue)
c. Standing time-out in White Noise Visual Screen (standing in bare feet on an uncomfortable rubber floor mat)
d. Ammonia (ammonia fumes sprayed near the nose)
e. Vapor Spray II (lasting approximately 15 seconds)
f. Vapor Spray II (lasting approximately 2 minutes)
g. Contingent physical exercise (series of sit-ups or toe-touches)
h. Remove Vapor Spray (vapor spray attached to the White noise Visual Screen)
i. Social punisher (student loosely tied to another student whom he/she finds aversive)
7. a. Hand squeeze
b. Wrist squeeze
8. Rubber band (snapped on wrist or inner arm)
9. Spank (applied to bare buttocks or thigh)
10. Muscle squeeze (applied to shoulder, tricep, pectoral, or thigh)
11. Rolling pinch (applied to buttocks, inner arm, inner thigh, bottom of feet, palms of hands, or stomach)
12. Finger pinch (applied to buttocks, inner arm, inner thigh, bottom of feet, palms of hands, or stomach)
13. Water Spray III (bucket of cold water poured over head)
14. Brief cool shower (1 min shower at approximately 50 degrees)
15. a. Automatic Vapor Spray Station (AVS) (wrists and ankles restrained while child wears Remote Vapor Spray Helmet; usually implemented in conjunction with other aversives)
b.Multiple Consequences
c.Combined Aversives

(Commonwealth of Massachusetts, Office for Children, Division of Administrative Law Appeals, OFC No. 1.54, 1985, p. 4-5).

The same document (p. 14-15) indicates that, ... on February 5, 1985, a letter from BRI staff physician to the Director of Student Services stated that larger students standing for 2 hours in the A.V.S. (No. 15 of the hierarchy actually used by BRI) would not present a problem, particularly if they are given a break in the middle and allowed to ride a bicycle for approximately 5 minutes... Prolonged standing can or may lead to varicosities, edema, leg ulcers and skin infections in the feet and legs when in combination with physical aversives to the feet and legs... During April, 1985, the OFC licensor review [*sic*] student "G"'s behavior charts and learned from March 9, 1985, to March 20, 1985, student "G" was placed in the A.V.S. on continuous, non-stop basis except for time-out of the A.V.S. for bathroom and water opportunities and sleeptime. Student "G" was required to wear a white noise visual screen with the noise turned off while sleeping.... In February, 1984, ... Student "AA" was placed in ankle cuffs with an eleven inch chain which student "AA" wore during all awake and sleep hours except for shower time... Efforts to place student "AA" in another facility have been unsuccessful and student "AA" was observed on August 28, 1985, at BRI in the restraint referred to above.

WHO? WHERE? HOW?

Who are the children, youth, and adults believed to require the use of severe punishment or aversives? They are the children, youth, and adults with whom, more than likely, every author in the present text has had some experience. They are the children, youth, and adults over whom parents and professionals have agonized for years. They are individuals who for a multitude of reasons, many unknown to parents and professionals, abuse themselves or another or both. They may hit themselves; beat their heads against a wall; pull their hair out; gouge their eyes, ears or genitalia. Oftentimes, these children, youth, and adults do not adhere to regular hours of sleep and can stay awake 5, 6, or 7 consecutive days and nights, pushing the significant-other adult(s) in their environment to enormous feelings of frustration and rage. They may threaten the life or physical well-being of a family member(s). More than likely, the older they become, the more difficulty they may cause to themselves or others.

Where have the children, youth, and adults who continue to abuse themselves and others been? More than likely, if not at home with their parents, these individuals have been on psychiatric wards of hospitals or in multiple institutions. Whether on psychiatric wards or in institutions, they have usually been in large congregate care with others who exhibit the same behavior or like behavior. Whether on psychiatric wards or in institutions, they often have been heavily medicated and placed in straitjackets or other forms of restraint. On psychiatric wards, they typically have been served by psychiatric nurses under doctors' orders and by nurses' aides who may or may not have 2 years of college preparation and who turn over frequently (George & Baumeister, 1981; O'Connor & Sitke, 1985). In institutions, they have been served by individuals with 4-year college degrees from a wide variety of occupations and by aides who in many, if not most, instances have only a high school diploma or a General Educational Development (GED) certificate offered through a junior or community college, and the turnover is high.

How have these children, youth, and adults who abuse themselves and/or others gotten to the point where parents, professionals, and others providing care and services view the use of severe punishment or aversives as a correct means to manage their behavior? Perhaps there are no straightforward answers to this question but, then again, perhaps there are. Consider parents who are so frustrated that they perceive no other alternative but to remove their children from their homes. Consider the entrepreneur who would seize an opportunity where a void exists. Consider services and alternatives that work but are not documented in traditional literature forms. Consider these collectively.

Parents' Frustration Leading to Removal

One only need be a parent of children not identified as having disabilities to realize that every parent has differing degrees of tolerance and frustration in response to the actions of their children. To be in a position to empathize with less fortunate parents, add the additional frustration of a child who does not respond to regular family contingencies;

cannot communicate needs, wants and desires; does not affirm the parents' love and role by reciprocation; and impedes the other family members' pursuit of achievement in adulthood. Traditional forms of help are not an option due to their heavy reliance on all family members' ability to communicate verbally. Depending on the parents' tolerance and frustration, the child may be removed from the home. Typically, this happens when the family situation is in crisis and not before. Families are advised that a "bed has opened" and they have to make a decision immediately. The bed that has opened is most often not in the community of the family. At the point of family crisis, parents typically accept any form of placement that reduces the family frustration and any form of treatment that provides a "ray of hope." Usually, parents begin to question the efficacy of the program only after their child has been out of the home for a period of time and they begin to see the effects of the removal when they visit. Rarely do they return their child to their home but, instead, they challenge the placement or try to make it better. Only rarely do, and can, parents of children with challenging behavior anticipate and assist with the development of services to maintain their children in their homes or in community alternatives.

Placements

Throughout the last two decades, our nation witnessed the treatment that individuals with developmental disabilities received in the institutions of America. We witnessed this on television, in pictorial exposés, and in the federal courtroom. Citizens were horrified and outraged over every instance of television and pictorial exposure, forcing state legislatures to take action. In the federal courtroom, this treatment was defined as abuse. Federal courts ordered states to provide guarantees that the practice of abuse would cease, the residents would be protected from harm, and developmental programs would be implemented.

As state-operated facilities and institutions increasingly have been prohibited from using severe means to control and manage the challenging behavior of residents, the private sector, or the entrepreneur, has moved in to fill the void. Of the 19 Massachusetts children and youth in placement at the BRI at the time of a young man's death, six were placed there by the Department of Mental Health; 11 were placed by the Department of Education or by local school systems; one was cost-shared by the Department of Social Services, the Department of Mental Health, and the local school system; and one was cost-shared by the Department of Education and the Department of Mental Health (Commonwealth of Massachusetts Office for Children, Division of Administrative Law Appeals, OFC No. 1.54, Insert 8a to 8, p.3). All placements from Massachusetts then were made by local or state agencies of government.

Alternatives That Work But Are Not Documented

The strategy of matching individuals with similar or like disabilities and actions, where one individual is served in a restrictive environment, such as an institution, and the other is served in a less restrictive environment in the community, has been successfully utilized in federal suits such as the 1977 *Halderman v. Pennhurst* (State Hospital and School); *Ronker et al. v. Walter et al.* (1983); and others. Additionally, one only need travel to local communities throughout many of the states of America to see that alternatives to the use of severe punishment or aversives do exist for individuals who present challenging behavior. Indeed, many individuals who, at one time or another, would have been candidates for the use of severe punishment or aversives are being served in local communities.

These are the communities and alternatives cited in federal deinstitutionalization suits, as well as in federal suits and due process hearings, when parents want their children to live in the community and/or attend the local public schools.

So why, when there are local communities that have developed alternatives for individuals who otherwise would have been sent to agencies such as the BRI, do we as professionals continue to debate the use of severe punishment or aversives and say there are no data or only weak data? Is it possible that, because these local successes are not documented in the literature using traditional research methods, we choose to ignore them? Is it possible that we, as a profession serving individuals with disabilities, have not yet merged research and technology with local community organization in concert with value and regard?

The discussion to this point has illustrated the circumstance in which individuals with disabilities who exhibit behavior that is identified as requiring extraordinary means find themselves. The circumstance reflects the following:

1. A society that does not value individuals with disabilities in the same manner as individuals without disabilities;
2. Multilevel agencies of government which practice segregation and exclusion versus integration, inclusion and supports for families and their local communities;
3. Families who are conditioned to justify the use of severe punishment or aversives as the only means to help their sons or daughters;
4. A community of professionals who are willing to debate the merits of exclusion versus inclusion in the literature, in the courts, and in educational due process instead of using collective energies to support families and their local communities.

THE RIGHT QUESTIONS

When a young man at BRI died and opponents of the use of severe punishment or aversives cried abuse, parents of young people at BRI answered the cry by asking, "So, where are the programs and where are the entrepreneurs who have demonstrated and would demonstrate another way?" The answer to this question is not unidimensional; it is multidimensional. To ask, "Where are the programs?" is unidimensional and a wrong question. To ask, "What assistance can we give families and local communities in order that they can support every individual, no matter how severely disabled or challenging, in their pursuit of growing up in a family, attending the local schools and working and recreating in the community?" is multidimensional and a right question. To ask, "Where are the entrepreneurs who have designed and can design specific programs?" is a wrong question. To ask, "What are professionals who earn their livelihood in service to my son or daughter doing?" is a right question. To ask, "What is my son or daughter learning about his or her life and the people in it when the program I agree to uses severe punishment or aversives?" is a right question. To ask, "What is my son or daughter learning if s(he) grows up in our family, attends the public schools, later lives in a home with significant others of his or her choice, and later works in an environment of his or her own selection?" is also a right question. All of the "right" questions are ones that parents deserve to have answered -- ones that individuals with disabilities deserve to be answered and acted upon.

THE RIGHT ANSWER(S)

Some are going to say that using the BRI case is not an appropriate example in academic discussions regarding the use of severe punishment or aversives with individuals who have developmental disabilities. They will say that this case is an aberration and no professionals "worth their salt" would recommend the practice of severe punishment or aversives being applied in this manner. The reality is, however, that the BRI case is an example of how some in a society will take an idea, a technology, or a practice with perceived credence and apply it in its extreme. The BRI case is an example of what is possible in a society when individuals are grouped and labeled by characteristics of their births.

What, then, are the right answers? The right answers, again, are not uni-dimensional but are multidimensional. The right answers are in the following collective statements representing the circumstance in which more and more individuals with developmental disabilities will find themselves in the future if parents, professionals, policymakers, and lawmakers come together as one:

1. A society that values every individual equally, no matter what the characteristics of birth;
2. Multilevel agencies of government that practice integration, and inclusion, and provide support for families and their local communities;
3. Parents who work with professionals to obtain and maintain the integrity of the family within the community;
4. A community of professionals who are willing to use collective energies in support of the integrity of the individual, the family, and the local community.

A Society That Values Every Individual Equally

Society's value of the individual, no matter what his or her characteristics of birth, is reflected in the laws passed at the federal, state, and local levels. These laws are civil, regulatory and criminal. They are designed to protect all the citizens and promote the democracy.

Federal law is made when some national goal is at stake. A national goal was at stake when Congress passed Section 504 of the Rehabilitation Act of 1973, providing access to individuals with disabilities all of the activities, services, programs, and facilities traditionally accessed by individuals without disabilities. A national goal was at stake when Congress passed Public Law 94-142, The Education of All Handicapped Children Act of 1975. The Act was in response to the issue that some children identified as having disabilities were not being provided the public education that children without disabilities were being offered in the schools of America. A national goal was at stake when Congress passed Part H of 99-457 and Section 619 of Part B, the 1986 Amendments to the Education of the Handicapped Act. Part H addressed the plight of those infants and toddlers who Congress realized would benefit from services at birth. Section 619 of Part B dealt with the provision of services for handicapped children ages three to five. By the 1990-1991 school year, states are mandated to provide services to preschoolers.

Desirable, of course, is federal law that is appropriately and accurately interpreted in its intent and implemented willingly by states and local communities. This desirable circumstance, however, is not the reality for many individuals with developmental disabilities. Public Law 94-142 is a good case in point.

Danielson and Bellamy (1989) have shown wide state variations in the placement of children and youth in segregated vs. integrated environments although the law mandates daily interactions with same-age peers without disabilities, even for those children living in institutions. Turnbull (1985) notes that the intent of the law will not be upheld to its fullest extent until the public is in consensus. The public affected by Public Law 94-142 in different states is not yet in consensus. The public is comprised of regular and special education administrators, teachers, related service personnel, university professionals, and parents.

Does this mean that federal laws are not an important element in the lives of individuals with disabilities? Absolutely not. Without federal laws, the inequities in the lives of individuals with disabilities would not draw the attention, elicit the outrage, and result in the subsequent protections and incentives. Does this mean that we have to keep defining the integrative intent of laws such as Public Law 94-142 in the courts? Absolutely. Does this also mean that we have to build a broader consensus among the public? Again, absolutely. Gent and Mulhauser (1988), after providing a comprehensive review of legal outcomes in recent years, suggest that courts rule more favorably for individual suits asking for school integration and community-based instruction than for class action suits. These authors also point out that *St. Louis Developmental Disabilities Treatment Center Parents' Association et al. v. Mallory et al.* (1984), a modified class action suit, where the judge believed a teacher who testified that "her students were so disabled that they could not differentiate between themselves and the environment and could not hold their heads up" (p. 193), so they would not benefit from interactions and integration into the public schools. He believed service providers over well-published and experienced professionals in The Association for Persons with Severe Handicaps (TASH).

Three suggestions become apparent when we consider how federal laws are made and implemented in relationship to achieving full citizenship for individuals with disabilities. First, instead of presenting cases as class action suits under Public Law 94-142 and/or other laws designed specifically for individuals, approaching group inclusion as a civil right, such as in *Brown vs. Board of Education* (1954), may have more success. Inclusion and access are civil rights, and the U.S. Office of Civil Rights in regional offices throughout the U.S. recently has had considerable success when monitoring compliance with Section 504 within the context of Public Law 94-142. Second, in cases where an individual is concerned, Public Law 94-142 has been a successful vehicle for achieving school integration, and suits should continue. Third, consensus-building among the stakeholding public is absolutely essential to all practices of inclusion, which is indicative of a society that values all its people. More consensus renders more acceptance renders more inclusion. Consensus-building is a tedious and time-consuming process. Parents and professionals alike must learn lessons from elected officials in the art of campaigning and of informing, educating, and convincing the general public and the identified stakeholders.

Finally, especially important for young children who demonstrate early signs of self-injury and aggression toward others is the mandating of services to all 3-to-5 year-olds in all states by the 1990-91 school year. If the behavior that leads to the use of severe punishment or aversives can be interrupted at an early age, the other increasingly effective societal systems of school integration, family supports and cash subsidies, positive programming, relevant instructional programs, and so on, will keep pace (see Chapter 19 by Dunlap, Johnson, & Robbins).

Multilevel Agencies Of Government Practicing

Agencies of federal, state, and local governments exist to serve the people. Multilevel agencies of government are generally responsible for implementing laws, monitoring compliance with laws, and distributing associated funds. Too often, these agencies are unwilling to implement services and programs commensurate with new laws, monitor compliance, and redirect funds toward implementation if the new law does not have enough associated funds. Agencies are typically unwilling because the politics of nonconsensus among the stakeholders may lead to undesirable consequences for the implementer, the enforcer, and the distributor of funds.

Absolutely crucial to moving forward with integration and inclusionary practices for individuals with disabilities within this climate are multiagency beliefs and values commensurate with enabling laws that are stated clearly in agency goals and objectives. Also crucial is leadership in the various agencies that is capable of implementing, monitoring and redistributing funds; leadership that is able to, so to speak, "withstand the heat." We have witnessed successful movement when agencies of government have these components (beliefs, values, and leadership) in place.

Finally, with no support from federal law, we have seen Michigan become the first state to actualize its value and regard for families with members who have disabilities by implementing a program of family support and cash subsidy. Family supports, such as local and ongoing respite services and cash subsidies that families can use to ease the financial burden by having additional monies to hire babysitters, replace tires for cars, purchase lifts for vans and so on, will go a long way to facilitate raising these children with their families. Experience tells us that providing integrated educational services and good individualized programs during the school-age years alone does not necessarily prevent children from placement outside the home. Family support and cash subsidy, then, may be the single most important innovation to date, especially when taken with the promising practice of integrating very young children with disabilities into day care centers and other places where children not identified as having disabilities are during these years. As noted in the earlier discussion, this innovation will be especially important for families with young children who present problem behaviors that are challenging, and runs the risk of pushing the family to decisions of removal. Experience also tells us that children who live with their families and are integrated during the early childhood years have an increased probability of being integrated during the public school years. Likewise, youth who live with their families and are integrated during the school-age years have an increased probability of being integrated during the adulthood years. Integration and family support contribute to conditions that prevent serious behavior problems from developing, and thus obviate the need for aversive programming.

Parents Working With Professionals

Helping parents work with professionals to maintain the integrity of the family within the community is undoubtedly the most effective strategy to accomplish integrated life-styles for persons with disabilities, no matter how challenging the behavior. If we as a society are going to realize a fully integrated life-style for persons with disabilities within our lifetime, the agenda for which we collectively work must be clear, concise, and attainable. The agenda must be presented to Congress and the federal government, to state legislatures and state agencies, to city councils and mayors, to school boards and superintendents, to employers and employees, to day care governing boards and day care administrators, to media personnel, and to judges and due process hearing officers.

Parents working alone run the risk of not being definitive enough. Professionals working alone run the risk of conveying self-interest and not recognizing the true needs of families and individuals with disabilities. Many federal, state, and local entities espouse parent involvement which usually means parent participation on an advisory board. Typical parent involvement is not enough to realize the agenda of full integration and effective programs. Realizing the agenda will require parent education and training, as well as a parent networking system. Parent education and training must not only provide procedures to exercise parental rights within specific laws, but must also include the determination of lifetime goals and expectations for their sons and daughters. Once parents have been educated and trained, they may be employed by agencies to educate and train other parents. Parents employed by agencies should be able to work from their homes and not from an agency. Parent networking systems should be supported financially by agencies and provide travel, telephone, and child care expenses.

If we as a society really do believe in the integrity of the family and the local community in which the family lives, then this type of support for parents is reasonable and warranted. This commitment to parent education, training, and networking would serve consensus-building well, in addition to adding prestige to the role of parents in their efforts with many diverse groups.

A Community Of Involved Professionals

As early as 1976, Bricker challenged researchers to stop conducting research meant to communicate solely with other researchers in order to enhance one's own status and visibility among colleagues. Twelve years later, Taylor (1988) writes:

> It seems incontestable that the agenda for the future of research in our field is filled with questions of daunting complexity. We seem to have answered all of the easy questions, and the questions that confront us today will demand sophisticated answers. For example, what does integration mean? Physical proof is no longer adequate proof ... to claim successful integration. Any definition of integration must take into account elements of friendship and affection. How does one measure emotional closeness (e.g., love or commitment) without distorting character? (p. 175).

In the 12 years between Bricker's assessment of the research on individuals with severe disabilities, and that of Taylor, it would appear on the surface that we have come a long way. Perhaps we have. Yet, we still have thousands of children educationally segregated, thousands of people still institutionalized, more than 60 youth in an agency that utilizes severe punishment and aversives, and probably many more receiving severe punishment and aversives in other agencies, although perhaps not as pervasively.

When we try to integrate those youngsters educationally, deinstitutionalize people, and provide another way for those in programs that use severe punishment or aversives, we hear that there are no data or there are only weak data. Perhaps we haven't answered the "easy" questions as sufficiently as needed. Perhaps we haven't examined closely enough the variables in successful community programs not reported in the literature. Perhaps the research is not disseminated widely enough to have an impact on those who provide barriers. Perhaps there are no data or only weak data because researchers find fault with each other's methods, rendering them invalid in each other's view. All these explanations are plausible and need to be considered. However, the most important consideration, for those of us who earn our livelihood in service to individuals with disabilities, whether that be research or the facilitation of applications in the field or both, is the obligation we *have* or *don't have* when we have knowledge, information, and skills that could directly influence the quality of life for thousands of individuals with disabilities, no matter how severe or challenging.

SUMMARY

Throughout this chapter, the effects on persons with disabilities and their families when society does not value them in the same manner as it values persons without disabilities have been illustrated. To argue the merits of using severe punishment or aversives with any person with developmental disabilities who exhibits self-injurious behavior, or behavior that is a danger to others, is immoral and unethical. Professionals who earn their livelihood in services for, or research with individuals with disabilities, incur a moral and ethical obligation to ensure that people who have disabilities have sufficient supports and protection in the community to allow them to grow up with their families, attend the public schools, later live in homes with a few significant others of their choice, and have jobs of their own selection. Strong infant, toddler, and early childhood programs are critical to the interruption of behavioral patterning leading to the perceived need for the use of severe punishment or aversives to manage behavior. The use of severe punishment or aversives needs to be defined as abuse, just as it is defined as abuse when applied with people without disabilities. If it walks like a duck and talks like a duck, it is a duck.

REFERENCES

Commonwealth of Massachusetts, Office for Children, Division of Administrative Law Appeals, OFC No. 1.54 (1985).

Bricker, W. (1976). The service of research. In M. A. Thomas (Ed.), *Hey don't forget about me! Education's investment in the severely, profoundly and multiply handicapped* (pp. 162-179). Reston, VA: Council for Exceptional Children.

Brown v. Board of Education, 347 US 483 (1954).

Danielson, L. C., & Bellamy, G. T. (1989). State variation in placement of children with handicaps in segregated environments. *Exceptional Children, 55*, 448-455.

Dunlap, G., Johnson, L. F., Robbins, F. R. (1990). Skill development and early interventions. In A. C. Repp & N. N. Singh (Eds.), *Current perspectives in the use of nonaversive and aversive interventions for persons with developmental disabilities.* Sycamore Publishing Co.: Sycamore, IL.

Gent, P. J., & Mulhauser, M. B. (1988). Public integration of students with handicaps: Where it's been, where it's going, and how it's getting there. *The Journal of the Association for Persons with Severe Handicaps, 13*, 188-196.

George, M. J., & Baumeister, A. A. (1981). Employee withdrawal and job satisfaction in community residential facilities for mentally retarded persons. *American Journal of Mental Deficiency, 85*, 639-647.

Halderman v. Pennhurst (State Hospital and School), 446 F. Supp. 1295 (E.D. Pa. 177).

O'Connor, G., & Sitke, G. F. (1975). Study of a new frontier in community services: Residential facilities for the developmentally disabled. *Mental Retardation, 13*(4) 35-38.

Ronker et al. v. Walter et al., 700 F. 2d 10058 (6th Cir. 1981), cert. denied S. Ct. 81 (1983).

St. Louis Developmental Disabilities Treatment Center Parents' Association et al. v. Mallory et al. 591 F. Supp. 14116 (W.D. Mo. 1984).

Taylor, S. J. (1988). Preface to generations of hope. *Journal of the Association for Persons with Severe Handicaps, 13*, 173-174.

Turnbull, H. R. (1985). Jay's story. In R. Turnbull & A. P. Turnbull (Eds.), *Parents speak out: Then and now* (2nd ed.) (pp. 109-118). Columbus, OH: Charles E. Merrill.

CHAPTER

11

TRANMISSION OF BEHAVIOR MANAGEMENT TECHNOLOGIES FROM RESEARCHERS TO PRACTITIONERS: A NEED FOR PROFESSIONAL SELF-EVALUATION

Doug Guess
University of Kansas

The primary assumption of this chapter is that insufficient attention has been directed toward how the use of behavior management techniques on persons with disabilities affects the behavior of both those persons using the procedures and those persons receiving the treatment. Discussion will center mainly on these concerns in relation to the use of aversive procedures and techniques designed to inflict pain and discomfort on the recipients, and which are not typically used or recommended in normal child-rearing practices in our society. In this discussion, historical practices of using aversive procedures with persons who have disabilities will be addressed, as well as the influences today of these practices on the behavior of researchers, personnel trainers, clinicians, teachers, parents, and others who directly or indirectly interact with these individuals. My position is not intended as a criticism of the many persons who, for various reasons, advocate the judicious use of aversive procedures in the education and treatment of persons with very severe behavior problems, including self-injurious behavior and violent aggression. I am, nevertheless, on written record as opposing the use of aversive procedures with persons who are disabled, and my rationale for assuming this position came only after considerable study and reflection. In doing so, I approached the issue from both an empirical and philosophical perspective, not only questioning the effectiveness and efficiency of aversive procedures to modify behavior perceived as deviant, but also attempting to understand the broad implications of how our practices influence attitudes and behavior toward persons with disabilities, including, of course, attempts to assimilate them into the mainstream of our society.

In reviewing the published literature over the past 25 years, one finds three identifiable groups targeted for the use of aversive procedures to modify perceived deviant behavior: prisoners, patients in psychiatric hospitals, and persons with disabilities including, especially, those with mental retardation (Guess, Helmstetter, Turnbull, & Knowlton, 1986). Both legal and personal protests from the first two groups effectively diminished the use of aversive procedures as part of their treatment regimes. The third group, however, those persons with disabilities, has continued to this day to receive interventions using a variety of aversive procedures that include punishment, negative reinforcement, and positive practice overcorrection. In many respects, this has been an "experiment" of unparalleled proportions in the history of delivering human services to a minority population identified as deviating from perceived societal norms and expectations--an experiment that has combined the quest for empirical knowledge in support of a particular theory of behavior, in combination with the training of countless numbers of clinicians and educators, to put into practice the assumptions of the theory; and both with the practical goal of improving the lives of these persons. One can only speculate on why there has been such a long history of using aversive procedures with persons with disabilities. Certainly, the effectiveness of the procedures is debatable, especially when considering the issues of generalization and maintenance of such treatments (cf., Clark, 1987; Guess et al., 1986; Lennox, Miltenberger, Spengler, & Erfanian, 1988).

We know also that B.F. Skinner, the architect of behaviorism from which the aversive procedures were derived, did not advocate the widespread use of punishers with persons with disabilities nor, indeed, any other group. In an August 16, 1987, interview with the *New York Times*, Skinner made the following statement: "What's wrong with punishments is that they work immediately, but give no long-term results. The responses to punishment are either the urge to escape, to counterattack, or a stubborn apathy. These are the bad effects you get in prisons or schools, or wherever punishments are used."

Perhaps the continued use of aversive procedures, at least with individuals identified as mentally retarded, was based on the nature of this population in combination with the institutional settings in which, several decades ago, most of them lived. Certainly, their behaviors were no more destructive to themselves (or others) than behaviors of the prison population, or patients in psychiatric hospitals. Unlike the prisoners or psychiatric patients, however, many persons with mental retardation are not capable of effectively protesting what is done to them, no matter how well meaning the actions might be. Additionally, a representative sample of published research studies using aversive procedures with these persons over the past 25 years shows that the large majority of these studies have been conducted in institutional and other segregated settings (Guess et al., 1986), removed thus from public scrutiny and monitored internally by those who, for the most part, would advocate their use. This observation is most important because these institutional-based research studies using aversive procedures provided both the basis for the development and later extensive dissemination of the technology that has continued to be used, and because (as will be discussed subsequently) both the procedures used and the behavior that they were intended to modify have influenced current perceptions and attitudes that are not necessarily positive toward these persons.

In many respects, both the development and application of a technology that uses, in part, aversive procedures was done mainly in the effort to verify empirically the procedures, themselves, without also considering the larger and possibly more important issues of the consequences that these efforts have had for both the users and recipients of these procedures. Questions that should have been asked early in this effort were rarely addressed, and possibly not even considered to be important. As argued earlier by Guess et al. (1986), the use of aversive procedures with persons with disabilities is more than an empirical issue; it also is a pervasive moral and ethical issue, this latter issue, until most recently has been neglected largely by professional and advocacy groups in the area of developmental disabilities.

We now, of course, find ourselves involved in a national effort to implement behavioral management strategies in integrated community settings with an extensive history of a technology and orientation based on the use of aversive procedures derived primarily from populations residing in segregated institutional environments. Overcoming this history and the orientation that it instilled in the professional arena likely will require some radical adjustments in thinking, in addition to the continued rapid development of nonaversive alternatives. In all likelihood, many members of the professional community will not fully accept the rationale for not using aversive procedures unless more pervasive arguments can be made that override the assumption that "punishment works" and is a necessary "right-to-treatment" option. With this assumption in mind, we must address the issue pertaining to important gaps in our current knowledge about behavior management. These "gaps" are not related specifically to the intervention procedures, per se, but to basic and long neglected areas of inquiry pertaining to the consequences of using aversive procedures on (a) possible negative changes in overall educational and treatment practices among persons using these procedures with this population, and (b) professional and societal perceptions of persons with disabilities. Central to both of these points is the issue of how the use of aversive procedures has emerged so strongly in our field and some of the assumptions that have been made in this development.

Use Of Aversive And Societal Perceptions

Friedman (1975) correctly observed that aversive treatments themselves are components of parental and educator child development practices, and that they are also important ingredients in intervention regimes with adults who are not disabled. Agreeably, punishment procedures are a common, and likely important, aspect of normal child-rearing practices, as well as a reality of life in our communities and society. At issue, however, is a departure from normal child-rearing practices in the types of aversive stimuli used to modify the behavior of persons with disabilities. In the developmental disabilities literature, one finds a variety of aversive stimuli that likely would not be used to manage the behavior of persons who are not disabled. These stimuli include, for example, electric shock, hair pulling, contingent tickling, pinching, ammonia capsules placed under the nose, forced exercise, white noise at 95 db, Tabasco sauce, vinegar, and lemon juice squirted into the mouth, the forced swallowing of vomitus, and so on. As pointed out by Guess et al. (1986), these stimuli resemble, at least in topography if not intensity, similar stimuli reported by Amnesty International (1984) to control the behavior of political prisoners. Obviously, of course, the motivations for using aversive procedures to manage the behavior of persons with disabilities are quite different from those used by governments to control the behavior of political prisoners. Nevertheless, the types of aversive stimuli used as part of the procedure to modify the behavior of persons with disabilities raise some interesting questions about the treatment of behavior problems in integrated community settings. At least two dilemmas can be identified.

First, as referenced earlier (Guess et al., 1986), the vast majority of published studies using the types of aversive stimuli described above (especially the more intensive ones) were conducted in institutional and other segregated settings. In addition, generalization of the targeted behavior, when it does occur, is necessarily programmed in those settings and situations most likely encountered by the recipients of the procedures. If our collective goal, then, is to implement behavior management programs in integrated community settings, would those persons advocating the use of aversive procedures and stimuli also be willing to use them with persons with disabilities in these settings and in full view of persons in the community? If the answer is "no," then one must ask them why? Would there be a double standard in which it is all right to use aversive procedures within the confines of a segregated facility, but not where the "nonprofessional" members of the community can observe what is being done to persons with disabilities. If this is the case, then one would find a treatment justification for the placement of persons with disabilities in segregated environments which, of course, is antithetical to current practices and philosophies (Hansen & Haring, 1981; Taylor, Racino, Knoll, & Lutfiyya, 1987).

In brief, the types of behavior management procedures used in integrated community settings must include a best-fit between what practitioners are willing to do, what other nonprofessional members of the community are willing to accept, and how such practices influence the acceptance of these persons into the mainstream of community life. If recommended professional practices deviate significantly from accepted community standards on how persons with disabilities should be treated, then a self-analysis by the profession seems warranted. This self-analysis also should include the possibility that many advocates for the continuation of segregated and highly restrictive environments for persons with disabilities (especially mental retardation) do so, at least in part, because these types of environments allow them to implement behavior control procedures that likely would not be condoned in community settings. This possibility is supported by the observation of Sarason (1985) who noted the current high rate of clinicians now working in bureaucratic settings (e.g., institutions for persons with mental retardation, mental hospitals, prisons, reformatories) that have long been known for their "...absence of caring and compassionate ambience" (p. 178). (Having previously worked 13 years as a behavioral psychologist and researcher in an institutional setting for children and youth with mental retardation, my own experiences would not contraindicate the above observations.)

Use Of Aversive Procedures And Perceptions Of Service Providers

In 1981, the Executive Board of The Association for Persons with Severe Handicaps passed what was then, and still is, a controversial resolution that called for no longer using aversive procedures with persons who have disabilities. The resolution was based in part on the still debatable effectiveness of these procedures to manage behavior and, importantly, on the observations among Board members that these procedures were being both abused and misused in a variety of settings that serve persons with disabilities. While the researchers, as pointed out earlier, have been reluctant to publish studies in which aversive procedures were used in integrated community settings, the practitioners possibly have been less hesitant to use these procedures in a much broader context--and with apparently fewer and less stringent systems to monitor their behavior. I have had many real life examples related to me to support this point, including the placement of a preschool child's face down in an ice packet to encourage head lifting behavior, the indiscriminate and widespread spraying of the face of students for very minor behavior infractions, the use of alum for a student who used foul language, and so on. These examples are what I, and other colleagues (cf., Guess et al., 1986), have referred to as the *spread effect* and *procedural decay*, both of which likely appear more frequently in classrooms and other applied settings, but which also can be found in literature where aversive procedures have been used with persons who are disabled. Together, they represent a potentially negative impact on the behavior of persons who use aversive technology, as well as on the recipients of the treatment.

The *spread effect* essentially involves the increasing escalation of aversive procedures to control behavior in applied settings, an observation that was made by Nietzel (1979) in reference to the use of punishers to control the behavior of prison inmates. Neisworth and Smith (1973) earlier expressed a similar concern about the spread effect when using aversive procedures with persons who are mentally retarded:

> Because punishment does produce at least immediate suppression of unwanted behavior, users of punishment may be negatively-reinforced to use punishment until it becomes their major strategy to change behavior. This explains why attendants, teachers, aides, and others who work with children with retarded behaviors often employ aversive tactics: punishment has its "rewards"--the immediate suppression of the unwanted behavior, the immediate compliance of the punished person....it tends to become habit forming. (p. 54)

One also can observe the spread effect in the published research where aversive procedures have been used with questionably valid target behaviors including, for example, the use of electric shock to reduce rocking behavior (Baumeister & Forehand, 1972); hand slapping for hands-in-mouth and finger movements (Romanczyk, 1977); and a comparison of water mist to the face and vinegar or lemon juice into the mouth to decrease hand clapping and hand and finger jabbing (Friman, Cook, & Finney, 1984).

The spread effect is also found in a related concept, *procedural decay*, where aversive procedures are actually used to teach new skills. The above example from a preschool classroom demonstrates this point where a negative reinforcement procedure (i.e., raising the head to avoid having the face in an ice packet) was being used to establish head control behavior in a young child with severely handicapping conditions. Again, however, the published literature shows similar examples where aversive procedures were used to teach skills to children and youth with handicapping conditions. Massey and Insalaco (1969) employed white noise at 95 db as a punisher for incorrect responses to a visual discrimination task among 40 children aged 7-21, and described as severely/profoundly retarded. Kircher, Pear, and Martin (1971) used a shock to punish inattention in a picture-naming task with two young children diagnosed as severely/profoundly retarded. An overcorrection procedure (forced hand and arm movements) was used by Hinerman, Jenson, Walker, and Petersen (1982) for incorrect responses by a child with autism being taught to sign words.

The potentially alarming aspect of the spread effect and procedural decay is the extent to which practitioners might have followed a similar path, using teaching and treatment regimens that encompass aversive procedures that have been legitimized by published research articles, textbooks, and likely in personnel training programs. This effect brings to issue a discussion of the transmission of knowledge and information related, in this case, to the use of aversive procedures.

Initially, we must recognize that the potential for the misuse and abuse of aversive procedures is something that the field of developmental disabilities cannot take lightly. There are likely some persons in our field who, given even the slightest pretense of professional legitimacy, will use aversive procedures in ways that are incongruent with the humane treatment of persons with disabilities, and especially with those persons with disabilities whose level of physical and/or cognitive impairment reduces their ability to effectively protest against what is being done to them. I would also include in this latter group some persons with profound mental retardation who might not even have a "cause-effect" concept, and thus would not be capable of perceiving the application of an aversive stimulus as being *contingent* on their preceding "unwanted" behavior.

There is, however, a majority of practitioners whose misuse or abuse of aversive procedures results not from a purposeful intent to inflict pain on others but from their own interpretations of our professional literature, academic courses, workshops, and conference presentations. Over the past several decades, for example, our field has been flooded with instructional textbooks, journal articles, training manuals, films, and other forms of print media that include the use of aversive procedures as standard practice in the management of behavior among persons with disabilities. Indeed, the majority of university personnel training programs probably have included aversive behavior management procedures as part of their curriculum. Instruction on using the procedures usually includes, of course, the necessity for concurrent positive programming and the caution to use aversive procedures as the last step in a continuum from least-to-most intrusive interventions. This massive dissemination effort is, nevertheless, subject to severe criticism when viewed from the perspective of how this information is passed down to on-line practitioners, and a failure to provide complete "truth in packaging," a problem that likely is in no small part responsible for the misuse (or even use) of aversive procedures in education and treatment settings serving persons with disabilities.

THE DISSEMINATION PYRAMID: FROM RESEARCHERS TO PRACTITIONERS

A pyramid model (Figure 1) is useful when conceptualizing the flow of the large amount of information on the use of aversive procedures that has been disseminated in our field. At the top pyramid is a relatively small number of researchers, followed next by a larger number of persons who both translate the research findings and teach others how to apply what has been learned. This group typically represents personnel trainers including, especially, university instructors. The next and even larger group in the pyramid represents the practitioners and service providers who, themselves, were "students" (formal or otherwise) receiving the technology from the instructors. Extending the pyramid even further, one finds parents and other care providers who are often trained to use the procedures and technology from the on-line practitioners or other service personnel.

In this chapter, I cannot even scratch the surface of the complex issue of how knowledge and information are obtained, interpreted, used, and disseminated in the

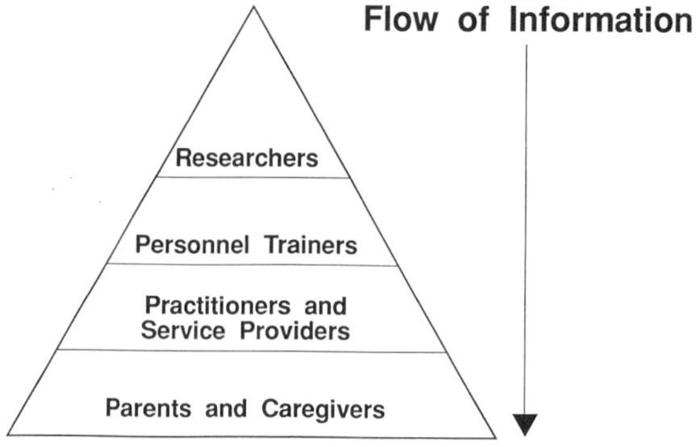

Figure 1: Dissemination and flow of information on aversive procedures from researchers to practitioners and parents.

scientific and educational communities (cf., Skrtic, 1986, 1988 for this discussion in relation to the field of special education). Below, however, is a brief sketch of some major problems and issues related to the flow of information down the pyramid, and how this flow might have contributed to both the overstated effectiveness attributed to aversive procedures, as well as the misapplication of this technology in applied settings for students with disabilities.

Problems With The Research Base

Earlier, I noted that a representative sample of published studies in major journals from 1965 to 1985 showed that most studies using aversive procedures were conducted in segregated environments that included institutions and university-based clinics (Guess et al., 1986). Further analyses of these data indicated that approximately one-third of the published research studies used experimental designs that controlled for both internal and external validity, and that systematic, reliable collection of both generalization and maintenance data was rare. Generalization data, when collected, typically included only a small subset of potentially controlling events and settings. Maintenance data were very infrequently collected for a period of over 12 months following the termination of treatment. Side effects from the treatment (both positive and negative) usually were described as anecdotal information, if discussed at all.

A more recent review of the literature (Lennox et al., 1988) on decelerative treatment practices among persons with mental retardation from 1981 to 1985 also found that few research reports addressed the variables of generalization, maintenance, and side effects. Importantly, these authors found that nearly two-thirds of the studies reviewed did not report pretreatment functional analyses to identify potential controlling variables. Lennox et al. (1988) also expressed surprise at the large number of aversive procedures still being evaluated in the literature. These findings raise a real question about the commitment of many applied behavior analysts to abandon the use of aversive treatments with persons who are disabled (cf., Mulick, in press).

In calling for a total ban on the use of punishment procedures, McGee (1988) takes the position that "...punishment is a tool that precludes the discovery of more humane positive approaches" (p. 78). She further points out that such a ban will initially cause a lot of confusion because so many programs and teachers rely on punishment procedures. She then concludes:

> The question becomes, then, does the good that will result from a ban on aversives justify the harm? If there must be a sacrifice involved in either the use or prohibition of aversives, the amount and duration of harm must be weighed against the benefits. In the long run, far fewer people will be hurt if aversive consequences are banned; thus, today's children will be protected from unnecessary punishment, and even more children of the future will be protected from obsolete aversives (p. 79).

The absence of critical information (and data) in most of the studies reviewed by Guess et al. (1986) and Lennox et al. (1988) is understandable, given the early dates in which some of these studies appeared in the literature and the lack of concern at that time for issues of generalization, maintenance, side effects, and so on. The primary purpose of these investigations was to demonstrate that punishers, negative reinforcers, and overcorrection procedures could, when used in combination with positive programming techniques (usually DRO), at least temporarily, suppress a variety of behaviors. Nevertheless, these investigations, regardless of their empirical and applied shortcomings, provided the basis for the extensive dissemination of a technology that was adopted as encompassing state-of-the-art practices for treating excess behavior among persons with disabilities.

Dissemination Of The Aversive Procedure Technologies By The Academic Community

The behavior of those persons next on the pyramid, the large variety of personnel trainers (including especially university instructors), is best understood through a discussion of paradigms, a concept made popular through the writings of Thomas Kuhn in his classic book, *The Structure of Scientific Revolutions* (1970). Although Kuhn's analysis was directed toward the physical sciences, some persons have currently extended his thinking to the field of special education (cf., Edgar, 1988; Heshusius, 1982, 1986; Skrtic, 1986, 1988). A paradigm, generally defined, encompasses a model or pattern by which researchers, educators, and practitioners operate. It provides, in many respects, an orientation and philosophy by which new knowledge is assimilated into a theoretical perspective on the nature of observed phenomena. A paradigm offers a central organizing *gestalt* for the identification of new research questions, the interpretation of wide and often varying research findings, and, importantly, a possible framework for a large world view. Within this context, it is important to note that all sciences are based on "ideologies" (cf., Guess, Turnbull, & Helmstetter, in press) and that in many cases these ideologies are used to further the social agendas and world views of those who adhere to a particular paradigm.

Behavioral psychology is widely acknowledged to have served as the primary paradigm in special education for at least 25 years, and it has been adopted almost exclusively as the primary instructional orientation by the majority of institutions that prepare teachers and other personnel to serve persons with disabilities. When considering the influence of paradigms on professional and scientific disciplines, it is easier to understand how and why the use of aversive procedures became so entrenched in the education and treatment of persons with disabilities. These individuals not only provided a subject base for attempts to validate the behavioral paradigm, but also did so within the context of a usually legitimate rationale; i.e., their behaviors often needed to be remediated. Even today, however, the controversy does not center on the perceived need to identify new paradigms for the treatment of unwanted behavior among persons with disabilities, but rather on whether the nonaversive technology within the behavioral paradigm is sufficient to the task

The cautions of Skinner on the long-term negative outcomes of punishers notwithstanding, many of those embracing the behavioral paradigm likely perceived the use of aversive technology not only as the best available procedure for decelerating very difficult problem behaviors, but also as confirmation, at least in part, of the overall empirical validation of the theory. This perception was true for the large number of personnel trainers who not only embraced behaviorism but who also were most eager to carry this message to potential converts, including students. Therefore, even though the empirical basis for the use of aversive procedures was incomplete, if not inadequate, it nevertheless was included as a widespread component of not only personnel training curricula but also in the vast amount of literature pertaining to the education and treatment of persons with disabilities--including training manuals for use by parents. The acceptance and eventual application of the technology by students and practitioners is due, in large measure, to the authoritative nature of institutionalized education.

As pointed out by Skrtic (1988), induction into a profession (e.g., special education, psychology, social work) is accomplished through *training*, involving the internalization of presumably objective knowledge, and *indoctrination*, involving internalization of values and norms. Skrtic maintains that this knowledge is actually "subjective" because it represents the accepted and unquestioned practices of a tradition. Nevertheless, the process of professional induction requires the student to submit to the authority of the instructor, as well as to the institutional legitimacy of the profession. "As such, professional education tends to be dogmatic and authoritarian, as well it might be, given its institutional context and the fact that the inductee initially lacks enough of the profession's specialized knowledge and skills to be able to evaluate it on its own terms" (Skrtic, 1988, p. 423).

As further observed by Skrtic (1988), this induction holds true also for the applied scientist and the practitioner of the profession, with each receiving knowledge from a higher authority in the hierarchy of professional knowledge, and each accepting the knowledge on faith (cf., Popper, 1970). As observed by persons analyzing professional induction (e.g., Kuhn, 1970; Skrtic, 1988), textbooks assume a special place in the indoctrination process because they contain not only the profession's theories and methods but also the primary mode for perceiving the world. They provide, in essence, the vehicle for maximizing the authority and credibility of the profession's knowledge; alternative positions to the established knowledge are avoided, thus strengthening the existing paradigm from which the knowledge base is derived.

Teaching a technology that includes, in part, aversive procedures to manage behavior among persons with disabilities thus was consistent with the theoretical assumptions of the predominant behavioral paradigm in special education and certain schools of psychology. Its dissemination to practitioners and service providers was accomplished through formal personnel training programs, instructional textbooks, and training manuals written primarily by those conducting the training (and, in many cases, also doing the applied research). Importantly, these textbooks and manuals essentially, and usually necessarily, presented the aversive techniques in a summarized and practical manner that gave the appearance of state-of-the-art practices with an established empirical basis. Students and other potential service providers were not always exposed to the severity of the problems associated with generalization, maintenance, or potential side effects resulting from the procedures. Interestingly, the negative side effects of aversive control procedures are widely acknowledged in the published literature pertaining to the theoretical assumptions of behavior modification and its general application in a variety of applied settings (Balsam & Bondy, 1983).

Additionally, future service providers were not usually told that much of the research base included inadequate experimental designs and that the studies were conducted in highly controlled segregated settings. They often were not made aware of a potential negative and long-term impact on persons who frequently use aversive procedures. Additionally, they were not often exposed in depth to explanations of unwanted behavior that might conflict with the assumptions of the behavioral paradigm.

The above observations are underscored by Skrtic (1988) who noted: "As long as there is no reason to doubt the conventional knowledge of a profession, textbook-based training and indoctrination is an effective way to prepare personnel to staff it. But when there is reason to question the adequacy of a profession's knowledge, professional autonomy and the effectiveness of the induction process itself make it difficult, if not impossible, for the profession to view its knowledge and itself critically" (p. 424). In essence, the premature widespread dissemination of a technology that used aversive procedures to control the behavior of persons with disabilities and the relatively weak empirical foundation for this technology rest primarily with those who provided the training through formal instruction, workshops, conferences, and the print media.

The misuse and abuse of the technology of using aversive procedures by an expanded base of practitioners and service providers was, in retrospect, an inevitable outcome of the professional induction process, combined with a failure of the profession to carefully research and monitor the everyday application of these procedures by persons who were not sufficiently trained to self-monitor the implications of their own behavior. There were, indeed, major gaps among the research findings, the instructional personnel who failed to interpret and question these findings adequately, and the on-line service providers who were expected to use them in a professional, responsible manner in settings and situations that often differed considerably from the original research sites. All of these problems and oversights provide the basis for some substantive recommendations for future research and practices that involve persons who have difficult to manage behavior and also have a disability. These recommendations include suggestions for both researchers and those who would translate and disseminate research findings into treatment practices.

RECOMMENDATIONS

Providing Straightforward Positions On Values And Philosophical Stances

Many of the current controversies pertaining to the use of punishment procedures are subserved by basic disagreements over "values" and the role, if any at all, values should play in the determination of such intervention practices with persons who are disabled. Regardless of one's values, or if there is indeed an honest commitment by many to perceive values separate from science (cf., Etzel, 1988), professionals and their organizations should forthrightly state their positions. This stance is taken with the belief that removing one's values from their particular theoretical paradigm or "world view" is impossible even if this world view arrives at the conclusion that values are separate from one's science, or that values are relative derivations of scientific findings and are subject to continual revision and change. An example is offered to help clarify this recommendation.

The Association for Persons with Severe Handicaps (TASH) (as well as several other professional and advocacy groups) adopted an official position that aversive procedures should not be used with persons who have disabilities and, especially, individuals with severe and profound disabilities. This position was based in part on the available data that suggested problems with both the efficacy and effectiveness of these procedures, and in part on the conclusion that the use of aversive procedures with person with disabilities is ethically and morally wrong--a statement of values. Whether one agrees or disagrees with the TASH position on aversive procedures (TASH Resolution, 1981), the organization leaves no doubt where it stands on the issue. Importantly, the resolution is interrelated with other similar value-laden positions, such as community integration for all persons with disabilities and a host of other recommendations described as "best-practices" or "program quality indicators" (Meyer, Eichinger, & Park-Lee, 1987). And, while it has been suggested (Zeph, 1989) that some of the best-practice recommendations (e.g., choice-making) embraced by TASH are philosophically incongruent with the behaviorally- based methodology and paradigm adopted by many of its members, this organization has at least endeavored to present unambiguously its "world view" and related value positions on controversial issues.

The strong and unequivocal position taken by The Association for Persons with Severe Handicaps against the use of aversive procedures relates to the earlier discussion on the nature of scientific paradigms, the translation of these paradigms into recommended practices, the influence of personal values, beliefs, and world views on the academic writings of professionals, and the subsequent positions that professionals take on controversial issues as a result of their world views. This behavior, quite obviously, is not limited to any single paradigm or theory, especially in the "softer" social sciences. The best that we can ask for is that our science, itself, be improved, and that the methodologies used and the questions asked more accurately approximate reality combined with a more intense effort to objectively report the findings therefrom, and thus enable us to clearly impart to others one's values and beliefs in relation to the *interpretation* of the data under review. This recommendation holds true for both professional groups and the individuals who comprise the professions. In essence, it is naive to assume that researchers and professionals are able to separate their value-laden world views from the areas of scientific inquiry that they both conduct and interpret--and to acknowledge this fact is a straightforward first step that needs to be taken in our field.

Research Guidelines For The Development Of Intervention Strategies

The long history of research using aversive procedures and the now controversial application of these procedures to persons with disabilities should serve as a strong forewarning to those researchers who are developing nonaversive intervention strategies that are applicable for use in integrated community settings. The research and development of nonaversive intervention strategies to modify problem behavior among persons with disabilities in community settings necessarily should include the following criteria for success: (a) significant changes in the targeted behavior as demonstrated with experimental designs that provide for both internal and external validity; (b) the identification and systematic measure of both positive and negative side effects resulting from the application of the procedures; (c) concurrent measures of generalization to a variety of stimulus subsets; and (d) long-term follow-up for maintenance of the initial treatment outcome. Professional journals should not even accept manuscripts for publication that do not provide empirically sound measures of generalization and maintenance unless the procedures used are especially innovative and promising.

In addition to the above criteria, the technologies developed to use nonaversive procedures should be closely evaluated for subsequent ease and accuracy in application by service providers and practitioners. This evaluation should include measures on the extent to which the procedures being used by practitioners match those that were designed initially as part of the technology. This type of social validity also should, and importantly, include potential misuse and abuse of the procedures in applied settings, as well as related behavioral changes in the overall performance of the users and their changes in perceptions toward persons with disabilities. Had these latter recommendations been followed in the development and application of aversive procedures, problems that were discussed earlier associated with the "spread effect" and "procedural decay" might have been avoided in many applied (and research) settings.

Guidelines For Reporting And Disseminating Research Findings

This recommendation relates to honesty and objectivity in reporting research results. Research reports and articles pertaining to the use of nonaversive technologies should be presented in a most conservative manner, with any observed limitations of the procedures, possible negative side effects, and potential for use or misuse by service providers made unequivocally clear to personnel trainers and other persons who would use the finding as the basis for curriculum and instruction.

Persons disseminating the technology should make this information evident to potential practitioners and service providers. Personnel trainers, writers of textbooks, workshop presenters, and so on have the responsibility to provide accurate and thorough reports from the researchers in their efforts to instruct others on the application of the procedures. As discussed earlier, this has been a major problem in the widespread dissemination of aversive procedures where the zeal in promoting the behavioral paradigm and ideology may have interfered with the accurate and objective interpretation of research findings (c.f., Kuhn's, 1971, discussion of textbook writing in the natural sciences), and it certainly is true in the application of these findings to settings that varied considerably from the original research sites, many of which were controlled laboratory environments (Guess et al., 1986).

New Approaches, Paradigms, And Disciplines

This final recommendation is based on the observation that the treatment of severe problem behaviors among individuals perceived as disabled is predominantly confined to the perspective of a single paradigm (behaviorism) within a single discipline (psychology). While the nonaversive behavioral technology being developed currently offers the best practical and humane solution to this difficult problem area, perhaps the complexity of these behaviors will require a multi-paradigmatic and cross-discipline effort for a total solution. Unfortunately, this expanded effort is far from reality. As a field, we have perpetuated paradigm inbreeding to the point where new, imaginative, and creative ideas are resisted, where students and proteges in the field are limited in their professional world view, and, moreover, where persons who stray from the paradigm are frequently the focus of professional ridicule, if not outright scorn. Unfortunately, as noted by Kuhn (1971), shifts in paradigms in the natural sciences (i.e., new ways at looking at the nature of reality) must often await either the retirement or actual demise of those in power.

As pointed out by Skrtic (1986), our present behavioral paradigm in special education is based on theoretical assumptions that "... demonstrate no recognition of the possibility of alternate frames of reference..." (p. 14). In addition, Iano (1987) maintains that behavioral practices in the severely handicapped area have achieved predominance "... by default rather than healthy competition with other approaches" (p. 59). Whether or not these statements reflect reality, the fact remains that our present world view on both the interpretation and treatment of behavior problems is indeed narrow--by anyone's standards--and the possibility of any new paradigm shift on the horizon is likely remote.

With this prospect, this final recommendation has called for the development of new approaches in the treatment of severe behavior problems, that will not supplant but will supplement and enhance the emerging behaviorally-based nonaversive technologies.

The first questions to be asked, of course, are what else is available and from what new paradigms are they derived? Most persons would answer, "I don't know," which, of course, is precisely the problem. As a field, we in fact do not know. More importantly, however, we have not really looked, nor have we prepared new researchers, theorists, and academicians to look, even in our own field, let alone other fields and disciplines. We know that solutions to other difficult problem areas in the human services field (e.g., child abuse, suicide, chronic depression, Alzheimer's disease, AIDS) are viewed through numerous and interrelated perspectives that involve participation by many sciences, social and governmental agencies, volunteer groups, etc. Does not the successful prevention and treatment of self-injurious behavior among persons with disabilities, for example, require the same effort, even though the incidence is much lower than these other difficult problem areas? While some effort has been made to study biochemical and other anatomical causes for self-injurious behavior (Cataldo & Harris, 1982), especially among persons with autism, we have not really sought the knowledge and involvement from other disciplines and fields in helping us better understand many of the behaviors that are considered "deviant" among persons with disabilities, these persons thus becoming targeted for interventions that often include the use of aversive stimuli and procedures.

What, for example, can anthropology teach us about cross-culture similarities or differences in how "deviant" behavior is defined, how mental retardation is described and viewed, or, especially, how problem behaviors associated with disabilities are perceived and treated? How many other countries use aversive stimuli to control problem behaviors? Do other countries and cultures use approaches and procedures to deal with problem behaviors that we have neither heard of nor tried? Can the disciplines of sociology or social psychology help us better understand why we use aversive procedures in treating problem behaviors of persons with disabilities? How do persons in the community perceive such procedures? How do persons with disabilities, themselves, view the use of aversive procedures on other persons who also are disabled? What can we learn from the disciplines of philosophy, ethics, and religion in the perception and treatment of problem behaviors among persons with disabilities? What contributions can be made from the field of gerontology, genetics, and nutrition? What can we learn from specialized areas of study such as sensory deprivation, biofeedback, sensory perception, and community and animal ecology? The point, of course, is that we have limited our perspectives on the prevention and treatment of problem behaviors among persons with disabilities to what Skrtic (1986, 1988) might view as a microcosm within a microcosm; and our answers and solutions derived from such a narrow world view will be similarly limited.

My final recommendation accordingly calls for a concerted commitment to expand the scope of available and potential knowledge from a variety of fields and disciplines in the study of problem behaviors among persons with disabilities. This will require provision for integrated, cross- and within-discipline dialogue, cooperative research investigations, and essentially, a willingness of professionals in our own field to expand their horizon and knowledge base.

CONCLUSIONS

In this chapter, an attempt has been made to direct attention to our own behavior as members of the helping professions who are committed to improving the quality of life for persons with disabilities. This has included the contributions of past history on our present behavior, as well as current contextual and societal influences on how we conduct our practices in applied settings, research environments, and academic communities. The time has come, I strongly believe, for the helping professions to intensely investigate, reflect upon, and thoroughly analyze how they, themselves, behave--both as groups and as individuals. While the current controversy over the use of aversive versus nonaversive procedures in the treatment of persons with disabilities serves as a pivotal point for this discussion, the issues raised are much broader and possibly even more important. These issues relate to how our science is interpreted by those who conduct it, how information is disseminated by those who analyze the findings from it, and how the consumers eventually apply it in real life settings and situations. Throughout this chain, we cannot fail to underscore the important role that personal biases, values, and ideologies play in the behavior and conduct of all persons who are concerned. For these reasons alone, our own professional "introspection" is urgently needed.

REFERENCES

Amnesty International Publications (1984). *Torture in the eighties*. London.

The Association for Persons with Severe Handicaps (1981). *Resolution calling for the cessation of aversive procedures with persons who are handicapped*. Seattle, WA.

Baumeister, A.A., & Forehand, R. (1972). Effects of contingent shock and verbal command on body rocking of retardates. *Journal of Clinical Psychology, 28*, 586-590.

Balsam, P., & Bondy, A. (1983). The negative side effects of reward. *Journal of Applied Behavior Analysis, 16*, 283-296.

Cataldo, M., & Harris, J. (1982). The biological basis for self-injury in the mentally retarded. *Analysis and Intervention in Developmental Disabilities, 2*, 21-39.

Clark, M. (1987). *A review of the literature regarding decelerative procedures*. Unpublished manuscript. University of Wisconsin, Madison, WI.

Edgar, E. (1988). Policy factors influencing research in early childhood special education. In S. Odom & M. Karnes (Eds), *Early intervention for infants and children with handicaps* (pp. 63-73). Baltimore: Paul H. Brookes.

Etzel, B. (1988). An empirical orientation when planning rehabilitation research. Proceedings from *Behavior management and community integration for individuals with developmental disabilities and severe behavior problems*. Washington, DC: Sponsored by the Office of Special Education and Rehabilitation Services, and Research and Training Center on Community-Referenced Behavior Management.

Friedman, P. R. (1975). Legal regulation of applied behavior analysis in mental institutions and prisons. *Arizona Law Review, 17*, 39-104.

Friman, P., Cook, J. W., & Finney, J. (1984). Effects of punishment procedures on the self-stimulatory behavior of an autistic child. *Analysis and Intervention in Developmental Disability, 4*, 39-46.

Guess, D., Turnbull, H. R., & Helmstetter, E. (in press). Science, paradigms, and values: A response to Mulick. *American Journal on Mental Retardation*.

Guess, D., Helmstetter, E., Turnbull, H. R., & Knowlton, S. (1986). *Use of aversive procedures with persons who are disabled: An historical review and critical analysis*, (Monograph #2) Seattle: The Association for Persons with Severe Handicaps.

Hansen, C., & Haring, N. (1981). *Integration of developmentally disabled in-*

dividuals into the community. Baltimore: Paul H. Brookes.

Heshusius, L. (1982). At the heart of the advocacy dilemma: A mechanistic world view. *Exceptional Children, 49*, 6-13.

Heshusius, L. (1986). Paradigm shifts and special education: A response to Ulman and Rosenberg. *Exceptional Children, 52, 461-465.*

Hinerman, P., Jenson, W., Walker, G., & Petersen, P. B. (1982). Positive practice overcorrection with additional procedures to teach signed words to an autistic child. *Journal of Autism and Developmental Disorders, 12*, 253-263.

Iano, R. (1987). Rebuttal: Neither the absolute certainty of prescriptive law nor a surrender to mysticism. *Remedial and Special Education, 8*, 52-87.

Kircher, A., Pear, J., & Martin, G. (1971). Shock as punishment in a picture-naming task with retarded children. *Journal of Applied Behavior Analysis, 4*, 227-233.

Kuhn, T. (1970). *The structure of scientific revolutions* (2nd Ed). Chicago: University of Chicago Press.

Lennox, D., Miltenberger, R., Spengler, P., & Erfanian, N. (1988). Decelerative treatment practices with persons who have mental retardation: A review of five years of literature. *American Journal on Mental Retardation, 92*, 492-501.

Massey, P., & Insalaco, C. (1969). Aversive stimulation as applied to discrimination learning in mentally retarded children. *American Journal of Mental Deficiency, 74*, 269-272.

McGee, G. (1988). Community integration for individuals with developmental disabilities and severe behavior problems. Proceedings from *Behavior management and community integration for individuals with developmental disabilities and severe behavior problems.* Washington, DC: Sponsored by the Office of Special Education and Rehabilitation Services, and Research and Training Center on Community-Referenced Behavior Management.

Meyer, L., Eichinger, J., & Park-Lee, S. (1987). A validation of program quality indicators in educational services for students with severe disabilities. *Journal of the Association for Persons with Severe Handicaps, 12*, 251-263.

Mulick, J. (in press). The ideology and science of punishment in mental retardation. *American Journal on Mental Retardation*.

Nietzel, M. T. (1979). *Crime and its modification: A social learning perspective*. New York: Pergamon Press.

Neisworth, J. T., & Smith, R. M. (1973). *Modifying retarded behavior*. Boston: Houghton Mifflin Co.

Popper, K. R. (1970). Normal science and its dangers. In I. Lakatos & A. Musgrave (Eds.), *Criticism and the growth of knowledge* (pp. 51-58). Cambridge: Cambridge University Press.

Romancyzk, R. (1977). Intermittent punishment of self-stimulation effectiveness during application and extinction. *Journal of Consulting and Clinical Psychology, 45*, 53-60.

Sarason, S. (1985). *Caring and compassion in clinical practice: Issues in the selection, training, and behavior of helping professionals*. San Francisco: Josey-Bass.

Skinner, B. F. (August 16, 1987) *The New York Times*.

Skrtic, T. (1986). The crisis in special education knowledge: A perspective on perspectives. *Focus on Exceptional Children, 18*(7), 1-16.

Skrtic, T. (1988). The crisis in special education knowledge. In E. L., Meyen & T. Skrtic (Eds.), *Exceptional children and youth: An introduction* (Third Ed.) (pp. 515-547). Denver: Love.

Taylor. S., Racino, J., Knoll, J., & Lutfiyya, Z. (1987). *The nonrestrictive environment: On community integration for people with the most severe disabilities*. Syracuse, NY: Human Policy Press.

Zeph, L. (1989). *A call for an exploration of the philosophical inconsistencies between values and methodologies in the education of students with severe handicaps*. Submitted for publication.

PART III

CHAPTER

12

CLIENT CHARACTERISTICS AND TREATMENT SELECTION: LEGITIMATE INFLUENCES AND MISLEADING INFERENCES

Timothy J. H. Paisey
Robert B. Whitney and Pamela M. Hislop
State of Connecticut Department of Mental Retardation

We accept as axiomatic the right of persons to receive effective behavioral treatment (Van Houten, Axelrod, Bailey, Favell, Foxx, Iwata, & Lovaas, 1988) to remediate severely inappropriate or dysfunctional conduct. There is considerable controversy among professionals, consumers, and advocates, however, regarding treatments labelled "aversive," or those that incorporate punishment principles -- especially when applied to persons with developmental disabilities.

Three major themes underlie the diverse arguments against use of aversives. The first may be categorized as the "*Unacceptable in Principle*" position, which maintains that aversive procedures, their efficacy notwithstanding, are coercive (Lovett, 1985; McGee, Menolascino, Hobbs, & Menousek, 1987), are morally or legally proscribed (Turnbull, Guess, Backus, Barber, Fiedler, Helmstetter, & Summers, 1986), and topographically resemble torture (Guess, Helmstetter, Turnbull, & Knowlton, 1987). Hence, they shock the conscience and "dehumanize" both the recipient and provider of the treatment. Discussion and rebuttal of such points fall properly within the arenas of ethics and law.

The empirical contributions of applied behavior analysis touch most directly on the remaining two perspectives. One of these, the "*Relative Efficacy*" argument, alleges that use of aversive strategies rests on a relatively narrow data base of poorly designed case studies demonstrating temporary efficacy, with limited follow-up and numerous adverse side effects (Guess et al., 1987). Nonaversive strategies of equal or greater efficacy are claimed to have been developed recently (e.g., Evans & Meyer, 1985; LaVigna & Donnellan, 1986) which reportedly do not suffer from these defects. However, such criticisms fail to account for either the extensive literature on the effects of punishment (Axelrod & Apsche, 1983; Matson & DiLorenzo, 1984) or recent analyses of data from published studies (Guess et al., 1987; Lennox, Miltenberger, Spengler, & Erfanian, 1988; Matson & Taras, 1989). While conceding that many older studies of punishment effects now can be faulted on methodological grounds, we find the same to be true for their nonaversive counterparts. Criticism of 20-year-old studies for failure to examine generalization and maintenance (while reporting reversibility as a demonstration of contingency control) surely misses the point. The point instead is that still so few published outcomes of nonaversive interventions with severely aberrant behavior are reported with a degree of methodological rigor sufficient to permit replication or comparison with contemporary studies of punishment.

Perhaps in implicit recognition of the futility of attempting "meta-analytic" approaches to research spanning almost a quarter-century of dramatic change in habilitative practices, a third argument against aversives invokes an idiographic perspective. This, which we might term the "*Wrong Strategy*" position, proposes that inappropriate behaviors which are the target of aversive interventions are often "communicative" or otherwise "functional." Since aversive interventions allegedly fail to generate functionally equivalent alternatives, their efficacy is doubted, as is any intervention which neglects the primary motivation for the client's problematic behavior. Accordingly, effective treatment includes a functional analysis, leading to the identification of functionally equivalent alternative behaviors to be shaped and strengthened. Aversive procedures are rendered superfluous as inappropriate conduct is replaced in this manner.

Upon close examination, the *Wrong Strategy* argument can be seen to affirm three nested propositions: (a) that treatment of behavior matched to analysis of its causes is superior to treatment selection on *a priori* grounds, (b) that analysis of the causes of behavior will facilitate exclusively nonaversive treatment interventions, and (c) (implicitly) that such analysis and prescriptive narrowing of treatment can be generalized to even the most extreme behavioral challenges. If tenable, the *Wrong Strategy* argument provides compelling reasons for behavior analysts to cease using aversives.

Elimination of all use of aversives requires that all three of the above propositions be supported. Obviously, a failure to demonstrate the superiority of treatments selected on the basis of functional analysis would return us to the sterile ground of the *Relative Efficacy* debate. A failure to demonstrate that effective nonaversive solutions can be sought for functionally analyzed problems or, worse, demonstration that functional analysis may support aversive remedies, would scarcely inspire confidence. Most assuredly, restriction of the method to the solution of only certain problems would not support elimination of aversive procedures.

There is evidence concerning each of the three propositions discussed above. For the first, prescriptive narrowing of treatment selection, there is moderate support. For the second, indication of exclusively nonaversive solutions, there is evidence to the contrary. For the third, generalization to challenging cases, there is again evidence to the contrary. In this chapter, we will review this and related evidence, primarily in the context of applied behavioral treatment of self-injury for which aversives frequently have been regarded as necessary. Part I examines published research on the motivation for aberrant behavior, together with implications for treatment selection and outcome. Part II presents applied examples of nonaversive interventions with severely aberrant behavior, while Part III reports large-scale data on client characteristics and interventions drawn from an entire service system. These various sources of data provide empirical perspectives on the strengths and limitations of nonaversive methods that are not limited to single cases or a single methodology. We draw on these data in Part IV to identify circumstances when nonaversive methods seem to fail, and when use of aversives therefore may be indicated.

ANALYSIS AND INTERVENTION RESEARCH

Functional Analysis and Treatment Selection

A series of studies have applied operant analysis to identify conditions that maintain aberrant behavior. Several (Carr, Newsom, & Binkoff, 1976; Gaylord-Ross, Weeks, & Lipner, 1980; Touchette, MacDonald, & Langer, 1985; Weeks & Gaylord-Ross, 1981) have demonstrated that demands or less-preferred instructional conditions may elicit self-injurious behavior (SIB). The importance of negative reinforcement mechanisms in both aggression (Carr, Newsom, & Binkoff, 1980) and tantrum behavior (Carr & Newsom, 1985) in demand settings has also been demonstrated. Such research extends earlier studies that identified the role of social reinforcement in maintenance of SIB (Lovaas, Freitag, Gold, & Kassorla, 1965; Lovaas & Simmons, 1969), and has led to the elaboration of a model for the motivation of aberrant behavior.

This model has been applied successfully to the analysis of SIB, although its postulated reinforcement mechanisms may be extended to other forms of behavior. Carr (1977) advanced three hypotheses for the genesis and maintenance of SIB which are amenable to operant analysis: SIB may be maintained by attention (positive reinforcement), escape from aversive demands (negative reinforcement), or by "self-stimulation" (intrinsic reinforcement). A distinction is immediately apparent between the two socially mediated mechanisms of attention and escape on the one hand and postulated internal reinforcement mechanisms on the other. Some researchers (e.g., Donnellan, Mirenda, Mesaros, & Fassbender, 1984) have attempted to extend this to a symmetrical model by postulating both "arousal induction" and "arousal reduction" sources for internally motivated aberrant behavior. But operational definition of these constructs requires demonstration of functional control through manipulation of stimulus conditions, and there is no clear distinction between these and more general positive and negative reinforcement mechanisms (other than on the narrow grounds of whether antecedent stimuli are social behaviors versus physical events or setting characteristics). While ecological variables do exert significant effects on SIB (Schroeder, Mulick, & Rojahn, 1980), large response classes of stereotypic behaviors (including SIB) nevertheless have been argued to be intrinsically maintained by either perceptual reinforcement (Lovaas, Newsom, & Hickman, 1987) or neurobiological mechanisms (Lewis, Baumeister, & Mailman, 1987) rather than by social or environmental stimuli.

Several assessment strategies have been derived from this model. One approach, pioneered by Iwata and his coworkers (Iwata, Dorsey, Slifer, Bauman, & Richman, 1982; Parrish, Iwata, Dorsey, Bunck, & Slifer, 1985), has exposed persons who exhibit SIB and stereotypic behaviors (Sturmey, Carlson, Crisp, & Newton, 1988) to a series of brief analogue conditions within multielement designs. Typical conditions have included "Social Disapproval," "Academic Demand," "Unstructured Play," and "Alone." Conditions consistently associated with the highest rates of aberrant behavior permit an operant analysis of maintaining contingencies. Thus, behavior exhibited primarily under Social Disapproval is inferred to be maintained by social reinforcement, while behavior exhibited primarily under Academic Demand is inferred to be maintained by negative reinforcement. By contrast, behavior exhibited in the absence of external contingencies may be self-stimulatory.

Such operant assessment techniques have been applied successfully in the development of functionally related interventions for SIB in several young persons with severe disabilities (Iwata, Pace, Willis, Gamache, & Hyman, 1986; Parrish et al., 1985). Repp, Felce, and Barton (1988) have extended this to classrooms serving severely retarded children who exhibited SIB or stereotypic behavior. Interventions derived from each of the three main motivational hypotheses were administered in different classrooms and matched to informal functional analysis. Treatments derived from the functional analyses were the most successful. Additionally, Paisey, Whitney, and Moore (1989) used lap-top computer software capable of storing multiple real-time observations for subsequent event-lag analysis (Repp, Harman, Felce, Van Acker, & Karsh, 1989) to determine conditional probability relationships between SIB and both antecedent and consequent stimuli in two profoundly retarded adults. Comparison of the effects of three behavioral interventions under analogue conditions suggested interactions with the subjects' differing motivations for SIB. Taken together, available data suggest that functional analysis may assist in the selection of effective behavioral intervention, and that treatments addressing one form of motivation for aberrant behavior may not be applicable universally to other forms.

A related approach involves analyzing the "communicative functions" or "pragmatics" of aberrant behavior (Donnellan et al., 1984). Carr and Durand (1985) and Durand and Carr (1987) manipulated levels of task difficulty and adult attention to demonstrate that high levels of task difficulty and low levels of adult attention were discriminative for higher rates of self-injury, aggression, tantrums, and stereotypic behavior. Their subjects subsequently were taught strategies to request assistance with difficult tasks or to obtain adult attention. Following training, negative response covariation was observed between verbal communications and aberrant behaviors. These data are frequently adduced as support for several principles, including the social motivation of certain aberrant behaviors, their communicative function, and the utility of weakening undesirable behaviors by differentially reinforcing a functionally equivalent alternative.

These studies are undoubtedly elegant and have important clinical implications, but their relevance to a critical examination of functional analysis should not pass unchallenged. First, all the subjects in these studies were selected for participation because they engaged in disruptive behavior under demand conditions, and subsequent interventions were also performed under demand conditions (academic tasks). Thus, the experimental manipulations did not strictly *generate* motivation-based interventions, but rather offered confirmation for the informal subject selection. Second, all the subjects had some verbal skills already within their repertoire, which raises obvious questions regarding the external validity of a "communicative" analysis when applied to persons without expressive language skills. Third, Parrish, Cataldo, Kolko, Neef, and Egel (1986) have demonstrated experimentally systematic inverse response covariation between classes of appropriate and inappropriate behaviors in mentally retarded children under demand conditions, irrespective of the class of behaviors to which specific contingencies were applied. Accordingly, demonstration of negative response covariation between appropriate speech and aberrant behavior when differential reinforcement is applied to the former does not prove functional *equivalence* between these response classes, since the postulated relationship is not transitive or logically reversible. Collateral increases in social behavior accompanying suppression of an aberrant behavior by punishment procedures are also frequently reported (see Newsom, Favell, & Rincover, 1983), but surely provide little evidence for functional equivalence of response classes. Analysis of concurrent operants, or perhaps "blocking effects" (Lovaas et al., 1987, pp. 56-57), seems more appropriate. There is also a clear risk of committing a teleologic error of the following type: If communication training reduces aberrant behavior, then the aberrant behavior must have been communicative in nature! Additional criticism of such apparently circular reasoning has been made by Lewis et al. (1987, p. 254) with regard to defining "self-stimulatory" behavior by its presumed function, and many of the same caveats apply to the literature on providing opportunities for alternative behaviors or sensory stimuli as interventions for stereotypic behavior (Lovaas et al., 1987). Here, too, demonstrating reductions in stereotypic behavior as a function of engagement in other forms of behavior does not necessitate a "self-stimulation" interpretation. Reinforcement theory can accomodate the results, just as the work of Carr and his associates (Carr & Durand, 1985; Carr et al., 1980; Durand & Carr, 1987) convincingly demonstrates that increasing negative reinforcement contingent on one response class -- even if arbitrarily selected (Carr et al., 1980) -- is likely to decrease the frequency of a concurrent negatively-reinforced response, provided reinforcement is withheld from the latter.

A third, largely atheoretical approach is represented by *structural analysis.* Touchette et al. (1985) have developed a data matrix in which aberrant behavior is plotted across the time of day over consecutive days. The matrix permits identification of the pattern of behavior across time and conditions. Such ecological factors as the staff on duty or the client's scheduled activities then may be matched to these patterns. Functional control can be arranged by systematically altering the sequence of these stimuli, and effective treatment may consist of simply changing or eliminating circumstances associated with aberrant behavior. Touchette et al. (1985) report case examples of this approach with developmentally disabled persons exhibiting aggression and SIB. A similar, yet more molecular, strategy is reflected in the work of Mace and his colleagues, reviewed by Axelrod (1987). This and derivative work (e.g., Paisey & Whitney, 1989) manipulates several conditions (e.g., level of protective equipment, level of social interaction) within analogue sessions in order to identify the conditions associated with the lowest frequencies of aberrant behavior, and has been applied successfully to the development of effective interventions for disruptive behavior and SIB. In its most general form, this ecobehavioral approach suggests simultaneous, concurrent recording of multiple environmental events and multiple client behaviors in order to determine functional relationships for both group (Schroeder, Rojahn, & Mulick, 1978) and single-person settings (Paisey, Whitney, Hislop, & Wainczak, in press).

It should be evident that these strategies are mutually complementary, differing primarily in the range and specificity of controlling variables that are examined and manipulated. All provide evidence that identification of discriminative or reinforcing stimuli contributes to the development of effective behavioral intervention for developmentally disabled populations. In all likelihood, increasing sophistication and precision in assessment procedures, informed by theories of the motivation for aberrant behavior, will decrease reliance on simple analogue assessments - perhaps in favor of multidimensional or even nonlinear analyses of interactions between multiple stimulus events and multiple response classes. Nevertheless, matching intervention strategies to the results of functional analysis does not logically necessitate narrowing the class of permissible interventions to exclude punishment. Whether this is accomplishable is largely an empirical matter.

Is Functional Analysis Incompatible with Punishment?

Axelrod (1987) has pointed out that functional analysis may lead to a recommendation to use punishment, and many of the interventions based on analyses reported above did, in fact, employ punishing stimuli. It will be convenient to recall the operant definition of aversive or punishing stimuli employed by LaVigna and Donnellan (1986); namely, any systematic response-contingent event (including extinction) leading to deceleration (see Chapter 5 by Luiselli). Clients whose SIB was determined to be nonsocial or self-stimulatory initially were treated by Iwata et al. (1986) and Parrish et al. (1985) with various combinations of nonaversive procedures indicated by the functional analyses. Although these interventions reduced SIB, brief contingent manual restraint, or contingent application of protective equipment, was required for clinically acceptable treatment effects. These contingencies obviously represent procedural punishment.

By contrast, Carr and his associates (Carr & Durand, 1985; Carr & Newsom, 1985; Carr et al., 1980; Durand & Carr, 1987) have been able to reduce escape-motivated SIB, aggression, tantrums and stereotypies by either decreasing the aversiveness of demands or by teaching alternative responses to request assistance. Other data tend to support the possible utility of nonaversive interventions for escape-motivated behavior in demand contexts. For example, in one of the conditions reported by Paisey, Whitney and Moore (1989), relatively high rates of SIB underwent significant reductions when instructional demands were noncontingently presented on an inescapable fixed-time schedule. This represents one aspect of manipulation of antecedent or concurrent stimuli. Weeks and Gaylord-Ross (1981) demonstrated that applying errorless learning principles to difficult discriminations resulted in both skill acquisition and reductions in negatively-reinforced SIB, and Smith (1985) has reported two cases in which curricular modifications, such as sequencing demands via picture prompts or reducing the duration of instruction, were successful in reducing aggressive behavior. Reduction of the aversiveness of instructional demands, therefore, appears to represent a common element in viable nonaversive intervention strategies for escape-motivated behavior, in conjunction with demand fading within an escape-learning paradigm (e.g., Bird, Dores, Moniz, & Robinson, 1989).

There are relatively few published data directly addressing the selection of appropriate interventions for aberrant behavior that is identified as attention-motivated via objective, reported, functional analysis (Repp, Singh, Olinger, & Olson, in press). Given the ubiquity of variants of differential reinforcement (which, by definition, include procedural extinction or brief time-out from attention) in the behavioral intervention literature (e.g., Matson & DiLorenzo, 1984), there is considerable evidence for the effectiveness of procedures that are implicitly derived from the attention-motivation hypothesis for aberrant behavior. However, procedures such as contingent mechanical chair restraint (Vukelich & Hake, 1971), or contingent manual restraint followed by 24-hour social isolation (Foxx, Foxx, Jones, & Kiely, 1980), each procedure being embedded within dense schedules of positive reinforcement, are equally consistent with the attention-reinforcement hypothesis, and yet certainly would not be regarded as nonaversive.

This points to a more general problem for attempts to proscribe certain classes of techniques because they lack functional relationships with the target behavior. Procedures such as time-out (Solnick, Rincover, & Peterson, 1977) and restraint (Favell, McGimsey, Jones, & Cannon, 1981; Singh, Winton, & Ball, 1984) may have either punishing or reinforcing properties in certain cases, depending on the context in which they are used and the learning history of the client. Such "paradoxical" effects can be easily reconciled with the principles of functional analysis, since manipulation of the relative reinforcing properties of "time-in" and "time-out" environments is analagous to addressing escape-motivated behavior by varying the aversiveness of instructional demands. Accordingly, time-out procedures would not be effective interventions for negatively-reinforced behavior, nor would alteration of instructional stimuli be a primary intervention for positively-reinforced behavior. Along similar lines, instances in which other nominally aversive techniques either fail to yield behavioral suppression or result in unplanned increases in the target behavior also may be attributable to interactions between unanalyzed aspects of the client's motivation and certain procedural components, as opposed to being "negative side effects" of the procedures themselves. By way of illustration, Measel and Alfieri (1976) report application of positive practice overcorrection in treatment of two young persons who exhibited SIB, but experienced dramatically different outcomes. Complete suppression was attained in one case, while SIB escalated in the other. In attempting to account for this, the authors raise the possibility that some elements of the overcorrection procedure, particularly the physical contact, may have been reinforcing. A good argument can be made that certain "failures" in the application of notionally aversive procedures are explicable by recourse to functional analysis, and that such motivational analysis may assist in selecting among various notionally aversive alternatives. In general, then, functional analysis may assist in developing any intervention - aversive or nonaversive - and the weight of evidence does not exclusively favor nonaversive prescriptions. Rather, functional analysis may assist in narrowing treatment selection primarily by rejecting alternatives that might interact with the client's motivation in an untoward manner. This clearly leaves the key choice between aversive and exclusively nonaversive strategies unresolved.

Client-treatment Interactions

Many of the studies described above, especially those of Carr and his associates, focused on younger persons who were systematically selected for inclusion primarily on the basis of displaying a clear, unitary motivation for their aberrant behavior, often under highly discriminated conditions. By contrast, analyses of less highly screened samples (Iwata et al., 1982; Sturmey et al., 1988) suggest that a significant proportion of persons displaying SIB or stereotypic behaviors may have either nonsocial motivations, or may exhibit multiply-determined responses (i.e., behaviors that are responsive to several concurrent contingencies). As previously discussed, functional analysis has not necessarily indicated nonaversive (or, perhaps more accurately, non-punishment) treatment interventions for these types of aberrant behaviors.

Given that the consummatory responses of stereotypic or multiply-determined chains of aberrant behavior may be essentially internal, contriving response deprivation, or otherwise altering reinforcement for such behavior in a positive manner, is inherently difficult. This notion is supported by the intervention literature for stereotypic responding (LaGrow & Repp, 1984), pica (Paisey & Whitney, 1989), and rumination (Starin & Fuqua, 1987), which offers limited evidence for the effectiveness of solely non-punishment strategies in treating nonsocial severely aberrant responding. Although there is a literature on provision of alternative sensory stimulation (Lovaas et al., 1987), it is important to note that successful treatment is primarily reported with milder forms of aberrant behavior, that mere provision of opportunities for alternative activities in the absence of social mediation has little effect on behavioral repertoires (Foxx, McMorrow, Bechtel, Busch, Foxx, & Bittle, 1986), and that caregiver mediation may reduce nonsocial aberrant responding because it is discriminative for socially-mediated punishment (Mace & Knight, 1986).

In summary, these data suggest that a significant percentage of aberrant behaviors may be nonsocial in motivation, or may have complex determinants. The current literature indicates that nonsocial SIB may be both dangerous and difficult to treat, and that functional analysis of such behavior is not complemented by an array of functionally-derived nonaversive interventions. Since basic research suggests that behavior under the control of internal cues may have a shallower stimulus generalization gradient (Hearst, 1969) than behavior under the control of external cues, it may be correspondingly more difficult to treat via nonaversive means. This is because basing nonaversive strategies on functional analysis of the problem behavior requires that the latter be highly discriminated (i.e., that it occurs under certain conditions but not others). By contrast, aversive procedures override maintenance contingencies that may be, in such cases, either difficult to detect or manipulate.

CASE EXAMPLES OF NONAVERSIVE INTERVENTIONS

If exclusive reliance is to be placed on nonaversive methods, there is an obvious question regarding the applicability of "functional-equivalence" strategies to the remediation of severely aberrant conduct, since well controlled studies support the utility of primary punishers in such cases (Foxx, McMorrow, Bittle, & Bechtel, 1986; Linscheid, Iwata, Ricketts, Williams, & Griffin, in press; Paisey & Whitney, 1989; Rojahn, McGonigle, Curcio, & Dixon, 1987). In these reports, problematic behaviors presented clear risk of injury to the participants or others. Numerous other treatments had been attempted without success, and the behaviors either resisted an analysis of social determinants or functionally-related nonaversive strategies were found wanting. These and many similar studies demonstrate reliable, replicable, durable suppression of the most severely aberrant behavior in applied settings without adverse side effects. We find it instructive to contrast such outcomes with attempts to provide comprehensive and sophisticated nonaversive behavioral treatment to persons who present the most extreme behavioral challenges.

Case Examples in Applied Settings

The following seven case examples reflect representative attempts to apply functionally derived nonaversive strategies to the solution of severe behavior problems across various settings. Importantly, these examples reflect an administrative commitment to renounce aversive options, matched by allocation of unlimited resources. All included continuous, direct observation and real-time data recording made by experienced, professional observers, and most included reversal designs or multiple baselines.

CASE 1. Shirley was a 33-year-old woman with profound mental retardation who lacked detectable expressive or receptive language skills. Data, collected during a 7-day baseline across all waking hours, showed head hitting at up to 18 rpm, head banging at up to 4 rpm, and aggression at up to 0.75 rpm, throughout the day. This behavior had led to damage to her jaw and dentition, extensive hair loss and contusions to her scalp, and massive overgrowth of scar tissue. Her head banging literally could be heard and felt throughout the house.

Previous interventions had included various forms of restraint and, most recently, a package described as "Gentle Teaching." Informal functional analysis unambiguously indicated demand-escape as a primary motivation. Prior to intervention, caregivers were attempting to "interpret" her "communicative intent," and no systematic contingencies were in effect.

Intervention included approximately 3500 hours of direct on-site services by up to four professionals at a time. Program components included continuous response blocking by two staff wearing protective gear, protective padding applied to environmental surfaces, cueing of demand and demand-free periods, spatial discrimination of demand and demand-free areas, shaping task performance by graduated guidance, escape-extinction, gradual demand fading by increasing the duration and complexity of tasks, errorless learning of tasks, and high-rate edible, social, and tactile reinforcement for task performance on a titrating DRO. Staffing supports, time intervals, protective gear, and response blocking were gradually faded, and instructional control generalized to regular staff. Within two months, this package resulted in a 77% decrease in "off-task," a ten-fold increase in work behavior, a 40% reduction in head hitting, an 80% reduction in head banging, and a 60% reduction in aggression. These improvements were maintained for at least an additional 3 months, during which support staff faded their involvement. Follow-up at one year suggested a lack of program maintenance by primary caregivers and a possible return to baseline frequencies, despite extensive training and gradual fading of supports.

CASE 2. Richard was a 24-year-old man with profound mental retardation who also exhibited escape-motivated SIB and aggression. His receptive language skills were adequate, and he could indicate requests by manual signs. SIB included head hitting, head banging, self-scratching, pinching and biting, and self-induced vomiting. Injuries to staff and residents had resulted from his aggressive behavior, which included severe biting. Unlike Shirley, Richard's behavior was highly discriminated and occurred mainly in response to demand presentations. As a consequence, staff avoided placing any demands on him, and he seldom participated in habilitative activities.

Intervention included 450 hours of on-site services by up to three professional staff at a time. Vocational tasks were taught by graduated guidance in time blocks of gradually increasing duration. Instruction was given by staff who wore protective gear for extinguishing and blocking both aggressive and self-injurious behavior. Completion of work was reinforced by praise and food items, and a token system was gradually introduced. Work periods were gradually extended to 30 minutes, alternating with 10-minute breaks, and a minimal demand schedule was developed for the remainder of the day. Within 30 days, his SIB and aggression were reduced to zero, "on-task" was up to 60% of the time, he was fully integrated into a community sheltered workshop, and intensive staffing supports had been withdrawn. Follow-up at 3 and 6 months revealed maintenance of these gains.

CASE 3. Bill was a 32-year-old man with severe mental retardation who possessed adequate receptive language and some expressive speech. Bill was referred in life-threatening crisis due to the effects of gouging his flesh, extracting his teeth and nails, scratching and picking himself (up to 10% of daily intervals), and severe weight loss. He also exhibited aggression and property destruction (10 - 25% of daily intervals) that presented considerable risks because of his stature.

Frequent use of restraint, numerous behavioral programs, and psychoactive medication had failed to reduce such conduct. Formal structural and functional analyses revealed these behaviors to be multiply determined. SIB was largely self-stimulatory and occurred almost exclusively when staff were not present. Aggression was determined under analogue conditions to be an escape response, while property destruction appeared to be reinforced by attention and its sensory consequences.

Intervention consisted of developing a customized single-person residence, with two specialist staff per shift, 24 hours per day. Interior doors were removed to permit continuous observation, and most habilitative demands initially were eliminated. Considerable environmental protection (over windows, electrical outlets, etc.) was added, and minor attempts at property destruction were ignored. Major episodes of property destruction resulted in Bill's being directed out of the house. Aggression was passively blocked, and social interactions were initiated predominantly at his discretion. Severe SIB and aggression were reduced to close to zero within the first month, and property destruction within 4 months, after approximately 5500 staff hours. Levels of all behaviors remained low, at non-life-threatening intensities, and Bill was transferred successfully to a group home after 8 months. Follow-up at 6 months revealed maintenance of these gains, although attempts to vary psychotropic medications subsequently resulted in some behavioral deterioration.

CASE 4. Mike was a 19-year-old profoundly retarded man with receptive but no expressive language skills, and with agitated and destructive behavior that mechanical restraint for 3 weeks and up to 40 mg. of Haldol per day had failed to control. Discharged to the same treatment environment as Bill, intervention included teaching by graduated guidance, demand fading, response prevention, stimulus satiation, negative practice, brief contingent withdrawal of attention, and a titrating DRO using edible and social reinforcers, which was run by six behavior specialist staff working in relays of 12 hours per day. Formal operant assessment under analogue conditions had indicated clearly that he was motivated by attention to his inappropriate behavior.

Over approximately 3 weeks, the following behaviors emerged, each with a characteristic "extinction burst:" screaming, sprawling on the floor, grabbing others' clothing, grabbing others in "choke" holds, tantrumming, damaging electrical sockets, stereotypic crawling, public disrobing and masturbation, self-slapping, head banging, self-biting, mouthing objects, running away, emptying closets, destroying property and fitments, climbing over stair rails, repeated toilet flushing, head dunking in the toilet, self-induced vomiting, hitting others, moving furniture from room to room, trichotillomania, destroying of plumbing fixtures, and tearing up carpeting. During this period, he continued to sleep at home, although his family resorted to continuous mechanical restraint during waking periods. After 1000 hours of staff intervention, head banging, head hitting, self-biting and mouthing had been eliminated, aggression had been reduced from 0.15 rpm, to 0.03 rpm, and grabbing others from 14% of the time to 4%, while time engaged in habilitative tasks increased from 40% to 80%. Despite efforts to train family members, there was little evidence of generalization, and he was admitted to an institution.

CASE 5. Ernie was a 19-year-old man with mild mental retardation and language skills developed to a level that permitted sustained conversation with others. Assessment under formal analogue conditions revealed negative attention (reprimands, warnings, and emotional distress) to be the principal reinforcers of his aberrant conduct, which included SIB (self-slapping) at up to 5 rpm. Other problematic behaviors included striking others, property destruction, exposing himself, public disrobing, public masturbating, and running away. If, in the course of routine conversation, he was asked why he engaged in such behavior, he would reply, "for attention." Continuous mechanical restraints, a seclusion room, and psychotropic medications had failed to curb this conduct, and he was referred to the same treatment environment developed for Bill and Mike.

A 1-week baseline showed the following data: aggression (6% of the observations), property destruction (10%), SIB (3%), public exposure or masturbation (0%), and running away (1%). A varied schedule of activities was provided by two staff at all times, and no consequation was delivered during baseline other than redirection. DRO, using snacks as reinforcers, had brief suppressive effects, as did contingency contracting and token systems. Given the variety and nature of Ernie's conduct, extinction in conjunction with self-control procedures proved both ineffective and emotionally exhausting for even highly motivated staff. Ernie frequently attained short-term behavioral objectives, earned his negotiated reinforcer, and then either rejected it or exposed himself. Eventually, he learned to urinate frequently on the residence carpeting, apparently because he realized that this behavior scarcely could be tolerated.

Within 1 month, the majority of his problematic behaviors occurred at frequencies greater than baseline, and this situation persisted, despite an additional 7 weeks of treatment efforts. After this, he was transferred to another residence and enrolled in a sheltered workshop. These two programs held widely contrasting treatment philosophies. The former facility attempted "progressive," exclusively nonaversive approaches, including differential reinforcement and extinction. At follow-up, his inappropriate behavior had escalated in this setting. By contrast, the sheltered workshop relied on more "traditional" behavioral methods, and reported that use of a time-out room during one morning had effectively suppressed his aberrant conduct.

CASE 6. Maureen was a 19-year-old woman who had profound mental retardation, severe auditory impairment, and a limited repertoire of manual signs. Her problematic behavior primarily consisted of severe skin picking and mouthing, which had led to tissue loss, infections, and scarring. Assessments at the residence and day program revealed a classic patterning to this high-frequency behavior, which apparently was self-stimulatory since it was least likely to occur under two conditions: when she was directly engaged in manipulating objects (e.g., work materials, eating utensils), and when she was aware of being observed by staff.

An array of textured, manipulable items was presented in forced-choice trials of two dissimilar objects, accompanied by a gestural request to return both items. The item returned first was scored as least-preferred. Within 2 hours, she spontaneously would hold and manipulate solid items with textured surfaces, provided they were large enough to require a full palmar grasp. Under a titrating DRO, with juice and ice cream as reinforcers, she was successfully shaped into holding and manipulating items for up to 30 minutes without any SIB. After 30 minutes, new items were substituted and the interval was reset. All of the residence staff were trained in these simple methods, including delivery of incidental reinforcement for object manipulation and maintenance of eye contact. Consultant staff were on site for an additional week to monitor implementation. Follow-up at approximately 1 month revealed apparent disregard for virtually all aspects of the procedure and return of the SIB (despite at least a 1:4 staff-to-client ratio).

CASE 7. George was a 23-year-old man with severe mental retardation and a large, muscular stature. He had adequate receptive language skills, but no functional expressive medium. He was transferred from institutional residence to a customized single-person community residence and vocational program, for which 20 staff were recruited, trained, and supervised by the first and second authors. This program (cf. Paisey, Whitney, Hislop, & Wainczak, in press) received direct consultation and peer review from prominent experts in behavioral analysis and SIB.

During baseline, George exhibited head banging (0.07 rpm), head hitting (0.41 rpm), aggression (0.13 rpm), tantrums (8% of the day), and was frequently off-task (71% of the day). Of numerous treatment efforts, only contingent aromatic ammonia had proven effective. At the time of the present study, he was receiving Thorazine and Dilantin, and was being placed in mechanical restraint or protective equipment 36% of the time.

In addition to a custom-designed program with planned activities every 15 minutes from 6:00 a.m. to 10:00 p.m., numerous nonaversive programs were implemented over a 12-month period (all were derived from structural and functional analyses). Continuous, real-time data recording across all settings permitted identification of naturally occurring events which were either antecedent to, concurrent with, or subsequent to SIB, aggression, etc. These were augmented by formal assessment of the discriminative properties of antecedent mands and other stimuli (Carr et al., 1976), and operant analysis of possible reinforcers (Iwata et al., 1982). Results showed that aggression and SIB were multiply determined. Certain tasks and settings, as well as most forms of social interaction, increased the rate. Instructional demands, however, did not increase inappropriate behavior, and negative attention (reprimands, emotional responses) emerged as a reinforcer. In addition to consistent withdrawal of all negative attention (extinction), high rates of incidental reinforcement were delivered, as well as formal reductive schedules (DRO, DRI, DRL, DRA) for the entire day. Reinforcers included praise, edible items, tokens, vibration, break periods, preferred activities, solitude, safety signals, brief restraint and full-body restraint (as reinforcers), sports activities, and vigorous hugs, squeezes or massage. An additional DRO procedure was mediated by the SIBIS sensor and microprocessor, using access to house lighting, the radio, television, and other electrically controlled events as reinforcers. Other contingencies included brief withdrawal of attention, negative reinforcement via removal of visual prompts, presentation of choices, stimulus narrowing, interpolated reinforcement, discriminated extinction, stimulus change, and simple extinction. All daily activities were task-analyzed and instructed via verbal, gestural or pictorial cues with prompt fading, modeling, forward or backward chaining, direct instruction, or delayed prompting. Extensive efforts were made to teach functional expressive communication using nonverbal behaviors, pictures, and a voice synthesizer. Activities that increased inappropritate behavior were either modified, eliminated, or transferred to community settings. Restraints and psychotropic medications were eliminated.

Over approximately a 12-month period, elements of the above procedures resulted in reductions in inappropriate behavior, but not to clinically acceptable levels. After approximately 35,000 staff hours, head banging occurred at 0.06 rpm, head hitting at 0.35 rpm, aggression at 0.04 rpm, and tantrums 6% of the time. Numerous adaptive behaviors were acquired, however, and George was actively engaged in age-appropriate tasks 70% of the time. Staff resources were then reduced by 50% (to two per shift), and simple extinction throughout the day was adopted as the sole program method for the following 12 months. This resulted in a continued gradual decrease in behavior to 0.01 rpm for head banging, 0.14 rpm for head hitting, 0.01 rpm for aggression, and 3% for tantrums. Loss of acquired adaptive skills, along with reduced task engagement and increased stereotypic behavior, occurred concurrently.

Practical Constraints on Nonaversive Interventions

Such interventions with severely challenging cases in applied settings point to several conclusions in addition to those customarily drawn from single-case treatment studies. First, reductions in target behaviors occurred (at least temporarily) in all cases, concurrent with measurable skill acquisition. This result attests to the integrity and validity of the interventions, but not necessarily to their clinically acceptable outcomes. In many instances, behavior reduction was gradual or incomplete, with limited generalization and significant risk of reversal following thinning or fading. We should note that these limitations are identical to those cited in the criticism of punishment strategies; perhaps they are inherent in treatment of the most severely aberrant behavior by any method that does not result in complete suppression.

Secondly, effective nonaversive intervention required two to four highly trained persons capable of managing multiple, concurrent, and subtle contingencies each day. Assuming a median of 1,000 professional staff hours per case (in addition to background staffing) during the initial suppression phase, the cost of comprehensive nonaversive intervention is likely to be formidable. Since multielement packages were usually required, we cannot assume that functional analysis (or even implementation of published methods) will necessarily assist the majority of program settings in the complex task of treatment development and evaluation; the full-time commitment of skilled behavior analysts will be needed. No matter how extensive the consultation or training, expecting regular caregivers to assume more than a maintenance role in such cases is unrealistic.

When aberrant behavior is under a relatively high degree of stimulus control (Shirley, Richard, and Maureen), nonaversive solutions appear both feasible and relatively effective, provided they can be implemented consistently. In more complex situations, however, identifying momentary motivation for multiply determined behavior is difficult. For example, the case of George revealed how multiple, concurrent schedules and stimuli maintain SIB and aggression for very long periods in the absence of apparent extrinsic reinforcement. Within open environments, the effects of multiple schedules are probably not additive. As the number and complexity of controlling variables increase, we may view the challenge of isolating and manipulating relevant stimuli as exponentially more difficult. Strategies indicated by one possible motivational construct inadvertently may reinforce similar-topography behavior which is maintained by different sources of motivation. Some sources of reinforcement with a strong affective component, such as negative attention, may be difficult or impossible to withhold or provide under contrived schedules (as in the cases of Mike, Ernie, and George).

Neither communicative ability nor intensity of aberrant behaviors were especially useful as predictors of treatment duration or outcome. The time course of treatment appeared more closely related to such factors as the nature, complexity, and degree of generalization of maintenance stimuli. Obviously, these factors may be elucidated only by formal operant analysis and not by superficial inspection. Assessments that neglect such analysis may run the risk of matching treatments to persons on the basis of potentially irrelevant attributes, such as topography or adaptive skills. The risk is that aversives may be advocated when they are not truly necessary or, contralaterally, that nonaversive procedures may be chosen in a doctrinaire fashion. Social attributions should not be permitted to masquerade as "functional analysis."

Finally, the degree of environmental control required for therapeutic deprivation, sensory extinction, response interruption, or continuous observation, may itself generate rather aversive conditions - perhaps more so than aversive contingencies brought to the natural environment. At some point, boundaries between the "aversiveness" of single-element punishment techniques and physically intrusive, multielement "nonaversive" treatment packages surely become somewhat blurred.

We suggest that the utility of functional analysis as an alternative to aversive procedures is ultimately susceptible to cost-benefit determination. Behaviors of increasing severity (cost to the client), complexity (cost to the behavior analyst), and trans-situational consistency (cost to the caregiver), rather than the more traditional indices of response frequency, history, and topography, will be more likely to indicate those circumstances under which aversive strategies are necessary. This need not be argued on the basis of notional effectiveness, but more on the grounds that as the costs of functional analysis increase (involving prolonged risks, failure to isolate and control relevant variables, partial effects, concurrent schedules, gradual outcomes, and lack of generalization or maintenance) the logic of using aversive procedures also grows. This is precisely because aversives (especially primary) do not *require* prior functional analysis to achieve their suppressive effects; they simply override all other prevailing contingencies. Conversely, the cost-benefit ratio may tilt increasingly in favor of nonaversive solutions as response risk and schedule complexity decrease and situational specificity increases. Logically, advances in the analysis and manipulation of multiple, concurrent variables (as in ecobehavioral assessment) will further erode the legitimate use of aversives by raising the "break-even" point, although some cases may continue to fall beyond this point.

LARGE-SAMPLE ANALYSIS OF PERSON AND TREATMENT VARIABLES

Given the extent of contemporary discussion regarding the appropriateness of certain behavioral procedures, we are surprised that relatively few empirical studies have addressed the extent and circumstances of their actual application in service settings. We assume, with Mulick and Linscheid (1988), that providers and sanctioners of aversive interventions are motivated by factors other than "professional ignorance" (p. 317) or "universal sadism" (p. 318). If they were improperly motivated, the application of aversives would be relatively haphazard (as many critics would have us believe). On the other hand, if the decision to employ aversives is informed, rational, and professional, what criteria are typically used?

From research that asks respondents to rate aspects of behavioral procedures along such dimensions as "restrictiveness," "potency," and "acceptability" (Morgan, 1989; Spreat, Lipinski, Dickerson, Nass, & Dorsey, 1989; Tarnowski, Rasnake, Mulick, & Kelly, 1989), we know that the stimulus characteristics of procedures themselves play a disproportionate role in determining their rankings, resulting in "a more bureaucratic, rather than clinical approach to the evaluation of treatment acceptability" (Spreat et al., 1989, p. 11). With few exceptions, critical appraisal of the appropriateness of aversives has largely neglected the role of client characteristics in the evolution of clinical decisions.

At a national level, a recent survey of 80 public residential facilities serving a total of more than 30,000 clients (Griffin, Keyes, Emerson, Paisey, Stark, Williams, Dayan, Ricketts, & Zukotynski, in press) found that almost 40% of the residents exhibit either SIB or aggression, but that only 6% are involved in formal, committee-approved aversive programs. Similarly, a statewide survey of approximately 10,000 clients of public residential facilities in Texas (Griffin, Williams, Stark, Altmeyer, & Mason, 1986) reported that only 7% of the 14% engaged in SIB were on formalized aversive programs (plus another 4% on overcorrection and 19% on some form of time-out). In both of these samples, the use of aversive procedures is restricted to a relatively small subset of clients, indicating a high degree of selectivity. More detailed examination of these possible relationships between client characteristics and treatment selection, as well as control for the potentially confounding influence of institutional residence, is provided by our own study of SIB among persons with mental retardation in Connecticut.

Connecticut Study

The survey methodology of Griffin et al. (1986) was employed to identify which of the 1400 persons registered as clients in one of the six Department of Mental Retardation regions in Connecticut engaged in SIB. The survey found 167 (12%) persons meeting our criteria. Respondents were asked to check all SIB topographies, to indicate whether clients were on a committee-approved aversive or nonaversive behavior program to reduce SIB, and whether they previously had been on an aversive program. They also were asked to identify the highest level of injury associated with the person's SIB.

Over the course of the following 12 months, additional data were collected. Using various methods (including a contingency analysis questionnaire, event-lag analysis, and assessment under analogue conditions), we classified the SIB of 86 individuals as attention-motivated, escape-motivated, or self-stimulatory (nonsocial). For 54 individuals, trained observers collected a minimum of 4.5 hours of continuously recorded data per individual. Collectively, these data permit an examination of possible relationships among the following: (a) mental retardation level, (b) severity of SIB-attributed injury, (c) functional analysis of SIB (attention-motivated, escape-motivated, self-stimulatory), and (d) program type (currently aversive, previously aversive, nonaversive, no program).

Client Characteristics and "Risk Factors"

SIB emerged as more commonly associated with increasing degrees of mental retardation and not simply as an artifact of living arrangements, since the entire regional client population was included. The relatively more common incidence of self-mouthing, pica, and rumination among severely and profoundly retarded persons with SIB suggests the potential importance of gustatory reinforcement in the genesis and maintenance of SIB in these persons, and it is noteworthy that such responses are predominantly nonsocial in function.

Pica and rumination, together with head banging, also were associated with increasing risk of actual injury to the person, and current risk was related to both earlier age of onset and a larger number of current SIB topographies. Both relationships illustrate potentially important client-specific variables, since neither age of onset nor number of SIB topographies for persons who are now predominantly adults are likely to be related in any direct fashion to the behavior of current caregivers. The mean age at which SIB was first documented for the population was 14 years, with a current mean age of 31, and it is likely that behavior with an average history of 17 years predates most contemporary habilitative practices.

In connection with programming decisions to address SIB, there was clear evidence that restraint and aversive procedures are used relatively more frequently with persons who exhibit more SIB topographies, as well as those who experienced moderate or severe SIB-attributed injuries. Grouping the sample by a functional analysis of SIB, 43% of the persons with self-stimulatory SIB were currently being treated by aversive interventions versus 16% by exclusively positive programs. The corresponding figures for escape-motivated and attention-motivated persons, respectively, were 19% versus 54% and 13% versus 48%. These data suggest that relevant client characteristics - rather than "professional ignorance" - are influencing program decisons.

On the basis of these data, we would expect to find relatively higher concentrations of aversive or intrusive program procedures among persons who have more severely handicapping conditions, as has been indicated by reviews of the behavior reduction literature (Guess et al., 1987). Such a correlational finding should not be taken as evidence of discriminatory practice, as some critics of aversive procedures would have us believe. Rather, the evidence suggests that certain types of severely aberrant behavior occur with disproportionate frequency among persons with severe or profound retardation, and that such behavior often tends to be resistant to simple, nonaversive intervention for reasons discussed above.

Client Characteristics and Caregiver Behavior

From these data, we found that caregivers apparently did not adjust their habilitative or incidental interactions with clients as a function of risk of injury attributable to SIB. Specifically, we could detect no differences in the nature or frequency of staff prompts, reinforcement, or negative attention delivered to persons who inflicted serious injuries on themselves versus those who did not. This finding suggests that severity of SIB is unlikely to be a simple function of differential attention, prompting or other common social determinants, and that alternative client-specific constructs (such as topography) are more relevant to a determination of risk.

By contrast, there were clear differences in the distribution of caregiver attention across groups of persons whose primary motivations for SIB differed. Caregivers interacted most frequently with individuals who were determined to be attention-motivated. However, relatively high rates of negative attention and demands (without greater task engagement) suggest that much of this attention was not delivered contingent on adaptive conduct. Similarly, despite the greater risk from their SIB, negatively-reinforced or escape-motivated individuals did not receive fewer habilitative demands than other persons, but did receive significantly less positive reinforcement. Staff attention again was delivered in an essentially non-therapeutic manner to such persons, perhaps thereby contributing to maintenance of their SIB. Finally, there was no evidence for relatively more frequent attempts to engage persons with self-stimulatory SIB in appropriate activities. Rather, staff seemed to respond to the SIB of attention-motivated persons by attending to it, to that of escape-motivated persons by persisting with demands and reprimands, and to persons with self-stimulatory SIB in a relatively undifferentiated manner.

Caregivers clearly do adjust their behavior as a function of client motivation for aberrant conduct, but not in ways suggested by fundamental principles of applied behavior analysis. Foxx (1985) has commented that "the act of reinforcement is an unnatural one for most people" (p. 193), and the present data indeed suggest that differential reinforcement is unlikely in applied settings. Such findings have important bearing on the practical utility of alternatives to punishment and aversives. As Iwata (1988) has argued, all formal reductive behavioral procedures are, in a sense, "default" responses by caregivers, in that such programs seek to reverse the effects of prior learning which has taken place under naturalistic social contingencies. The present data, together with other observational studies of interactions in naturalistic settings (Felce, Saxby, de Kock, Repp, Ager, & Blunden, 1987; Repp & Barton, 1980; Repp, Felce, & de Kock, 1987; Rosenthal, Underwood, & Martin, 1969) clearly suggest that caregivers, irrespective of setting, pervasively behave in ways which inadvertently may maintain existing aberrant behavior of their charges. More than 20 years of empirically demonstrable progress in applied behavior analysis apparently has exerted relatively limited influence over the day-to-day behavior of primary service providers.

The likely reasons for this are not hard to discern. Problems of staff turnover, motivation, and training are well-known (Repp et al., 1987) and affect services in both public- and private-sector settings; parents typically receive little formal training or professional supports, except in exemplary demonstration programs. The result is a broad gap between research on the one hand and actual practice on the other. Since "positive programs," especially those derived from principles of functional analysis, require re-arrangement of existing social contingencies, direct competition inevitably is set up with the latter. In the absence of convincing evidence for durable change in the social ecology of a person's setting, positive programs are unlikely to compete successfully with prevailing naturalistic contingencies. This is less of a problem for aversive methods, especially those which provide salient, novel sensory stimulation, since these are largely not confounded with prevailing social contingencies and are not dependent on them for their efficacy. Such procedures are also "self-eliminating," since they are faded, thinned, or withdrawn as the target behavior is suppressed. By contrast, the caregiver effort requirement of positive programs may persist almost indefinitely.

RECONCILING FUNCTIONAL ANALYSIS AND AVERSIVE PROCEDURES

We have not sought to argue that positive procedures "do not work," or that aversive interventions are mandated for certain classes of aberrant behavior. Rather, we have attempted to show that, in principle, nonaversive reduction strategies can be developed only for those behaviors in which the controlling variables can be identified and manipulated. When these conditions are met, interventions based on functional or operant analyses are generally more effective than those selected on *a priori* grounds.

The arguments, intervention research, and data presented and reviewed in this chapter converge on a common theme: Aberrant behavior exhibited by some persons with developmental disabilities is genuinely more resistant to functionally-derived, nonaversive interventions than that of others. Five sources of evidence point to this conclusion:

1. More elegant and effective nonaversive interventions based on

principles of stimulus control have been reported for negatively-reinforced behavior than for either attention-motivated or self-stimulatory forms of aberrant conduct.

2. Unscreened groups of persons exhibiting severely aberrant conduct include a significant proportion whose behavior is self-stimulatory (nonsocial) or multiply determined. Nonaversive treatment typically is not successful for this sample.
3. Persons exhibiting multiply-determined SIB, multiple SIB topographies, and certain forms of self-stimulatory SIB, are at objectively greater risk of serious injury.
4. In practice, aversive or restrictive interventions are more likely to be used with persons who exhibit self-stimulatory SIB, multiple SIB topographies, or who are otherwise at greater risk of serious injury.
5. Observational data suggest that more severe forms of SIB are not simply attributable to differential caregiver interactions.

Undoubtedly, insufficient attention is being paid to social ecology in the development of many programs designed to prevent or ameliorate challenging behavior. However, we would argue that many identifiable "risk factors" are rooted in idiosyncratic reinforcement histories, and that interventions targeted at currently prevailing extrinsic or social contingencies may have a tangential bearing in such instances. Expecting an operant analysis to perform a task for which it was not developed, namely, to serve as a generator of nonaversive interventions for all cases, is inherently unrealistic.

While some claim that functional analysis prescriptively narrows treatment selection, this assertion requires an inductive leap, since the decision rules needed to guide selection from the array of treatment options have not been developed. Both assessment and intervention technologies have matured to the point where matching interventions to persons seems theoretically within our grasp. Yet this goal is likely to remain a tantalizingly elusive one as long as advocates of fundamentally obscurantist and reactionary perspectives insist through the "aversives debate" on focusing primarily on the stimulus properties of interventions themselves rather than on operant analysis of the effects of the entire array of possible intervention methods.

Some circumstances simply do not favor nonaversive interventions. If the person's current behavior or environment resists analysis and intervention under prevalent, typical contingencies, then radical change may be necessary. From this perspective, stimuli of increasing aversiveness and corresponding novelty properly may be restricted to a relatively narrow range of applications:

1. When there is a significant risk of injury associated with emission of even a single response.
2. When the behavior is highly generalized.
3. When the behavior appears to be endogenously reinforced.
4. When the behavior is maintained by multiple contingencies.
5. When multiple aberrant response topographies are concurrently emitted.

As more of these characteristics apply in a particular case, the justification for introducing radically changed contingencies also may increase. Consequently, objective identification of such risk elements may operationally define "client need" and "right to effective treatment," and hence identify those circumstances when aversive procedures indeed are warranted.

CONCLUSIONS

Critics of aversive procedures have stressed functional analysis as an alternative leading to elimination of these practices. In this chapter, we have argued that this perspective is oversimplified and misleading, suggesting as it does that, if only we have enough information we always will be able to find positive solutions. In practice, severely aberrant behavior is often complex, multiply determined, or maintained by relatively remote or inaccessible stimuli. Nonaversive solutions may not be functionally derived for all instances of problem behavior, and aversive interventions may be indicated logically by functional analysis itself.

There are also certain practical constraints. Because the contingencies in nonaversive programs typically incorporate familiar ("normative") stimuli, their momentary power is relatively lower than that of salient aversive contingencies which superimpose novel consequences. Nonaversive interventions, consequently, introduce skill and effort requirements that may be difficult to attain or maintain in many applied settings, particularly in cases of severely aberrant behavior where only partial or gradual response suppression is achieved. Since the daily interactions of caregivers with such persons is typically distributed in a non-therapeutic manner, universal application of positive programming requires nothing less than comprehensive change in the very fabric of social behavior. This is probably a utopian ideal, unattainable in all but a few specialized, segregated settings. By contrast, learning under aversive motivation is ubiquitous, and may be a prerequisite of socialization and rule-governed conduct in general. Exclusive reliance on non-punishment strategies may be both impractical and non-normative.

Interdisciplinary teams of professionals who actually provide services in applied settings appear to be influenced by these principles. Data suggest that their program decisions are implicitly rule-governed, with a high correspondence between objective indices of client risk or behavior complexity and program restrictiveness. Claims that aversives are used indiscriminately are without current foundation. Subject to appropriate oversight, there is a recognized need for their application in certain instances. Since contemporary regulations and professional judgment appear to function adequately, where is the empirical justification for prohibition?

REFERENCES

Axelrod, S. (1987). Functional and structural analyses of behavior: Approaches leading to reduced use of punishment procedures? *Research in Developmental Disabilities, 8*, 165-178.

Axelrod, S., & Apsche, J. (1983). *The effects of punishment on human behavior.* New York: Academic Press.

Bird, F., Dores, P. A., Moniz, D., & Robinson, J. (1989). Reducing severe aggressive and self-injurious behaviors with functional communication training. *American Journal on Mental Retardation, 94*, 37-48.

Carr, E. G., (1977). The motivation of self-injurious behavior: A review of some hypotheses. *Psychological Bulletin, 84*, 800-816.

Carr, E. G., & Durand, V. M. (1985). Reducing behavior problems through functional communication training. *Journal of Applied Behavior Analysis, 18*, 111-126.

Carr, E. G., & Newsom, C. (1985). Demand-related tantrums. *Behavior Modification, 9*, 403-426.

Carr, E. G., Newsom, C. D., & Binkoff, J. A. (1976). Stimulus control of self-destructive behavior in a psychotic child. *Journal of Abnormal Child Psychology, 4*, 139-153.

Carr, E. G., Newsom, C. D., & Binkoff, J. A. (1980). Escape as a factor in the aggressive behavior of two retarded children. *Journal of Applied Behavior Analysis, 13*, 101-117.

Donnellan, A. M., Mirenda, P. L., Mesaros, R. A., & Fassbender, L. L. (1984). Analyzing the communicative functions of aberrant behavior. *Journal of the Association for Persons with Severe Handicaps, 9*, 201-212.

Durand, V. M., & Carr, E. G. (1987). Social influences on "self-stimulatory" behavior: Analysis and treatment application. *Journal of Applied Behavior Analysis, 20*, 119-132.

Evans, I. M., & Meyer, L. H. (1985). *An educative approach to behavior problems: A practical decision model for interventions with severely handicapped learners.* Baltimore, MD: Paul H. Brookes.

Favell J. E., McGimsey, J. F., Jones, M. L., & Cannon, P. R. (1981). Physical restraint as positive reinforcement. *American Journal of Mental Deficiency, 85*, 425-432.

Felce, D., Saxby, H., de Kock, U., Repp, A., Ager, A., & Blunden, R. (1987). To what behaviors do attending adults respond?: A replication. *American Journal of Mental Deficiency, 91*, 496-504.

Foxx, C. M., Foxx, R. M., Jones, J. R., & Kiely, D. (1980). Twenty-four hour social isolation: A program for reducing the aggressive behavior of a psychotic-like retarded adult. *Behavior Modification, 4*, 130-144.

Foxx, R. M. (1985). The Jack Tizzard Memorial Lecture. Decreasing behaviours: Clinical, ethical, and environmental issues. *Australia and New Zealand Journal of Developmental Disabilities, 10*, 189-199.

Foxx, R. M., McMorrow, M. J., Bechtel, R., Busch, L., Foxx, C. L., & Bittle, R. G. (1986). The lack of effects of enriched and automated environments on the adaptive and maladaptive behavior of mentally retarded persons. *Behavioral Residential Treatment, 1*, 105-124.

Foxx, R. M., McMorrow, M. J., Bittle, R. G., & Bechtel, D. R. (1986). The successful treatment of a dually-diagnosed deaf man's aggression with a program that included contingent electric shock. *Behavior Therapy, 17*, 170-186.

Gaylord-Ross, R. J., Weeks, M., & Lipner, C. (1980). An analysis of antecedent, response, and consequence events in the treatment of self-injurious behavior. *Education and Training of the Mentally Retarded, 15*, 35-42.

Griffin, J. C., Keyes, J. B., Emerson, J. H., Paisey, T. J., Stark, M. T., Williams, D. E., Dayan, M., Ricketts, R. W., & Zukotynski, G. (in press). Survey on the use of aversive therapy: National Association of Superintendents of Public Residential Facilities. *Superintendent's Digest.*

Griffin, J. C., Williams, D. E., Stark, M. T., Altmeyer, B. K., & Mason, M. (1986). Self-injurious behavior: A statewide prevalence survey of the extent and circumstances. *Applied Research in Mental Retardation, 7*, 105-116.

Guess, D., Helmstetter, E., Turnbull, H. R., & Knowlton, S. (1987). *Use of aversive procedures with persons who are disabled: An historical review and critical analysis.* Seattle, WA: The Association for Persons with Severe Handicaps.

Hearst, E. (1969). Aversive conditioning and external stimulus control. In B. A. Campbell & R. M. Church (Eds.), *Punishment and aversive behavior* (pp. 235-277). New York: Appleton-Century-Crofts.

Iwata, B. A. (1988, May). *The development and adoption of controversial default technologies*. Presidential Address to the Association for Behavior Analysis, Philadelphia, PA.

Iwata, B. A., Dorsey, M. F., Slifer, K. J., Bauman, K. E., & Richman, G. S. (1982). Toward a functional analysis of self-injury. *Analysis and Intervention in Developmental Disabilities, 2*, 3-20.

Iwata, B. A., Pace, G. M., Willis, K. D., Gamache, T. B., & Hyman, S. L. (1986). Operant studies of self-injurious hand biting in the Rett Syndrome. *American Journal of Medical Genetics, 24*, 157-166.

LaGrow, S. J., & Repp, A. C. (1984). Stereotypic responding: A review of intervention research. *American Journal of Mental Deficiency, 88*, 595-609.

LaVigna, G. W., & Donnellan, A. M. (1986). *Alternatives to punishment: Solving behavior problems with non-aversive strategies*. New York: Irvington.

Lennox, D. B., Miltenberger, R. G., Spengler, P., & Erfanian, N. (1988). Decelerative treatment practices with persons who have mental retardation: A review of five years of the literature. *American Journal on Mental Retardation, 92*, 492-501.

Lewis, M. H., Baumeister, A. A., & Mailman, R. B. (1987). A neurobiological alternative to the perceptual reinforcement hypothesis of stereotyped behavior: A commentary on "self-stimulatory behavior and perceptual reinforcement." *Journal of Applied Behavior Analysis, 20*, 253-258.

Linscheid, T. R., Iwata, B. A., Ricketts, R. W., Williams, D. E., & Griffin, J. C. (in press). Clinical evaluation of SIBIS: The Self-Injurious Behavior Inhibiting System. *Journal of Applied Behavior Analysis*.

Lovaas, O. I., Freitag, G., Gold, V. J., &Kassorla, I. C. (1965). Experimental studies in childhood schizophrenia: Analysis of self-destructive behavior. *Journal of Experimental Child Psychology, 2*, 67-84.

Lovaas, O. I., Newsom, C., & Hickman, C. (1987). Self-stimulatory behavior and perceptual reinforcement. *Journal of Applied Behavior Analysis, 20*, 45-68.

Lovaas, O. I., & Simmons, J. Q. (1969). Manipulation of self-destruction in three retarded children. *Journal of Applied Behavior Analysis, 2*, 143-157.

Lovett, H. (1985). *Cognitive counseling and persons with special needs: Adapting behavioral approaches to the social context.* New York: Praeger.

Mace, F. C., & Knight, D. (1986). Functional analysis and treatment of severe pica. Journal of Applied Behavior Analysis, 19, 411-416.

Matson, J. L., & DiLorenzo, T. M. (1984). *Punishment and its alternatives: A new perspective for behavior modification.* New York: Springer.

Matson, J. L., & Taras, M. E. (1989). A 20-year review of punishment and alternative methods to treat problem behaviors in developmentally delayed persons. *Research in Developmental Disabilities, 10*, 85-104.

McGee, J. J., Menolascino, F. J., Hobbs, D. C., & Menousek, P. E. (1987). *Gentle teaching: A non-aversive approach to helping persons with mental retardation.* New York: Human Sciences.

Measel, C. J., & Alfieri, P. A. (1976). Treatment of self-injurious behavior by a combination of reinforcement for incompatible behavior and overcorrection. *American Journal of Mental Deficiency, 81*, 147-153.

Morgan, R. L. (1989). Judgments of restrictiveness, social acceptability, and usage: Review on procedures to decrease behavior. *American Journal on Mental Retardation, 94*, 121-133.

Mulick, J. A., & Linscheid, T. R. (1988). Review of "Alternatives to punishment: Solving behavior problems with nonaversive strategies." *Research in Developmental Disabilities, 9*, 317-321.

Newsom, C., Favell, J. E., & Rincover, A. (1983). The side effects of punishment. In S. Axelrod & J. Apsche (Eds.), *The effects of punishment on human behavior* (pp. 285-316). New York: Academic Press.

Paisey, T. J. H. & Whitney, R. B. (1989). A long-term case study of analysis, response suppression, and treatment maintenance involving life-threatening pica. *Behavioral Residential Treatment, 4*, 191-211.

Paisey, T. J. H., Whitney, R. B., Hislop, M., & Wainczak, S. (in press). *Case study 5: George*. In R. Romanczyk (Ed.), *Self-injurious behavior: Etiology and treatment*. New York: Plenum.

Paisey, T. J. H., Whitney, R. B., & Moore, J. (1989). Person-treatment interactions across nonaversive response deceleration procedures for self-injury: A case study of effects and side effects. *Behavioral Residential Treatment, 4*, 69-88.

Parrish, J. M., Cataldo, M. F., Kolko, D. J., Neef, N. A., & Egel, A. L. (1986). Experimental analysis of response covariation among compliant and inappropriate behaviors. *Journal of Applied Behavior Analysis, 19*, 241-254.

Parrish, J. M., Iwata, B. A., Dorsey, M. F., Bunck, T. J., & Slifer, K. J. (1985). Behavior analysis, program development, and transfer of control in the treatment of self-injury. *Journal of Behavior Therapy and Experimental Psychiatry, 16*, 159-168.

Repp, A. C., & Barton, L. E. (1980). Naturalistic observations of institutionalized retarded persons: A comparison of licensure decisions and behavioral observations. *Journal of Applied Behavior Analysis, 13*, 333-341.

Repp, A. C., Felce, D., & Barton, L. E. (1988). Basing the treatment of stereotypic and self-injurious behaviors on hypotheses of their causes. *Journal of Applied Behavior Analysis, 21*, 281-289.

Repp, A. C., Felce, D., & de Kock, U. (1987). Observational studies of staff working with mentally retarded persons: A review. *Research in Developmental Disabilities, 8*, 331-350.

Repp, A. C., Harman, M. L., Felce, D., Van Acker, R., & Karsh, K. G. Conducting behavioral assessments on computer-collected data. *Behavioral Assessment, 11*, 249-268.

Repp, A. C., Singh, N. N., Olinger, E., & Olson, D. R. (in press). Using functional analysis to test hypotheses of the causes of self-injurious behavior: Rationale, current status, and future directions. *Journal of Mental Deficiency Research*.

Rojahn, J., McGonigle, J. J., Curcio, C., & Dixon, M. J. (1987). Suppression of pica by water mist and aromatic ammonia: A comparative analysis. *Behavior Modification, 11*, 65-74.

Rosenthal, T. L., Underwood, B., & Martin, M. (1969). Assessing classroom incentive practices. *Journal of Educational Psychology, 60*, 370-376.

Schroeder, S. R., Mulick, J. A., & Rojahn, J. (1980). The definition, taxonomy, epidemiology, and ecology of self-injurious behavior. *Journal of Autism and Developmental Disorders, 10*, 417-432.

Schroeder, S. R., Rojahn, J., & Mulick, J. A. (1978). Ecobehavioral organization of developmental day care for the chronically self-injurious. *Journal of Pediatric Psychology, 3*, 81-88.

Singh, N. N., Winton, A. S. W., & Ball, P. M. (1984). Effects of physical restraint on the behavior of hyperactive mentally retarded persons. *American Journal of Mental Deficiency, 89*, 16-22.

Smith, M. D. (1985). Managing the aggressive and self-injurious behavior of adults disabled by autism. *Journal of The Association for Persons with Severe Handicaps, 10*, 228-232.

Solnick, J. V., Rincover, A., & Peterson, C. R. (1977). Some determinants of the reinforcing and punishing effects of timeout. *Journal of Applied Behavior Analysis, 10*, 415-424.

Spreat, S., Lipinski, D., Dickerson, R., Nass, R., & Dorsey, M. F. (1989). A paramorphic representation of the acceptability of behavioral programming. *Behavioral Residential Treatment, 4, 1-13.*

Starin, S. P., & Fuqua, R. W. (1987). Rumination and vomiting in the developmentally disabled: A critical review of the behavioral, medical and psychiatric treatment research. *Research in Developmental Disabilities, 8*, 575-605.

Sturmey, P., Carlson, A., Crisp, A. G., & Newton, J. T. (1988). A functional analysis of multiple aberrant responses: A refinement and extension of Iwata et al.'s (1982) methodology. *Journal of Mental Deficiency Research, 32*, 31-46.

Tarnowski, K. J., Rasnake, L. K., Mulick, J. A., & Kelly, P. A. (1989). Acceptability of behavioral interventions for self-injurious behavior. *American Journal on-Mental Retardation, 93*, 575-580.

Touchette, P. E., MacDonald, R. F., & Langer, S. N. (1985). A scatter plot for identifying stimulus control of problem behavior. *Journal of Applied Behavior Analysis, 18*, 343-351.

Turnbull, H. R., Guess, D., Backus, L., Barber, P., Fiedler, C., Helmstetter, E., & Summers, J. A. (1986). A model for analyzing the moral aspects of Special Education and behavioral interventions: The moral aspects of aversive procedures. In P. Dokecki & R. Zaner (Eds.), *Ethics and decision-making for persons with severe handicaps: Toward an ethically relevant research agenda* (pp. 167-210). Baltimore, MD: Paul H. Brookes.

Van Houten, R., Axelrod, S., Bailey, J. S., Favell, J. E., Foxx, R. M., Iwata, B. A., & Lovaas, O. I. (1988). The right to effective behavioral treatment. *Journal of Applied Behavior Analysis, 21*, 381-384.

Vukelich, R., & Hake, D. F. (1971). Reduction of dangerously aggressive behavior in a severely retarded resident through a combination of positive reinforcement procedures. *Journal of Applied Behavior Analysis, 4,* 215-225.

Weeks, M., & Gaylord-Ross, R. (1981). Task difficulty and aberrant behavior in severely handicapped students. *Journal of Applied Behavior Analysis, 14*, 449-463.

CHAPTER

13

FLASH BONDING OR COLD FUSION? A CASE ANALYSIS OF GENTLE TEACHING

F.J. Barrera and George M. Teodoro
Applied Behaviour Analysis Program
Southwestern Regional Centre MCSS

The history of modern psychology shows that reaction to novel approaches or unorthodox interpretations predictably assumes at least two forms. In one, the new methodology or philosophy is shunned by the mainstream school of thought and becomes a fringe movement, and an outsider that falls quick prey to adversarial victimization. Witness, for example, our treatment of parapsychology. In the other, novel conceptions or techniques tend to become appraised by a Kuhnian process of paradigmatic assimilation. Unorthodox methodologies are broken down into acceptable and digestible variations of prevailing theoretical trends: New wine is easily poured into old bags. The field of behavior analysis seems particularly to be littered with many carcasses of this assimilative gluttony.

The appearance of Gentle Teaching (McGee, Menolascino, Hobbs, & Menousek, 1987) as a radical new treatment philosophy for all severely challenging behavior of developmentally disabled individuals seems to have already suffered the same historical fate that we have bestowed on other novel conceptions. We have sneered at Gentle Teaching's ungentle criticisms of behaviorism and of the scientific, principles of lawfully determined behavior, and we have shunned it as biased, unscientific, and naive. We also have conducted revisionistic armchair analysis of Gentle Teaching, dismissing it more often than not as a mere recombinant of positive reinforcement, manual guidance, prompting, and extinction.

This chapter relates our experiences during 15 months while we attempted to develop an effective Gentle Teaching treatment program for an individual with self-injurious behavior (SIB). Our initial assumption was that if Gentle Teaching claims were true, we should learn this new method and use it instead of traditional behavior modification techniques. We also believed that by using the tools of behavior analysis -- objective measurements, reliable observations, experimental manipulations -- we could attain a more fruitful understanding of how Gentle Teaching works.

METHOD

Participant

Richard, a 33-year-old profoundly retarded male had a protracted history of self-injury, institutionalization, hospitalizations, and highly restricted life-style. Clinical diagnoses included epilepsy and erythroblastosis fetalis, and during the course of the study pharmacological treatment included chlorpromazine (Largactil) 100 mg h.s. (hora somni) to assist sleeping, and carbamazepine (Tegretol) CR 300 mg b.i.d. (bis in die) for anti-epileptic control. A small number of occasionally needed p.r.n. (pro re nata) medications, including chlorpromazine, chloral hydrate (Noctec), and diazepam (Valium) for settling extreme agitation, and numerous topical treatments for injuries.

Richard's body showed the effects of long-standing self-injury, first reported at 3 years of age. His ears were severely lacerated and cauliflowered from fist punches and from striking his ears on the shoulder bone; his forehead was disfigured by cuts from hitting it with objects as well with as his knee; teeth were missing from striking his face with his foot; and significant hair loss had occurred from pulling it out or from forcefully rubbing his scalp on objects. Richard also displayed numerous scars, bruises, ulcerations, and open sores along arms, legs, and torso from severe bites, scratches, kicks, and dropping to the floor. During the course of the study, Richard severely avulsed his right auricle; required a number of restraint changes to reduce swelling of wrists, hands, and ankles or to prevent further injury to specific areas (e.g., knees, elbows, heels); underwent dental surgery twice; and ripped out a toenail. These and other incidents required stopping our treatment sessions for various periods of time, as noted later.

Following his admission to our treatment unit, Richard was exposed for 5 months to a wide array of positive and intrusive procedures, including various differential reinforcement schedules, self-restraint training, different types of brief contingent physical restraint, fading of mechanical restraints (straitjacket, wrist-cuffs), skill teaching, various types of time-outs, and water sprays. None proved to have any significant or lasting effect. Detailed functional analyses of different daily activities and preferred reinforcers (which included playing with running water, smoked oysters, proximity to staff, restraints, chocolates, and blondes) suggested that neither conditional nor unconditional access to these affected his rate of SIB.

Setting, Dependent Variables, And Data Collection

Treatment sessions were conducted within the SIB Trauma Unit, a specialized 10-bed treatment residence operated within a provincial facility for developmentally disabled persons. Nearly all sessions in the first three phases (see Experimental Procedures) were conducted in a large, carpeted, well-ventilated room that was furnished with a long table, chairs, simple educational materials, toys and games. Baselines and the fourth-phase sessions were conducted in various parts of the residence (dining area, sleeping bays, living room).

We chose as the main dependent variables two of Richard's most frequently occurring SIB topographies: closed-fist punches to the side of the head (temple, ears) with either hand, referred to as "head bangs" (HBs); and cocked strikes with his head on either shoulder bone (humerus-clavicle joint), referred to as "ear-to-shoulder bangs" (ESBs). Throughout the sessions, we systematically attempted to block hits by interposing the therapist's hands between Richard's ears and fists or by shadowing his hands (for HBs) and by outfitting Richard with a thick towel around his neck (for ESBs). Hits were recorded regardless of whether or not actual contact was made; blocks were not. During several sessions, we also recorded other collateral SIB topographies, such as body-dropping, biting, crying, kicking and foot-stomping -- all associated with periods of agitation, resistance and temper tantrums.

The preceding behaviors were recorded either with tally counters or with a hand-held electronic recorder (Human Technologies, Inc.), and with both in some cases. Sessions typically involved a minimum of three staff (therapist, blocker and recorder). In approximately 29% of the sessions, extra staff manning videotaping equipment also were present. From these videotaped sessions, 5-min samples were recorded for an average of 53% of the sessions of each experimental phase. Sampling was randomly determined by recording for 5 min and resting for the following 5 min, or vice versa. This sampling schedule was the basis for interobserver reliability checks, as well as for recording the dependent variables listed below. Videotaped sampling occasionally was complemented with dual recordings made directly from sessions, as noted above.

Two sets of dependent variables, one for Richard and one for the therapists, were defined and recorded as follows. Richard's *responsive behaviors* included eye contact with the therapist, smiling, laughing, accepting hugs, self-initiating touching of or turning toward the therapist(s), shaking hands, and reciprocating with any of these behaviors in response to therapist behavior. These forms of social activity are referred to as bonding behaviors by McGee et al. (1987, p. 127), and their emergence is the central outcome goal of Gentle Teaching (McGee et al., 1987, p. 15, p. 39).

Therapists behaviors included rewards and demands of a verbal, physical, or gestural nature. *Task rewards* were delivered for being on-task or for completing a small task. Examples included commanding phrases (such as "good work," "you did that puzzle really well," "you're doing that very nicely") and physical displays of affection (such as hugs, smiles, or caressing the hand with which Richard was doing a task).

Person rewards were not contingent on any specific behavior, and consisted of affectionate phrases such as "you're a great guy," "very good, Richard," "you're really neat;" and actions such as "thumbs-up" signs and pats. Many task and person rewards were necessarily identical, differing only in their contingency to Richard's behavior or in their semantic content.

Therapists' *demands* could be verbal, physical, or gestural actions that requested some response from Richard. Demands included behaviors such as gesturing to a specific task material or presenting a task item to Richard. Also included in this category were physical attempts to keep his fists away from his ears, such as placing the therapist's hand on Richard's wrist, or guiding and redirecting his hands with some measure of force away from his head toward task materials. Verbal demands, which staff were instructed to avoid as much as possible, included phrases such as "put this over here", or "now let's try this."

Interobserver Reliability

Two observers recorded the occurrence of specific dependent variables during prescribed intervals. The number of agreements was then divided by the total of agreements and disagreements (x 100) to yield a standard percentage reliability figure. Recording interval size varied depending on the frequency of the variable. For low-rate behaviors such as social responsiveness items, interval size was 15 sec. For medium-rate variables such as verbal task rewards, demands, and both types of SIB, interval size was 5 sec. For high-rate behaviors (all other rewards), the interval size was 3 sec. The mean percentage agreement for HBs was 92% (range: 85-98%); ESBs, 91% (range: 86-96%); demands, 82% (range: 73-94%); responsive behaviors, 99% (range: 80-100%); and for all rewards, 87% (range: 79-93%).

Experimental Procedures

The study consisted of a single-case A-B1-B2-B3-B4-A design in which A's were baseline periods with no Gentle Teaching intervention, and phases B1 through B4 entailed four formats of Gentle Teaching. Throughout the study, Richard's normal daily routine involved a significant use of restraints when not involved in any activity. These were removed prior to each session and normally reapplied at its conclusion.

BASELINES (A): These two phases consisted of three pre-intervention and three post-intervention sessions 25 min in length. Each baseline session consisted of an unstructured situation during which restraints were removed, edible and social reinforcers were made available, and simple routine tasks, attempts to teach communication, or meals were present. The last pre-intervention session was conducted a few days before phase B1; the first post-intervention session took place over a month after phase B4 was terminated.

TASK CENTERED PHASE (B1): This phase consisted of 36 sessions, each 30 min in length, usually conducted 5 days per week. Richard was freed of his restraints and seated at a table across from the therapist and in front of the staff assigned to block SIB blows. An extensive array of educational materials (sorting, inserting, matching) and games (puzzles, building toys) were arranged to provide variety and choice of tasks and to eliminate down-time between tasks. The ignore-redirect-reward paradigm (McGee et al., 1987) was used throughout. Attempted or actual SIB was gently blocked as much as possible, but otherwise was given no heed by staff; non-verbal efforts were made to redirect Richard continuously to the task; and any task completion, however minor, was followed by encouraging, enthusiastic remarks and affectionate physical and tactile contacts. A 5-day break was scheduled after Session 5 to ensure recovery from dental surgery.

DELAYED REWARD PHASE (B2): In reviewing the outcome of the previous phase, especially from analyses of videotaped material, we noticed that, given our high density of rewards and his moderately high and persistent rates of responding, many of the therapists' rewards occurred close in time to Richard's SIB. To control for possible adventitious reinforcement (Greenspoon, 1955; Skinner, 1948) of SIB, special efforts were made in this phase to prevent temporal contiguity of rewards and HBs. Thus, for example, if Richard punched himself the therapists would interrupt or withhold their rewards until he was back on-task or HBs were successfully redirected. By delaying rewards in this manner, we hoped that we would be able to convey to Richard more clearly what activities were associated with rewards, as well as ensuring that SIB was not inadvertently "valued" (McGee et al., 1987, pp. 39-54). To simplify the implementation of this procedure, ESBs were not included in the delay contingency.

This phase consisted of 19 sessions, scheduled and conducted as before in the same setting and with the same materials. A 7-day break was required following Session 2 for recovery from dental surgery.

PERSON VALUING PHASE (B3): Due to our continuing negative outcomes, we assumed that further expertise and guidance were needed to improve our clinical effectiveness. Hence, Gentle Teaching sessions were discontinued for a period of approximately 2 months, during which videotaped samples of our sessions were forwarded to Dr. John McGee for review and analysis. A consultation with the junior author was arranged, and correspondence summarizing the reviews and recommendations subsequently were received (McGee, *personal communications*, July 6, 1988, and August 9, 1988). Based on an analysis of three 2-min samples of the videotaped material, the following major criticisms and suggestions were made to us:

1. Rewarding (or value-giving) was too contingent on task com-

pletion and should be given on a more noncontingent human valuing basis. Tasks were to be used as vehicles for participation, not merely as objects to be completed.

2. The reward-to-demand ratio was too low and it was necessary to decrease the ratio of demands (or dominative interactions) to rewarding or value-giving interactions several-fold. A rate of 10 to 15 rewards for each demand was suggested.

3. Reciprocation seeking (i.e., eliciting prosocial responses from Richard) of therapists and the authenticity and warmth of some of their interactions were felt to be lacking and in need of correction.

The above recommendations were incorporated into our training protocol for this phase. Emphasis on task completion and task rewards was curtailed in favor of person rewards, reward sharing, and teaching human rewards. In addition, demands were sharply reduced, thereby affecting the reward-to-demand ratio in the recommended direction. Greater effort was placed on seeking reciprocation from Richard, and staff whose tone of reward delivery was deemed flat or mechanistic were excluded from the study.

This phase consisted of 16 sessions, scheduled in much the same way as before and in the same setting, except that session durations were increased to an average of 55 min. Following Session 4, Richard inflicted a deep avulsion on his ear which could not be sutured and which required one month's rest -- he managed to reopen the cut four times during this period. A further 2-week break was required by a ward-wide quarantine order.

SCHEDULED CARE-GIVING PHASE (B4): Following the last session of the preceding phase, the Gentle Teaching study was discontinued for a period of 6 months. During this time, we corresponded again with Dr. McGee seeking further suggestions, and inquired about the possibility of sending Richard to Nebraska for directly supervised treatment (Teodoro, *personal communication*, Oct. 27, 1988). However, this time we received no response.

We spent the balance of this break seeking and meeting with other Ontario clinicians using Gentle Teaching, trying to learn from their experiences. We finally made contact with a Detroit-based consulting agency, Paradigmetrics, which provided us with a 3-day intensive staff training practicum on Gentle Teaching techniques for Richard. From this practicum, our treatment team developed the somewhat unusual format of this phase, that differed significantly from Gentle Teaching in three ways: One, the use of edibles, including meals, was incorporated into many sessions. Two, Richard was placed in a form of social isolation (Foxx et al., 1980) between sessions, typically sitting in an empty bay and facing away from other clients and staff. Three, restraints were not totally removed for sessions, but were gradually shed across sessions on a limb-by-limb basis.

This format also differed from previous phases as follows. No sessions were conducted within the confines of the training room used before. Sessions were scheduled several times per day (up to 10 sessions initially) and were conducted 7 days per week. Session duration varied from only a few minutes at first to several hours during the final part of this phase. Cumulative session time per day rose from about 33 min (range 6 min to 1.2 hr) in the first 10 days to about 4.2 hr (range 12 min to 7.8 hr) in the last 10 days.

In the typical early sessions, Richard's chair would be wheeled out of the bay toward staff; one hand would be freed from restraints, and he would be encouraged and praised for brief task participation. He then would be restrained again and isolated until the next session.

Special efforts were made to ensure that restraint reapplication was done in a reassuring manner and was not contingent on SIB. No staff contact was allowed while he was fully restrained. This phase was conducted for 44 days, and only two breaks occurred, each lasting one or two days.

Staff Participation

The junior author was present in all sessions, either as therapist, blocker, or occasionally recorder. Two other staff alternated as therapist during phase B1, and four additional unit staff assisted in specific occasions. During phase B2, assistance was provided primarily by two staff, with occasional help from three other individuals. Phase B3 was conducted by only four individuals, including the junior author. Phase B4 involved seven different staff from two shifts, in addition to the brief initial assistance of the Paradigmetrics trainers. Data recording was undertaken by staff (all trained in recording techniques) with the assistance of three university-level students.

Independent Validation of Gentle Teaching Formats

To determine how similar or dissimilar our application of Gentle Teaching methodology was to that of McGee et al. (1987), we conducted three separate validation tests with groups of direct-care students (N= 21) from a local college. Each group first was given a short lecture on the main principles of Gentle Teaching and written summaries of these. Next, they screened a section from McGee's (1986) video training package and completed a questionnaire. The questions (N= 18) were grouped under three topics: the theoretical bases of Gentle Teaching (e.g., dependence vs. independence, distance vs. warmth, person-centered vs. behavior-centered); the therapist's behavior (e.g., mechanistic vs. enthusiastic, varied vs. repetitive rewards, conditional vs. unconditional delivery); and the participant's behavior (e.g., accepting rewards, initiating contact, reciprocating). Next, they were shown, one at a time, eight samples of our training sessions (the order was randomized across groups), and were asked to complete the same questionnaire after each sample. Each sample was rescreened several times until all students completed their questionnaires. Samples were selected from phases B1, B2, B3 of the study and, unbeknown to the students, they included what we and other behavior specialists familiar with the technique deemed to be one of our best and one of our worst examples of Gentle Teaching.

RESULTS

Figure 1 shows the results for our major dependent variables, head bangs (HBs) and ear-to-shoulder bangs (ESBs) across all conditions in terms of SIB's per min (numbers in parenthesis in the text indicate rates unless otherwise noted). Data show that no SIB-free sessions occurred in any condition, though very low rates were noted in specific sessions. The lowest points for HBs occurred in the initial Baseline and Task Centered conditions (0.07 and 0.13 rpm); for ESBs, in the Task Centered, Scheduled Care-Giving, and first Baseline conditions (0.03, 0.03, and 0.18 rpm, respectively).

Results from the Task Centered phase (B1) show an initial decrease after the first dental surgery recovery period, followed by a slowly ascending trend in both responses for the remainder of this condition. By the last three sessions, HBs had climbed to the same level as in the first three sessions (3.17, 3.19), while ESBs more than doubled in rate for the same sessions (3.38, 7.71). While no data were collected for on-task behavior, videotaped material indicated that

Richard was on-task with his hands fairly constantly. ESBs were not, of course, incompatible with on-task behavior. During Richard's few attempts to leave the table, the therapists followed him with the task material (e.g., working on the floor). By the last few sessions, however, Richard began showing signs of agitation (looking at the exit door, tugging at his clothes, engaging in tantrums).

Results from the Delayed Reward phase (B2), during which efforts were made to put some temporal distance between HBs and therapist rewards, seem to show the same effects as in the previous condition. That is, there was a gradual, though slightly more accelerated, increase in SIB responding across sessions. For both behaviors, rates more than doubled from the first three to the last three sessions (HBs: 2.19, 5.53; ESBs: 6.81, 15.28). The sharp rise of ESBs, which in this condition were neither incompatible with on-task behavior nor included in the delay contingency, was particularly notable and exceeded by far any other condition, including Baseline points. The relatively marked increase in HBs also suggests that the combination of rewards for task and reward delays for HBs (a best-test case for reinforcer effectiveness) had a weak impact on Richard's behavior, and even might have aggravated it. Again, signs of agitation and resistance appeared to increase in this condition, especially during the later sessions.

The results for the Person Valuing phase (B3), in which procedural strategies were modified to provide the most faithful and precise format of Gentle Teaching, show a pattern of accelerated increase similar to those of previous conditions. The main remarkable difference was that the increase occurred predominantly for HBs rather than for ESBs. Comparisons between the first 3 and last 3 sessions of this phase indicated a greater than four-fold increase in HBs (2.37, 10.90), but a sizeable reduction of ESBs (2.17, 0.53). These high rates of HBs, which on the average overshot even Baseline levels, could reflect the fact that task demands were reduced significantly in this phase, thus allowing Richard freer use of his hands to engage in SIB. This situation also may have been exacerbated

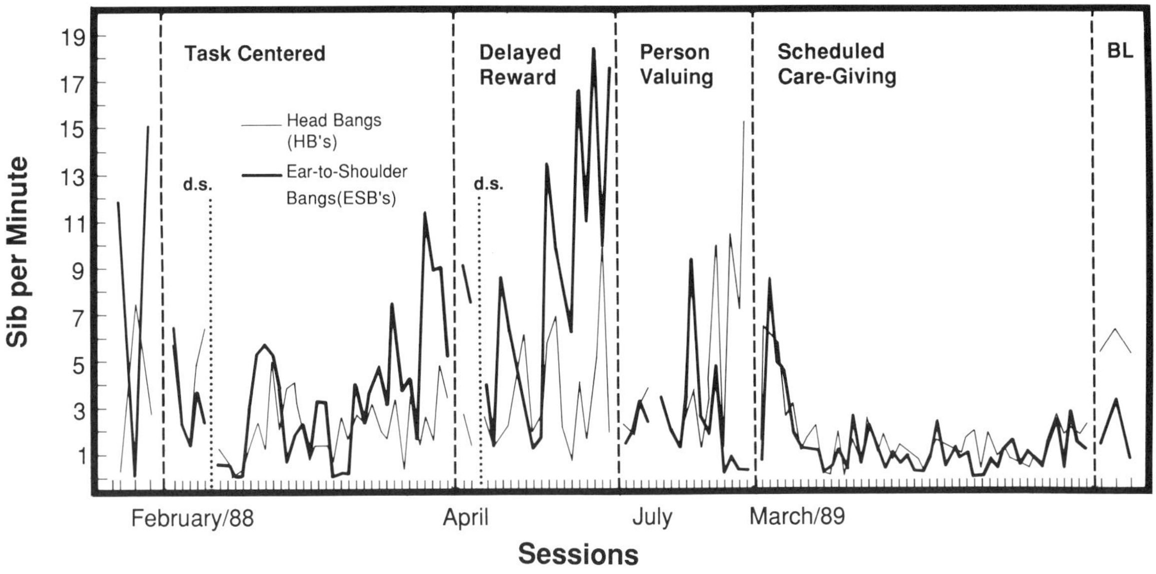

Figure 1: Daily response rate per min of Richard's self-injurious behaviors during baselines (BL) and the four intervention conditions. HBs refers to head bangs and ESBs to ear-to-shoulder bangs. Short vertical broken lines indicate dental surgery (d.s.) breaks during conditions.

by the very high rates of noncontingent rewards used throughout this condition. As in previous phases, signs of agitation were noted frequently and perhaps more so in this case because Richard tended to gravitate toward the door. On one occasion, the door was finally opened and the therapists continued working outside the room, following Richard. This proved to be one of the most disillusioning sessions.

Our final intervention, the Scheduled

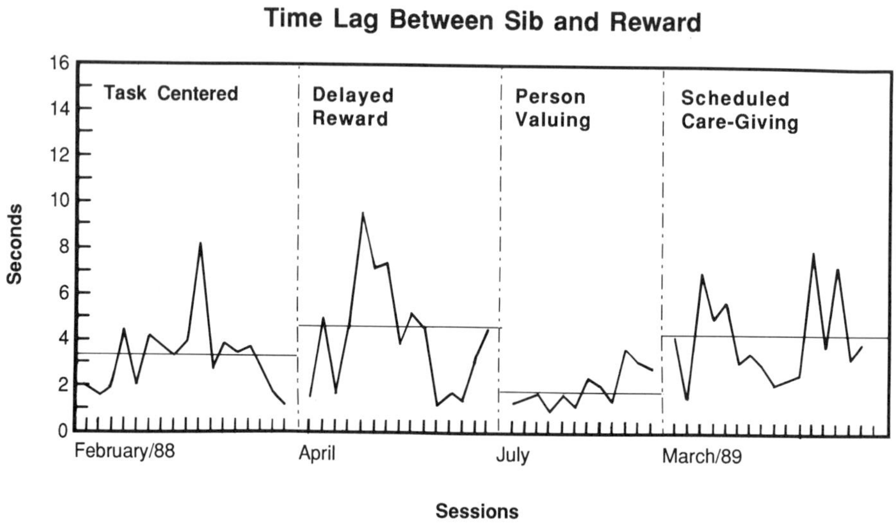

Figure 2: Time lags (Response-reinforcer intervals) between SIB occurrence and reward delivery during the four intervention conditions. Only data for HBs (head bangs) are shown. Solid horizontal lines indicate median values per condition.

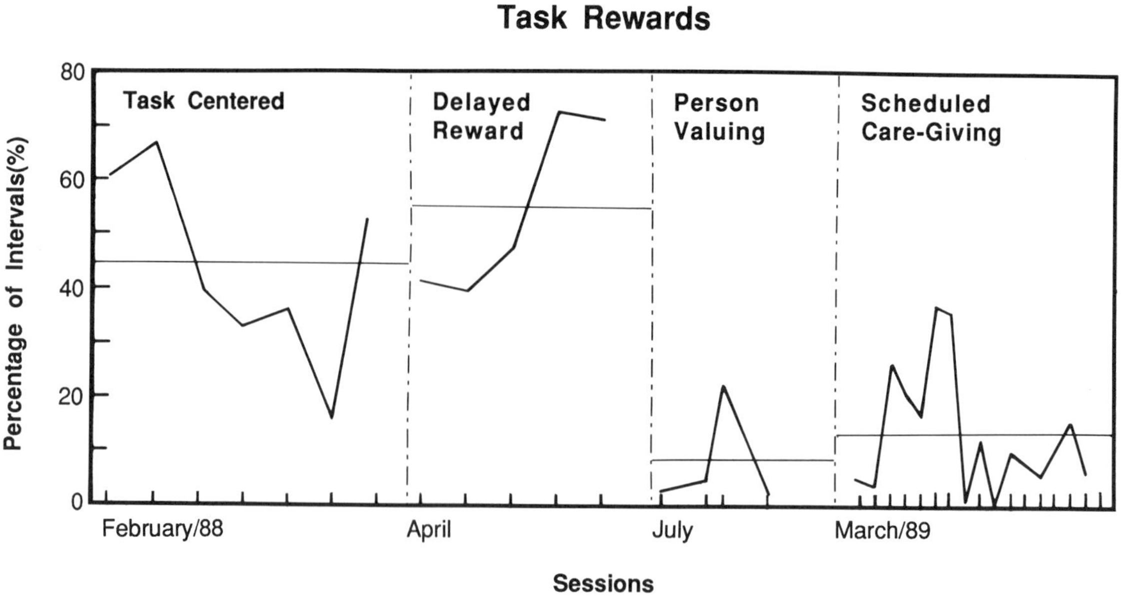

Figure 3: Percentage of intervals with task rewards during the four intervention conditions. Solid horizontal lines represent mean values per condition.

Care-Giving phase (B4), departed radically from acceptable Gentle Teaching boundaries and yet, as the results show, generated the lowest rates of SIB. Except for a sharp spike during a few early sessions (unrelated to session durations), rates for both HBs and ESBs remained very much at the level of the first session (HBs 1.61; ESBs 0.78) and close to the entire condition means (HBs 1.60; ESBs 1.44). There was a small cluster of slightly higher rates in the last few sessions, but this was not necessarily predictive of the terminal accelerations seen in previous

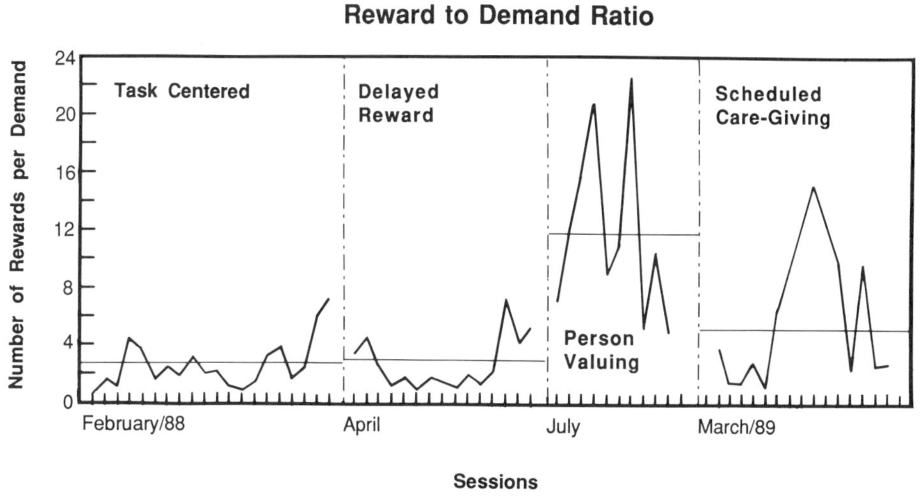

Figure 4: Reward-to-demand ratios (number of rewards administered for each demand presented) during the four intervention conditions. Solid horizontal lines indicate mean condition values.

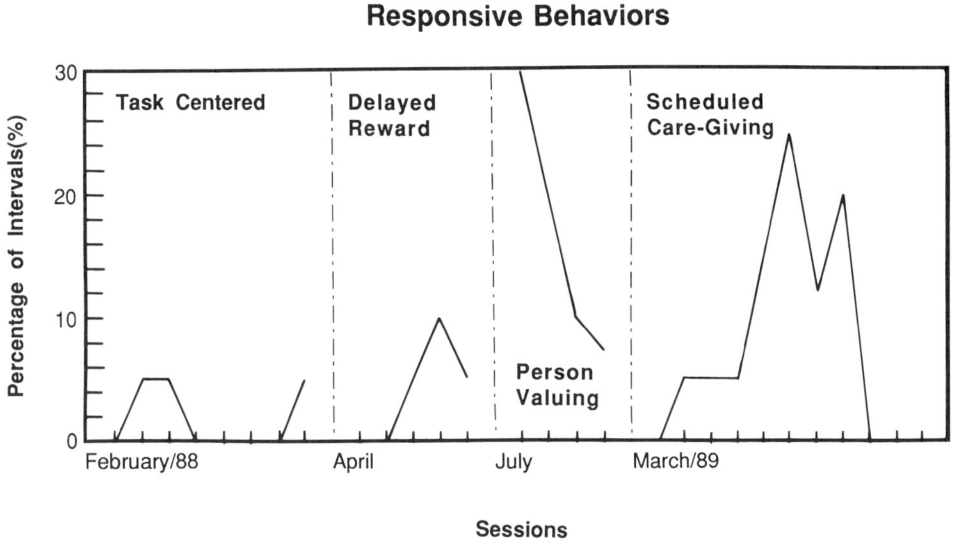

Figure 5: Percentage of intervals with responsive behaviors manifested by Richard during the four intervention conditions.

phases. The low, stable rates seen throughout are all the more remarkable in view of the fact that cumulative session durations increased, on average, eightfold from the first to the last portions of this condition. Equally notable are the observations that few agitations or temper tantrums occurred during sessions, and that Richard seemed generally relaxed and peaceful during this phase. In three isolated instances, Richard was reported to remain without restraints by himself (i.e., without self-restraining staff) for considerable periods of time with few incidents of SIB.

Although this phase demonstrated much greater effectiveness in reducing SIB than any of the previous Gentle Teaching formats, which tended generally to worsen Richard's behavior, the level of responding still was deemed clinically unacceptable. By the end of this phase, Richard had self-inflicted over 16,500 instances of different SIBs while out of restraints.

Results from the post-intervention Baseline showed an increase in both SIBs to about 60% of the pre-intervention Baseline levels (HBs 5.67; ESBs 1.90), suggesting that generalization across time was not strong. Rate of HBs was generally close or within the terminal ranges of Task Centered and Delayed Reward conditions, but only about half of the Person Valuing mean terminal rate. Rate of ESBs remained close to the levels seen in the Scheduled Care-Giving condition.

In addition to the main results depicted in Figure 1, we collected secondary sets of data on both therapist and participant behavior to assess the integrity of our interventions and corroborate whether or not we met our intended procedural goals.

First, Figure 2 shows an analysis of the average time elapsed between SIB occurrence and delivery of reward for session samples of our four intervention conditions (only data for HBs are shown). The data indicate that the median lag was highest in the Delayed Reward phase. In this condition, nearly 70% of the data points exceeded a 3-sec lag. The figure also shows that the lowest median lag occurred in the Person Valuing phase, in which less than 20% of the samples exceeded a 3-sec response-reward lag. The other two conditions fell between these extremes, although the Scheduled Care-Giving phase also resulted in an unexpected preponderance of lag times exceeding the 3-sec level.

Figure 3 shows the proportion of task rewards given by therapists during session samples in each intervention phase. As would be expected, the highest conditions with task rewards were the Task Centered and Delayed Reward phases, with averages of 44% and 55% of the intervals. In the Person Valuing condition, characterized by a predominance of person rewards, the mean proportion of intervals with a task reward was only 8%. Lastly, the Scheduled Care-Giving condition showed an increase to about 40% of the intervals during the early, shorter sessions, and a decrease to about 8% of the intervals during the later, longer sessions. The mean proportion of intervals with task rewards in this phase was 13%.

Figure 4 shows an analysis of the "reward-to-demand ratio", i.e., the number of rewards given by the therapists for each demand presented to Richard. As indicated, Richard received about 3 rewards per demand in the first two task-oriented phases. In the Person Valuing phase, rewards per demand increased markedly, up to a 22:1 ratio. This translated to close to 3,500 rewards per session or about 40/min. The overall mean number of rewards for this condition was about 12 for each demand, well within the high range recommended by Dr. McGee. For the final phase, Scheduled Care-Giving, the reward-to-demand ratio fluctuated across sessions as a consequence of varying session lengths.

To avoid confusion, we should note that the absolute rate of all rewards (task and person), irrespective of demands, remained fairly constant on the average across the four intervention conditions. For the Task Centered phase, the condition mean was 26.9 rewards/min (range: 19.4 - 33.6/min); for the Delayed Reward condition, the mean was 28.2 rewards/min (range: 19.5 - 35/min); for the Person Valuing phase, 26 rewards/min (range: 13.9 - 40.1/min); and for the Scheduled Care-Giving phase, 29.2 rewards/min (range: 11.7 - 57.7/min).

Figure 5 shows that the rate of responsive behaviors (smiling, eye contact, reciprocation, etc.) displayed by Richard was surprisingly very low throughout conditions. Scattered and typically transient instances were noted on isolated occasions, with the stronger effect noted in two early Person Valuing Sessions (session sample condition mean: 17% of intervals), and a small cluster of Scheduled Care-Giving sessions (session sample condition mean: 8% of intervals). It seems rather inconceivable that after so many sessions and different formats, we only accrued such low levels of social responsiveness from Richard. However, lest one be left with the impression that he is a dour individual, we have documented elsewhere (Teodoro & Barrera, 1989) that Richard shows many signs of social responsiveness (including happy playfulness, seeking and accepting kisses, and hearty laughs), but only when he is fully restrained.

Finally, the results from our independent validation tests disclosed the following findings. When students' ratings were analyzed to determine if they could discriminate between our good and bad examples of Gentle Teaching, significant differences occurred on 75% of the selected items (two-tailed, paired sample t-tests with p.001 on 7 items; p.01 on the remaining items). When our videotaped samples were compared against McGee's (1986), excluding our best and worst samples, students' ratings found both sets highly comparable, except that (a) our therapists seemed to be having more fun and enjoyment interacting with Richard than McGee had with his participant (p.001); and (b) Richard was surprisingly more responsive than McGee's subject (e.g., he smiled more often, p.001). When our best sample was compared to McGee's segment, students rated us superior in 50% of the items (p.001 on 4 other items; p.01 or p.05 on the remaining ones), and very similar in the other 50% of the cases. And when our worst sample was compared to McGee's, students rated us only marginally worse, with no significant differences in 85% of the items. In this specific sample, we were deemed more "distanced" (p.01) and "mechanistic" (p.05).

DISCUSSION

The results of our study do not bode well for Gentle Teaching. We believe that we have conducted a systematic, exhaustive, and honest exploration of this approach, and yet we have come up empty-handed. Our initial curiosity of how Gentle Teaching worked has evolved into the more skeptical and severe question of whether it actually works. As the outcomes of our different intervention phases indicated, within-condition increases consistently emerged in nearly all cases, especially for HBs. When conditions closely approximated those described by McGee et al. (1987) and McGee (1986), no rapid elimination of SIB occurred. When special efforts were made to ensure the best possible implementation of newer Gentle Teaching strategies (e.g., McGee, *personal communications*, 1988; McGee, 1989), HB levels took a turn for the worse, quadrupling in rate and surpassing non-treatment baselines. Moreover, moderately low rates were maintained only when Gentle Teaching was combined with methods entailing food reinforcers, restraints, and intrusive isolation, all denounced as proscribed practices by the

Gentle Teaching approach. Lastly, our participant's attempts to resist and terminate sessions, as well as to escape from the training area in most phases, suggest that this approach acquired undeniably aversive properties. Taken together, these results indicate that, at least for our subject, Gentle Teaching was an ineffective, counterproductive, and aversive intervention.

Why did our attempts result in such a resounding failure? One possibility that we implemented the procedures incorrectly seems seriously questionable in light of our secondary data analyses. Reward-demand ratios were favorably tilted in the correct, desirable direction (Figure 4). Person rewards were made optimally noncontingent (Figure 2) to facilitate human valuing. Task-reward and task-centeredness were reduced sharply in favor of equitable, prosocial interactions and reward sharing (Figure 3). Additionally, evaluation of our implementation by external independent raters indicated that we were very comparable to teaching exemplars (McGee, 1986) and, in some cases, actually superior by Gentle Teaching criteria. These results suggest that we complied with all recommendations, met all criticisms, and conducted a legitimate high-quality and committed version of Gentle Teaching. Hence, we believe that the failure was not one of treatment delivery, but a failure of the methodological and conceptual approach itself.

One also could argue that other less obvious reasons were behind this failure. For example, our value base and solidarity posture (McGee et al., 1987, pp. 29-38; 173-175) might be seriously disputed on the grounds that we accept the use of intrusive and aversive measures as a means of providing compassionate care (to which list we must now add Gentle Teaching). However, we contend that if Gentle Teaching requires that one must suspend one's beliefs -- in our case, 50-odd years of empirical behavioral knowledge -- in order to attain clinical effectiveness, we must wonder whether this request emanates from a cult rather than an emerging revolutionary paradigm. Intellectual honesty would dictate that acceptance of the value base presupposition requires rather more compelling evidence than a simple leap of faith (Lakatos, 1970).

Similarly, one also could argue that *any* negative case of Gentle Teaching is an incorrect application of this procedure and that, in this sense, it can never fail. From a philosophical viewpoint, however, we should remember that negative results are scientifically important, even if they involve only a single case as in this study, because they may have the veto power to disconfirm and *falsify* theoretical positions (e.g., Lakatos, 1970; Popper, 1959). This is especially true with positions that claim to be all-encompassing, or that have staked their superiority on the proposition that all other viewpoints are essentially wrong and can be replaced by the new approach. If Gentle Teaching assumes the posture that it cannot fail, it would then assume the status of an unfalsifiable claim outside the rules of empirical evidence.

One of the most damaging outcomes of our study was the failure of the procedures to elicit a reasonable degree of socially responsive behaviors, i.e., of bonding as termed by McGee et al. (1987, e.g., p. 127). The object of Gentle Teaching is to teach bonding, and its emergence is the pivotal therapeutic outcome of this approach. Thus, the fact that our intense and indisputably extensive attempts to reward, value, and seek reciprocations did not result in significant bonding seriously questions one of Gentle Teaching's main precepts. There seem to be, however, some recurring difficulties with Gentle Teaching's use of this term. For example, as noted by Love (1988), no empirical evidence has been provided to support such a central concept. The concept of bonding has also lacked the clear-cut objective definitions and limiting operational conditions necessary to ascertain its validity (see Jordan et al., 1989). In addition, Gentle Teaching often makes the incorrect assumption that bonding works quickly (Klaus & Kennell, 1982).

A closer reading of Gentle Teaching's conceptualization of bonding suggests, moreover, that there are two serious internal flaws. One, from McGee et al.'s (1987, pp. 43-45, 155, 170-171) descriptions of the therapist or caregiver as signaling and representing safety and security, *attachment* may have been confused with bonding. Attachment is the child-to-parent (or client-to-therapist) relationship marked by preferential responding to a figure that provides a secure base, whereas bonding is the parent-to-child (or therapist-to-client) relationship marked by a one-way affectional commitment (Ainsworth, 1989; Bowlby, 1988; Klaus & Kennell, 1982). Hence, what Gentle Teaching describes as signs of bonding in clients are in reality only expressions of attachment, and it is only the therapist or the caregiver --and not the client -- who can become truly bonded. In light of this analysis, Gentle Teaching's numerous claims about client bonding may be incorrect.

The other conceptual flaw is the tandem assumptions that (a) Gentle Teaching leads to bonding, and (b) that bonding in turn leads to the reduction or disappearance of SIB or other problem behaviors. The first link already has been questioned by our data, as well as by other investigators (Jordan et al. 1989; Singh & Jones, 1989). With regard to the second link, the literature seems to cast serious doubts on this assumed cause-effect relation, in that evidence strongly suggests that the direction of the relation is in fact the other way around: The reduction or elimination of problem behaviors is what leads, or may lead, to the appearance of socially responsive behaviors (Foxx et al., 1989; Lichstein & Schreibman, 1976; Matson & Taras, 1989; Mudford, 1985; Newsom, Favell, & Rincover, 1983). Indeed, fine-grained analyses of SIB and social behavior patterns suggest that significant SIB reduction is an antecedent condition for the emergence of prosocial behaviors (Barrera, Teodoro,& Labadie, 1989). Thus, the rather simplistic notion that social responsivity by itself can somehow permanently displace deeply ingrained problem behaviors remains at this point conjectural and difficult to validate scientifically.

The treatment failures and conceptual errors of Gentle Teaching that we have reported here raise numerous questions. In what remains of this section, we will attempt to address the question What is Gentle Teaching?

We can begin to answer this by submitting that Gentle Teaching likely cannot be reduced and digested into a behavioral fold as nothing more than a repackaged version of familiar operant procedures (i.e., shaping, differential reinforcement, graduated guidance, etc.). Although the phraseology of Gentle Teaching appears in *similitude* behavioral, and although McGee (1989) acknowledges the use of certain non-consequential techniques (errorless learning, fading, prompting), our results suggest that, as a clinical method, Gentle Teaching is irreducible to common operant variables. For one thing, its heavy reliance and emphasis on unconditional human valuing, i.e., on noncontingent reinforcers, would circumvent such assimilation. In addition, we noted that when Gentle Teaching was improved with reward delays, it fared no better in the best-test case than when reward delays were not used. If Gentle Teaching's mechanism was operant in nature, then even a slight improvement should have been detectable. Similarly, we could conclude that adventitious reinforcers likely were not influential in other phases, as it is doubtful that incidental reinforcers would have more impact than deliberately scheduled ones.

It also strikes us as odd that Gentle Teaching would choose such a relatively weak package, producing at best modest and mediocre results (e.g., Jordan et al., 1989; Paisey et al., 1989; Singh & Jones, 1989), as the edifice upon which Gentle Teaching's claims could stand. We believe, instead, that much of this approach's effectiveness seems to center on the effectiveness of the reinforcers that it was using and that pre-intervention reward potency might be the best predictor of success or failure. This view naturally runs contrary to Gentle Teaching's claim that it is a vehicle for teaching reward valorization and the value of human interaction, but then it clearly failed to do so in our study. At the very least, this interpretation sheds some light on puzzling findings that we have seen in a number of unpublished studies, such as improved outcomes when aversive motivators are combined with Gentle Teaching, poor post-session generalization, and occasional and transient attenuation of behavior intensity. In our study, this view also would suggest that stimulus conditions associated with inescapable, implosive, and possibly satiating or confusing rewards would fare much worse than those in which social reward was escapable, had its dosage highly controlled, and was combined with other reinforcers.

Finally, any answer to what is Gentle Teaching must include the fact that, in a certain sense, it is not a treatment and is not even client-centered, but is instead an approach aimed at reeducating caregivers. Much of Gentle Teaching's appeal seems to be based on not whether it works, and in many cases this seems unimportant (e.g., Kelley & Stone, 1989), but instead on its ability to help caregivers cope with and accept the chronic and seemingly intractable traits of their charges. Caregivers are taught to make attitudinal changes and lifelong commitments, i.e., true parental or therapist bonds, seemingly sharing many of the attributes of positive healing or palliative care. These life choices presumably reduce the daily stress of dealing with problem behaviors and the guilt of inefficacy and defeat, and thus strengthen acceptance of disabling conditions with some dignity and self-respect. Apparently, these commitments can be reinforced by even minute signs of social responsiveness, even in the absence of therapeutic behavioral changes, because they justify in the caregivers' perceptions their new faith. For much of Gentle Teaching, the question of whether it works or not is thus meaningless, and it is not surprising that in the face of negative treatment results some caregivers will reply that it really does not matter, while others will argue that it does *appear* to work.

In closing, we can draw an analogy between the recent debates surrounding Cold Fusion (e.g., Hively, 1989) and Gentle Teaching (e.g., Mudford, 1985), in that for us Gentle Teaching remains an elusive creature that resists both assimilation and verification. The latter problem would seem to rule out Gentle Teaching as a legitimate universal treatment alternative, and it is unfortunate that groups advocating sole use of nonaversiveness, at least in Canada (e.g., see Lipovenko, 1989), have invested so much faith in this one option. With regard to assimilation, we doubt that such a process will be easily completed: Gentle Teaching has too many changing components that make it difficult to validate experimentally. Additionally, some components involve issues of faith and commitment that are not data-based and may escape altogether the purview of behavioral science and applied research. Thus, while there is a clinical fascination with commitment (e.g., see Costanzo, 1989), Gentle Teaching's combination of faith and ineffectiveness might be considered cruel and dishonest, making its acceptance and adoption by the clinical community at this point remote. These and other problems, such as external validity, indirect inferential measures, credibility, and internal conceptual flaws, make unlikely the prospect that Gentle Teaching will bring in the new day.

NOTE

The authors wish to thank the many staff from the SIB Trauma Unit, A.B.A. Program, who assisted and participated in this study, with special thanks to Kim Boundy, Brian Labadie, Doreen Martin, Andy Murray, Jack Polland, Joel McPhail, Barb Vangassen, Dolores Newham, Paul Gagnon, and Richard's favorite blonde, Shelley Brown. Thanks are also due to Jim Lewandoski and Stephanie Brady of Paradigmetrics; to Tom Lloyd of St. Clair College; to Neil Garbe, Donna Fohkens, and Heather Praill of Guelph University; to Trixie Jenner, Department of Psychology; and to Mr. Lloyd Jackson, Administrator, Southwestern Regional Centre.

REFERENCES

Ainsworth, M. D. S. (1989). Attachments beyond infancy. *American Psychologist, 44*, 709-716.

Barrera, F. J., Teodoro, G. M., & Labadie, B. D. (1989, May). *Social bonding outcomes in a clinical trial of SIBIS*. Invited address presented at the 15th Annual International Convention of the Association for Behavior Analysis, Milwaukee.

Bowlby, J. (1988). *A secure base: Clinical applications of attachment theory*. London: Routledge.

Costanzo, P. R. (1989). A thought-wrenching epitaph: Commitment and meaning [Review of *Commitment, Caring and Conflict*]. *Contemporary Psychology, 34*, 727-730.

Foxx, C. L., Bittle, R. G., & Faw, D. G. (1989). A maintenance strategy for discontinuing aversive procedures: A 52-month follow-up of the treatment of aggression. *American Journal on Mental Retardation, 94*, 27-36.

Foxx, C. L., Foxx, R. M., Jones, J. R., & Kiely, D. (1980). Twenty-four hour isolation. *Behavior Modification, 4*, 130-144.

Greenspoon, J. (1955). The reinforcing effect of two spoken sounds on the frequency of two responses. *American Journal of Psychology, 68*, 409-416.

Hively, W. (1989). Science observer. *American Scientist, 77*, 327.

Jordan, J., Singh, N. N., & Repp, A. C. (1989). An evaluation of gentle teaching and visual screening in the reduction of stereotypy. *Journal of Applied Behavior Analysis, 22* 9-22.

Kelley, B., & Stone, J. (1989). Gentle teaching in the classroom. *entourage, 4*, 15-19.

Klaus, M. H. & Kennell, J. H. (Eds.). (1982). *Parent-infant bonding* (2nd ed.). St. Louis: Mosby.

Lakatos, I. (1970). Falsification and the methodology of scientific research programmes. In I. Lakatos & Musgrave (Eds.), *Criticism and the Growth Knowledge* (pp. 91-196). London: Cambridge University Press.

Lichstein, K., & Schreibman, L. (1976). Employing electric shock with autistic children: A review of the side effects. *Journal of Autism and Childhood Schizophrenia, 1*, 163-173.

Lipovenko, D. (1989). Gentle teaching stresses emotional bonds. *The Globe and Mail*, Toronto, March 6, p. 5.

Love, S. R. (1988). Review of gentle teaching: A nonaversive approach to helping persons with mental retardation. *Research in Developmental Disabilities, 9*, 441-445.

Matson, J. L., & Taras, M. E. (1989). A 20-year review of punishment and alternative methods to treat problem behaviors in developmentally delayed persons. *Research in Developmental Disabilities, 10*, 85-104.

McGee, J. J. (1986). *Gentle approach: A four part video series on gentle teaching.* Omaha: Meyer Children's Rehabilitation Institute.

McGee, J. J. (1989). *Gentle teaching: Behavioral change through respect and justice*. Toronto: G. Allan Roeher Institute.

McGee, J. J., Menolascino, F. J., Hobbs, D. C., & Menousek, R. E. (1987). *Gentle teaching: A nonaversive approach for helping persons with mental retardation*. New York: Human Sciences Press.

Mudford, O. C. (1985). Treatment selection in behaviour reduction: Gentle teaching versus the least intrusive treatment model. *Australia and New Zealand Journal of Developmental Disabilities, 10*, 265-270.

Newsom, C., Favell, J. E., & Rincover, A. (1983). Side effects of punishment. In S. Axelrod & J. Apsche (Eds.), *The effects of punishment on human behavior* (pp. 285-316). New York: Academic Press.

Paisey, T. J. H., Whitney, R. B., & Moore, J. (1989). Person-treatment interactions across nonaversive response-deceleration procedures for self-injury: A case study of effects and side-effects. *Behavioral Residential Treatment, 4*, 69-88.

Popper, K. R. (1959). *The logic of scientific discovery*. New York: Basic Books.

Singh, N. N., & Jones, L. J. (1989). *Comparative effects of gentle teaching and visual screening on self-injurious behavior.* Paper presented at the 97th Annual Convention of the American Psychological Association, New Orleans.

Skinner, B. F. (1948). "Superstition" in the pigeon. *Journal of Experimental Psychology, 38*, 168-172.

Teodoro, G. M., & Barrera, F. J. (1989, March). *An experimental analysis of gentle teaching*. Presented at the Annual Convention of the American Association of Mental Retardation (Ontario Chapter), Toronto.

CHAPTER

14

EFFECTS OF GENTLE TEACHING AND ALTERNATIVE TREATMENTS ON SELF-INJURY

Linzi J. Jones
University of Otago

Nirbhay N. Singh and Kathy A. Kendall
Medical College of Virginia
Commonwealth Institute for Child and Family Studies

Gentle Teaching is a humanistic approach to the care of persons with mental retardation. The central proposition of Gentle Teaching is that caregivers should eschew the use of punishment and adopt a liberating posture toward persons with severe behavioral challenges such as aggression and self-injury (McGee, 1988a). Bonding is seen as the primary vehicle for establishing new values in therapists and their clients. Indeed, bonding is not only the vehicle, but also the goal of Gentle Teaching (McGee, Menolascino, Hobbs, & Menousek, 1987). The proponents of Gentle Teaching assume that through bonding with caregivers, the client will prefer to participate in activities and engage in appropriate interactions with others instead of engaging in maladaptive behaviors.

Bonding can be described as a teaching process that aims at helping the client to realize that (a) the caregiver symbolizes safety and security, (b) the caregiver's words and physical contacts are intrinsically rewarding, and (c) participation with the caregiver generates reward (McGee et al., 1987). During the client-caregiver interaction, the caregiver may provide an environment that sets the occasion for the realization of these goals, individually or in combination, depending on the characteristics of the client. For example, if a client fears caregivers' then the primary emphasis may be placed on teaching that human presence denotes safety. However, in the process of achieving this, it is likely the client will come to realize that interaction with the caregiver is intrinsically rewarding, thereby increasing the probability of further positive interactions. The proponents of Gentle Teaching hypothesize that such client-caregiver bonding teaches the client the value and reward of positive human interactions.

Although caregivers are responsible for initiating bonding, changes in the value system should lead to attitudinal and behavioral changes in both the clients and the caregivers. To have maximum impact, the caregivers must be tolerant, warm, and affectionate throughout their interactions with the client, demonstrating that human presence is in itself rewarding.

The ignore-redirect-reward process is the basic strategy used in the Gentle Teaching paradigm (McGee et al., 1987).

The three components are not used sequentially because they are considered as a single process, requiring the caregiver to implement all three almost concurrently. In theory, caregivers' use of these techniques will promote bonding and, consequently, instill values in the client that influences him/her to participate and interact appropriately. Not only is the client expected to develop new values toward people, but caregivers are presumed to benefit in this respect as well (McGee et al., 1987).

Ignore requires caregivers to avoid or minimize their responses that typically occur after a client has begun to display maladaptive behavior. By ignoring the behavior, caregivers withhold the reward of human interaction that might have provided the initial motivation for engaging in maladaptive behavior. Throughout such an episode, caregivers continue to maintain their posture of solidarity with the client while simultaneously appearing oblivious to the client's actual maladaptive behavior. Essentially, caregivers attempt to teach the client that human interaction is rewarding, but only if they display adaptive behavior. While maladaptive behavior is not reinforced, the client is certainly not subjected to punishment for it. Indeed, the goal is not to eliminate the behavior per se, but to instill in the client a new set of values that will result in mutually humanizing and liberating interactions between the client and the caregiver.

Interrupt is used when ignoring alone would not be potent enough to control the client's behavior and if the behavior would result in the client or others (e.g., staff, peers) being at risk for injury, or if ignoring would lead to property damage. Interrupting occurs with minimum attention to the behavior, and caregivers are required to interrupt (i.e., block punches or head bangs) only until the client is calm and will not cause any harm to self or others. The essence of *interrupt* is that it is used only for the purpose of preventing harm and not for controlling the client. Interruption is followed immediately by redirection in order to return the client's attention to the task so that rewarding interactions can continue. The teaching experience is never terminated as a result of inappropriate behavior as this reinforces the client's maladaptive behavior that is used as a means of avoiding participation in a task.

Redirect is the most important element of the Gentle Teaching paradigm and is "the key response of the caregiver that refocuses the interactional flow from undesirable to rewarding interactions" (McGee, 1988a, p. 208). Caregivers attempt to nonverbally refocus the client's attention on rewarding interactions. By limiting the amount of client-caregiver verbal interaction during the display of maladaptive behavior, it is less likely that the client will be reinforced for negative behaviors. Instead, the client receives verbal as well as tactile rewards only while engaged in positive human interaction. Rewards such as praise and shoulder touches are given for the client's slightest attempts at appropriate behavior. Not only does this show that reward is available, but how it can be gained. It tells the client that despite past behavior, he/she can still earn rewards.

Punishment is proscribed in the Gentle Teaching philosophy because it not only makes client-caregiver bonding impossible to achieve, but also leaves the client submissive and "devoid of human feelings" (McGee, 1988a). Proponents of Gentle Teaching are against the use of such procedures as extinction, time-out, visual screening, overcorrection, and physical restraints, among others (McGee, 1988b), because these procedures are seen only as attempts to decrease the frequency of the client's maladaptive behaviors without creating new values in the client and caregivers.

An important characteristic of Gentle Teaching is the flexibility in its implementation. The caregivers' posture of solidarity directs their interactions with the clients, allowing for a variety of ways to implement the Gentle Teaching techniques. For example, if a client engages in stereotypy, caregivers are responsible for generating a means to redirect the client to other positive behaviors. The only guidelines they have to follow is that the client is not rewarded verbally or physically, and a posture of solidarity is communicated to the client. Although this flexibility may have certain advantages, such as allowing for creativity and perhaps greater commitment on the part of the caregiver, it can lead to a change in the fundamental goals of the treatment, especially when the situation is stress provoking (Thomas, 1984).

Furthermore, there is no standard methodology for implementing Gentle Teaching because its proponents have not operationally defined their procedures which would enable caregivers to use them in a consistent manner. Indeed, this may be one of the major drawbacks of the Gentle Teaching paradigm, leading to confusion in its use by various professionals. If Gentle Teaching procedures cannot be easily replicated by caregivers, it means the procedures are so highly specialized that they are beyond daily use by those who need to use them the most. In addition, it poses immense problems to social scientists who wish to independently evaluate its efficacy because there will be little agreement between the proponents of Gentle Teaching and independent evaluators on even the most fundamental issues, such as the nature of the independent variable (Jordan, Singh, & Repp, 1989; Singh & Jones, 1989).

McGee and his colleagues have published a small number of studies attesting to the effectiveness of Gentle Teaching in treating severe behavior problems of persons with mental retardation (e.g., McGee, 1985a; Menolascino & McGee, 1983). The most common methodology used in these reports is a B design (Barlow & Hersen, 1984) where B is the treatment phase of the study. As others have noted (e.g., Mudford, 1985; Singh, 1983), the lack of a robust experimental methodology precludes an evaluation of the data presented in these studies. Indeed, these studies do not meet any of the criteria currently used for evaluating the reliability and validity of investigations in this area. However, McGee's own work (e.g., McGee, 1988a) suggests that Gentle Teaching may be effective and that attempts should be made to independently evaluate its effectiveness.

In the first independent evaluation of Gentle Teaching, Jordan et al. (1989) used an alternating treatments design to compare Gentle Teaching, visual screening, task training and a no-treatment control condition in the reduction of stereotypy of three persons with mental retardation. The results showed a modest decrease in stereotypy during task training. Both Gentle Teaching and visual screening procedures were more effective than task training and the no-treatment control condition, with visual screening being more effective than Gentle Teaching. Indeed, stereotypy increased in one client under the Gentle Teaching condition. Contrary to the predictions of the proponents of Gentle Teaching, bonding occurred at the same low levels under both Gentle Teaching and visual screening.

In a related study, Singh & Jones (1989) replicated the Jordan et al. (1989) study, but focused on the self-injury of a man with profound mental retardation. The results showed a modest reduction in self-injury with task training. As in the earlier study, both procedures were more effective than the task training and the no-control conditions, with visual screening being more effective than Gentle Teaching. In addition, bonding occurred at the same low levels under both treatment conditions.

Paisey, Whitney, and Moore (1989) evaluated the effects and side effects of three procedures on the self-injury and collateral behaviors of two persons with profound mental retardation while they were engaged in an analogue task similar to that found in prevocational settings. They compared the effects of Gentle Teaching, graduated guidance, and differential reinforcement of incompatible behavior combined with brief interruption (DRI+ I) with both subjects. The self-injury of the first subject was maintained by negative reinforcement and by attention in the second subject. It was found that DRI+I was superior to the other two procedures with the first subject and graduated guidance was marginally more effective than DRI+I and Gentle Teaching with the second. Although all three procedures were effective to some degree in decreasing the self-injury of the two subjects, Gentle Teaching was not found to be the most effective with either subject.

Unlike Gentle Teaching, the visual screening procedure used by Jordan et al. (1989) and Singh & Jones (1989) is a mildly intrusive punishment procedure which has been extensively and rigorously evaluated in the treatment outcome literature (see Rojahn & Marshburn, in press). Screening procedures have been used successfully to treat self-injurious and a variety of other maladaptive behaviors of children with developmental disabilities (Demetral & Lutzker, 1980; McGonigle, Duncan, Cordisco, & Barrett, 1982; Singh & Winton, 1984). The procedure involves blocking the client's vision for a few seconds, contingent on each occurrence of the target behavior. Typically, caregivers use their hands to momentarily cover the client's eyes although other variations, such as terry cloths and screens, have been used (e.g., Singh, Beale, & Dawson, 1981; Singh, Winton, & Dawson, 1982). It has been reported that although clients often react by crying, struggling, or trying to pull the caregiver's hands away, most cases show that this only occurs during the first few applications (Singh, 1980; Singh et al., 1981).

The aim of the study reported in this chapter was to further evaluate the effectiveness of Gentle Teaching. Like the two previous studies in this series (Jordan et al., 1989; Singh & Jones, 1989), a comparative analysis paradigm was used to evaluate the effectiveness of Gentle Teaching and traditional behavioral procedures.

METHOD

Subjects

SUBJECT 1. Jeff was a 10-year-old boy who had been diagnosed as profoundly mentally retarded on the American Association on Mental Deficiency criteria (Grossman, 1983), and had been institutionalized for the past six years. His age-equivalent score on the Vineland Adaptive Behavior Scale (revised) was 0.9 month. He had engaged in self-injury for a number of years although the exact age at which he began self-injury could not be determined. He had minimal receptive language and no expressive language.

He had few self-care skills, being able to finger-feed himself and assist with dressing and undressing. He enjoyed being cuddled and tickled. Jeff exhibited no play behaviors, but engaged in frequent stereotypic behaviors with favored objects. He had participated in a training group, but had to be removed from it because of his self-injury and screaming and the need for constant supervision to control his behavior. Jeff's self-injury took the form of head banging which was restricted to banging against doors and the floor. His head banging was often accompanied by high-pitched screaming, crying, and whining. If Jeff engaged in these behaviors, his direct care staff would typically place him in his room, give him a hot bath (one of his favorite activities), give him some food, or take him for a walk. A helmet had been used previously to prevent injury from head banging; however, Jeff would bang his head, scream if the helmet was placed on his head, and then attempt to remove it. In addition, the use of the helmet resulted in the reopening above his eye of a scar that was always present due to his seizures. For these reasons, the use of the helmet was discontinued.

An informal functional analysis indicated that Jeff's head banging was probably maintained by self-stimulation and escape from planned activities. If Jeff was left alone for any length of time, he would head bang and scream and would stop only if nursing staff interacted with him. This was most likely to occur if Jeff heard voices within or outside his room. Jeff also was observed to use head banging and screaming to escape from activities such as toileting, lunch, dinner, or tasks in the training area. If the demands were removed, he would cease these behaviors.

During the study, Jeff received the following medication: valproic acid (Depakene) 400 mg/10mls three times a day; nitrazepam (Mogadon) 5 mg twice a day; and diazepam (Valium) 5 mg on an as-needed basis for status epileptic. Medication was kept constant throughout the course of the study.

SUBJECT 2. Jillian was a 20-year-old woman who had been diagnosed as profoundly mentally retarded on the American Association on Mental Deficiency criteria (Grossman, 1983), and had been institutionalized for the past 15 years. Her retardation was caused by a subdural hemorrhage 5 days after birth which resulted in hemiplegia of the left side. She had a 17-year history of mouthing and rumination. Her mouthing resulted in red, swollen, calloused hands, and there was evidence of breakdown of tissue and infection. Rumination had resulted in low body weight (37 kg) and bad breath. There was no record of any treatments being carried out for her self-injurious mouthing prior to this study. Verbal reprimands and physical restraints (splints applied for an hour after each meal) were used by nursing staff to prevent rumination, but they had not decreased the behavior.

Jillian had minimal receptive language and no expressive language. She had no self-care skills. Jillian had never been included in any training groups because of her disruptive behavior and non-performance of tasks. During the study, she received the following medication: diazepam (Valium) 5 mg twice a day; amitriptyline (Elavil) 50 mg daily; temazepam (Restoril) 20 mg at night on an as-needed basis. Medication was kept constant throughout the course of the study.

Settings

The baseline and treatment sessions for both subjects were held in a sparsely furnished activity room and in their residential ward. Toys and activities that were to be used in the study were freely available, and only functional age-appropriate tasks (Brown, Branston, Hamre-Nietupski, Pumpian, Certo, & Gruenewald, 1979; Reid, Parsons, McCarn, Green, Phillips, & Schepis, 1985) were used.

Therapists' Training

As in the Singh and Jones (1989) study, four therapists were trained in behavioral observation techniques, in the art of Gentle Teaching, and in the use of visual screening. The training procedures used were as described by Jordan et al. (1989), and included modeling and role-play of the procedures, as well as viewing several tapes of Gentle Teaching which featured Dr John McGee (McGee, 1986), and reviewing of a number of his research papers (e.g., McGee, 1985a; Menolascino & McGee, 1983).

Response Definitions

Self-injury and a number of collateral behaviors were recorded. Self-injury was broadly defined as behavior that causes, or at least has the potential to cause, manifest damage to the person's own body. The specific self-injurious behavior recorded for Jeff was *head banging* which was defined as hitting the head against any surface, and the collateral behavior was *screaming* which was defined as a loud noise that changes in pitch or volume. The specific self-injurious behavior recorded for Jillian was *mouthing*, defined as placing hand(s) or finger(s) in the mouth so that the fingernail is not visible.

In addition, the collateral behaviors recorded for both Jeff and Jillian were: (a) *on task*: any activity directed toward completion of the task and includes active manipulation of materials in the manner directed by the therapist, without assistance; excludes throwing, dropping, mouthing, hitting surfaces, passing objects repetitively from hand to hand, or manipulation of objects in any way other than as directed by therapist; (b) *task training*: active manipulation of materials with full or partial guidance; and (c) *bonding*: smiling -- directed at the therapist either spontaneously or in response to therapist; physical approach -- subject moves to within 0.5 m of the therapist, demonstrating eye contact for more than 2 sec, touching, hugging, or shaking the hand of the therapist.

Data Collection and Reliability

Data were collected 5 days a week in three 30-minute sessions separated by a 5-minute changeover break. Data were collected using a partial-interval recording technique, with each session divided into 90 10-second intervals. Behavioral categories occurring within each interval were recorded. Free response time available to the subject during the comparison of the two procedures was equated.

Reliability checks were conducted on 25% of the sessions by an independent observer. An agreement was defined as both observers recording the presence or absence of target responses during the same 10-second interval. Reliability was calculated for both occurrences and nonoccurrences of the target behaviors. The mean inter-observer agreements for occurrences and nonoccurrences, respectively, for Jeff were: head banging -- 92% and 87%; screaming -- 97% and 97%; on task -- 88% and 97%; task training -- 90% and 77%; and bonding -- 91% and 99%; and for Jillian they were: mouthing -- 85% and 95%; rumination -- 85% and 95%; on task -- 73% and 96%; task training -- 86% and 77%; and bonding -- 83% and 99%.

Experimental Design

The effectiveness of Gentle Teaching and visual screening were compared, using an alternating treatments design (Barlow & Hayes, 1979; Kazdin, 1982). A no-treatment control condition was included to demonstrate experimental control. In addition, the effects of task training, a nonaversive positive intervention procedure, was evaluated immediately following the baseline phase.

As in the other two studies in this series (i.e., Jordan et al., 1989; Singh & Jones, 1989), a number of steps were taken to avoid or reduce the risk of multiple treatment interference. These included alternating each member of each pair of therapists following every session and presenting condition-specific cues to the subjects prior to the commencement of each treatment session. The study consisted of the following phases.

BASELINE 1. Due to the severity of Jeff's head banging, his baseline was conducted for five 10-minute sessions over 2 days. However, 30-minute sessions were scheduled in all other phases. Only those toys or tasks to be used in the study were available to avoid confounding factors such as novelty of the toys. For Jeff, these involved a bike with training wheels, a jigsaw depicting a fire engine, a ball, and a plastic snake. Jillian's tasks included a hairbrush to brush her hair, a sanding board and sandpaper, a shoe, and a polishing cloth. No experimental manipulations were in effect during baseline. However, as Jillian's activities were to be carried out at a table, she was directed verbally and/or physically back to her seat if she left it. Jeff was not required to be seated as his primary activity was to learn to ride the bike which involved using the entire floor space.

BASELINE 2. The effects of active task training on self-injury were evaluated in two of the three daily sessions in this phase, with the third being a control condition which was identical to baseline 1 conditions. The task training procedures used were adapted from Singh and Millichamp (1987), and included the following components: verbal instructions, modeling, graduated physical guidance, and the use of verbal and tactile reinforcement contingent on compliance with therapist directions or appropriate behavior. A task training phase was included to determine the effects of a differential reinforcement procedure on self-injury and on task behavior. No consequences were provided for self-injury other than redirecting Jeff and Jillian to their tasks.

ALTERNATING TREATMENTS 1. In this condition, Gentle Teaching, visual screening, and a no-treatment control were introduced in a counterbalanced order each day. Their toys and equipment were available during all sessions.

a). *No-Treatment Control.* This was identical to the control conditions in Baseline 1 and Baseline 2.

b). *Gentle Teaching.* This condition involved using Gentle Teaching methods to teach bonding and to prevent self-injury. Each occurrence of self-injury resulted in the interrupt-ignore-redirect-reward techniques being used (McGee et al., 1987). For Jeff, this involved using an open palm between the head and surface used to head bang. For Jillian, an open palm was used to block attempts to strike the head, body parts, or hard surfaces. Each subject was redirected to the task and socially reinforced for appropriate behavior.

The Gentle Teaching procedures used in this phase approximate the procedures used during task training (e.g., interrupt, redirect), except that the procedures now were used in accordance with the principles of Gentle Teaching, and additional supportive techniques were used (e.g., teaching in silence; McGee et al., 1987). The procedures corresponded closely to the guidelines suggested by McGee et al. (1987, p. 142) for the treatment of self-injury.

c). *Visual Screening.* The task training procedures used in Baseline 2 were continued throughout this phase, making this, in essence, a task training plus visual screening condition. Following each self-injurious response, the subject's eyes were either covered with both of the therapist's hands to block vision, or one hand was placed over the eyes and the other hand was placed at the back of the head to hold it still (McGonigle et al., 1982). Release from visual screening occurred after 5 seconds had elapsed with no resistance (e.g., screaming, struggling, self-injury, or aggression) from the subject.

ALTERNATING TREATMENTS 2. As the effects of both treatments, visual screening and Gentle Teaching, were neither clinically significant, nor differentially effective for Jeff, we decided to use the less restrictive intervention in this phase during two of the three daily sessions. Thus, for Jeff, Gentle Teaching was used during two sessions and a no-treatment control condition was in effect in the other session. Neither Gentle Teaching nor visual screening was clinically effective in reducing Jillian's mouthing. Consequently, we decided to use an oral hygiene procedure that had been demonstrated to be effective in the treatment of rumination and mouthing (Singh, Manning, & Angell, 1982). The task training procedures and the no-treatment control condition were identical to that in previous phases; however, only one oral hygiene intervention session was scheduled daily. On the occurrence of mouthing, Jillian was instructed to brush her teeth for 2 minutes with a Listerine-soaked toothbrush. If no response was made, full manual guidance was provided by the therapist. This was later faded to partial guidance. During the oral hygiene treatment, recording ceased and the duration of the procedure was timed with a stopwatch.

FINAL PHASE. Gentle Teaching was used in all three daily sessions with Jeff to establish clinical control over self-injury. The average length of each use of the Gentle Teaching procedure was 6 seconds, based on an average of two uses per session. Oral hygiene was used in both sessions to control the mouthing of Jillian.

RESULTS

Jeff

Figure 1 shows the occurrence of head banging and bonding across all experimental phases. Jeff's average rate of head banging during Baseline 1 was 22% and decreased to 8% during the no-treatment control condition during Baseline 2. Head banging decreased to 7% during task training in the Baseline 2 phase, but this rate was not clinically different from the no-treatment control condition. Head banging continued to decrease under both the treatment and the control conditions in the Alternating Treatments 1 phase, with equal reductions being evident under Gentle Teaching and visual screening. Head banging decreased substantially (to 1%) with the introduction of Gentle Teaching alone in two of the three daily sessions, but it increased during the no-treatment control condition to 9%. Head banging was maintained at near-zero levels under Gentle Teaching in the final phase when Gentle Teaching was used during all three daily sessions.

Jeff engaged in low levels of bonding during Baseline 1 (6%) and the no-treatment control condition in Baseline 2 (7%). Bonding decreased during Baseline 2 when the task training condition was in effect (2%) and decreased further across all conditions during the Alternating Treatments 1 phase when the effects of Gentle Teaching and visual screening were compared. It increased again during Alternating Treatments 2 phase, with the no-treatment control condition showing the highest level (7%). As shown in Figure 1, bonding increased to 5% during the final phase when Gentle Teaching was used across all three daily sessions.

Jeff's screaming occurred at a moderate but variable level (13%) during Baseline 1 and increased 16% during the no-treatment control condition in Baseline 2. Screaming was at its worst during one of the task training conditions in this phase, reaching an average of about 27% of the sessions. There was a differential effect on screaming when visual screening and Gentle Teaching procedures were used for head banging, with less screaming occurring during the visual screening sessions. Further reductions in screaming occurred during the Alternating Treatments 2 phase when Gentle Teaching was used in two of the three daily sessions. Screaming remained at low levels during the final phase, but became more variable across days.

Jeff did not engage in any on-task behavior during Baseline 1 or during the no-treatment control condition of Baseline 2. On-task behavior increased during Baseline 2 to very low levels (1%) when task training was provided. It

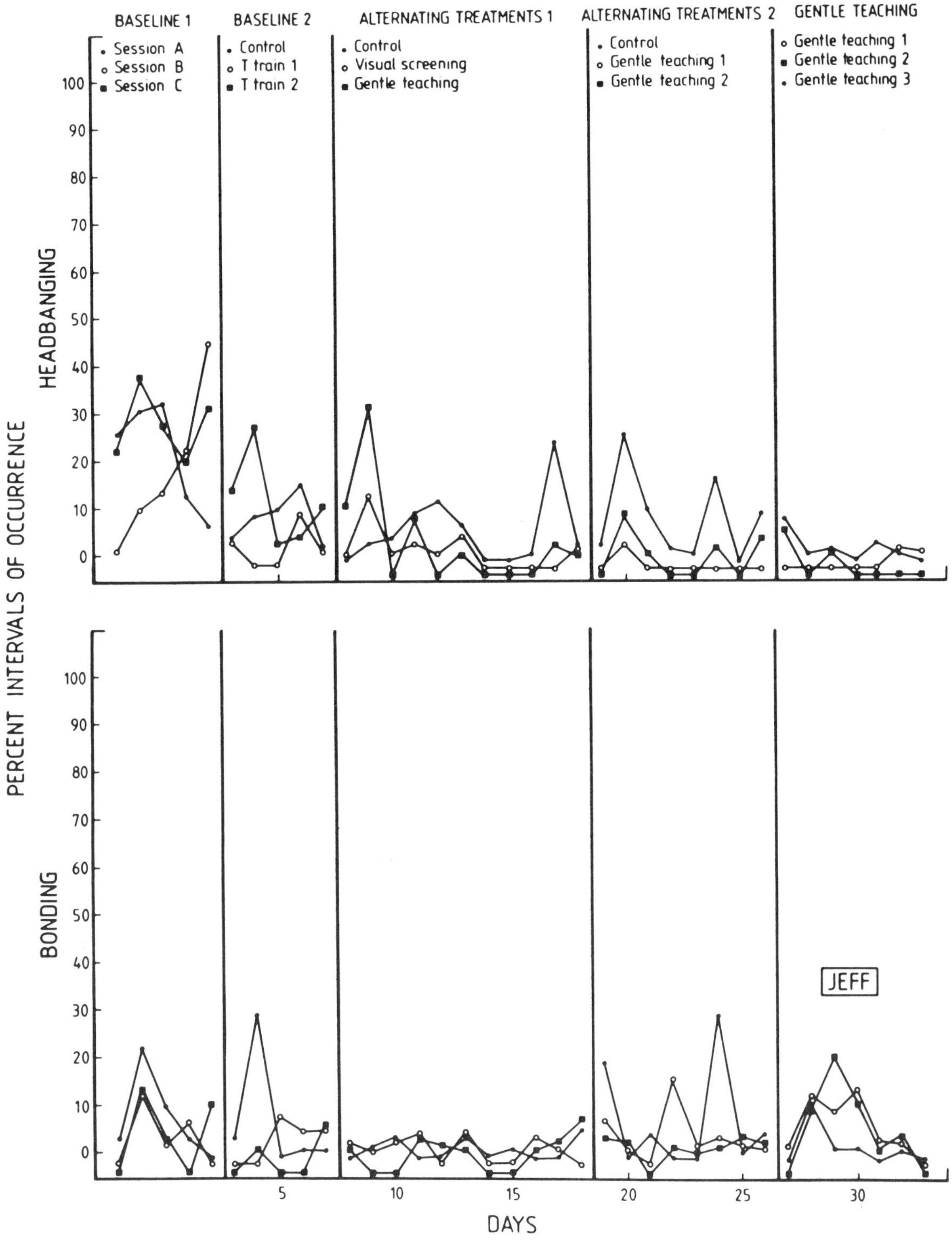

Figure 1: Percentage of intervals of occurrence of headbanging and bonding behavior across experimental phases by Jeff.

gradually increased under both the visual screening (9%) and Gentle Teaching (10%) procedures during the Alternating Treatments 1 phase. Further increases were noted in the Alternating Treatments 2 phase when Gentle Teaching (21%) was used during two of the three daily sessions. Little change was noted in the no-treatment control condition until the last phase when on-task behavior reached an average of about 26% across the three daily sessions.

Task training was introduced during Baseline 2 and was required throughout the rest of the study. Jeff required task training between 45% to 75% of the sessions across the two treatment conditions. There were no differential effects of the two treatment conditions on the level of task training required during the Alternating Treatments 1 condition.

Jillian

Figure 2 shows the percentage of intervals of occurrence of mouthing and bonding across all experimental phases. Jillian's average rate of mouthing during Baseline 1 was 48% and about 41% during the no-treatment control condition in Baseline 2. Mouthing decreased to an average of 32% during Baseline 2 when task training was in effect during two of the three daily sessions. No differential effects on mouthing were evident when Gentle Teaching and visual screening procedures were used contingent on the behavior. Not only did the occurrence of mouthing fail to decrease, but it showed a marked increasing trend during the last three sessions. When oral hygiene procedures were used instead, the occurrence of mouthing decreased to 6% of the sessions. There was a moderate decrease in mouthing in the no-treatment control condition, but it still occurred during 20% of the sessions. The occurrence of mouthing decreased even further (to 3%) when oral hygiene was used during both sessions in the final phase.

Bonding occurred at clinically insignificant levels during the first three phases and not at all when oral hygiene was used.

Jillian did not engage in on-task behavior throughout the study except for the last phase when she was on-task for less than 2% of the sessions. Jillian required task training at a variable level, ranging from 42% to 64% of the sessions across phases.

DISCUSSION

Results of the present study show few clinically significant differences in the effectiveness of Gentle Teaching and visual screening. This was true for both the reduction of targeted behaviors and for bonding. Contrary to the findings in previous studies (Jordan et al., 1989; Singh & Jones, 1989), the two procedures appeared to be equally effective with one subject and ineffective with the other.

Jeff

Both Gentle Teaching and visual screening were equally effective in reducing SIB to near-zero levels when compared to the baseline and a no-treatment control condition. Following the least restrictive model, Gentle Teaching was selected as the treatment of choice for the final two phases of the study; Jeff's self-injury remained at low levels during these phases.

Prior to treatment, the therapists and staff hypothesized that Jeff's head banging was maintained by both social attention and avoidance behavior. Jeff's head banging was frequently accompanied by screaming, crying, and whining. His behavior during baseline and the treatment sessions appeared to support this hypothesis. In addition, Jeff engaged in a number of other behaviors during the baseline and no-treatment control conditions, including sleeping and stereotypy.

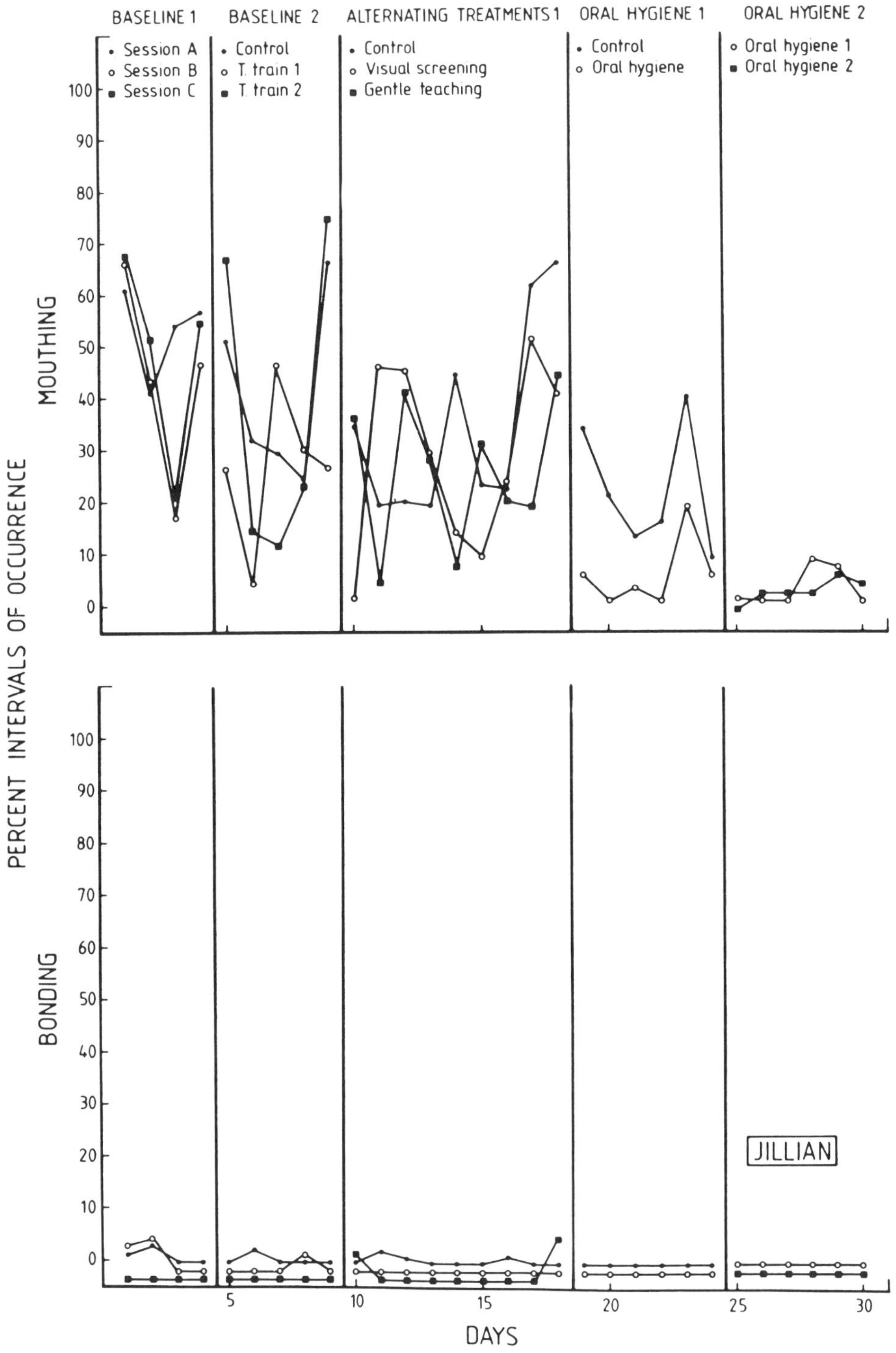

Figure 2: Percentage of intervals of occurrence of mouthing and bonding behavior across experimental phases by Jillian.

Staff observed that Jeff would head bang and scream when he heard voices outside the door, and also when a therapist was in the room. This behavior occurred for the most part during Baseline 1 and tended to decrease across treatment phases. The therapists hypothesized that Jeff's need for social attention had been met during the treatment conditions, and that this was responsible for the observed decrease in his head banging during the control condition.

It was also noted that during treatment sessions Jeff was less likely to head bang and/or scream in the first of the three daily treatment sessions and would tend to show avoidance behavior in the following sessions. As biking was his age-appropriate task requirement, he would try to avoid riding the bike by head banging and screaming when he was led to it. However, as soon as the therapist released his hand or he was free to get off the bike, he would immediately cease head banging and screaming.

Both on-task and task training conditions tended to be inversely related to screaming and head banging. When head banging stabilized at near-zero levels, on-task and task training behaviors increased and stabilized at their highest levels.

There were no differential effects of Gentle Teaching and visual screening on bonding. In both treatment conditions, bonding occurred at near-zero levels. The highest levels of bonding occurred during the baseline and no-treatment control condition.

Jillian

The results showed that visual screening and Gentle Teaching did not have a clinically significant effect on mouthing when compared to a no-treatment control and task training conditions. Mouthing was reduced to moderate levels but did not stabilize under both treatment conditions. When an alternative procedure, oral hygiene, was introduced, there was a dramatic reduction in mouthing which was maintained at near-zero levels thereafter. Generalization to the control condition also occurred, with mouthing decreasing to substantially lower levels. In addition, on-task behavior emerged for the first time, once mouthing was reduced, to near-zero levels in the final phase.

As with Jeff, no differential effects of Gentle Teaching and visual screening were observed in Jillian's bonding. Indeed, bonding did not occur at all with Gentle Teaching and only occurred during 1% of the sessions with visual screening.

Fulcher (1984) has suggested that visual screening may be effective only in treating external forms of self-injury, such as that displayed by Jeff. He suggested that mouthing, pica, and rumination, all of which are internal/ingestion types of self-injury, may not be treatable with visual screening. However, data to the contrary are available showing excellent control of such behaviors with visual screening (e.g., Singh & Winton, 1984). It is more likely that treatments are differentially effective given specific motivations for the problem behavior (Repp, Singh, Olinger, & Olson, in press).

On the contrary, the proponents of Gentle Teaching do not make any such distinctions, as they have reported success with 540 consecutive cases with its use (Casey, McGee, Stark, & Menolascino, 1985). However, empirical support for this claim is lacking, and no data from methodologically rigorous studies have been published that show that Gentle Teaching is effective regardless of the motivation for the problem behavior. We have predicted elsewhere that Gentle Teaching will be most successful with those clients whose behavior is motivated by social attention (Jordan et al., 1988). Indeed, it is difficult to see how Gentle Teaching will be effective with those behaviors that are reinforced by automatically produced interoceptive perceptual reinforcers (Lovaas, Newsom, & Hickman, 1987), or self-injury that is neurobiologically based (Harris, in press; Lewis, Baumeister, & Mailman, 1987).

It can be argued by the proponents of Gentle Teaching that the methods used in the present study did not meet the requirements of their procedure. For example, it can be argued that the daily 30-minute session of Gentle Teaching may have been too short. Menolascino and McGee (1983) have recommended 60-to 90-minute daily sessions for persons with severe or profound mental retardation who engage in self-injury. While this would not have been experimentally practical, it must be remembered that Gentle Teaching was successful in treating Jeff's self-injury to near-zero levels with only the daily half-hour sessions.

In addition, it can be argued that Gentle Teaching was unsuccessful because the therapists were required to carry out both the Gentle Teaching *and* visual screening procedures. This might have jeopardized the development of bonding, the goal of Gentle Teaching, due to the aversive nature of visual screening. However, this would not explain why Gentle Teaching was successful for Jeff, despite the absence of bonding. In future studies, researchers might consider using a multiple baseline across settings (or subjects) design to evaluate the effectiveness of Gentle Teaching without having the confound of an aversive procedure.

The present study does not confirm McGee's assumptions regarding bonding. McGee (1985b) has claimed that individuals who engage in SIB have not bonded, but bonding occurred during baseline for both subjects. McGee (1985b) also claimed that although punishment procedures may suppress SIB behavior, the individuals will not bond. While Jillian did not show any instances of bonding during the visual screening and oral hygiene conditions, Jeff displayed similar levels of bonding during the visual screening and Gentle Teaching treatment conditions.

It might be argued further that the reason Gentle Teaching was not effective in Jillian's case was due to the near-zero levels of bonding by her throughout the study. However, this is a circular argument, and it may well be that inadequacies of the Gentle Teaching procedures precluded the development of bonding. The definition of bonding used in this study may have been too strict. However, other examples of bonding include eye contact, which was impractical to measure in this study, and teasing, which is difficult to define. Handholding was excluded because it was often used to get demands met, and handshaking was excluded as it was viewed as an artificial display of affection. Therefore, smiling and touching were the only behaviors used to measure bonding. A more clearly operationalized definition of bonding is necessary for further analysis of client bonding.

In sum, although Gentle Teaching and visual screening were equally effective in reducing one subject's self-injurious behavior, both treatments failed to treat the self-injury of another. It is clear that due to the nature of the experimental design used, studies of comparative treatments will have methodological weaknesses. However, this should not preclude attempts to evaluate a method of treatment that appears to be in line with the current zeitgeist for the humane and benevolent care of persons with developmental disabilities.

NOTES

Preparation of this chapter was supported by the Commonwealth Institute for Child and Family Studies.

We wish to thank the nursing staff at Templeton Hospital and Training School for their generous assistance throughout the study. Special thanks are due to Jim Marshal, Eric Lundin, and Jenny Jordan.

Gay Tyler-Merrick, Lorinda Creighton, and Joy Rogers served as therapists. We also wish to thank Peggy Smith and Judy Singh for their editorial input.

REFERENCES

Barlow, D.H., & Hersen, M. (1984). *Single case experimental designs.* New York: Pergamon Press.

Barlow, D.H., & Hayes, S.C. (1979). Alternating treatments design: One strategy for comparing the effects of two treatments in a single subject. *Journal of Applied Behavior Analysis, 12*, 199-210.

Brown, L., Branston, M.B., Hamre-Nietupski, S., Pumpian, I., Certo, N., & Gruenewald, L. (1979). A strategy for developing chronological age-appropriate and functional curricular content for severely handicapped adolescents and young adults. *The Journal of Special Education, 13*, 81-90.

Casey, K., McGee, J., Stark, J., & Menolascino, F. (1985). *A community-based system for the mentally retarded: The ENCOR experience*. Lincoln, NE: University of Nebraska Press.

Demetral, G.D., & Lutzker, J.R. (1980). The parameters of facial screening in treating self-injurious behavior. *Research in Severe Developmental Disabilities, 1*, 261-277.

Fulcher, G. (1984). A review of self-injurious behavior. *Australia and New Zealand Journal of Developmental Disabilities, 10*, 51-67.

Harris, J.C. (in press). Neurobiological factors in self-injurious behavior. In J. Luiselli, J.L. Matson, & N.N. Singh, (Eds.), *Assessment, analysis, and treatment of self-injury.* New York: Springer-Verlag.

Grossman, H.J. (1983). *Classification in mental retardation*. Washington: American Association on Mental Deficiency.

Jordan, J., Singh, N.N., & Repp, A.C. (1989). An evaluation of gentle teaching and visual screening in the reduction of stereotypy. *Journal of Applied Behavior Analysis, 22*, 9-22.

Kazdin, A.E. (1982). *Single-case research designs: Methods for clinical and applied settings*. New York: Oxford University Press.

Lewis, M.H., Baumeister, A.A., & Mailman, R.B. (1987). A neurobiological alternative to the perceptual reinforcement hypothesis of stereotyped behavior: A commentary on "self-stimulatory behavior and perceptual reinforcement." *Journal of Applied Behavior Analysis, 20*, 253-258.

Lovaas, O.I., Newsom, C., & Hickman, C. (1987). Self-stimulatory behavior and perceptual reinforcement. *Journal of Applied Behavior Analysis, 20*, 45-68.

McGee, J.J. (1985a). Examples of the use of gentle teaching. *Mental Handicap in New Zealand, 9*, 11-20.

McGee, J.J. (1985b). Bonding as the goal of teaching. *Mental Handicap in New Zealand, 9*, 5-10.

McGee, J.J. (1986). *Gentle approach: A four part video series on gentle teaching*. Omaha, NE: Media Resource Center, Meyer Children's Rehabilitation Institute.

McGee, J.J. (1988a). Issues related to applied behavioral analysis. In J.A. Stark, F.J. Menolascino, M.H. Albarelli, & V.C. Gray (Eds.), *Mental retardation and mental health*, (pp. 203-212). New York: Springer-Verlag.

McGee, J.J. (1988b). Ethical issues of aversive techniques: A response to

Thompon, Gardner, and Baumeister. In J.A. Stark, F.J. Menolascino, M.H. Albarelli, & V.C Gray (Eds.), *Mental retardation and mental health*, (pp. 218-228). New York: Springer-Verlag.

McGee, J.J., Menolascino, F.J., Hobbs, D.C., & Menousek, P.E. (1987). *Gentle teaching*. New York: Human Sciences Press.

McGonigle, J.J., Duncan, D., Cordisco, L., & Barrett, P. (1982). Visual screening: An alternative method for reducing stereotypic behaviors. *Journal of Applied Behavior Analysis, 15*, 461-467.

Menolascino, F.J., & McGee, J.J. (1983). Persons with severe mental retardation and behavioral challenges: From disconnectedness to human engagement. *Journal of Psychiatric Treatment and Evaluation, 5*, 187-193.

Mudford, O.C. (1985). Treatment selection in behavior reduction: Gentle teaching versus the least intrusive treatment model. *Australia and New Zealand Journal of Developmental Disabilities, 10*, 265-270.

Paisey, T.J.H., Whitney, R.B., & Moore, J. (1989). Person-treatment interactions across nonaversive response deceleration procedures for self-injury: A case study of effects and side effects. *Behavioral Residential Treatment, 4*, 69-88.

Reid, D.H., Parsons, M.B., McCarn, J.E., Green, C.W., Phillips, J.F., & Schepis, M.M. (1985). Providing a more appropriate education for severely handicapped persons: Increasing and validating functional classroom tasks. *Journal of Applied Behavior Analysis, 18*, 289-301.

Repp, A.C., Singh, N.N., Olinger, E., & Olson, D.R. (in press). A review of the use of functional analyses to test causes of self-injurious behavior: Rationale, current status, and future directions. *Journal of Mental Deficiency Research*.

Rojahn, J., & Marshburn, E. (in press). Facial screening and visual occlusion. In J. Luiselli, J.L. Matson, & N.N. Singh, (Eds.), *Assessment, analysis, and treatment of self-injury*. New York: Springer-Verlag.

Singh, N.N. (1980). The effects of facial screening on infant self-injury. *Journal of Behavior Therapy and Experimental Psychiatry, 11*, 131-134.

Singh, N.N. (1983). Behavioral dimensions of the de Lange syndrome: Attribution of mystique and a question of cause and effect. *Journal of Mental Deficiency Research, 27*, 237-238.

Singh, N.N., Beale, I.L., & Dawson, M.J. (1981). Duration of facial screening and suppression of self-injurious behavior: Analysis using an alternating treatments design. *Behavioral Assessment, 3*, 411-420.

Singh, N.N., & Jones, L.J. (1989). *Comparative effects of gentle teaching and visual screening on self-injurious behavior.* Paper presented at the American Psychological Association Convention, New Orleans.

Singh, N.N., Manning, P.J., & Angell, M.J. (1982). Effects of an oral hygiene punishment procedure on chronic rumination and collateral behavior in monozygous twins. *Journal of Applied Behavior Analysis, 15*, 309-314.

Singh, N.N., & Millichamp, C.J. (1987). Independent and social play in profoundly mentally retarded adults: Training, maintenance, generalization, and long-term follow-up. *Journal of Applied Behavior Analysis, 20*, 23-34.

Singh, N.N., & Winton, A.S.W. (1984). Effects of a screening procedure on pica and collateral behaviors. *Journal of Behavior Therapy and Experimental Psychiatry, 15*, 59-65.

Singh, N.N., Winton, A.S.W., & Dawson, M.J. (1982). The suppression of antisocial behavior by facial screening using multiple baseline and alternation treatments design. *Behavior Therapy, 13,* 511-520.

Thomas, E.J. (1984). *Designing interventions for the helping profession*. Beverly Hills, CA: Sage Publications.

CHAPTER

15

RESPONSIBILITY AND QUALITY OF LIFE

Jay S. Birnbrauer
Murdoch University

If contingencies of reinforcement are integral to socialization, then punishment and aversives are inevitable. This assertion is especially true when the aim is to maximize quality of life in social, nonsegregated settings. While positive reinforcement and non-reinforcement are essential for behavior change, they alone are not sufficient when persons are free to avoid lessons, free to leave the teaching environment, and when several are living and learning together. Positive reinforcement also presupposes deprivations. Environments of noncontingent plenty are the circumstances in which punishment and negative reinforcement are the only remaining means of teaching. But, of course, such environments will not last. The more fundamental issue of the development of responsibility needs to be resolved. The quality of our lives is necessarily diminished to the extent that responsibility is not shared by all -- caretakers, advisors, advocates, and clients.

A child spills her milk down her front and on the floor. Joan, a caretaker, says, "Never mind," calmly fills another glass, shows the child how to use two hands, instructs her to be careful, and cleans up the mess. Maureen, on the other hand, says, "Look what you have done, naughty girl!", fills another glass, encourages use of two hands, and cleans up the mess. Diane reprimands, says that there shall be no more milk, and cleans up the mess. Melissa likewise says "no more milk," and, in addition, prompts the child to clean up the mess. Shirley says, "We'll have to clean that up, won't we? And then see about getting you some more." The child is prompted to help and does, sort of; then she is given a second glass, is shown how to use two hands, and is told to be careful.

Incidents like this are replayed at dinner tables with great regularity, and in the eyes of many are trivial and should not be a problem. Yet, frequently they do escalate into aversive exchanges and outcomes that are incorrect and completely devoid of any consideration of effects on the offender and others in the setting in the short or long term. In some homes, and certainly in the same home on subsequent occurrences (depending upon who is present, the age of the person, the individual's disabilities, and the kind of day they have been having to that point), such incidents will culminate in harsher words and actions such as smacks, spankings, and being sent away from the table. In other words, how such incidents are resolved is determined by the caretaker's social environment, as well as the child's response to the initial reaction, plus whatever training the caretaker may have had and the proximity of supervision.

In this debate about aversives, we give too little attention to the fact that the behavior of all parties -- client or child, caretaker (parent, teacher, direct care worker, work supervisor, and so on), siblings, co-residents or co-workers, and consultants and experts -- is subject to the same laws of behavior and requirements of community living. Thus, while experts argue, committees meet, and we write papers, caretakers and clients in the meantime continuously influence each other's behavior for better or worse. What committees decide and I write here has trivial effects in comparison. The debate also proceeds as if *any* of the ways recommended to handle incidents is free of cost and other aversive aspects to one or more of the persons present.

The debate misses the important points completely. The choice is not between using or not using aversives. The choices are: (1) Shall we use aversives correctly and advantageously to punish behavior or pretend that they do not occur? (2) What type of punishment do we use? (3) Whose behavior is to be punished or, more correctly, who shall live under continuing aversive conditions? (4) Which objectives are most important in the short and long term? The underlying solution is to institute and maintain contingencies of reinforcement that maximize positives and minimize negatives for each member of the group. Achieving this goal is no mean task; it is in the realm of dreams and fantasy. It is likely that the enormity of designing and maintaining good teaching-living environments explains our having become entangled in the wrong questions which, in turn, has compounded the problems.

Often we hear "if only caretakers would do as they have been taught," and I agree that better training and, more importantly, better maintenance conditions are needed. It seems to me, though, that systematic training in empirically proven methods and principles is decreasing. Indeed, in some circles the suggestion that empirical data be heeded and gathered is treated with disdain. The result is that caretakers receive inconsistent and incorrect advice. These are not the circumstances conducive to their behaving positively, unstintingly, and consistently with clients.

Psychologists and other team members do not agree on best answers; however, we must agree upon a method for selecting and evaluating options that not only protects individuals but also permits our learning. Certainly, legislating for or against options is not the method to choose. Nor is there a place for committees of uninformed persons and decisions based upon the good will and common sense of caretakers. By acquiescing to arguments other than valid evidence, we preempt conducting the research that is needed and we fail to model appropriate behavior.

We will acquiesce because social-political realities require that; but, our responsibility remains to inform, to monitor the effects of decisions, and to continue to work toward more systematic decision making processes. Sometimes I think that we have fallen into the trap of making a virtue out of necessity and have re-defined what may be good public relations and politics as behavioral principles.

Problems are compounded from another source: namely, defining problems, choosing objectives, and establishing their priority. Often we don't agree that there is a problem and sometimes people even ask: "Whose problem is it?" In my example, is there a problem because spilled milk has to be cleaned up, or because glasses cost money and effort to replace? Is there a problem because the child or someone else forgoes milk as the supply of money or milk is limited? Or, is it because the client will be excluded naturally from social situations if such behavior continues? Or, is it because the incident disrupts what is meant to be a pleasant meal together? Regardless of our answer, socialized caretakers will do something about the mess, if nothing else, and whatever is done has aversive effects on someone in the group.

Is it in the best interests of persons to be excluded from sharing in the costs and pain their behavior causes? I think not, unless they are going to live in isolation. In families and communities, problems are co-owned.

If living-learning environments are to change in the desired directions, discussion should be brought back to the factors necessary for the maintenance of individual *and* group behaviors. Framing issues in the form of "rights," "least restrictive," or "least intrusive," "normalization" and "acceptability" with only one group member in mind is shortsighted. In the past, the balance was tipped against individuals with disabilities and offenders. They were placed in institutions where protection, order, and our convenience were paramount. "Quality of life," "least restrictive environment," and other such concepts were unheard of, but were applied implicitly to families, caretakers, and the rest of us. Now in our effort to correct the balance, and correct it we should, we may have gone too far. Long-term objectives for the clients are important, but so are the immediate and long-term effects upon others in the clients' social environments. We need to get the pendulum to come to rest at the midpoint.

As a psychologist, I understand my responsibility to be (1) to conduct a careful assessment of appropriate and problematic behavior and the environments in which they occur; (2) to select methods of fostering and maintaining prosocial behavior and reacting to aversive incidents in ways that will be most effective in (a) decreasing the likelihood of recurrence, and (b) generalizing to other situations in which the behavior causes inconvenience, loss, and danger to others and to the client; and (3) to arrange a monitoring and data collection system to guide decision making after the program has been implemented. These steps apply no matter what names are attached to the methods chosen.

I have not included notions of "least restrictive," "least intrusive," and "acceptability," because they apply only when choosing among alternatives with similar probabilities of success. Almost without saying they enter the decision making tree last. We must also accurately estimate the undesirable effects of implementing programs that do not succeed; failing does make problems more difficult to solve later.

We should cease behaving as if caretakers have boundless supplies of time, energy, and resistance to extinction and punishment. Given that they do not, planning priorities should be placed upon instituting and maintaining contingencies of reinforcement, both positive and negative, so that (a) the need for punishment is diminished, (b) the unsystematic use of aversives is diminished, and (c) aversives are employed only in contexts that maximize effectiveness in the shortest period of time.

There are many situations in which the least intrusive method measured against the duration of treatment, the effects upon others, and the morale of caretakers will be one that includes punishment. Ironically, those situations increase as we become more concerned about clients' quality of life, which I take to include freedom, and that, in turn, requires individual responsibility.

But we do have genuine alternatives, and are our concerns about punishment well-founded? Some advocate benign environments; but, completely benign environments will not teach new repertoires or develop existing ones. All living environments that go beyond merely controlling or stopping unwanted behavior must include non-reinforcement of some client behavior all of the time and some behavior some of the time. Non-reinforcement, if discriminable, is a situation people will avoid; signaled periods of non-reinforcement are called time-out and are frequently used to punish behavior; i.e., decrease some behavior. When non-reinforcement is a sudden change in program rather than part of a continuing shaping program, it elicits negative emotional behavior. Aggressive and destructive behaviors often ensue. Non-reinforcement is painful to the individual, and it can be said to be cruel (as many parents and teachers will have been told by their children) although no blows have been struck.

Those unwanted effects of non-reinforcement, however, are entirely avoidable by anticipating the longer term and by fading in noncontingent (free) access to all reinforcers. Moreover, unwanted effects are temporary, just as they are with punishment, when rules are clear and alternatives are reinforced. Indeed, no enduring harmful effects of punishment, when used properly, have ever been documented. Proper use means placing highest priority on contingencies of positive reinforcement, not unconditionally benign environments.

I am reminded of a youth, called George. He was about 14 years old, classified as severely retarded, mute, and strong enough to have taught all of the staff to respect his signals that he did not want to do something. He was residing on a special unit in which the staff had been trained to reinforce with socials and tokens, to give instructions and assign tasks commensurate with current functioning level, and to ignore inappropriate behavior that did not represent a threat. A warning followed by brief exclusionary time-out if necessary was employed in the event of dangerous behavior. In the interest of staff safety, time-out was not attempted with George. Consequently, he was excluded -- some might say he chose to exclude himself -- from many of the opportunities for learning and recreation that were available. His parents visited only infrequently and were too afraid to take him home. They were resigned to the situation and George showed no signs of being concerned about the quality of his life. Given his well-being, there was no reason in the present for any further intervention.

At the same time, there was nothing in his treatment plan to teach him alternatives to physical aggression when frustrated; nor was accommodating him likely to last indefinitely. So, we implemented exclusionary time-out about 5 times; thereafter, George's progress on all fronts was remarkable.

In making this decision, we chose long-term objectives, and we chose a method the literature showed was effective in the context of rich reinforcement contingencies (which was the case) and for children who preferred the company of others (which George did). Undoubtedly, other interventions would have worked; indeed, continuing with no intervention might have worked. The anecdote after all is an AB study. We considered also that special concessions for George meant depriving his peers of opportunities and attention, an option which is often unwittingly taken. Finally, we had to consider relief staff who did not know how to read George's gestures or had not experienced the results of calling his bluff.

Some who agree that completely benign environments are neither possible nor desirable argue that natural contingencies, verbal explanations, modeling, and other procedures that are acceptable and respectable will suffice. They are sufficient with clients who have learned the prerequisites of these methods, but these clients are not the ones whose behavior challenges us. The people whose behavior is of great concern require planned interventions and, more often than not, *unnatural* reinforcement programs.

Another difficulty with this position is the concept of natural reinforcement. In most teaching situations, there are no natural consequences that are differential. Consider, for example, teaching a child to play a musical instrument or to read and do sums. What are the immediate natural consequences of learning these skills? Of what consequence is it to have clean hands, brushed teeth, or to be in bed by 7 p.m.? So, we use social reinforcers (or I should say, social reactions that we hope will be positively reinforcing) in the form of approval, praise, hugs and kisses, opportunities to participate in preferred activities, and so on. Such consequences are commonly used and generally acceptable, but there's nothing natural about many of them and they do require being withheld until the desired behavior occurs.

The natural consequences of offensive behavior are usually positive for the offender and only negative to others. In the spilled milk example, the only naturally aversive consequences are the loss of milk and possibly having a wet shirt. But, caring people are likely to interfere with both of those. I am not suggesting we should not. I am merely pointing out that in our caring and protecting, natural negative consequences are not allowed to operate.

I will close where I began and summarize with "the problem" of how to deal with a client's milk spilling. Of the reactions listed, only one (Shirley's) deals with the incident presently in a way that considers teaching the child to be responsible for her actions in the future. Shirley attempted to use additional milk to reinforce cleaning up, but even this method could misfire because its success depends upon cleaning up and the accompanying attention being punishing. It also is problematic because it is the most time intensive procedure and thus diminishes attention to others in the group. It also may impinge on the caretaker's own meal break and that of colleagues. Generally speaking, the natural contingencies affecting the caretaker's behavior are quite likely to work against consistent use of this alternative.

Joan's approach, on the other hand, is the easiest. It takes little time and avoids aversive reactions that might be obtained by either depriving the child of more milk or making her clean up the mess. One also could argue that the caretaker was not giving social attention to the behavior and, thus, if spilling the milk was attention seeking, Joan's reaction constituted an extinction trial. Given that this analysis is correct, that intervention in no way makes matters worse and permits the caretaker to attend to other duties and the needs of others in her care. Learning to clean up can be taught at another time. Lessons taught at other times, however, do not teach responsible behavior.

Maureen's alternative, which is perhaps the most common, is the worst of the lot. It demonstrates inconsistent verbal and motor reactions on the caretaker's part and thus teaches that reprimands have no meaning. Since the child received both attention and more milk, nothing instructive for the child would have been accomplished. It is common because it is maintained by others in the social setting; it looks like something is being done with the least amount of interference.

The approaches by Diane and Melissa illustrate the several ways deprivations and aversives are used unwisely. Neither provides a second trial of milk drinking, and both might evoke tantrums and escalate the situation into either the adult's conceding or ending the crisis with a harsher penalty, none of which teaches the child anything socially useful. While Melissa attempts to have the child clean up, she does so without the assistance of a reinforcer. Thus, it is appropriate to describe this method as "making" the child clean up the mess.

In conclusion, my argument is that it is to glib to dismiss or accept interventions on the grounds of their being aversive or not, or intrusive or not, acceptable or not, or natural or unnatural. The following questions have greater priority: What are the short- and long-term objectives? Whose rights and quality of life are uppermost? Which patterns of caretaker behavior are likely to be sustained by social environments including their clients?

What should and ought to be is not what is and will be. The best approach to preventing improper and unnecessary use of aversives is sound and careful instruction in contingencies of reinforcement and providing social environments for caretakers that will sustain responsible and appropriate behavior.

CHAPTER

16

GENTLE TEACHING AND THE PRACTICE OF HUMAN INTERDEPENDENCE: A PRELIMINARY GROUP STUDY OF 15 PERSONS WITH SEVERE BEHAVIORAL DISORDERS AND THEIR CAREGIVERS

John J. McGee and Liliana Gonzalez
Creighton University

Considerable attention has been given to behavioral interventions designed to decrease aberrant behavior in individuals with mental retardation. Recent reviews have evaluated procedures for the treatment of self-injury (Johnson & Baumeister, 1978; Favell et al., 1982; Gorman-Smith & Matson, 1985; Rincover 1986); aggression and disruption (Fehrenbach & Thelen, 1982; Lennox, Miltenberger, Spengler, & Erfanian, 1988); and self-stimulation and stereotypies (Gorman-Smith & Matson, 1985; LaGrow & Repp, 1984; Schraeder, Shaull, & Elmore, 1983). These strategies encompass a wide range of aversive and nonaversive procedures. Yet, in an analysis of punishment procedures, Guess, Helmstetter, Turnbull, and Knowlton, (1987) urged further research in the area of nonaversive interventions so that severe and even life-threatening behaviors might be more effectively and non-intrusively modified.

Research related to intervention strategies that focus on the communicative dimension of behaviors has offered new insights into their nature and possible remediation. The function of maladaptive behavior has been pointed out by Donnellan, Mirenda, Mesaros, and Fassbender (1984) and Carr and Durand (1986). Self-injury has been studied as having an escape function maintained by negative reinforcement (Carr, Newsom, & Binkoff, 1976) or a reinforcing function maintained through its sensory consequences (Rincover & Devany, 1982). Self-stimulation and stereotypic behaviors also have been analyzed relative to their reinforcing qualities (Hung, 1978; Lovass, Newsom, & Hickman, 1987; Rincover & Devany, 1982) and their function as an escape from aversive conditions (Durand & Carr, 1987). Aggression and other disruptive behaviors also have been examined for their escape and avoidance functions (Iwata, 1987). Although their communicative function has become more clearly established, aberrant behavioral patterns have been shown often to be multiply determined (Wahler, 1976; Carr, 1977), such as through a combination of organic factors and positive reinforcement (Carr & McDowell, 1980).

Beyond the communicative significance, little research has pointed toward the interactional nature of behavioral change and the role that caregivers play in this change process. However, Bateson (1951) and Watzlawick et al. (1967) pointed out that relationships are based on either control or reciprocity, and concluded that those based on complementary conditions result in healthy emotional states. Sluzki and Beavin (1965) urged the study of the factors that constitute reciprocal relationships. In the care of persons with mental retardation, little research emphasis has been given to the analysis of dyadic relationships, even though such studies might broaden and deepen the current understanding of the communicative nature of aberrant behaviors, both in relation to persons with special needs and their caregivers. Ainsworth and Bell (1979) examined the formation of affection in dyads through the bonding process, and Sroufe and Waters (1976) indicated that bonded relationships were observable through mutual contact seeking and signaling behaviors such as hugs, smiles, vocalizations, maintained eye contact, and reaching out. Although these studies have centered on mother-infant relationships, they might offer potential benefit in the analysis of caregiving interactional patterns at any age. By identifying, defining, and evaluating the nature and role of dyadic interactions, we might be able to isolate those caregivers' interactions that facilitate the expression of reciprocal relationships in persons with special needs.

Gentle Teaching (McGee, Menolascino, Hobbs, & Menousek, 1987; McGee, 1988) analyzes behavior from an interactional perspective, and asks caregivers to identify and significantly decrease any dominative interactions and to adopt or substantially increase value-centered ones. Its purpose is to help marginalized persons turn from feelings of apartness to those of union expressed through participatory interactions and human interdependence. It requires caregivers to initiate and establish new interactional patterns based on unconditional and authentic valuing.

METHODOLOGY

This preliminary group study evaluated the effects of Gentle Teaching in an AB design among 15 individuals with clinical histories of multiple and severe behavioral problems reported as highly disruptive, destructive, or life-threatening. It made four assumptions: (a) The continuous delivery of noncontingent value-centered interactions is critical to the deceleration of target behaviors; (b) The meaning of these interactions can be taught even to those reported to be unresponsive to positive reinforcement; (c) The deceleration of the use of punishment, restraint, and other dominative interactions tends to remove the barriers that impede bonding, friendship, and interdependence; and (d) The concurrent acceleration of the caregiver's value-giving and warm assistance facilitates and leads to mutual and reciprocal prosocial relationships (McGee, 1988).

Subjects

The 15 persons who participated in this study (see Table 1) were referred by their parents or guardians due to the severity and refractory nature of their behavioral problems. Each had a diagnosis of mental retardation based on standardized intelligence tests. They included all levels of mental retardation and various allied developmental and emotional disorders, such as deafness, blindness, non-ambulation, cerebral palsy, epilepsy, autism, organic brain disorders, depression, and schizophrenia. They presented complex behaviors often described as life threatening or as dangerous to others. They bore stigmata such as scars, bruises, burns, scratches, tissue calcification, and detached retinas. Their average age was

22 years, with a range of 7 to 41 years. All had been involved in a range of nonaversive and aversive behavioral interventions. Most had been subjected to mechanical restraint devises, such as locked and masked helmets, and restraint chairs in which they were immobilized by their arms, legs, and stomachs; others had been involved in physical restraint procedures during times of aggression or self-injury. Other recent interventions had included seclusion, time-out, response cost, water mist sprayed in the face, overcorrection, verbal reprimands, and forced exercise. One child had been subjected to contingent electric shock for 18 months immediately prior to this study due to life-threatening self-injurious behavior. Based on case conferences, review of clinical records, and the inspection of programmatic charts, we found none of these interventions to have been successful.

Caregivers

Thirty caregivers participated in this study in their roles as parents, primary caregivers, or participants in a Gentle Teaching training program. Included along with parents and house parents were social workers, psychologists, and teachers. Their average number of years of formal education was 16, with a range of 10 to 22. Their average number of years of experience was 9, with a range of 2 to 25. Their average age was 37, with a range of 23 to 60 years. They reported prior training in behavior modification and had previously participated in aversive and nonaversive behavioral programs. Human rights standards were safeguarded for all participants, both caregivers and persons with mental retardation.

Settings

Both baseline and treatment occurred in natural environments and were conducted in structured and non-structured sessions. The same type of setting was used for each person. Activities used in the baseline conditions consisted of tasks that were described as routine parts of each person's individual program plans and were often age-inappropriate and limited in range (e.g., adults sorting sticks

Table 1: Subject Characteristics

Subject	Age	Level of MR	Primary Behavioral Patterns	Most Recent Prevalent Aversive Intervention
01	08	Moderate	SIB - Aggression	Forced Feeding and Time-out
02	37	Severe	Aggression - SIB	Seclusion and Social Reinforcement
03	40	Profound	SIB - Aggression	Restraint Chair, Forced Relaxation
04	39	Profound	SIB - Aggression	Restraint Chair
05	19	Severe	Aggression - SIB	Forced Relaxation and Visual Screening
06	07	Severe	SIB - Active Withdrawal	Restraint Chair
07	17	Profound	SIB - Passive Withdrawal	Locked Masked Helmet & Primary Reinforcement
08	07	Mild	Aggression - Active Withdrawal	Water Mist Spray and Token Economy
09	17	Mild	Aggression - SIB	Restraint Chair
10	34	Profound	SIB - Aggression	Time-Out and Token Economy
11	10	Mild	Aggression - SIB	Arm Tubes and Physical Restraint
12	07	Profound	SIB - Active Withdrawal	Seclusion
13	40	Severe	Aggression - Active Withdrawal	Overcorrection and Forced Relaxation
14	41	Severe	Aggression - SIB	Verbal Reprimands and Token Economy
15	08	Moderate	SIB - Aggression	Contingent Electric Shock and Mechanical Restraint

Table 2: Categories, Operational Definitions, and Examples: Caregiver Interactional Observation System (CIOS)

1. VALUE GIVING (VG). Physical (P), verbal (V), or gestural (G) caregiver interactions that convey non-contingent social approval and are expressed at any time with or without reference to how the individual is interacting. They appear to express sincere friendship, warmth, acceptance, and the desire to share. Typical examples include: smiles; nods of approval; signing "thumbs up;" warm eye contact; facial expressions appearing to express joy, pleasure, or approval; playful interactions; giving "five;" pats on the back; embraces, compliments such as "Good!" or "I like what you are doing!;" reflective commentaries related to the person or the caregiver in the form of story-telling or personal sharing, such as describing interests, relationships, or concerns related to the caregiver or the person.

2. RECIPROCITY ELICITING (RE). Verbal, gestural, or physical interactions on the part of the caregiver that appear to be specifically aimed at creating opportunities for the person to reciprocate valuing toward the caregiver so that the relationship might become mutual. They are intended to teach the person to receive and accept valuing as well as to reciprocate it. The caregiver seeks to evoke these valuing responses through words, gestures, or physical interactions. These depend on the caregiver's elicitation, not on the person's response. Typical examples include: extending one's hand as a signal for a handshake or one's arms outward as a signal for an embrace, touching the person's face as an indication to smile, placing one's hand in the person's for a handshake, placing the person's arms over one's shoulders for a hug, asking the person to smile, and soliciting verbal comments.

3. ASSISTING WARMLY (AW). Verbal, physical, or gestural caregiver interactions that enable the person to participate in tasks and activities with the caregiver, others, or alone. The primary purpose is to effectuate participation, not skill acquisition or task completion. The caregiver appears to express this helping relationship in a spirit of friendship and equality, and thereby diminishes any perception of an emotional or physical tug-of-war that might result in withdrawal, aggression, or self-injury. The expression of warmth is indicated in personalizing the assistance, helping the person start, being attuned to slight frustrations, working alongside the person, and disregarding the "functional level" of the person. The type and degree of assistance can change from moment to moment, since the central focus is on participation and its use as a vehicle for structured interactions with the caregiver. For example, if a caregiver says, "Let's start!" and the person screams and runs away, warm assistance would indicate that a less "forceful" prompt be used, such as accompanying individuals to wherever they might be doing the task with them. This variable is also accompanied by VG, VE, and when necessary, protective interactions. Although the type of warm assistance can change from moment to moment, other typical examples include prompting techniques, such as working side by side with the person, placing material in the person's hand, moving materials closer to signal an opportunity for initiation, passing materials to the person, insertingmaterials into the hand, working hand over hand, and verbally guiding the person through the task.

4. PROTECTING (PR). Verbal, physical, or gestural caregiver interactions used to prevent harm or disruption without immobilizing the person, and expressed in a warm, non-forceful manner. They are responses directly related to potentially harmful behaviors. They are brief and can be accompanied by VG, VE, and AW. Typical examples are: holding one's forearm out to block an attempt at hitting, placing one's hand between the person's forehead and a wall when self-injury is the intent, "shadowing" a person's movements as ongoing attempts at self-injury occur; i.e., moving one's arm(s) or hand(s) in unison with the person's attempts at injury, scooting objects away to prevent them from being thrown, and conveying soothing messages, such as, "Everything is fine. Nobody is going to hurt you."

5. ASSISTING DEMANDINGLY (AD). Verbal, physical, or gestural caregiver interactions intended to help the person initiate, engage in, or complete a task or activity. They are similar to AW in that they occur during tasks and activities; however, they appear to be focused on compliance, task performance, or skill acquisition. AW expresses a friendly and equal relationship with the person and the willingness of the caregiver to focus on mutual participation, whereas AD indicates a cold, intolerant, or distanced relationship, and the focus of the interaction is on the task, its correctness or orderliness, rather than on a flow of participation as in AW. The person's refusal to comply can result in the withholding of further instructions or social interactions for a fixed period of time, the repetition of instructions with no positive social interactions, or the escalation of the restrictiveness of the "assistance." Typical examples are: delivering verbal commands in a neutral or depersonalized tone; forceful physical movements, such as pulling a person's hand to accomplish a task; graduated guidance when it results in an emotional or physical tug-of-war; forced physical movements, such as taking a person by the chin and ordering, "Look at me!;" sternly pointing; firm or mechanistic instructions, such as telling the person, "Hands down!;" and verbally or gesturally warning or threatening the person.

6. RESTRAINT AND PUNISHMENT (RP). Restraint consists of any physical or verbal caregiver interactions or environmental arrangements that might partially or totally immobilize the person, whether done immediately after the display of a particular target behavior or as an ongoing part of the person's life condition through restrictive devices or settings. Punishment consists of the presentation of aversive events or the removal of positive events after a response. Typical examples of restraint as an ongoing life condition are the use of tubes on arms, mittens on hands, helmets, straitjackets, locked wards, seclusion, and the use of chemicals. Typical examples of its use as an immediate consequence can be any of the above, plus a

Table 2 (cont.)

range of traditional procedures, such as physical holds and verbal demands, such as ordering someone, "Go to your room!" The use of punishment includes procedures such as electric shock, white noise, slapping, pinching, placing noxious substances in the mouth, verbal reprimands, water squirted in the face, forced body movements, contingent exercise, contingent restraint, restitution, overcorrection, visual screening, and time-out.

Table 3: Categories, Operational Definitions, and Examples: Person's Interactional Observation System (PIOS)

1. VALUE RECIPROCATION (VR). Physical, verbal, or gestural interactions on the part of the person that convey the return of valuing toward the caregiver as a response to the caregiver's elicitation. They are directly dependent on the caregiver's seeking them and include any degree of approximation, such as simply allowing the caregiver to place his or her hand in the individual's as a "handshake." They are intended to teach the person not only to receive and accept valuing, but also to reciprocate it. Typical examples are warm gestures, smiles, vocalizations, hugs, handshakes, reaching out, gazing, cooing, and friendly verbal answers or comments.

2. VALUE INITIATION (VI). Any spontaneous physical, verbal, or gestural valuing toward the caregiver. These interactions are not direct responses to RE. They are similar to those indicated in VR above, but are independent of any direct value elicitation. If the person accepts the caregiver's gestural offer of a handshake but also warmly gazes at the caregiver, the handshake is measured as a VR and the gaze as a VI. Other examples include self-initiated interactions, such as smiling, reaching out, talking in a friendly manner, offering to help, and looking at the caregiver in a friendly manner.

3. PARTICIPATING CORRECTLY (PC). Any correct responses to the approximation, initiation, performance, completion, or constructive manipulation of a prescribed task or activity with full, partial, or no caregiver assistance. Skill acquisition, task performance, and orderliness are secondarily important; the primary focus is on the value of social interactions with the caregiver since participation is a vehicle for VG, VE, VR, and VI. It is the caregiver's responsibility to facilitate PC by providing whatever degree of warm assistance might be necessary regardless of the individual's "functional level." Typical examples of PC without help are putting the pieces of a puzzle together, setting the table, playing a game, and answering questions in a classroom setting. Typical examples of PC with help are performing a task side by side with the caregiver in an assembly-line fashion, initiating a task by having the caregiver place the first piece of material in one's hand, any physical movement toward the task with the caregiver pointing to the next step, and approximating any level of participation in any step of the task with any degree of assistance.

4. INTERDEPENDENCE-CENTERING (IC). Task-shared (IC-T) or person-centered (IC-P) interactions beyond the primary caregiver that are based on sharing activities or directly valuing others beyond the dyad. These involve the integration of other caregivers or peers into the relationship. Typical examples of task-shared IC are (a) three children playing a game involving passing pictures to one another in turn or (b) a group of adults working together in an assembly line. Task-shared IC involves observations of each step of the particular joint activity, wherein each movement related to the joint activity comprises a shared experience. Typical examples of person-centered IC are (a) one child giving warm eye contact to another while playing a game, (b) or two adults, while working on a task, making friendly comments to one another. Both types of IC can occur concurrently.

5. PARTICIPATING INCORRECTLY (PI). Incorrect responses that a person makes while participating on a prescribed task or activity. These can occur with or without caregiver assistance. These errors are observed in any step of a task. Typical examples of PI without assistance are (a) a person is supposed to place silverware in a tray, but places it on the counter, or (b) a person is asked to sort cards by colors in pre-specified piles, but dumps them all together. Typical examples of PI with assistance are the same as the above, but with the caregiver providing prompts. In spite of caregiver effort, the person nevertheless makes errors.

6. SEVERE INTERACTIONAL PROBLEMS (SIP). Acts of aggression, self-injury, active withdrawal, or passive withdrawal. These also include attempts of same. Self-injury consists of behaviors that potentially or actually cause harm to self. Aggression consists of attempts to inflict or actually inflicting harm or severe discomfort upon others. Active withdrawal consists of physical movement away from the caregiver. Passive withdrawal consists of self-stimulatory, stereotypic, or passively resistant behaviors. Typical examples of self-injurious behaviors are head banging, face slapping, hitting walls, hand biting, pulling out fingernails, tearing flesh from body, choking self, eye gouging, ear gouging, rectal digging, kicking self, eye poking, and pica. Typical examples of aggression toward others are biting, hitting, slapping, pulling hair, scratching, kicking, aggressive comments, throwing objects at others, poking others, spitting at people, and projectile vomiting. Typical examples of active withdrawal are moving from one's chair, sliding onto the floor, rolling under or climbing on tables, throwing materials on the floor, running away, stompingfeet, public masturbation, pounding fist on table, and yelling. Typical examples of passive withdrawal are mouthing hands or objects, body rocking, finger flicking, arm waving, staring out of windows or at lights, moving head from side to side, echolalic speech, feigning sleep, folding one's arms, looking away, licking self, playing with spittle, rumination, and regurgitation.

on pegboards or stringing beads). However, in the intervention, caregivers were instructed to use more practical, age-appropriate, and varied activities, such as placing silverware in a container, folding towels, washing and ironing, sorting household materials, and labeling envelopes. During both conditions, other individuals were present in the settings and no environmental modifications were made. The average staffing ratio in both conditions was 1:1.

Observational Instruments and Behavioral Definitions

Interactional patterns were assessed through two measurement instruments (see Tables 2 and 3). The Caregiver's Interactional Observation System (CIOS) and the Person's Interactional Observation System (PIOS) were designed to categorize, code and record dyadic interactions in order to reflect the nature and frequency of observed dyadic sequences. These were field tested and revised in two pilot projects supervised by the author involving 50 dyads over a 24-month period in order to correct ambiguities and assure consistency. Tables 2 and 3 contain the interactional variables, subvariables, operational definitions, and examples.

The six categories in CIOS and PIOS were subdivided into 18 and 16 subvariables, respectively (see Table 4), and data

Table 4: Interactional Variables and Subvariables

CAREGIVER: VALUE-CENTERED DIMENSION (VCD)	PERSON: PARTICIPATORY DIMENSION (PD)
Value Giving (VG)	**Value Reciprocation (VR)**
Physical (VG-P)	Physical (VR-P)
Verbal (VG-V)	Verbal (VR-V)
Gestural (VG-G)	Gestural (VR-G)
Reciprocity Eliciting (RE)	**Value Initiation (VI)**
Physical (RE-P)	Physical (VI-P)
Verbal (RE-V)	Verbal (VI-V)
Gestural (RE-G)	Gestural (VI-G)
Assisting Warmly (AW)	**Participating Correclty (PC)**
Physical (AW-P)	With Help (PC-WH)
Verbal (AW-V)	Without Help (PC-WoH)
Gestural (AW-G)	
Protecting (PR)	**Interdependence Centering (IC)**
Physical (Pr-P)	Task-Shared (IC-T)
Verbal (PR-V)	Person-Centered (IC-P)
Gestural (PR-G)	
CAREGIVER: DOMINATIVE DIMENSION (DD)	**PERSON: NON-PARTICIPATORY DIMENSION (NPD)**
Assisting Demandingly (AD)	**Participating Incorrectly (PI)**
Physical (AD-P)	With Help (PI-WH)
Verbal (AD-V)	Without Help (PI-WoH)
Gestural (AD-G)	
Restraint-Punishment (RP)	**Severe Interactional Problems (SIP)**
Physical (RP-P)	Aggression (SIP-AGG)
Verbal(RP-V)	Self-Injury(SIP-SIB)
Environmental(RP-E)	Active Withdrawal (SIP-ActW)
	Passive Withdrawal (SIP-PasW)

sheets were used to record frequencies. The variables and subvariables were grouped into two broad caregiver categories: the value-centered dimension (VCD), VG + RE + AW + PR and the dominative dimension (DD), AD + RD. Similarly, the person variables and subvariables were collapsed into the participatory dimension (PD), VR + VI + PC + IC and the nonparticipatory dimension (NPD), PI + SIP. Both coding systems require content and process analyses to measure the nature and modality of the interactions, as well as to infer the type of interaction taking into account observed affective states. For example, when a caregiver assists a person in a task, it is necessary to differentiate whether the assistance is verbal, physical, or gestural and whether it is expressed warmly (AW) or demandingly (AD); or, if a person is making a vocalization, the observer has to determine whether it is VR, VI, or perhaps SIP as in the case of passive withdrawal. Or, if the caregiver is engaged in VG on a continuous basis through words and touch and at the same time is involved in AW-V as well as in PR-P, the observer has to evaluate each interaction in terms of its occurrence and meaning. Likewise, the person could be engaged in multiple forms of other interactions, such as VR or VI while also being involved in PC or PI as well as in SIP.

Due to the complexity of these interactional processes, this study established seven parameters to minimize discrepancies in scoring: (a) The variables could only be recorded if directly observed. (b) Interactions were recorded separately for each member of the dyad in the same time intervals. (c) Interactions lasting more than 10 sec, such as a conversation or the use of a masked helmet, were counted as 1 occurrence each 10 sec. (d) Discrete interactions such as a single pat on the back (e.g., the caregiver's hand touching the person's back in a momentary movement cycle) or a verbal reprimand (e.g., the caregiver saying, "Hands down!") were counted according to their number of occurrences. (e) The frequency of multiple verbal interactions lasting less than 10 sec was determined by their syntax (i.e., each sentence sequence was counted as one occurrence). For example, if the caregiver gave apparently gruff commands, such as "Look at me! Pick it up! Put your hands here!", three AD-V interactions would be counted. (f) Two or more simultaneous interactions were coded as separate events; e.g., when a caregiver smiled (VG-G), and verbally praised a person (VG-V). (g) All interactions were categorized and counted regardless of their degree of intensity (e.g., tap on the face [SIB] and a severe head bang [SIB]).

Data Collection and Reliability

Dyads were videotaped in their settings from approximately 9:00 a.m. to 11:00 a.m. and 1:00 p.m. to 3:00 p.m. each weekday. A Sony mini-camera was placed unobtrusively in a corner of the setting, typically 3 to 4M from the dyad. If the dyad's location changed, the camera was moved to the new location or was handheld. Random 2-min observation samples were selected from these twice-daily sessions, and these comprised the data recording intervals in both conditions.

A graduate student in psychology participated in the original field testing of CIOS and PIOS, and then received observer training over an 80-hour period by coding and recording 15 varied analogous videotaped vignettes. The primary author provided instruction and feedback to achieve a consistent level of accuracy. Reliability checks were conducted by observing and recording occurrences distributed evenly across approximately 15% of the observation intervals for each dyad. The percentage of agreement was calculated for each variable and subvariable by dividing the number of agreements by the number of agreements plus disagreements and multiplying by 100. Average overall reliability was 87%.

Design

An AB design was utilized, with one case also having follow-up observations. In the baseline condition, caregivers carried out routine behavioral intervention programs in natural settings. The intervention phase consisted of the implementation of Gentle Teaching. The following factors were introduced to strengthen internal validity (Kazdin, 1981): objective data based on videotaped observations, continuous assessment in both phases through random time samples, multiple and heterogeneous cases, identification of target behaviors unresponsive to other interventions as verified in clinical histories and case conferences, measurement of immediate and final effects, and various statistical analyses using the SPSS-X computer package. To verify the nature and severity of the behaviors and the type of procedures used, clinical histories were thoroughly reviewed. The types of procedures previously utilized varied in their intrusiveness and were classified using criteria established by Lennox et al. (1988): Level I (58%) -- environmental control, antecedent control, reinforcement, instructions, and physical assistance; Level II (70%) -- extinction, social disapproval, overcorrection, response cost, physical restraint, and visual screening; Level III (62%) -- time-out, mechanical restraint, spray mist, and contingent electric shock. (Note that some subjects were exposed to several procedures and most subjects also were involved in positive programs. Also, 33% of the individuals were receiving psychoactive medications.)

Observations averaged 4.8 sessions during baseline and 8.3 during intervention. The following criteria were established: (a) a minimum of three baseline observations, (b) at least seven treatment sessions, (c) the computation of videotaped data on a session-by-session basis based on randomly selected 2-min time intervals, and (d) the use of CIOS and PIOS to categorize and record the observed frequencies. Prior to the intervention phase, each caregiver received 8 hr of hands-on didactic training in Gentle Teaching conducted by the author (McGee et al., 1987; McGee, 1988). The Gentle Teaching phase involved approximately two caregivers per person in alternating shifts. Besides training in Gentle Teaching, caregivers were also specifically instructed (a) to preclude the use of restraint and punishment, even though target behaviors occasionally appeared to momentarily escalate (e.g., when a person was freed from a restraint chair); (b) to use protective interactions to prevent harm without immobilizing the person; (c) to avoid the use of edible reinforcers or tokens; and (d) to use age-appropriate and functional tasks, while maintaining a similar level of difficulty as observed in the baseline (e.g., sorting silverware in a kitchen instead of sorting chips in a dayroom, or folding towels in a laundry room instead of folding paper in a classroom).

Gentle Teaching Intervention

In order to decelerate the targeted behavioral classes and to accelerate participatory interactions, Gentle Teaching simultaneously focuses on the deceleration of dominative caregiver interactions and the substantive acceleration of value-centered ones. The central strategy is to resignify dyadic interactions through unconditional value-giving and its frequent elicitation, while giving warm assistance and protection when necessary. The basic paradigm is that caregiver interactions begin with, center on, and effectuate human valuing and its reciprocation. While establishing new interactional meanings, the power of past interactional patterns is designified; i.e., attempts at aggression, self-injury, or withdrawal are given little or no attention or meaning, except to prevent them or protect the particular individual or others. The central purpose of the paradigm is to resignify interactions; i.e., to create bonded relationships, friendships, and a spirit of human interdependence as inferred in the caregiver's value-centered interactions and the person's participatory ones.

Several supportive techniques are employed throughout the intervention in order to effectuate the central paradigm: (a) errorless teaching strategies (Cronin & Cuvo, 1979) to increase PC, facilitate AW and highlight VG; (b) task analysis (Gold, 1972) to facilitate PC and decrease PI and SIP; (c) precise and conservative prompting (Stokes & Baer, 1977) in order to increase PC and differentiate VG and RE from skill acquisition or task performance; (d) co-participation on tasks with the person (McGee, 1988) to decrease PI and create increased opportunities for VG, RE, VR, VI, and IC; (e) the use of tasks as vehicles to focus interactions on VCD and PD (McGee et al., 1987; McGee, 1988); (f) the identification of precursors to target behaviors to decrease their intensity or duration and to signal the need for increased VG, AW, or PR (McGee, 1988); (g) the reduction of verbal instructions or verbal and physical demands (Gold, 1972) in order to concurrently increase and highlight VG and RE; (h) choice-making (Shevin & Klein, 1984) to increase opportunities for VR and IC; (i) fading assistance (Becker et al., 1975) and integrating other caregivers and peers into the relationship to facilitate IC; (j) the use of dialogue; i.e., personalized verbal interactions throughout the process (McGee, 1988) to facilitate VG, VE, and VR as well as to increase the possibility of VI. The use of these supportive techniques involves a moment-to-moment decision-making process in which the caregiver determines which teaching condition might immediately help to decrease dominative interactions and increase value-centered ones, while concurrently increasing the person's participation and decreasing the occurrence of target behaviors.

Intervention effectiveness was evaluated according to the following interactional criteria: (a) near zero-level dominative interactions, (b) a ratio of 30:1 value-centered interactions to dominative ones, (c) a ratio of 8:1 participatory interactions to nonparticipatory ones, and (d) a deceleration of targeted behavioral classes by 75% in the total intervention process. To achieve these results, caregivers were expected to identify, analyze, and diminish dominative interactions, such as reprimands, the use of physical, chemical, or mechanical restraint, time-out, overcorrection, and other similarly punitive actions found in aversive therapy. In addition, they had to significantly decrease any interactions that appeared to convey mechanistic or authoritarian expressions, emotional tugs-of-war, or any form of interaction that appeared to place compliance or skill acquisition over valuing the person. Protective interactions were sometimes necessary due to the severity of the behaviors; yet, these had to be done without immobilizing the person. Simultaneously, caregivers were expected to express unconditional valuing in order to bring about participation and give feelings of safety and security. As caregivers centered themselves on this personal and social change process, they also assumed a commitment to help the marginalized person move from a state of nonparticipation toward that of participation by decreasing incorrect engagement in tasks and activities and other distancing interactions, such as acts of aggression, self-injury, running from the caregiver, or engaging in self-stimulation.

Concurrently, the individuals with behavioral difficulties had to learn to reciprocate valuing toward the caregiver, as well as to participate in tasks and activities. This mutual transformation required sharp, ongoing caregiver values and praxis. Thus, the intervention process involved definitions of caregiver values and purposes, the dynamic use of a range of supportive techniques, and interactional change.

RESULTS

Visual Inspection

A visual inspection (Kazdin, 1982) of the charts shows clear differences related to frequency changes between baseline and intervention (see Figures 1 and 2).

Figure 1 depicts the acceleration of the caregivers' value-centered interactions and the deceleration of dominative ones. Figure 2 reveals similar acceleration of participatory interactions and the deceleration of nonparticipatory ones. The baselines indicate that the interactional levels were fairly constant in each case and dimension. Caregivers displayed almost no value-centered interactions and high frequencies of dominative ones, whereas, the subjects showed almost no participatory interactions and relatively high nonparticipatory ones. The intervention phase shows relatively rapid decreases in dominative and nonparticipatory interactions and similar increases in value-centered and participatory interactions.

Case 15 includes an 18-month follow-up as well as three observations of a caregiver previously unexposed to the intervention. This adolescent had been unsuccessfully subjected to contingent electric shock prior to the intervention due to high frequency self-injurious behaviors. The figure reveals that his life-threatening behaviors were at a high level in the baseline and, at the same time, his caregiver engaged in high levels of dominative ones. In the first treatment phase, a caregiver skilled in Gentle Teaching was able to decrease the self-injury to near-zero while simultaneously increasing value-giving. In phase two, the child's mother and teacher continued the intervention with similar results. Eighteen months later, they were observed carrying out the procedure in the child's classroom with continued success. However, in the child's institutional residence, another caregiver who was unexposed to the intervention, was observed, and these data revealed a return to baseline levels in all dimensions. Thus, the child seemed to be able to interact without any significant self-injury among those who were capable of high frequency value-centered interactions, but was unable to maintain his progress when confronted with dominative interactions. Follow-up studies are being conducted on all cases. The other cases showed similar intervention effects; i.e., rapid deceleration of dominative caregiver interactions and each person's nonparticipatory ones. The totality of the charts indicate that caregiver change is related to each person's change and that a dynamic interactional process occurred.

Percentage of Change Between Conditions

The percentage of change between phases in all interactional variables was noteworthy (see Table 5). Caregivers increased their interactions in all value-centered variables: value-giving, 72%; value eliciting, 100%; assisting warmly, 85%; and protecting, 57%. They decreased their demanding assistance and restraint and punishment by 64% and 89%, respectively. At the same time, the group increased each variable in the participatory dimension and decreased all nonparticipatory interactions. In the intervention sessions, the decreases in aggression (86%), self-injury (76%), active withdrawal (70%), and passive withdrawal (63%) showed substantial impact and indicated that Gentle Teaching holds promise for persons with these severe needs. The average percentage of decrease in the constellation of aggression, self-injury, and withdrawal was 74%. Clinical observation indicated that the remaining behavioral difficulties were non-harmful and non-disruptive. Our operational definitions of aggression, self-injury, and withdrawal included even minor attempts or mild occurrences. For example, "self-injury" observed during the

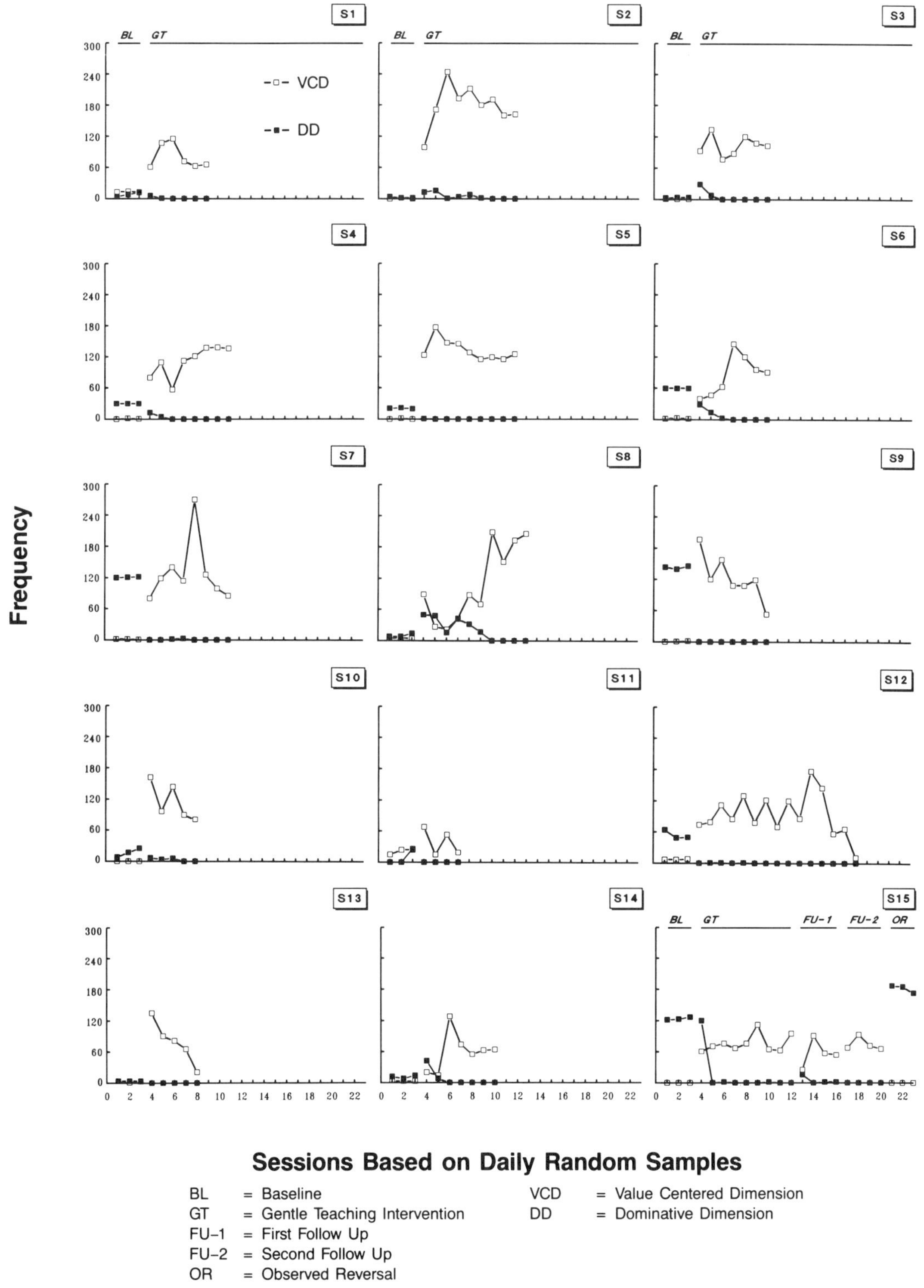

Figure 1: Caregiver Interactional Dimensions

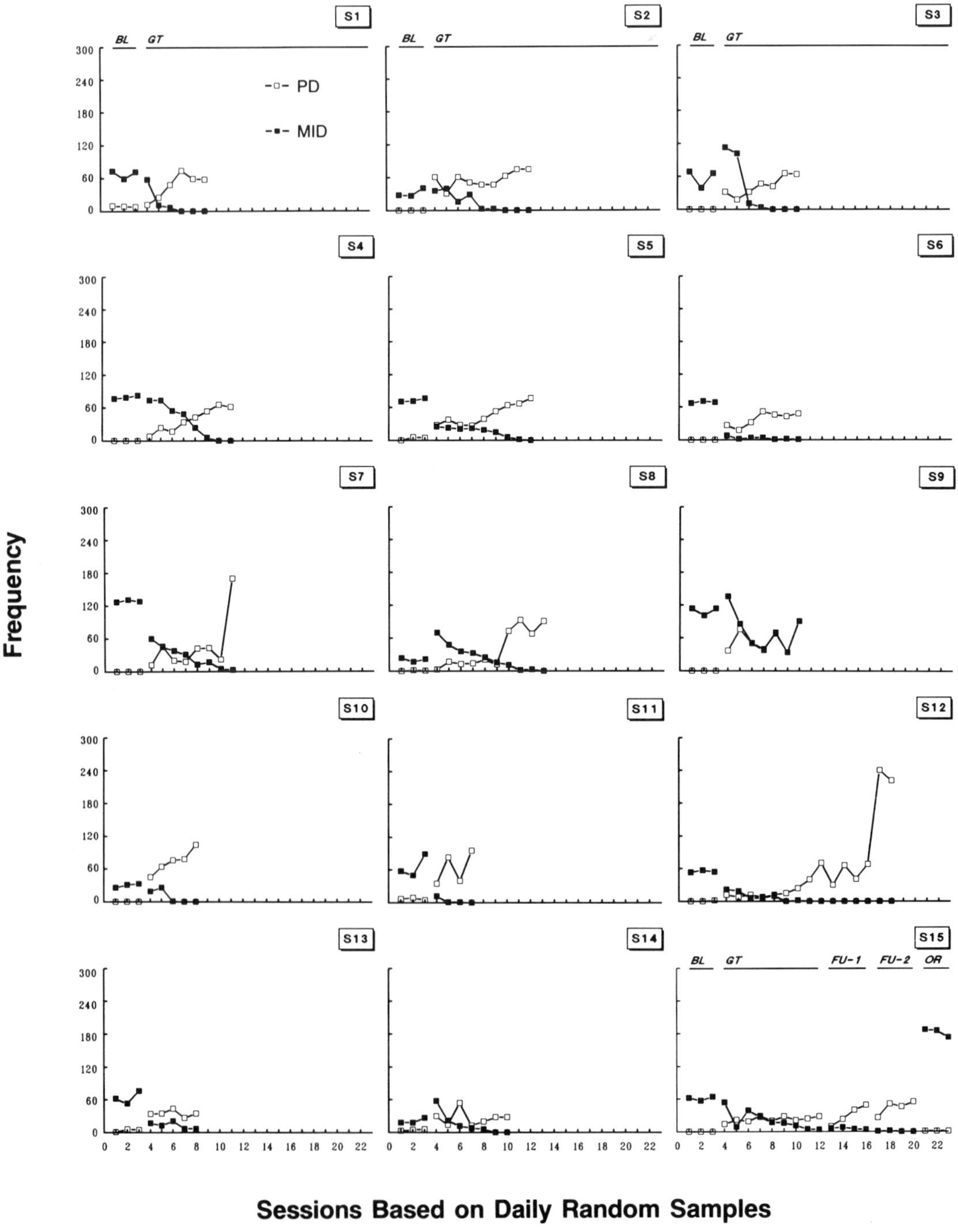

BL = Baseline
GT = Gentle Teaching Intervention
FU-1 = First Follow Up
FU-2 = Second Follow Up
OR = Observed Reversal
PD = Participatory Dimension
MID = Maladaptive Interactive Dimension

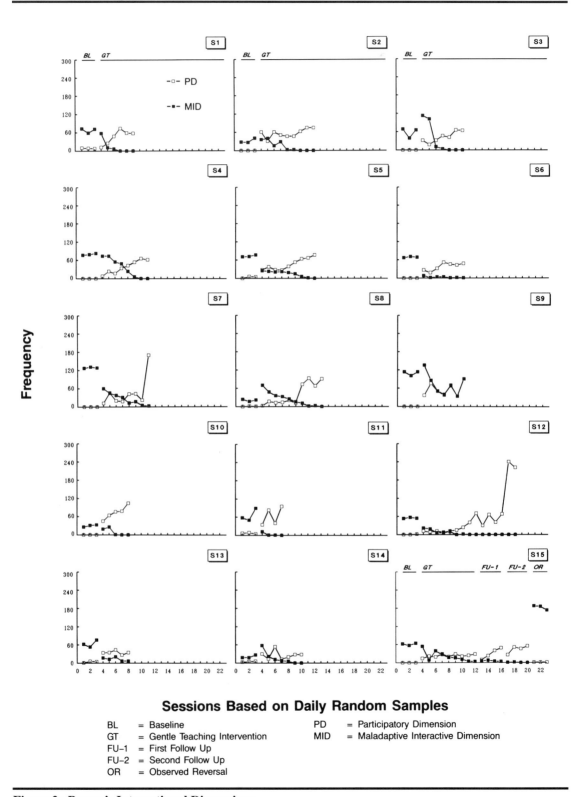

Figure 2: Person's Interactional Dimensions

last treatment sessions consisted of mild tapping of the cheeks or touching one's sore ears instead of head banging or gouging. Similarly, aggression involved observations that indicated mild attempts or gestures at hitting or biting. Thus, even though there was a noted 76% decrement in self-injury and an 85% decrement in aggression, the balance of those interactions in the final intervention sessions were qualitatively different from those observed in the baseline and were not considered to be major clinical preoccupations.

Statistical Significance of the Effect

Differences in the four interactional groups were evaluated and significant differences were observed between both conditions (See Table 6). The target behavioral classes showed significant decrease. The baseline for nonparticipatory behaviors was significantly higher (M = 61.8 +/- 30.1) than the intervention (M = 5.6 +/- 5.0), p .001. At the same time, the intervention revealed significantly higher participatory interactions (M = 56.4 +/- 22.8) than the baseline (M = 1.9 +/- 2.9), p .001. Equally striking differences were seen in the caregivers' interactions. In the baseline, dominative interactions were high (M = 41.3 +/- 49.0) and in the intervention, these decreased significantly (M = 0.6 +/- 1.2), p .001; at the same time, baseline value-centered interactions (M = 3.0 +/- 5.1) increased significantly (M = 108.1 +/- 37.9), p .001. Thus, these data indicate that the intervention had significant effects on dyadic performance.

DISCUSSION

The results of this preliminary study provide tentative support that Gentle Teaching effectuates substantial change in both caregivers and persons

Table 5: Percentage of Change for Each Variable Between Both Conditions

Caregiver				Person			
VCD	% Increase	DD	% Decrease	PD	% Increase	MID	% Decrease
Value Giving	72.0	Assisting Demandingly	64.0	Value Reciprocating	100.0	Participating Incorrectly	6.2
Value Elicition	100.0	Restraint-Punishment	89.4	Value Initiating	100.0	Aggression	86.0
Assisting Warmly	84.5			Participating Correctly	89.4	Self-Injury	76.0
Protecting	57.3			Interdependence Centering	100.0	Active Withdrawal	70.0
						Passive Withdrawal	63.0

VCD = value centered diemsnsion DD = dominative dimension
PD = participatory dimension MID = maladaptive interactional dimension

Percentages were calcuated based on change between baseline and intervention for total sessions.

with behavioral difficulties. Inspection of the charts indicates striking impact. The statistical analyses showed significant differences with a high level of confidence. The positive evaluation of treatment effectiveness, both in regard to the group's acceleration of participatory interactions and deceleration of nonparticipatory ones, was evidenced in the interactional analyses. These findings are consistent with our clinical experiences in recent years (McGee, 1988).

The baseline sessions presented a major issue relative to the frequency of aggression and self-injury in a group historically subjected to various forms of restraint and punishment. In order to design a study that would reflect the actual conditions of the group, baseline data consistent with each person's actual intervention procedure was utilized. Due to the restrictiveness of the interventions in the baseline condition, most individuals were unable to display as high a frequency or as intense a level of aggression or self-injury as they typically might have since their bodily movements often were limited through the use of tubes on their arms, masked helmets, locked rooms and wards, arms and legs tied to chairs, and immobilization in wheelchairs. However, based on their documented histories of extreme punishment and restraint-based procedures, observations of initial attempts at self-injury or aggression provided clear evidence of high frequency aggression and self-injury. Similarly, the baseline sessions might not have reflected the individual's ability to participate, both due to the restraint used and the reluctance of their caregivers to interact with them. Indeed, in several instances, caregivers refused to approach some of the individuals, while others only half-heartedly attempted to engage them in activities.

A significant finding in this study was that, as caregivers rapidly accelerated their value and focused on eliciting it, each individual began to gradually reciprocate it. However, caregivers had to learn that valuing was not just a matter of "delivering reward," but rather the expression of genuine caring and companionship, even in the worst moments. Clinical observations indicated that caregivers were generally accustomed to giving rewards "contingent on appropriate behaviors." They reported great difficulty in unconditionally valuing the individuals, especially when in turmoil. They initially tended to give value

Table 6: Group Interactional Means for Baseline (A) and Intervention (B)

	M		SD		$\underline{t}$
Dimension	A	B	A	B	
Maladaptive	61.8	5.6	30.1	5.0	7.4**
Participatory	1.9	56.4	2.9	22.8	8.6**
Dominative	41.3	0.6	49.0	1.2	3.1*
Value-Centered	3.0	108.1	5.1	37.9	-9.9**

* $p < .01$
** $p < .001$

$n_A = 48$, $n_B = 124$

for deeds done. By concentrating on a relationship based on companionship, they helped themselves express more natural and authentic value-centered interactions. Future studies should report the effects of various subvariables and other qualitative analyses.

Another significant observation related to the need for caregivers to participate in tasks and activities with each person rather than just "instructing" them to participate. This distinction helped caregivers to recognize that they were as initially disconnected in the relationship as the behaviorally involved person. Co-participation seemed to signal a common ground for the dyads rather than a mandatory deed to be done. Initial sessions also often centered on protective interactions consisting of blocking attempts at hits or shadowing attempts at self-injury. However, it was most vital for caregivers to simultaneously resignify the interactions through warm assistance and ongoing valuing. This process helped give a new meaning to the emerging relationship. Thus, the burden for initial change in the relationships fell on the shoulders of caregivers rather than on the mere application of a technique.

In spite of the current limitations, the present study enables us to conclude that the Gentle Teaching paradigm can be an effective intervention strategy for the well-being of persons with mental retardation and their caregivers. In essence, it indicates that domination should give way to valuing and that nonparticipation can be replaced by participation. Further studies will concentrate on larger groups, more precise analyses of variables and subvariables, relationships between them, and the qualitative dimensions of this change process.

The intervention process utilized many behavioral techniques and its findings were consistent with many past studies relative to them. Yet, it also asked caregivers to reflect on their values and their relationship with persons with severe behavioral difficulties, to adopt values based on human interdependence, and translate these into value-centered actions. The intervention required a mutually humanizing perspective relative to the human condition, and expected caregivers to look at human needs and hopes based on not only what was seen, but also on what was felt. Skinner (1969) defined a binary system of reward and punishment as the central principle in human behavior; this intervention asked caregivers to give human valuing freely and unconditionally. Behaviorism's rejection of the inner-being (Skinner, 1978) has been periodically reconfirmed through admonitions to caregivers to close their eyes to mentalistic interpretations of human existence (Baer et al., 1987). The findings in this study are inconsistent with such assumptions. Gentle Teaching does not deny the power of reward and punishment; rather, it seeks to create relationships based on the assumption that all people long for interdependence and justice in spite of their observed behaviors. It requires caregivers to reflect on the mind-body-spirit wholeness of those whom they serve. More specifically, the findings in this study are inconsistent with past research that has supported contingent electric shock for persons with life-threatening behaviors (Lovass et al., 1965; Linsheid, 1988; Favell et al., 1982) as well as the control-by-contingency orientation often reported in the treatment of aggressive and disruptive behaviors (Lennox et al., 1988) through punitive practices such as time-out, overcorrection, physical restraint, mechanical restraint, noxious taste, and water mist sprayed in the face in order to deal with aggression.

Lastly, these findings critically question behavioral psychology and many of its resultant practices which represent a psychology based on an emotionally neutral view of personkind and the belief that the human consists of nothing more than a set of stimuli and responses (Bakan, 1966; O'Donnell, 1985). Gentle Teaching is a value system, as well as a teaching approach, and as such does not promise quick and yet easy solutions to individual and social problems. It urges caregivers to recognize and deal with the inner-being and interdependence of marginalized people (Chomsky, 1971). The initial purpose of Gentle Teaching is the convergence of the "I" and the "Thou" (Buber, 1955) and a recognition of the dialectic that exists within and between persons as they struggle to balance the fear of union with the innate hunger for interdependence (Unger, 1984). It asks caregivers to critically question their own intentions and to move toward feelings of solidarity with marginalized people. It recognizes the vulnerability that exists in both caregivers and persons with special needs. Its ongoing and ultimate purpose is mutual liberation, impacting not only on observable behaviors, but on the very roots of human spirituality (Boff & Boff, 1987). It requires actions based on values that strive for the hope of interdependence and the transformation of the self and the other. It highlights characteristics such as companionship, commitment, freedom from dominative beliefs, joyfulness, reflection, and dialogue as crucial expressions of personal and social change processes. The ultimate test lies in the extent to which all persons are integrated into the confluence of family and community life. These findings tend to validate the possibility that caregivers and persons with severe behavioral difficulties can change; however, statistics alone cannot measure the total effects of an interaction. Hopefully, these findings will serve as a vehicle for further dialogue on the wholeness and interdependence of each person.

REFERENCES

Ainsworth, M. D. S., & Bell, S. M. (1979). Attachment exploration and separation illustrated by the behavior of one-year-olds in a strange situation. *Child Development, 41*, 49-67.

Baer, D. M., Wolf, M. M., & Risley, T. R. (1987). Some still current dimensions of applied behavior analysis. *Journal of Applied Behavior Analysis, 20*, 313-327.

Bakan, D. (1966). Behaviorism and American urbanization. *Journal of the History of the Behavioral Sciences, 2*, 5-28.

Bateson, G. (1951). Information and codification: A philosophical approach. In J. Ruesch & G. Bateson (Eds.), *Communication: The social matrix of psychiatry*. New York: Norton & Company.

Becker, W. C., Engelmann, S., & Thomas, D. R. (1975). *Teaching 2: Cognitive learning and instruction*. Chicago: Science Research Associates.

Boff, L., & Boff, C. (1987). *Introduction to a theology of liberation*. Maryknoll, NY: Orbis Books.

Buber, M. (1955). *Between man and man*. Boston: Beacon Press.

Carr, E. G. (1977). The motivation of self-injurious behavior: A review of some hypotheses. *Psychological Bulletin, 84*, 800-816.

Carr, E. G., & Durand, V. M. (1986). The social-communicative basis of severe behavior problems in children. In S. Reiss & R. Bootuzi (Eds.), *Theoretical issues in behavior therapy*. New York: Academic Press.

Carr, E. G., & McDowell, J. J. (1980). Social control of self-injurious behavior of organic etiology. *Behavior Therapy, 11*, 402-409.

Carr, E. G., Newsom, C. D., & Binkoff, J. A. (1976). Stimulus control of self-destructive behavior in a psychotic child. *Journal of Abnormal Child Psychology, 4*, 139-153.

Chomsky, N. (December, 1971). The case against B. F. Skinner. *New York review of books*.

Cronin, K. A., & Cuvo, A. J. (1979). Teaching mending skills to mentally retarded adolescents. *Journal of Applied Behavioral Analysis, 12*, 401-406.

Donnellan, A. M., Mirenda, P. L., Mesaros, R. A., & Fassbender, L. L. (1984). Analyzing the communicative functions of aberrant behavior. *Journal of The Association for Persons with Severe Handicaps, 9*, 201-212.

Durand, V. M., & Carr, E. G. (1987). Social influences on "self-stimulatory" behavior: Analysis and treatment application. *Journal of Behavior Analysis, 20, 119-132.*

Favell, J. E., Azrin, N. H., Baumeister, A. A., Carr, E. G., Dorsey, M. F., Lovaas, O. I., Rincover, A., Risley, T. R., Romanczyk, K. R. G., Russo, D. C., Schroeder, S. R., & Solnick, J. V. (1982). The treatment of self-injurious behavior. *Behavior Therapy, 13*, 529-554.

Fehrenbach, P. A., & Thelen, M. A. (1982). Behavioral approaches to the treatment of aggressive disorders. *Behavior Modification, 6*, 465-497.

Gold, M. W. (1972). Stimulus factors in skill training of retarded adolescents on a complex assembly task: Acquisition, transfer and retention. *American Journal of Mental Deficiency, 76*, 517-526.

Gorman-Smith, D., & Matson, J. L. (1985). A review of treatment research for self-injurious and stereotyped responding. *Journal of Mental Deficiency Research, 29*, 295-308.

Guess, D., Helmstetter, E., Turnbull, H. R., & Knowlton, S. (1987). Use of aversive procedures with persons who are disabled: An historical review and critical analysis. *TASH Monograph Series, No. 2*. Seattle, WA: The Association for Persons with Severe Handicaps.

Hung, D. W. (1978). Using self-stimulation as reinforcement for autistic children. *Journal of Autism and Childhood Schizophrenia, 8*, 355-366.

Iwata, B. A. (1987). Negative reinforcement in applied behavior analysis: An emerging technology. *Journal of Applied Behavior Analysis, 20*, 361-378.

Johnson, W. L., & Baumeister, A. A. (1978). Self-injurious behavior: A review and analysis of methodological details of published studies. *Behavior Modification, 2*, 465-487.

Kazdin, A. E. (1981). Drawing valid inferences from case studies. *Journal of Consulting and Clinical Psychology, 49*, 183-192.

LaGrow, S. J., & Repp, A. C. (1984). Stereotypic responding: A review of intervention research. *American Journal of Mental Deficiency, 88*, 595-609.

Lennox, D. B., Miltenberger, R. F., Spengler, P., & Erfanian, N. (1988). Decelerative treatment practices with persons who have mental retardation: A review of five years of literature. *American Journal of Mental Retardation, 92*, 492-501.

Linsheid, T. R. (1988). *Treatment of the Self-Injurious Behavior Inhibiting System (SIBIS): A report on three cases*. Paper presented at the meeting of the Association for Behavior Analysis, Philadelphia, PA.

Lovaas, O. I., Newsom, C., & Hickman, C. (1987). Self-stimulatory behavior and perceptual reinforcement. *Journal of Applied Behavior Analysis, 20*, 45-68.

Lovass, O. I., Schaeffer, B., & Simmons, J. Q. (1965). Building social behavior in autistic children by use of electric shock. *Journal of Experimental Research in Personality, 1*, 99-109.

McGee, J. J. (1988). *Gentle teaching: Behavior change through respect and justice*. Toronto: G. Allan Roeher Institute.

McGee, J. J., Menolascino, F. J., Hobbs, D. C., & Menousek, P. E. (1987). *Gentle teaching: A non-aversive approach to helping persons with mental retardation*. New York: Human Sciences Press.

O'Donnell, J. M. (1985). *The origins of behaviorism*. New York: University Press.

Rincover, A. (1986). Behavioral research in self-injury and self-stimulation. *Psychiatric Clinics of North America, 9*, 755-765.

Rincover, A., & Devany, J. (1982). The application of sensory extinction procedures to self-injury. *Analysis and Intervention in Developmental Disabilities, 3*, 67-81.

Schraeder, C., Shaull, J., & Elmore, B. (1983). Behavioral treatment of self-stimulation in the developmentally disabled: A methodological review. *Behavior Modification, 7*, 267-294.

Shevin, M., & Klein, N. K. (1984). The importance of choice-making skills for students with severe disabilities. *Journal of the Association for Persons with Severe Handicaps, 9*, 159-166.

Skinner, B. F. (1969). *Contingencies of reinforcement: A theoretical analysis*. New York: Appleton-Century-Crofts.

Skinner, B. F. (1978). *Reflections on behaviorism and society*. Englewood Cliffs, NJ: Prentice-Hall.

Sluzki, C. E., & Beavin, J. (1965). Symmetry and complementarity: An operational definition and typology of dyads. *Acta Psiquiatrica y Psicological de America Latina, 11*, 321-330. @REFERENCE = Sroufe, L. A., & Waters, E. (1976). The ontogenesis of smiling and laughter: A perspective on the organization of development in infancy. *Psychological Review, 83*, 173-189.

Stokes, T. F., & Baer, D. M. (1977). An implicit technology of generalization. *Journal of Applied Behavior Analysis, 10*, 349-367.

Unger, R. M. (1984). *Passion: An essay on personality*. New York: Free Press.

Wahler, R. C. (1976). Deviant child behavior within the family: Developmental speculations and behavior change strategies. In H. Leitenberg (Ed.), *Handbook of behavior modification and behavior therapy* (pp. 516-543). Englewood Cliffs, NJ: Prentice-Hall.

Watzlawick, P., Beavin, J. H., & Jackson, D. D. (1967). *Pragmatics of human communication*. New York: W. W. Norton & Co.

CHAPTER

17

SERIOUS SELF INJURY: THE ETHICS OF TREATMENT AND RESEARCH

Earl C. Butterfield
University of Washington

Might it be possible, when treating serious -- repeated, intense, and non-accidental -- self-injury, to allow ethically for both clinical and research considerations? As I tried to answer this question, I found help in thinking concretely about self-injurious people and in the deliberations of two human experimentation committees, one of which approved and one of which disapproved an experiment on nursing care for people who had suffered myocardial infarctions (Cromwell, Butterfield, Brayfield, & Curry, 1977).

In this paper, I will describe my thoughts about self-injurious persons whom I have known, the deliberations of those two committees, and parallels between the care of people with heart attacks and people who injure themselves. I conclude that serious self-injury can be treated ethically, with the highest standards of clinical practice and maximal yield of scientific information upon which to base improved, ethically unimpeachable treatments, even punishing and coercive treatments.

Because I was having considerable difficulty answering the question whether it is possible to allow ethically for both clinical and research considerations when treating serious self-injury, I thought more concretely. I imagined a young man who was blinding himself by gouging his eyes. I imagined a young woman who was deafening herself by clapping her ears. I imagined a boy who was receiving too little nourishment to sustain life because he made himself vomit after every meal by forcing his fingers down his throat. I imagined a girl who was disfiguring herself by striking her face against tables and other hard objects. To prevent the gouging, would I punish it with electric shock? If the shock would save the young man's sight, and informed consent was given, I thought that I would not hesitate: I would shock a consenting person to save his vision, or her hearing, or his sustenance, or her face.

A clinically relevant rule was dawning on me: A treatment is ethical if it and the treated condition result in less physical damage or longer life for the client than the untreated condition alone[1]. But the rule needed to be broadened. Although electric shock can be intense enough to damage one physically, only milder, aversive shock would be used in an effort to

1In this paper, I mean different things by damaging, harmful, and aversive. By damaging, I mean physically injurious. By harmful, I mean socially or psychologically impairing. By aversive, I mean unpleasant or painful. Many beneficial and ethical treatments damage patients physically, or harm them psychologically, or are aversive, or all three, just less so than the conditions themselves left untreated.

reduce eye gouging. Again, thinking concretely helped.

Physically undamaging but painful shock applied as punishment is not guaranteed to reduce or eliminate self-injury permanently. How long would I be willing to shock self-injuring clients? The rest of their lives? What made me ask? A little introspection showed that I asked because knowing how long I might need to continue shock before deciding whether it would work would allow me to estimate better the nonphysical harm that could be done by arrangements necessary for shocking. A permanent arrangement to shock could restrict a person's chances for social and intellectual growth. These sorts of harm, as well as physical damage, should be weighed when choosing among treatment options.

What if simply putting goggles on the young man would prevent eye gouging? Compared to arrangements needed for long-term electric shock, goggles are probably socially and developmentally less harmful, and therefore preferable. What if earmuffs would prevent deafness even if the ear clapping continued? What if a dental appliance would allow eating but not self-inflicted vomiting? What if a boxer's headgear would prevent damage from beating one's head on hard objects? The rule evolved: The treatment that minimizes physical damage and psychological harm is the clinically ethical choice. Thus, using shock to treat eye gouging would be justified only if wearing goggles did not stop the gouging (goggles can be removed and so might earmuffs, a dental device, and boxer's headgear), because long-term shock adds harm that goggles, muffs, and appliances do not. Generalizing the argument, the use of efficacious treatments that nevertheless cause some physical damage or psychological harm is clinically ethical if they result in less damage or harm than any other efficacious treatment and less than no treatment at all.

I turned next to research ethics. Again, it helped to think concretely. I recalled my experience in directing a research project (Cromwell et al., 1977) which, after approval by the National Institute of Mental Health, was reviewed in 1965 by two human experimentation committees, one for the sponsoring university and one for the hospital where the work was to be done. The grant application reviewed by the two committees proposed that patients hospitalized for heart conditions be randomly assigned to one of eight different nursing care conditions, representing all of the possible combinations of high or low information about heart attacks, high or low diversionary stimulation in the form of TV, visitors, etc., and high or low participation in one's own treatment. Random assignment to these research conditions was ethical to us as researchers because expert clinical opinion was divided and pertinent data were lacking.

Some cardiologists believed that more information was better for their patients; others believed less was better; no data were available to resolve this disagreement nor the following ones. Some intensive care physicians believed that heart patients would recover faster if they participated in their own treatment; others believed participation would damage their patients. Some internists were certain that diversion was healthy; others believed it was stressful. Other physicians, and quite a few psychologists, believed that stress was a product of personal characteristics interacting with environment characteristics, so that some patients would be stressed by a lot of information, others by the absence of information; some by a lot of participation, others by passive receipt of care; and some by diversion, and others by maximal opportunity to reflect upon their condition. If these latter professionals were correct, there would be no uniformly correct combination of nursing care for all patients. Indeed, depending upon the personality characteristics of the patient, any of the eight combinations that we investigated could have been the best care.

Both human experimentation committees noted the substantial disagreement among experts about which clinical treatment is minimally damaging. Both determined that there were no valid data with which to resolve the clinicians' disagreement. Both accepted the scientific ethic that under such conditions patients should be assigned to treatments that maximized knowledge for the treatment of patients in the future. In our case, that meant random assignment. Both committees approved random assignment. In other words, both committees decided that when we do not know which of several possibly effective treatments will minimize physical damage and psychological harm to patients, the ethical choice is to let scientific considerations guide treatment. Any human experimentation committee might decide that same way.

Despite their agreement on the propriety of our proposal to determine randomly which treatment a patient would receive, only one committee approved our project. The reasoning of the two committees provides a productive analogy for answering ethical questions about medical and behavioral treatments -- for example, whether to treat self-injury with punishment.

We proposed several ways to evaluate the efficacy of our experimental treatments of heart patients. One was to analyze patients' blood for chemical indications of healing of damaged heart tissue. The question arose whether drawing blood samples for our research purpose would damage patients. To provide appropriate medical care for patients with heart attacks, blood samples must be taken, but drawing too much blood is damaging, even life threatening. Failing to draw blood necessary for medical treatment would be unethical. Would the drawing of additional blood for research purposes jeopardize the patients? We had provided the University Committee with too little information about the amount of blood that needed to be drawn for clinical reasons to answer this question, so it did not approve our proposal. The Hospital Committee had detailed information about the amounts of blood drawn for clinical reasons, and this committee determined that drawing additional blood for research purposes would not damage patients or threaten their lives.

Both committees' actions were consistent with the principle that it is ethical by scientific standards to use potentially damaging conditions with some patients in order to provide sound evidence about which treatments to choose for future patients. Only the Hospital Committee had the information needed to implement that principle. The Hospital Committee approved the project, and we conducted it as proposed.

The purpose of our experiment was to compare the eight treatments that different clinicians advocated, while measuring personality characteristics that many felt would determine which condition would be least stressful to patients. As it turned out (Cromwell et al., 1977), none of the experts advocated correctly. One of our measures was the number of people who died between admission to the hospital and six months after discharge. Death rate was not changed by any care variable or in interaction with any personality variable. Two other measures were time from admission with suspicion of a myocardial infarction until time of discharge and time from discharge to resumption of normal activity (work, etc.). Neither of these measures was influenced by any of the nursing care variables alone or in interaction with personality, but both were influenced by the interaction of nursing care factors. Receiving three high or three low conditions (information, participation, and diversion) resulted in longer stays in the hospital and more months before resumption of normal activity than any one or two high conditions. Our research showed that until better evidence is available, the clinically ethical choices are any one or two of the high conditions.

I see two parallels between the present situation with respect to use of punishers for treatment of serious self-injury and the prior situation with respect to treatment of recovery from heart attacks. First, knowledge was indefinite then, as it is now. Because of important advances in our understanding of punishing treatment procedures (Azrin, Besalel, Jamner, & Caputo, 1988; Iwata, 1988; Mulick, in press), we know that punishers can help some self-damaging people under some conditions, but we are still not clear about who the people are or what the conditions might be. Second, there are strong differences of opinion now, as there were then. Some physicians were certain that information about their heart condition is bad for patients who have had heart attacks. Others were certain that information is helpful. Those who now believe punishing treatment is sometimes helpful are confident that it should be used sometimes (Iwata, 1988); others believe it should never by used (Guess, Helmstetter, Turnbull, & Knowlton, 1987).

I see a difference between the situations too. Those of us who wished to do the experiment on nursing care agreed among ourselves how to answer questions on ethics posed by the human experimentation committees that would decide whether we could do it. The shared goal was to increase the chances of future patients' recovery while minimizing the chances of physical damage for present patients. Civil rights issues and personal judgments about pain and suffering from the drawing of blood were not pitted against clinical and research ethics as the committees decided whether we should study recovery from heart attack. We all adopted a utilitarian view of ethics (Mulick, in press). We did not debate whether low diversion -- no reading material, TV, radio, or unessential visitors -- was an infringement of rights. There was no need to debate these issues because patients, their families, and their physicians were informed about the standard clinical conditions to which the patients would be assigned if they did not participate in our experiment and about the experimental conditions to which the patients might be assigned if they did participate. Both the physicians and the patients -- or their relatives -- decided whether to participate in the experiment.

The chief questions for the committees and for us as researchers were whether knowledge was complete enough to allow a decision about the best form of nursing without further experimentation (it was not, although there was substantial agreement about non-nursing aspects of the patients' medical care), whether our experimental nursing procedures posed any established threat to the physical well-being of the patients (they did not), and whether patients or their families and their physicians could decline to participate in the experiment (they could).

With respect to punishers in the treatment of self-injury by mentally retarded people, civil rights issues and personal beliefs about pain and suffering are invoked against further experimentation, regardless of informed consent. The argument is that aversive conditions are unacceptable as long as there are untried nonaversive procedures, regardless of knowledge about their efficacy. The argument is not compelling, first, because it assumes that particular treatments are inherently punishing. Actually, whether a condition is punishing depends upon the context in which it occurs (Holburn & Dougher, 1986; Konarski, 1987; Premack, 1971). The argument is not compelling, second, because more painful treatments are routinely sanctioned for less damaging conditions -- root canal therapy, hair transplants, amphetamines for obesity, etc. The argument is not compelling, third, because we fine and imprison people for inflicting the kind of punishment on others that some people inflict on themselves. The argument is not compelling, fourth, because informed consent must be obtained for treating mentally retarded people, just as it must be obtained for treating people who are not mentally retarded.

Such considerations suggest that aversiveness is not the issue. The issue is the relative efficacy of physically damaging and psychologically harmful treatments to one another and to no treatment at all. The efficacy, physical damage, and psychological harm done by most conceivable treatments of serious self-injury have not been established. Whether some self-damaging behaviors respond more fully to harmless procedures and others to harmful ones is unknown. Whether some conditions of administration of harmful procedures reduce self-injury more rapidly than others is not known. Whether harmful treatments can sometimes be fully and completely withdrawn without resumption of self-injury is unknown. The list is remarkably long of what we do not know and may not be allowed to investigate because of non-utilitarian ethical arguments about the use of punishment.

According to the utilitarian view of ethics, research should continue until the relative efficacy for reducing self injurious behavior of various treatments has been established. Clinical practice should be determined by the results of such research as is available when a treatment is given. If research has revealed a non-damaging and harmless procedure that is usually more effective than damaging or harmful procedures, the harmless and non-damaging one should be used first, on the clinical principle of minimizing damage and harm. Harmful treatments should be tried only if usually efficacious harmless ones fail to eliminate serious self-injury, and then only if it is judged that a typical long course of effective treatment using the harmful procedure will result in less damage and harm than the untreated self-injurious behavior, and if appropriate informed consent is obtained. If a procedure is usually more effective so that it results overall in less damage or harm to the client, it should be used first, provided that informed permission is given. No treatment should be continued longer than its established time for positive results unless there is no reasonable alternative treatment to be applied. When alternatives are not available, treatment with already tried procedures should be used for a longer period than usual, provided that they result in no increase in physical damage or psychological harm relative to no treatment of the self-injury. When alternative treatments are available, they should be tried as long as self-injury continues or seems likely to recur.

When there is no satisfactory evidence on efficacy or degree of harm, treatments should be tried in the order that will be most revealing of useful information for the treatment of the people in question and others who injure themselves. In other words, if there are no reliable and valid data to guide clinical practice, scientific concerns should dictate treatment choices. Experimental investigation will provide objective guides to treatment for self-injurious behavior more quickly than ideological disputation and paternalistic denial of the right to receive experimental treatments for which informed consent is obtained

Haggling about appropriate informed consent must be avoided. Guidelines for who can give informed consent are well established, and wrangling needlessly delays the onset of treatment that might reduce self-damaging and self-harming behaviors. The result is an unethical increase in damage and harm to clients who cannot themselves give informed consent.

To summarize, I conclude that treatment of all seriously self-injurious people, whether they are mentally retarded or not, should be guided by utilitarian ethics of the sort that are applied when deciding about any medical or behavioral treatment. Informed consent should be required for any treatment. Treatments having established efficacy should be tried first. When there is more than one such treatment, they should be tried in the order that minimizes physical damage and psychological harm. If no treatment of known efficacy works, other plausible treatments should be applied in accordance with established rules of science for maximizing information about how to treat people who do not respond to known treatments. Following these guidelines, serious self-injury can be treated ethically, with the highest standards of clinical practice, and additional treatments can be investigated, with maximal yield of scientific information upon which to base improved, ethically unimpeachable treatments, even punishing and coercive treatments of mentally retarded people.

REFERENCES

Azrin, N. H., Besalel, V. A., Jamner, J. P. & Caputo, J. N. (1988). Comparative study of behavioral methods of treating self-injury. *Behavioral Residential Treatment, 3*, 119-152.

Cromwell, R. L., Butterfield, E. C., Brayfield, F. M., & Curry, J. M. (1977). *Acute myocardial infarction: Reaction and recovery.* St. Louis: Mosby.

Guess, D., Helmstetter, E., Turnbull, H. R., & Knowlton, S. (1987). *Use of aversive procedures with persons who are disabled: An historical review and critical analysis.* Seattle, WA: The Association for Persons with Severe Handicaps.

Holburn, C. S., & Dougher, M. J. (1986). Effects of response satiation procedures in the treatment of aerophagia. *American Journal of Mental Deficiency, 91*, 72-77.

Iwata, B. A. (1988). The development and adoption of controversial default technologies. *Behavior Analyst, 11*, 149-157.

Konarski, E. A. (1987). Effects of response deprivation on the instrumental performance of mentally retarded persons. *American Journal of Mental Deficiency, 91*, 537-542.

Mulick, J. A. (in press). The ideology and science of punishment in mental retardation. *American Journal of Mental Retardation.*

Premack, D. (1971). Catching up with common sense or two sides of generalization: Reinforcement and punishment. In R. Glaser (Ed.), *The nature of reinforcement*, pp. 121-150. New York: Academic Press.

NOTE

Nancy Jackson, Alvin Eller, Bob Howenstine, and Craig Jensen provided valuable suggestions about how to improve an earlier draft of this paper. I thank them for their help, while accepting responsiblity for what is said.

CHAPTER

18

BALANCING FREEDOM FROM HARM AND RIGHT TO TREATMENT FOR PERSONS WITH DEVELOPMENTAL DISABILITIES

Maurice A. Feldman
Surrey Place Centre and the University of Toronto

Practitioners in the field of developmental disabilities are often faced with an ethical and practical dilemma of helping someone who is exhibiting severe behavior disorders such as self-injury and aggression: defending the individual's right to effective treatment and education, and protecting him/her from unnecessary intrusion, discomfort, or pain.

To date, the most effective techniques for teaching persons with developmental disabilities are primarily based on behavioral procedures such as contingencies of reinforcement, shaping, and stimulus control. Behavioral instruction has been used to teach skills so that persons can experience a higher quality of life in minimally restrictive settings. Likewise, behavioral procedures have been used to eliminate maladaptive behavior and to replace it with alternative, functional behavior. For the most part, behavior reduction programs use not only positive reinforcement, but also punishment.

The use of punishment is the subject of much recent controversy. Some authors (e.g., Guess, Helmstetter, Turnbull, & Knowlton, 1987; LaVigna & Donnellan, 1986; McGee, Menolascino, Hobbs, & Menousek, 1987; Sobsey, 1987; Turnbull et al., 1986) and groups (e.g., American Association on Mental Retardation, Association for Retarded Citizens, Canadian Association for Community Living, The Association for Persons with Severe Handicaps) consider the use of therapeutic punishment to be totally without moral justification and are calling for a ban of any treatment that inflicts pain, is discomforting, or is restrictive. This "anti-punishment" or "freedom from harm" faction also maintains that there is never any need to use punishment as positive-based, nonpunitive methods are available that are as, if not more, effective than punitive procedures in treating severe behavior problems.

On the other hand, others argue that denying persons with handicaps access to effective interventions is morally wrong and discriminatory and the asserting that punishment is always unnecessary is premature. This "right to effective treatment" group (e.g., Matson, 1988; Van Houten et al., 1988) argues that the combination of punitive and positive-based strategies is currently the most effective treatment for those individuals who exhibit severe and dangerous behavior disorders.

This paper will (a) examine the validity of the claims made by both groups, (b) describe the positive and negative impact that each position has or could have on the treatment of persons with developmental disabilities, and (c) outline a model that attempts to balance and protect both the right to be free from harm *and* the right to receive effective treatment.

ISSUES

The "Freedom from Harm" Position

CLAIMS. Advocates of this position maintain that the use of punishment with persons who have developmental disabilities is unethical and unnecessary. They profess that nonpunitive methods, such as reinforcing alternative behavior, produce better generalization and maintenance of therapeutic and educational gains than punishment and that, unlike punishment, there are no negative side effects.

How valid are these claims? Recently published reviews (Favell et al., 1982; Gorman-Smith & Matson, 1985; Lennox, Miltenberger, Spengler, & Erfanian, 1988; Matson & Gorman-Smith, 1986; Matson & Taras, 1989) have consistently revealed that most research indicates that combinations of positive reinforcement and punishment strategies are more effective than reinforcement alone in treating *severe* behavior problems. Also, some recent studies that supposedly illustrate the effectiveness of a nonpunitive approach either did not deal with severe behavior disorders or were found to be methodologically weak, or included in fact, potential punishment components (e.g., Berkman & Meyer, 1988; McGee et al., 1987; Santarcangelo, Dyer, & Luce, 1987; Wells & Smith, 1983). Thus, the claims of those that advocate the exclusive use of nonpunitive procedures may be premature, given the current technology and research (See Axelrod, 1987a; Bailey, 1987; Love, 1988; Mudford, 1985).

Second, the claim that reinforcement-based reductive procedures lead to better generalization and maintenance than punishment is also not clearly supported in the literature (Matson & Taras, 1989). It is recognized (Stokes & Baer, 1977) that generalization of positively reinforced behavior requires explicit programming by using such strategies as multiple exemplars, common stimuli, and loose training. Theoretically and logistically, these techniques also could be applied to enhance the generalization of punishment effects.

The effects of positive reinforcement and punishment also are symmetrical with respect to maintenance. That is, while the discontinuation of a punishment procedure is likely to result in an increase in the target behavior, termination of a reinforcement program likely will decrease the newly learned behavior; in fact, this is the rationale behind single-subject withdrawal designs (Hersen & Barlow, 1976). The perception that the behavior suppressing effects of punishment do not persist as long as positively reinforced behaviors may exist because of a tendency to notice the re-emergence of a previously punished high-rate and salient maladaptive behavior (e.g., head banging) more readily than the gradual extinction of previously reinforced low-rate unobtrusive adaptive behavior (e.g., on-task, playing). Effective maintenance strategies (e.g., thinning schedules, transferring control to natural contingencies) are needed for both reinforcement and punishment interventions.

Third, the view that positive reinforcement strategies are free of negative side effects is not entirely justified. For example, Balsam and Bondy (1983) described several unwanted side effects of positive reinforcement, such as aggression, ritualistic behaviors, distraction from the learning task, and dependency on the reinforcing agent. Those authors who are promoting positive-based approaches do not make reference to the potential for these undesirable side effects of reinforcement.

In summary, the claims of the anti-punishment group are not supported by the weight of current research findings. Although there are some promising developments in the areas of ecobehavioral and functional analyses, reinforcer identification, differential reinforcement of alternative behavior, extinction, and stimulus control (e.g., Axelrod, 1987b; Carr & Durand, 1985; Iwata, Dorsey, Slifer, Bauman, & Richman, 1982; Repp, Felce, & Barton, 1988; Rincover & Devany, 1982; Steege, Wacker, Berg, Cigrand, & Cooper, 1989; Touchette, MacDonald, & Langer, 1985), the effectiveness of all-positive approaches in eliminating serious maladaptive behavior, without requiring an accompanying punitive procedure, has yet to be clearly substantiated. Moreover, some of the problems that plague punishment techniques (e.g., generalization, maintenance, unwanted side effects) may occur with nonpunitive methods as well.

IMPACT. The anti-punishment movement has had both positive and negative repercussions. On the plus side, it has led to a rejuvenation of interest and research in nonpunitive procedures; this is clearly in the best interests of clients. The renewed emphasis on positive strategies discourages the use of a "cookbook" approach in favor of ecological and functional analyses (Axelrod, 1987b; Iwata et al., 1982; LaVigna & Donnellan, 1986). A systematic and thorough behavioral assessment helps identify the controlling and maintaining variables for the maladaptive behavior; this information is crucial in designing effective nonintrusive programs primarily aimed at teaching functional and socially appropriate behaviors to replace the maladaptive behavior (e.g., Carr & Durand, 1985; Steege et al., 1989; Repp et al., 1988). While functional analysis has been long recommended in behavior modification textbooks (e.g., Martin & Pear, 1978; Sulzer-Azaroff & Mayer, 1975), it has yet to become standard practice in many settings.

There also have been some negative effects of the anti-punishment crusade which ostensively calls for the banning of punitive procedures (although it is often not clear which specific procedures are being denounced). If certain techniques that would effectively eliminate harmful behaviors such as self-injury are banned, what happens to those individuals, however few in number they may be, who do not respond to the best efforts at nonpunitive intervention? The outcomes are bleak: To be expected is prolonged suffering, not just of the individual, but also of the family, friends, and care providers; a lifetime of physical and/or chemical restraint; placement in a more restrictive environment; rejection; and lost opportunities to engage in meaningful social, educational, vocational, and recreational activities.

There may be some other negative aspects of denying access to treatment. Some individuals, because of their current behavior disorders, will be considered "unteachable;" ironically, they may be denied access to the very training programs that would teach them alternative functional behavior due to an unwillingness on the part of administrators or program staff to use certain procedures that would have allowed such a person to function successfully in that environment and benefit from instruction.

If formal punishment programs are discouraged, there may be an increased risk of nonprogrammatic and unrecognized use of intrusive procedures. To avoid charges of promoting intrusive programs, some practitioners may re-label contingent restraint, social isolation, and other potentially punishing consequences as "crisis intervention," or give them pretty names (e.g., "relaxation room" instead of time-out room). In such a climate, agencies may claim an absence of punishment programs, when in effect the front-line staff may be (inconsistently) applying intrusive and aversive stimuli in order to prevent injury, destruction, and disruption. This may result in de facto use of aversives without appropriate safeguards typical of sanctioned behavioral programs (i.e., informed consent, accompanying positive reinforcement, review, and evaluation). Increased likelihood of abuse to clients is also possible due to the staff's lack of recognition, documentation, understanding, and training in the procedures being employed. For example, the consistent application of restraint as a form of crisis intervention to "calm" the aggressive client actually may be functioning as a punisher (i.e., reducing the future probability of the response on which it is contingent). No amount of "psychobabble" or good intentions will turn off the laws of nature. In effect, the so-called crisis intervention procedure is no different operationally or functionally from the contingent restraint prohibited by the agency because it is too intrusive. However, the reinforcement contingencies for the verbal behavior of directors and managers to maintain publicly that no punishment programs are operating in their organizations are not necessarily the same as the contingencies for front-line staff actually responsible for maintaining control of client behavior in service settings. Safeguards to protect the clients from unnecessary harm need to be put in place regardless of whether restrictive, intrusive, and aversive procedures are considered behavioral programs or not (Blake et al., 1987).

The reluctance to acknowledge the use of punitive procedures also is found in the treatment literature. Two examples are provided. The first paper (Wells & Smith, 1983), touted without qualification (Sobsey, 1987) as providing evidence for the effectiveness of nonpunitive intervention, describes the results of an application of sensory integration to the treatment of self-injury. The study reported that self-injury decreased in four persons with mental retardation when stimulation (e.g., vibration) was provided, particularly to affected body areas. While the demonstration of treatment effectiveness is questionable, given such obvious methodological flaws as a lack of an experimental design in 3 of the 4 subjects, non-naive observers, and no reliability data, what is most pertinent to the present discussion is the fact that "when ... SIB occurred ... the trainer then intervened by *holding the subject's hands until a decrease in resistance... occurred*" (p. 665, emphasis added). No further mention is made of the use and potential effects of hand restraint although there are many examples in the literature of the punishing effects of contingent restraint. Ironically, the very next study in the same issue of the journal (Richmond, 1983) provides evidence that a treatment package including brief hand restraint decreased stereotypic behavior. Unlike the previous article, Richmond described the programmed consequence for stereotypic behavior (reprimand and hands down) in the abstract and refers to it throughout the article. He operationalized duration of restraint (2-3 sec), and, in the discussion, he acknowledged the multicomponent aspect of the treatment package consisting of both reinforcement and punishment.

The second example of "hidden punishment" (Santarcangelo et al., 1987), published in the *Journal of The Association for Persons with Severe Handicaps* (an organization that lobbies against punishment), claims to show a decrease in the disruptive behavior of four children with autism "through reinforcement of appropriate play behaviors," but fails to acknowledge the possible punishing effects of an accompanying verbal reprimand procedure (Van Houten, Nau, MacKenzie-Keating, Sameoto, & Colavecchia, 1982).

The two *published* papers cited above illustrate the inhibition to accept the role of punishment in a professional environment where people who use punishment may be punished themselves. Rather than avoiding the issue by hiding, de-emphasizing, or renaming intrusive or aversive procedures, their use should be clearly documented and be subject to legal, professional, and ethical standards and safeguards (e.g., Blake et al., 1987; Repp & Deitz, 1978).

In summary then, the recent efforts to promote positive procedures and decry punitive methods has had both positive effects (e.g., the development and promotion of research on new nonpunitive approaches, re-emphasis on functional analysis), and potentially negative effects (e.g., denial of right to treatment, exclusion from less restrictive settings, failure to document active treatment variables).

The "Right to Effective Treatment" Position

CLAIMS. On the other side of the continuum, there are practitioners (e.g., Van Houten et al., 1988) who argue that when dealing with severe behavior problems that are causing injury, the client should receive the most effective treatment as soon as possible and that clients should not be exposed to treatments, although less intrusive, which are not likely to be effective and which would simply prolong the suffering experienced by the individual.

Advocates of this approach argue that the aversiveness of a program cannot be judged in isolation; a thorough analysis must include an examination of the total amount of suffering experienced because of the continuing behavior problem; and that the decision to use a particular strategy should be based on the technique that will add the least aversiveness but still result in the largest overall reduction in suffering experienced by the person. For the most part, the right-to-treatment group argues, that existing evidence suggests that the combination of punishment of the maladaptive behavior and positive programming for alternative behavior is currently the most effective intervention for severe behavior problems and, therefore, should be the treatment of choice.

With its focus on magnitude and speed of behavior change, this position is perceived as having a constricted view of effectiveness (LaVigna, 1987). More consideration should be given to other important outcome measures, such as generalization, maintenance, clinical significance, side effects, and social validity/acceptability (Favell et al., 1982).

Also, this group downplays the fundamental and generally accepted model of treatment which calls for the use of the least restrictive/intrusive intervention. The model is the standard of practice in medicine and has served that profession well (although not perfectly). This approach recommends a continuum of empirically tested interventions for a particular ailment, starting with ones that are likely to cause the least risk and disruption to the person's life, are least discomforting and stressful, and have the fewest negative side effects. If initial results are discouraging, then more restrictive treatments are prescribed as necessary to eliminate the illness.

The right-to-effective treatment group maintains (e.g., Matson, 1988) that the least restrictive but most effective treatment be employed. As this group also argues that behavioral programs incorporating punishment are the most effective, logic dictates that punishment be used in the initial stages of treatment. This decision-making model, however, is currently operating in an empirical vacuum. While there is considerable evidence documenting the effectiveness of punitive procedures, there is still little research identifying pretreatment variables which would allow for an accurate prediction that, *for a particular client in a particular circumstance*, nonpunitive procedures are not likely to be effective and so intrusive procedures are needed at the outset of treatment. At this time, initial interventions for individual clients are often chosen more on the basis of the individual clinician's bias, judgment, and institutional constraints than by reference to scientific or actuarial predictor variables.

IMPACT. Like the anti-punishment view, this approach has had positive and negative effects on the field. An obvious benefit of going directly to the most powerful suppressive treatment is seen with life-threatening situations where continued self-injury or aggression could cause death or serious harm. Expeditious elimination of a behavior problem decreases reliance on chronic restraint, isolation, and psychotropic medication; it allows increased participation in less restrictive and more positive environments that promote the learning of alternative behavior.

There are potential negative aspects of using intrusive procedures. There are concerns (Guess et al., 1987; LaVigna & Donnellan, 1986; McGee et al., 1987; Turnbull et al., 1986) about the degrading and controlling aspects of punishment, lack of social acceptability (Irvin & Lundervold, 1988), emotional side effects (Newsom, Favell, & Rincover, 1983), narrow stimulus control (Birnbrauer, 1968), and poor maintenance (Foxx & Livesay, 1984). As indicated earlier, the latter three problems are not unique to punishment and may also occur with reinforcement-based programs.

Another important issue raised by the anti-punishment faction is that the punishers may be highly reinforced for using punishment (Turnbull et al., 1986). This may result in increasing reliance on more and more intrusive procedures for more and more clients; correspondingly, there would be less effort directed at trying alternative nonpunitive approaches.

Thus, there is a trade-off when a consideration is made to use the most effective intervention for the treatment of severe behavior problems in persons with developmental disabilities. Rapid reductions in aberrant behavior may be achieved through the use of intrusive and/or aversive procedures, but the overall and long-term impact on the person's quality of life, as well as the social context in which the intervention takes place, must be considered also when making treatment decisions.

Balancing Freedom from Harm and the Right to Treatment

The two approaches represented here, the "freedom from harm" view on the one hand and the "right to effective treatment" view on the other, garner moral, clinical, and scientific arguments in defense of their positions. As described above, although each position offers potential benefits, the extreme and mostly unsubstantiated aspects of their arguments may have detrimental effects on individuals and on the field. The majority of practitioners no doubt try to balance these opposing views, incorporate their strengths, and spurn their weaknesses. This model maintains the least restrictive/intrusive treatment alternative; it emphasizes preventive approaches and a substantive behavioral assessment looking at, among other things, ecological/functional analyses and reinforcer identification (Axelrod, 1987b; Iwata et al., 1982; LaVigna & Donnellan, 1986; Steege et al., 1989). Initially, the information from the behavioral assessment is used to develop a comprehensive positive program (LaVigna & Donnellan, 1986) which may include such nonpunitive strategies as stimulus control (Touchette et al., 1985), differential reinforcement (Repp & Deitz, 1974), extinction (Rincover & Devany, 1982), and functional communication/skill training (Carr & Durand, 1985).

The above methodology is obviously compatible with the freedom- from-harm view. However, unlike the position taken by the anti-punishment group, a more balanced approach does not call for the banning of punitive procedures. Instead, it recognizes that no matter how sophisticated we become in deploying nonpunitive interventions, certain clients still may not improve; their behavior problems, however, may be amenable to other treatments that incorporate punishment.

Until such time, however, as prognostic indicators are identified that allow for accurate predictions of the potential effects of different interventions for different individuals, the application of the least restrictive model should start with nominally nonpunitive and socially acceptable interventions. If the severity of the client's behavior warrants the use of protective devices and procedures (e.g., response blocking, physical restraint), then the possible function (i.e., reinforcing or punishing) of these events should be determined, acknowledged, and perhaps incorporated into the treatment (e.g., Favell, McGimsey, & Jones, 1978).

Explicit punishment procedures should be used only after reasonable attempts to use nonpunitive strategies have been unsuccessful. As with the selection of nonpunitive procedures, the choice of the punishment also should be derived from the functional analysis; e.g., positive practice may be more effective than time-out for escape-motivated behavior.

Intrusive and aversive procedures should be used only with appropriate consents, safeguards, and review (i.e., under a set of government-sanctioned regulations and standards) by trained and supervised mediators, and only as a last resort. Any program incorporating punishment should provide careful monitoring of side effects, emotional preparation of significant others in the person's life, and strategies to facilitate generalization and maintenance (preferably with natural reinforcement contingencies). A punitive procedure should be implemented only as part of a larger program aimed at increasing functional alternative skills. The lack of resources to conduct an effective reinforcement-based program or institutional expedience should not serve as justifications to implement a more intrusive program.

NEEDED RESEARCH

The above approach attempts to strike a balance between the least restrictive model and the right-to-effective treatment, given the current treatment technology. The fact that reviewers [e.g., Favell et al. (1982) and Matson and Taras (1989) on the one hand versus LaVigna and Donnellan (1986) and Sobsey (1987) on the other] have reached virtually opposite conclusions about the relative efficacy of punitive and nonpunitive interventions attests to the inconclusiveness of the current literature. Certainly more research and development is needed in the areas of prevention, behavioral assessment, prognosis, diagnosis-treatment interactions, and positive-based interventions. There is a dearth of well-designed intervention comparison studies (see Jordan, Singh, & Repp, 1989, for an exception), particularly those employing between-group designs. Indeed, most of the studies evaluating behavioral interventions rely on single-case designs which have limited external validity (Lovaas & Favell, 1987). Current empirical support for the effectiveness of punishment comes primarily through replication across a wide range of clients, behaviors, settings, and mediators.

The most important question in this area of research is not which "works" better, nonpunitive or punitive procedures, but rather which interventions work best with which kinds of persons, for which problems, with the least negative side effects (Kazdin & Wilson, 1978). Between-group studies with large sample sizes are needed to address this issue. This is the approach used in most branches of medicine to evaluate and compare treatments. In evaluating treatments for severe behavior disorders, however, ambitious studies are hampered by lack of adequate numbers of subjects to generate sufficient statistical power. To overcome this obstacle, researchers from different treatment centers should be encouraged to pool their subjects and resources and collaborate on large-scale multi-site projects. Another problem with conducting between-group studies is the ethical dilemma posed by assigning persons with dangerous behaviors to control groups. In reality, however, as many clinics are unable to treat all referred clients at any one time, waiting list control groups already exist.

CONCLUSION

In conclusion, the development of a treatment technology that is both morally *and* scientifically based will not be achieved by oversimplifying complex issues; i.e., positive reinforcement (good) versus punishment (bad) (Axelrod, 1987a), but rather through research designed to identify the intricate interactions that likely exist between the efficacy of different interventions (and combinations), presenting problems, client characteristics, and setting variables. We should maintain a positive bias reflecting the least restrictive model; we should not expose clients to unnecessary punishment programs. On the other hand, we also do them a disservice if we provide them only those programs that have an emotional appeal or that look good, but are totally ineffective. Our good intentions must be tempered by empirical results.

Continued research should make punitive procedures less necessary than they are now; however, therapeutic punishment should still be available for those, hopefully, fewer and fewer individuals who may need them.

REFERENCES

Axelrod, S. (1987a). Doing it without arrows: A review of Lavigna and Donnellan's "Alternatives to punishment: Solving behavior problems with non-aversive strategies." *Behavior Analyst, 10*, 243-251.

Axelrod, S. (1987b). Functional and structural analyses of behavior: Approaches leading to reduced use of punishment procedures? *Research in Developmental Disabilities, 8*, 165-178.

Bailey, J.S. (1987). Misguided alternatives. *Contemporary Psychology, 32*, 571-572.

Balsam, P.D., & Bondy, A.S. (1983). The negative side effects of reward. *Journal of Applied Behavior Analysis, 16*, 283-296.

Berkman, K.A., & Meyer, L.H. (1988). Alternative strategies and multiple outcomes in the remediation of severe self-injury: Going "all out" nonaversively. *Journal of The Association for Persons with Severe Handicaps, 13*, 76-86.

Birnbrauer, J. (1968). Generalization on punishment effects: A case study. *Journal of Applied Behavior Analysis, 1*, 201-211.

Blake, M., Feldman, M., Keller, M., Moore, C., & Munn, F. (1987). *Standards for the use of behavioural training and treatment procedures in settings for developmentally handicapped persons.* Toronto: Ontario Ministry of Community and Social Services.

Carr, E.G., & Durand, V.M. (1985). Reducing behavior problems through functional communication training. *Journal of Applied Behavior Analysis, 18*, 111-126.

Favell, J.E., Azrin, N.H., Baumeister. A.A., Carr, E.G., Dorsey, M.F., Forehand, R., Foxx, R.M., Lovaas, O.I., Rincover, A., Risley, T.R., Romanczyk, R.G., Russo, D.C., Schroeder, S.R., & Solnick, J.V. (1982). The treatment of self-injurious behavior. *Behavior Therapy, 13*, 529-554.

Favell, J.E., McGimsey, J.F., Jones, & M.L. (1978). The use of physical restraint in the treatment of self-injury and as positive reinforcement. *Journal of Applied Behavior Analysis, 11*, 225-242.

Foxx, R.M., & Livesay, J. (1984). Maintenance of response suppression following overcorrection: A 10-year retrospective examination of eight cases. *Analysis and Intervention in Developmental Disabilities, 4*, 65-79.

Gorman-Smith, D., & Matson, J.L. (1985). A review of treatment research for self-injurious and stereotyped responding. *Journal of Mental Deficiency Research, 29*, 295-308.

Guess, D., Helmstetter, E., Turnbull, H.R., & Knowlton, S. (1987). Use of aversive procedures with persons who are disabled: An historical review and critical analysis. TASH Monograph Series, No. 2. Seattle, WA: The Association for Persons with Severe Handicaps.

Hersen, M., & Barlow, D.H. (1976). *Single case experimental designs: Strategies for studying behavior change*. New York: Pergamon Press.

Irvin, L.K., & Lundervold, D.A. (1988). Social validation of decelerative (punishment) procedures by special educators of severely handicapped students. *Research in Developmental Disabilities, 9*, 331-350.

Iwata, B.A., Dorsey, M.F., Slifer, K.J., Bauman, K.E., & Richman, G.S. (1982). Toward a functional analysis of self-injury. *Analysis and Intervention in Developmental Disabilities, 2*, 3-20.

Jordan, J., Singh, N.N., & Repp, A.C. (1989). An evaluation of gentle teaching and visual screening in the reduction of stereotypy. *Journal of Applied Behavior Analysis, 22*, 9-22.

Kazdin, A.E., & Wilson, G.T. (1978). *Evaluation of behavior therapy: Issues, evidence, and research strategies.* Cambridge, MA: Ballinger.

LaVigna, G.W. (1987). *The case against aversive stimuli: A review of the clinical and empirical evidence.* Paper presented at the Association for Behavior Analysis 13th Annual Convention, Nashville, TN, May 1987.

LaVigna, G.W., & Donnellan, A.M. (1986). *Alternatives to punishment: Solving behavior problems with nonaversive strategies*. New York: Irvington.

Lennox, D.B., Miltenberger, R.G., Spengler, P., & Erfanian, N. (1988). Decelerative treatment practices with persons who have mental retardation: A review of five years of the literature. *American Journal on Mental Retardation, 92*, 492-501.

Lovaas, O.I., & Favell, J.E. (1987). Protection for clients undergoing aversive/restrictive interventions. *Education and Treatment of Children, 10*, 311-325.

Love, S.R. (1988). Review of "Gentle Teaching: A Non-aversive Approach in Helping Persons with Mental Retardation." *Research in Developmental Disabilities, 9*, 441-443.

Martin, G., & Pear, J. (1978). *Behavior modification: What it is and how to do it.* Englewood Cliffs, NJ: Prentice-Hall.

Matson, J.L. (1988, March 30). *Statement of Philosophy and Goals*. International Association for the Right to Effective Treatment.

Matson, J.L., & Gorman-Smith, D. (1986). A review of treatment research for aggressive and disruptive behavior in the mentally retarded. *Applied Research in Mental Retardation, 7*, 95-103.

Matson, J.L., & Taras, M.E. (1989). A 20 year review of punishment and alternative methods to treat problem behaviors in developmentally delayed persons. *Research in Developmental Disabilities, 10*, 85-104.

McGee, J.J., Menolascino, F.J., Hobbs, D.C., & Menousek, P.E. (1987). *Gentle teaching: A non-aversive approach to helping persons with mental retardation*. New York: Human Sciences Press.

Mudford, O.C. (1985). Treatment selection in behavior reduction: Gentle teaching versus the least intrusive treatment model. *Australia and New Zealand Journal of Developmental Disabilities, 10,* 265-270.

Newsom, C., Favell, J.E., & Rincover, A. (1983). The multiple effects of punishment. In J. Apsche and S. Axelrod (Eds.), *Punishment: Its effects on human behavior* (pp. 285-316). New York: Plenum Press.

Repp, A.C., & Deitz, D.E.D. (1978). On the selective use of punishment. *Mental Retardation, 16,* 250-254.

Repp, A.C., & Deitz, S.M. (1974). Reducing aggressive and self-injurious behavior of institutionalized retarded children through reinforcement of other behaviors. *Journal of Applied Behavior Analysis, 7*, 313-315.

Repp, A.C., Felce, D., & Barton, L.E. (1988). Basing treatment of stereotypic and self-injurious behaviors on hypotheses of their causes. *Journal of Applied Behavior Analysis, 21*, 281-290.

Richmond, G. (1983). Evaluation of a treatment for a hand-mouthing stereotypy. *American Journal of Mental Deficiency, 87*, 667-669.

Rincover, A., & Devany, J. (1982). The application of sensory extinction procedures to self-injury. *Analysis and Intervention in Developmental Disabilities, 2*, 67-81.

Santarcangelo, S., Dyer, K., & Luce, S. (1987). Generalized reduction in disruptive behavior in unsupervised settings through specific toy play. *Journal of The Association for Persons with Severe Handicaps, 12,* 38-44.

Sobsey, D. (1987). Non-aversive behavior management: The verdict is in. *News and Notes (American Association on Mental Retardation). 1*, pp. 2, 8.

Steege, M.W., Wacker, D.P., Berg, W.K., Cigrand, K.K., & Cooper, L.J. (1989). The use of behavioral assessment to prescribe and evaluate treatments for severely handicapped children. *Journal of Applied Behavior Analysis, 22*, 23-33.

Stokes, T. F., & Baer, D. M. (1977). An implicit technology of generalization. *Journal of Applied Behavior Analysis, 10*, 349-367.

Sulzer-Azaroff, B., & Mayer, G.R. (1975). *Applying behavior-analysis procedures with children and youth*. New York: Holt, Rinehart and Winston.

Touchette, P.E., MacDonald, R.F., & Langer, S.N. (1985). A scatter plot for identifying stimulus control of problem behavior. *Journal of Applied Behavior Analysis, 18*, 343-351.

Turnbull, H.R., Guess, D., Backus, L., Barber, P.A., Fiedler, C.R., Helmstetter, E., & Summers, J.A. (1986). A model for analyzing the moral aspects of special education and behavioral interventions: The moral aspects of aversive procedures. In P.R. Dokecki and R.M. Zaner (Eds.), *Ethics of dealing with persons with severe handicaps* (pp. 167-216). Baltimore: Paul H. Brookes.

Van Houten, R., Axelrod, S., Bailey, J.S., Favell, J.E., Foxx, R.M., Iwata, B.A., & Lovaas, O.I. (1988). The right to effective behavioral treatment. *Journal of Applied Behavior Analysis, 21*, 381-384.

Van Houten, R., Nau, P.A., MacKenzie-Keating, S.E., Sameoto, D., & Colavecchia, B. (1982). An analysis of some variables influencing the effectiveness of reprimands. *Journal of Applied Behavior Analysis, 15*, 65-83.

Wells, M.E., & Smith, D.W. (1983). Reduction of self-injurious behavior of mentally retarded persons using sensory-integrative techniques. *American Journal of Mental Deficiency, 87*, 664-666.

CHAPTER

19

PREVENTING SERIOUS BEHAVIOR PROBLEMS THROUGH SKILL DEVELOPMENT AND EARLY INTERVENTION

Glen Dunlap, Lynn Foster Johnson, and Frank R. Robbins

Florida Mental Health Institute
University of South Florida

A powerful movement in the field of developmental disabilities has focused on the development and dissemination of positive, "nonaversive" approaches for solving serious behavior problems (Horner, Dunlap, Koegel, Carr, Sailor, Anderson, Albin, & O'Neill, in press). This movement has emerged in concert with efforts to promote community integration and human rights, and also as a response to the common technologies that seek to suppress problem behaviors through aversive contingencies (cf. Evans & Meyer, 1985; LaVigna & Donnellan, 1986). Proponents of positive perspectives have described a diverse array of strategies that are difficult to subsume under one orientation (e.g., Durand, in press; McGee, Menolascino, Hobbs, & Menousek, 1987; Meyer & Evans, 1989). However, one common theme that tends to characterize positive approaches is the focus on preventing behavior problems by building repertoires of adaptive, functional skills (e.g., Carr & Durand, 1985), by incorporating ecological and antecedent manipulations (e.g., Dyer, Dunlap, & Winterling, in press; Kern, Koegel, & Dunlap, 1984; Singer, Singer, & Horner, 1987), and by promoting social integration and enriched lifestyles (e.g., Berkman & Meyer, 1988; Horner, 1989). This emphasis on prevention is a clear departure from techniques that stress punishment contingencies and behavioral suppression.

The thesis of this chapter is that prevention of serious behavior problems can be accomplished best by initiating systematic, functional skill development at a very early age. Furthermore, the authors believe that comprehensive programs of early intervention (followed by well-designed, longitudinal programs of education and behavioral support) should be capable of preventing the later occurrence of serious behavior problems in the vast majority of cases (McGee, 1988). While there are no experimental studies that address this thesis directly, there is an extensive array of convergent data and logic that are supportive of this position. The purpose of this chapter is to discuss the advantages and to highlight the promise of early intervention as an avenue for habilitation and prevention of behavior problems in persons with severe developmental disabilities.

Before discussing specific arguments, we would like to clarify some key terms.

First, by *behavior problems,* we are referring to responses such as severe aggression, self-injury, disruptive tantrums, destruction of property, bizarre stereotypies, and other behaviors that cause injury or are so violent and stigmatizing that they are incompatible with regular community participation. We are not suggesting that early intervention (or any other approach) can serve to prevent all undesirable behavior. Our concern is with those topographies that demand intervention because they produce obvious harm to a person's physical or social well-being. The focus of the chapter is on *persons with developmental disabilities*, especially those with severe mental retardation and autism. However, we expect that the message and implications of this chapter pertain equally to individuals with less severe handicaps. Finally, by *early intervention*, we are referring to individualized assessment and treatment that is comprehensive, that focuses on functional skill development (especially in the domains of communication and socialization), and that is begun during or before the preschool years. In particular, we are referring to "state-of-the-art" services that incorporate professional and family participation, transdisciplinary expertise, and the latest information in instructional technology, child development, and applied behavior analysis.

The remainder of this chapter will be divided into four sections. In the first, we will discuss the concept of prevention and skill development. We then will delineate general advantages of early intervention and show how effective early intervention may contribute importantly to the prevention of future behavior problems. In the third section, summary data from a regional training and consultation program will be presented to illustrate positive effects of an early intervention service that focused on establishing functional skills and positive interpersonal relationships. In the final section, we will summarize the discussion and offer suggestions for developing early intervention as a pivotal component in the service agenda for persons with developmental disabilities.

PREVENTING SERIOUS BEHAVIOR PROBLEMS

In recent years, there has been an increased emphasis on interventions that are designed to affect behavior problems indirectly. That is, instead of emphasizing specific consequences to apply when problem behaviors are actually occurring, interventions are being focused increasingly on what to do during those times when behavior problems are *not* occurring. The general idea is that behavior problems can be solved more durably, and in a way that preserves a person's rights to dignity, if the emphasis of intervention is placed on developing functional competencies and providing environmental contexts that encourage socially acceptable responses. If such desirable patterns of responding are functionally redundant with, or topographically incompatible with, behavior problems, the intervention serves both habilitative and preventive purposes.

"Preventing" serious behavior problems can be viewed from very different perspectives. Head banging, for example, can be prevented by employing physical or chemical restraints. Such procedures, however, are highly negative in that they simultaneously inhibit other forms of responding. The use of restraints is viewed by many as unacceptable, except in dangerous crises when they might be necessary on a temporary basis (Horner et al., in press). More positive preventive approaches include stimulus-based manipulations (Carr, Taylor, Carlson, & Robinson, in press). This set of procedures involves changing those stimuli that are associated with problem behaviors, and/or arranging for the presence of stimuli that are correlated with desirable patterns of responding (e.g., Carr, Newsom, & Binkoff, 1976; Dyer et al., in press; Kern et al., 1984; Singer et al., 1987; Touchette, MacDonald, & Langer, 1985; Winterling, Dunlap, & O'Neill, 1987). The stimuli to be manipulated may include instructions, curricular activities, people, materials, or any number of other antecedent or setting events. Stimulus-based interventions often produce rapid and dramatic effects, and they represent an important and growing part of positive behavior management (Carr et al., in press). However, one limitation of stimulus-based procedures is that their effects can be expected to apply only to the immediate contexts in which they are used.

A more comprehensive approach to prevention is *skill development.* This, too, is a central component of positive behavior management, and it is particularly germane from the perspective of early intervention. Skill development is a broad behavior management tactic which seeks to preclude the subsequent occurrence of problem responses by establishing behavioral competencies that are socially desirable and that facilitate access to reinforcers in the individual's natural environment. The essential logic holds that if a person has learned to use efficient, appropriate responses which serve the functions that otherwise might be served by problem behaviors, there will be a much greater probability that the desirable responses will be performed and, conversely, a much reduced likelihood that problem behaviors will be exhibited. The skill development approach views behavior problems more as manifestations of behavioral deficiencies than as behavioral excesses. With habilitative education designed to overcome these deficiencies, behavior problems (or the future potential for the emergence of behavior problems) can be effectively prevented.

Skill development includes interventions that are designed for immediate and longitudinal purposes. Skills that are established to respond to immediate needs are usually identified through functional analyses of prevailing behavior problems (O'Neill, Horner, Albin, Storey, & Sprague, in press). Such analyses are conducted in order to determine the functional operations of specifically identified behavior problems, with the expectation that the findings will suggest some alternative response(s) that might be taught as an appropriate replacement. For example, Horner and Budd (1985) assessed the disruptive yelling and grabbing of a nonverbal boy with severe handicaps and determined that these problem behaviors regularly were associated with the presentation of certain stimulus items (e.g., juice). The authors eliminated (prevented) future occurrences of the problem behavior by teaching the child to use manual signs as an effective and efficient form of requesting the identified stimuli. Analogous relationships between many problem behaviors and communication have been confirmed by numerous authors (e.g., Bird, Dores, Moniz, & Robinson, 1989; Carr, 1988; Carr & Durand, 1985; Donnellan, Mirenda, Mesaros, & Fassbender, 1984; Durand & Carr, 1987), suggesting that the most common target for skill development must be functional communication (Durand, in press). Attempts to establish desirable, communicative equivalents, based on systematic functional analyses, are becoming acknowledged as extremely positive and productive directions for the management of serious behavior problems (Horner et al., in press).

While training in functional communication skills is the most common educative approach for reducing behavior problems, other instructional efforts have met with similar success. For example, Santarcangelo, Dyer, and Luce (1987) examined the disruptive responding of four children with autism in unstructured play settings. When the authors taught the children to play appropriately with specific toys, they found that the children's disruptions were reduced significantly. In another study (Hunt, Alwell, & Goetz, 1988), strategies were developed for increasing the duration of positive social exchanges between students with handicaps and their nondisabled peers. As the "conversational" interactions were established, inappropriate and disruptive problem behaviors declined. These and other investigations (e.g., Eason, White, & Newsom, 1982; Favell, McGimsey, & Schell, 1982; Koegel, & Koegel, 1990) illustrate the generalized reduction in problem behaviors that can be attributed to programs of skill acquisition.

From the same skill development perspective, one may expect that a comprehensive and longitudinal program of functional education should be capable of preventing, in addition to remediating, serious behavior problems. Given that many behavior problems occur because of deficient repertoires of appropriate responding, one can reasonably assume that increased competencies could provide an individual with opportunities and reinforcers that would reduce substantially the "need for" disruptive behavior patterns. If a person is provided with proficiencies in adaptive life skills and communication, and if these expressions are reinforced, problem behaviors that serve such purposes would be redundant and unnecessary. Effective training in self-care routines, leisure and recreation skills, self-management, relaxation, mobility, independence, tolerance, social interactions and negotiations, and vocational adjustments could increase the probability of successful outcomes in a wide range of typical life circumstances. The greater the competencies in functional adaptations, the less chance there should be that intransigent, serious problem behaviors would develop.

Continuing advances in instructional technology and in the design of supportive environments are making such comprehensive educational programs increasingly feasible. However, for persons who experience severe disabilities, such efforts still must be viewed as very long-term endeavors. It is, in fact, logical to begin such programs at the earliest possible point in time. There are many reasons to believe, in particular, that a comprehensive program of functional skill development that is begun during or before the preschool years should be capable of establishing a broad foundation for competent performance and, indirectly, an effective deterrent to the later occurrence of serious behavior problems.

While the authors' conviction is that early intervention can represent an effective behavioral "inoculation," we acknowledge that there is no direct evidence in support of this position. This is probably the case, in part, because of the difficulties in conducting research on prevention over long periods of time. Also, the perspectives that would guide such hypotheses have not been well established until recently. However, despite the absence of direct experimentation, there are many logical arguments and data that converge to support quality early intervention as an avenue for both effective habilitation and prevention. Therefore, our aim in the following section will be to delineate some of the general advantages of an early intervention approach.

ADVANTAGES OF EARLY INTERVENTION

Too often, systematic intervention is initiated at a time when it is most likely to fail; that is, when the behavior problem has progressed to the point that it is extremely intense, its history is long and complex, and service providers have become fearful or otherwise have become hesitant to undertake time-consuming, educative interventions. In contrast, early intervention services may have a much greater likelihood of short-term success and long-term impact. Some of the most obvious advantages of early intervention may be described as (a) a relative receptivity to instructional programs, (b) a relative simplicity of learning histories and functional analyses, (c) facilitating characteristics of caregivers and ecologies, and (d) facilitating physical characteristics.

Receptivity to Instruction

Although the empirical support for this assertion is still developing (Casto & Mastropieri, 1986; Simeonsson, Olley, & Rosenthal, 1987), there is nevertheless a prevalent belief that instructional programs for persons with severe developmental disabilities are more effective and easier to conduct when the students are still in early childhood. There are also studies that demonstrate the relative educability of very young children. In a retrospective analysis, Fenske, Zalenski, Krantz, and McClannahan (1985) reported significantly greater improvements when children with autism entered treatment before the age of five in comparison with those children who began intervention after they had turned five. Similarly, a number of authors have reported substantial gains in cognitive and curricular performance when interventions were initiated during or before the preschool years (e.g., Anderson, Avery, DiPietro, Edwards, & Christian, 1987; Dunlap, Robbins, & Plienis, 1989; Groden, Dominque, Chesnick, Groden, & Baron, 1983; Lovaas, 1987). The magnitude of these gains is not paralleled in studies with older individuals.

When children are provided with early educational services, they begin to acquire skills and competencies that can be functional immediately, as well as serving as an important foundation for the development of more advanced skills in later years. This may be true especially in the related domains of communication and socialization. Numerous authors, for example, have indicated that a child who has not learned to speak or use language before kindergarten may have a relatively poor prognosis, especially in the realm of speech and language development (e.g., Rutter, 1978). While the exact reasons for such a "critical period" are not yet completely understood, several authors have pointed to the processes of neurological maturation and cerebral lateralization (e.g., Krashen, 1975; Lenneberg, 1967). From this perspective, Wetherby and her colleagues (e.g., Wetherby, 1984; Prizant & Wetherby, 1988) have emphasized the importance of early communication intervention and have noted that such intervention may have significant collateral effects on aberrant behavior. In their discussion of the relationship among communication, social development, and problem behaviors, Prizant and Wetherby (1988) noted that an "obvious implication is that early communication intervention may serve to preclude the development of potentially dangerous and disruptive behavior" (pg. 6).

Simplicity of Learning Histories and Functional Analyses

Common sense suggests that young children have brief learning histories. They have not been exposed to large numbers of treatment plans or environments and, thus, the functions of their problem behaviors tend to be accessible to more immediate and straightforward interpretation. Our own experience has been that functional analyses of the self-injurious and aggressive responding of preschool-aged children, as opposed to older individuals, usually can be accomplished with simple observations and interviews. As a result, alternative behaviors can be identified and taught with a simplicity that is not common in work with older individuals.

Lovaas (1980) noted further that the inexperience of young children seems to facilitate the process of generalization. He attributed this greater generalization to the fact that preschool-aged children have not learned to discriminate readily between training and natural environments. Generalization also may be easier to arrange because young children tend to have fewer previously learned behaviors that might compete with desired responses in generalization settings (Horner & Billingsley, 1988). Regardless, the propensity for generalization to occur could have tremendous implications for the spread of competent performances across natural community environments.

Facilitating Characteristics of Caregivers and Ecologies

An additional set of advantages experienced by young children and early interventionists relates to the characteristics of the children's principal caregivers and to the settings that they inhabit. Predominantly, the principal caregivers of young children are their parents. In many instances, parents of a young child, regardless of the child's disability, are deeply committed to providing an optimal context for the child's development. Such parents are receptive to recommendations for intervention and are eager to participate in productive parent-professional partnerships. The natural family context can offer an ideal environment for the young child's cognitive, social, and emotional development.

In contrast, the caregiving environments for developmentally disabled individuals who are older are not always so supportive. Parents tend to have less contact, and they often may be mentally and physically exhausted from many years of contending with challenging behaviors and uncompromising service systems. Group homes and other residential programs may have sophisticated intervention systems, but their direct care staff are typically underpaid, shift-work personnel who cannot have the level of personal commitment experienced by natural families. Longitudinal consistency is very difficult to engineer in settings that are operated by service agencies.

Young children also may have the benefit of participating in a much wider range of integrated programs and typical community environments. Preschool programs that include children with and without disabilities are becoming common, and their supporting empirical base is growing (Odom & McEvoy, 1988; Strain, Hoyson, & Jamieson, 1985). Such programs provide opportunities for children to learn functional, social, communication, and other life skills, and how to access reinforcers from these experiences. Young children also may be exposed to more typical community activities than older individuals because their behaviors tend to be less conspicuous (Lovaas, 1987).

Caregiver and ecological characteristics can be seen as having important implications for a child's development in many ways. Young children may experience greater continuity and commitment in their interpersonal relationships, and they may encounter a more typical array of community life experiences on a routine basis. While these assumptions are certainly general, the significance of these ecological considerations should not be minimized. Caregiving and setting characteristics are instrumental from the perspective of longitudinal skill development.

Physical Characteristics

Finally, a most obvious distinction of young children is their physical size. Children who are preschool-aged or younger are usually small, and their problem behaviors are rarely very threatening. On the other hand, the same topographies performed by an adult might be extremely intimidating and potentially dangerous.

This important difference suggests a number of advantages: (a) more people are willing (and eager) to work and interact with young children; (b) many of the problem behaviors displayed by young children are possible to ignore, thus permitting more opportunity to focus on the development of functional skills; and (c) young children are easier to include in a wider range of activities because their behaviors do not tend to be as stigmatizing.

The advantages of early intervention, including the fact that young children are small (and cute), suggests that systematic and functionally-oriented intervention should not only result in relatively rapid gains, but also that the gains can be a pivotal starting point for a life of competent performance in which problem behaviors should be an incongruous and very low probability event. Of course, this promise cannot be realized until high quality early intervention services are provided for those persons who have developmental disabilities and are "at risk" for serious problem behaviors. In the following section, a program is described that attempted to provide such services to a large rural region of Appalachia where few specialized services were available.

A DEMONSTRATION PROGRAM

The Preschool Training Project (PTP) was a federally funded demonstration program that provided advocacy, training, and consultation services for young children with autism and their families within a 30,000-square-mile region of West Virginia, Ohio, and Kentucky. The PTP did not provide direct intervention for the children. Instead, the program offered individualized training, support, and consultation for families, along with periodic assistance and consultation for community-based service providers. This training was designed to provide parents, other family members, and service providers with information and specific skills needed to teach and interact positively with the children. The curricular emphasis was on communication and skill development. Behavior problems were addressed indirectly through the establishment of functional equivalents or through stimulus-based interventions.

In general, participating families received approximately 50 hours of in-clinic assessment and individualized training over the first 3 months of program involvement. The training process began by having one of the program's staff interact with the child to establish rapport, to sample preferences and reinforcers, and to establish the rudiments of cooperative responding. Throughout this early part of the training process, the child's parent(s) observed through a one-way mirror, a second staff member providing a description and rationale for the procedures that were being employed. The observations were accompanied by some readings (e.g., Koegel & Schreibman, 1982) that helped to provide an introduction to the "hands-on" training that followed. During the hands-on part of training, the child's parent(s) conducted short instructional sessions with their children after a demonstration by the staff member. Parents received some feedback during the session regarding their use of instructional techniques and management of their child's inappropriate behavior. More detailed feedback was provided after the session as the parents and staff member reviewed a videotape of the preceding session. As the parents' proficiency and confidence increased, they conducted more of the instructional sessions. By the end of the 3 months, the parents were conducting the sessions without assistance.

Following the initial 3 months, the program's direct involvement with the child and family was reduced to periodic assessments and regularly scheduled consultation in the local community. More frequent contact was maintained by telephone. In addition, families were assisted in their interactions with service agencies, and information and consultation were provided for the children's service providers. For more detailed descriptions of the full program, readers are referred to Dunlap, Robbins, Morelli, and Dollman (1988), and to Dunlap, Robbins, Dollman, and Plienis (1988).

A total of 15 children and their families participated in the program. Each of the families completed the 3-month training phase, and 13 started early enough to continue through at least 1 year of involvement. All of the children were between the ages of 2 and 4.5 years at intake, and all were diagnosed as having autism or a related handicap involving significant deficits in social and communication skills. Thirteen of the children were nonverbal, and all but one functioned in the moderate to severe range of mental retardation. Most of the families lived in rural Appalachian communities that were located at least 30 miles from the site of the program's facility. Families spanned the range of the socioeconomic strata, with 10 of the children being members of two-parent families.

As part of the project's program evaluation efforts, an extensive battery of measures was collected on the children and families at various points in the training process (Plienis, Robbins, & Dunlap, 1988). Data on child developmental gains and the variables related to outcome have been reported elsewhere (Dunlap, Robbins, & Plienis, 1989; Robbins, Dunlap, & Plienis, in press) and will not be addressed here. The data of particular relevance for this chapter concern levels of serious problem behaviors that were gathered from videotaped mother-child interactions. These videotaped interactions were collected at three intervals: (a) at intake, before any training was provided; (b) immediately following the 3-month training period; and (c) 1 year following intake; i.e., 9 months of follow-up. At each assessment period, the child and mother were videotaped while they were alone in a room engaged in dyadic, instructional interactions with activities appropriate for the child's developmental level. Data were collected every 10 seconds on a variety of child and mother variables (Robbins, Plienis, & Dunlap, 1988), including a child behavior category labeled as *seriously disruptive.* This category included aggression, self-injury, and severe tantrums.

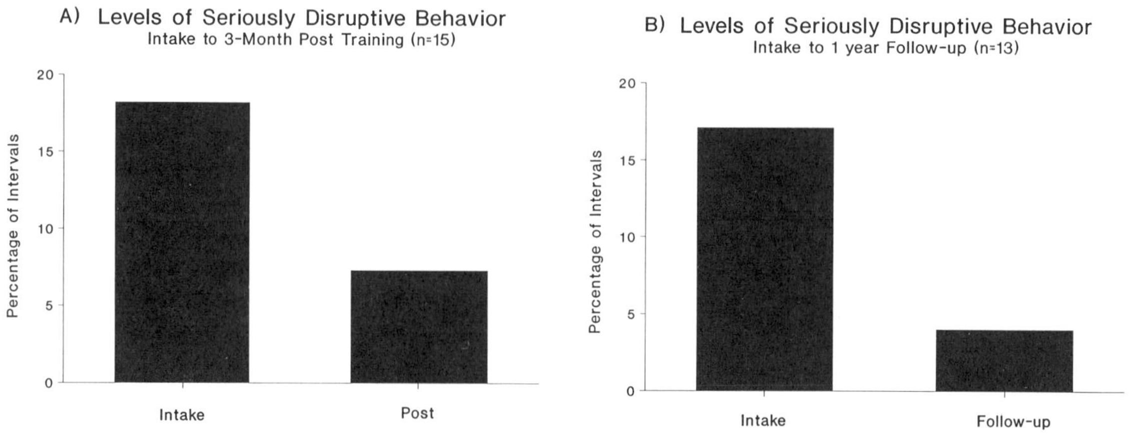

Figure 1: Summary data on behavior problems from the Preschool Training Project. The left panel (A) shows levels of seriously disruptive responding for 15 children at intake and following 3 months of family training. The right panel (B) shows levels of seriously disruptive behavior for 13 children at intake and at a 1-year follow-up.

Figure 1 presents group summary data for the participating children in the project. The left panel shows the seriously disruptive responding of the 15 children at intake and immediately following the 3-month family training program. As can be seen, the percentage of intervals with seriously disruptive behavior decreased substantially over this 3-month period. Of greater importance are the data collected following 1 year of program involvement (right panel). These data, showing the seriously disruptive behavior of the first 13 children, indicate that the positive effects of the mothers' intervention not only maintained but also resulted in even further decreases over time.

While these results do not represent experimentally controlled outcomes, the data are nonetheless highly encouraging. The reductions in serious problem behavior were maintained, despite a virtual absence of direct contact between program personnel and the participating children after the first 3 months of involvement. Furthermore, the reductions were accomplished with a positive approach and without any intrusive or punishment-based interventions.

Although the 1-year follow-up data are encouraging, individual analyses indicate that not all of the problem behaviors were eliminated entirely. In particular, two of the children continued to demonstrate significant behavior problems at home. One of these children suffered from severe, uncontrolled otitis media and the other from a seizure disorder. We believe that improved medical care and continuing efforts to build functional behaviors would be needed to completely eliminate these problem responses. On the other hand, most of the children progressed to the point where they displayed virtually no disruptive responses at all. Further anecdotal reports from these children's families (e.g., at a 2-year follow-up) indicate that the children are continuing to show improvements, with few or no occurrences of serious behavior problems at home or in the community. In addition, most of the children are participating in typical community settings, including integrated preschool, kindergarten, and first grade classrooms. These results, especially those on the reduced levels of problem behaviors, lend some additional support to the notion that early intervention and functional skill development may constitute an effective impediment in circumventing a possible later history of serious problem responding.

SUMMARY

In this chapter, we have argued that a skill-building orientation to early intervention can eliminate most behavior problems in an efficient and durable manner. We also have suggested that such services have the potential to prevent the later emergence of serious behavior problems in persons with developmental disabilities. In this concluding section, we would impose some caveats and some recommended directions.

First, the authors support of their positions in this chapter is largely in the form of logic, common sense, and experimental data that are limited in their evaluations of follow-up. We would acknowledge that our principal thesis, having to do with prevention and early intervention, is not supported directly by longitudinal data. Therefore, we recommend that experimentally controlled investigations be conducted to test the assumptions put forth in this chapter, especially those pertaining to long-term prevention. Furthermore, we acknowledge that we do not yet have complete knowledge of the etiology or epidemiology of serious behavior problems (Cataldo, 1988). While substantial data are attesting to the role of functional skill deficiencies, complete solutions for some severe problem behaviors probably will not be available until more knowledge is obtained on physiological factors (e.g., Cataldo &

Harris, 1982; Gedye, 1989) and other determinants.

Second, our position is not that just any early intervention service will produce meaningful prevention or significant educational outcomes. We feel strongly that the focus should be on skill development and, in particular, on the establishment of repertoires that are functional, that facilitate communication and social interactions, and that have a likelihood of generative effects (e.g., Koegel & Koegel, 1988). Early intervention programs must work closely and cooperatively with the children's families and the children's individual ecologies (Dunlap Robbins, Morelli, & Dollman, 1988). Third, we do not believe that early intervention can work as an invincible vaccine. Although it may be pivotal, early intervention is just a first step in a longitudinal plan of habilitation. Subsequent services must also provide functional education, comprehensive support, and a positive orientation if the early intervention foundation is to have ultimate value.

While there is a tremendous need for ongoing research, we believe that there are also compelling reasons to advocate an early skill development approach to serious behavior problems. Such an emphasis is supported by a burgeoning data base, is consistent with social values, and holds promise as an effective preventive. If functional skill development is initiated early and supported longitudinally, future considerations of aversive or disrespectful interventions may be irrelevant.

The advent of PL 99-457 and its mandate for individualized early intervention programs offer great opportunities for meaningful service development. As early intervention services proliferate, we can expect, too, that accompanying efforts will occur in research and quality program development. Our hope is that this growth will reveal the full potential of functional skill development for the future well-being of persons with severe disabilities.

NOTE

Preparation of this paper was supported by Cooperative Agreement No. G0087C0234 from the National Institute on Disability and Rehabilitation Research. Collection of the data reported herein was supported by U.S. Department of Education (Handicapped Children's Early Education Program) Grant No. G008530082. The opinions expressed in this paper do not necessarily reflect the positions of the supporting agencies, and no official endorsement should be inferred.

REFERENCES

Anderson, S. R., Avery, D. L., DiPietro, E., K., Edwards, R.L., & Christian, W. P. (1987). Intensive home-based early intervention with autistic children. *Education and Treatment of Children, 10,* 352-366.

Berkman, K. A., & Meyer, L. H. (1988). Alternative strategies and multiple outcomes in the remediation of severe self-injury: Going "all out" nonaversively. *Journal of The Association for Persons with Severe Handicaps, 13*, 76-86.

Bird, F., Dores, P. A., Moniz, D., & Robinson, J. (1989). Reducing severe aggressive and self-injurious behaviors with functional communication training. *American Journal on Mental Retardation, 94,* 37-48.

Carr, E. G. (1988). Functional equivalence as a mechanism of response generalization. In R. H. Horner, G. Dunlap, & R. L. Koegel (Eds.), *Generalization and maintenance: Life-style changes in applied settings* (pp. 221-241). Baltimore: Paul H. Brookes.

Carr, E. G., & Durand, V. M. (1985). Reducing behavior problems through functional communication training. *Journal of Applied Behavior Analysis, 18*, 111-126.

Carr, E. G., Newsom, C. D., & Binkoff, (1976). Stimulus control of self-destructive behavior in a psychotic child. *Journal of Abnormal Child Psychology, 4*, 139-153.

Carr, E. G., Taylor, J. C., Carlson, J. I., & Robinson, S. (in press). Reinforcement and stimulus-based treatments for severe behavior problems in developmental disabilities. *Proceedings of the Consensus Conference on the Treatment of Severe Behavior Problems and Developmental Disabilities.* Washington, DC: National Institute of Health..

Casto, G., & Mastropieri, M. A. (1986). The efficacy of early intervention programs: A meta-analysis. *Exceptional Children, 52*, 417-424.

Cataldo, M. F. (1988). Knowledge based approaches toward assisting the developmentally disabled and other considerations. In R.H. Horner & G. Dunlap (Eds.), *Behavior management and community integration for individuals with developmental disabilities and severe behavior problems* (pp. 91-107). Monograph from a symposium sponsored by the Office of Special Education and Rehabilitative Services and the Research and Training Center on Community-Referenced Behavior Management. Washington, DC.

Cataldo, M. F., & Harris, J. H. (1982). The biological basis for self-injury in the mentally retarded. *Analysis and Intervention in Developmental Disabilities, 2,* 21-39.

Donnellan, A. M., Mirenda, P. L., Mesaros, R. A., & Fassbender, L. L. (1984). Analyzing the communicative functions of aberrant behavior. *Journal of The Association for Persons with Severe Handicaps, 9*, 201-212.

Dunlap, G., Robbins, F. R., Dollman, C., & Plienis, A. J. (1988). *Early intervention for young children with autism: A regional training approach.* Huntington, WV: Marshall University.

Dunlap, G., Robbins, F. R., Morelli, M. A., & Dollman, C. (1988). Team training for young children with autism: A regional model for service delivery. *Journal of the Division for Early Childhood, 12*, 147-160.

Dunlap, G., Robbins, F. R., & Plienis, A. J. (1989). *Follow-up results from a rural family training program for young children with autism*. Paper presented at the annual meeting of the Association for Behavior Analysis, Milwaukee.

Durand, V. M. (in press). *Functional communication training: An intervention program for severe behavior problems*. New York: Guilford Press.

Durand, V. M., & Carr, E. G. (1987). Social influences on "self stimulatory" behavior: Analysis and treatment application. *Journal of Applied Behavior Analysis, 20*, 119-132.

Dyer, K., Dunlap, G., & Winterling, V. (in press). The effects of choice-making on the problem behaviors of students with severe handicaps. *Journal of Applied Behavior Analysis*.

Eason, L. J., White, M. J., & Newsom, C. (1982). Generalized reduction of self-stimulatory behavior: An effect of teaching appropriate play to autistic children. *Analysis and Intervention in Developmental Disabilities, 2*, 157-169.

Evans, I. M., & Meyer, L. H. (1985). *An educative approach to behavior problems: A practical decision model for interventions with severely handicapped learners*. Baltimore: Paul H. Brookes.

Favell, J. E., McGimsey, J. F., & Schell, R. M. (1982). Treatment of self-injury by providing alternate sensory activities. *Analysis and Intervention in Developmental Disabilities, 2*, 83-104.

Fenske, E. C., Zalenski, S., Krantz, P. J., & McClannahan, L.E. (1985). Age at intervention and treatment outcome for autistic children in a comprehensive intervention program. *Analysis and Intervention in Developmental Disabilities, 5*, 49-58.

Gedye, A. (1989). Extreme self-injury attributed to frontal lobe seizures. *American Journal on Mental Retardation, 94*, 20-26.

Groden, G., Dominque, D., Chesnick, M., Groden, J., & Baron, G.(1983). Early intervention with autistic children: A case presentation with pre-program, program and follow-up data. *Psychological Reports, 53*, 715-722.

Horner, R. H., (1989). Discussion of Oregon Community Support and community-referenced behavior management. In G. Dunlap (Chair), *Community-referenced research on behavior management*. Symposium presented at the annual meeting of the Association for Behavior Analysis, Milwaukee.

Horner, R. H., & Billingsley, F. F. (1988). The effect of competing behavior on the generalization and maintenance of adaptive behavior in applied settings. In R. H. Horner, G. Dunlap, & R. L. Koegel (Eds.), *Generalization and maintenance: Life-style changes in applied settings* (pp. 197-220). Baltimore: Paul H. Brookes.

Horner, R. H., & Budd, C. M. (1985). Acquisition of manual sign use: Collateral reduction of maladaptive behavior, and factors limiting generalization. *Education and Training of the Mentally Retarded, 20*, 39-47.

Horner, R. H., Dunlap, G., Koegel, R. L., Carr, E. G., Sailor, W., Anderson, J., Albin, R. W., & O'Neill, R. E. (in press). Toward a technology of "nonaversive" behavioral support. *Journal of The Association for Persons with Severe Handicaps*.

Hunt, P., Alwell, M., & Goetz, L. (1988). Acquisition of conversation skills and the reduction of inappropriate social behaviors. *Journal of the Association for Persons with Severe Handicaps, 13*, 20-27.

Kern, L., Koegel, R. K., & Dunlap. G. (1984). The influence of vigorous vs. mild exercise on autistic stereotyped behaviors. *Journal of Autism and Developmental Disorders, 14*, 57-67.

Koegel, R. L., & Koegel, L. K., (1988). Generalized responsivity and pivotal behaviors. In R. H. Horner, G. Dunlap, & R. L. Koegel (Eds.), *Generalization and maintenance: Lifestyle changes in applied settings* (pp. 41-66). Baltimore: Paul H. Brookes.

Koegel, R. L., & Koegel, L. K. (1990). Extended reductions in stereotypic behavior through a self-management treatment package. *Journal of Applied Behavior Analysis, 23*, 119-127.

Koegel, R. L., & Schreibman, L. (1982). *How to teach autistic and other severely handicapped children*. Lawrence, KS: H & H Enterprises, Inc.

Krashen, S. (1975). The critical period for language acquisition and its possible basis. *Annals of the New York Academy of Sciences, 263*, 211-224.

LaVigna, G. W., & Donnellan, A. M. (1986). *Alternatives to punishment: Solving behavior problems with non-aversive strategies.* New York: Irvington.

Lenneberg, E. H. (1967). *Biological foundations of language*. New York: Wiley.

Lovaas, O. I. (1980). Behavioral teaching with young autistic children. In B. Wilcox & A. Thompson (Eds.), *Critical issues in educating autistic children and youth.* (pp. 220-233). U.S. Department of Education: Office of Special Education: Washington, DC.

Lovaas, O. I. (1987). Behavioral treatment and normal educational and intellectual functioning in young autistic children. *Journal of Consulting and Clinical Psychology, 55*, 3-9.

McGee, G. G. (1988). Community integration for individuals with developmental disabilities and severe behavior problems. In R. H. Horner & G. Dunlap (Eds.), *Behavior management and community integration for individuals with developmental disabilities and severe behavior problems* (pp. 68-82). Monograph from a symposium sponsored by the Office of Special Education and Rehabilitative Services and the Research and Training Center on Community-Referenced Behavior Management. Washington, DC.

McGee, J. J., Menolascino, F. J., Hobbs, D. C., & Menousek, P. E. (1987). *Gentle teaching: A non-aversive approach to helping persons with mental retardation.* New York: Human Sciences Press.

Meyer, L. H., & Evans, I. M. (1989). *Non-aversive intervention for behavior problems: A manual for home and community.* Baltimore: Paul H. Brookes.

Odom, S. L., & McEvoy, M. A. (1988). Integration of young children with handicaps and normally developing children. In S. Odom & M. B. Karnes (Eds.), *Early intervention for infants and children with handicaps: An empirical base*, (pp. 241-267). Baltimore: Paul H. Brookes.

O'Neill, R. E., Horner, R. H., Albin, R. W., Storey, K., & Sprague, J. R. (in press). *Functional analysis: A practical assessment guide*. Sycamore, IL: Sycamore Publishing Company.

Plienis, A. J., Robbins, F. R., & Dunlap. G. (1988). Parent adjustment and family stress as factors in behavioral parent training for young autistic children. *Journal of the Multihandicapped Person, 1,* 31-52.

Prizant, B. M., & Wetherby, A. M. (1988). Providing services to children with autism (ages 0 to 2 years) and their families. *Topics in Language Disorders, 9*, 1-23.

Robbins, F. R., Dunlap, G., & Plienis, A. J. (in press). Family characteristics, family training, and the progress of young children with autism. *Journal of Early Intervention.*

Robbins, F. R., Plienis, A. J., & Dunlap. G. (1988). *The code for the assessment of teaching skills (CATS).* Unpublished manuscript, Marshall University, Huntington, WV.

Rutter, M. (1978). Developmental issues and prognosis. In M. Rutter & E. Schopler (Eds.), *Autism: A reappraisal of concepts and treatment* (pp. 497-505). New York: Plenum Press.

Santarcangelo, S., Dyer, K., & Luce, S. C. (1987). Generalized reduction of disruptive behavior in unsupervised settings through specific toy training. *Journal of The Association for Persons with Severe Handicaps, 12*, 38-44.

Simeonsson, R. J., Olley, J. G., & Rosenthal, S. L. (1987). Early intervention for children with autism. In M. J. Guralnick & R. C. Bennett (Eds.), *The effectiveness of early intervention for at risk and handicapped children* (pp. 275-296). New York: Academic Press.

Singer, G. H. S., Singer, J., & Horner, R. H. (1987). Using pretask requests to increase the probability of compliance for students with severe disabilities. *Journal of The Association for Persons with Severe Handicaps, 12,* 287-291.

Strain, P. S., Hoyson, M., & Jamieson, B. (1985). Normally developing preschoolers and intervention agents for autistic-like children: Effects of class deportment and social interaction. *Journal of the Division for Early Childhood, 9,* 105-115.

Touchette, P., MacDonald, R., & Langer, S. (1985). A scatter plot for identifying stimulus control of problem behavior. *Journal of Applied Behavior Analysis, 18,* 343-351.

Wetherby, A. M. (1984). Possible neurolinguistic breakdown in autistic children. *Topics in Language Disorders, 4,* 19-33.

Winterling, V., Dunlap, G., & O'Neill, R. E. (1987). The influence of task variation on the aberrant behaviors of autistic students. *Education and Treatment of Children, 10,* 105-119.

CHAPTER

20

WHEN AND WHEN NOT TO CONSIDER THE USE OF AVERSIVE INTERVENTIONS IN THE BEHAVIORAL TREATMENT OF AUTISTIC CHILDREN

Tristram Smith
University of California

Autistic children display a variety of severe behavior problems. They have little or no language, attachment to others, play, or self-help skills. They also may be extremely inattentive to their environment, preferring to occupy themselves with self-stimulatory behaviors, such as repetitively flapping their hands. In addition, they may exhibit dangerously high rates of tantrums and aggression toward themselves or others (Lovaas & Smith, 1988).

Although a wide range of treatments have been attempted with autistic children, only behavioral treatments have been demonstrated scientifically to improve the children's functioning (Rutter, 1985). Behavioral treatments are complex, but, as a very general statement, one may say that they emphasize the use of positive reinforcement procedures (Lovaas, 1981). Positive reinforcement procedures often have been highly effective in strengthening adaptive behaviors while alleviating the severe behavior problems presented by autistic children. However, the procedures have not been effective in all cases; in fact, they have sometimes failed to produce any reduction in behavior problems (Matson & Taras, 1989). Such failures have proved troublesome because they give rise to the dilemma of whether to allow a behavior problem to continue or whether to introduce aversive interventions contingent upon the behavior. This dilemma constitutes the focus of the present chapter.

At the outset, it should be noted that some professionals have argued against the existence of such a dilemma. Their arguments have taken two main forms (e.g., LaVigna & Donnellan, 1986): (a) Aversive interventions are not a viable option because they fail to suppress behavior problems or because they produce negative side effects; and (b) Nonaversive interventions always can be found to suppress behavior problems, thereby precluding any need to consider aversives. The first argument may appear plausible, but it has consistently been found to be inaccurate. If aversives are implemented properly (as described later in this section), they often produce rapid and permanent elimination of behavior problems, and negative side effects are rare - rarer, in fact, than positive side effects (Carr & Lovaas, 1983; Matson & Taras, 1989; Lichstein & Schreibman, 1976; Newsom, Favell, & Rincover,

1983). The second argument, however, requires more careful consideration.

Certainly, as research on behavioral treatments for autistic children has progressed, effective positive reinforcement procedures have been developed to handle many severe behavior problems that previously had been manageable only with aversive interventions. For example, electric shock was, unfortunately, a component of the first procedure that was empirically shown to establish social stimuli (approval and physical closeness) as reinforcement in extremely isolated autistic children. Although this procedure established positive social reinforcement without adverse side effects, it was abandoned almost immediately because its effects were situation-specific and because procedures that relied exclusively on positive reinforcement were sought and soon found (Lovaas, Freitag, Kinder, Rubinstein, Schaeffer, & Simmons, 1966). At about the same time, positive reinforcement procedures began to emerge for reducing highly disruptive behaviors, such as severe aggression or self-stimulation. Lovaas, Freitag, Gold, and Kassorla (1965) found a strong inverse correlation between the rate of such disruptive behaviors and the rate of adaptive behaviors. High rates of disruptive behaviors were associated with low rates of adaptive behaviors, and vice versa. This suggested that, in some instances, disruptive behaviors might be reduced by reinforcing more adaptive behaviors, a procedure referred to as the differential reinforcement of alternative behaviors (DRA). A number of investigators (e.g., Peterson & Peterson, 1968) showed that DRA was, in fact, an effective behavior reduction procedure in some cases. Carr (1977) then pointed out that the selection of which alternative behaviors to reinforce in DRA procedures could be guided by a functional analysis. For example, Carr and Durand (1985) demonstrated that, for some autistic individuals, aggressive behaviors served a communicative function (i.e., enabled these individuals to express some of their needs) and that, their behaviors could be reduced by building language skills. Procedures for conducting a functional analysis have been refined by Van Houten (1989) and his associates, and procedures for reducing behavior problems with positive reinforcement have been summarized by Donnellan, LaVigna, Negri-Shoultz, and Fassbender (1988).

Intervening in an autistic child's life during the preschool years is another strategy that has emerged from behavioral work on preventing aversives (see Chapter 19 by Dunlap, Johnson, & Robbins). Early intervention may allow teachers to bring behavior problems under control before the problems have accumulated a long reinforcement history and before children grow large enough to inflict severe damage on themselves or others. This strategy also may increase the effectiveness of DRA procedures, since preschool autistic children appear to acquire new, adaptive behaviors more readily than older autistic children (Lovaas & Favell, 1987).

In addition to studying nonaversive interventions, investigators have explored interventions that, though aversive, may be more socially acceptable than stimuli that were used in earlier studies such as electric shock. Some interventions that have been studied consist of administering an aversive stimulus that is considered to be less intense than shock, such as slapping a child on the thigh or wrist (Koegel & Covert, 1972), spraying water mist (Singh, Watson, & Winton, 1986), or saying "no" in a loud, stern voice (Van Houten, 1989). Other procedures that have been advanced include time-out, response cost, and overcorrection (Axelrod & Apsche, 1983). These three procedures differ from the aversive interventions that were previously mentioned because they do not involve physical punishment (i.e., do not include the administration of a stimulus that causes physical pain or discomfort). Consequently, they have been regarded as preferable, but further research is needed to support this view.

These various advances have been spurred by the hope that aversive interventions one day would be rendered obsolete, and they provide grounds for optimism that this hope will be realized. Regrettably, however, some autistic children still appear to have severe behavior problems that at present can be reduced only with aversive interventions (cf., Axelrod, 1987).

The existence of such behavior problems was confirmed by a recent study (Ackerman, Reed, Smith, & Lovaas, 1989). The subjects in this study were four preschool children who were receiving a very intensive behavioral intervention (40 hours of one-to-one treatment per week that was provided in the home for two or more years under the close supervision of highly experienced therapists). Each child exhibited 2-5 behaviors that were identified as severely disruptive and that were targeted for reduction. Initially, all of the targeted behaviors were placed in a baseline condition, during which only DRA was provided. The treatment program was 40 hours per week, and baseline lasted up to 24 weeks. Thus, the DRA was much more extensive than any other DRA program previously reported in the literature. Nevertheless, all of the targeted behaviors were unchanged during the baseline (DRA) condition and remained at high rates until an aversive intervention was introduced. The intervention consisted of a slap on the thigh after the occurrence of a targeted behavior, and the intervention was used in conjunction with intensive DRA procedures. Consistent with previous studies (reviewed by Matson & Taras, 1989), the introduction of this aversive intervention was associated with sharp reductions in almost all of the targeted behaviors; negative side effects were minimal and positive side effects were observed for all subjects.

The study of Ackerman et al. (1989) strongly suggests that professionals may continue to face the dilemma of whether to allow a behavior problem to continue or whether to introduce an aversive intervention. This is a very difficult dilemma indeed, and the literature on aversive interventions contains few discussions of how the dilemma may be resolved appropriately. However, several guidelines have emerged. First, aversive interventions should be considered only as a very last resort when all other interventions have failed (Griffith, 1983). Second, aversive interventions should be considered only if the treatment staff are highly skilled at shaping complex behaviors such as language using positive reinforcement procedures (Lovaas & Favell, 1987). Such skill is required to ensure that positive reinforcement procedures are adequately attempted before considering aversive interventions and to facilitate teaching new behaviors that can replace those suppressed with the interventions. Finally, if aversives are administered, they must be administered in the following manner to maximize their effectiveness and to minimize the risk of negative side effects (Favell et al. 1982; Lovaas & Favell, 1987; Matson & Kazdin, 1981): (a) No more than one or two specific behaviors should be targeted at a time for an aversive intervention; (b) The aversive intervention should be administered every time the targeted behavior occurs; (c) Positive reinforcement should be used concurrently to build adaptive behaviors that may replace the targeted behaviors; and (d) The effects of the aversive intervention should be monitored carefully with behavioral data to check for suppression without negative side effects.

These considerations are important, but they do not cover the full range of issues confronting a service provider who must decide whether to employ an aversive intervention. Three basic issues that are left untouched follow. First, one needs to know what is aversive and what is not for each individual autistic child. As will be seen, however, this distinction can be difficult to make. Second, the potential benefits of aversive interventions must be large, as administering aversives for trivial problems clearly would be inappropriate; yet, there has been little consideration of exactly how large the benefits should be. Finally, caretakers should have an important role in the decision on whether or not to use aversives, but their role in this decision has not been explored adequately. The neglect of these three issues creates an important gap, and I will attempt to provide a start toward filling this gap in the remainder of the present chapter.

WHAT IS AVERSIVE TO AN AUTISTIC CHILD?

A stimulus is defined as aversive if it is a negative reinforcer or a punisher. As a negative reinforcer, a stimulus increases escape or avoidance behavior; as a punisher, a stimulus reduces the likelihood that a behavior will recur. In principle, then, a stimulus is defined as aversive on the basis of its effect on those who receive it. In practice, however, it is often defined on the basis of its effect on those who *administer* it. For example, Donnellan, LaVigna, Negri-Shoultz, and Fassbender (1988) wrote, "By punishment, we do not usually include standard classroom or household disciplinary actions... even though these technically might be considered punishment" (p. 1). Instead, they continued, "We are concerned with certain behavior change techniques that often are used in classrooms and programs" which "may raise serious legal and ethical questions" and which could expose treatment staff to "civil and sometimes criminal sanctions" (pp. 1-2).

Note that these authors define punishment in terms of society's effect on them, rather than in terms of the consequence on the autistic person. Undoubtedly, legal and ethical considerations, as well as any other factors that may deter professionals from adopting an intervention, need to be taken into account in evaluating the intervention (Bernstein, 1989). There is no point in developing an intervention that no one is willing to use. Nevertheless, the main focus should remain on what is aversive to the client since it is the client, and not the treatment staff, whose welfare is of paramount concern when evaluating an intervention.

Adherence to a client focus leaves ample reason to be hesitant about aversive interventions. These interventions can be and have been used in such a way as to harm clients (Donnellan et al., 1988), and it is thus critically important to minimize the risk of harm. Nevertheless, it is unclear to what extent efforts to avoid aversives actually have reduced clients' risk. For example, as noted earlier, efforts have been made to replace physical aversives with interventions that professionals regard as less aversive. However, these alternative interventions may do more to satisfy professionals than to help autistic children avoid aversives (Newsom, Favell, & Rincover, 1983). We do not know, for example, whether removing all social and environmental reinforcement (as in time-out) or compelling a client to make restitution and practice a more adaptive but possibly unpleasant alternative to the behavior (as in overcorrection) is more unpleasant than a physical aversive. Even if such interventions are more unpleasant, they may take longer to yield a desired behavior change. Again, we do not know whether a long course of a less unpleasant intervention is preferable to a short course of a more unpleasant but functionally aversive intervention. These issues are not resolvable at present, primarily because of a lack of information about interventions that are advanced as alternatives to physical aversives. The functional properties of such interventions have received little research attention, whereas the functional properties of physical aversives have been studied extensively and are fairly well understood (cf., Azrin & Holz, 1966; Carr & Lovaas, 1983).

The uncertainties involved in weighing the relative aversiveness of different interventions become particularly troubling if one considers individual characteristics of clients such as autistic children. For example, autistic children commonly form extreme attachments to certain objects and may become very upset if these objects are removed. What, then, would be the effect on such children of taking away preferred possessions (as in response cost)? These children also become very upset by even minor changes in the environment, such as the rearrangement of furniture (Kanner, 1943). What would be the impact on such children of making major environmental changes, such as admitting them into a psychiatric hospital or requiring them to undergo therapy sessions in a clinical setting? Still another common behavior of autistic children is struggling to escape situations in which adults place requests on them or initiate other social interactions. This behavior is often displayed in parent-child interactions (Kanner, 1951), psychological assessments (Schopler, Reichler, & Rochin, 1986), and behavioral treatments (Lovaas, 1981).

Escape behavior may become especially severe in "relationship therapies," even though these therapies aim to help adults form connections with autistic children by accepting them as they are and imposing minimal demands. For example, working in the context of the psychoanalytic framework developed by Bettelheim (1967), Schopler (1962) described a case in which, for 30 therapy sessions, an autistic girl destroyed objects in his therapy office, ruined his clothes, masturbated on his leg, and yelled "No" repeatedly while attempting to run out the door, a behavior that Schopler prevented by physically blocking her. In *holding* therapy, the purpose of which is to establish a bond between an autistic child and the mother (Tinbergen & Tinbergen, 1983), the primary intervention consists of having the mother hold the child for extended periods of time until the child stops trying to escape. The objective is to cause "the autistic defense...to crumble" (Welch, 1987; p. 48). Thus, many instructional or therapeutic efforts, however well-intentioned, may possess substantial aversive properties for autistic children. On the other hand, many autistic children are remarkably unperturbed by stimuli that cause physical pain for most other individuals. As a result, although physical aversives certainly should be avoided as much as possible, they actually may be less aversive to some autistic children than a whole range of generally accepted interventions.

These considerations show that professionals cannot make an intervention nonaversive for autistic children simply by refraining from the use of physical aversives as well as other aversives (e.g., timeout. Indeed, some autistic children may experience components of virtually all interventions as aversive. It is also evident that when professionals do choose to administer aversive interventions, they have few guidelines for keeping the aversiveness to a minimum. This is because scanty information exists on the relative aversiveness of different interventions and on the effect that the level of aversiveness has on the rate of behavior change. Thus, at the present state of knowledge, there is, unfortunately, little basis for determining how to set up a nonaversive or minimally aversive treatment program for autistic children, short of providing no treatment at all. To fill this gap in knowledge, researchers will have to study a wider range of topics than how to avoid physical aversives, which has been the primary focus of investigations thus far.

WHAT BEHAVIORS MAY WARRANT THE USE OF PHYSICAL AVERSIVES?

When nonaversive interventions fail, the limited use of physical aversives may be in the child's best interests under the following circumstances: (a) The aversives suppress behaviors such as severe aggression or self-injury that pose an immediate danger to the client or others (Favell et al., 1982); or (b) The aversives eliminate behaviors that prevent successful integration into normal settings; e.g., bizarre self-stimulatory behaviors that socially isolate a client otherwise ready to learn to interact with normal peers (Lovaas & Favell, 1987). On the other hand, aversives seem contraindicated if behaviors respond to nonaversive interventions or if behaviors show only a slight or fleeting reduction with aversives.

These parameters may serve as general guidelines for determining when aversives merit consideration, but they are difficult to apply in some clinical situations. For example, an autistic child may display a behavior that does not present an immediate danger but does pose a potential threat because it is becoming worse (e.g., self-injury that currently causes only minor damage but is increasing in frequency or severity). Or an autistic child may show behavior problems that, if removed, would improve functioning substantially but would fall short of facilitating "recovery" from autism. This is illustrated by Ackerman et al.'s (1989) study of an intensive behavioral intervention that strongly emphasized the use of positive reinforcement and made limited use of physical aversives.

In this study, aversives produced a clearly positive outcome for one client (eliminating disruptive behaviors and enabling the client to attain a normal IQ, successful integration into normal classes, and satisfactory adjustment as measured by tests of personality and adaptive functioning). However, more ambiguous outcomes were observed in two cases. One client attained normal levels of intellectual functioning, as well as integration into normal classes, and he maintained this level of functioning at the time of a follow-up several years later; however, he was experiencing high levels of adjustment difficulties such as depression . Although these adjustment difficulties emerged many years after the withdrawal of aversive interventions and hence are probably not attributable to them, they indicate that the client cannot be said to have "recovered." Another client showed a 48-point IQ increase which was maintained over time, but he continued to require placement in a special education class. This client and others who achieve a similar outcome, in all likelihood, will require supervision for the remainder of their lives. As Lovaas and Favell (1987) pointed out, this requirement places the clients at risk for relapsing because they are usually segregated into settings where few demands are placed on them and where other residents model inappropriate behaviors.

A comparable outcome was achieved for clients in a study on aversive interventions reported by McEachin and Leaf (1984). For example, one client showed a substantial improvement following aversive interventions, including making friendships and becoming indistinguishable from peers in a class for language-delayed children. However, the client continued to score in the mentally retarded range on tests and, therefore, was likely to require life-long supervision with the attendant risks described above. Thus, there are a number of "gray areas" in which aversives produce desirable behavior changes, but the changes, may not be of great enough magnitude to justify their use.

Significant normalization in functioning have so far been reported only for preschool autistic children who participate in a highly intensive behavioral program (Simeonnson, Olley, & Rosenthal, 1987). At present therefore, the use of aversives to promote such normalization should be restricted to very young autistic clients in intensive treatment programs. If this general requirement is met, the decision to use aversives to promote normalization should be made individually, based on a prediction of overall treatment outcome and a prediction of the outcome of the aversive intervention for a particular client. That is, the client should be considered likely to achieve normal functioning and to benefit from the aversive intervention. Unfortunately, however, little is known about how to make such a prediction (Lovaas & Smith, 1988). Even in hindsight, the success or failure of an intervention may be open to different interpretations.

For example, Ackerman et al. (1989) reported one case in which aversives failed. They noted that this failure occurred with the subject who had the lowest level of intellectual functioning of any subject in the study. They also noted that, for this client, the investigators had targeted some very subtle behaviors such as failing to look on request. Finally, they observed that the client was unresponsive to aversives as applied to several behaviors, rather than to only one behavior.

These observations suggest three possible ways to predict whether the use of an aversive intervention to promote normalization will be effective. First, the intervention may be likely to fail for clients with low levels of intellectual functioning, partly because they may be unable to discriminate why they are receiving the aversive, and partly because they may be slow in acquiring the adaptive behaviors necessary for normalized functioning. Second, an aversive intervention may have a higher probability of success when behaviors involving major muscle groups (e.g., aggression) are targeted than when more subtle behaviors are targeted. Third, a history of failing to respond satisfactorily to aversives may contraindicate the use of aversives.

WHAT IS THE ROLE OF PARENTS IN THE DECISION OF WHETHER OR NOT TO EMPLOY AVERSIVE INTERVENTIONS?

Several authors have noted that professionals do not, and should not, decide by themselves whether to use aversive interventions (Bernstein, 1989; Griffith, 1983; Lovaas & Favell, 1987). For the most part, these accounts have emphasized the need for peer review to supplement professionals' decisions. However, the autistic child's parents also should be involved in the decision-making process. In many treatment programs, parents are explicitly placed in charge of their child's treatment (Baker, 1989), and, in all programs, they have the final say in determining whether to proceed with aversives.

Informed consent should be obtained from the parents, and the following information should be conveyed: (a) Aversives are used as a last resort; (b) When used, they will be delivered contingent on only one or two specific behaviors at a time, while the vast majority of the interventions in the program will involve positive reinforcement; (c) The main potential benefit of aversives is that they may reduce behavior problems that are not reducible with any other available intervention; (d) The main potential risks are that the aversives may not reduce the behavior problems they target or may produce negative side effects; and (e) The problems mentioned in (d) are infrequent, but should be monitored carefully by collecting comprehensive behavioral data on the client's functioning. In order for parents to evaluate this information properly, two additional requirements must be met. First, parents should be taught to collect data from behavioral observations. This skill enables them to verify that nonaversive interventions have failed and to monitor the effects of aversive interventions if they are introduced. Second, with their permission, parents should participate in a "test session" to determine whether the aversive intervention is acceptable to them and is likely to reduce their child's behavior problem, in their judgment and in the judgment of the treatment staff. For example, Ackerman et al. (1989) introduced aversive interventions in a meeting where the child, the parents, and the entire treatment staff were present. Initially, when the child was out of the room, the adults practiced the aversive intervention (a slap on the thigh) on each other to ensure that it was comparable to what most normal parents use on their normal children (Lichstein & Schreibman, 1976). Then the intervention was begun by the most experienced therapists, followed by the rest of the treatment team (parents and staff) if the intervention appeared to be reducing the child's behavior problem. The intervention was continued beyond this session only if the entire team was comfortable with the intervention and unanimously agreed that it was reducing the child's behavior problem. Even then, it continued to be monitored very closely, with data collected hour-by-hour.

During the informed-consent process, parents, of course, have two options: consenting or refusing to allow the aversives. If they refuse, it seems best to accept their decision, but not because our acceptance is the only available option. Some professionals, especially physicians, have put legal pressure on parents to allow their child to receive a treatment that goes against the parents' beliefs. For example, some religious groups oppose medical procedures such as blood transfusions, but physicians have obtained court orders to require children in these groups to receive treatment, despite the objections of parents. However, in the case of aversives, such action seems inappropriate because the aversive intervention probably will fail under these circumstances. To be successful, an aversive intervention requires the cooperation of all those who regularly interact with the child, most importantly the parents (Carr & Lovaas, 1983). Such cooperation is highly unlikely if the parents have been forced to allow aversives. Thus, a refusal from the parents should rule out the use of aversives.

In addition, parents sometimes either ask that their autistic child receive physical aversives or ask a professional to assist or sanction their use of aversives. This creates an awkward situation for professionals who have expended considerable energy in finding alternatives to aversive interventions. However, it is probably more common than parents' refusing aversives, since the vast majority of parents already use physical aversives with their children, (Lichstein & Schreibman, 1976). The situation arises frequently in clinical work, not only with parents of autistic clients, but also with parents of other children who pose behavior management problems (Patterson, 1976). In such situations, therapists generally oppose any use of physical aversives and redirect parents toward alternative interventions, especially DRA. For most client populations, this approach has considerable merit because DRA has been found to be more effective than aversives in managing most behavior problems (Patterson, 1976). Still, one should recognize that this approach runs counter to standard child-rearing practices, which typically include some use of aversives. Moreover, even if DRA is often more effective than aversives, DRA may not *always* be more effective. Therefore, it may not always be in the child's best interest for parents to avoid aversives entirely. Ideally, aversives would be unnecessary, but, realistically, this may not be the case until further advances are made in DRA procedures.

Some autistic individuals display behaviors that are currently manageable only with aversive procedures (Ackerman et al., 1989). Therefore, parents should be supported if they use aversives with some behaviors. Certainly, aversives should be viewed as a last resort, and this should be conveyed to the parents. However, no other effective intervention may be available for controlling an autistic child's behavior, and the behavior could be highly dangerous or disruptive, perhaps necessitating removing the child from the home unless the behavior is stopped. Thus, if parents ask that their child receive aversives in a treatment program, such a request may merit serious consideration. In addition, if parents request help in administering aversives themselves, certain precautions should be taken. First, professionals should determine whether the parents have the skills to program positive reinforcement procedures (e.g., teaching alternative behaviors) and aversive procedures correctly. Second, professionals should rule out factors that might place the parents at risk for abusing aversives (e.g., drug addiction). Third, a mechanism should exist for providing ongoing, in-home supervision of the use of aversives to make sure that they are being administered properly. Thus, parents' initiatives with regard to physical aversives should be met very cautiously but perhaps should not be discouraged altogether.

SUMMARY AND CONCLUSION

Nonaversive, DRA procedures are the preferred method for dealing with behavior problems (cf. Sidman, 1989). Much progress has been made and continues to be made toward utilizing DRA procedures effectively to manage the extreme behavior problems presented by autistic children. The goal has been to enable exclusive reliance on nonaversive procedures (ruling out any need to consider aversive interventions) but, unfortunately, this goal has not yet been reached. Until it is reached, some professionals and parents may be in the unenviable position of deciding whether to accept a behavior problem or to implement an aversive intervention. A number of implicit or explicit assumptions have arisen in connection with this decision, such as those that follow. First, aversive interventions are easily distinguished from nonaversive interventions, enabling professionals to avoid aversive interventions if they so choose. Second, aversive interventions can be ranked from most to least aversive, with physical aversives generally constituting the most aversive interventions. Third, behaviors that warrant consideration of the use of aversives can be reliably identified. Finally, parents should be discouraged from initiating aversives themselves. As the accumulated knowledge about the behavioral treatment of autistic children increases, some of these assumptions may prove to be correct, while others may not. Therefore, further exploration is needed. The present chapter was intended to provide a start in this direction and to examine in more detail the relative aversiveness of different interventions, the behaviors that may warrant consideration of using aversives, and the role of parents in making informed decisions about their use.

REFERENCES

Ackerman, A., Reed, G., Smith, T., & Lovaas, O. I. (1989). *The contribution of contingent aversives to the treatment of very young autistic children*. Manuscript submitted for publication.

Axelrod, S. (1987). Doing it without arrows: A review of LaVigna & Donnellan's *Alternatives to punishment: Solving behavior problems with non-aversive strategies. The Behavior Analyst, 10*, 243-251.

Axelrod, S., & Apsche, J. (1983). *The effects of punishment on human behavior*. New York: Academic Press.

Azrin, N. H., & Holz, W. C. (1966). Punishment. In W. K. Honig (Ed.), *Operant be-*

havior: Areas of research and application (pp. 380-447). New York: Appleton-Century-Crofts.

Baker, B. L. (1989). *Parent training.* Manuscript submitted for publication.

Bernstein, G. S. (1989). Social validity and the debate over use of aversive/intrusive procedures. *The Behavior Therapist, 12,* 123-125.

Bettelheim, B. (1967). *The empty fortress.* New York: Free Press.

Carr, E. G. (1977). The motivation of self-injurious behavior: A review of some hypotheses. *Psychological Bulletin, 84,* 800-816.

Carr, E. G., & Durand, V. M. (1985). Reducing behavior through functional communication training. *Journal of Applied Behavior Analysis, 18,* 111-126.

Carr, E. G., & Lovaas, O. I. (1983). Contingent electric shock as a treatment for severe behavior problems. In S. Axelrod & J. Apsche (Eds.), *The effects of punishment on human behavior* (pp. 221-246). New York: Academic Press.

Donnellan, A. M., LaVigna, G. W., Negri-Shoultz, N., & Fassbender, L. L., (1988). *Progress without punishment.* New York: Teachers College Press.

Favell, J. E., Azrin, N. H., Baumeister, A. A., Carr, E. G., Dorsey, M. F., Forehand, R., Foxx, R. M., Lovaas, O. I., Rincover, A., Risley, T. R., Romanczyk, R. G., Russo, D. C., Schroeder, S. R., & Solnick, J. V. (1982). The treatment of self-injurious behavior. *Behavior Therapy, 13,* 529-554.

Griffith, R. G. (1983). The administrative issues: An ethical and legal perspective. In S. Axelrod & J. Apsche (Eds.), *The effects of punishment on human behavior* (pp. 247-284). New York: Academic Press.

Kanner, L. (1943). Autistic disturbances of effective contact. *Nervous Child, 2,* 181-197.

Kanner, L. (1951). The conception of wholes and parts in early infantile autism. *American Journal of Psychiatry, 108,* 23-26.

Koegel, R. L., & Covert, A. (1972). The relationship of self-stimulation to learning in autistic children. *Journal of Applied Behavior Analysis, 5,* 381-387.

LaVigna, G. D., & Donnellan, A. (1986). *Alternatives to punishment: Solving behavior problems with nonaversive strategies.* New York: Irvington.

Lichstein, K. L., & Schreibman, L. (1976). Employing electric shock with autistic children: A review of the side-effects. *Journal of Autism and Childhood Schizophrenia, 6,* 163-173.

Lovaas, O. I. (1981). *Teaching developmentally disabled children: The ME Book.* Austin, TX: Pro-Ed.

Lovaas, O. I., & Favell, J. E. (1987). Protection for clients undergoing aversive/restrictive interventions. *Education and Treatment of Children, 10,* 311-325.

Lovaas, O. I., Freitag, G., Gold, V. J., & Kassorla, I. C. (1965). Experimental studies in childhood schizophrenia: Analysis of self-destructive behavior. *Journal of Experimental Child Psychology, 2,* 67-84.

Lovaas, O. I., Freitag, G., Kinder, M. I., Rubinstein, B. D., Schaeffer, B., & Simmons, J. Q. (1966). Establishment of social reinforcers in two schizophrenic children on the basis of food. *Journal of Experimental Child Psychology, 4,* 109-125.

Lovaas, O. I., & Smith, T. (1988). Intensive behavioral treatment with young autistic children. In B. B. Lahey & A. E. Kazdin (Eds.), *Advances in clinical child psychology, Volume 11* (pp. 285-324). New York: Plenum Press.

Matson, J. L., & Kazdin, A. E. (1981). Punishment in behavior modification: Pragmatic, ethical, and legal issues. *Clinical Psychology Review, 1*, 197-210.

Matson, J. L., & Taras, M. E. (1989). A 20-year review of punishment and alternative methods to treat problem behaviors in developmentally delayed persons, *Research in Developmental Disabilities, 10*, 85-104.

McEachin, J. J., & Leaf, R. B. (1984). *The role of punishment in the motivation of autistic children*. Paper presented at the annual meeting for The Association of Behavior Analysis. Milwaukee, WI.

Newsom, C., Favell, J. E., & Rincover, A. (1983). Side effects of punishment. In S. Axelrod & J. Apsche (Eds.), *The effects of punishment on human behavior* (pp. 285-316). New York: Academic Press.

Patterson, G. R. (1976). *Living with children*. Champaign, IL: Research Press.

Peterson, R. F., & Peterson, L. R. (1968). The use of positive reinforcement in the control of self-destructive behavior in a retarded boy. *Journal of Experimental Child Psychology, 6*, 351-360.

Rutter, M. (1985). The treatment of autistic children. *Journal of Child Psychology and Psychiatry, 26*, 193-214.

Schopler, E. (1962). The development of body image and symbol formation through bodily contact with an autistic child. *Journal of Child Psychology and Psychiatry, 3*, 191-202.

Schopler, E., Reichler, R. J., & Rochin, B. R. (1986). *The childhood autism rating scale (CARS)*. New York: Irvington.

Sidman, M. (1989). *Coercion and its fallout.* Boston, MA: Authors Cooperative.

Simeonnson, R. J., Olley, J. G., & Rosenthal, S. L. (1987). Early intervention for children with autism. In M. J. Guralnick & F. C. Bennett (Eds.), *The effectiveness of early intervention for at-risk and handicapped children* (pp. 275-296). Orlando, FL: Academic Press.

Singh, N. N, Watson, J. E., & Winton, A. S. (1986). Treating self-injury: Water mist versus facial screening or forced arm exercise. *Journal of Applied Behavior Analysis, 19*, 403-410.

Tinbergen, N., & Tinbergen, E. A. (1983). *Autistic children: New hope for a cure*. London: Allen and Unwin.

Van Houten, R. (1989). The use of the functional teaching model to treat self-injury and aggression in a group treatment setting. In J. L. Malenfant (Chair), *The functional teaching model: Treating severe behavior in the context of re-enacting the behavior in a clinical setting through an analysis of its function*. Symposium conducted at the meeting of the Association for Behavior Analysis, Milwaukee, WI.

Welch, M. G. (1987). Toward prevention of developmental disorders. *Pennsylvania Medicine, 90*, 47-52.

PART IV

CHAPTER

21

THE EXPERIMENTAL (FUNCTIONAL) ANALYSIS OF BEHAVIOR DISORDERS: METHODOLOGY, APPLICATIONS, AND LIMITATIONS

Brian A. Iwata, Timothy R. Vollmer, and Jennifer R. Zarcone

University of Florida

A great deal of research has focused on the treatment of aggressive, destructive, and self-injurious behaviors over the past 25-30 years, and the most significant contributions to date have been based on principles of learning, formally known as applied behavior analysis (Baer, Wolf, & Risley, 1968). It has been shown repeatedly that undesirable behavior can be reduced in frequency and can even be replaced by more appropriate forms of behavior by using differential reinforcement, extinction, or punishment, and much of the current controversy in this area centers around the relative effectiveness and social acceptability of these techniques. Do reinforcement-based procedures (e.g., DRO or DRA combined with extinction) produce reductions in severe behavior disorders similar to those seen with punishment? Even if not as effective as punishment, will adequately designed reinforcement-based procedures produce consistent and clinically significant reductions in such behaviors? Is punishment necessary to successfully treat serious behavior disorders in the developmentally disabled? These questions have been posed for a number of years and have occasioned every conceivable response, based on support ranging from experimental data to personal views regarding what is right or wrong. Although debate no doubt will continue, federal agencies recently have acknowledged the fact that punishment, although intrusive, constitutes effective and legitimate therapy, and may be justified under certain conditions (Consensus Development Panel on Destructive Behaviors in Persons with Developmental Disabilities, 1989; U.S. Department of Health and Human Services, Health Care Financing Administration, 1988).

An important corollary in the punishment controversy is the renewed interest in the origins of behavior disorders and the question of whether "functional analysis" approaches to assessment and treatment can eliminate the apparent need for punishment and related "aversive" interventions. All "nonaversive" approaches to behavioral reduction necessarily entail the application of differential reinforcement and extinction in some combination. Interestingly, the very use of these procedures requires certain assumptions about conditions that promote and maintain disorders such as aggression and self-injurious behavior (SIB). Realization of this fact has led to the development of methods for identifying the motivational properties of behavior disorders and for designing treatment programs that either correct or nullify the effects of an individual's motivational history with respect to that disorder. Although still in its formative stages, this functional analysis approach has been suggested as an important element in the effective management of severe behavior problems (Consensus Development Panel on Destructive Behaviors in Persons with Developmental Disabilities, 1989). It is unlikely that research in this area will yield definitive answers to the questions posed above, but it may provide a basis for determining what types of intervention should be attempted before considering the use of punishment.

This chapter will review historical and contemporary research on the functional analysis of behavior disorders. The motivational properties (functions) of problems such as SIB and aggression will be described, and methods by which these functions may be identified will be examined. Finally, treatment implications, as well as potential limitations of the functional analysis model, will be discussed.

THE LEARNED FUNCTIONS OF BEHAVIORDISORDERS

Although there is evidence suggesting that some forms of behavioral pathology in the developmentally disabled may be induced through biological mechanisms (e.g., Cataldo & Harris, 1982), the results of both basic and applied research clearly indicate that a majority of behavior problems are learned responses (e.g., Bachman, 1972; Carr, 1977). A brief discussion of the contingencies that may account for behavioral acquisition and maintenance will provide a context for identifying the components of a functional analysis.

Environmental Positive Reinforcement

Events that are presented contingent on the occurrence of behavior may serve as positive reinforcement and strengthen the behavior. This process typically is associated with skill acquisition, but it could easily account for the development of behavior problems as well. Parents, teachers, and other caretakers often respond to a "disruption" by attempting to redirect or distract the misbehaver through the provision of attention, preferred activities or materials, food, or even reprimands. Although these consequences cause the problem to cease temporarily, they ultimately may increase its rate. Developmentally disabled individuals are particularly at risk for inadvertent strengthening of behavior problems through positive reinforcement because: (a) they have few appropriate behaviors at their disposal by which they can gain access to preferred events, and (b) their social environments may be relatively deprived to the point where the appropriate behaviors that they do exhibit often are ignored. Smolev (1971) provided an early account of how these factors play a role in the development of SIB.

Environmental Negative Reinforcement

Events that are removed, attenuated, or prevented contingent on the occurrence of behavior may strengthen behavior through the process of negative reinforcement. Escape from and avoidance of "undesirable" events may take a number of forms, some of which are at least tolerable even if not socially acceptable (e.g., refusing to do something, failing to show up when expected, leaving, etc.). Unfortunately, many developmentally disabled individuals have not acquired these behaviors and must rely on other means to terminate aversive situations, including general noncompliance, tantrums, and other forms of disruption, destructive behavior, aggression, and SIB (see Iwata, 1987, for a more extensive discussion of how severe behavior disorders may be inadvertently shaped by using negative reinforcement).

Automatic Reinforcement

Some behaviors appear to develop and persist independent of environmental factors. Several labels have been used to describe these behaviors in the developmentally disabled over the years, including "mannerisms," "self-stimulation," and "stereotypy" (Baumeister, 1978), and a variety of underlying mechanisms have been suggested. For example, some behaviors may be biologically induced, others may provide positive reinforcement (i.e., "pleasurable" stimulation), and still others may provide negative reinforcement by attenuating an "aversive" physiological state. To the extent that these behaviors are strengthened by consequences they directly produce, the term "automatic reinforcement" (Skinner, 1969) seems most desirable as a description of the maintaining contingency because it connotes the fact that behavior occurs independent of the social environment, as well as the fact that either positive or negative reinforcement may be involved.

RELEVANCE OF THE FUNCTIONAL ANALYSIS APPROACH TO ASSESSMENT AND TREATMENT

As the above discussion suggests, behavior disorders may be learned in a number of ways. Thus, mere examination of a behavior's topographic features (e.g., head banging vs. scratching vs. self-biting) may provide little information about factors responsible for the behavior. Similarly, the continued classification of disorders by topography for the purpose of treatment selection, as well as research attempting to identify the most effective treatment for a given behavior problem (e.g., aggression), may be unproductive because the same behavior exhibited by two individuals can be maintained through different mechanisms. One individual's aggressive acts may be a function of positive reinforcement in the form of attention, materials, or food; whereas, another individual's aggression may be negatively-reinforced by escape from work, educational tasks, or other aversive events. It is unlikely that any one behavioral intervention will have the same suppressive effect on these different functions. For example, traditional uses of extinction and time-out generally take the form of "ignoring" the misbehavior, terminating an activity, or removing the individual from the immediate environment. These procedures are designed to eliminate access to the *delivery* of stimulation and may be effective if the behavior is, in fact, maintained by positive reinforcement. By contrast, the identical procedures applied as treatment for negatively-reinforced behavior will only serve to exacerbate the problem (Solnick, Rincover, & Peterson, 1977). A less critical but similar difficulty is encountered when developing treatment programs based on differential reinforcement. The event used as a reinforcer in such programs usually is selected in an arbitrary manner and almost always is presented as positive reinforcement. In the case of behavior disorders maintained by positive reinforcement, this approach may be effective if the event selected as the reinforcer competes successfully with (i.e., is more potent than) the event maintaining the behavior. A higher likelihood of success may be expected if the therapeutic reinforcer is the event maintaining the behavior. In the case of behavior disorders maintained by negative reinforcement, the arbitrary delivery of positive reinforcers in either DRO or DRA/DRI contingencies may be unnecessary and add little to the effectiveness of a treatment program.

Thus, aside from providing basic information on the etiology of behavior disorders, the analysis of behavioral function or, alternatively, the "functional analysis" approach to assessment, may yield the following benefits:

1. In identifying the contingency that is most relevant to the occur-

rence of a behavior problem, a pre-treatment functional analysis will suggest: (a) the antecedent conditions that give rise to the behavior problem; (b) the source of reinforcement that should be eliminated; (c) the general reinforcement contingency, as well as the specific reinforcing events, that should form the basis for treatment; and (d) the reinforcement-based approaches to treatment that are either irrelevant or perhaps even countertherapeutic. In providing this information, functional analyses have the potential for increasing the effectiveness of reinforcement-based approaches to treatment, thereby decreasing the situations in which punishment is necessary.

2. Through additional research, it should be possible to develop a system for classifying behavioral interventions based on the functions of behavior for which they are effective. Any approximation to such a system would be superior to random selection or classification based on either behavioral topography or arbitrary placement in a hierarchy ranging from "least" to "most" intrusive.

3. Through identification of the ways in which behavior disorders are acquired and maintained, a more comprehensive and systematic approach to prevention is possible.

The use of punishment provides a limiting case for the relevance of behavioral function. The effectiveness of punishment is based solely on the fact that the event used as the punishing stimulus is strong enough to override whatever source of reinforcement may be maintaining the behavior. This fact suggests that, given the arbitrary use of reinforcement-based versus punishment procedures as treatment, one would expect a higher degree of success with punishment, a finding that has been supported repeatedly in the literature (e.g., Axelrod & Apsche, 1983; Matson & DiLorenzo, 1984). Because the design of effective punishment procedures requires no information about the function of a behavior disorder, the topic will be covered only briefly at the end of this chapter.

METHODS FOR IDENTIFYING THE LEARNED FUNCTIONS OF BEHAVIOR DISORDERS

In the most general sense, a functional analysis of a behavior "...requires a believable demonstration of the events that can be responsible for the occurrence or non-occurrence of that behavior (Baer et al., 1968). This approach has been taken by both basic and applied researchers in an attempt to identify the environmental determinants of behavior, and the model generally adopted involves establishing a new relationship between a change in the environment and a subsequent change in behavior. In other words, the question most often asked is, "How can the environment be changed to affect the future occurrence of the behavior?" Through replication and extension, it is theoretically possible to identify all of the environmental changes that produce, maintain, or abolish behavior. Such an achievement, however, yields little information about which specific relationships (out of all those identified in past research) account for a given behavior in a given individual. Thus, a different question is asked when attempting to identify the current functions of a behavior: "What, if anything, in the environment maintains this particular behavior as it now exists in this individual?" Although this question is of central importance to the study of all behavior and has particular significance to the treatment of behavior disorders, the emergence of formal approaches to the analysis of behavioral function is a recent phenomenon.

The basic task in attempting to identify the current motivational functions of behavior involves collecting information about the behavior and how it both affects and is affected by the environment. A number of methods for obtaining such information have been described in the literature, and they can be distinguished by the type of data collected and the conditions under which assessment takes place (see Table 1 for a summary). Although designed to serve the same purpose, these methods vary considerably in terms of both precision and complexity, and each method contains inherent strengths and weaknesses.

Indirect Methods

The simplest approaches to learning about behavior do not require the collection of any firsthand data and are, therefore, considered indirect or anecdotal methods of assessment. In essence, the therapist or researcher asks a series of questions about the behavior and other events having potential significance. In the case of severe behavior disorders exhibited by developmentally disabled individuals, the process is one step further removed from the actual behavior because the individual who exhibits the behavior does not provide the verbal report. Instead, parents, teachers, or other relevant persons are asked either to describe events as they have witnessed them in the past or to make conclusions about the causes of an individual's behavior based on their past observations. Questions may be general in nature, such as those suggested by Gambrill (1977) and Reese (1978), or they may be asked in a standard format, as in the A-B-C (Antecedents-Behavior-Consequences) questionnaire described by Sulzer-Azaroff & Mayer (1977). In either case, an assessment interview focusing on behavioral function should attempt to produce a clear description of: (a) the behavior, (b) the situations in which it does and does not occur, (c) antecedent events that may precipitate the behavior, and (d) the typical reactions of others.

A refinement of the A-B-C questionnaire was developed recently by Durand and Crimmins (1988). These authors designed a 16-item rating scale called the MAS (Motivation Assessment Scale) which attempts to isolate one of four possible functions for SIB: positive reinforcement through attention, positive

Table 1: Summary of Methods for Identifying the Functions of Behavior Disorders

	INDIRECT ASSESSMENT	DESCRIPTIVE ANALYSIS	FUNCTIONAL ANALYSIS
Procedure	Subjective verbal report of behavior under naturalistic conditions	Quantitative direct observation of behavior under naturalistic conditions	Quantitative direct observation of behavior under preselected and controlled conditions
Advantages	Efficiency and ease of application	Objectivity, relevance to everyday events	Objectivity, high degree of control allowing for identification of functional relations
Disadvantages	Questionable reliability and validity	Complexity, inability to identify effects of subtle or intermittent variables, potential "masking" by irrelevant events	Complexity, potential insensitivity to highly idiosyncratic events, potential risk of establishing new behavioral function

reinforcement through access to materials, negative reinforcement through escape, or sensory (i.e., automatic) reinforcement. Each item consists of a question about specific aspects of SIB (e.g., topography, frequency, conditions of occurrence or nonoccurrence) which is answered on a numeric scale ranging from zero (never) to six (always). The scaled responses can be summed or averaged according to a simple formula, yielding a ranked score for each of the four functions.

There are several advantages to indirect approaches, including ease of application, cost, and efficiency (administration requires only a few minutes). Information gained through such methods, however, may provide unreliable estimates of behavior and lead to invalid conclusions about its controlling variables. There have been very few attempts to establish the reliability or validity of indirect assessments of behavioral function, and the available data do not provide strong support for their use. For example, Durand and Crimmins (1988) had pairs of teachers and aides complete the MAS for each student whose SIB was assessed in several classroom contexts and then compared the results obtained by the two independent verbal reports. Although interrater reliability scores were considered to be within an acceptable range, the calculations were based on correlational analyses rather than on point-by-point comparison of the teachers' scores. Thus, the extent to which the teachers provided the same ranking for any given question is unknown. In a related study, Green, Reid, White, Halford, Brittain, and Gardner (1988) attempted to determine whether institutional staff could identify positive reinforcers for the behavior of profoundly retarded clients. The authors compared the results obtained from staff reports with those derived from direct assessments of client approach behavior toward a variety of stimuli, and they found little correspondence between the two sets of data. Subsequently, Green et al. assessed the effectiveness of stimuli identified through either process as positive reinforcement during training sessions. They found that staff-identified stimuli did not function as reinforcers unless clients had exhibited approach behavior toward these items during direct assessment.

In light of the potential limitations of verbal report measures, they cannot be considered adequate for the purpose of behavioral assessment. Their use might be recommended, however, as a first step in the assessment process. Data gathered through interviews, questionnaires, rating scales, and checklists can provide preliminary information about the severity and scope of the problem, and also can form a basis for further inquiry.

Descriptive Analysis Through Direct, Naturalistic Observation

A more objective and systematic approach to assessment involves firsthand observation of an individual's behavior in environmental contexts that are relevant to the problem. One of the earliest examples of this approach was reported by Bijou, Peterson, and Ault (1968). Beginning with a narrative account (i.e., written record) of ongoing behavior, they proposed some basic rules for: (a) generating response definitions and categories, (b) developing interval-based observation procedures, (c) gathering objective data on behavior, and (d) assessing interobserver reliability. Various aspects of the procedures described by Bijou et al. since have become standard methodology for the general conduct of behavioral research, but the actual model they presented exemplifies perfectly a descriptive approach to the analysis of behavioral function. Their methods allow for precise behavioral specification and a quantitative account of behavior (including its antecedents and consequences) across time and environments. Data records can be summarized as amount of behavior (e.g., rate, duration, or percent of intervals) observed, given known prevailing conditions. In addition, although not demonstrated by Bijou et al., data from descriptive analyses can be used to calculate conditional probabilities between behavior and both antecedent and consequent events (e.g., the probability that an adult's instruction is followed by a child's tantrum within a given amount of time, or that an instance of a client's SIB is followed by either caregiver attention or termination of instruction).

The descriptive analysis model described by Bijou et al. has been extended across a wide range of subject populations, behaviors, and environments. For example, Cataldo, Bessman, Parker, Pearson, Reid, and Rogers (1979) applied a descriptive analysis to ongoing behavior in pediatric intensive care units. Based on the data they obtained, Cataldo et al. were able to identify those aspects of the environment that most easily could be modified to increase positive behaviors and reduce the inappropriate behaviors of the patients.

The most recent adaptation of the descriptive analysis approach was reported by Touchette, MacDonald, and Langer (1985). Called the "Scatter Plot" method, this procedure involves specification of several levels of a target behavior (e.g., none vs. 1 or 2 instances vs. 3 or more instances) and coding a data sheet according to the level of behavior observed within half-hour intervals throughout the day. The advantages of the scatter plot are its relative simplicity compared to ongoing data collection and the fact that the actual data record produces a visual distribution of behavior across time. Although the authors suggested that the scatter plot is superior to traditional line graphs because stimulus events associated with a response can be easily noted, the data collection and recording procedures do not allow for any notation of a behavior's environmental correlates. The system could be modified to accommodate such recording, but the contiguity between environmental events and behavior would be lost over the half-hour interval. Further refinements to the scatter plot method necessarily result in a system resembling that described by Bijou et al. (1968). Thus, the scatter plot can be useful in determining the temporal parameters of a behavior problem (i.e., when the behavior occurs most and least), but a more complete descriptive analysis would be required to determine the potential causes for temporal patterning.

Although time-consuming, descriptive analyses based on direct observation possess a number of advantages over indirect methods of assessment. First, they are inherently more objective than verbal report measures because they reflect actual ongoing behavior. Second, they are quantitative in nature, thereby permitting conclusions about the *degree* of correspondence between behavior and other events transpiring in the environment. Finally, because observation is conducted directly in the natural environment, a wide range of events-everything that occurs-is subject to scrutiny and not just that which is "remembered."

The major disadvantage of this approach is the fact that naturally occurring events do not necessarily reveal functional relationships. For example, it is possible that some behavior disorders are followed by highly intermittent reinforcement (e.g., the probability of escaping an ongoing educational session following tantrums or aggression is no greater than 1 in 20 or 30) that, nevertheless, is sufficient to maintain the problem. Such low levels of correlation may be decreased even further as a function of sampling procedures because it is not possible to observe behavior continuously over long periods of time. The resulting correlation between inappropriate behavior and escape may be so low as to be dismissed as unimportant. This problem may be further compounded by a high correlation between the behavior and other completely unrelated events. Continuing with the same example, it is possible that client tantrums during educational sessions reliably are followed by reprimands or redirection by the teacher (schedule = VR2), but are maintained by highly intermittent escape (schedule = VR25). An analysis of these data, based on either frequency of occurrence or conditional probabilities, would suggest that the behavior is maintained by positive reinforcement (attention) when the behavior, in fact, was maintained by negative reinforcement (escape). Thus, naturalistic observations of behavior may not allow detection of the effects of intermittent events and, at the same time, may suggest the presence of a functional relationship where none exists. For these reasons, conclusions based on this approach to assessment should be made cautiously; this fact must be emphasized because the data resulting from direct observation are much more convincing than those generated through subjective verbal reports. Also, for these reasons, the term "descriptive" rather than "functional" more accurately describes the type of analysis performed.

Functional Analysis Through Direct, Controlled Observation

An adequate demonstration of the effects of subtle, suspected, or even obvious variables on behavior requires control over those variables while observation is conducted. This approach to assessment constitutes an experimental or "functional" analysis of behavior, in that the relationship of interest is verified directly through manipulation and replication. Although some would consider this definition overly restrictive, it is the only definition consistent with standard rules of evidence that have defined our field since its inception. Baer et al. (1968) succinctly described one of these rules by noting that "...a non-experimental (functional) analysis is a contradiction in terms" (p. 92).

The components of a functional analysis involve constructing at least one condition (experimental) in which the variable of interest is present (e.g., contingent attention for inappropriate behavior), and another condition (control) in which the variable is absent (e.g., no attention, noncontingent attention, DRO, etc.). Observation of behavior then proceeds while the experimental and control conditions are alternated, usually by way of multielement or reversal designs. In these respects, the functional analysis model of assessment uses an evaluation methodology identical to that found in treatment research. The difference lies in the types of manipulations that are used. The goal of treatment is to eliminate the behavior disorder using procedures that might be adapted for general use. By contrast, the goal of assessment is to demonstrate sensitivity to a given environmental event. Therefore, variables selected for examination in a functional analysis assessment will probably have the effect of increasing the frequency of the behavior problem, at least temporarily. Similarly, assessment conditions selected because they may be associated with a decrease in the behavior might never be undertaken as treatment due to their impracticality.

Two variations of the functional analysis model have been exemplified in research conducted to date. The first approach involves verifying the effects of a single variable whose influence on behavior is suspected based on previous information (e.g., anecdotal report or naturalistic observation). An early example of this approach was reported by Lovaas and Simmons (1969). In attempting to account for a high degree of instability in baseline levels of SIB, the authors exposed one subject to several conditions that differed with respect to the variable of attention: social deprivation, social satiation (continuous attention), and social attention contingent on occurrences of SIB. They found much higher levels of SIB during the contingent attention condition, thereby providing one of the first demonstrations that this serious disorder can be strengthened directly through positive reinforcement. Carr, Newsom, and Binkoff (1976, 1980) examined a different function for behavior disorders. They showed that their subjects' inappropriate behaviors served as escape responses by comparing levels of SIB and aggression exhibited during demand versus no-demand conditions. In both of these examples, it was possible to demonstrate unequivocally that a specific environmental event played an important role in the maintenance of a problem behavior by isolating and then manipulating that event while observing its effects. These studies also showed that control procedures used during assessment (e.g., continuous attention, no demands), although adequate for the purpose of comparison, would not necessarily be used as treatment even though they produced low levels of behavior.

In some situations (e.g., short-term residential settings, outpatient clinics), the collection of background information required to conduct the types of singular analyses just described may not be possible or may yield little benefit. In addition, it is conceivable that a given behavior disorder may serve more than one function. For these reasons, a second method of analysis has emerged that can be best characterized as a general model for determining which of several variables may be maintaining a behavior problem. Iwata, Dorsey, Slifer, Bauman, and Richman (1982) exposed subjects to a series of four conditions designed to assess the sensitivity of SIB to positive reinforcement (attention contingent on SIB), negative reinforcement (escape from demands contingent on SIB), automatic reinforcement (placement in a barren environment with no access to either attention or toys), and a control (no attention for SIB, no demands, play materials available, and attention contingent on the absence of SIB). Results showed reliable patterns of responding for 6 of 9 subjects, whose SIB was noticeably higher in a specific condition (differing across subjects), indicating a functional relationship between the variable manipulated and the behavior disorder. Results from subsequent studies have supported the utility of this approach with SIB (Day, Rea, Schussler, Larsen, & Johnson, 1988; Iwata, Pace, Cowdery, Kalsher, & Cataldo, 1990; Mason & Iwata, in press; Steege, Wacker, Berg, Cigrand, & Cooper, 1989), as well as with other problems such as aggression (Mace, Page, Ivancic, & O'Brien, 1986), multiple disruptive behaviors (Carr & Durand, 1985), pica (Mace & Knight, 1986), and stereotypic behavior (Durand & Carr, 1987; Sturmey, Carlsen, Crisp, & Newton, 1988).

The obvious strengths of functional analysis assessments include a high degree of quantitative precision and a clear demonstration of how contingencies and stimuli associated with them can affect behavior. A unique feature of functional analyses is the ability to examine the effects of several variables, either singly or in combination. For example, a behavior problem maintained by positive reinforcement may occur at a low rate generally, but may be exacerbated when reinforcement is not available for appropriate behaviors. This possibility can be explored by implementing a functional analysis that includes both types of conditions. Finally, control conditions within a functional analysis that produce low levels of problem behavior might suggest some short-term strategies for management. The elimination of all demands for an individual whose behavior problem serves as escape, for example, does not constitute effective or practical treatment. However, curtailment of training demands for a highly aggressive or self-injurious individual temporarily might reduce the risk of serious injury until a treatment program is developed and implemented.

Because rather stringent control must be exercised, not only over the measurement process but also over environmental events and their relationship to the target behavior, some have suggested that functional analyses may be too complex for use in typical treatment settings (e.g., Durand & Crimmins, 1988). This criticism is unwarranted because precisely the same requirements must be met in order to develop and implement most treatment programs with any degree of consistency.

A more significant limitation of the functional analysis is that it may not reveal all of the events that maintain a behavior problem in its natural environment. An analysis that examines only the negative reinforcement aspects of aggression (e.g., Carr et al., 1976) does not address the possibility that the behavior also is maintained by positive reinforcement. Likewise, an analysis showing that behavior is maintained by positive reinforcement may not identify all of the specific events serving as reinforcers. Tarpley and Schroeder (1979), for example, described the behavior of one subject whose SIB apparently was reinforced by having a particular ball returned to him. Although a functional analysis may well have demonstrated that the subject's SIB was sensitive to positive reinforcement generally, it is unlikely that the function of a particular ball would have been delineated without the aid of naturalistic observation. A functional analysis can reveal a range of events that serve as specific reinforcers, but only if these events are examined systematically. This limitation illustrates the benefit of combining information obtained from additional background sources to determine how a functional analysis might be best constructed.

Another potential problem with functional analyses is the possibility of establishing a *new relation* by exposing an existing behavior problem to a different reinforcement contingency. Consider, for example, an individual whose aberrant behavior is *currently maintained by positive reinforcement*. This person's behavior already is sensitive to environmental contingencies, and through contact with an escape contingency during assessment, a *transfer of control to negative reinforcement* might occur. Because of this possibility, it is advisable to carry out assessment procedures for the briefest amount of time needed to show control. This solution is not ideal, but it reduces the likelihood of teaching the client a new behavioral relationship that he or she may carry into the natural environment.

In summary, of the three methods for identifying the functions of behavior disorders (indirect assessment, descriptive analysis, functional analysis), only the functional analysis provides an adequate demonstration of causal relationship. It is, therefore, recommended as a standard component of the treatment-development process in order to: (a) confirm the utility of information obtained through other means, or (b) identify or isolate the role played by different environmental events when naturalistic observations do not yield obvious results. The development of a functional analysis may be aided through information already obtained using one or both of the other methods.

VARIABLES AFFECTING THE OUTCOME OF A FUNCTIONAL ANALYSIS

Although indirect and descriptive approaches to behavioral assessment require some decision making about questions to be asked or data to be collected, no attempt is made to exert any particular influence over behavior or the environmental contexts in which it occurs. In a functional analysis, on the other hand, variables are manipulated so as to increase or decrease the behavior under examination; therefore, predictions must be made about how a behavior will be affected by a specific manipulation. For example, positively-reinforced behavior often responds quite differently than negatively-reinforced behavior, given an identical change in the environment. Similarly, more than one variable might be manipulated in order to establish the fact that a behavior disorder is maintained by the same contingency (e.g., positive reinforcement). In this section, we will focus on how the different functions of behavior disorders are affected by separate classes of variables.

Positive, negative, and automatic reinforcement differ with respect to the nature of the maintaining contingency (stimulus presentation vs. removal) and whether or not the contingency is mediated through the external (social) environment. In addition, several correlated variables may produce changes in the rate of responding. These variables can be classified as antecedent and consequent events, and each can be further subdivided. Antecedent events include establishing operations and discriminative stimuli. An establishing operation, such as deprivation or satiation, is an event that increases or decreases the effectiveness of a given reinforcer. A discriminative stimulus or S^D is an event in whose presence a behavior has been reinforced previously; and the opposite of a discriminative stimulus or S^{Δ} is an event in whose presence a behavior has not been reinforced (see Michael, 1982, for an extended discussion of the establishing and discriminative functions of stimuli). Consequent events that affect behavior include the contingency itself and its associated schedule, as well as the existence of contingencies for competing behaviors (concurrent reinforcement). Table 2 shows how these variables, for a given function of behavior, can be manipulated to increase or decrease behavior. Although antecedent events necessarily occur first in any environment-behavior sequence, they exert influence over behavior due to their relationship with consequent events. Thus, our discussion of how variables may be manipulated so as to bring about differential responding begins with the endpoint of behavior; namely, its consequences.

Behavior Maintained by Positive Reinforcement

CONSEQUENT EVENTS. The use of positive reinforcement to demonstrate the function of behavior was exemplified in the Lovaas and Simmons (1969) study cited previously where contingent attention increased SIB. The continuous attention condition also used provided an appropriate comparison because if the SIB was maintained by positive reinforcement, one would expect it to decrease as a result of this operation. The social deprivation condition that they included could be considered an example of extinction, and it apparently functioned in that manner by producing a decrease in SIB. It is important to note, however, that extinction may be associated with an initial increase rather than a decrease in the behavior, suggesting that the use of extinction as a comparison for contingent positive reinforcement may lengthen unnecessarily the amount of time required for assessment.

The schedule of reinforcement also affects the frequency of behavior. This fact was demonstrated by Lovaas, Freitag, Gold, and Kassorla (1965) who examined the effects of continuous versus intermittent social reinforcement on SIB. During one condition, the authors followed every instance of SIB with the comment, "I don't think you're bad" (schedule= FR1); during another condition, the same comment was made following approximately every fifth response (schedule= VR5). Higher frequencies of SIB occurred during the latter condition. Although appropriate for the purpose of assessment, one should consider the potential disad-

Table 2: Expected Outcomes of a Functional Analysis Based on Manipulations of Variables that Affect Behavior Maintained by Positive, Negative, or Automatic Reinforcement

BEHAVIORAL FUNCTION AND VARIABLE	MANIPULATIONS THAT INCREASE BEHAVIOR	MANIPULATIONS THAT DECREASE BEHAVIOR
Positive Reinforcement		
Consequent Events:		
Contingency for target behavior	Contingent stimulus delivery	Satiation or No stimulus presentation
Reinforcement schedule	Intermittent reinforcement	Continuous reinforcement
Concurrent reinforcement	No reinforcement for competing beh.	DRO/DRA/DRI
Antecedent Events:		
Discriminative stimulus (S^D)	S^D present	S^D absent or S Delta present
Establishing operation	Specific deprivation	Noncontingent stimulus delivery
Negative Reinforcement		
Consequent Events:		
Contingency for target behavior	Contingent stimulus removal	No stimulus removal (Extinction)
Reinforcement schedule	Same as positive reinforcement function	Same as positive reinforcement function
Concurrent reinforcement	Same as positive reinforcement function	Same as positive reinforcement function
Antecedent Events:		
Establishing operation	Aversive stimulation present	Aversive stimulation absent
Discriminative stimulus	Same as positive reinforcement function	Same as positive reinforcement function
Automatic Reinforcement		
Consequent Events:		
Contingency for target behavior	Not subject to external control	Not subject to external control
Reinforcement schedule	Not subject to external control	Not subject to external control
Concurrent reinforcement	Same as positive reinforcement function	Same as positive reinforcement function
Antecedent Events:		
Establishing operation	Idiosyncratically determined	Idiosyncratically determined
Discriminative stimulus	Not subject to external control	Not subject to external control

vantages of intermittent schedules. First, if differential responding is sufficient to reveal a functional relationship, a comparison between noncontingent reinforcement versus continuous (contingent) reinforcement should provide an adequate analysis. Thus, further increases in behavior associated with intermittent schedules may be both unnecessary and unsafe from the standpoint of client risk. Second, intermittent reinforcement during assessment subsequently may make the behavior more resistant to extinction (e.g., Neisworth, Hunt, Gallop, & Madle, 1985; although cf. Wylie & Grossman, 1988).

Finally, the availability of reinforcement for competing behaviors (concurrent reinforcement) may affect the level of the target behavior. For example, Carr, Schreibman, and Lovaas (1975) decreased echolalia in three autistic children by presenting praise and food contingent on appropriate responses to questions and discontinuing reinforcement for inappropriate responses. This study exemplifies the therapeutic use of DRI, and it is possible that either DRA or DRI contingencies may be applied for the purpose of assessment. However, the behavior-reducing effects of differential reinforcement do not necessarily reveal the function of a behavior because events that are sufficient to decrease a behavior (e.g., DRA) may not be the same as those which maintain behavior.

ANTECEDENT EVENTS. When access to a known positive reinforcer is limited through either deprivation or reinforcement removal, the effectiveness of that reinforcer is enhanced or established (hence, the term "establishing operation"). By contrast, excessive amounts of positive reinforcement, delivered either noncontingently or contingently (as in satiation), decrease the subsequent effectiveness of the reinforcer. Several studies have used establishing operations to reveal how behavior problems are maintained. Day et al. (1988) deprived self-injurious children (subjects) of access to preferred toys during brief play sessions, while free access was available to the subjects' peers. The subjects received toys contingent on the occurrence of SIB, but the toys were removed again after a short period of time. The SIB of two subjects increased during this condition, particularly following removal of the toys, suggesting that the items served as positive reinforcers for SIB. Similarly, in studies where attention was delivered contingent on the occurrence of inappropriate behavior (e.g., Iwata et al., 1982, 1990; Mace et al., 1986; Steege et al., 1989), subjects were relatively deprived because no other behaviors were followed by attention.

Other antecedent events affect behavior because they have been paired previously with reinforcement. Vukelich and Hake (1971) demonstrated discriminative control over aggressive behavior. In one condition, a therapist provided attention to the subject (S^D) condition); in another condition, a different therapist provided attention only when the subject behaved appropriately (S^D condition). The subject's aggressive behavior reliably increased in the presence of the first therapist but not the second. This study exemplifies a situation in which a behavior problem is reinforced in some situations but not others (e.g., home vs. school), and where one would expect to see increases in the problem with the persons or places associated with reinforcement.

Behavior Maintained By Negative Reinforcement

CONSEQUENT EVENTS. Several studies have shown that the contingent postponement or removal of known aversive events can produce an increase in inappropriate behavior. For example, Day et al. (1988), Iwata et al. (1982, 1990) and Steege et al. (1989), while conducting educational sessions with self-injurious subjects, followed occurrences of SIB with brief escape from tasks and found that SIB was higher during this condition when compared to several controls. It is interesting to note that the contingent escape was operationally identical to a traditional extinction procedure, and this illustrates a critical distinction between behavior maintained by positive versus negative reinforcement. The former class of behaviors is weakened through contingent stimulus removal, whereas, the latter is directly strengthened.

The Iwata et al. (1990) study also illustrated the fact that negative reinforcers may be just as idiosyncratic as positive reinforcers. They found differences across subjects with respect to events that produced escape behavior. One subject exhibited SIB only when demands of a medical nature were presented; no SIB occurred during academic demand sessions. A second subject reliably exhibited SIB during academic demand sessions, but only when the demands were relatively effortful (e.g., self-care tasks) and not when the task requirements involved simply pointing, sorting, etc.

Other variables associated with negative reinforcement contingencies (i.e., reinforcement schedules and concurrent reinforcement) have not been studied extensively. There is some evidence, however, that concurrent reinforcement for appropriate behavior may not compete successfully with ongoing escape or avoidance. In two of the studies cited above (Iwata et al., 1982,1990; Steege et al., 1989), praise was provided contingent on task performance (compliance), yet contingent task removal was a more effective reinforcer. Thus, it appears that positive reinforcers typically delivered by therapists are not sufficient to override the aversive aspects of some task situations.

ANTECEDENT EVENTS. Establishing operations for negatively-reinforced behavior are the inverse of those for positively-reinforced behavior. That is, the presence of (aversive) stimulation establishes escape as a negative reinforcer, whereas, the absence of stimulation eliminates the basis for escape. Other stimuli that have been paired with escape (e.g., people, places, etc.) also can occasion the inappropriate behavior by acquiring discriminative properties for avoidance. A number of studies have shown that aggressive and self-injurious behavior may be associated with antecedent, demand-related conditions: demands vs. no demands (Carr et al., 1976, 1980; Carr & Durand, 1985), or difficult vs. easy tasks (Weeks & Gaylord-Ross, 1981). It is often impossible to determine, however, the exact function that these antecedent conditions served. It is not clear whether the demands per se were aversive events (i.e., the demands were an establishing operation for escape from demands) or whether they were discriminative stimuli (i.e., the demands occasioned avoidance of other events that usually followed demands, such as physical prompting, remedial trials, etc.). The distinction between these demand functions is perhaps subtle, but it identifies which aspect of an aversive instructional situation needs to be modified.

Behavior Maintained By Automatic Reinforcement

Situations in which automatically-produced reinforcers account for the development or maintenance of behavior disorders are the most difficult to identify for several reasons. First, by definition, the reinforcing events are not provided by an external environment that is readily observable. Second, the antecedent events that occasion such behavior also may occur independent of the environment (e.g., physiological deprivation or aversive stimulation) or may consist of events that do not operate in a discrete fashion. Third, it is possible that the automatic response products serve as either positive or negative reinforcement. For example, SIB that provides sensory stimulation can be viewed as positively-reinforced behavior (Lovaas, Newsom, & Hickman, 1987), whereas SIB that attenuates pain associated with a medical condition (e.g., head banging by an individual who has a headache) is negatively-reinforced behavior (Cataldo & Harris, 1982). Thus, there are few means by which one can exert external control over factors that determine the occurrence or nonoccurrence of automatically reinforced behavior.

CONSEQUENT EVENTS. By providing or withholding reinforcement for incompatible or competing behaviors (concurrent reinforcement), it is possible to affect indirectly the frequency of the problem behavior. When used as the sole method for determining whether a behavior is maintained by automatic consequences, concurrent reinforcement is problematic because similar effects might be seen with behavior that is maintained through environmental sources. Nevertheless, this strategy has been used occasionally and is exemplified in a study by Mulhern and Baumeister (1969). They developed an apparatus that could detect body rocking in a seated subject, and used the device to reinforce sitting still by way of a DRO contingency. Whenever a subject sat still for a predetermined amount of time, the machine dispensed an edible reinforcer. Sessions were run at a time of day when the subjects were mildly food deprived (mid-to late afternoon), and the authors found that the subjects' frequency of body rocking decreased over time as the effect of the reinforcer was established. Similar findings have been reported by Berkson and Mason and colleagues (e.g., Berkson & Mason, 1965; Davenport & Berkson, 1963) who found that the availability of toys decreased the occurrence of stereotyped behavior. Although described by Berkson and Mason as an example of providing alternate sources of stimulation, the presence of toys per se probably does not alleviate a state of deprivation (establishing operation). Rather, the availability of toys makes possible another behavior--toy manipulation--whose reinforcement might compete with that obtained through "nonfunctional" stereotypic behavior.

ANTECEDENT EVENTS. Situations in which there is little stimulation are likely to serve as establishing operations for aberrant behaviors that provide automatic positive reinforcement. A number of studies have shown that deprivation, including a general lack of stimulation (Horner, 1980), the absence of play materials (Berkson & Mason, 1965; Davenport & Berkson, 1963; Guess & Rutherford, 1967), or a lack of social interaction (Moseley, Faust, & Reardon, 1970) can be associated with increases in stereotyped behavior. Conversely, noncontingent stimulation, which presumedly reduces a state of deprivation, should decrease the frequency of such behaviors. Forehand and Baumeister (1970), for example, found that a variety of stereotypic behaviors decreased when subjects were shown colorful slides.

Behavior that produces automatic negative reinforcement terminates or attenuates ongoing aversive stimulation. Although some behaviors of this type may be associated with discrete environmental stimulation (e.g., covering one's ears or yelling loudly to attenuate or drown out another individual's screaming), aberrant behaviors, typically in the form of SIB, are most likely to be associated with internal aversive states (i.e., biological conditions). A functional analysis in such cases involves combining behavioral measures with medical diagnostic techniques in an attempt to determine whether or not the presence of a medical problem produces behavior that alleviates some of the annoying symptoms. Although there are no clear demonstrations that SIB has been caused by a specific medical problem, correlational analyses suggest that the behavior may be associated with several conditions, including dermatitis, ear infections, and headaches (Cataldo & Harris, 1982).

THE DEVELOPMENT OF TREATMENT PROGRAMS BASED ON FUNCTIONAL ANALYSIS ASSESSMENT

When the maintaining contingencies (and associated stimuli) for a problem behavior have been identified through a functional analysis, a systematic approach to treatment is possible. The focus of intervention becomes the selection or development of therapeutic techniques that will eliminate, reverse, or in some other way alter the maintaining contingencies. As with the behavior disorder itself, the function of treatment, rather than its form, becomes an important consideration.

Reinforcement-based approaches to treatment can serve three general functions: (a) alleviating conditions that give rise to the behavior problem by altering an establishing operation, (b) eliminating reinforcement for the behavior through extinction, or (c) combining extinction with differential reinforcement for the absence of the target behavior (DRO) or the occurrence of alternative behaviors (DRA or DRI). These functions are listed in Table 3 and are described in greater detail below.

Table 3: Summary of Methods for Treating Behavior Disorders Based on Their Functional Properties

BEHAVIORAL FUNCTION	FOCUS OF TREATMENT	EXAMPLE
Positive Reinforcement	Establishing Operation	Noncontingent reinforcement (Lovaas & Simmons, 1969) Satiation (Allyon & Michael, 1959)
	Extinction	Withholding positive reinforcement (Mace et al., 1986) Time-out (Mason & Iwata, 1990))
	Differential Reinforcement	DRO (Steege et al., 1989) DRA - Establishing mands for positive reinforcement (Day et al., 1988)
Negative Reinforcement	Establishing Operation	Reduction of aversive stimulation (Weeks & Gaylord-Ross, 1981)
	Extinction	Prevention of escape (Iwata et al., 1990)
	Differential Reinforcement	DRA - Increased positive reinforcement for compliance (Mace et al., 1988) DRA - Escape as negative reinforcement for compliance (Heidorn & Jensen, 1984) DRA - Establishing mands for escape (Day et al., 1988)
Automatic Reinforcement	Establishing Operation	Noncontingent stimulation (Bailey & Meyerson, 1970)* General enrichment of physical and social environment (Horner, 1980)* Satiation (Rast et al., 1981)* Reduced aversive stimulation**
	Extinction	Attenuation of response-produced stimulation- (Rincover & Devaney, 1982)*
	Differential Reinforcement	Establishing alternative (automatically reinforced) behavior (Favell et al., 1982)*

* Applies when the behavior produces positive reinforcement
** Applies when the behavior produces negative reinforcement

Behavior Maintained By Positive Reinforcement

Anderson, Dancis, and Alpert (1978) compared the effects of several attention manipulations on SIB exhibited by individuals with Lesch-Nyhan syndrome. One of the conditions involved the delivery of noncontingent attention and exemplifies a situation where an establishing operation--deprivation--was modified to decrease SIB. The continuous attention condition described by Lovaas and Simmons (1969) also alleviated an apparent state of deprivation, and in all likelihood replaced it with a temporary condition of satiation. Ayllon and Michael (1959) described one of the earliest and clearest examples of satiation. Working with psychiatric patients who hoarded magazines that were generally scarce, the authors included a condition in which the ward was flooded with magazines, and found that rates of hoarding decreased markedly. Although treatment was not preceded by a functional analysis of the behavior, Ayllon and Michael confirmed the positive reinforcing effect of magazines and the decreased value of these items when they were more freely available.

When an individual is deprived of reinforcers to the point of exhibiting inappropriate behaviors in order to obtain them, the delivery of noncontingent reinforcement would seem to be an important component of ethical treatment. However, when the amount or schedule of reinforcement necessary to reduce the problem behavior is excessive (e.g., as in having to provide continuous attention in order to eliminate SIB or aggression), this approach to treatment becomes impractical and it may be effective only on a temporary basis. Furthermore, although the behavior may decrease in response to noncontingent reinforcement, it remains a functional part of the individual's behavioral repertoire and can be expected to reappear.

The most direct way to reduce a behavior is to eliminate the maintaining reinforcement contingency through extinction. Although simple in theory, successful application requires correct identification of both the contingency (i.e., positive vs. negative reinforcement) and the specific stimuli serving as reinforcers. Occasionally, it is possible to speculate about both of these and guess right. For example, Harmatz and Rasmussen (1969) presumed that adult attention served as positive reinforcement for their subject's SIB, and they demonstrated that by ignoring (i.e., not attending to) the behavior, it could be extinguished. The treatment manipulation in this study verified the initial hypothesis regarding the maintaining variable for SIB. However, if treatment had proved unsuccessful, the cause for failure would be difficult to determine. Was the procedure implemented inconsistently? Was the event withheld--attention--the wrong reinforcer? Or, was the procedure aimed at the wrong contingency (positive reinforcement)? The literature contains many examples of ineffective extinction programs, and it is certain that each of the above possibilities accounts for a proportion of the failures. The first possibility (inconsistent application) can be remedied through appropriate training and monitoring, but ruling out the second and third possibilities requires a functional analysis. Such an analysis takes the guesswork out of decisions about which consequences to remove, and it reduces the possibility of negative treatment results. The functional reinforcer will have been identified already, and its systematic removal from the operative contingencies becomes matter of procedural and practical implementation.

Indeed, research utilizing data from functional analyses to prescribe extinction procedures has begun to emerge. Mace et al. (1986), after identifying contingent attention (disapproving comments) as a reinforcer for aggressive and disruptive behaviors, eliminated the consequence and found that the behaviors decreased. Similarly, Day et al. (1988) found that the SIB of two clients appeared to be positively-reinforced through contingent access to toys. Treatment involved making these items unobtainable contingent on SIB. It is important to note that Day et al. included another treatment component (DRA) by requiring subjects to make vocal and nonvocal responses in order to receive the items. Thus, the role played by extinction per se is not clear in the Day et al. study. It is likely, that extinction was a critically important aspect of treatment, however, because there is no reason to believe that one behavior would be eliminated merely as a result of reinforcing a second behavior.

Time-out is a procedure derived from and similar to extinction, in that both eliminate opportunities for reinforcement. The general distinction between the two is that extinction refers to the removal of the reinforcer(s) maintaining the behavior, whereas, time-out involves contingently removing access to reinforcers that may or may not be involved in maintenance of the behavior. Time-out procedures vary considerably in their relative intrusiveness, and include removal of a discrete stimulus, such as removing a plate of food from the table contingent on inappropriate behavior (e.g., Barton, Guess, Garcia, & Baer, 1970); physical removal of an individual from a reinforcing environment (e.g., Porterfield, Herbert-Jackson, & Risley, 1976); placement of an individual in a less reinforcing environment (e.g., Bostow & Bailey, 1969); and physical containment through either mechanical or manual restraint (e.g., Rolider & Van Houten, 1985). As these descriptions suggest, the procedural differences among extinction, time-out, and punishment are sometimes unclear.

A time-out procedure specifically derived from the functional analysis of a behavior disorder would involve contingent termination of an ongoing event whose contingent presentation had been demonstrated to maintain the behavior. This type of time-out was exemplified in two studies on the treatment of SIB. Tate and Baroff (1966) and Mason and Iwata (in press) provided relatively continuous adult attention and/or physical contact to their subjects, which was temporarily interrupted contingent on SIB. This variant of time-out is relatively "nonintrusive," and the specific situations in which it might be effective could be determined empirically by demonstrating that the behavior is positively-reinforced by the stimulus class that will be contingently removed, or from which the client will be removed.

Differential reinforcement procedures necessarily include an extinction or time-out component. Additionally, they involve the use of positive reinforcement. A typical distinction among such procedures is based on whether reinforcement is delivered contingent on the absence of the target behavior (DRO), the occurrence of an alternative behavior (DRA), or the occurrence of an incompatible behavior (DRI). Taking into account the functional properties of behavior disorders, it is possible to make an additional and more important distinction.

The events selected as reinforcers in behavior reduction programs may or may not play a role in maintaining the problem behavior. The use of arbitrarily selected reinforcers is a common practice (e.g., Poling & Ryan, 1982). Even when it is demonstrated that certain events function as positive reinforcers for *some* behaviors (e.g., as in Steege et al., 1989), it is not necessarily the case that these same events maintain the problem behavior. Two potential limitations may result from the exclusive use of arbitrary reinforcers. As noted previously, it is likely that arbitrary reinforcers, if effective, must be more powerful than the reinforcer currently maintaining the behavior disorder. A functional analysis may reveal which specific reinforcers (out of all those exerting some influence over an individual's behavior) account for the occurrence of the problem behavior. These relevant reinforcers, when used in DRO, DRA, or DRI schedules, should be effective due to their preexisting relationship with the disorder. The second limitation is based on a prediction that the behavior disorder will continue at some level if differential reinforcement procedures do not include relevant reinforcers. For example, even if food items (arbitrary) used in a differential reinforcement program are generally more powerful than attention (relevant), one would expect to see the behavior problem occur in situations where the client has been relatively deprived of attention. This fact was demonstrated by Carr and Durand (1985) who initially determined that attention in the form of praise was responsible for maintaining multiple behavior problems in two of their subjects. During two treatment conditions, an alternative response was followed by either attention (relevant reinforcer) or assistance with the ongoing task (irrelevant reinforcer), and results showed that attention was more effective. The Day et al. (1988) study provided a particularly interesting example of the use of relevant reinforcers in a DRA contingency. By pairing specific reinforcers (toys) with specific responses (requests), the authors established mands for positive reinforcement (Skinner, 1957), which are basic functions of verbal behavior that determine the reinforcer produced by a given response.

Behavior Maintained By Negative Reinforcement

Escape behavior is reduced most easily by eliminating the events that establish escape as a negative reinforcer. Procedurally, this involves identifying situations in which the inappropriate behavior terminates ongoing events or postpones their occurrence, and either eliminating the events or modifying them so as to reduce their apparent aversive qualities. When it appears, for example, that demand-related contexts provoke aggressive or self-injurious behavior, the establishing operation--aversive tasks--may be modified in several ways. One component of a program described by Heidorn and Jensen (1984) involved reducing the number of demands presented to their subject, initially to one. By contrast, Weeks and Gaylord-Ross (1981) reduced the complexity of the situation by presenting easy tasks. Finally, Carr et al. (1976) embedded demands (which formerly produced SIB) within entertaining stories. As expected, each of these changes in the training context was associated with a rapid decrease in the target inappropriate behaviors. Their use, however, should be limited to situations in which the behavior is intolerable and even then should be considered as a temporary means of reducing behavior, because treatment based solely on the modification of establishing operations poses two significant problems. First, the situations in which inappropriate escape behaviors occur often are related to an individual's habilitative needs. By eliminating or greatly curtailing these activities, long-term educational goals may be sacrificed for short-term reductions in inappropriate behavior. One often encounters individuals for whom training demands have been reduced or even entire educational programs eliminated because they are associated with dramatic increases in severe behavior disorders. This undesirable outcome might be prevented through the use of stimulus fading techniques, in which the original, problem-provoking situation is first eliminated and then reinstated through gradual change. For example, Heidorn and Jensen (1984) successfully faded in the number of demands, whereas, Weeks and Gaylord-Ross (1981) faded across the dimension of task difficulty. The second problem with removal of an establishing operation is that the behavior is reduced indirectly by delivering reinforcement--elimination of an aversive event--before the behavior occurs. The behavior remains functional, however, and will recur, because it is unlikely that all sources of aversive stimulation can be (or should be) eliminated. This problem can be solved only by reducing the behavior directly through extinction.

Traditional uses of extinction (e.g., ignoring the behavior) and time-out are not only ineffective but actually countertherapeutic as treatment for negatively-reinforced behavior. Escape behavior is extinguished by eliminating its reinforcing consequence; namely, the termination or postponement of the aversive events (Hineline, 1977). For example, if aggression had been reinforced previously by the cessation of training activities, escape-extinction would involve no longer allowing the behavior to serve that function by requiring completion of the task at hand, or by not terminating the training session contingent on aggressive behavior.

A number of studies have used escape-extinction to reduce the following inappropriate behaviors that previously functioned to terminate ongoing instruction: aggression (Carr et al., 1976), SIB (Iwata et al., 1990; Repp, Felce, & Barton, 1988; Steege et al., 1989), tantrums (Sailor, Guess, Rutherford, & Baer, 1968), and other stereotypic responses (Mace, Browder, & Lyn, 1987). However, the extent to which extinction alone was responsible for observed behavior changes in these studies is not clear because other procedures were included in the treatment programs. For example, one of the subjects in the Carr et al. study initially was restrained in a chair, and instruction did not begin until aggressive behavior ceased. In other studies, inappropriate behavior produced immediate physical guidance to complete the assigned task (Iwata et al. and Steege et al.). An interesting contingency directly related to the function of the target behavior was included in the Sailor et al. study. After identifying difficult and easy tasks, the authors presented more difficult tasks contingent on the occurrence of tantrum behavior. In these studies, the contingent presentation of restraint, physical guidance, or more difficult tasks may have served as punishment for the target behavior.

Differential reinforcement as treatment for escape behavior can be applied in several ways. One option, positive reinforcement for appropriate behavior, may not be very effective in the forms it usually takes (i.e., praise or food items) because these are routinely included in most situations where demands are placed on clients and yet escape behaviors persist. Positive reinforcement procedures may be enhanced by: (a) increasing presession deprivation from positive reinforcement (Corte, Wolf, & Locke, 1971), (b) varying reinforcers during training so as to minimize satiation (Egel, 1981), or (c) increasing the density of reinforcement during training sessions (Mace, Hock, Lalli, West, Belfiore, Pinter, & Brown, 1988). The Mace et al. study was particularly interesting because it did not involve the use of either deprivation or additional reinforcers. Instead, the authors first identified demands for which compliance was either likely (high-probability commands) or unlikely (low-probability commands). During treatment, compliance to low-probability commands was increased when each low-probability command was preceded by rapid presentation of three high-probability commands. The increase in reinforcement density was thus achieved through task selection and sequencing.

Differential reinforcement also can be delivered as negative reinforcement. The fact that escape from task demands can strengthen problem behavior suggests that the same consequence could be used to strengthen appropriate behavior. For example, training situations could be arranged so that the only means of terminating the session is to refrain from engaging in disruptive behaviors or to exhibit specific appropriate behaviors (i.e., compliance); these contingencies could be described, respectively, as *escape DRO* and *escape DRA*. Task requirements could be simple at first and extended later, as in the Heidorn and Jensen (1984) study where treatment began with a single demand.

A third example of differential reinforcement, also involving negative reinforcement, focuses on the establishment of appropriate escape behavior. The reinforcer remains the same (termination of the task), but a new behavior is substituted for the inappropriate response (e.g., aggression, SIB). This approach was taken by Day et al. (1988), who prompted one of their subjects to say "No," which was followed by a short break from the training activity. The availability of an appropriate escape response is an extremely important training goal because it can be generalized to new situations, whose aversive aspects may be unpredicted by caretakers, parents, etc.

Behavior Maintained By Automatic Reinforcement

Bailey and Meyerson (1970) found that noncontingent vibratory stimulation produced a decrease in their subject's self-injurious head banging. In a related study, Rast, Johnston, Drum, and Conrin (1981) found that when their subjects were given additional portions of food (i.e., as much as they freely would consume), rates of rumination decreased. In both of these studies, behavior was reduced by providing noncontingent access to an event that may have been functionally similar to the consequence produced by the behavior itself. For example, head banging may have been maintained by response-produced kinesthetic or vibratory reinforcement, and rumination may have been maintained by the presence of food in the mouth, swallowing, etc. If the behaviors were automatically reinforced in this manner, the procedures implemented by Bailey and Meyerson and Rast et al. amounted to noncontingent reinforcement. Even if the behaviors were not maintained by these specific reinforcers, the procedures still may have affected an establishing operation by providing a sufficient amount of competing stimulation to make the target behavior less reinforcing (Bailey & Meyerson) or to induce satiation (Rast et al.). Additional research has shown that noncontingent stimulation need not be specific in order to have beneficial effects on behavior. To the extent that overall social and environmental enrichment eliminate general states of deprivation (e.g., Horner, 1980; Moseley et al., 1970), reductions in a variety of stereotypic behaviors might be seen.

When specific response-reinforcer relationships are identified (or, as is often the case, presumed), the development of treatment programs based on extinction becomes possible.

For example, Rincover (1978) hypothesized that one of his subject's stereotyped object twirling was maintained by the auditory stimulation it produced. By carpeting the table on which the objects were spun, Rincover reduced the auditory stimulation and the subject's twirling decreased. The general process--behavior reduction through attenuation of response-produced stimulation--has been called sensory extinction (Rincover, 1978; Rincover, Cook, Peoples, & Packard, 1979), and has been applied to the treatment of stereotypic SIB by having subjects wear equipment (e.g., helmets, gloves, padding) that did not prevent the behavior from occurring, but reduced the stimulation (Dorsey, Iwata, Reid, & Davis, 1982; Parrish, Iwata, Dorsey, Bunck, & Slifer, 1985; Rincover & Devany, 1982).

Although the results of these studies are promising, there are both practical and theoretical questions that remain unanswered. First, behaviors can produce several types of stimulation, and the process of identifying the relevant and unique response-reinforcer relationship seems to be one of trial-and-error. The behavior of object twirling could be maintained by auditory, visual, or tactile stimulation, and it is not clear how Rincover (1978) isolated the auditory factor as most relevant. Second, some procedural applications of sensory extinction (e.g., eliminating visual stimulation) may be extremely impractical unless they can be used on an intermittent or response-contingent basis (e.g., Dorsey et al., 1982). Finally, the SIB-reducing effects of protective equipment may be attributable to processes other than sensory extinction (e.g., time-out from environmental positive reinforcement). Additional research is needed to clarify these issues and to establish the generality of sensory extinction procedures across a wider range of behaviors.

Differential reinforcement applied as treatment for automatically reinforced behavior involves considerations similar to those for positively-reinforced behavior. Treatment may focus on the strengthening of arbitrary responses using arbitrary reinforcers; often, however, this approach has had limited success. Harris and Wolchik (1979), for example, found that food and praise delivered in a momentary DRO contingency were relatively ineffective in suppressing hand stereotypies exhibited by four subjects. An approach more consistent with a functional analysis of automatic reinforcement would focus on strengthening behaviors that compete successfully with stereotypic behavior because these new behaviors produce their own reinforcing stimuli; that is, the new behaviors are themselves stereotypic or self-stimulatory (i.e., automatically reinforcing). Isolate play behavior--toy manipulation--is essentially stereotypic in nature, and the studies by Berkson cited earlier (Berkson & Mason, 1965; Davenport & Berkson, 1963) demonstrated behavioral replacement through competing, response-produced reinforcement. More recently, Favell, McGimsey, and Schell (1982) used this strategy in the treatment of SIB by providing visual toys to a client who engaged in eye poking and popcorn to a client who engaged in pica.

Discussion so far has been limited to automatic positive reinforcement, but behavior disorders also can produce automatic negative reinforcement. The establishing operations for such behavior almost always are associated with a medical condition, and the function of the behavior is to attenuate one or more of its aversive symptoms. The most direct and ethical approach to treatment would involve: (a) identifying and eliminating the medical condition, and (b) teaching the individual either an appropriate means of signaling the presence of a medical condition or alternative methods for alleviating its symptoms.

COMPARATIVE RESEARCH

The research reviewed on treatment development generally indicates that interventions derived from the functional analysis of a behavior disorder can be highly effective. Support for this conclusion, however, provides little justification for the functional analysis model of assessment and treatment because conceivably *any intervention* (i.e., one either randomly selected or completely irrelevant to the function of the target behavior) could have produced an identical outcome. A basic and important question, therefore, is whether interventions based on functional analyses are more effective than those selected through some other means.

Very little research has addressed this question directly, although several studies have included conditions that serve as adequate comparisons. For example, some studies on the treatment of escape behavior (Iwata et al., 1990; Mace et al., 1988; Steege et al., 1989) contained two conditions that provided a comparison between extinction/time-out for positively-reinforced behavior (contingent termination of ongoing activities) versus negatively-reinforced behavior (continuation of ongoing activities and prevention of escape). The former condition was associated with an increase in responding above that seen during several other control conditions, whereas, the latter was associated with response reduction; this finding was consistent across seven subjects in one study (Iwata et al.). Data from the three studies indicate very clearly that knowledge about a behavior's maintaining variables is necessary in order to select an appropriate extinction procedure.

A study containing multiple comparisons was reported recently by Repp et al. (1988). After determining that two subjects' inappropriate behaviors were self-stimulatory and a third subject's was escape-motivated, the authors developed three treatments: extinction for positively-reinforced behavior, extinction (combined with compliance training) for negatively-reinforced behavior, and increased task presentation (combined with compliance training) for self-stimulatory behavior. The following comparisons were then made: (a) the positive reinforcement treatment versus the negative reinforcement treatment for the subject whose behavior was negatively-reinforced, (b) the self-stimulation treatment versus the positive reinforcement treatment for one subject whose behavior was self-stimulatory, and (c) the self-stimulatory treatment versus the negative reinforcement treatment for the other self-stimulatory individual. In each case, the treatment derived from the authors' initial analysis was more effective.

Mason and Iwata (in press) also conducted several comparisons in an attempt to identify the active components of sensory-integrative therapy (Dura, Mulick, & Hammer, 1988). They exposed three subjects, whose SIBs were maintained by different contingencies (positive, negative, and automatic reinforcement) to sensory-integrative therapy. In the two cases where treatment was effective, the results were shown to be artifactual (i.e., related to noncontingent attention for the attention-motivated subject, and to the elimination of demands for the escape-motivated subject). Subsequently, a treatment related to the function of each subject's SIB was designed and successfully implemented.

The Mason and Iwata study also illustrates the use of the functional analysis model to evaluate differential effects of any intervention program, not just those involving the application of environmental contingencies. For example, Jordan, Singh, and Repp (1989) found that visual screening (McGonigle, Duncan, Cordisco, & Barrett, 1982) was much more effective than Gentle Teaching (McGee, 1985 a,b) in the treatment of stereotypic behavior. An extension of that study would involve examining the effects of Gentle Teaching (or components of it) on behavior problems maintained by different variables. Another case in which comparative research would be improved through the use of functional analyses is the evaluation of drug effects; specifically, the use of opioid antagonists as treatment for SIB. A common theory underlying the use of such drugs is that SIB is maintained by the reinforcing release of endogenous opioids known as endorphins, and that the uptake of these substances is blocked through the administration of naloxone or naltrexone (Cataldo & Harris, 1982). This theory clearly points toward a specific function of SIB (automatic reinforcement through self-administration of endorphin) and a drug action based on extinction; yet, none of the research conducted to date (Barrett, Feinstein, & Hole, 1989; Davidson, Kleene, Carroll, & Rockowitz, 1983; Richardson, & Zaleski, 1983; Sandman, et al., 1983; Szymanski, Kedesdy, Sulkes , & Cutler, 1987) has identified the function of SIB in subjects who received the drug, and perhaps this accounts for the conflicting findings that have been reported.

ADDITIONAL PROBLEMS IN IMPLEMENTATION, AND LIMITATIONS, PROFESSIONAL ISSUES

Assessment-Induced Risk

When conducting a functional analysis of maintaining variables for problem behaviors, it is usually necessary to reinforce the continued occurrence of those behaviors on a temporary basis. Therefore, the assessment process induces a certain amount of risk. The mere occurrence of aggression and SIB, for example, increases the likelihood of injuries, and other factors may worsen the problem. Response topographies may become more severe during assessment because the behavior is often prevented in the natural environment, whereas, particular conditions during assessment might require the behavior to be carried out (i.e., no therapist intervention). Rate, intensity, and latency of response all can be affected by specific aspects of the assessment process (e.g., stimuli, contingencies, schedules, etc.), and steps should be taken to minimize injury to self or others. Some of these may include protective equipment for clients (e.g., helmets for head hitting or boxing gloves for face punching), special clothing for therapists (e.g., Carr et al., 1980), and development of criteria for terminating sessions due to unacceptable risk (e.g., Iwata et al., 1982, 1990).

Multiple Control

There is no reason to assume that a given behavior problem serves one and only one function. Severe SIB and aggression normally require a response from the environment, and the contexts in which these behaviors occur may allow them to contact both positive and negative reinforcement. For example, a child with a limited behavioral repertoire might bite his or her hand when socially deprived because the behavior produces caregiver attention (positive reinforcement), but, during training activities, the hand biting may be maintained as an escape response (negative reinforcement).

If behavior is multiply controlled, it will occur in more than one natural environment or specifically designed assessment condition, and the correct identification of maintaining variables may require a series of progressively more refined assessments. In addition, multiply controlled behavior may require multiple treatments that change across situations. This can become quite difficult when intervention consists of withholding attention in one context (attention extinction), while continuing to provide attention and guidance in another (escape extinction). Such a treatment program requires highly trained therapists who can quickly discriminate contextual differences and their effects on behavior, because even occasional errors might result in intermittent reinforcement and further strengthening of the behavior.

Implications For The Definition And Use Of Restrictive Interventions

Aside from the fact that there is no agreed upon definition of what constitutes restrictive or aversive treatment, the placement of treatments in a hierarchy from least to most restrictive usually is based on some subjective determination of relative dislike for one procedure compared to another. The greatest danger in developing any system that emphasizes the form of treatment is that the function of treatment may be overlooked. Extinction, for example, may take numerous forms (e.g., attention-extinction, escape extinction, sensory-extinction), but none have been differentiated in any published hierarchy of recommended treatment procedures. Even if these three variants were included in a future hierarchy, their relative positions based on intrusiveness probably would be irrelevant. It is likely that both attention-extinction and sensory extinction would be viewed as less intrusive than escape-extinction; nevertheless, only escape-extinction should be used as treatment for negatively-reinforced behavior. Thus, current research on the development of treatments derived from the functional analysis of behavior disorders indicates that our preference for least restrictive approaches to intervention should include another criterion: "likely to be effective, given the function of the behavior problem."

A potential advantage of the functional analysis model noted at the beginning of this chapter was the possibility that it might reduce the situations where punishment techniques are required. There are several problematic situations, however, that will continue to present treatment challenges. First, the very nature of some behavior disorders (i.e., dangerously aggressive behavior or high-risk SIB) precludes the exclusive use of treatments whose effects are gradual (e.g., differential reinforcement and extinction). Second, the rate of some behaviors may require the use of very rich schedules of reinforcement, but the implementation of such schedules with any degree of consistency may be practically impossible. Third, inconsistent application of complex treatment programs for multiply controlled behavior may do little more than further enmesh our clients into a life of dangerous behavior if intermittent reinforcement increases resistance to treatment. Finally, the question of cost-benefit is relevant to any discussion of complex technologies and certainly applies to the technology described throughout this chapter.

SUMMARY

Research on severe behavior disorders in the developmentally disabled has shown that many of these problems are learned responses that can be acquired and maintained in different ways. A review of these basic functions of behavior disorders suggests how one might differentiate one function from another in a given individual. Based on information obtained through several sources (e.g., indirect sources or naturalistic observation), a functional analysis requires systematic observation of behavior while variables known to affect behavior in certain ways are manipulated. The resulting data often will reveal the current function of the behavior and will allow the development of treatment programs uniquely matched to that particular function.

REFERENCES

Anderson, L., Dancis, J., & Alpert, M. (1978). Behavioral contingencies and self-mutilation in Lesch-Nyhan disease. *Journal of Consulting and Clinical Psychology, 46*, 529-536.

Ayllon, T., & Michael, J. (1959). The psychiatric nurse as a behavioral engineer. *Journal of the Experimental Analysis of Behavior, 2,* 323-334.

Axelrod, S., & Apsche, J. (1983). *The effects of punishment on human behavior.* New York: Academic Press.

Bachman, J.A. (1972). Self-injurious behavior: A behavioral analysis. *Journal of Abnormal Psychology, 80*, 211-224.

Baer, D.M., Wolf, M.M., & Risley, T.R. (1968). Some current dimensions of applied behavior analysis. *Journal of Applied Behavior Analysis, 1,* 91-97.

Bailey, J., & Meyerson, L. (1970). Effect of vibratory stimulation on a retardate's self-injurious behavior. *Psychological Aspects of Disability, 17,* 133-137.

Barrett, R.P., Feinstein, C., & Hole, W.T. (1989). Effects of naloxone and naltrexone on self-injury: A double-blind placebo-controlled analysis. *American Journal on Mental Retardation, 93*, 644-651.

Barton, E.S., Guess, D., Garcia, E., & Baer, D. (1970). Improvement of retardates' mealtime behaviors by timeout procedures using multiple baseline techniques. *Journal of Applied Behavior Analysis, 3,* 77-84.

Baumeister, A.A. (1978). Origins and control of stereotyped movements. In C.E. Meyers (Ed.), *Quality of life in severely and profoundly retarded people* (pp. 353-384). Washington, D.C.: American Association on Mental Deficiency.

Berkson, G., & Mason, W.A. (1965). Stereotyped movements of mental defectives: IV. The effects of toys and the character of the acts. *American Journal of Mental Deficiency, 68,* 511-524.

Bijou, S.W., Peterson, R.F., & Ault, M.H. (1968). A method to integrate descriptive and experimental field studies at the level of data and empirical concepts. *Journal of Applied Behavior Analysis, 1,* 175-191.

Bostow, D.E., & Bailey, J.S. (1969). Modification of severe disruptive and aggressive behavior using brief timeout and reinforcement procedures. *Journal of Applied Behavior Analysis, 2,* 31-37.

Carr, E.G. (1977). The motivation of self-injurious behavior: A review of some hypotheses. *Psychological Bulletin, 84,* 800-816.

Carr, E.G., & Durand, V.M. (1985) Reducing behavior problems through functional communication training. *Journal of Applied Behavior Analysis, 18,* 111-126.

Carr, E.G., Newsom, C.D., & Binkoff, J. (1976). Stimulus control of self-destructive behavior in a psychotic child. *Journal of Abnormal Child Psychology, 4,* 139-153.

Carr, E.G., Newsom, C.D., & Binkoff, J. (1980). Escape as a factor in the aggressive behavior of two retarded children. *Journal of Applied Behavior Analysis, 13,* 101-117.

Carr, E.G., Schreibman, L., & Lovaas, O.I. (1975). Control of echolalic speech in psychotic children. *Journal of Abnormal Child Psychgology, 3,* 331-351.

Cataldo, M.F., Bessman, C.A., Parker, L.H., Pearson, J., Reid, J.E., & Rogers, M.C. (1979). Behavioral assessment for pediatric intensive care units. *Journal of Applied Behavior Analysis, 12,* 83-97.

Cataldo, M.F., & Harris, J. (1982). The biological basis for self-injury in the mentally retarded. *Analysis and Intervention in Developmental Disabilities, 2,* 21-39.

Consensus Development Panel on Destructive Behaviors in Persons with Developmental Disabilities. (1989). *Consensus statement on destrructive behaviors in persons with developmental disabilities (preliminary draft).* Bethesda, MD: The National Institutes of Health.

Corte, H.E., Wolf, M.M., & Locke, B.J. (1971). A comparison of procedures for eliminating self-injurious behavior of retarded adolescents. *Journal of Applied Behavior Analysis, 4,* 201-213.

Davenport, R.K., & Berkson, G. (1963). Stereotyped movements of mental defectives: II. Effects of novel objects. *American Journal of Mental Deficiency, 67,* 879-882.

Davidson, P.W., Kleene, B.M., Carroll, M., & Rockowitz, R.J. (1983). Effects of naloxone on self-injurious behavior: A case study. *Applied Research in Mental Retardation, 4,* 1-4.

Day, R.M., Rea, J.A., Schussler, N.G., Larsen, S.E., & Johnson, W.L. (1988). A functionally based approach to the treatment of self-injurious behavior. *Behavior Modification, 12,* 565-589.

Dorsey, M., Iwata, B.A., Reid, D., & Davis, P. (1982). Protective equipment: Continuous and contingent application in the treatment of self-injurious behavior. *Journal of Applied Behavior Analysis, 15,* 217-230.

Dura, J.R., Mulick, J.A., & Hammer, D. (1988). Rapid clinical evaluation of sensory-integrative therapy for self-injurious behavior. *Mental Retardation, 26,* 83-87.

Durand. V.M, & Carr, E.G. (1987). Social influences on "self-stimulatory" behavior: Analysis and treatment application. *Journal of Applied Behavior Analysis, 20,* 119-132.

Durand, V.M., & Crimmins, D.B. (1988). Identifying the variables maintaining self-injurious behavior. *Journal of Autism and Developmental Disorders, 18,* 99-117.

Egel, A.L. (1981). Reinforcer variation: Implications for motivating developmentally disabled children. *Journal of Applied Behavior Analysis, 14,* 345-350.

Favell, J.E., McGimsey, J.F., & Schell, R.M. (1982). Treatment of self-injury by providing alternate sensory activities. *Analysis and Intervention in Developmental Disabilities, 2,* 83-104.

Forehand, R., & Baumeister, A.A. (1970). The effect of auditory and visual stimulation on stereotyped rocking behavior and general activity of severe retardates. *Journal of Clinical Psychology, 26,* 426-429.

Gambrill, E.D. (1977). *Behavior modification: Handbook of assessment, intervention, and evaluation.* San Francisco: Joscy-Bass.

Green, C.W., Reid, D.H., White, L.K., Halford, R.C., Brittain, D.P., & Gardner, S.M. (1988). Identifying reinforcers for persons with profound handicaps: Staff opinion versus systematic assessment of preferences. *Journal of Applied Behavior Analysis, 21,* 31-43.

Guess, D., & Rutherford, G. (1967). Experimental attempts to reduce stereotyping among blind retardates. *American Journal of Mental Deficiency, 71,* 984-986.

Harmatz, M.G., & Rasmussen, W.A. (1969). A behavior modification approach to head banging. *Mental Hygiene, 53,* 590-593.

Harris, S.L., & Wolchik, S.A. (1979). Suppression of self-stimulation: Three alternative strategies. *Journal of Applied Behavior Analysis, 12,* 185-189.

Heidorn, S.D., & Jensen, C.C. (1984). Generalization and maintenance of the reduction of self-injurious behavior maintained by two types of reinforcement. *Behaviour Research and Therapy, 22,* 581-586.

Hineline, P.N. (1977). Negative reinforcement and avoidance. In W.K. Honig & J.E.R. Staddon (Eds.), *Handbook of operant behavior* (pp. 364-414). Englewood Cliffs, NJ: Prentice-Hall.

Horner, R.D. (1980). The effects of an environmental "enrichment" program on the behavior of institutionalized profoundly retarded children. *Journal of Applied Behavior Analysis, 13,* 473-491.

Iwata, B.A. (1987). Negative reinforcement in applied behavior analysis: An emerging technology. *Journal of Applied Behavior Analysis, 20,* 361-387.

Iwata, B.A., Dorsey, M.F., Slifer, K.J., Bauman, K.E., & Richman, G.S. (1982). Toward a functional analysis of self-injury. *Analysis and Intervention in Developmental Disabilities, 2,* 1-20.

Iwata, B.A., Pace, G.M., Cowdery, G.E., Kalsher, M.J., & Cataldo, M.F. (1990). Experimental analysis and extinction of self-injurious escape behavior. *Journal of Applied Behavior Analysis, 23,* 11-27.

Jordan, J., Singh, N.N., & Repp, A.C. (1989). An evaluation of gentle teaching and visual screening in the reduction of stereotypy. *Journal of Applied Behavior Analysis, 22,* 9-22.

Lovaas, O.I., Freitag, G., Gold, V.J., & Kassorla, I.C. (1965). Experimental studies in childhood schizophrenia: Analysis of self-destructive behavior. *Journal of Experimental Child Psychology, 2,* 67-84.

Lovaas, O.I., Newsom, C.D., & Hickman, C. (1987). Self-stimulatory behavior and perceptual reinforcement. *Journal of Applied Behavior Analysis, 20,* 45-68.

Lovaas, O.I., & Simmons, J.Q. (1969). Manipulation of self-destruction in three retarded children. *Journal of Applied Behavior Analysis, 2,* 143-157.

Mace, F.C., Browder, D., & Lyn, Y. (1987). Analysis of demand conditions associated with stereotypy. *Journal of Behavior Therapy and Experimental Psychiatry, 18,* 25-31.

Mace, F.C., Hock, M.L., Lalli, J.S., West, B.J., Belfiore, P., Pinter, E., & Brown, D.K. (1988). Behavioral momentum in the treatment of noncompliance. *Journal of Applied Behavior Analysis, 21,* 123-141.

Mace, F.C., & Knight, D. (1986). Functional analysis and treatment of severe pica. *Journal of Applied Behavior Analysis, 19,* 411-416.

Mace, F.C., Page, T.J. Ivancic, M.T., & O'Brien, S. (1986). Analysis of environmental determinants of aggression and disruption in mentally retarded children. *Applied Research in Mental Retardation, 7,* 203-221.

Mason, S.A., & Iwata, B.A. (in press). Artifactual effects of sensory-integrative therapy on self-injurious behavior. *Journal of Applied Behavior Analysis.*

Matson, J.L., & DiLorenzo, T.M. (1984). *Punishment and its alternatives: New perspectives for behavior modification.* New York: Springer.

McGee, J.J. (1985a). Examples of the use of gentle teaching. *Mental Handicap in New Zealand, 9 (4),* 11-20.

McGee, J.J. (1985b). Gentle teaching. *Mental Handicap in New Zealand, 9 (3),* 13-24.

McGonigle, J.J., Duncan, D., Cordisco, L., & Barrett, R.P. (1982). Visual screening: An alternative method for reducing stereotypic behaviors. *Journal of Applied Behavior Analysis, 15,* 461-467.

Michael, J. (1982). Distinguishing between discriminative and motivational functions of stimuli. *Journal of the Experimental Analysis of Behavior, 37,* 149-155.

Moseley, A., Faust, M., & Reardon, D.M. (1970). Effects of social and nonsocial stimuli on the stereotyped behaviors of retarded children. *American Journal of Mental Deficiency, 74,* 809-811.

Mulhern, T., & Baumeister, A.A. (1969). An experimental attempt to reduce stereotypy by reinforcement procedures. *American Journal of Mental Deficiency, 74,* 69-74.

Neisworth, J.T., Hunt, F.M., Gallop, H.R., & Madle, R.A. (1985). Reinforcer displacement: A preliminary application of the CRF/EXT effect. *Behavior Modification, 9,* 103-115.

Parrish, J.M., Iwata, B.A., Dorsey, M.F., Bunck, T.J., & Slifer, K.J. (1985). Behavior analysis, program development, and transfer of control in the treatment of self-injury. *Journal of Behavior Therapy and Experimental Psychiatry, 16,* 159-168.

Poling, A., & Ryan, C. (1982). Differential reinforcement of other behavior schedules: Therapeutic applications. *Behavior Modification, 6,* 3-21.

Porterfield, J.K., Herbert-Jackson, E., & Risley, T.R. (1976). Contingent observation: An effective and acceptable procedure for reducing disruptive behavior of young children in a group setting. *Journal of Applied Behavior Analysis, 9,* 55-64.

Rast, J., Johnston, J.M., Drum, C., & Conrin, J. (1981). The relation of food quantity to rumination behavior. *Journal of Applied Behavior Analysis, 14,* 121-130.

Reese, E. (1978). *Human behavior: Analysis and application.* Dubuque, IA: Wm. C. Brown.

Repp, A.C., Felce, D., & Barton, L.E. (1988). Basing the treatment of stereotypic and self-injurious behaviors on hypotheses of their causes. *Journal of Applied Behavior Analysis, 21,* 281-289.

Richardson, J.S., & Zaleski, W.A. (1983). Naloxone and self-mutilation. *Biological Psychiatry, 18,* 99-101.

Rincover, A. (1978). Sensory extinction: A procedure for eliminating self-stimulatory behavior in developmentally disabled children. *Journal of Abnormal Child Psychology, 6,* 299-310.

Rincover, A., Cook, R., Peoples, A., & Packard, D. (1979). Sensory extinction and sensory reinforcement principles for programming multiple adaptive behavior changes. *Journal of Applied Behavior Analysis, 12,* 221-233.

Rincover, A., & Devany, J. (1982). The application of sensory extinction procedures to self-injury. *Analysis and Intervention in Developmental Disabilities, 2,* 67-81.

Rolider, A., & Van Houten, R. (1985). Movement suppression timeout for undesirable behavior in psychotic and severely developmentally delayed children. *Journal of Applied Behavior Analysis, 18,* 275-288.

Sailor, W., Guess, D., Rutherford, G., & Baer, D.M. (1968). Control of tantrum behavior by operant techniques during experimental verbal training. *Journal of Applied Behavior Analysis, 1,* 237-243.

Sandman, C.A., Datta, P.C., Barron, J., Hoehler, F.K., Williams, C., & Swanson, J.M. (1983). Naloxone attenuates self-abusive behavior in developmentally disabled clients. *Applied Research in Mental Retardation, 4,* 5-11.

Skinner, B.F. (1957). *Verbal behavior.* Englewood Cliffs, NJ: Prentice-Hall.

Skinner, B.F. (1969). *Contingencies of reinforcement: A theoretical analysis.* New York: Appleton-Century-Crofts.

Smolev, S.R. (1971). Use of operant techniques for the modification of self-injurious behavior. *American Journal of Mental Deficiency, 76,* 295-305.

Solnick, J.V., Rincover, A., & Peterson, C.R. (1977). Some determinants of the reinforcing and punishing effects of timeout. *Journal of Applied Behavior Analysis, 10,* 415-424.

Steege, M.V., Wacker, D.P., Berg, W.K., Cigrand, K.K., & Cooper, L.J. (1989). The use of behavioral assessment to prescribe and evaluate treatments for severely handicapped children. *Journal of Applied Behavior Analysis, 22,* 23-33.

Sturmey, P., Carlsen, A., Crisp, A.G., & Newton, J.T. (1988). A functional analysis of multiple aberrant responses: A refinement and extension of Iwata et al.'s methodology. *Journal of Mental Deficiency Research, 32,* 31-46.

Sulzer-Azaroff, B. & Mayer, G.R. (1977). *Applying behavior-analysis procedures with children and youth.* New York: Holt, Rinehart, & Winston.

Szymanski, L., Kedesdy, J., Sulkes, S., & Cutler, A. (1987). Naltrexone in treatment of self-injurious behavior: A clinical study. *Research in Developmental Disabilities, 8,* 179-190.

Tarpley, H.D., & Schroeder, S.R. (1979). Comparison of DRO and DRI on rate suppression of self-injurious behavior. *American Journal of Mental Deficiency, 84,* 188-194.

Tate, B.G., & Baroff, G.S. (1966). Aversive control of self-injurious behavior in a psychotic boy. *Behaviour Research and Therapy, 4,* 281-287.

Touchette, P.E., MacDonald, R.F., & Langer, S.N. (1985). A scatter plot for identifying stimulus control of problem behavior. *Journal of Applied Behavior Analysis, 18,* 343-351.

U.S. Department of Health and Human Services, Health Care Financing Administration (1988, June 3). Medicaid program; Conditions for intermediate care facilities for the mentally retarded; Final rule. *Federal Register, 53,* (107), 20447-20505.

Vukelich, R., & Hake, D.F. (1971). Reduction of dangerously aggressive behavior in a severely retarded resident through a combination of positive reinforcement procedures. *Journal of Applied Behavior Analysis, 4*, 215-225.

Weeks, M., & Gaylord-Ross, R. (1981). Task difficulty and aberrant behavior in severely handicapped students. *Journal of Applied Behavior Analysis, 14*, 449-463.

Wylie, A.M., & Grossman, J.A. (1988). Response reduction through superimposition of continuous reinforcement : A systematic replication. *Journal of Applied Behavior Analysis, 21*, 201-206.

CHAPTER

22

A TAXONOMIC APPROACH TO THE NONAVERSIVE TREATMENT OF MALADAPTIVE BEHAVIOR OF PERSONS WITH DEVELOPMENTAL DISABILITIES

Alan C. Repp and Kathryn G. Karsh
Northern Illinois University
and
Educational Research & Services Center

There are nearly 6,000,000 individuals in the United States with developmental disabilities, the largest number of which have mental retardation (National Institutes of Health, 1989). Of these individuals, 750,000 are enrolled in public school programs for persons with mental retardation (U.S. Department of Education, 1988).

The prevalence of serious maladaptive behaviors among mentally retarded person in public school programs is difficult to determine. Available epidemiological data published since 1980 (Borthwick, Meyers, & Eyman, 1981; Corbett & Campbell, 1981; Griffen, Williams, Stark, Altmeyer, & Mason, 1986; Hill & Bruininks, 1984; Jacobson, 1982; Oliver, Murphy, & Corbett, 1987; Repp & Barton, 1980) suggest that as many as 14 to 38% of these persons engage in aggressive and destructive behaviors (e.g., hitting, biting others, throwing furniture), 6 to 40% engage in self-injurious behavior (e.g., head banging, biting one's hand, eye gouging), and 40 to 60% engage in stereotypic behavior (e.g., body rocking, arm flapping) at a rate high enough to be problematic.

These serious maladaptive behaviors have been studied extensively by both basic and applied researchers. This research attention has been fostered by (a) the incidence of the behaviors among persons with mental retardation; (b) the negative effects of the maladaptive behavior on the acquisition and display of adaptive behavior; and (c) the failure to develop treatment interventions that have shown consistent, long-lasting results in reducing or eliminating these behaviors.

MALADAPTIVE BEHAVIOR: EFFECTS AND TREATMENT

Negative Effects Of Maladaptive Behavior

The reduction or elimination of maladaptive behaviors is important for both the educational and social consequences of the behaviors. Educationally, severe maladaptive behaviors interfere with adaptive responding and with learning new skills (Koegel & Covert, 1972; Lovaas, Litrownink, & Mann, 1971; Repp, Deitz, & Deitz, 1976; Watkins &

Konarski, 1987). In addition, severe maladaptive behaviors result in decreased interaction with the environment, as staff interact with individuals less often during their educational program when they engage in maladaptive behaviors (Baumeister, 1978).

Socially, severe maladaptive behaviors lead to avoidance by others because of the conspicuousness and inappropriateness of these behaviors (Kelly & Drabman, 1977). These behaviors may lead to increased negative interaction with staff (Paisey, Whitney, & Hislop, Chapter 12), and they are the single most important factor leading to institutionalization or, at the very least, to placement in a more restricted setting (Eyman, O'Connor, Tarjan, & Justine, 1972). These behaviors may prevent parents from caring for their children in their natural home settings, as well as seeing their children participate in regular education environments and the community (Biklen, 1987).

Physically, these behaviors may result in bruising, bleeding, or tissue damage to the individual or similar damage to others in the environment. Many individuals receive psychiatric drugs for their severe behavior problems (Cohen & Sprague, 1977; Hill, Balow, & Bruininks, 1985) which may have deleterious effects on their overall functioning.

Treatment Programs

In response to the need to reduce serious maladaptive behaviors, numerous research studies have been conducted (cf., LaGrow & Repp, 1984; Romanczyk, 1986; Schroeder, Rojahn, & Oldenquist, 1989). Many of the methods devised to reduce these behaviors are based on principles of behavioral learning theory (applied behavior analysis), and include either punishment procedures (e.g., overcorrection, brief physical restraint, time-out) or positive reinforcement strategies (e.g., DRO, DRI, or functional equivalence training).

Some of the available treatment interventions have shown immediate effects, but the results have not been maintained over time or generalized to other settings (Carr, Taylor, Carlson, & Robinson, 1989; LaGrow & Repp, 1984; O'Brien & Repp, in press; Repp, Singh, Olinger, & Olson, 1990; Schroeder et al., 1989). Additionally, positive results have not always been replicated across individuals. Reviews of the effectiveness of both punishment (Cataldo, 1989) and positive reinforcement procedures (Carr et al., 1989) have not revealed consistent success rates for either type of procedure. The efficacy of treatments has not been adequately measured with respect to the covariation of behaviors, negative side effects, consumer satisfaction, clinical significance, or community acceptance of the intervention (Schroeder et al., 1989).

Nonaversive Treatments

One of the most controversial issues today involves the types of intervention programs used to treat severe maladaptive behaviors and whether they should be restricted to nonaversives (e.g., DRO, DRI) or whether aversives (e.g., overcorrection, time-out, restraint) also should be used. Some objections to punishment procedures are based on ethical and legal reasons, and these have contributed to some dissatisfaction with currently available aversive treatment interventions (e.g., Biklen, 1987; Evans & Meyer, 1985).

In an analysis of the comparative effectiveness of four nonaversive treatments, Carr et al. (1989) reported that all four procedures (i.e., skills acquisition, stimulus-based interventions, DRO, and DRI) had some measure of success. However, skills acquisition (59% success) and stimulus-based interventions (48% success) were superior overall to DRO (28% success) and DRI (33% success). The authors suggested that treatment outcome could be improved if a more systematic and sophisticated use of functional analysis was employed as an aid to treatment selection and treatment planning.

The purpose of this paper is not to enter the debate over whether aversives should or should not be used. Rather, the purpose is to advocate a scientific approach to the problem, and to suggest a way that more effective nonaversive treatments can be implemented.

Functional Analysis and Hypothesis-driven Treatments

One option for improving the efficacy of treatment interventions is to conduct a functional analysis of the maladaptive behavior. A functional analysis is an attempt to identify the conditions that are maintaining the behavior. For example, several studies have based treatment on a functional analysis of self-injurious behavior (SIB). Carr, Newsom, and Binkoff (1976) found that self-injury increased when commands were given but decreased when simple declarative sentences were directed toward a student. Other studies showed that SIB was related to the type of task presented (Gaylord-Ross, Weeks, & Lipner, 1980), and that SIB could be reduced by decreasing demands, by employing easy tasks, and by using errorless teaching procedures (Weeks & Gaylord-Ross, 1981). Another study (Iwata, Dorsey, Slifer, Bauman, & Richman, 1982) showed that self-injury could be related to other conditions as well (e.g., presence of materials, type of demand, and type of attention). The authors argued that a functional analysis of the maladaptive behavior should be a part of the treatment procedure, and that specific treatments should be based on such an analysis.

We believe there is a need to conduct functional analyses and to use hypothesis-driven interventions as treatment procedures (Repp, Felce, & Barton, 1988). To this end, we propose that a taxonomy should be developed that will allow us to base nonaversive treatments on a functional analysis of the conditions maintaining severe behavior problems. From this taxonomy, nonaversive procedures may be selected that match treatment interventions to hypotheses of the causes of the behavior problem.

Environmental Dependence And Independence

Severe behavior problems can occur for many reasons, and various interventions have been developed to treat them. Relatively few research studies, however, have attempted to match those interventions to the reasons the behavior problem might be occurring (LaGrow & Repp, 1984). We believe that this approach can be addressed through a taxonomy that will help us determine the reasons for a specific individual's behavior problems, reasons that will lead directly to more effective treatment.

Before presenting the taxonomy, we would like to discuss the terms *environmentally dependent* and *environmentally independent*, terms that are central to the operation of a taxonomy. By *environmentally dependent*, we mean behaviors whose rate, duration, or topography are affected by the naturally occurring environment. With the proposed taxonomy, and with the methods of recording and data analysis we have developed (Repp, Felce, & Karsh, in press; Repp, Harman, Felce, Van Acker & Karsh, 1989; Repp, Karsh, Van Acker, Felce, & Harman, 1989), we may be able to determine which behaviors of each individual are affected by the environment; namely, the *environmentally dependent behaviors*. Therapists then can manipulate the indicated parts of the environment as a part of the treatment program.

Although some behaviors are environmentally dependent, others are independent of either the current or past environment. Behaviors not shown to be affected by the environment *may* be considered *independent of the current environment.* These can be identified through the proposed taxonomy in a default sense, but treatment would not be suggested by the cells themselves. These behaviors may be better treated through other means (e.g., psychopharmacology). Scientifically, however, the important point is that a test can be made of whether we can classify behavior problems in a way that will (a) separate environmentally dependent from environmentally independent behaviors, and then (b) classify environmentally dependent behaviors into cells of the taxonomy. From the taxonomy, we should be able to identify hypothesis-derived treatments, the efficacy of which can be tested.

TAXONOMY

In this section, we will present a taxonomy based upon the relationship of behavior to *antecedent events* and *consequences* in the environment that would be maintaining the behavior. The taxonomy is based upon the relationship of behavior to the environment, with this relationship being a functional one. Thus, this taxonomy will determine which behaviors are *environmentally dependent* and the *part of the environment* on which they are dependent. With this information, we will learn why the behavior is being maintained, and we may be able to decrease the behavior by a natural, nonaversive manipulation of the maintaining environment.

Antecedent Events

Antecedent events are those parts of the environment that exist prior to behavior and affect its rate or duration. Although most agree that settings, and events within these settings, affect behavior, there is relatively little discussion of setting events within our literature. Important exceptions have been provided by Bijou and Baer (1961, 1965), Kantor (1959), Wahler and Fox (1981), and Willems (1974).

These authors have provided our current understanding of setting events and considered them to have (a) a *functional* relationship to behavior (i.e., to increase or decrease behavior) and (b) a *temporal* relationship to behavior (i.e., to precede or to exist concurrent with behavior). These considerations are central to our taxonomy (Repp & Deitz, 1990) which describes both the environment (a condition, a short-term event, and a stimulus-response interaction) and its temporal relationship to the environment. The latter describes environments that are (a) temporally *distant* from the response (more than 1 minute), (b) temporally *proximate* (from 1 to 60 seconds), and (c) temporally *concurrent* (at the same time). The taxonomy also considers the functional relationship of the environment to the behavior, and it describes either increases or decreases as a result of any of the three parts of the environment. This schema is presented in Table 1.

A taxonomy can also classify the relationship between behavior and its consequences. Such a taxonomy is presented in Table 2, and it differentiates (a) consequences that are a function of response *emission or omission*, (b)consequences that involve stimulus *presentation or removal*, and (c) consequences that *increase or decrease* responding.

The taxonomy presented in Table 2 can be analyzed in the same way as the taxonomy in Table 1. In this case, the analysis is of the probability that any response emission (or periodic omission) leads to a subsequent event (e.g., praise, task cessation, attention). The conditional probability of the subsequent event, given the target behavior, is compared with its overall or unconditional probability. If the event occurs only after a particular behavior, then that behavior is

TABLE 1 **A TAXONOMY OF ANTECEDENT EVENTS THAT *INCREASE (R+) OR DECREASE (R-) BEHAVIOR***

	ENVIRONMENT					
Temporal relation to target behavior	Condition		Short-Term Event		Stimulus-Response Interaction	
Distant	R+	R-	R+	R-	R+	R-
Proximate	R+	R-	R+	R-	R+	R-
Concurrent	R+	R-	R+	R-	R+	R-

an operant for that event (Skinner, 1938). This analysis, however, is more problematic than the one for Table 1 because the behavior may well be on a complex schedule of reinforcement.

We can, however, address both the positive reinforcement and the negative reinforcement hypotheses through Tables 1 and 2. If the stimuli are associated with positive or negative reinforcers, they will become discriminative stimuli or conditioned aversive stimuli, and will correlate with a change in the rate of behavior occurring in their presence. In the positive reinforcement paradigm, the target behavior will function to continue these environmental events, while in the negative reinforcement paradigm, the target behavior will function to discontinue the environmental events. In either case, the lag analysis described in the following section provides a suitable means for making the determination.

We believe that using these taxonomies will help us learn whether some persons' behaviors are environmentally dependent or independent, and, if dependent, on which parts of the environment they are dependent. However, severe behavior problems cannot be classified in the taxonomy without a methodology for collecting data within this framework. Our experience with this type of work over the last 5 years has led us to abandon data

TABLE 2 **A TAXONOMY OF SUBSEQUENT EVENTS CONTINGENT ON RESPONSE EMISSION OR OMISSION WHICH *INCREASE* (R+) OR *DECREASE* (R-) A TARGET BEHAVIOR**

Consequence contingent on response emission or omission	Stimulus Presented as Consequence		Stimulus Removed as Consequence	
Response Emission	R+	R-	R+	R-
Response Omission	R+	R-	R+	R-

collection that relies on paper and pencil and on time-sampling procedures. Instead, we have chosen to develop a system that uses portable computers to collect and analyze data that will provide us with more useful information. While this system initially was used to examine institutional and group home environments of persons with mental retardation (e.g., Felce, deKock, & Repp, 1986; Felce, Saxby, deKock, Repp, Ager, & Blunden, 1987; Felce, Thomas, deKock, Saxby, & Repp, 1985), it more recently has been refined and used to study the maladaptive behaviors of these individuals. In the next section, we will discuss some of this methodology.

DATA COLLECTION: THE PCS SYSTEM

In the prior section, we presented a taxonomy that relates behavior to either those events happening before the behavior (antecedent conditions and events) or those events happening after the behavior (subsequent events). Use of the taxonomy is dependent upon a data collection system that will allow the analysis of a behavior-environment interaction in real time, so that each specific behavior can be placed in its proper cell of the taxonomy. In this section, we will discuss a research methodology that allows us to develop this taxonomy.

For the last 5 years, we have been developing a computer-based data collection system (PCS) that records events in real time in the order in which they occur (Repp & Felce, 1990; Repp, Felce, & Karsh, in press; Repp, Harman, Van Acker, Felce, & Karsh, 1989; Repp, Karsh, Felce, Van Acker, & Harman, 1989). This technology has allowed us to address research questions that we previously have been unable to answer either because of technical problems, such as the complexity of the recording codes, or because of practical problems, such as the time required to analyze data. With our present technology, we can (a) simultaneously record up to 45 events in real time in the sequence in which they have occurred, and (b) summarize and analyze data by the computer programs we have developed. With this technology, we can record behaviors in the environment, determine the temporal relationship of the environment to behavior, and determine the *functional relationship of behavior to the environment*.

Hardware

Various programs have been written for several computers, including the Epson HX-20 which is a portable computer, weighing a few pounds, and capable of being held while being operated. The computer has a built-in printer that produces session totals and some data analyses, and an internal clock that keys each code's occurrence to the nearest second and provides the means by which the temporal relationships for the taxonomy can be identified. While the Epson is a superb computer for data collection, the data analysis programs are too sophisticated to be done by this computer (which has 32K). As such, the analysis is done on a Zenith desk-top model (with 1 megabyte RAM). Programs also have been written for MS-DOS portable computers which can perform both the data collection and data analysis functions.

Software

There are two major types of programs: those for data collection and those for data analysis (Karsh, Repp, & Ludewig, 1989). The data collection system includes two collection and two reliability programs, while the data analysis system is divided into four subgroups. Each of these will be explained briefly.

RECORDING PROGRAMS. The observer can simultaneously record up to 45 events in a code (i.e., conditions, events, stimulus-response interactions, and behaviors). Four sets of keys may be operated as mutually exclusive sets, with each set consisting of as many as 15 members. For these sets, the operator presses a key to indicate that an event is in effect, and then another key to indicate that the first event has terminated and a second one has begun. With this option, we can develop the taxonomy of setting events described in Table 1. For example, we can have five mutually exclusive task-related *conditions* for a student (e.g., overt demand, covert demand with and without opportunity to respond adaptively, and no demand with and without opportunity to respond adaptively). We also could have six mutually exclusive *conditions* that describe the class structure (e.g., isolation, one-to-one instruction, small group with instruction and with no instruction, and large group with instruction and with no instruction). We could have another set of codes that describes the type of activity (e.g., self-help, functional academic, free time, other). These conditions or events are examples of what might be used for the taxonomy of Table 1.

A program of analysis (*nesting*) allows us to determine the frequency and duration of each behavior in our code under each separate condition (e.g., under demand, structure, and activity), as well as under combinations of conditions (e.g., overt demand in small-group instruction during functional academics). Then, with this information, we may be able to determine which conditions increase or decrease the rate and duration of each behavior of interest.

DATA ANALYSIS PROGRAMS. The data collection programs have done two things for us with respect to Table 1. The first is that they have automatically formatted data so that we can know the effects on behavior of conditions, events, or stimulus-response interactions that are *concurrent* with the target behavior. Thus, the third row of Table 1 can be addressed. The second is that programs have formatted data so that we can learn the extent to which something (i.e., a condition, event, or stimulus-response interaction) *temporally proximate* to the target response affects that behavior. This is done with contingency tables that provide the information necessary to complete the second row of Table 1 and all of Table 2. A brief explanation of these programs follows.

Our thinking in this area has been greatly influenced by the work of Bakeman and Sackett on lag sequential analysis (e.g., Bakeman, 1978; Bakeman & Brownlee, 1980; Bakeman & Gottman, 1986; Sackett, 1978, 1979). This analysis of conditional probabilities determines whether the probability that one event leads to another is significantly different from that which would be expected by chance. The specific procedures used to analyze sequences have been recently modified somewhat by Bakeman (Bakeman, Adamson, & Strisik, in press) who has served as our statistical consultant in the development of some of our analyses. Now, a log-linear approach is used; however, the basic concept remains the same and will be explained in terms of event- and time-based lag analyses.

The *event* program describes the probability that any particular event (e.g., a task demand) leads to another event (e.g., self-injury), either directly (lag 1) or after any number (1, 2, etc.) of intervening events (lag 2, lag 3, etc.). This conditional probability is then compared to the overall or unconditional probability of the target behavior. In addition, the lag can be calculated from the beginning of a condition or antecedent event *(onset event lag)*, only during its occurrence (*co-occurrence event lag*), or only upon its offset (*offset event lag*). These programs then allow the researcher to complete the second and third rows of Table 1 (a *condition, event,* or *stimulus-response interaction* that is *proximate* or *concurrent* with the target response and either *increases* or *decreases* the probability of that behavior). The programs also allow the completion of rows one and two of Table 2, where the behavior (or its non-occurrence) becomes the antecedent and the consequence becomes the event to be lagged. The *event x time* program is a variation of the event program, and provides a lag analysis of the probability of a contingency on a second-by-second basis. With this information, we can determine whether any setting event increases or decreases the probability of severe maladaptive behavior. These data can fill the cells of the taxonomy and thereby indicate what parts of the environment should be manipulated in order to decrease the behavior.

The point we have addressed here is not whether we have to use aversives or whether nonaversives are sufficient. Rather, we have addressed the methodology that we use in conducting functional analyses, and have proposed a taxonomy that may provide a direct relationship between data collected and treatment selected within the constructs most commonly used to explain the behaviors in question. In this way, we would be using what Carr et al. (1989) have called *hypothesis-derived interventions*.

Although we use data collected in naturalistic settings, data for this taxonomy could just as easily be collected in analogue situations (Iwata et al., 1982). In both cases, the relationship between maintaining conditions and treatment selection can be established. Through this procedure, we hope that we can improve our ability to select and design effective nonaversive programs for the treatment of the behaviors at the center of this issue.

GENERAL METHODOLOGY FOR TREATMENT

Hypothesis-Derived Interventions

Baumeister (1989) has described seven theories of etiologies for maladaptive behavior: (a) neural oscillation, (b) developmental stage, (c) biology/neurochemistry, (d) psychodynamics, (e) homeostasis/arousal, (f) communication, and (g) conditioning. Of these, the last three are particularly useful as constructs for environmentally dependent behaviors.

The *homeostasis or arousal theory* states that we seek an optimal level of stimulation (probably for survival reasons), that when we are understimulated we engage in various behaviors (e.g., stereotypy) to increase our arousal state, and that when we are overstimulated we engage in the same or other types of behavior to decrease our arousal state. The *communication theory* states that these behaviors have communicative intent which happen to be socially unacceptable means of communication. Several studies, for example, have shown that persons who engage in stereotypy or self-injury stop these behaviors when taught alternative ways to communicate their desire to receive the same consequences that their maladaptive behavior was producing (e.g., adult attention). The *conditioning theory* states that maladaptive behaviors are learned and maintained through positive reinforcement (i.e., the response produces an event that reinforces the behavior) or negative reinforcement (i.e., the response removes an aversive event and is thereby reinforced).

Several authors (e.g., Carr et al., 1989; Repp, Singh, Olinger, & Olson, 1990; Schroeder et al., 1989) have subsumed the communication theory under conditioning, relabeled the homeostasis theory as stimulation, and have suggested that three theories or hypotheses cover the *environmentally dependent* behaviors: (a) *negative reinforcement* (b) *positive reinforcement*, and (c) *stimulation*. As shown in Table 3, each of these procedures fits one or more of the environmental schema of the taxonomy in Table 1.

While the relationships will be described in the next section, at this point we will say that when *conditions* affect

TABLE 3 TAXONOMY OF ANTECEDENT EVENTS

Condition	Short-term Event	Stimulus-Response Interaction
1. negative reinforcement	1. negative reinforcement	1. negative reinforcement
2. positive reinforcement	2. positive reinforcement	2. positive reinforcement
3. stimulation		

environmentally dependent behaviors, they may do so for the following hypothesized reasons: (a) negative reinforcement, (b) positive reinforcement, or (c) stimulation. When *events* affect behavior, the reasons may be (a) negative reinforcement, or (b) positive reinforcement. When *stimulus-response interactions* affect behavior, the reasons may be (a) negative reinforcement, or (b) positive reinforcement.

Treatments Indicated by the Hypotheses

NEGATIVE REINFORCEMENT HYPOTHESIS. The empirical research suggests that some maladaptive behavior is maintained by avoidance of aversive stimuli (Carr, 1977; Durand & Carr, 1987; Iwata et al., 1982; Repp et al., 1988). For example, an individual may engage in SIB in order to avoid a demand from the teacher. If the teacher withdraws the demand, the individual's SIB is negatively-reinforced, and the probability that the individual will engage in SIB under the same or similar conditions is increased.

A wide variety of stimuli may assume aversive properties and may be functionally linked to an individual's increase in maladaptive behavior. Aversive *conditions* may include crowding (McAfee, 1987), lighting (Frankel, Freeman, Ritvo, & Pardo, 1978), noise levels (Berkson & Stewart, 1986), or a monotonous, repetitive task (Winterling, Dunlap, & O'Neill, 1987). Aversive *antecedent events* may include physical guidance from a staff member (see chapter 12 by Paisey et al.), a difficult task demand (Carr & Durand, 1985), or a bell that signals a change in activities or staff (Kaufman & Levitt, 1965). *Stimulus-response interactions* which could be aversive might include engagement in a nonpreferred activity (Baumeister, MacLean, Kelly, & Kasari, 1980) or a series of incorrect responses during instruction (Weeks & Gaylord-Ross, 1981). The point here is not to provide an exhaustive list of aversive conditions, events, and stimulus-response relationships that can be functionally related to maladaptive behavior, but to suggest that these stimuli, once identified, may be considered in developing a hypothesis-driven treatment.

TREATMENT 1. If a functional analysis of the maladaptive behavior identifies specific events or conditions related to the behavior, this knowledge can be used in designing an intervention. For example, if instructional demands are functionally related to the behavior from a negative reinforcement perspective, then functional equivalence training (FET) could be an indicated treatment.

This intervention assumes that some maladaptive behavior can be viewed as a nonverbal form of communication. Through a functional analysis of the behavior, we may identify the behavior as a nonverbal request to be removed from the instructional demand. The indicated treatment then would be to teach the individual a more adaptive request behavior. For example, the individual might be taught to sign or gesture when he is ready for the activity to end.

TREATMENT 2. A necessary precursor to a stimulus-based treatment is the identification of the conditions or events that are correlated with high and low rates of the maladaptive behavior. One possible treatment, following the functional analysis, is to increase the individual's exposure to conditions or events that are associated with lower rates of the maladaptive behavior. Examples of environmental manipulations include increasing opportunities for social interaction (Hollis, 1965), increasing time spent in preferred activities (Repp, Singh, Karsh, & Deitz, 1990), increasing the amount of time spent in enriched environments (Horner, 1980), and decreasing the density of classrooms or residences (Barton & Repp, 1981; Repp, Barton, & Gottlieb, 1983).

TREATMENT 3. Another indicated treatment that may follow a functional analysis is the modification of the aversive stimuli that are functionally related to high rates of the behavior. One approach could be to make the task easier by employing an errorless learning strategy (Repp & Karsh, in press; Weeks & Gaylord-Ross, 1981). Other approaches could be to change the staff member who delivers the instructional demands or to shorten the teaching session.

TREATMENT 4. An alternative treatment procedure involves interspersing stimuli associated with low rates of the behavior (e.g., easy task demands) among activities associated with high rates of the behavior (e.g., difficult tasks) (Carr, Newsom, & Binkoff, 1976). The task variation procedure (Dunlap & Koegel, 1980; Rowan & Pear, 1985), where difficult task demands are interspersed among easy ones, has proven effective in reducing maladaptive behaviors (Winterling et al., 1987).

TREATMENT 5. A functional analysis may indicate that a certain educational curriculum may be correlated with high rates of maladaptive behavior. For example, a repetitive, nonfunctional task, such as taking pegs in and out of a pegboard, may produce high rates of the behavior (Green, Canipe, Way, & Reid, 1986; Meyer & Evans, 1986). Modifying the curriculum so that a variety of both functional, and interesting tasks are presented may lead to decreases in the maladaptive behavior. Finally, a certain combination of stimuli (e.g., time of day, room location, task, and staff members present) may create a setting event that is functionally related to the behavior. Modifying the components of the setting event or allowing the individual to become gradually familiar with this discriminative complex (Carr et al., 1989) may reduce the behavior.

POSITIVE REINFORCEMENT HYPOTHESIS. The positive reinforcement hypothesis suggests that some maladaptive behavior is maintained by positive reinforcers that increase the probability of the behavior. These reinforcers may be social or tangible. They also may be conditions, events, or stimulus-response relationships. For example, an individual's maladaptive behavior may be functionally related to staff social attention and proximity (Carr & Durand, 1985); to the presentation of toys, snacks, or manipulable objects (Durand & Crimmins, 1988); to part of a chain where the maladaptive behavior precedes a reinforced adaptive response; or to a stimulus-response relationship of teacher demands and correct responding.

TREATMENTS 1 AND 2. Conceptually, *DRO* (reinforcing periods in which the behavior is *omitted*) would be an indicated treatment because it can provide the same reinforcement that the maladaptive behavior previously obtained; as such, the maladaptive behavior is no longer reinforced and becomes nonfunctional (Barmann, 1980; Luiselli, Miles, Evans, & Boyce, 1985). A *DRI* (reinforcing behavior *incompatible* with the maladaptive behavior) procedure also provides reinforcement, but reinforcement is contingent upon the occurrence of a single incompatible adaptive behavior rather than the absence of the maladaptive behaviors as in DRO (Friman, Barnard, Altman & Wolf, 1986; Steege, Wacker, Berg, Cigrand, & Cooper, 1989). It, too, can be programmed so that the reinforcer can be obtained by a means other than the maladaptive behavior. In this case, reinforcement can be provided on a richer schedule for the adaptive, incompatible response.

TREATMENT 3. Skills acquisition training also can be considered an indicated treatment for maladaptive behavior that is functionally related to positive reinforcement. If an individual is taught a broad range of adaptive behaviors within vocational, leisure, domestic, and community curricular domains, then these skills constitute a new means of gaining social and tangible reinforcers. The maladaptive behavior that has been maintained previously by positive reinforcement is no longer necessary.

STIMULATION HYPOTHESIS. The stimulation hypothesis suggests that maladaptive behaviors are maintained by the sensory stimulation that they generate. The assumption is that a certain level of stimulation is optimal for an individual, and that an individual will engage in compensatory behaviors in order to maintain that optimal level. Therefore, some individuals engage in maladaptive behaviors when environmental stimulation is low.

TREATMENTS. Conditions that may be functionally related to maladaptive behaviors according to the stimulation hypothesis include barren rooms (Horner, 1980), passive leisure activities (Baumeister et al., 1980), and instruction that offers little opportunity for active responding (Repp & Karsh, in press). An indicated treatment would be to provide the individual with *alternative sources of stimulation* through exercise (Kern, Koegel, Dyer, Blew, & Fenton, 1982), toy play (Eason, White, & Newsom, 1982), enriched classrooms and living environments (Horner, 1980), or an instructional procedure that produces a high rate of student responding (Repp & Karsh, in press).

CONCLUSION

We have suggested that three hypotheses [(a) negative reinforcement, (b) positive reinforcement, or c) stimulation)] can explain the maintaining conditions of maladaptive behaviors that are environmentally dependent. We propose, however, that none of these hypotheses applies to all individuals. We also propose that more effective treatments can be implemented if a taxonomy is used to identify the functional relationship between the maladaptive behavior and conditions, events, or stimulus-response relationships in the environment. If a procedure based on a hypothesis suggested by the taxonomy is implemented, then treatment of maladaptive behaviors may be more effective.

REFERENCES

Bakeman, R. (1978). Untangling streams of behavior: Sequential analyses of observational data. In G. P. Sackett (Ed.), *Observing behavior: Data collection and analysis methods. Vol 2.* (pp 63-78). Baltimore, MD: University Park Press.

Bakeman, R., Adamson, L. B., & Strisik, P. (in press). Lags and logs: Statistical approaches to interaction. In M. H. Bornstein & J. Bruner (Eds.), *Interaction in human development*. Hillside, NJ: Erlbaum.

Bakeman, R., & Brownlee, J. R. (1980). The strategic use of parallel play: A sequential analysis. *Child Development, 51*, 873-878.

Bakeman, R., & Gottman, J. M. (1986). *Observing interaction: An introduction to sequential analysis*. New York: Cambridge University Press.

Barmann, B.C. (1980). Use of contingent vibration in the treatment of self-stimulatory hand-mouthing and ruminative vomiting behavior. *Journal of Behavior Therapy and Experimental Psychiatry, 11*, 307-311.

Barton, L. E., & Repp, A. C. (1981). Naturalistic studies of institutionalized retarded persons: Relationship between stereotypic responding, secondary handicaps, and population density. *Journal of Mental Deficiency Research, 25*, 257-264.

Baumeister, A. A. (1978). Origins of control of stereotypic movements. In C. E. Meyers (Ed.), *Quality of life in severely and profoundly retarded people: Research foundations for improvements* (pp. 353-384). Washington, DC: Monograph #3 of the American Association on Mental Deficiency.

Baumeister, A. A. (1989). Etiologies of self-injurious and destructive behavior. *Proceedings of the Consensus Conference on the Treatment of Severe Behavior Problems and Developmental Disabilities*. Bethesda, MD: National Institutes of Health.

Baumeister, A. A., MacLean, W. E., Kelly, J., & Kasari, C. (1980). Observational studies of retarded children with multiple stereotyped movements. *Journal of Abnormal Child Psychology, 8*, 501-521.

Berkson, G., & Stewart, J. (1986). *Sound level and stereotypic body rocking*. Paper presented at the Gatlinburg Conference on Developmental Disabilities, Gatlinburg, TN.

Bijou, S. W., & Baer, D. M. (1961). *Child development I: A systematic and empirical theory*. Englewood Cliffs, NJ: Prentice-Hall.

Bijou, S. W., & Baer, D. M. (1965). *Child development II: Basic stages of infancy*. Englewood Cliffs, NJ: Prentice-Hall.

Biklen, D. (1987). In pursuit of integration. In M.S. Berres & P. Knoblock (Eds.), *Program models for mainstreaming: Integrating students with moderate to severe disabilities* (pp. 19-39). Rockville, MD: Aspen.

Borthwick, S. A., Meyers, C. E., & Eyman, R. K. (1981). Comparative adaptive and maladaptive behavior of mentally retarded clients of five residential settings in three western states. In R. H. Bruininks, C. E. Meyers, B. B. Sigford, & K. C. Lakin (Eds.), *Deinstitutionalization and community adjustment of mentally retarded people* (pp. 351-359). Washington, DC: Monograph #4 of the American Association on Mental Deficiency.

Carr, E. G. (1977). The motivation of self-injurious behavior: A review of some hypotheses. *Psychological Bulletin, 84*, 800-816.

Carr, E. G., Newsom, C. D., & Binkoff, J. A. (1976). Stimulus control of self-destructive behavior in a psychotic child. *Journal of Abnormal Child Psychology, 4*, 139-153.

Carr, E. G., Taylor, J. C., Carlson, J. S., & Robinson, S. (1989). Reinforcement and stimulus-based treatments for severe behavior problems in developmental disabilities. *Proceedings of the Consensus Conference on the Treatment of Severe Behavior Problems and Developmental Disabilities*. Bethesda, MD: National Institutes of Health.

Carr, E. G., & Durand, V. M. (1985). Reducing behavior problems through functional communication training. *Journal of Applied Behavior Analysis, 18*, 111-126.

Cataldo, M. F. (1989). The effects of punishment and other behavior reducing procedures on the destructive behaviors of persons with developmental disabilities. *Proceedings of the Consensus Conference on the Treatment of Severe Behavior Problems and Developmental Disbilities*. Bethesda, MD: National Institutes of Health.

Cohen, M. N., & Sprague, R. L. (1977). *Survey of drug usage in two midwestern institutions for the retarded*. Paper presented at the Gatlinburg Conference on Research in Mental Retardation, Gatlinburg, TN.

Corbett, J. A., & Campbell, H. J. (1981). Causes of self-injurious behavior. In P. Mittler (Ed.), *Frontiers of knowledge in mental retardation: Vol 2. Biomedical aspects* (pp. 285-292). Baltimore, MD: University Park Press.

Dunlap, G., & Koegel, R. L. (1980). Motivating autistic children through stimulus variation. *Journal of Applied Behavior Analysis, 13*, 619-627.

Durand, V. M., & Carr, E. G. (1987). Social influence on "self stimulatory" behavior: Analysis and treatment application. *Journal of Applied Behavior Analysis, 20*, 119-131.

Durand, V. M., & Crimmins, D. B. (1988). Identifying the variables maintaining self-injurious behavior. *Journal of Autism and Developmental Disorders, 18*, 99-117.

Eason, L. J., White, M. J., & Newsom, C. (1982). Generalized reduction of self-stimulatory behavior: An effect of teaching appropriate play to autistic children. *Analysis and Intervention in Developmental Disabilities, 2*, 157-169.

Evans, I. M., & Meyer, L. H. (1985). *An educative approach to behavior problems*. Baltimore, MD: Paul H. Brookes.

Eyman, R. K., O'Connor, G., Tarjan, G., & Justine R.S. (1972). Factors determining residential placement of mentally retarded children. *American Journal of Mental Deficiency, 76*, 692-698.

Felce, D., deKock, U., & Repp, A. C. (1986). An eco-behavioral analysis of small community-based houses and traditional large hospitals for severely and profoundly mentally handicapped adults. *Applied Research in Mental Retardation, 7*, 393-408.

Felce, D., Saxby, H., deKock, U., Repp, A. C., Ager, A., & Blunden, R. (1987). To what behaviors do attending adults respond?: A replication. *American Journal of Mental Deficiency, 91*, 496-504.

Felce, D., Thomas, M., deKock, U., Saxby, H., & Repp, A. C. (1985). An ecological comparison of small community-based houses and traditional institutions: II. *Behaviour Research and Therapy, 23*, 337-348.

Frankel, F., Freeman, B. J., Ritvo, E., & Pardo, R. (1978). The effect of environmental stimulation upon the stereotyped behavior of autistic children. *Journal of Autism and Childhood Schizophrenia, 8*, 389-394.

Friman, P. C., Barnard, J. D., Altman, K., & Wolf, M. M. (1986). Parent and teacher use of DRO and DRI to reduce aggressive behavior. *Analysis and Intervention in Developmental Disabilities, 6*, 319-330.

Gaylord-Ross, R. S., Weeks, M., & Lipner, C. (1980). An analysis of antecedent, response, and consequent events in the treatment of self-injurious behavior. *Education and Training of the Mentally Retarded, 15*, 35-42.

Green, C. W., Canipe, V. S., Way, P. J., & Reid, D. H. (1986). Improving the functional utility and effectiveness of classroom services for students with profound multiple handicaps. *The Journal of The Association for Persons with Severe Handicaps, 11*, 162-170.

Griffen, J. C., Williams, D. E., Stark, M. T., Altmeyer, B. K., & Mason, M. (1986). Self-injurious behavior: A state-wide prevalence survey of the extent and circumstances. *Applied Research in Mental Retardation, 7*, 105-116.

Hill, B. K., Balow, E. A., & Bruininks, R. H. (1985). A national study of prescribed drugs in institutions and community residential facilities for mentally retarded people. *Psychopharmacology Bulletin, 21*, 279-284.

Hill, B. K., & Bruininks, R. H. (1984). Maladaptive behavior of mentally retarded individuals in residential facilities. *American Journal of Mental Deficiency, 88*, 380-386.

Hollis, J. H. (1965). The effects of social and non-social stimuli on the behavior of profoundly retarded children: Parts I and II. *American Journal of Mental Deficiency, 69*, 755-789.

Horner, R. D. (1980). The effects of an environmental "enrichment" program on the behavior of institutionalized profoundly retarded children. *Journal of Applied Behavior Analysis, 13*, 473-491.

Iwata, B. A., Dorsey, M. G., Slifer, K. J., Bauman, K. E., & Richman, G. S. (1982). Toward a functional analysis of self-injury. *Analysis and Intervention in Developmental Disabilities, 2*, 3-20.

Jacobson, J. (1982). Problem behavior and psychiatric impairment within a developmentally disabled population I: Behavior severity. *Applied Research in Mental Retardation, 3*, 121-139.

Kantor, J. R. (1959). *Interbehavioral psychology*. Granville, OH: Principia Press.

Karsh, K. G., Repp, A. C., & Ludewig, D. (1989). PCS: *Portable computer systems for observational research*. DeKalb, IL: Communitech International.

Kaufman, M. E., & Levitt, H. (1965). A study of three stereotyped behaviors in institutionalized mental defective. *American Journal of Mental Deficiency, 69*, 467-473.

Kelly, J. A., & Drabman, R. S. (1977). Generalizing response suppression of self-injurious behavior through an overcorrection procedure: A case study. *Behavior Therapy, 8*, 468-472.

Kern, L., Koegel, R.L., Dyer, K., Blew, P.A., & Fenton, L.R. (1982). The effects of physical exercise on self-stimulation behavior and appropriate responding in autistic children. *Journal of Autism and Developmental Disorders, 12*, 399-419.

Koegel, R. L., & Covert, A. (1972). The relationship of self-stimulation to learning in autistic children. *Journal of Applied Behavior Analysis, 5*, 381-387.

LaGrow, J., & Repp, A. C. (1984). Stereotypic responding: A review of intervention research. *American Journal of Mental Deficiency, 88*, 595-609.

Lovaas, O. I., Litrownik, A., & Mann, R. (1971). Response latencies to auditory stimuli in autistic children engaged in self-stimulatory behavior. *Behavior Research and Therapy, 9*, 39-49.

Luiselli, J. K., Miles, E., Evans, T. P., & Boyce, D. A. (1985). Reinforcement control of severe dysfunctional behavior of blind, multihandicapped students. *American Journal of Mental Deficiency, 90*, 328-334.

McAfee, J. K. (1987). Classroom density and the aggressive behavior of handicapped children. *Education and Treatment of Children, 10*, 134-145.

Meyer, L. H., & Evans, I. M. (1986). Modification of excess behavior: An adaptive and functional approach for educational and community contexts. In R. H. Horner, L. H. Meyer, & H. D. B. Fredericks (Eds.), *Education of learners with severe handicaps: Exemplary service strategies* (pp. 315-350). Baltimore, MD: Paul H. Brookes.

National Institutes of Health (1989). Consensus development conference statement: Treatment of destructive behaviors in persons with developmental disabilities. *Proceedings of the Consensus Conference on the Treatment of Severe Behavior Problems and Developmental Disabilities*. Bethesda, MD: AUTHOR.

O'Brien, S., & Repp, A. C. (in press). A review of 30 years of research on the use of differential reinforcement to reduce inappropriate responding. *Behavior Modification*.

Oliver, C., Murphy, G. H., & Corbett, J. A. (1987). Self-injurious behavior in people with mental handicap: A total population study. *Journal of Mental Deficiency Research, 31*, 147-162.

Repp, A. C., & Barton, L. E. (1980). Naturalistic observations of retarded persons: A comparison of licensure decisions and behavioral observations. *Journal of Applied Behavior Analysis, 13*, 333-341.

Repp, A. C., Barton, L. E., & Gottlieb, J. (1983). Naturalistic studies of institutionalized profoundly and severely mentally retarded persons. *American Journal of Mental Deficiency, 87*, 441-447.

Repp, A. C., & Deitz, D. E. D. (1990). An ecobehavioral taxonomy for stereotypic responding. In S. Schroeder (Ed.), *Ecobehavioral analysis and developmental disabilities: The twenty-first century* (pp. 122-140). New York: Springer-Verlag.

Repp, A. C., Deitz, S. M., & Deitz, D. E. D. (1976). Reducing inappropriate classroom and prescriptive behaviors through DRO schedules of reinforcement. *Mental Retardation, 14*, 11-15.

Repp, A. C., & Felce, D. (1990). A microcomputer system used for evaluative and experimental behavioural research in mental handicap. *Mental Handicap Research, 3*, 21-32.

Repp, A. C., Felce, D., & Barton, L. E. (1988). Basing the treatment of stereotypic and self-injurious behavior on hypotheses of their causes. *Journal of Applied Behavior Analysis, 21*, 281-289.

Repp, A. C., Felce, D., & Karsh, K. G. (in press). The use of a portable microcomputer in the functional analysis and modification of maladaptive behaviour. In R. Remington (Ed.), The *challenge of severe mental handicap: A behaviour analytic approach*. Chichester: John Wiley & Sons.

Repp, A. C., Harman, M. L., Felce, D., Van Acker, R., & Karsh, K. G. (1989). Conducting behavioral assessments on computer-collected data. *Behavioral Assessment, 11*, 249-268.

Repp, A. C., & Karsh, K. G. (in press). The task demonstration model: A program for teaching persons with severe handicaps. In R. Remington (Ed.). *The challenge of severe mental handicap: A behaviour analytic approach.* Chichester: John Wiley & Sons.

Repp, A. C., Karsh, K. G., Van Acker, R., Felce, D., & Harman, M. (1989). A computer-based system for collecting and analyzing observational data. *Journal of Special Education Technology, 9*, 207-217.

Repp, A. C., Singh, N. N., Karsh, K. G., & Deitz, D. E. D. (1990). Ecobehavioral analysis of stereotypic and adaptive behaviors: Activities as setting events. Paper submitted for publication.

Repp, A. C., Singh, N. N., Olinger, E., & Olson, D. R. (1990). The use of functional analyses to test causes of self-injurious behaviour: Rationale, current status, and future directions. *Journal of Mental Deficiency Research, 34*, 95-106.

Romanczyk, R. G. (1986). Self-injurious behavior: Conceptualization, assessment, and treatment. In K. Gadow (Ed.), *Advances in learning and behavioral disabilities* (pp 29-56). Greenwich, CT: JAI.

Rowan, V. C., & Pear, J. J. (1985). A comparison of the effects of an interspersal and a concurrent training sequence on acquisition, retention, and generalization of picture names. *Applied Research in Mental Retardation, 6*, 127-145.

Sackett, G. P. (1978). Measurement in observational research. In G. P. Sackett (Ed.), *Observing behavior: Data collection and analysis methods: Vol. 2* (pp 25-43). Baltimore, MD: University Park Press.

Sackett, G. P. (1979). The lag sequential analysis of contingency and cyclicity in behavioral interaction research. In J. Osofsky (Ed.), *Handbook of infant development* (pp. 623-649). New York: John Wiley & Sons.

Schroeder, S. R., Rojahn, J., & Oldenquist, A. (1989). Treatment of destructive behaviors among people with developmental disabilities. *Proceeding of the Consensus Conference on the Treatment of Severe Behavior Problems and Developmental Disbilities.* Bethesda, MD: National Institutes of Health.

Skinner, B. F. (1938). *The behavior of organisms.* New York: Appleton-Century-Crofts.

Steege, M. W., Wacker, D. P., Berg, W. K., Cigrand, K. K., & Cooper, L. J. (1989). The use of behavioral assessment to prescribe and evaluate treatments for severely handicapped children. *Journal of Applied Behavior Analysis, 22*, 23-33.

U.S. Department of Education (1988). *Tenth annual report to congress on the implementation of the education of the handicapped act.* Washington, DC: AUTHOR.

Wahler, R. G., & Fox, J. J. (1981). Setting events in applied behavior analysis: Toward a conceptual and methodological expansion. *Journal of Applied Behavior Analysis, 14*, 327-338.

Watkins, K. M., & Konarski, E. A. (1987). Effect of mentally retarded persons' level of stereotypy on their learning. *American Journal of Mental Deficiency, 91*, 361-365.

Weeks, M., & Gaylord-Ross, R. (1981). Task difficulty and aberrant behavior in severely handicapped students. *Journal of Applied Behavior Analysis, 14*, 449-463.

Willems, E. P. (1974). Behavioral technology and behavioral ecology. *Journal of Applied Behavior Analysis, 7*, 151-166.

Winterling, V., Dunlap, G., & O'Neill, R. E. (1987). The influence of task variation on the aberrant behaviors of autistic students. *Education and Treatment of Children, 10*, 105-119.

CHAPTER

23

USE OF FUNCTIONAL ANALYSIS AND ACCEPTABILITY MEASURES TO ASSESS AND TREAT SEVERE BEHAVIOR PROBLEMS: AN OUTPATIENT CLINIC MODEL

David Wacker, Mark Steege, John Northup, Thomas Reimers, Wendy Berg, and Gary Sasso
The University of Iowa

OVERVIEW

The purpose of this chapter is to describe an outclinic assessment model, based on functional analysis procedures, for prescribing treatment recommendations in cases involving individuals who engage in self-injury and aggression. The question of whether aversives should be used is not directly addressed in this chapter. Rather, our purpose is to describe an assessment approach that we believe is applicable across most outclinic settings to increase the probability that recommended nonaversive treatments will be effective. This probability is increased because the results of the functional analysis are used to (a) identify the maintaining conditions for both inappropriate and appropriate behavior, and (b) match the recommended treatment with the identified maintaining condition.

The Stereotypic, Self-Injurious, and Aggressive Behavior Service at The University of Iowa was initiated as an outclinic within the Department of Pediatrics approximately 2 years ago in response to an increasing demand for behavioral assessment and consultation services. This service is unique to the extent that functional analyses of behavior are conducted on an outclinic basis, with routine follow-up provided locally. This was necessary because the clinic is intended to provide a tertiary level of service; i.e., patients frequently travel from 100 to 200 miles to receive clinic services, prohibiting ongoing weekly outclinic treatment services. Instead, as will be discussed more fully in later sections, we attempt to identify maintaining conditions for target behaviors, develop proactive (nonaversive) treatment plans based on the results of assessment, and then provide specific recommendations for primary care providers. Currently, two patients are evaluated each week in the clinic, with each patient receiving a 90-minute functional analysis procedure concurrent with behavioral interviews conducted with direct care staff. A schematic of the procedures is presented in Figure 1.

As shown in Figure 1, once a referral is made to the clinic, the history of the client and target behavior data are gathered through survey and checklist information. The service team, composed of two staff

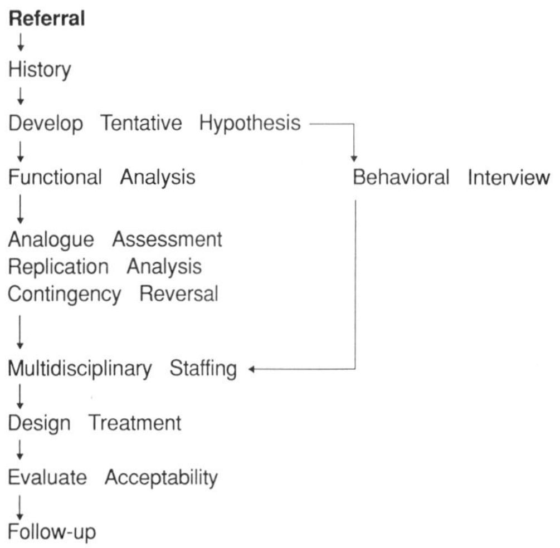

Figure 1: Schematic overview of the sequence of activities occurring in outpatient service for self-injurious and aggressive behaviors.

psychologists, two special education staff, and two graduate or undergraduate students, reviews the information and develops tentative hypotheses regarding the maintaining conditions of behavior. These are reviewed and further developed at a morning staffing, followed by an interview of primary caretakers and the completion of a functional analysis.

The interview, which lasts from 30 to 60 minutes, is conducted concurrently with the functional analysis and focuses specifically on current reinforcers, punishers, and other environmental events. The functional analysis is based specifically on the work of Iwata, Dorsey, Slifer, Bauman, and Richman (1982) and Carr and Durand (1985), and involves an analogue assessment of maintaining conditions. Depending on the target behavior and historical information, different assessment protocols are used to focus on the conditions maintaining both inappropriate and appropriate behavior. For aggression and self-injury, three basic phases of assessment are conducted: (a) *analogue assessment*, in which various 10-minute analogue conditions (e.g., alone, demand, and social attention) are presented in a counterbalanced order, with contingent application of consequences presented for inappropriate behavior; (b) *replication analysis*, in which the conditions producing the highest and lowest occurrences of target behavior are repeated; and (c) *contingency reversal*, in which the conditions maintaining inappropriate behavior are differentially provided for appropriate behavior, thus constituting an initial treatment session. If successful, the contingency reversal provides initial support for our recommended treatment and is the first step of treatment.

Following our assessment, a multidisciplinary staffing is held with other professionals who evaluated the patient (usually a pediatrician, speech/language therapist, and social worker); recommendations are provided, and follow-up is conducted by phone or by community outreach to determine the integrity of the procedures and the acceptability of the recommendations.

The empirical basis for this service was derived from previous evaluations of functional analysis, and was based specifically on the results obtained from our inpatient unit. We have found that the first treatment session following the functional assessment has resulted in immediate decreases in inappropriate behavior once reinforcement is provided for an appropriate behavior and withheld for inappropriate behavior (Steege, Wacker, Berg, Cigrand, & Cooper, 1989). An example of these findings is provided in Figure 2. As shown in the top panel of Figure 2, the inpatient's self-injurious behavior (eye poking) occurred primarily during alone conditions and was hypothesized to be maintained by positive reinforcement (arousal induction). Treatment (bottom panel of Figure 2), which consisted of Differential Reinforcement of Appropriate Behavior (pressing a pressure-sensitive microswitch that activated a tape player with music), resulted in an immediate decrease of self-injurious behavior.

Based on the results from our inpatient unit, we thought that similar results might be obtained within an outpatient clinic.

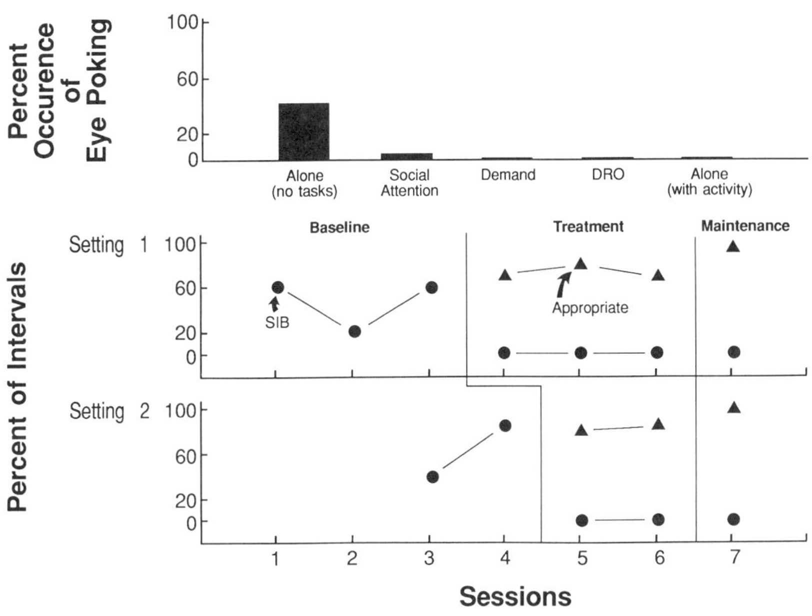

Figure 2: Results of a functional analysis and treatment program implemented for one child on an inpatient unit.

Given the time restrictions (90 minutes) of outclinic evaluations, determining how to evaluate the results of assessment was problematic. Our solution was to use a rapidly changing reversal or multielement design (Northup, Wacker, Steege, Cigrand, Sasso, & Cook, 1989), in which replication of initial results (analogue assessment) was obtained through the replication or reversal contingency phases of evaluation. Two case examples of this approach follow.

Case Example 1

Roy was a 20-year-old male referred for evaluation of self-injurious behavior. He had been diagnosed previously as functioning within the severe to profound range of mental retardation, was nonambulatory and nonverbal, and had no formal means of communication. Roy's 10-year history of self-injurious behavior consisted of head banging and arm and hand biting. Self-injurious behavior was reported to occur at least daily, and it was rated by local staff as being of severe intensity. Previous interventions included stroking his face with a fluffy mitt, relaxation, and time-out. Evidence of mixed success was reported with the use of relaxation. Based on this information, our initial hypothesis was that Roy's behavior was maintained by negative reinforcement because relaxation permitted him to escape tasks and time-out resulted in an escalation of self-injury.

Assessment sessions ranged from 5 to 10 minutes. During each session, two observers simultaneously but independently recorded the occurrence of Roy's self-injurious behaviors (head banging and arm and hand biting) and appropriate behaviors. Appropriate behavior was defined as engagement in a functional or age-appropriate task or activity. Observations were recorded using a 6-second partial interval recording procedure. The analogue sessions were conducted within a rapidly changing reversal design; that is, assessment conditions changed following the termination of each 10-minute session. Assessment for Roy began with the following three analogue conditions:

1) ALONE. Roy was directed to the therapy room and left alone with the verbal instruction to wait. The therapist then left the room and had no other interaction or contact with him; no tasks or activities were provided. This condition served as a control for four variables: the presence of the therapist, the absence of preferred items, the absence of social interaction or attention, and the absence of demands. This condition also simulated the situation in which an individual is left unattended and provided with no activities. A high frequency (relative to other analogue conditions) of self-injury in this condition suggests that behavior is maintained by sensory or automatic reinforcement (Iwata et al., 1982).

2) ESCAPE. During this condition, Roy was required to participate in folding and sorting towels and washcloths. The therapist initially provided verbal instructions, modeling, and physical prompts. Towels and washcloths were presented continuously at a stable rate and, because Roy did not complete the task independently, hand-over-hand guidance was used nearly continuously throughout the session. Contingent upon the occurrence of self-injury, the task was immediately removed, and the therapist turned or moved away from Roy for 15 to 30 seconds. If self-injury persisted, the folding and sorting task was withheld until termination of the behavior, at which time the task was immediately reinstated. All therapist interactions were limited to providing task instructions and guidance. Neutral or appropriate behavior displayed by Roy was ignored. This condition was designed to represent the situation in which tasks or activities are terminated when an individual engages in self-injury (e.g., time-out). If Roy's self-injury was maintained by negative reinforcement (i.e., escape from unpleasant tasks or activities), one would expect the frequency of occurrence to be highest in this condition.

3) SOCIAL ATTENTION. Throughout this condition, the therapist sat in a seat near Roy and appeared to read a magazine. No tasks or activities were provided. Contingent upon the occurrence of self-injury (all other behavior was ignored), the therapist immediately provided attention for 10 to 15 seconds. Attention consisted of verbal reprimands (e.g., "Please don't do that."), a light touch on the shoulder, or redirection. This condition was intended to simulate the situation in which caregivers attend to self-injury, but provide little or no attention for appropriate behavior. If Roy's self-injury was maintained by social attention, a relatively high frequency would be expected during this condition. For Roy, these three conditions constituted the analogue assessment. The primary purpose was to identify the conditions that functionally controlled his self-injury and, specifically, whether his self-injury was maintained by negative reinforcement as hypothesized.

The results for Roy are presented in Figure 3. Self-injury occurred with a substantially higher frequency during the escape condition (35% of the recorded intervals) than in the other two conditions (less than 10%).

Following completion of the analogue assessment, the highest (escape) and the lowest (alone) conditions were repeated in order to replicate the initial results; these findings are also displayed in Figure 3. Again, the frequency of self-injury was substantially higher in the escape condition (42% of the recorded intervals) than during the alone condition, providing a replication of our initial results.

Roy was then observed during three additional conditions that constituted a contingency reversal. These began with a presentation of the condition in which the highest percentage of self-injurious be-

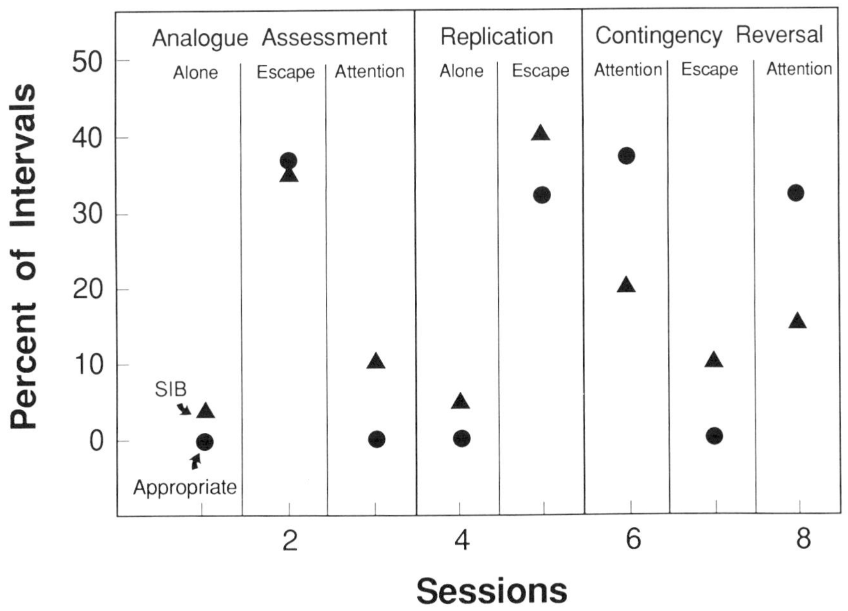

Figure 3: Results of an outpatient evaluation for Roy.

havior occurred during the analogue assessment (escape). However, in this contingency-reversal condition, escape (negative reinforcement) was provided immediately following the occurrence of appropriate behavior rather than following the occurrence of self-injury. Specifically, a DRA schedule of reinforcement was provided in which a break identical to the one in the initial escape condition was provided upon completion of folding a towel, and self-injury was ignored. Following completion of this condition, an additional reversal component was implemented by repeating a condition from the initial assessment (social attention). As before, all inappropriate behavior resulted in immediate social attention. Escape from task contingent upon appropriate behavior was then repeated to form a modified reversal design.

The results of the three contingency reversal conditions, as shown in Figure 3, indicate that the two conditions in which escape from task was provided for appropriate behavior resulted in a decrease in occurrence of self-injurious behavior to 18% and 14%, respectively. The contingency reversal sessions also provided a direct analysis of events controlling appropriate as well as inappropriate behavior. The substantially lower frequencies of self-injury during the contingency reversal condition provided direct empirical support for our recommended treatment (Differential Reinforcement of Appropriate Behavior and extinction for self-injury).

Case Example 2

Alicia was a 4-year-old female who was referred for evaluation of self-injurious and aggressive behavior. Alicia had been diagnosed previously as functioning within the severe range of mental retardation; she presented no significant medical problems. Her self-injury consisted of hand biting, which was reported to occur daily, and it was rated as being moderate to severe in intensity. Prior to the outpatient evaluation, a Differential Reinforcement of Communication program (signing) had been implemented in the home, but both self-injury and signing were ignored at school. No other prior intervention programs for self-injury were reported. Although the program for differentially reinforcing communication achieved initial success at home, at the time of our evaluation, hand biting had increased to levels in excess of original frequencies. Her mother reported that Alicia continued to sign "please" to briefly escape tasks at home.

Our analogue assessment with Alicia used the following four conditions: (a) free play, (b) escape, (c) social attention, and (d) tangible. All sessions were conducted within a special education classroom in the clinic that was equipped with a one-way mirror. The free play condition was conducted in a manner similar to that of Roys', except that toys were available for play. During the escape condition, Alicia was engaged in several grooming tasks, including brushing her teeth and hair and washing her hands and face. As with Roy, brief breaks were provided contingent upon the occurrence of self-injury, while all appropriate behavior was ignored. The social attention condition was conducted as described for Roy. During the tangible condition, Alicia was allowed access to preferred toys (based on parent report) for 15 to 30 seconds contingent upon the occurrence of hand biting. The tangible condition represented the naturally occurring situation in which individuals are redirected to known reinforcers or are given preferred items in an attempt to calm or soothe them following self-injurious behavior. As in all the other analogue conditions, appropriate behavior was ignored.

The results of the standard assessment for Alicia are displayed in Figure 4. Self-injurious behavior occurred only during the escape condition and with low frequency (7% of the intervals); however, each occurrence was of high intensity. This condition also resulted in frequent screaming and tantrums. During all other conditions, Alicia remained cooperative and generally appropriate.

The escape and free play conditions

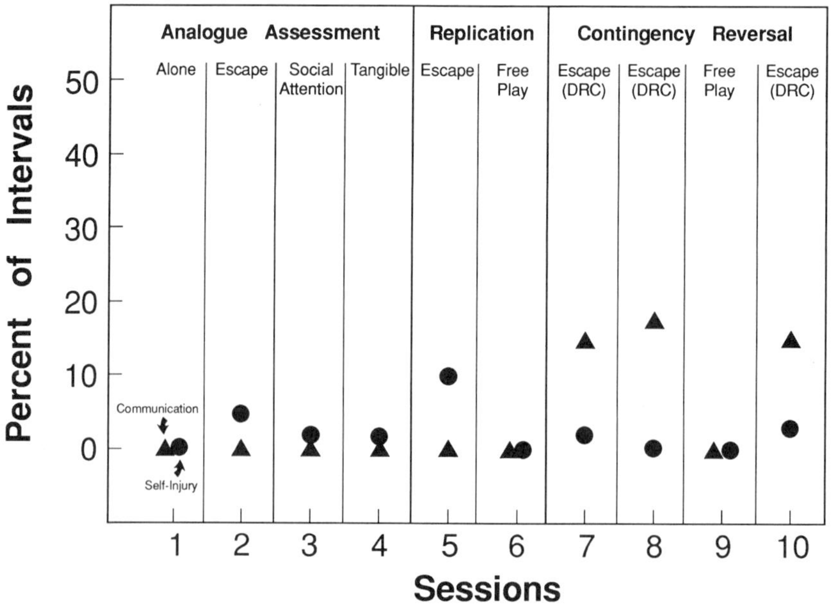

Figure 4: Results of an outpatient evaluation for Alicia across the analogue, replication, and contingency reversal phases of assessment.

then were repeated to replicate the results of the analogue assessment. As displayed in Figure 4, self-injurious behavior occurred only during the escape condition at a rate similar to the original condition (10%). The contingency reversal was conducted for Alicia with the addition of a functional communication treatment component (Differential Reinforcement of Communication). Three additional escape conditions were implemented in which grooming was continued; however, Alicia could obtain a brief (10- to 15-second) break by signing "please." Approximately every 15 to 30 seconds, a least-to-most restrictive prompt sequence (verbal instruction, partial physical assistance, complete physical assistance) was used to prompt the "please" sign. All self-injurious behaviors resulted in graduated guidance to prompt her to continue the task. Following the two initial escape conditions, the initial free play condition was implemented again to replicate previous results and to provide a control condition. A final demand condition then was conducted to form a modified reversal design.

During the contingency reversal conditions, Alicia's self-injury dropped to zero or near zero percentages of occurrence. In addition, during the first treatment condition, she signed "please" 14 times in 10 minutes. During the two subsequent escape conditions, similar results occurred. Interestingly, her signing decreased immediately during the free play condition, but increased again when the final escape condition was reinstated. These results supported her mother's claim that signing could serve as a replacement response (Carr, 1988) for Alicia's self-injury.

These two case examples illustrate the range of treatments recommended in the clinic. In all cases, differential reinforcement is recommended to increase or shape an appropriate response (participation in a task or communication). In most cases, differential reinforcement is combined with a second contingency (time-out for behavior maintained by positive reinforcement and graduated guidance for negative reinforcement) to form a treatment package. We utilize the contingency for inappropriate behavior with individuals who currently display high frequencies or intensities of inappropriate behavior, or those who have long histories of displaying inappropriate behavior. This is necessary if the objective is to decrease the frequency or intensity of behavior relatively quickly--a constant pragmatic requirement in the outclinic setting. The use of mild punishment contingencies, such as time-out or graduated guidance, in conjunction with positive techniques, also has proven to be acceptable to most referring consumers, an important consideration for long-term use of the recommended treatments. Our long-term goal is to fade the use of mild punishment, but, to date, we have not systematically evaluated fading approaches.

PROMOTING CONTINUED USE OF TREATMENT AND MAINTENANCE OF CLIENT BEHAVIOR

The functional analysis phase of the outpatient evaluation provides an efficient method for identifying the class of maintaining contingencies (positive or negative reinforcement) of the target behavior, and thus provides the basis for establishing an initial treatment program for use in local school and home settings. To date, over 45% of the patients evaluated in the clinic have demonstrated substantial decreases in maladaptive behavior 6 months following assessment, with no additional consultation. However, the extent to which a proposed treatment results in long-term behavior changes is determined not only by the initial effectiveness of the treatment procedure as demonstrated by the contingency reversal, but also by the generalizability of the treatment across different settings and people and over time.

At least two variables affect the continued use of the treatment to maintain client behavior. First, the proposed treatment will be effective within the client's home and school environment only to the extent that the conditions used within the assessment reflect the maintaining conditions typically available within the local environment. Normally occurring antecedents and consequences to the client's behavior are identified prior to the outpatient evaluation through the historical data collected and are confirmed through the behavioral interview. Once identified, these antecedent and consequent conditions are simulated within analogue conditions to assess their impact on the client's behavior. Antecedents and consequences that are routinely available to the client within his or her local setting are emphasized using a common stimuli approach (Stokes & Baer, 1977) to assessment and treatment. Second, when the antecedent and consequence conditions currently maintaining the client's inappropriate behavior are identified and their effects replicated, the client usually is taught a more appropriate alternative behavior to obtain the identified maintaining contingencies.

In addition to the effects in the clinic, the effects in the client's natural environment also must be considered. A treatment that may be effective in the clinic setting may not be effective in the normal environment if the resources that are typically available within that environment (e.g., caregiver-to-client ratio, client scheduling constraints) are not considered. For example, teaching a client to sign "please" may result in an immediate break within the clinic setting because of the high staff-to-client ratio. However, if the client's normal environment has the typically high client-to-staff ratio, the signing behavior may not be noticed by those in control of the contingencies or it may, at best, result in the delayed presentation of reinforcement, thus reducing the effectiveness of treatment.

The importance of matching the proposed treatment with the natural environment is shown in Case Example 2. Alicia's display of the sign "please" within the clinic setting, and reportedly within the home setting, resulted in an immediate break from the assigned activity. However, according to her mother's report at the outpatient evaluation, Alicia's signing was ignored within the school setting, thus demonstrating the need to consider the contingencies that will be available routinely within the local setting. In addition to incorporating the naturally available contingencies within the client's environment, the proposed treatment also must be acceptable to direct caregivers before we can determine that the treatment is applicable to the local setting.

ASSESSING THE ACCEPTABILITY OF RECOMMENDED TREATMENTS

Lack of compliance to recommended treatment approaches can make the management of behavioral problems difficult, particularly in outpatient settings where the professional typically has less control over behavior than in an inpatient unit. Evaluating the effectiveness of a given treatment is frequently difficult, not necessarily because of inherent difficulties with the treatment itself, but because of a failure by the consumer to carry out the treatment as intended (Reimers, Wacker, & Koeppl, 1987). As Witt and Elliott (1985) pointed out, "A treatment that is not used, is no treatment at all" (p. 253). For this reason, we are placing increased emphasis on the acceptability of recommended treatments to the consumer.

The term "acceptability" originally referred to "judgments by persons, clients, and others of whether treatment procedures are appropriate, fair, and reasonable for the problem or client" (Kazdin, 1981). Consumer satisfaction, or the rated acceptability of a proposed treatment, may be an especially important issue when several procedures are available for treatment. For example, several treatments may be equally effective (based on studies in controlled settings), but may not be perceived as equally effective by the consumer. If acceptability affects the consumer's compliance with a recommended treatment, then the most acceptable treatment may be the most successful (Kazdin, 1981). Assessing the acceptability of a treatment also may help in determining those factors that lead to the treatment's success or failure and may assist in modifying treatment to make it more effective (Reimers et al., 1987).

Several aspects of proposed treatments have been identified as affecting treatment acceptability by consumers. Variables include (a) perceived severity of the behavior problem (Elliott, Witt, Galvin, & Peterson, 1984), (b) understanding of the treatment procedures (Singh & Katz, 1985), (c) effectiveness (Reimers & Wacker, 1988), (d) side effects (Kazdin, 1981), and (e) time needed to implement the treatment and overall disruption to one's routine (Witt & Martens, 1983). These findings suggest that if consumers do not find a particular treatment acceptable, they will be less likely to continue implementing it. Thus, assessing consumer's acceptability may provide some indication of how likely they are to carry out the treatment. If we are able to establish a positive relationship between ratings of acceptability and treatment compliance, we can then develop treatment recommendations that have the highest probability of being implemented by consumers.

Acceptability measures are used in our outpatient service for two reasons. The first is to assess acceptability prior to local implementation of the treatment procedures. The purpose of these ratings is to determine whether consumers view the recommendations as too time-consuming, too disruptive to scheduled routines, having too many side effects, or being ineffective. Additional therapist time is spent with consumers who express concerns with one or more of these factors. When consumers express concerns, attempts are made by staff to clear up any misconceptions or to modify the treatment procedures.

The second and primary function of assessing acceptability is to determine obstacles to adherence with treatment recommendations. Ratings are obtained 1, 3, and 6 months following initial assessment to provide an indication of the consumer's success in implementing the treatment recommendations.

In summary, recent research suggests that acceptability ratings can indicate to clinicians why maintenance effects were or were not achieved. Obtaining acceptability ratings from consumers, in addition to obtaining more objective assessments of behavior, has helped us conduct a more thorough assessment of maintenance. Our hope is that continued research will increase success in selecting effective treatment packages in order to maintain positive treatment gains over extended periods of time in local settings.

SUMMARY

In this chapter, we describe an outpatient model for evaluating and initiating treatment of self-injurious behavior. Other outpatient approaches have been reported in the literature, with the results being generally positive (e.g., Charlop, Parrish, Fenton, & Cataldo, 1987). Our approach is based on direct observation, using a functional analysis (Iwata et al., 1982) to identify maintaining conditions, with built-in replication evaluated through a rapidly changing reversal design. Our final phase of evaluation, the contingency reversal, provides at least partial confirmation that the treatment derived from assessment will be effective; we then attempt to establish the acceptability (Reimers et al., 1987) of treatment to the consumers who will deliver treatment. Follow-up, both locally and within our clinics, suggests that this approach to assessment and treatment can be successful, with about 50% of the clients making substantial treatment gains.

Why 50% of the cases have not resulted in long-term gains is unclear. One variable may be the length of time clients have engaged in maladaptive behavior, which on the average is about 10 years. Also, procedures recommended for appropriate behavior, for inappropriate behavior, or for both, may not have been implemented consistently or may have been discontinued prematurely, perhaps because the initial success achieved was not maintained over time. Because our recommended treatments usually involve packages of distinct components, we are currently unable to identify the active component for any given individual over time. We now need to establish better the conditions under which this approach to assessment and treatment can be successful over extended periods of time. For some cases, inpatient treatment is needed; for others, a different approach may be indicated. What does seem clear is that a functional analysis approach to assessment is viable, even under the restrictions imposed by outclinic settings. Functional analyses of maintaining conditions provide a basis for treatment by identifying classes of reinforcers. Even if the analogue situation does not match the natural environment exactly, it nevertheless provides an indication of maintaining conditions that may be utilized within the natural environment. By matching the treatment to the maintaining condition (Iwata, Pace, Kalsher, Cowdery, & Cataldo, 1990), an effective treatment is more likely to be found. Functional analysis procedures are not used to prescribe specific treatments or only nonaversive treatments, however. Nevertheless, the completion of a functional analysis appears to increase the probability that an effective nonaversive treatment will be identified. Our intent is to continue to develop and evaluate proactive treatments that are delivered primarily in community settings. Our initial results suggest that such a model can be successful, and that further analysis is warranted.

REFERENCES

Carr, E. (1988). Functional equivalence as a mechanism of response generalization. In R. Horner, R. Koegel, & G. Dunlap (Eds.), *Generalization and maintenance: Life style changes in applied settings* (pp. 221-241). Baltimore: Paul H. Brookes.

Carr, E., & Durand, V. M. (1985). Reducing behavioral problems through functional communication training. *Journal of Applied Behavior Analysis, 18*, 111-126.

Charlop, M., Parrish, J., Fenton, L., & Cataldo, M. (1987). Evaluation of hospital-based outpatient pediatric psychology services. *Journal of Pediatric Psychology, 12*, 485-503.

Elliott, S., Witt, J., Galvin, G., & Peterson, R. (1984). Acceptability of positive and reductive behavioral interventions: Factors that influence teachers' decisions. *Journal of School Psychology, 22*, 353-360.

Iwata, B., Dorsey, M., Slifer, K., Bauman, K., & Richman, G. (1982). Toward a functional analysis of self-injury. *Analysis and Intervention in Developmental Disabilities, 2*, 3-20.

Iwata, B., Pace, G., Kalsher, M., Cowdery, G, & Cataldo, M. 1990). Experimental analysis and extinction of self-injurious escape behavior. *Journal of Applied Behavior Analysis 23*, 11-27.

Kazdin, A. (1981). Acceptability of child treatment techniques: The influence of treatment efficacy and adverse side effects. *Behavior Therapy, 12*, 493-506.

Northup, J., Wacker, D., Steege, M., Cigrand, K., Sasso, G., & Cook, J. (1989). *Outpatient evaluation of self-injurious and aggressive behavior using functional analysis*. Paper presented at the annual meeting of the Association for Behavior Analysis, Milwaukee, WI.

Reimers, T., & Wacker, D. (1988). Parents' ratings of acceptability of behavioral treatment recommendations made in an outpatient clinic: A preliminary analysis of the influence of treatment effectiveness. *Behavioral Disorders, 14*, 7-15.

Reimers, T., Wacker, D., & Koeppl, G. (1987). Acceptability of behavioral interventions: A review of the literature. *School Psychology Review, 16*, 212-227.

Singh, N., & Katz, R. (1985). On the modification of acceptability ratings for alternative child treatments. *Behavior Modification, 9*, 375-386.

Steege, M., Wacker, D., Berg, W., Cigrand, K., & Cooper, L. (1989). The use of behavioral assessment to prescribe and evaluate treatments for severely handicapped children. *Journal of Applied Behavior Analysis, 22*, 23-33.

Stokes, T., & Baer, D. (1977). An implicit technology of generalization. *Journal of Applied Behavior Analysis, 10*, 349-367.

Witt, J., & Elliott, S. (1985). Acceptability of classroom management strategies. In T. Kratochwill (Ed.), *Advances in school psychology* Vol. 4. (pp. 251-288). Hillsdale, NJ: Erlbaum.

Witt, J., & Martens, B. (1983). Assessing the acceptability of behavioral interventions used in classrooms. *Psychology in the Schools, 20*, 510-517.

CHAPTER

24

THE WRONG ISSUE: AVERSIVE VERSUS NONAVERSIVE TREATMENT THE RIGHT ISSUE: FUNCTIONAL VERSUS NONFUNCTIONAL TREATMENT

Edward G. Carr, Sarah Robinson, and Laura Wray Palumbo
SUNY at Stony Brook
and
Suffolk Child Development Center

For a number of years, the central question in the field has been whether there are circumstances in which the use of aversive treatment is justified because nonaversive treatment has failed. That is the wrong question. We will argue that the question is wrong because it has caused the field to focus on crisis management at the expense of long-term treatment, reactive strategies at the expense of proactive ones, technology at the expense of understanding, and behavior control at the expense of education. There is a better question. The essence of this question concerns whether there are things that we can do, that indeed we must do, when behavior problems are not occurring so that there will be far fewer crises to manage and, therefore, no need to continually raise the question of when extraordinary procedures are justified.

We have deliberately taken the tack of challenging the question posed at the outset because asking a particular question inherently limits the boundaries of debate and discussion. Our point is that the field, by agreeing to devote its efforts to answering the aversives versus nonaversives question, has tacitly agreed that other questions are less central, or less of a priority. We believe quite the opposite. We believe that the question concerning whether there are things that we should do when an individual is not misbehaving (in order to reduce or eliminate behavior problems) is, in fact, the central question and the major priority. We will argue that this question is scientifically and theoretically interesting quite apart from any appeal it may have from a values perspective.

A VIGNETTE

The field always has paid at least lip service to the idea of dealing with behavior problems by providing nonaversive treatment to individuals who are, for example, self-injurious or aggressive. The field also has been quick to challenge advocates of nonaversive approaches by presenting a vignette much like the following prototype:

> We have a 35-year-old man, Mr. Brown, diagnosed as severely

> retarded, who is 6'4" and weighs 250 lbs. Brown is a severe head banger who recently hospitalized his 11th group home staff member this year by head-butting that unfortunate individual when the staff member tried to restrain him during an episode of self-injury. We have used a large number of positive approaches, but still have daily crises that pose serious threats to the safety of both Brown and the staff. Although we have the deepest commitment to and greatest affection for positive approaches, it is now clear that they have their limits, and the time has come to consider ammonia, pinches, slaps, shock, etc. It is fine for others to talk about values, ethics, and humanism, but we're on the front lines. We need more than self-righteous talk. We need to know what to do when Brown is putting his head through a closed window or choking one of the staff.

This vignette typifies the predicament faced by advocates of nonaversive methods. It would seem foolhardy to believe that one could address the crisis described by using nonaversive methods and, indeed, it is foolhardy. The problem is that the vignette traps us into the seemingly inevitable conclusion that aversives are called for, but it does so by presenting a misleading perspective. The real issue is not whether (at the moment the staff member is being choked) one should debate the merits of aversive versus nonaversive approaches; it is too late then for such a debate. The real issue, the issue that the field has not focused on for the past 25 years, is why the crisis was allowed to develop in the first place. That is, what was done when Brown was not choking people or shattering glass with his head? The field has not adequately addressed the issue of whether the amorphous educational programming that frequently occurs between crises is as objectionable and disadvantageous as the intrusive interventions that sometimes occur at the moment of crisis. Further, and of greatest importance, how would one know exactly what procedures to choose when Brown is not a problem in order to ensure that he will continue not to be a problem? The answer to this last question depends on the reasons why Brown is misbehaving or, in technical terms, on the nature of the variables of which his behavior problems are a function. This focus inevitably leads to a consideration of functional analysis and hypothesis-driven treatment.

HYPOTHESIS-DRIVEN TREATMENT: BIRTH, OBLIVION, RESURRECTION

Hypothesis-driven treatment involves choosing interventions that are based on one's knowledge of the variables controlling the behavior problems (Repp, Felce, & Barton, 1988). These variables can be identified through formal functional analysis. That is, antecedents and/or consequences can be experimentally manipulated in order to identify what factors produce systematic changes in the level of behavior problems (Skinner, 1953, 1959). There are also less formal ways of identifying controlling variables. These include direct observation of environment-behavior interactions (without any attempt at manipulation) or the use of structured interviews with people (e.g., parents, teachers) who have had an opportunity to interact with the individual of interest over long periods of time (Durand & Crimmins, 1988; Groden, 1989; O'Neill, Horner, Albin, Storey, & Sprague, 1989). Whether the assessment is made formally or informally, the result is the same: Specific hypotheses are derived from the information gathered, and these hypotheses are used to choose and construct treatments designed to alter the controlling variables in such a manner as to minimize or eliminate behavior problems. That is what we were taught in graduate school (Baer, Wolf, & Risley, 1968; Bandura, 1969; Kanfer & Saslow, 1969; Sulzer-Azaroff & Mayer, 1977; Ullmann & Krasner, 1965). Reality is another matter.

When the field was born, it seemed as if hypothesis-driven treatment might become the norm. Aggression, self-injury, noncompliance, operant vomiting, and a host of other serious behavior problems were shown to be lawfully related to environmental variables, and plausible treatment strategies were suggested based on experimental analyses (Hawkins, Peterson, Schweid, & Bijou, 1966; Lovaas, Freitag, Gold, & Kassorla, 1965; Patterson, Littman, & Bricker, 1967; Wahler, 1969; Wolf, Birnbrauer, Williams & Lawler, 1965). But, to quote some lines by Dowson,

> They were not long, the days of wine and roses
> Out of a misty dream
> Our path emerged for a while, then closed
> Within a dream.

Hypothesis-driven treatment died out from the literature. For many years now, functional analysis has been teetering on the edge of oblivion, a development that has been amply documented in reviews of the literature (Deitz, 1978; Hayes, Rincover, & Solnick, 1980; Lundervold & Bourland, 1988). A de facto set of values has emerged in which technology (the desire for a cure or, at least, substantial improvement) has taken precedence over understanding (the desire to know the variables of which behavior is a function). In view of the vignette presented earlier, it is easy to see why there might be an emphasis on cure. Faced with a dangerously aggressive and self-injurious individual, a parent, teacher, or psychologist may conclude that functional analysis is a purely academic exercise that pales beside the necessity for immediate action; that is, the necessity for quick, effective technology. This conclusion begs the question, however. The issue is that one must determine whether it is indeed true that technology applied in the absence of understanding really constitutes treatment at all. There is a growing suspicion, which will be discussed later, that it does not.

This suspicion has led to the resurrection of functional analysis. There is now an increasing interest in reexamining and extending our understanding of the antecedent and consequent variables that control behavior problems, and, most importantly, there is an attempt to deduce treatment interventions based on this understanding (Bachman, 1972; Baumeister & Rollings, 1976; Carr, 1977; Carr & Durand, 1985a; Cataldo & Harris, 1982; Demchak & Halle, 1985; Frankel & Simmons, 1976; Horner et al., 1989; Iwata, Dorsey, Slifer, Bauman, & Richman, 1982; Romanczyk, Gordon, Crimmins, Wenzel, & Kistner, 1980; Schroeder, Rojahn, Mulick, & Schroeder, in press). On the consequence side, a variety of factors have been shown to influence severe behavior problems. Specifically, self-injury, aggression, and related behaviors have been demonstrated to be maintained by positive reinforcers, including attention (Carr & Durand, 1985b; Carr & McDowell, 1980; Lovaas et al., 1965; Lovaas & Simmons, 1969; Martin & Foxx, 1973), tangible events (Durand & Crimmins, 1988; Edelson, Taubman, & Lovaas, 1983), sensory stimuli (Favell, McGimsey & Schell, 1982; Rincover & Devany, 1982), and biochemical factors (Barrett, Feinstein, & Hole, 1989; Sandman, Datta, Barron, Hoehler, Williams, & Swanson, 1983; Thompson, Hackenberg, & Schaal, in press). Behavior problems have also been demonstrated to be maintained by negative reinforcers involving escape from or avoidance of aversive stimuli (Carr & Newsom, 1985; Carr, Newsom, & Binkoff, 1976, 1980; Iwata, 1987; Plummer, Baer, & LeBlanc, 1977; Sailor, Guess, Rutherford, & Baer, 1968; Weeks & Gaylord-Ross, 1981). On the antecedent side, the emission of severe behavior problems has been demonstrated to be systematically related to a variety of factors, including demands (e.g., Carr et al., 1980), crowding (e.g., Boe, 1977; McAfee, 1987), staff change (e.g., Touchette, MacDonald, & Langer, 1985), vestibular stimulation (e.g., Dura, Mulick, & Hammer, 1988), exercise (e.g., Baumeister & MacLean, 1984), clothing configuration (e.g., Rojahn, Mulick, McCoy, & Schroeder, 1978), and task repetition (e.g., Winterling, Dunlap, & O'Neill, 1987). Thus, there are well documented reasons (controlling variables) indicating why individuals engage in severe behavior problems. Because of this fact, the question now is whether it is still acceptable to focus most of our energies on developing treatment strategies and adhering to treatment philosophies that stress purely technological solutions to crisis situations.

WHAT IS WRONG WITH PURE TECHNOLOGY?

Pure technology, as noted already, is defined by its emphasis on cure (elimination or, at least, dramatic reduction in behavior problems to negligible levels) rather than any emphasis on understanding the variables of which behavior is a function (Deitz, 1978). Interestingly, as this definition makes clear, a variety of interventions, nonaversive as well as aversive, fall into the category of technology.

Let us consider the use of an aversive procedure, such as shock, to treat the individual described earlier in the vignette. Whenever Brown strikes his head against a glass window, he is given a shock. There is a temporary suppression of self-injury. Two months later, his head banging returns to its baseline level. How might this failure be accounted for? Consider that Brown, who is nonverbal and does not sign, has no way of indicating that he has to go to the bathroom, a room that cannot be entered for safety reasons, without staff supervision. Normally, this situation is not a problem because the staff toilet the residents every few hours. Today, however, two staff are out sick, and Brown earlier had drunk a large quantity of juice. Consider also that Brown has a long history of being punished for wetting himself. In short, he is in a bind. After a period of generalized agitation, during which staff massage his back to get him to calm down, he still has to go to the bathroom, and then severe self-injury begins. He bloodies himself, and staff rush him into the bathroom to apply cold compresses. At this point, Brown breaks loose from the staff and uses the toilet. This scenario shows that no matter how many times Brown is shocked for head banging, he still will be frustrated whenever he has to go to the bathroom. At best, shock will delay the next inevitable bout of self-injury. Staff then meet with a consultant who tells them that their positive habilitative program, while commendable, is too general to deal with the problem of self-injury. The consultant recommends that a program using the differential reinforcement of other behavior (DRO) be added to the general positive procedures now in place. Whenever Brown has begun to engage in a bout of self-injury, he is to receive half a glass of his favorite juice contingent on every 15-second block of time in which there is no self-injury. Now his situation has become even more complicated. In addition to getting shocked for head banging, which is itself under stimulus control of a full bladder, he is receiving large amounts of fluids that further challenge the limits of his bladder capacity. This situation seems destined to drive self-injury to record levels, a prediction later confirmed in the staff notes that make reference to a catastrophic day and the necessity to consider the introduction of several additional aversive procedures.

There are a number of issues worth considering with respect to the worst case scenario that we have just described. One issue pertains to the possibility of staff incompetence. It seems obvious that the staff should have developed a treatment program around the problem of toileting. Since no functional analysis was carried out, however, why is this idea obvious? It is only obvious because our description of the situation made it obvious. The staff is not incompetent at all. They made use of two widely discussed and much researched technologies. Scientific data existed on other cases involving people with retardation who exhibited severe self-injury. These data demonstrated that DRO and shock were plausible procedures. What else need one know? One needs to know that self-injury is not a random act; that is, in lay terms, it usually has a purpose, and that purpose will never be determined by the blind application of pure technology, but only by the systematic identification of controlling variables, or, in other words, by a functional analysis. Pure technology is not designed to address the variables of which behavior problems are a function and, therefore, is vulnerable to the kinds of failure just described. Our example also indicates that pure technology can be nonaversive as well as aversive. In the absence of functional analysis, either procedure can be problematic. The major point that we wish to make in this chapter is that the real debate in developmental disabilities is ultimately not about the use of aversive versus nonaversive procedures. The real debate is about the use of functional versus nonfunctional procedures; that is, the use of procedures based on a knowledge of the variables of which problem behavior is a function versus procedures not based on such knowledge.

Of course, one could argue that the field has done reasonably well in applying a variety of standard treatment technologies in the absence of functional analysis. This statement is only partly true, however, since a number of literature reviews document numerous treatment failures and weak effects following the application of these technologies. In the area of nonaversive treatment, for example, a review of 96 studies determined that the success rate (defined as 90% or more suppression in the level of behavior problems relative to baseline) was much lower for procedures not based on functional analysis than it was for those procedures based on such an analysis (Carr, Taylor, Carlson, & Robinson, in press). Interestingly, no such comparison data are available for the literature on aversives for the simple reason that the application of aversive procedures does not depend on a knowledge of the variables controlling behavior problems. That is, shock or ammonia inhalation, for example, could be applied to instances of self-injury irrespective of whether the behavior was motivated by escape, attention, tangibles, or sensory variables and also independent of what specific stimulus factors might be operating. On this basis, one can categorize aversive intervention as nonfunctional (i.e., not tied to the variables of which the behavior problems are a function). Interestingly, the data on punishment procedures often indicate good short-term effects (Cataldo, in press; Guess, Helmstetter, Turnbull, & Knowlton, 1987). However, one point is well worth emphasizing; namely, that any interpretation of the effects of aversive procedures is greatly complicated by the fact that these procedures are almost invariably accompanied by a variety of nonaversive and educational interventions conducted over protracted periods of time. It is reasonable to consider the possibility that long-term treatment effectiveness may be more a function of the accompanying educational and nonaversive procedures than the aversive procedures themselves (Foxx, in press; Foxx, Bittle, & Faw,

1989). One could only test this notion by withholding educational treatments for long periods of time in order to see whether aversives by themselves produced good maintenance. This test would be both unethical and illegal. In the absence of such a test, a meaningful working hypothesis would be that it is the functional components of the long-term educational procedures that are responsible for maintenance. If so, then it is clear once again that even if aversives have short-term effects, one is inevitably forced to consider functional treatments to produce long-term effects. The virtue of the hypothesis that we have been discussing is that functionality can be operationally defined and procedures based on the concept can be tested in a systematic and empirical manner in the best tradition of our field. But if functionality is a relevant concept for long-term treatment, why cannot it also be relevant to addressing the issue of drastically reducing or eliminating altogether the crises with which we are so often confronted?

THE ALTERNATIVE TO PURE TECHNOLOGY

How might we deal with crises in the short run without being dependent on standard, nonfunctional technology? Ironically, the negative lessons learned from applications of pure technology may be helpful. In examining the treatment literature based on such technologies, one is struck by the fact that a systematic rationale is rarely provided on why one procedure is chosen over another. For example, with respect to aversive procedures, why choose ammonia pellets rather than shock, or slaps rather than pinches? The situation is no better in the case of nonfunctional procedures that are nonaversive. Why choose DRO rather than differential reinforcement of incompatible behavior (DRI)? Nonfunctional procedures typically are justified, if at all, by the fact that other studies exist in which a similar type of individual who had a similar type of problem was successfully treated with the procedure. In other words, diagnostic category and behavior topography, two factors that represent the antithesis of the behavioral treatment philosophy, are repeatedly given as the reasons for selecting a behavioral treatment. How far we have come from our roots! Pure technology is, in fact, the diametric opposite of clinical behaviorism, an approach that stresses the idea that treatment must be based on a knowledge of the variables of which behavior is a function. Therefore, it follows that the alternative to pure technology involves incorporating knowledge of controlling variables in the initial selection and systematic elaboration of treatment procedures.

It is best to illustrate the strategy by referring again to the vignette. Having replaced our consultants because their nonfunctional treatments had no long-term effect, we are still confronted with a number of instances each day in which Brown rushes toward the window to bang his head. This event constitutes a crisis. Do we need some new aversives, such as ammonia pellets or slaps, or perhaps a change from DRO to DRI? No, we do not. Common sense and professional responsibility dictate that several staff need to physically pull Brown away from the window so that he does not hurt himself. Is this treatment? No, it is not. It is crisis management. Does Brown enjoy this procedure? Judging from the struggle he puts up and the accompanying screaming, one could infer that he does not find the procedure enjoyable. But, as is commonly the case, he eventually settles down. *Now*, when the crisis has ended, we are in a position to do treatment. *Now*, when there are no behavior problems, we need to implement our treatment for behavior problems. *Now*, in contrast to the past 25 years when so many behaviorists have handed all of the calm Browns back to teachers and parents and told them, "It's your turn," it is time for these same behaviorists to change and become educators themselves. It is time to ask the question, "What do we know about the factors controlling his behavior problems?" It is time to act on that knowledge by designing treatments based on the results of our functional analyses.

Reinforcement-Based Treatments

To continue with our example, analyses indicate that Brown's self-injury and aggression are under multiple motivational and setting event control. It appears that many instances of such behavior arise when he is unable to access certain tangible reinforcing stimuli, including food (especially soda, coffee, and second helpings of meal items) and selected activities (especially walking in the neighborhood and going to the bathroom). In lay terms, his behavior problems seem to be primitive attempts to get what he wants. In behavioral terms, self-injury and aggression are operants maintained by a variety of tangible reinforcers given intermittently by the staff contingent on Brown's problem behavior. Based on this analysis, it makes no sense to administer shocks, ammonia pellets, or pinches contingent on undesirable behavior. Equally so, it makes no sense to set up a DRO in which candy is dispensed for every 15 seconds in which self-injury does not occur since there is no evidence that candy was a maintaining variable for the behavior problem. Nor does it make sense to set up a DRI in which Brown receives praise for sitting quietly with hands folded on his lap since hands thus positioned will not access any of the critical reinforcers. The aversive and nonaversive procedures are identical in one important respect: They are both nonfunctional. A procedure needs to be selected that has some rational and systematic connection to the variables known to control the problem. The functional analysis allows us to deduce what the features of such a procedure might be. Above all, the procedure should involve teaching Brown a new behavior that serves the same function as the self-injury and aggression (i.e., accesses the same reinforcers). One procedure could involve teaching him to request the relevant reinforcers. The fact that Brown is nonverbal is no problem since sign training procedures are available (e.g., Carr, Binkoff, Kologinsky, & Eddy, 1978; Carr & Kologinsky, 1983; Horner & Budd, 1985; Wacker, Steege, Berg, Reimers, Sasso, Northup, & Hays, 1989). Thus, within the toileting context, he could be taught to sign "bathroom," a response that serves the same function as the behavior problems. Since Brown is highly motivated to make this request, acquisition of the sign should be rapid. Likewise, depending on the context, he could be taught to request soda, coffee, second helpings at mealtime, and neighborhood walks. In short, developing a functionally equivalent response would constitute one part of the treatment plan (Carr, 1985, 1988; Carr & Durand, 1985a, 1987). It would probably not be enough, however. In developing a new desirable response to compete with an old undesirable one, it is also necessary to take steps to ensure that the new response is more efficient at generating the relevant reinforcers than the old one (Billingsley & Neel, 1985; Carr & Kemp, in press; Carr & Lindquist, 1987; Horner & Billingsley, 1988). Simply stated, the new response should access the relevant reinforcer with a shorter delay, greater consistency, and less effort. Practically, this idea translates into rearranging the social environment so that people with whom Brown interacts are knowledgeable about his communication system, and also are prepared to act consistently and rapidly when requests are made. Once the new communicative repertoire is well established, it becomes possible to introduce some intermittency and delay of reinforcement in the contingency. In summary, response efficiency is also a factor in treatment planning.

A hallmark of behavioral conceptualization is that a single set of responses can have multiple functions (e.g., Carr, 1977). Thus, Brown's self-injury and aggression, as noted previously, is under multiple motivational and setting event control. Nonfunctional treatments, aversive as well as nonaversive, are not sensitive to this fact. Functional treatments must be. Thus, when analysis indicates that Brown's problems are also set off in situations that, in lay terms, would be labeled frustrating or boring, it is clear that additional treatments must be designed that are linked to these variables. Further, these treatments will be different from the ones already described. Consider first the case of frustration, contextually operationalized as the emission of behavior problems following repeated incorrect responding on an academic task. Here, an appropriate treatment might be to rearrange the presentation of academic instruction so that it conforms to an errorless learning paradigm (Weeks & Gaylord-Ross, 1981). In addition, one could teach Brown to request assistance whenever he receives negative feedback (Carr & Durand, 1985b). Consider next the case of boredom, contextually operationalized as the emission of behavior problems in the presence of a repetitive task. One could approach this problem simply by varying the task (Winterling, Dunlap, & O'Neill, 1987). In addition, some data suggest that encouraging people with developmental disabilities to make choices produces general behavior improvement (Guess, Benson, & Siegel-Causey, 1985; Koegel, Dyer, & Bell, 1987). More specifically, recent data demonstrate that allowing an individual to make choices produces a reduction in disruptive problem behavior (Dyer, Dunlap, & Winterling, 1989). On this basis, our treatment also should involve allowing Brown to choose periodically the task on which he would like to work. To sum up, the putatively aversive characteristics of the instructional situation can be altered in such a way as to make escape and avoidance (i.e., behavior problems) unnecessary. The alteration is made by implementing multiple procedures that are functionally linked to the multiple variables controlling self-injury and aggression.

Further functional analyses also may implicate attention-seeking as a factor in Brown's problems. Again, a treatment with different specifications than any described so far must be designed in order to address this aspect of the behavior problem. A reasonable treatment might be to teach Brown to request attention from others (Carr & Durand, 1985b), thereby obviating the necessity for engaging in self-injury or aggression as a way of accessing attention. However, the treatment would need to be more sophisticated than it sounds; that is, the social situation would have to be restructured so that individuals for whom Brown had some affection would be the ones to respond to his communicative efforts. Strangers might well be nonfunctional in this regard (i.e., their attention would not serve as a reinforcer) and, yet, it is surprising how often it is the case that strangers (i.e., unfamiliar psychologists and staff) dispense praise and other forms of attention that, from a functional perspective, amount to no more than neutral stimuli. In addition, attention would itself need to be analyzed into its component parts. Praise and/or random chatter may not be a reinforcer for Brown. Thus, it may turn out that a specific social game is the reinforcer, in which case Brown would have to be taught to request this particular social activity rather than a more generic type of interaction. Again, treatment would need to be carefully tailored to address the variables controlling the problem.

Stimulus-Based Treatments

One sometimes reads in the published literature, or hears during a consultation, that a functional analysis of consequences was carried out to no avail; that is, the variables maintaining the behavior could not be identified. Although it is always possible that the analysis failed because it was carried out poorly, one should not disregard the possibility that the analysis may have failed because our assessment methodology is still in an embryonic state and/or that there may be constellations of variables that control behavior of which we know little. The long-term solution to this problem would be to refocus our efforts toward systematic assessment and away from pure technology. One short-term approach, which may also become a long-term approach as we gain more knowledge, is to realize that functional analysis refers to a consideration of antecedent and setting events as well as consequences.

Returning to our vignette, it may be that certain instances of Brown's self-injury and aggression cannot be definitively linked to specific consequences. This outcome should not be used to justify the application of nonfunctional treatment. Rather, it should prompt a detailed analysis of antecedent and setting events. This idea has been part of the folklore of the field for quite some time. It is, therefore, surprising that only recently has there been a concerted and systematic effort to explore in detail the promise of a stimulus-based methodology. A good example of this methodology is illustrated in the approach developed by Touchette, MacDonald, and Langer (1985). In their approach, the presence or absence of behavior problems is correlated with time of day in settings in which environmental events repeat themselves in a fairly predictable fashion across time. For example, it is possible to correlate the presence of certain staff with low levels of behavior problems and the presence of others with high levels. Touchette et al. demonstrated that, in the short run, judicious staff substitutions could be made in such a manner that behavior problems were quickly reduced. From a conceptual perspective, it would be important to analyze why some staff evoke behavior problems while others do not. This understanding would likely lead to further improvements in treatment strategy. Such research remains to be done. Nonetheless, from a clinical perspective, the observed correlations lend themselves to formulating a plan to redesign the environment. Thus, if it is found that Brown behaves well in the presence of certain staff, the hours of those staff might be rearranged when feasible to ensure that these staff are on duty when Brown is awake and active. The staff in whose presence Brown misbehaves could be reassigned to a different set of duties or assigned to those hours in which Brown is sleeping or otherwise inactive. These changes can be cumbersome and are, therefore, meant only as a short-term approach to the problem. Their virtue, a point that we wish to stress strongly, is that they, like all stimulus control approaches, produce rapid behavior change. In other words, treatments derived from stimulus-based functional analyses may be one important alternative to nonfunctional treatment as a way of dealing quickly with crises. Two points are worth emphasizing. First, the fact that there is a need for crisis management procedures does not mean that these procedures have to be nonfunctional. Crisis management can *become* treatment if it is based on an analysis of controlling variables, an approach that the field ought to be pursuing with vigor. Second, crisis procedures, whether functional or nonfunctional, cannot continue to be the mainstay of intervention for behavior problems. Behavior enhancement, skill building, and maintenance constitute the central issues in treatment but traditional crisis management fails to address any of these concerns.

Other analyses of setting events may suggest that Brown, like many people with developmental disabilities, responds poorly to crowded living conditions. In fact, there are data showing that aggression in people without handicaps is more probable in crowded conditions (Epstein, 1981; Ginsberg, Polman, Yanson, & Hope, 1977; Loo, 1978). Although we may not know the motivational (consequence) variables underlying these observations, the correlational data imply that a rational strategy would be to restructure the environment to produce less crowding. An irrational and nonfunctional strategy would be to force Brown to endure crowded living conditions by making aversive stimuli contingent on any aggression that he displayed in this context. Interestingly, data suggest that reducing crowded conditions also may reduce aggressive behavior in people diagnosed as retarded (Boe, 1977; McAfee, 1987).

To continue, Brown, as is unfortunately the case for so many persons with developmental disabilities, lives a sedentary existence. He passes long hours each evening just sitting on the couch or in the kitchen. Correlational data suggest that, following protracted periods of inactivity, Brown is more likely to engage in self-injury and aggression. Based on this analysis, one might deduce that a rational treatment strategy would involve systematically programming exercise periods at home or, better from an integration perspective, enrolling Brown in local community gym activities with appropriate supervision. Data exist demonstrating that the provision of exercise programs can be an important setting event in ameliorating stereotypy (Kern, Koegel, Dyer, Blew, & Fenton, 1982). More germane still to the present problem are data demonstrating that exercise programs also may reduce aggression and self-injury (Baumeister & MacLean, 1984).

Finally, and somewhat paradoxically, we may note that even a procedure such as DRO, typically implemented in a nonfunctional manner, may have promise as a stimulus-based treatment strategy. The key element in such a strategy involves reconceptualizing DRO. Traditionally, DRO has been viewed as a procedure in which behaviors other than the undesirable ones are gradually strengthened so that they come to compete with, and perhaps eliminate altogether, the undesirable behaviors. There is no systematic evidence in the clinical literature that this process ever occurs. It is taken on faith that it does. Perhaps there is an alternative way of viewing DRO that may have heuristic value. Specifically, consider the typical case in which DRO involves delivering a number of tangible reinforcers such as food. To many individuals, food is a powerful discriminative stimulus that evokes a variety of behaviors (e.g., looking at the food, apprehending it, eating it) that may be functionally, if not topographically, incompatible with behavior problems. As long as the DRO interval is reasonably short, the individual may be engaged almost continuously in food-related responding, a situation that is likely to make the performance of undesirable behavior improbable. In short, the repetitive delivery of food during DRO could be conceptualized as an antecedent variable; namely, a stimulus complex that controls low rates of behavior problems. The stimulus-based dimension of DRO may be related to the distraction strategy employed in desperation by many clinicians faced with a behavior crisis. One often finds that when an individual suddenly becomes self-injurious, concerned staff begin to offer the individual a variety of toys, foods, and activities as distractions in the hope that engagement with some or all of these events will quickly limit the duration and severity of the self-injurious episode. Perhaps DRO is not so much a reinforcement-based procedure as it is a systematic way of providing discriminative stimuli (distraction) for behavior that will actively compete with the undesired behavior. If so, then the lesson to be learned from DRO and nonsystematic attempts at distraction is that we may be able to deal with crises more effectively by identifying, through functional analysis, those classes of stimuli that are powerfully discriminative for nonproblem behavior. The one thing that all of the stimulus-based interventions that we have discussed (judicious staff selection, reduced crowding, ample exercise, and some instances of DRO) have in common is that they may set the occasion for nonproblem behavior. Ultimately, the treatment of severe behavior problems may benefit just as much from the systematic identification of stimulus classes that control desirable (nonproblem) behavior as from the systematic identification of stimulus classes that control problem behavior (Evans & Meyer, 1985). Until recently, the field has shown little concern for using setting events and antecedent stimuli in this manner (Wahler & Fox, 1981). Even now, we lack an assessment methodology for systematically identifying clinically important classes of stimulus events, relying instead on the fortuitous findings of others. Just as much to the point, we have no coherent theory to guide us in our search for these stimulus classes. This search should be an important scientific priority, especially in view of the demonstrated clinical utility of those few stimulus-based procedures already reported in the literature. We need systematic assessment methodologies and a coherent theory to guide the assessment process so that we may use the results of such an assessment to elaborate treatment strategies that are functionally linked to the controlling variables. In other words, stimulus-based interventions need to be individualized to reflect the results of specific functional analyses.

Maintenance Issues

Thus far, we have suggested that functional stimulus-based procedures can play a role in the short-term treatment of behavior problems, as can functional reinforcement-based procedures. The next question, intimated earlier, concerns whether the same procedures are also relevant to long-term treatment goals, for example, maintenance. In a recent review of the literature dealing with the procedures that we have been discussing, we discovered that only a handful of published studies dealt with the issue of maintenance; however, several of these studies did demonstrate maintenance effects of up to a year (Carr et al., in press). Clearly, this issue deserves more attention than it has received.

Consider stimulus-based interventions. At a conceptual level, one could predict that some of these procedures would typically have to be in effect for indefinite periods in order to generate treatment durability. Hence, any return to crowded conditions, lack of exercise, or inappropriate staff might well trigger a return to baseline levels of behavior problems. Such programmed maintenance is hardly an unreasonable goal, however, in light of the fact that none of us, for instance, would accept inadequate living space, limited exercise, and inappropriate staff for our own nonhandicapped children.

The use of reinforcement-based procedures best exemplifies the promise of functional analysis with respect to the issue of maintenance. Because the skills taught with these procedures serve the same purpose (in lay terms) as the problem behaviors that they are designed to replace and, further, do so more efficiently, one might expect that these skills would be exhibited indefinitely, given a socially responsive environment. One might expect them to produce long-term effects with respect to the elimination of behavior problems since they make the emission of such behavior problems unnecessary for accessing the relevant reinforcers. Interestingly, in spite of the fact that these procedures have not been available until recently, there are already a number of studies documenting long-term treatment effects (Bird, Dores, Moniz, & Robinson, 1989; McConnachie, Levin, Kemp, Carlson, Berotti, & Carr, 1989; Durand & Carr, 1983; Durand & Kishi, 1987). Perhaps these long-term positive outcomes should not be surprising. After all, if an individual can reliably get what he or she wants simply by making requests, then why should that individual ever stop making such requests and revert to the potentially less efficient mode of requesting represented by self-injury and aggression?

FUNCTIONAL VERSUS NONFUNCTIONAL TREATMENT: SUMMARY OF DISTINCTIVE FEATURES

Table 1 summarizes the major differences between functional and nonfunctional approaches to treatment as we have been discussing them. These differences emerge most clearly in answer to four questions that can be posed concerning the nature of treatment.

How Are Treatments Selected?

All functional approaches stress the necessity for selecting treatments based on a knowledge of the variables, both antecedent and consequent, of which behavior is a function. A premium is placed on understanding the nature of behavior, and this understanding derives from systematic functional analysis. In contrast, nonfunctional approaches do not depend on the identification of the variables controlling behavior. That is, they represent pure technology. They are cure-oriented and not understanding-oriented. Implicit in the literature on nonfunctional approaches is a set of selection criteria that emphasize choosing treatments based on behavior topography and\ or general diagnostic category. For example, a given procedure may be selected because previous studies demonstrated that the procedure worked when applied to self-injury (topographical consideration) or to persons with developmental disability (general diagnostic consideration). It is worth emphasizing that nonfunctional treatments can be nonaversive, as well as aversive, in nature. Thus, DRO and electric shock are the same in the sense that the decision to use either one typically does not depend on any prior functional analysis.

When Is The Treatment Implemented?

Functional approaches are proactive. They are implemented, ironically, when no behavior problems are occurring. For example, a reinforcement-based intervention, such as communication training, takes place when the individual is calm and can attend to the acquisition of new skills. Likewise, a setting event intervention, such as that involving an exercise regimen, would take place during a time of day that was convenient and during which the individual was well behaved. In contrast, nonfunctional aversive approaches are reactive. Treatment is implemented only when the individual has

Table 1: Distinctive Features of Functional Versus Nonfunctional Approaches to Treatment

	Functional Treatment		Nonfunctional Treatment
1.	Treatment selection is explicitly based on functional analysis. The focus is on understanding.	1.	Treatment selection is implicitly based on behavior topography and/or general diagnostic category. The focus is on technology.
2.	Treatment is proactive. It takes place when the individual is not engaging in behavior problems.	2.	Aversive treatment is reactive. It takes place when the individual is engaging in behavior problems.
3.	The purpose of treatment is to make desirable responses more probable. The focus is on education and behavior enhancement. Behavior problem reduction is an important side effect.	3.	The purpose of treatment is to make undesirable responses less probable. The focus is on crisis management and behavior control. Behavior problem reduction is the main effect.
4.	Treatment is carried out indefinitely (long-term focus) because the main concern is with maintenance of increases in desirable behavior.	4.	Treatment is carried out for relatively brief periods of time (short-term focus) because the main concern is with crisis management of undesirable behavior.

begun to engage in serious behavior problems. For example, the application of either ammonia pellets or shock would occur only after an individual had started to self-injure or aggress. Quiescent periods would be devoid of these interventions. Interestingly, with respect to the issue of timing of treatment implementation, there is an asymmetry between nonfunctional approaches that are nonaversive as opposed to those that are aversive. Nonaversive approaches are implemented proactively. For example, DRO, once initiated, may continue to occur even during long time periods in which the individual is exhibiting no behavior problems. In this limited sense, nonaversive procedures, whether functional or nonfunctional, are similar.

What Is The Main Purpose Of Treatment?

All functional approaches are focused on making socially desirable responses more probable. Reinforcement-based approaches focus on making desirable responses more probable by arranging for reinforcement to be made contingent on these responses. For example, specific communication skills may be taught or preexisting skills enhanced. Stimulus-based treatments focus on making desirable responses more probable by arranging for stimuli that control nonproblematic behavior to be presented more often or by altering stimuli that control high rates of behavior problems so that they no longer do so but, instead, evoke nonproblematic behavior. For example, certain staff may be discriminative for nonproblem behavior. Therefore, by increasing an individual's exposure to such staff, one may increase the probability of socially desirable responses. Likewise, by altering a difficult curriculum using an errorless teaching paradigm, one is less likely to engender failure and frustration and more likely to evoke constructive academic behavior. In sum, the focus of functional treatment is on education and behavior enhancement. The reduction in behavior problems that occurs following this type of treatment is a side effect, albeit a critical one, of the main treatment goal.

In sharp contrast to what has just been said, all nonfunctional approaches are focused on making undesirable responses less probable. Nonfunctional aversive approaches achieve this effect by arranging for punishing stimuli (e.g., ammonia pellets) to be made contingent on undesirable responses. Nonfunctional nonaversive approaches (e.g., DRO) achieve this affect by arranging for reinforcing stimuli to be made contingent on desirable responses that almost certainly would not be defined as skill acquisition in an educational sense. In sum, the focus of nonfunctional approaches is on crisis management. The goal is not education or behavior enhancement, but rather behavior control, defined in this context as the rapid elimination of undesirable responses.

How Long Should Treatment Be Carried Out?

Because functional approaches are primarily educational in nature, they are intended, for the most part, to be carried out indefinitely. Thus, if an individual has been taught to request tangibles, attention, and assistance as a way of minimizing aggression and self-injury, the intent is to continue to add new communicative skills over time and to support those skills that already have been taught in order to give the individual more and more functional alternatives to behavior problems. This intent also operates, albeit somewhat differently, in the case of stimulus-based procedures. For example, if the introduction of an exercise regimen is found to be an effective treatment, one would probably continue the exercise program indefinitely for health reasons, as well as to enhance the likelihood of continued good behavior. Likewise, if providing less crowded living conditions proved beneficial, one would not return to crowded conditions once the individual's behavior improved. This treatment is not educational (in a skills training sense), but it does act to increase the likelihood of nonproblem behavior and is not meant to be a temporary solution. In sum, functional approaches constitute long-term treatment.

In contrast, because nonfunctional approaches are primarily a form of crisis management, they are intended to be carried out for brief periods of time, or only until the crisis has ended. For example, consider an aversive procedure such as electric shock. There is no intent to continue to use shock indefinitely. Rather, as soon as the individual's behavior is brought under control, shock is discontinued. In all probability, aversive procedures, particularly intrusive ones, would enjoy no popularity at all if it were believed that they had to be used throughout the life of the individual. Nonfunctional nonaversive procedures are also meant to be used briefly, again, for somewhat different reasons than those just discussed. Thus, DRO and DRI both require a great investment of personnel. Staff must be constantly present to monitor the behavior of the individual (DRO and DRI), to time the interval (DRO), and to dispense reinforcement (DRO and DRI). This level of involvement cannot be long sustained due to the personnel and administrative costs involved. In sum, nonfunctional approaches constitute short-term treatment.

A CLOSING PERSPECTIVE

Treatment failure is a bad thing, but being directionless is worse. Functional analysis offers us the possibility of learning from our failures so that we can pursue new directions rationally and systematically. Do we really know all the variables of which severe behavior problems are a function? No, we do not. It is a certainty that we will never know them if we continue to focus our energies on crisis management and debate the merits of aversive versus nonaversive treatment instead of the theoretically and clinically more meaningful issue of functional versus nonfunctional treatment. Ironically, if we devote ourselves to managing crises, then there always will be more crises to manage. Nonfunctional procedures, whether aversive or nonaversive, do not teach the kinds of skills or enhance the classes of responses that are needed to compete successfully with severe behavior problems in the long run. The field needs to look beyond crises in order to deal with crises. Functional treatment looks beyond crises. Functional treatment, the desire to understand, is the core of behaviorism and represents the proudest tradition of our field.

NOTE

Preparation of this chapter was supported in part by Cooperative Agreement #G0087C0234 from the U.S. Department of Education, "A Rehabilitation Research and Training Center on Community-Referenced Technologies for Nonaversive Behavior Management." We thank Rob Horner for his helpful critique.

REFERENCES

Baer, D.M., Wolf, M.M., & Risley, T.R. (1968). Some current dimensions of applied behavior analysis. *Journal of Applied Behavior Analysis, 1*, 91-97.

Bachman, J.A. (1972). Self-injurious behavior: A behavioral analysis. *Journal of Abnormal Psychology, 80*, 211-224.

Bandura, A. (1969). *Principles of behavior modification*. New York: Holt, Rinehart, & Winston.

Barrett, R.P., Feinstein, C., & Hole, W.T. (1989). Effects of naloxone and naltrexone on self-injury: A double-blind, placebo-controlled analysis. *American Journal on Mental Retardation, 93*, 644-651.

Baumeister, A.A., & MacLean, W.E. (1984). Deceleration of self-injurious and stereotypic responding by exercise. *Applied Research in Mental Retardation, 5*, 385-393.

Baumeister, A.A. & Rollings, J.P. (1976). Self-injurious behavior. In N.R.Ellis (Ed.), *International Review of Mental Retardation, Volume 8* (pp. 1-34). New York: Academic Press.

Billingsley, F.F., & Neel, R.S. (1985). Competing behaviors and their effects on skill generalization and maintenance. *Analysis and Intervention in Developmental Disabilities, 5*, 357-372.

Bird, F., Dores, P.A., Moniz, D., & Robinson, J. (1989). Reducing severe aggressive and self-injurious behaviors with functional communication training. *American Journal on Mental Retardation, 94*, 37-48.

Boe, R.B. (1977). Economical procedures for the reduction of aggression in a residential setting. *Mental Retardation, 15, 25-28.*

Carr, E.G. (1977). The motivation of self-injurious behavior: A review of some hypotheses. *Psychological Bulletin, 84*, 800-816.

Carr, E.G. (1985). Behavioral approaches to language and communication. In E. Schopler & G. Mesibov (Eds.), *Current issues in autism: Volume 3. Communication problems in autism* (pp. 37-57). New York: Plenum.

Carr, E.G. (1988). Functional equivalence as a mechanism of response generalization. In R. Horner, R.L. Koegel, & G. Dunlap (Eds.), *Generalization and maintenance: Life-style changes in applied settings* (pp. 194-219). Baltimore: Paul H. Brookes.

Carr, E.G, Binkoff, J.A., Kologinsky, E., & Eddy, M. (1978). Acquisition of sign language by autistic children. I: Expressive labeling. *Journal of Applied Behavior Analysis, 11*, 489-501.

Carr, E.G., & Durand, V.M. (1985a). The social-communicative basis of severe behavior problems in children. In S. Reiss & R. Bootzin (Eds.), *Theoretical issues in behavior therapy* (pp. 219-254). New York: Academic Press.

Carr, E.G., & Durand, V.M. (1985b). Reducing behavior problems through functional communication training. *Journal of Applied Behavior Analysis, 18*, 111-126.

Carr, E.G., & Durand, V.M. (1987, November). See me, help me. *Psychology Today*, pp. 62-64.

Carr, E.G., & Kemp, D.C. (in press). Functional equivalence of autistic leading and communicative pointing: Analysis and treatment. *Journal of Autism and Developmental Disorders*.

Carr, E.G., & Kologinsky, E. (1983). Acquisition of sign language by autistic children: II. Spontaneity and generalization effects. *Journal of Applied Behavior Analysis, 16*, 297-314.

Carr, E.G., & Lindquist, J.C. (1987). Generalization processes in language acquisition. In T.L. Layton (Ed.), *Language and treatment of autistic and developmentally disordered children* (pp. 129-153). Springfield, IL: Charles C. Thomas.

Carr, E.G., & McDowell, J.J. (1980). Social control of self-injurious behavior of organic etiology. *Behavior Therapy, 11*, 402-409.

Carr, E.G., & Newsom, C.D. (1985). Demand-related tantrums: Conceptualization and treatment. *Behavior Modification, 9*, 403-426.

Carr, E.G., Newsom, C.D., & Binkoff, J.A. (1976). Stimulus control of self-destructive behavior in a psychotic child. *Journal of Abnormal Child Psychology, 4*, 139-153.

Carr, E.G., Newsom, C.D., & Binkoff, J.A. (1980). Escape as a factor in the aggressive behavior of two retarded children. *Journal of Applied Behavior Analysis, 13*, 101-117.

Carr, E.G., Taylor, J.C., Carlson, J.I., & Robinson, S. (in press). Reinforcement and stimulus-based treatments for severe behavior problems in developmental disabilities. *Proceedings of the Consensus Conference on the Treatment of Severe Behavior Problems in Developmental Disabilities*. Washington, DC: National Institutes of Health.

Cataldo, M.F. (in press). The effects of punishment and other behavior reducing procedures on the destructive behaviors of persons with developmental disabilities. *Proceedings of the Consensus Conference on the Treatment of Severe Behavior Problems in Developmental Disabilities*. Washington, DC: National Institutes of Health.

Cataldo, M.F., & Harris, J. (1982). The biological basis for self-injury in the mentally retarded. *Analysis and Intervention in Developmental Disabilities, 2*, 21-39.

Deitz, S.M. (1978). Current status of applied behavior analysis: Science versus technology. *American Psychologist, 33*, 805-814.

Demchak, M.A., & Halle, J.W. (1985). Motivational assessment: A potential means of enhancing treatment success of self-injurious individuals. *Education and Training of the Mentally Retarded, 20*, 25-38.

Dura, J.R., Mulick, J.A., & Hammer, D. (1988). Rapid clinical evaluation of sensory integrative therapy for self-injurious behavior. *Mental Retardation, 26*, 83-87.

Durand, V.M., & Carr, E.G. (1983, October). *Differential reinforcement of communicative behavior: Classroom intervention and maintenance*. Paper presented at the meeting of the Berkshire Association for Behavior Analysis and Therapy, Amherst, MA.

Durand, V.M., & Crimmins, D.B. (1988). Identifying the variables maintaining self-injurious behavior. *Journal of Autism and Developmental Disorders, 18*, 99-117.

Durand, V.M., & Kishi, G. (1987). Reducing severe behavior problems among persons with dual sensory impairments: An evaluation of a technical assistance model. *Journal of The Association for Persons with Severe Handicaps, 12*, 2-10.

Dyer, K., Dunlap, G., & Winterling, V. (1989, May). The effects of making choices on the disruptive problem behaviors of students with severe disabilities. In G. Dunlap (Chair), *Community-referenced research on behavior management*. Symposium presented at the meeting of the Association for Behavior Analysis, Milwaukee, WI.

Edelson, S.M., Taubman, M.T., & Lovaas, O.I. (1983). Some social contexts of self-destructive behavior. *Journal of Abnormal Child Psychology, 11*, 299-312.

Epstein, Y.M. (1981). Crowding stress and human behavior. *Journal of Social Issues, 37*, 126-144.

Evans, I.M., & Meyer, L.H. (1985). *An educative approach to behavior problems: A practical decision model for interventions with severely handicapped learners*. Baltimore: Paul H. Brookes.

Favell, J. E., McGimsey, J. F., & Schell, R. M. (1982). Treatment of self-injury by providing alternate sensory activities. *Analysis and Intervention in Developmental Disabilities, 2*, 83-104.

Foxx, R.M. (in press). "Harry": A ten-year follow-up of the successful treatment of a self-injurious man. *Research in Developmental Disabilities*.

Foxx, R.M., Bittle, R.G., & Faw, G.D. (1989). A maintenance strategy for discontinuing aversive procedures: A 52-month follow-up of the treatment of aggression. *American Journal on Mental Retardation, 94*, 27-36.

Frankel, F., & Simmons, J.Q. (1976). Self-injurious behavior in schizophrenic and retarded children. *American Journal of Mental Deficiency, 80*, 512-522.

Ginsberg, H.J., Polman, V.A., Yanson, M.S., & Hope, M.L. (1977). Variation of aggressive interaction among male elementary school children as a function of changes in spatial density. *Environmental Psychology and Non-verbal Behavior, 2*, 67-75.

Groden, G. (1989). A guide for conducting a comprehensive behavioral analysis of a target behavior. *Journal of Behavior Therapy and Experimental Psychiatry, 20*, 163-169.

Guess, D., Benson, H.A., & Siegel-Causey, E. (1985). Concepts and issues related to choice-making and autonomy among persons with severe disabilities. *Journal of The Association for Persons with Severe Handicaps, 10*, 79-86.

Guess, D., Helmstetter, E., Turnbull, H. R., & Knowlton, S. (1987). Use of aversive procedures with persons who are disabled: An historical review and critical analysis. *Monographs of the Association for Persons with Severe Handicaps, 2*(1).

Hawkins, R.P., Peterson, R.F., Schweid, E., & Bijou, S.W. (1966). Amelioration of problem parent-child relations with the parent in a therapeutic role. *Journal of Experimental Child Psychology, 4*, 99-107.

Hayes, S.C., Rincover, A., & Solnick, J.V. (1980). The technical drift of applied behavior analysis. *Journal of Applied Behavior Analysis, 13*, 275-285.

Horner, R.H., & Billingsley, F.F. (1988). The effect of competing behavior on the generalization and maintenance of adaptive behavior in applied settings. In R.H. Horner, R.L. Koegel, & G. Dunlap (Eds.), *Generalization and maintenance: Life-style changes in applied settings* (pp. 197-220). Baltimore: Paul H. Brookes.

Horner, R.H., & Budd, C.M. (1985). Acquisition of manual sign use: Collateral reduction of maladaptive behavior, and factors limiting generalization. *Education and Training of the Mentally Retarded, 20*, 39-47.

Horner, R.H., Dunlap, G., Koegel, R.L., Carr, E.G., Sailor, W., Anderson, J., Albin, R.W., & O'Neill, R.E. (1989). *Toward a technology of "nonaversive" behavioral support*. Manuscript submitted for publication.

Iwata, B.A. (1987). Negative reinforcement in applied behavior analysis: An emerging technology. *Journal of Applied Behavior Analysis, 20*, 361-378.

Iwata, B.A., Dorsey, M.F., Slifer, K.J., Bauman, K.E., & Richman, G.S. (1982). Toward a functional analysis of self-injury. *Analysis and Intervention in Developmental Disabilities, 2*, 3-20.

Kanfer, F.H., & Saslow, G. (1969). Behavioral diagnosis. In C.M.Franks (Ed.), *Behavior therapy: Appraisal and status* (pp. 417-444). New York: McGraw-Hill.

Kern, L., Koegel, R.L., Dyer, K., Blew, P.A., & Fenton, L.R. (1982). The effects of physical exercise on self-stimulation and appropriate responding in autistic children. *Journal of Autism and Developmental Disorders, 12*, 399-419.

Koegel, R.L., Dyer, K., & Bell, L.K. (1987). The influence of child-preferred activities on autistic children's social behavior. *Journal of Applied Behavior Analysis, 20*, 243-252.

Loo, C.M. (1978). Density, crowding, and preschool children. In A. Baum & Y.M. Epstein (Eds.), *Human response to crowding* (pp. 371-388). Hillsdale, NJ: Erlbaum.

Lovaas, O.I., Freitag, G., Gold, V.J., & Kassorla, I.C. (1965). Experimental studies in childhood schizophrenia: Analysis of self-destructive behavior. *Journal of Experimental Child Psychology, 2*, 67-84.

Lovaas, O.I., & Simmons, J.Q. (1969). Manipulation of self-destruction in three retarded children. *Journal of Applied Behavior Analysis, 2*, 143-157.

Lundervold, D., & Bourland, G. (1988). Quantitative analysis of treatment of aggression, self-injury, and property destruction. *Behavior Modification, 12*, 590-617.

Martin, P.L., & Foxx, R.M. (1973). Victim control of the aggression of an institutionalized retardate. *Journal of Behavior Therapy and Experimental Psychiatry, 4*, 161-165.

McAfee, J.K. (1987). Classroom density and the aggressive behavior of handicapped children. *Education and Treatment of Children, 10*, 134-145.

McConnachie, G., Levin, L., Kemp, D., Carlson, J., Berotti, D., & Carr, E.G. (1989, May). Global functional communication training: A nonaversive treatment to reduce severe behavior problems. In G. Dunlap (Chair), *Community-referenced research on behavior management*. Symposium presented at the meeting of the Association for Behavior Analysis, Milwaukee, WI.

O'Neill, R.E., Horner, R.H., Albin, R.W., Storey, K., & Sprague, J.R. (1989). *Functional analysis: A practical assessment guide*. Unpublished manuscript, University of Oregon, Eugene, OR.

Patterson, G.R., Littman, R.A., & Bricker, W. (1967). Assertive behavior in children: A step toward a theory of aggression. *Monographs of the Society for Research in Child Development, 32* (5, Whole No. 113).

Plummer, S., Baer, D.M., & LeBlanc, J.M. (1977). Functional considerations in the use of procedural timeout and an effective alternative. *Journal of Applied Behavior Analysis, 10*, 689-706.

Repp, A.C., Felce, D., & Barton, L.E. (1988). Basing the treatment of stereotypic and self-injurious behaviors on hypotheses of their causes. *Journal of Applied Behavior Analysis, 21*, 281-289.

Rincover, A., & Devany, J. (1982). The application of sensory extinction procedures to self-injury. *Analysis and Intervention in Developmental Disabilities, 2*, 67-81.

Rojahn, J., Mulick, J.A., McCoy, D.E., & Schroeder, S.R. (1978). Setting events, adaptive clothing, and the modification of head banging and self-restraint in two profoundly retarded adults. *Behavioral Analysis and Modification, 2*, 185-196.

Romanczyk, R.G., Gordon, W.C., Crimmins, D.B., Wenzel, A.M., & Kistner, J.A. (1980). Childhood psychosis and 24-hour rhythms: A behavioral and psychophysiological analysis. *Chronobiologia, 7*, 17-24.

Sailor, W., Guess, D., Rutherford, G., & Baer, D.M. (1968). Control of tantrum behavior by operant techniques during experimental verbal training. *Journal of Applied Behavior Analysis, 1*, 237-243.

Sandman, C.A., Datta, P.C., Barron, J., Hoehler, F.K., Williams, C., & Swanson, J.M. (1983). Naloxone attenuates self-abusive behavior in developmentally disabled clients. *Applied Research in Mental Retardation, 4*, 5-11.

Schroeder, S.R., Rojahn, J., Mulick, J.A., & Schroeder, C.S. (in press). Self-injurious behavior: An analysis of behavior management techniques. In J.L. Matson & J.R. McCartney (Eds.), *Handbook of behavior modification with the mentally retarded* (2nd ed.). New York: Plenum.

Skinner, B. F. (1953). *Science and human behavior*. New York: The Free Press.

Skinner, B. F. (1959). Current trends in experimental psychology. In B. F. Skinner, *Cumulative record* (pp. 223-241). New York: Appleton-Century-Crofts.

Sulzer-Azaroff, B., & Mayer, G. R. (1977). *Applying behavior analysis procedures with children and youth*. New York: Holt, Rinehart, & Winston.

Thompson, T., Hackenburg, T., & Schaal, D. (in press). Pharmacological treatments for behavior problems in developmental disabilities. *Proceedings of the Consensus Conference on the Treatment of Severe Behavior Problems and Developmental Disabilities*. Washington, DC: National Institutes of Health.

Touchette, P. E., MacDonald, R. F., & Langer, S. N. (1985). A scatter plot for identifying stimulus control of problem behavior. *Journal of Applied Behavior Analysis, 18*, 343-351.

Ullmann, L. P., & Krasner, L. (Eds.). (1965). *Case studies in behavior modification*. New York: Holt, Rinehart, & Winston.

Wacker, D., Steege, M., Berg, W., Reimers, T., Sasso, G., Northup, J., & Hays, B. (1989, May). *A further evaluation of DRC: Communication response or schedule of reinforcement*. Poster presented at the meeting of the Association for Behavior Analysis, Milwaukee, WI.

Wahler, R. G. (1969). Oppositional children: A quest for parental reinforcement control. *Journal of Applied Behavior Analysis, 2*, 159-170.

Wahler, R. G., & Fox, J. J. (1981). Setting events in applied behavior analysis: Toward a conceptual and methodological expansion. *Journal of Applied Behavior Analysis, 14*, 327-338.

Weeks, M., & Gaylord-Ross, R. (1981). Task difficulty and aberrant behavior in severely handicapped students. *Journal of Applied Behavior Analysis, 14*, 449-463.

Winterling, V., Dunlap, G., & O'Neill, R. E. (1987). The influence of task variation on the aberrant behaviors of autistic students. *Education and Treatment of Children, 10*, 105-119.

Wolf, M. M., Birnbrauer, J. S., Williams, T., & Lawler, J. (1965). A note on apparent extinction of the vomiting behavior of a retarded child. In L. Ullman & L. Krasner (Eds.), *Case studies in behavior modification* (pp. 364-366). New York: Holt, Rinehart, & Winston.

CHAPTER

25

DIAGNOSING SEVERE BEHAVIOR PROBLEMS

David A.M. Pyles and Jon S. Bailey
Behavior Management Consultants, Inc. and Florida State University

As applied behavior analysts, we are confronted daily with clients engaging in physical aggression, verbal aggression, self-injury, property destruction, and disruption of the environment. Most often, systematic behavior programming is required to reduce the frequencies of these behaviors so that the clients eventually may be placed in less restrictive settings.

Traditionally, the approach to reducing these undesired responses has been the application of reinforcement and punishment contingencies to increase the frequencies of more appropriate behaviors and reduce the rates of inappropriate behaviors. Early on, researchers discovered that dramatic changes could be achieved through contingency management by applying consequences without regard to the function that the behavior served. Critics who argued that behavior change would be transient if the underlying causes of the behavior were not addressed were dismissed or ignored by behaviorists.

FUNCTION VERSUS TOPOGRAPHY OF BEHAVIOR

Historically, the causes of maladaptive behaviors were ignored or assumed to be unimportant, having occurred too remote in the client's past to be of current use. As long as a treatment was successful in affecting the rates of the targeted behaviors, it was considered successful. The sole focus was the *topography* of the behavior; i.e., the physical characteristics of the response, rather than its *function*, or the variables controlling the response.

The topography of a response is what makes a behavior appropriate or inappropriate. Examples of topography include a client's verbalizations, head banging or aggression. As such, a measure of the topography (such as rate, frequency, duration or percentage of intervals) is typically the dependent variable when a behavior is targeted for acquisition or reduction. The operational definition of a behavior, used to determine whether a behavior has or has not occurred, is a description of its topography.

The *function* of the behavior, on the other hand, is comprised of the antecedent and consequence variables occurring in relation to a response. Function determines whether a response will occur, as well as its probability. The function that a behavior serves also determines which specific treatment programs should be designed to eliminate the problematic behaviors. It is possible to eliminate problematic topographies through the use of aversive stimulation, such as electric shock, contingent upon head banging. However, if the head banging occurs because the client has a communication deficit (e.g., not being able to signal that attention is wanted), electric shock would not be the ethical treatment of choice.

The early concentration on topography rather than function is somewhat surprising, considering the field's emphasis on the importance of *functional* variables related to a behavior. According to Skinner's terminology, the field was training behavior*alists*, rather than behavior*ists*--people who emphasize the topography over the function of the response (Skinner, 1969).

Recently, research has shown that behaviors of similar topographies can be controlled by very different environmental stimuli (Carr & Durand, 1985; Iwata, Dorsey, Slifer, Bauman, & Richman, 1982; Repp, Felce, & Barton, 1988). Carr and Durand (1985) and Repp et al. (1988) demonstrated that addressing the wrong function can lead to ineffective treatment. The recent focus on the variables controlling a behavior for designing interventions is certainly a step forward for the field, and it can only lead to more efficient and ethical treatment of clients.

Concentrating only on either function *or* topography does not seem reasonable, however. Behavior does not occur in a vacuum. A response cannot occur without controlling variables, and controlling variables without a response are not useful for explaining behavior. Rather, a given act is a combination of topography *and* function. As such, they are inseparable. There may be a spatial or temporal delay between a behavior and its controlling variables, making control difficult to determine, but one cannot occur without the other.

What is more difficult to determine is how the function of a response leads to its specific topography. A related issue is how other functions can take control of the same topography of the behavior at a later time. One possibility is that initially a behavior is under the control of a given set of stimuli, and through adventitious pairing later with other stimuli, the behavior becomes an operant controlled by a second set of stimulus conditions. For example, an infant could experience some sort of discomfort, such as a wet diaper, and begin to cry, tantrum, and slap his face lightly. These behaviors may prompt the attention of his parent, who then changes the diaper. If the parent is not especially attentive to the child when he is wet again, the crying and face slapping may escalate and become more severe until he hits himself very hard to get the same message to the parents: "I'm wet!" Eventually, the child may become toilet trained, but the head hitting may continue, controlled by a new reinforcer: attention.

Initially, controlling variables of behavior were considered external environmental events, with the consequences of the behavior considered most important in determining whether a behavior would recur. Recently, however, we have begun to learn that antecedent events play a much larger role in the control of behavior than previously thought. We have observed maladaptive behaviors occurring as a function of illness, weight-reduction diets, premenstrual syndrome, and side effects or toxic levels of medications. As such, with the advent of Behavioral Diagnostics (Bailey & Pyles, 1989; Pyles & Bailey, in press), more attention is being paid to antecedent conditions than ever before.

IMMEDIATE TREATMENT VERSUS UNDERSTANDING BEHAVIOR

When encountering clients engaging in severely problematic behaviors such as aggression or self injury, applied behavior analysts face a unique predicament. Do we act immediately to gain control of the situation, or do we wait to intervene while gathering data essential for proper, ethical treatment? Can we do both simultaneously?

Determining the causal variables for maladaptive responding can be a lengthy, time-consuming process. Conducting a functional analysis, searching for medical causes of the behavior, or performing other types of behavioral diagnoses can take days, weeks, or even months. Designing programs without regard to these variables, however, can lead to ineffective or unethical treatment for the client engaging in these responses. At the same time, we cannot allow clients or staff to become injured because staff do not have a means of controlling the aberrant behaviors.

One guideline we can provide involves preventing a client from engaging in behavior endangering himself, others, or property. Many facilities have emergency procedures designed to provide staff with a means of addressing severe, unexpected behavioral events. These emergency procedures usually progress in an hierarchy ranging from separating the client from others to mechanical and chemical restraints.

One means of resolving the conflict between providing immediate treatment versus understanding the causes is to carry out emergency procedures that prevent injury or damage while searching for the causal variables. The Federal Habilitation Facilities (formerly known as ICF/MR--Intermediate Care Facilities/Mental Retardation) Guidelines and the regulations of some states require documentation demonstrating that the behavioral event could not have been predicted. Furthermore, in some states, there are strict limits on the number of times a month or year an emergency procedure can be used without implementation of a formal reduction program. While using the emergency procedure, we can collect baseline and diagnostic data for formal programming. The treatment program may entail contingencies used in the emergency procedures; in addition, the program should address the behavior's function (e.g., teaching a client to comply with requests to reduce escape-related self-injurious behavior).

Another approach to resolving the conflict between immediate treatment versus understanding the problem is to begin taking baseline data immediately and then to implement procedures described in the research literature. This approach differentiates behavior modification from behavior analysis. Behavior modification is a "cookbook" approach to addressing maladaptive behaviors, and it is not recommended in lieu of careful diagnosis of the problem and resulting differential treatment based on that analysis.

Is Behavioral Treatment Necessary?

Sometimes, a behavioral treatment is *not* the answer for addressing behavior problems. For example, if a mother wanted to reduce her baby's crying, that behavior could be put on extinction, and the baby could be reinforced with a bottle or attention when quiet. However, most parents would opt for a more commonsense approach: Discover why the child is crying and base the intervention on the cause of the behavior--if the baby was wet, the diaper would be changed; if hungry, the baby would be fed. Using a behavioral intervention such as extinction to reduce a baby's crying in this situation probably would be ineffective, is clearly negligent, and could permanently affect the relationship between parent and child.

One question that should be asked before designing behavioral interventions is this: What would happen if the behavior were left untreated? Often, when clients are placed in new settings, they engage in maladaptive behaviors. Many individuals who are mentally retarded do not adjust well to changes in their routines, and they respond by aggressing or attempting to escape the situation. Often, these problems take care of themselves and do not require aggressive behavioral intervention. We still may collect baseline and diagnostic data in the event that the problem does not resolve itself; we may also train the client to adapt to new situations without incident. However, some problems are transitory and do not require such an expenditure of resources.

A second and related question is: Do we need to be more tolerant? If a client engages in an annoying behavior (such as odd vocalizations) that does not result in injury to persons or property, and does not interfere with training or disrupt the environment, an alternative to active intervention may be to teach staff to ignore the behavior and to be more tolerant. Everyone has his own idiosyncrasies which are tolerated by the general public without censure.

Many stereotypic behaviors fall into this category. There is an extensive research literature detailing procedures that decrease the rates of these behaviors. However, once the contingencies are no longer in effect, the stereotypies recur. Providing a more appropriate topographical form of the behavior, while allowing the client to receive the same stimulation, is often the best means of addressing these responses. For example, rather than attempting to reduce a client's body rocking, perhaps placing him or her in a rocking chair would be a more suitable approach.

In general, behavioral intervention is probably *not* indicated if the behavior is a function of placement in a new environment, signals a medical or physiological condition, does not result in injury to others or damage to property, does not disrupt the environment, or does not interfere with educational programming.

Active And Passive Behavior Management

Historically, behavioral procedures have focused on the manipulation of consequences to effect behavior change, minimizing the role of antecedent stimuli. However, in the past 6 years, we have encountered a number of clients whose inappropriate behaviors functioned to escape antecedent aversive stimuli, such as requests made of them, diet restrictions, etc. We have found it necessary to differentiate between behaviors controlled by consequences (e.g., attention) and those occurring in relation to antecedent aversive stimulation (e.g., escape due to pain). An important implication of this differentiation is that different treatment strategies are indicated for each situation.

For behaviors controlled by consequent stimuli, operant intervention, or *Active Behavior Management,* is indicated (Bailey & Pyles, 1989; Pyles & Bailey, in press). Active behavior management involves acting upon the inappropriate behavior *directly* by manipulating consequences to effect a change in its rates. Procedures like differential reinforcement, response cost, and time-out are all forms of active behavior management used in the literature to address maladaptive behaviors.

A different approach is required for behaviors *not* controlled by consequences. For those behaviors occurring due to antecedent variables, removing the aversive antecedent stimulus, *Passive Behavior Management*, is preferred (Bailey & Pyles, 1989; Pyles & Bailey, in press). The typical approach used is to relieve the client's discomfort, interrupt antecedent chains leading to the terminal maladaptive behavior, adjust medication dosages, etc.

Pyles and Bailey (in press) described a client who jumped out of his wheelchair, resulting in bumps and bruises on his head. Observation of the client indicated that whenever he jumped out of the chair, staff gave him attention for the behavior. A typical active behavior management approach would be to train the staff to ignore his jumping behavior and provide reinforcement for sitting calmly in his chair. But, when we asked, "*Why* is this client jumping out of his wheelchair?", we discovered it was due to his sitting in the chair for extended periods of time. The indicated approach was to take him out of the wheelchair when he got home from school and place him on a mat or a couch-a passive behavior management solution. This intervention decreased his jumping out of the wheelchair to zero; he made no other attempts to hurt himself in any way, and appeared relieved to be out of the chair. In the example of the crying baby discussed earlier, extinction would be an example of an active behavior management approach to the problem; feeding the baby or changing the baby's diaper would be an example of a passive behavior management approach.

THE DECISION MAKING PROCESS

Many professionals agree that treatment of severe behavior problems should be based on the wealth of applied behavior analysis research conducted over the past 25 years. Without a research basis for implementing a procedure, therapists run the risk of using ineffective and possibly harmful treatments. The research conducted to date has not been carried out in any systematic or coordinated fashion. Thus, the behavior analyst confronted with a severe behavior problem must consult a myriad of texts and journals to determine possible treatments. The field is so new that often only one study may be found for any given treatment, and close examination of that experiment often reveals a narrow range of applicability. Any given study is usually carried out with only one target behavior and with one carefully selected subject population. The behavior analyst is then required to extrapolate from this study to address the presenting client problem. Rarely do the target behavior and subject match exactly with the problem at hand, so considerable judgment must be exercised. Limiting conditions of the research are often overlooked (Pyles & Bailey, in press). Under pressure, and in an effort to produce rapid behavior change, therapists may use procedures that are totally inappropriate for the client and behavior under consideration. Results may range from simple ineffectiveness to physical harm.

There is no guiding behavioral theory to suggest which treatment, from among the dozens available, should be used in any given set of circumstances. The Association for Behavior Analysis International recently issued a position statement on clients' right-to-treatment issues (Van Houten, Axelrod, Bailey, Favell, Foxx, Iwata, and Lovaas, (1988) which may lead to generally adopted guidelines. Alarmed at the misuse of behavioral procedures (particularly aversive treatments), advocates have demanded guidelines to prevent abuse. Guidelines for the use of behavioral procedures in Federal Habilitation Facilities currently exist, and many states have enacted their own guidelines (e.g., California, Georgia, Florida).

The Least Restrictive Model

Presently, most agree that the "least restrictive model" is appropriate (Mori & Masters, 1980) for the treatment (and protection) of retarded persons. As shown in Figure 1, this model seeks to

Level I

° Ignoring specific behaviors
° Counterconditioning

Level II

° Satiation
° Desensitization
° Response cost
° Nonisolated time-out
° Limited time-out
° Overcorrection
° Positive practice

Level III

° Punishers--loud noise, sour tastes, blowing air in the face, squirting a water mist in the face
° Isolated time-out
° Electric shock
° Chemical intervention
° Physical and equipment restraints

Source: Mori & Masters (1980)

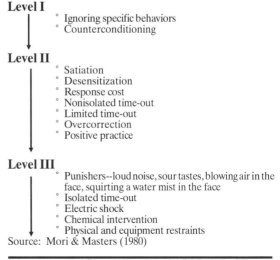

Figure 1: The "Least Restrictive" Model of Treatment

prevent the use of severe aversive consequences (e.g., electric shock) by requiring practioners to try less "restrictive" (more appropriately, less *aversive*) procedures. Many states have adopted this conceptual model, and have elaborated upon and institutionalized the levels implying sound moral or scientific grounds for determining which treatment is appropriate for a client. [Georgia has just released its "Behavior analysis and programming guidelines" (Gates & Kimber,1990), categorizing 35 procedures into four levels of restrictiveness.] Such a strategy presumably prevents therapists, teachers, parents, or behavior analysts from needlessly using aversive consequences where less aversive procedures would work as well.

Unfortunately, there are serious drawbacks in this formulation. First, there is no empirical foundation for placing procedures at the various levels. There is no basis, for example, for the determination that satiation is more restrictive or aversive than extinction. Electric shock can be extremely aversive, but it is certainly *less restrictive* than overcorrection or limited time-out. Second, there is an assumption that this hierarchy can be applied similarly to given individual clients. Research has shown, however, that time-out is usually reinforcing for an autistic child, although it is considered a Level III procedure. Third, if the procedures are ranked in degree of aversiveness, clients could be desensitized at each level to tolerate even more aversive stimuli. We may be programming our clients to require more and more aversive consequences to manage their behavior. Fourth, the use of a least restrictive hierarchy suggests that any given behavior problem should be approached using this method; i.e., start by ignoring the target behavior and reinforcing (counterconditioning) the opposite behavior. Totally disregarded is the *cause* or the *function* of the behavior. Finally, the least restrictive model was not developed by behavior analysts out of a need to determine the *most appropriate treatment,* but rather by advocates wishing to reduce the possibility of client abuse. There is clearly a need for a model of treatment that will guide practice decisions and retain some integrity with general principles of behavior.

The least restrictive model appears, at best, to be more of an administrative and regulatory convenience than a therapeutic tool. Behavioral procedures can be regulated simply by requiring all therapists to start with Level I and proceed to more restrictive or aversive levels if success is not achieved. Some states (Georgia and Florida) require permission and oversight to advance from one level to another (in an attempt to prevent abuse).

An Alternative To The Least Restrictive Model

We believe that Behavioral Diagnostics (Bailey & Pyles, 1989; Pyles & Bailey, in press) presents a viable alternative to the Least Restrictive model. As shown in Figure 2, this is a five-step process that is

Step 1: Diagnose the problem
- ° BEHAVIORAL DIAGNOSTIC Questions asked
- ° Direct observation of client in environment
- ° Examination of client for physical "causes" of behavior problems

Step 2: Develop the plan based on diagnosis
- ° PASSIVE BEHAVIOR MANAGEMENT if appropriate (consider limiting conditions)
- ° ACTIVE BEHAVIOR MANAGEMENT if appropriate (consider limiting conditions)

Step 3: Test the plan under controlled conditions
- ° Run Special Sessions--well controlled
- ° Make environmental changes

Step 4: Evaluate results
- ° Measure target behavior
- ° Measure related behaviors

Step 5: Put program in place
- ° Inservice staff
- ° Expand staff & settings
- ° Continue controlled observations

Figure 2: An alternative to the "Least Restrictive" model, Behavioral Diagnostics

compatible with behavior analysis practice and research procedures.

Step 1. Central to this approach is the notion that we must discover what causes the behavior to occur or determine the function that the behavior serves for the client in the environment. This analysis is best done through three distinct procedures. First, diagnostic questions are asked of staff and professionals to determine factors in the environment that may set the occasion for the behavior. Does the behavior occur at certain times of the day? Does it occur only with certain people? Is it more likely to happen when the client is in a demand or training situation? Next, direct observation of the client in the environment where the behavior problem occurs is carried out. Probe sessions may be implemented where the environment is changed under controlled conditions to determine, for example, the effects of eliminating demands, reducing the noise level, or allowing the client to eat more at mealtime. Third, possible physical causes for the behavior are given thorough examination by nursing, nutrition, dental, and medical personnel. We have discovered numerous cases of self-injury, destruction, and aggression related to food deprivaton, premenstrual syndrome, and medication side effects. In each case, we were assured initially that the clients had had recent physicals and that no known organic cause of the problem could be found. These discoveries were made only through careful, direct observation, extensive data collection, and intensive interactions with medical personnel. This slow, painstaking process of eliminating alternative explanations is in contrast to the more common dramatic interven-tion,s employed in behavior modification studies (Dorsey, Iwata, Ong, & McSween, 1980; Epstein, Doke, Sajwaj, Sorrell, & Rimmer, 1974; Foxx & Azrin, 1973; Lovaas & Simmons, 1969).

Step 2. This step is common to most standard behavioral programming, except that an emphasis is placed on employing Passive Behavior Management strategies where possible. A client who stripped and destroyed her clothes was given an opportunity to choose from her closet the clothes she would like to wear that day. A client who stole food and was aggressive at mealtime was given double portions of food. A client who was disruptive, aggresive, and self-injurious at shift-change was taken for a walk each day just prior to shift change. These interventions have in common the manipulation of behavior by changing the *antecedents* to the behavior. They are not only easier to implement since staff do not have to react differentially to client behavior, but they also appear more humane. The client who stole food had been placed on a diet by the nutritionist and was clearly hungry. Punishment for stealing food would be, in our opinion, be unethical. In those cases where contingency management is clearly the appropriate treatment, Active Behavior Management (standard behavior modification) is employed. Our experience has been that getting staff to carry out contingency-based treatments correctly and consistently is difficult. Reinforcement errors (e.g., delivering the reinforcer *before* the behavior) abound, and punishment errors (e.g., not punishing every time) occur with alarming frequency.

Step 3. In this step, we test the treatment plan under controlled conditions. Before expecting the staff to carry out the treatment, try it yourself. This case is particularly important with Active Behavior Management. Short sessions of an hour or less, carried out by a qualified person, will help determine the feasibility of treatment.

Step 4. The next step involves evaluating the results. Data collected should not only include the target behavior, but also other related or collateral behaviors. Aggression may be reduced, but self-stimulation or destruction may increase.

Step 5. If treatment is successful, we can train other staff and expand the length of the session. Not every treatment plan, particularly Active Behavior Management strategies, can be carried out all day long by regular direct care staff. As treatment is expanded from 2 to 4 hours per day, it should be monitored closely to determine if it is still effective.

Functional Categories Of Behavior

Ideally, behavioral treatment would be tailored for each individual client. Since there are vast individual differences from one client to the next (different degrees of retardation, different histories of reinforcement), and since clients experience widely different environments, treating behaviors categorically (e.g., "use time-out for aggression, use response cost for stealing, use DRO for self-stimulation") is clearly fraught with problems. An analysis of the recent treatment literature (Carr & Durand, 1985; Durand & Carr, 1987; Iwata, Dorsey, Slifer, Bauman, & Richman, 1982; Lewis, Baumeister, & Mailman, 1987; Lovaas, Newsom, & Hickman, 1987; Repp, Felce, & Barton, 1988; Touchette, MacDonald, & Langer, 1985) and our own clinicial case studies suggest the seven functional categories of behavior, as shown in Figure 3. Within each type of behavior, the therapist must determine what is to be done to treat the target behavior, to increase alternative behaviors, and to train the staff or change the environment. We will discuss each category briefly.

SELF-STIMULATION. Hand mouthing, hand flapping, repetitive vocalizations, and so on are examples of behaviors that are most likely maintained by the naturally occurring sensory stimulation that they produce. Origins of these behaviors may be developmental (e.g., head banging), due to sensory deficiencies (e.g., head weaving in blind clients), or due to environmental deprivation in the past or present. We should test for escape-related behaviors here since some clients may have a history of being excused from training if they exhibited unusual behaviors. Other medical and physiological factors also must be ruled out (e.g., certain medications can produce tinnitus and result in ear poking which may appear to be a self-stimulation behavior; seizures can cause head banging, etc.). Of course, we also must show that the client is not reinforced for the behavior when alone.

Once the behavior has been shown to be related to sensory stimulation, a variety of procedures may be appropriate. Preventing the sensory reinforcer (sensory extinction), combined with teaching an alternative, acceptable method of achieving the stimulation, is the most common strategy. Clients exhibiting self-stimulatory behaviors appear to have a "need" (a state of deprivation in behavioral terms) for certain types of sensory input. Therapists should focus on acceptable means of providing this stimulation rather than simply eliminating the behavior. Punishing a client who hums loudly or vocalizes continually is inappropriate; teaching the client to use a radio or Walkman for auditory stimulation is more likely to succeed and is ethically appropriate.

We have a client (blind, deaf, nonambulatory, profoundly mentally retarded) who had his hand in his mouth about 80% of the observed intervals. Combined with his occasional biting, this behavior presents a formidable treatment problem as he constantly had skin infections. All attempts to reduce the hand mouthing through DRO and mild contingent aversive stimuli failed. Recently we discovered that applying petroleum jelly to his hands several times each day caused the skin to heal and reduced hand mouthing to about 30%. While he still is labeled a "hand mouther" by the staff, he is now out of the protective gloves that he wore for almost 2 years.

We discourage the use of punishment except as a last resort in cases where tissue

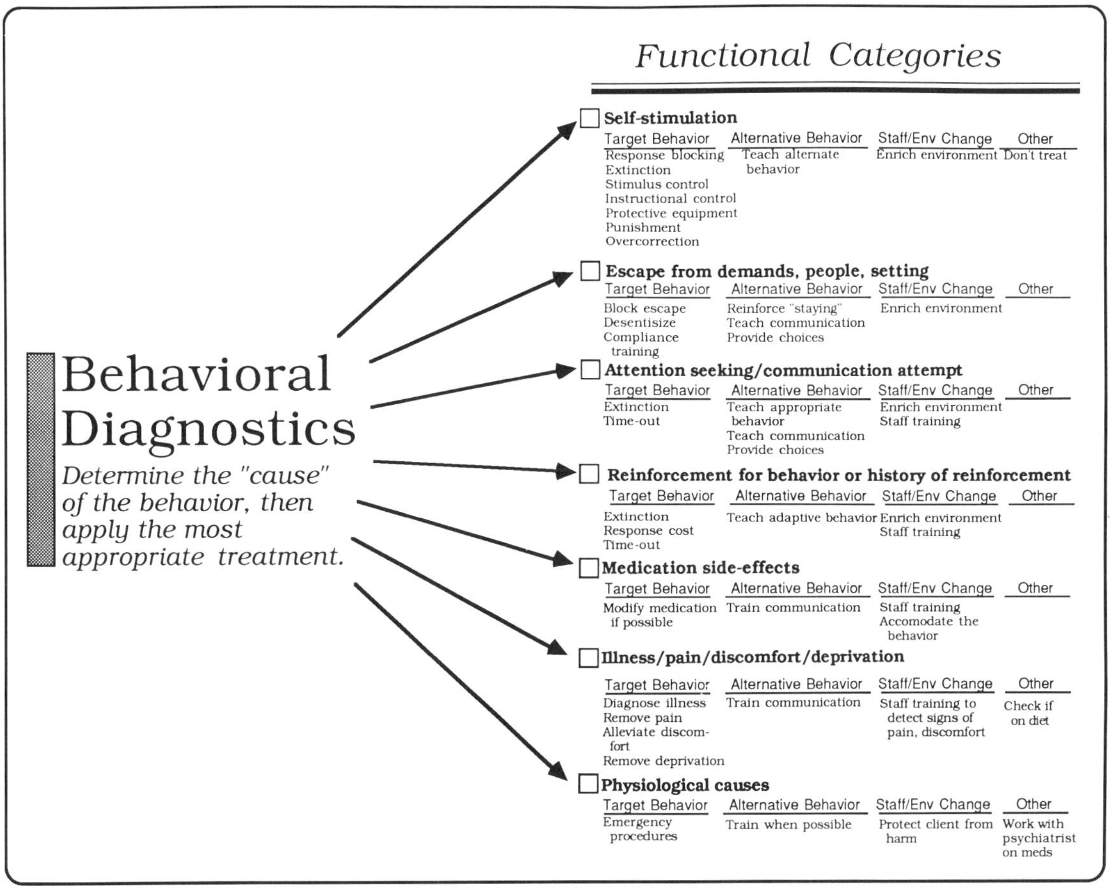

Figure 3: Functional categories of behavior according to the Behavioral Diagnostic Model

damage is involved. Clients may be entitled to engage in behaviors, despite the fact that they may annoy others. Improving the living environment by adding stimulting devices (e.g., response-operated radios, TVs, fans, light boxes, etc.) gives clients an opportunity to engage in appropriate forms of stimulation, and also reinforces operant responding which may be useful at other times. If there is no tissue damage resulting from the self-stimulation, consider simply not treating.

ESCAPE FROM DEMANDS, PEOPLE, OR SETTINGS. This behavior is fairly easy to determine since it occurs under specific stimulus control conditions. Often, staff will report, "He does it every time I ask him to sit down." The most direct solution (although unpopular with many staff) is simply to stop making the specific request. Then, the problematic request, or an approximation to it, can be introduced gradually under circumstances where compliance can be assured and reinforcement given immediately. In some circumstances, escape must be treated by blocking the response to prevent the reinforcement.

A client who refused to ride the school bus was placed on the bus in a wheelchair to prevent her from escaping. Reinforcement was given for riding on the bus, and the wheelchair was eventually faded. A client, who hit his trainer whenever hand-over-hand guidance was provided, was treated with desensitization. The trainer would stand behind the client, touch him, and lightly rub him on the shoulders. Over time, this procedure was extended to putting his hand on his upper arm, and then his lower arm, and then his hand. After several weeks of this gradual desensitization to touch, the client tolerated the hand-over-hand guidance. Some aggressive behavior is a way of saying, "I don't want to do this," and research has shown (Carr & Durand, 1985) that teaching a communication skill to replace the escape response is effective in these cases.

ATTENTION SEEKING/COMMUNICATION ATTEMPT. Some clients have a considerable "need" for staff attention and will do anything to get it. In poorly staffed environments, this situation can become a serious problem. The easiest solution, and perhaps the most appropriate, is to find other sources of social contact for the client. Volunteers may be recruited to spend time with the client, or the client may be placed in community activity groups, or in supported employment jobs with significant customer contact (Park & Gaylord-Ross, 1989).

One client banged his chest loudly and often, and was referred for self-injurious behavior. Staff reported that he did it to get attention. "He just wants us to take him to the bathroom," was their explanation. Two options present themselves in this case. The client could be trained to take himself to the bathroom, or he could be trained to signal his need in some more appropriate manner. In addition, staff had to block, ignore, and extinguish the inappropriate behavior that was intermittently reinforced by taking him to the bathroom only after he had banged his chest for a lengthy period. In some cases, attention-seeking can be reduced by enriching the environment, taking the client out of the facility often for field trips, or simply changing activities often.

REINFORCEMENT HISTORY. Some behavior problems result directly from the outcomes that they produce. One client, for example, searched the nurses' purses for gum or candy. Another was aggressive around staff and usually got his way. Most of the traditional behavior modification procedures are relevant for such cases. The target behavior must be stopped, and extinction, along with response cost or some other form of punishment (a consequence which will decrease the behavior), may need to be applied. In addition, if an appropriate alternative behavior can be found (e.g., asking for candy, working for gum), a program to teach the behavior and maintain it with the known reinforcer should be established. Care must be taken not to confuse this category with some deprivation or a medication side effect. A client who frequently ran from the classroom and down the hall was found to be drinking copiously from the drinking fountain because he was thirsty from his medication. Punishing this behavior clearly would be inappropriate.

MEDICATION SIDE EFFECTS. This category is often determined by ruling out the other categories. After an examination of the client's medication history reveals the behavior to be unrelated to the presence of staff or clients, or to occur at regular intervals (e.g., 2 hours after ingesting the medication), or to be a suggested side effect in the Physicians' Desk Reference, you may wish to consult with nurses or the facility physician. Nurses are often so busy dispensing medications that they have little time to spend with direct care staff who may observe symptoms. Furthermore, the staff who spend the most time with clients may have *no* training or instructions to identify side effects. The effects that we see most often are noncompliance or "spacy" behavior.

Occasionally, thirst-driven behavior also is observed. Some of the psychotropic medications appear to make clients hungry, causing them to take or steal food, or to become aggressive around mealtime.

Imposing a behavior program to reduce the problem appears to be adding insult to injury. Seizure medications can increase the likelihood of noncompliance since they make some clients feel nauseous. In this condition, they may not want to get up in the morning, may lose their appetite, or may prefer to stay in bed rather than participate in therapeutic activities. The behavior analyst can serve an important role in these cases by documenting the behavior changes resulting from medication changes and then presenting them to the nurse and physician for review.

In many cases, either alternative versions of the drugs can be found that do not have the side effects, or the medications can be scheduled at different times of the day to produce different effects. One client who began having many sleepless nights had his medication time changed so that it was administered at dinner rather than at bedtime. He had been referred for behavior programming because he was causing problems during the day; i.e., he was noncompliant and became aggressive. Within a few days of the change, he began sleeping at night and the daytime problems disappeared.

ILLNESS/PAIN/DISCOMFORT/DEPRIVATION. Our clients who are mentally retarded suffer from the same illnesses, pain, and discomfort as the rest of us. Unfortunately for them, they do not always have the means of correcting these problems. Lack of communication skills may prevent them from telling us that they are having menstrual cramps, a headache, or low back pain. Those who are also nonambulatory are literally unable to escape aversive situations. Such clients who exhibit severe behavior problems become prime candidates for "behavior modification." In an effort to make dramatic changes in behavior, the therapist may overlook one of the major causes. Ill-fitting shoes caused aggression in one client who refused to keep them on and, each day, fought the staff who tried to make the client keep them on. Another client cried and sobbed the majority of the day, and was placed in time-out. An analysis that extended over several months revealed that she was hungry, thirsty, wet, fatigued, and suffered from PMS. Her "behavior modification" program was dropped and replaced with a daily care routine that emphasized offering her something to eat and drink on regular intervals, checking her clothing frequently for urination, and offering her morning and afternoon naps. As each element was put in place, the crying and sobbing occurred less and less. She eventually graduated from our case management review when none of the maladaptive behaviors occurred for a 3-month period.

Finally, we have discovered a consistent relationship between dietary changes and disruptive, aggressive and noncompliant behavior. The sedentary life-styles of most clients predispose them to gain weight, which prompts nutritionists (perhaps in response to misguided federal guidelines) to put them on reduced-calorie diets. Within a month of such dietary management practices, these clients may be referred to behavioral staff for treatment of emerging behavior disorders. We now routinely inquire whether any given client who is referred is on a diet and, if so, attempt to reverse it prior to behavioral intervention. If placing the client back on the original diet reverses the behavior problem, we then demur from developing any further treatment, arguing that our place is not to solve problems caused by another professional. We believe clients are entitled to enough food to keep them from being hungry and enough exercise to keep them healthy.

We have participated in several behavior programs that involve reinforcing clients for active involvement in daily exercise routines.

PHYSIOLOGICAL CAUSES. Complex biological and physiological factors unrelated to the environment play a role in some severe behavior problems. One client went through cycles of deep depression, alternating with manic periods. For weeks at a time, she would not speak or make eye contact with anyone, and she would stand motionless for up to an hour, apparently oblivious to those around her. Then, after a 2-or 3-day transition period, she would begin pacing rapidly back and forth, approaching staff and grabbing them by the arm. She would speak in full sentences and, at these times, would read magazines aloud. We have charted these cycles over the past 2 years, and are working with the facility psychiatrist to evaluate appropriate medications. Another client who was elderly posed similar problems. For a few weeks, she would refuse food, strip off her clothes, race down the halls, and would not sleep or tolerate training. Then, suddenly, she would initiate social contact, adopt normal eating and sleeping patterns, and appear to be almost normal for approximately 6 weeks. We see no purpose in developing elaborate active behavior management programs for clients such as these, since they are clearly responding to internal physiological states. Staff must be trained to provide physical comfort and to protect the client from injury, as well as to identify when they are in a trainable condition. At those times, standard training is carried out in an attempt to teach adaptive skills. Staff are specifially trained not to punish clients when they are experiencing their manic phase. Clearly, more research is required before we understand this category of behavior (see Lewis, Baumeister, & Mailman, 1987, for a description of the neural oscillator model).

By closely examining the functional and causal basis for severe behavior problems, we are convinced that behavioral analysts can provide highly effective, although not always dramatic, treatments that are also ethically appropriate. Focusing on topography may yield dramatic changes at a cost to the client that may be too high.

A DATA-BASED APPROACH FOR DETERMINING CAUSES OF INAPPROPRIATE BEHAVIORS

When clients engage in infrequently occurring maladaptive behaviors, determining the variables that are maintaining them can be difficult. Often, the best information is obtained from staff reports of the incident. A common attempt to determine the causes is to ask the parent or staff to provide a written record of what happened immediately before, during, and after the episode. This procedure is used often by those working with clients in their home environments, the behavior analyst only being present a few hours per week. The drawback to this procedure is that it may require too much effort from the people reporting the event to collect adequate data; consequently, many events are not recorded. The caretaker may be busy, forget to record the incident, have difficulty writing clearly, etc. Often, when asking to see the data, the behavior analyst will hear such comments as, "Joe has been hitting a lot, but I wasn't able to write down any of the events."

We have found making checklists to be a useful, practical means of collecting data in these situations (Pyles, Taplac, & Bailey, 1989). If a behavior analyst is unable to observe the maladaptive episodes personally, or if the observations yield ambiguous information regarding causal variables, checklists can be used as a low-effort means of data collection when the traditional method of writing the antecedent, behavior, and consequences has failed. We used such a checklist in the case of attempting to diagnose Tom's inappropriate behaviors.

Tom was a profoundly retarded, verbal, ambulatory client who moved to a facility where we provide consultation. After he had been there a few months, he began engaging in frequent verbal aggression, noncompliance, and infrequent physical aggression. Staff reports and personal observations did not yield any conclusive data to direct us toward a treatment based on the variables. The behavior appeared to be occurring in relation to demands made of him, attention he received when acting inappropriately, or boredom. We also had informal reports that maladaptive behaviors occurred more often when he was having seizures, which were not completely controlled by anticonvulsive medication.

In order to obtain information to design an intervention, we made a checklist of what appeared to be the most common antecedent events, behaviors, and consequences (see Fig. 4). Whenever any of the behaviors on the data sheet occurred, staff checked all relevant conditions. If one was not present on the data sheet, then staff would describe it in the "other" category. If more than one of the events occurred, staff would record all events. For example, if he had been stopped from doing something *and* a toileting accident also had occurred, both were recorded; if he engaged in both physical and verbal aggression, both were recorded. The dates and times of the events also were recorded and plotted on a scatterplot in an attempt to determine whether there were times that the behavior did or did not reliably occur.

We collected data using this data sheet for approximately 6 weeks. We analyzed the data by setting up a graph listing the frequency of occurrence on the ordinate, and all of the environmental and behavioral events from the data sheet on the abscissa. A separate graph was made for each behavior. Each time a maladaptive behavior was recorded, a horizontal mark was made on the graph over the applicable environmental events; on the far left of the graph by the ordinate, we tallied the total number of times that each behavior occurred so that we could determine the number of times each environmental event occurred in relation to the total frequency. When the next event was recorded, marks were recorded on the next available line above the previous mark.

In this way, a tally of the number of times that each event occurred was recorded. After data collection was complete, high points on the graph indicated events occurring immediately before and after the maladaptive behavior. This measure is correlational, not necessarily causal, and thus should be regarded as a *guide* for determining treatment rather than a definitive statement of cause. This form of data collection allowed us to collect baseline and diagnostic data simultaneously.

The analysis revealed that (a) physical aggression, verbal aggression, and noncompliance were the most frequently occurring problems; (b) all three behaviors occurred most often when requests were made of him; (c) staff paid little attention when he engaged in these behaviors; and (d) no episodes occurred in relation to seizures. The maladaptive behaviors appeared to be a means of escaping from demands, and they did not appear to be maintained by attention.

The treatment package that we designed had the following components: hourly differential reinforcement for compliance (Pyles & Bailey, in press) where, each hour, we made a request, and reinforced him with a token (to be traded for preferred reinforcers) for complying, and we walked away without further interaction if he did not comply; a response cost of 10 tokens for verbal and physical aggression; manual restraint until he had been calm for 1 minute for physical ag-

Inappropriate Behavior Record

Instructions: Each time Tony engages in inappropriate behavior, check ALL boxes that apply describing the events occuring before, during and after the behavior.

Definitions:
- Physical Aggression: any occurrence of hitting, scratching, kicking, etc. directed at staff or clients.
- Verbal Aggression: any occurrence of cursing, yelling, or threatening others.
- Noncompliance: refusing to follow requests made of him by staff, not following directions within 30 seconds of request.
- Stealing: taking or having possession of any item not belonging to him without owner's permission.
- Public Masturbation: masturbating or fondling genitals any place other than in his bedroom

Date:____________ Time:__________a.m./.p.m. Staff:____________________

What Happened BEFORE Episode?
- ☐ Nothing--happened "out of the blue"
- ☐ Asked to do something (not training)
- ☐ Asked to do something (training)
- ☐ Asked to go somewhere
- ☐ Asked to move out of the way
- ☐ Stopped from doing something
- ☐ Had toileting accident
- ☐ Had a seizure
- ☐ Other (specify)_______________ ____________________________

Inappropriate Behavior
- ☐ Physical aggression
- ☐ Verbal aggression
- ☐ Noncompliance
- ☐ Stealing
- ☐ Public masturbation Location:_______________
- ☐ Other problematic behavior (Specify)______________ _____________________

What Happened AFTER Episode?
- ☐ Separated within environment
- ☐ Taken to room
- ☐ He calmed down on his own
- ☐ Had to make restitution (pay back something stolen, clean mess, etc.)
- ☐ Staff ignored his behavior
- ☐ Staff lectured/got in argument with him.
- ☐ Other (Specify)____________ ________________________

Date:____________ Time:__________a.m./.p.m. Staff:____________________

What Happened BEFORE Episode?
- ☐ Nothing--happened "out of the blue"
- ☐ Asked to do something (not training)
- ☐ Asked to do something (training)
- ☐ Asked to go somewhere
- ☐ Asked to move out of the way
- ☐ Stopped from doing something
- ☐ Had toileting accident
- ☐ Had a seizure
- ☐ Other (specify)_______________ ____________________________

Inappropriate Behavior
- ☐ Physical aggression
- ☐ Verbal aggression
- ☐ Noncompliance
- ☐ Stealing
- ☐ Public masturbation Location:_______________
- ☐ Other problematic behavior (Specify)______________ _____________________

What Happened AFTER Episode?
- ☐ Separated within environment
- ☐ Taken to room
- ☐ He calmed down on his own
- ☐ Had to make restitution (pay back something stolen, clean mess, etc.)
- ☐ Staff ignored his behavior
- ☐ Staff lectured/got in argument with him.
- ☐ Other (Specify)____________ ________________________

Date:____________ Time:__________a.m./.p.m. Staff:____________________

What Happened BEFORE Episode?
- ☐ Nothing--happened "out of the blue"
- ☐ Asked to do something (not training)
- ☐ Asked to do something (training)
- ☐ Asked to go somewhere
- ☐ Asked to move out of the way
- ☐ Stopped from doing something
- ☐ Had toileting accident
- ☐ Had a seizure
- ☐ Other (specify)_______________ ____________________________

Inappropriate Behavior
- ☐ Physical aggression
- ☐ Verbal aggression
- ☐ Noncompliance
- ☐ Stealing
- ☐ Public masturbation Location:_______________
- ☐ Other problematic behavior (Specify)______________ _____________________

What Happened AFTER Episode?
- ☐ Separated within environment
- ☐ Taken to room
- ☐ He calmed down on his own
- ☐ Had to make restitution (pay back something stolen, clean mess, etc.)
- ☐ Staff ignored his behavior
- ☐ Staff lectured/got in argument with him.
- ☐ Other (Specify)____________ ________________________

Figure 4: The Inappropriate Behavior Record used to determine functional and causal relationships between environment and behavior.

gression, followed by another 4 minutes to calm down without being held. A chair time-out procedure was not feasible because he resisted the procedure strongly and was sometimes able to escape. Following an episode of physical aggression, he would be required to complete the request made of him as a condition of release. If a safety-related request was made of him (e.g., evacuate a building during a fire drill) and he refused, physical guidance was provided to ensure his safety.

Figure 5 shows the analysis data for verbal aggression and the resulting treatment data. During baseline, he averaged three episodes of verbal aggression per month. When the treatment package was introduced in House 1, the average decreased to two per month. In the middle of month 5, he was moved to House 2, where there were more male staff to run the program (House 1 included several small, pregnant women who were reluctant to run the physical aggression component of the program). The rates of verbal aggression increased initially after he was moved to House 2, but then steadily decreased to zero episodes for 2 consecutive months.

Tom's noncompliance data are presented in Figure 6. During baseline, he averaged approximately six episodes per month. Initially, the treatment package resulted in an increase in noncompliance until he was moved to House 2. There, the rates rose sharply, then decreased to zero for 2 consecutive months.

Physical aggression data are presented in Figure 7. Treatment was not implemented for physical aggression until he had moved to House 2. Baseline data are collapsed for Houses 1 and 2 (he moved to the other house during that month). After the treatment package was implemented again, the rates rose sharply, then decreased to zero for 2 consecutive months.

We use the diagnostic data sheet as a means of collecting data when the causes of a behavior are not directly observable or are obscured by many variables occurring simultaneously. Collecting the antecedent, behavioral, and consequence data necessary to determine appropriate treatment requires only a few seconds. Generic data sheets can be used across clients, or data sheets can be tailored to individual clients. The information provided can be invaluable for streamlining the diagnostic process. The data presented demonstrate the efficacy of using these data to form treatments based upon the function that the behavior serves.

CHRONIC BEHAVIOR PROBLEMS

Some clients engage in maladaptive behaviors not easily addressed by reduction programming. Hand mouthing, for example, is a particularly difficult behavior to eliminate. Left untreated, this behavior can result in extensive skin breakdown, with the ever present danger of infection in the open wounds. Head hitting/head banging, picking sores, and pica in some clients are other examples of chronic behavior problems--persistent, pervasive, maladaptive behaviors that do not easily respond to reduction programming contingencies. Often, they look as if they serve a self-stimulatory function.

Foxx and Azrin (1973) successfully reduced hand mouthing using an overcorrection procedure with two severely mentally retarded clients. However, the majority of clients who engage in hand mouthing are *profoundly* mentally retarded with few, if any, adaptive behaviors. Because they also have few or no identified reinforcers, they make minimal progress in skill acquisition training programs, and often become agitated and resistant when physical guidance is used.

With these clients, reduction programming is often not much more effective than skill acquisition training. Short-lived treatment gains can be obtained with intensive programming. However, effective intervention requires nearly a 1-to-1 staff ratio, with constant supervision to block, interrupt, or consequate the occurrence/nonoccurrence of the response. Often, when staff intervene, the client becomes extremely agitated and resistive, posing a risk to himself or others. When staff are not present, the behavior recurs.

The issue of chronic maladaptive behaviors and the lack of an effective technology to eliminate them poses unique problems for our field. There is little in the research literature discussing chronic behavior problems to guide professionals; journals seldom publish research not having positive results. On the one hand, we are ethically bound to prevent the clients from injuring themselves. On the other, programming attempts are usually ineffective and, often, the best we can do is to provide protective equipment such as gloves or helmets. Such devices are considered restraints under the Federal Habilitation Facilities Guidelines, and must be implemented only as part of a behavior *reduction* program. Most of these programs have a criterion for termination: the highest acceptable rate of the behavior. With these clients, this criterion must be considered carefully as the program is often a never-ending one.

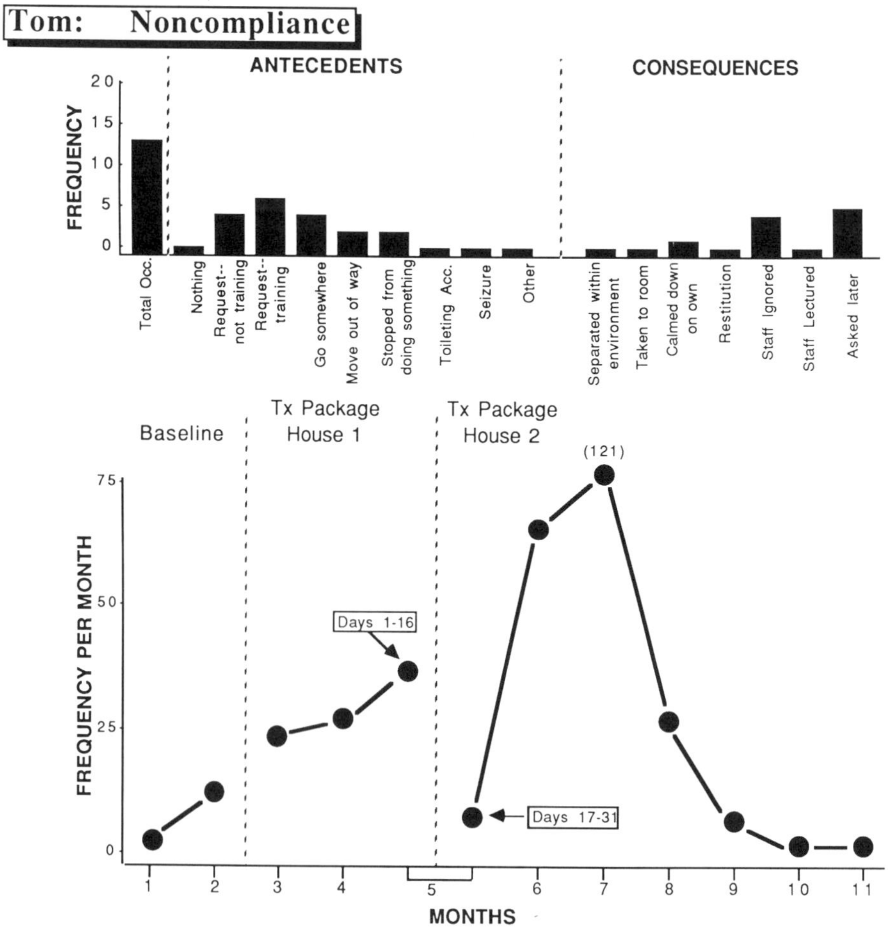

Figure 5: The analysis and treatment of Tom's verbal aggression.

The lack of effective programming, coupled with the need to protect the client, calls for a new conceptualization of the problem. In some cases, we may need to admit that there is no ethical behavioral treatment for the client and, instead, try to minimize the effects of the behavior. For example, the focus in such situations may be the reduction of the amount of skin damage the client has rather than the rates of the behavior.

Behavioral Treatment For Chronic Behavior Clients

There is little to draw from the research literature about chronic behavior problems. The Federal Habilitation Facilities Guidelines do not discuss them, either. As such, not much information exists about appropriate treatment modalities. The best we can do is to offer some suggestions for attempting treatment. Steps to follow when encountering a client with chronic behavior problems are:

1. *Conduct a behavioral diagnosis.* Determine the reason that the behavior is occurring, if possible. If causative variables are discovered, base interventions on these variables, using an Active Behavior Management or Passive Behavior Management approach (Bailey & Pyles, 1989, Pyles & Bailey, in press).

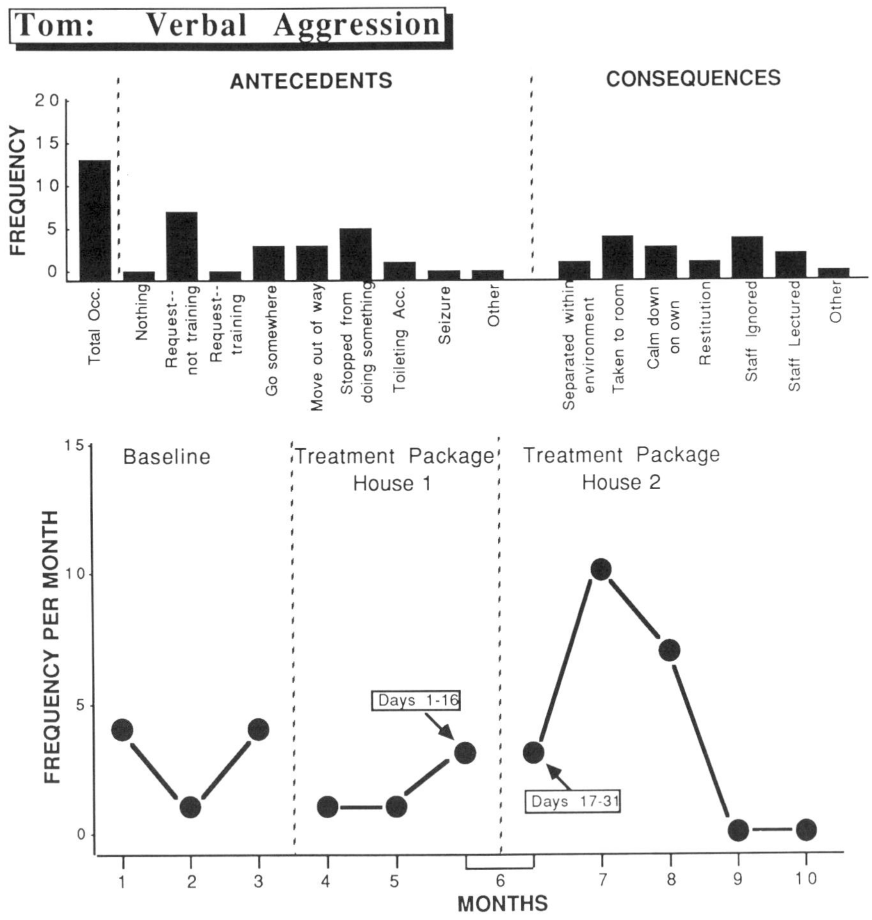

Figure 6: The analysis and treatment of Tom's noncompliance.

2. *Minimize damage to client or others.* Use protective equipment, restraints, or whatever is necessary within relevant guidelines to prevent injury.

3. *Attempt to reduce problematic behaviors.* After collecting appropriate baseline data, implement intervention programs. If these interventions are unsuccessful, modify the procedures and document all treatment attempts. Also, continue attempts to determine causal variables.

4. *Determine if the behavior problem is chronic.* If qualified behavior analysts are not able to treat a maladaptive behavior successfully after exhausting all reasonable avenues, perhaps it is a chronic behavior problem. We can offer few guidelines for what the determining characteristics of a chronic behavior problem are other than the resistance to successful programming, despite modifications by competent, experienced behavior analysts. In many cases, the clients engaging in these acts are individuals who are extremely low functioning, multiply handicapped (often nonambulatory, profoundly mentally retarded), and have no identified reinforcers that ethically can be used. They typically make no progress in training, despite fine-grained task analyses and heroic training efforts. Many also may have

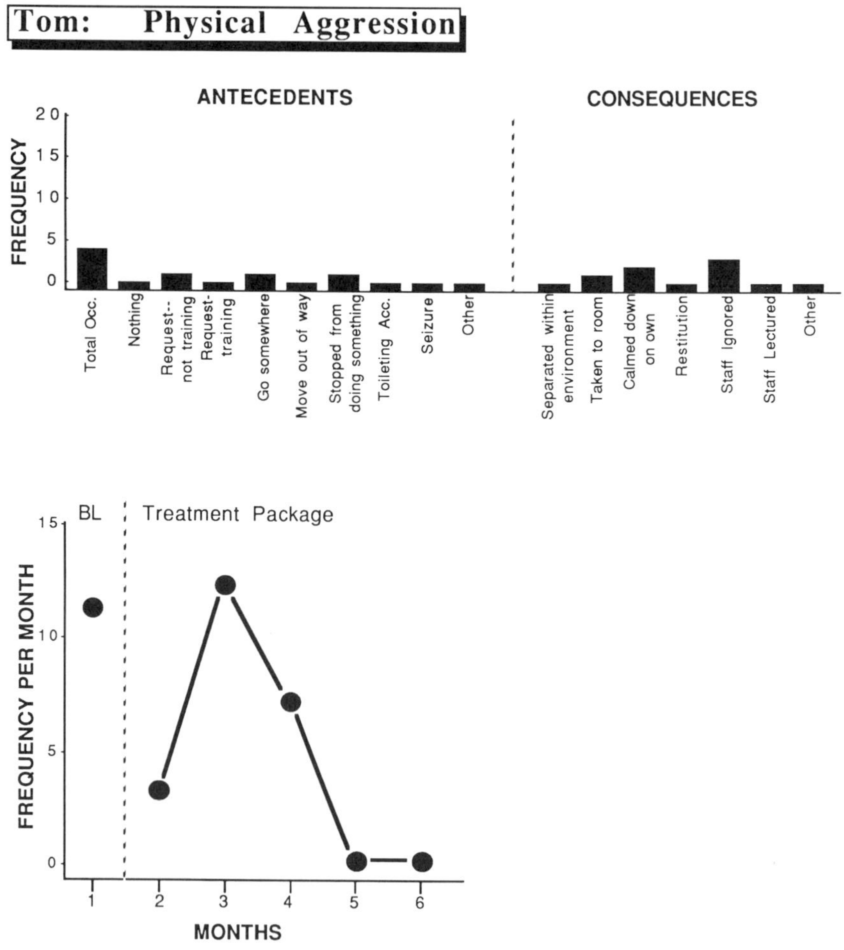

Figure 7: The analysis and treatment of Tom's physical aggression.

seizure disorders. Chronic behavior problems are not discussed in any facility, state, or federal behavior management guidelines. As such, we cannot offer any statutory guidelines for treatment.

5. *If chronicity is determined, use appropriate protection procedures.* Rather than labeling strategies for addressing chronic behavior problems "reduction programs," we suggest the use of a terminology such as "Client Protection Procedure." Write the program accordingly, following applicable facility, state and federal guidelines. If a measure is used as a protection procedure, we further suggest collecting data on measures, such as amount of tissue damage, as well as rate of the behavior.

Other Issues Regarding Chronic Behavior Problems

As stated earlier, the notion that some behavior problems may not be amenable to treatment by operant procedures is new and not well understood. Furthermore, it may represent an unpopular viewpoint in some circles: Our technology of behavior change may not be as encompassing as we had once believed. Some view our field as the one that could treat those whom no one else could. Any admission on our part that we do not have the tools necessary to treat all problems could be tantamount to admitting defeat. Thus, we would fail by causing people to give up hope and stop trying before all practicable avenues have been explored. We need to remember, however, that we are first and foremost *scientists*, and that we need to seek truth through our data. Our responsibility is not to give hope to others in the field; it is to report our data as accurately and objectively as possible. We must admit when we do not have the answers to a given problem.

Also relevant to the concept of chronic behavior problems is the need to revise the applicable federal and state guidelines for behavioral procedures. For example, protective equipment may be necessary to prevent injury, and guidelines would need revision to accommodate such procedures, provided other means of humane treatment have proven ineffective.

We do not claim to have all the answers involving clients with chronic behavior problems. There are other issues needing discussion that will not be permitted by the space available here. However, we *do* know some of the questions, and that is a start. As our technology advances, and some of these issues are resolved, some of the answers needed will become apparent.

SUMMARY

Behavioral Diagnostics is an approach to assessing and treating problematic behaviors with an emphasis on antecedent variables rather than on consequences to effect behavior change. Based on this approach, new conceptualizations of problems faced by behavior analysts must be developed.

In order to provide the most ethical and effective treatment, active and passive behavior management strategies must be based upon the reasons that the behaviors are occurring. It is no longer considered "best-practice" simply to intervene in a given situation; interventions must be tailored to the causes of behavior for that individual client.

This approach also requires new conceptualizations of issues such as determining when to intervene, how to manage clients who engage in chronic behavior problems, an alternative approach to the concept of least restrictive treatment, and ways of providing active treatment for those who do not benefit from skill acquisition training, despite numerous interventions. A Behavioral Diagnostics approach has required us to reformulate many of the questions we ask, and has highlighted issues requiring attention.

We look forward to applications of this new technology, paired with the current technologies now in existence. Only after such issues are taken into account can the most humane, ethical, and effective treatment be provided for these clients.

NOTE

We would like to thank Mary R. Burch for her editorial comments and suggestions on an earlier draft of this manuscript.

REFERENCES

Bailey, J. S., & Pyles, D. A. M. (1989). Behavioral diagnostics. *Monographs of the American Association on Mental Retardation, 12*, 85-106.

Carr, E. G., & Durand, V. M. (1985). Reducing behavior problems through functional communication training. *Journal of Applied Behavior Analysis, 18*, 111-126.

Dorsey, M. F., Iwata, B. A., Ong, P., & McSween, T. (1980). Treatment of self-injurious behavior using a water mist: Initial response suppression and generalization. *Journal of Applied Behavior Analysis, 13,* 343-353.

Durand, V. M., & Carr, E. G. (1987). Social influences on "self-stimulatory" behavior: Analysis and treatment application. *Journal of Applied Behavior Analysis, 20,* 119-132.

Epstein, L. H., Doke, L. A., Sajwaj, T. E., Sorrell, S., & Rimmer, B. (1974). Generality and side effects of overcorrection. *Journal of Applied Behavior Analysis, 7*, 385-390.

Foxx, R. M., & Azrin, N. H. (1973). The elimination of autistic self-stimulatory behavior by overcorrection. *Journal of Applied Behavior Analysis, 6*, 1-14.

Gates, J. J., & Kimber, C. (1990). *Behavior analysis and programming guidelines*. Atlanta: Georgia Division of Mental Health, Mental Retardation, and Substance Abuse.

Iwata, B. A., Dorsey, M. F., Slifer, K. J., Bauman, K. E., & Richman, G. S. (1982). Toward a functional analysis of self-injury. *Analysis and Intervention in Developmental Disabilities, 2*, 3-20.

Lewis, M. H., Baumeister, A. A., & Mailman, R.B. (1987). A neurobiological alternative to the perceptual reinforcement hypothesis of stereotyped behavior: A commentary on "self-stimulatory behavior and perceptual reinforcement." *Journal of Applied Behavior Analysis, 20*, 253-258.

Lovaas, O. I., & Simmons, J. Q. (1969). Manipulation of self-destruction in three retarded children. *Journal of Applied Behavior Analysis, 2*, 143-157.

Lovaas, O. I., Newsom, C., & Hickman, C. (1987). Self-stimulatory behavior and perceptual reinforcement. *Journal of Applied Behavior Analysis, 20*, 45-68.

Mori, A. A., & Masters, L. F. (1980). *Teaching the severely mentally retarded.* Germantown, MD: Aspen.

Park, H., & Gaylord-Ross, R. (1989). A problem-solving approach to social skills training in employment settings with mentally retarded youth. *Journal of Applied Behavior Analysis, 22*, 373-380.

Pyles, D. A. M., & Bailey, J. S. (in press). Behavioral diagnostic interventions. In J. Matson, J. K. Luiselli, & N. N. Singh (Eds.) *Analysis, Assessment, and Treatment of Self-Injury*. New York: Springer.

Pyles, D. A. M., Taplac, N., & Bailey, J. S. (1989). *A behavioral diagnostic approach to analyzing and treating maladaptive behaviors of a profoundly retarded male.* Paper presented at the meeting of the Florida Association for Behavior Analysis, Tampa, FL.

Repp, A. C., Felce, D., & Barton, L. E. (1988). Basing the treatment of stereotypic and self-abusive behaviors on hypotheses of their causes. *Journal of Applied Behavior Analysis, 21,* 281-289.

Skinner, B. F. (1969). *Contingencies of reinforcement: A theoretical analysis.* Prentice-Hall. NJ: Englewood Cliffs.

Touchette, P. E., MacDonald, R. F., & Langer, S. N. (1985). A scatterplot for identifying stimulus control of problem behavior. *Journal of Applied Behavior Analysis, 18*, 343-341.

Van Houten, R., Axelrod, S., Bailey, J. S., Favell, J. E., Foxx, R. M., Iwata, B. A., & Lovaas, O. I. (1988). The right to effective behavioral treatment. *Journal of Applied Behavior Analysis, 21*, 381-384.

CHAPTER

26

THE ECLIPSE OF AVERSIVE TECHNOLOGY: A TRIADIC APPROACH TO ASSESSMENT AND TREATMENT

Carl Schrader
Spectrum Center and Behavioral Consulting and Research Center

Robert Gaylord-Ross
San Francisco State University

The aversive treatment of egregious behavior like self-injury represents an acute intersection of science and human values. Scientific research might demonstrate particular treatment effects. Yet, society's acceptance (value) of certain treatments will largely determine their usage or elimination. Striking images of a child hitting his face to the point of bruises, blindness, or bleeding evokes a human response that this behavior must be curtailed. Yet, the sight of an adult shocking a child with a cattle prod evokes an equally strong response of censure.

During the past 30 years, the behavior modification field has developed a number of postures with respect to aversive treatment. Early on, it was assumed that aversive treatment was not appropriate for milder problem behaviors, since an emerging data base was showing that positive contingency management could reduce these behaviors (Favell, 1978). Soon, Lovaas and his colleagues (e.g., Lovaas & Simmons, 1969) were demonstrating that the most intractable cases of self-injury could be treated successfully with aversive stimuli like contingent electric shock. Although these findings were impressive, they also drew a humanistic response of disdain toward aversive procedures. Subsequently, in order to avoid the excessive use of aversives, professionals recommended a two-phase treatment model (e.g., Gaylord-Ross, 1980). In this approach a number of positive procedures were first attempted. If none of these successfully reduced the problem behavior, then, and only then, would an aversive procedure be tried.

The two-phase model appeared plausible and was embraced by many practitioners. At the same time, though, there was a growing human rights movement that advocated the banning of aversive procedures, particularly the most intrusive ones like contingent electric shock. Resulting legislation truncated the second part of the two-phase model. Such statutory controls often served the good purpose of curtailing bad practice or malpractice by professionals. In addition, the threat of a lawsuit greatly limited the use of severe aversive stimuli in residential and school settings, and also resulted in a greatly attenuated data base on the effectiveness of aversives.

At the same time, a call came out to develop nonaversive technology. If the second phase of the two-phase model was to be restricted, then there had to be a powerful positive program in place. Also, the belief emerged that all problem behaviors, no matter how serious, could be handled by nonaversive techniques. The last decade thus has witnessed an expanding body of literature demonstrating the effectiveness of nonaversive procedures. Perhaps the most exciting of these approaches has imputed a communicative intent to problem behaviors (Carr & Durand, 1985 a,b). For example, a behavior like head banging may produce attention from others. Carr and Durand (1985a) taught a child appropriate communicative responses (e.g., signing for help), which led to assistance and the reduction of head banging to gain attention. While such advances in nonaversive procedures have been striking, it still has not been demonstrated whether such approaches can successfully handle all cases of severe problem behavior, now or in the future.

THE TREATMENT TRIAD

The Treatment Triad defines a set of procedures and teaching strategies developed from working with atypical populations. In this model, behavioral programming with individuals manifesting challenging behavior problems is viewed within a dynamic, skills-oriented framework. In order to be truly comprehensive in our change efforts, we must assess and program across all relevant environmental and behavioral dimensions. These dimensions, although interdependent, can be broken into their component parts for purposes of clinical decision-making and the design of prescriptive treatment modules.

Assessment

The efficacy of the Triadic Treatment Model rests firmly on the ability of the practitioner to assess the relevant dimensions of the target behavior to be modified. The general aim of the assessment is to obtain all relevant information that has a bearing on the performance and maintenance of the target behavior (Gaylord-Ross, 1980). Specifically, we are interested in gathering information in the following areas:

(a) antecedent stimulus and setting events observed/reported prior to target behavior onset;
(b) a risk analysis delineating situations in which the individual is most and least at risk for target behavior performance;
(c) an analysis of the maintaining consequences for the target behavior and for alternative behaviors, and, in particular, the schedule on which each of these responses is maintained;
(d) a description of the total repertoire of the individual, with emphasis upon relevant skill deficits, collateral behaviors, and relative strengths; and
(e) an analysis of the function of the target behavior for the individual.

Our assessment areas correspond to the information contained in the traditional functional analysis with two important differences. First, a much greater emphasis is placed on discovering antecedent events occurring prior to or concurrent with the target behavior, and, secondly, information is gathered that enables us to interpret the function of the behavior for the individual. This information can be obtained best through a combination of direct observation of the individual and reports based upon mediator responses to a variety of behavioral checklists or inventories.

ASSESSING ANTECEDENTS. In our practice, we have found that this area is the most neglected of all the assessment domains. Answers to the question of what was going on just prior to the event or concurrent to the event are routinely met by a shrug of the shoulders and the cryptic response, "It just came out of the blue." Our assessment techniques are designed to prompt mediators' identification of antecedents by providing them with a structured format around which to evaluate. We use the Risk Profile (see Schrader & Levine, 1987) to assist the mediator in determining the presence or absence of specific hypothesized antecedents. The Risk Profile represents an extension of the work of Paul Touchette with the scatter plot (Touchette, MacDonald, & Langer, 1985). While the scatter plot asks responders to note the times that the behavior in question occurs, the Risk Profile provides mediators with a list of over 100 potential antecedents and requires them to decide which of these antecedents seem to be correlated with the presence of the target behavior. Responses are rated on a 3-point scale (never, sometimes, frequently), and provide the clinician with a profile of those situations in which the individual is at greatest and least risk for engaging in the target behavior. We have combined the scatter plot with the Risk Profile to form a Risk Plot which tracks a selected number of antecedents over time, thereby enabling the clinician to analyze patterns across both time and specific classes of antecedents (see Table 1).

In addition to the Risk Profile and the Risk Plot, we have employed two other tools. The first is the Setting Event Checklist (Gardner, Cole, Davidson, & Orv, 1986), which attempts to track distal antecedents or those events which may have occurred a *considerable* time before the actual target behavior, but are nevertheless thought to contribute to the performance of the behavior. Examples include disruptive behavior on the bus, prior temper outburst, or a change in the usual routine. A second tool, the Antecedent Assessment Scale (Schrader & Levine, 1989), was patterned after the work of Durand (1988). It consists of 20 questions concerning events which may be occurring at the time that the target behavior is observed. The questions are answered on a 5-point frequency-based scale, and are arranged to give the assessor a picture of the prevalence of five classes of antecedents: ecological, demand-based, interpersonal, intrapersonal, and event-based. Knowledge of the relative strength of each of these classes of stimulus events can help the clinician plan a more generalizable risk-reduction program by planned modifications of stimulus classes rather than singular events.

SKILLS ASSESSMENT. An important component of skills assessment is a determination of the degree to which an individual performs an appropriate alternative behavior that can take the place of the undesirable target response. To the extent that alternative behaviors are absent or weak, training must be included.

Skills assessments on the individual's functioning can be undertaken in the following domains: self-help skills; self-regulation (i.e., self-monitor, self-evaluate, and self-reinforce); social skills; leisure skills; understanding and compliance with instructions, vocational skills, and communication. These assessments are performed through direct observation and mediator report, and are designed to answer the question: "If this particular target behavior were eliminated, what behavior(s) would take its place?" If the assessment indicates that the individual does not have an appropriate alternative behavior in his or her repertoire, then skills teaching is indicated and prescribed as a part of the comprehensive treatment program.

Of all the skill domains, communication skills are the most critical. Severely handicapped individuals are invariably deficient in their ability to communicate basic needs, choose from alternative options, reject unwanted events or materials, and carry

Table 1

Table 1
Risk Plot

Student ____________________ Date ____________________

Instructions

1. Codify each of the Target Behaviors you are going to track.
2. When Target Behavior occurs, write the Antecedent Code in the space that intersects the Behavior Code and the time it occurred.
3. Record the Antecedent Code each time the Target Behavior occurs (the Antecedent Codes take the place of frequency slashes).

Behavior Codes

1 =	6 =
2 =	7 =
3 =	8 =
4 =	9 =
5 =	10 =

	Behavior									
Time	1	2	3	4	5	6	7	8	9	10
8:00										
8:30										
9:00										
9:30										
10:00										
10:30										
11:00										
11:30										
12:00										
12:30										
1:00										
1:30										
2:00										
2:30										
3:00										
3:30										
4:00										

Antecedent Code

a = in a novel place	n = during location transition time
b = in a noisy environment	o = prior engagement in self-stimulatory behavior
c = when given initiating instruction	p = prior engagement in lower level chained behavior
d = when given a terminating instruction	q = when need cannot be made known
e = after denial of request	r = during leisure time activities
f = during a novel or difficult task	s = on the bus
g = after making error(s)	t = while staff is occupied by others
h = with new or substitute staff	u = while waiting
i = during disruptive behaviors of others	w =
j = after peer provocation	x =
k = absence of structured work/leisure activities	y =
l = during familiar work tasks	z =
m = during activity transition times	

Behavioral Counseling and Research Center 1537A Fourth St., San Rafael, Calif. 94901

on rudimentary conversations. In the assessment of communicative ability, checklist assessments, such as the Communication Interview (Schuler & Goetz, 1981), can be used for clinical decision-making. The Communication Interview asks respondents to record how the individual expresses a variety of communicative functions, such as making requests for affection, indicating a desire for adult action, making requests for food or other objects, voicing a protest, and making declarations or comments. A choice of communicative behaviors that range from crying to appropriate speech is provided, from which the respondent can choose the individual's predominant form of expression. The subsequent function *x* behavior matrix provides the individual's communicative profile. Viewing excess behavior as a form of communication leads directly to interventions designed to remediate this deficit, thereby providing the individual with alternative strategies for negotiating wants (Carr, 1988; Donnellan, Mirenda, Mesaros, & Fassbender, 1984).

ASSESSING CONSEQUENCES. The third area of assessment involves the environmental events which follow a given behavior and alter or maintain its rate. Much has been written on the analysis of consequences and, for the most part, our work follows along traditional lines. However, adopting an approach that emphasizes the need to substitute appropriate and functionally equivalent alternative behavior for the target behavior leads us to a greater investigation of the availability of, and the environmental response to, these alternative behaviors. In particular, we are interested in obtaining information on the effectiveness, efficiency, and reliability of both the target behavior and the alternative behavior (Favell & Reid, 1988). Data gathered on the ability of both behaviors to obtain reinforcement (effectiveness), the ease of performance of the behaviors (efficiency), and the schedule of reinforcement that the behaviors receive (reliability) are vital to the concept of functional equivalence and the subsequent change programs that are designed.

In practice, we are interested in obtaining information on the following questions:

(a) What events follow the target behavior?
(b) What events follow the alternative, functionally equivalent (if any) behaviors?
(c) How easy is it for each of these behaviors to be performed?
(d) What is the schedule of reinforcement that these behaviors receive?
(e) What is the latency of reinforcement between response and reinforcement?
(f) Considering all of the above, what might the target behavior be communicating?

We have been aided in our pursuit of the hypothesized communicative message by the employment of the Motivation Assessment Scale (Durand, 1988). This device asks respondents to answer 16 consequent-based questions along a 6-point frequency scale ranging from Never to Always. Answers are then grouped into 4 categories that correspond to the most common types of consequent events seen with a developmentally disabled population. These categories, Sensory, Escape, Attention, and Tangible reflect the fact that responses, although different in form, may have very similar functions. Grouping behavior by classes corresponding to their hypothesized function (e.g., attention-based or escape-based behaviors) permits us to find functionally equivalent behaviors, within that response class, that are appropriate. Through differential reinforcement procedures, we then can increase the likelihood that they, rather than the target behavior, will occur when environmental conditions dictate. If there is no appropriate, functionally equivalent behavior to be found within that response class, then instructional training programs can be instituted to provide the individual with additional options for communicating his or her intent.

In summary, the primary goal of assessment is to delineate the events that exert stimulus control over the target and alternative behaviors and the variables that maintain these behaviors in the individual's repertoire. Our assessments also are characterized by an interest not only in the form of the target behavior, but also in its function. The doctrine of functional equivalence suggests that to the extent that an appropriate alternative behavior can be found or taught which provides the individual with the same function and reinforcement as the target behavior, the more lasting and generalizable the change will be.

Components of the Treatment Triad

The Treatment Triad is a comprehensive decision-making guide to behavior change programming. The intervention is divided into three components which, while interdependent, represent different procedural approaches to changing target behaviors. The triadic model is presented in Figure 1. As the figure illustrates, the model provides three broad categories of intervention: antecedent changes, curricular interventions, and contingency-based interventions. Once the assessment is completed, information is available that has direct application for each component of the model. While some problems will lend themselves more readily to one class of procedural options than to others, in general, all individuals

Figure 1. The Components of the Treatment Triad

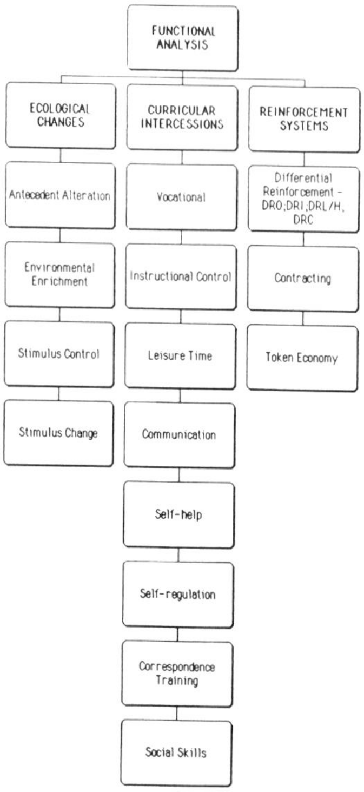

Figure 1: The Components of the Treatment Triad

can benefit from programming carried out across all of the intervention domains.

ECOLOGICAL/ANTECEDENT CHANGES. This category involves rearrangements of the environment that are designed to circumvent or prevent aberrant behavior from occurring (Meyer & Evans, 1986). Our assessment has provided information on high and low risk situations for the individual. A high risk situation is one in which the target behavior has a history of occurring, leading to a greater than average probability of recurrence. Correspondingly, a low risk situation is one in which the target behavior rarely, if ever, occurs. While the distinction between these two extremes occasionally can become blurred, there usually is agreement between mediators on what are high and low risk situations for a given individual.

There are two generic risk-reduction procedures: (a) decreasing the time spent in high risk situations while increasing time spent in low risk situations, and (b) changing the character of the high risk event so that it no longer sets the occasion for aberrant behavior. The first strategy, referred to as creating a zero baseline (Touchette, 1988), involves eliminating as many of the antecedent stimuli as are known in order to produce an environment that is as "errorless" as possible. In practice, this usually means the removal of most, if not all, demands (for a demand-based or escape responder), the provision of 1:1 attention (for the attention-based responder), and the availability of virtually unlimited tangible items (for the tangible responder). In short, the environment is manipulated until the behavior reaches a zero or near zero level.

In some cases, treatment can be terminated at this point. If the changes made in the environment can be maintained without undue disruption to educational progress, then the zero baseline program may be sufficient. In the majority of cases, however, risk factors must be introduced back into the environment. This necessitates the design of programs that modify the characteristics of the high risk situation so that it no longer engenders aberrant responding. There are a variety of interventions that can successfully modify high risk situations to the point where the individual is no longer at risk for aberrant behavior.

1. Environmental enrichment. Enrichment refers to the provision of a wide range of activities and materials that create a stimulating and reinforcing environment. As Horner (1980) clearly demonstrated, the availability of a variety of recreational materials, along with training in the use of these materials, can be a dramatically effective means of reducing aberrant behaviors. For practical purposes, an enriched environment is one that provides availability of and reinforcement for interacting with materials and activities, opportunity and reinforcement for the use of language and other forms of communication, a high interest curriculum, novelty in available stimuli, frequent reinforcement for adaptive behaviors, opportunities for structured and incidental social interaction, an adequate amount of personal space, choices within a predictable schedule, and the opportunity for community participation.

2. Stimulus change. This involves a change of stimulus conditions within the environment (LaVigna & Donnellan, 1986). As a risk reduction strategy, it relies upon the novelty of the new stimulus *configurations* to change established responses. Examples of stimulus change procedures include changing seat arrangements within a classroom, changing furniture arrangements within a group home, having staff wear different clothing, and changing the path of a community walk. Stimulus change procedures are useful for temporarily disrupting the individual's typical pattern of responding while giving the professional time to design a more comprehensive plan.

3. Stimulus Fading. Stimulus fading involves an alteration in some dimension of the antecedent stimulus. In the typical stimulus fading paradigm, the stimulus is altered to the point where responding is at zero or near zero rates (via elimination or substantial modification), a phase which is then followed by a gradual return to the stimulus's original state (Iwata, 1987). If the shaping procedure has been performed carefully enough, then responding should remain at low levels, provided that the motivation for escape behavior is lessened or eliminated as well. Stimulus fading occurs across activities (Touchette et al., 1985), task demands (Heidorn & Jensen, 1984), behavior reduction procedures (Pace, Iwata, Edwards, & McCosh, 1986), and staff (Schrader & Levine, 1989). This category of stimulus alteration is frequently employed when task difficulty (Weeks & Gaylord-Ross, 1981) or task boredom (Evans & Voeltz, 1982) appear to be correlated with high rates of aberrant behavior. By altering the instructional strategy to include less difficult material (Weeks & Gaylord-Ross, 1981), more functional routines (Evans & Voeltz, 1982), or more enjoyable presentations (Carr, Newsom, & Binkoff, 1980), control can be established over the target behavior. Fading to the original instructional modality may or may not be attempted once behavioral control is achieved. Often the originally problematic stimuli can be returned in unaltered form with a subsequent maintenance of low levels of the problem behavior. Whether this is due to the buildup of positive behavioral momentum, to the breakdown of the recency effect, or to other variables, it deserves further research attention.

4. Stimulus Interruption. This approach involves the discovery and subsequent breakdown of behavioral chains that terminate in the target behavior. We refer to this procedure as stimulus (rather than response) interruption because of the fact that each behavior in the chain functions as the stimulus for the next behavior in the chain. The discovery of lower level or intensity behaviors which proceed the target behavior can pay handsome dividends. Examples of this procedure can be found in the work of Zlutnick, Mayville, and Moffat (1975) and Hamlet, Axelrod, and Kuerschner (1984).

5. Stimulus Control. While all of the strategies in this section can be seen as employing the principle of stimulus control, a special case of stimulus control programming has been identified. This approach involves permitting the aberrant behavior to occur, but only under mediator-prescribed conditions. In practice, this procedure suggests that certain levels of a target behavior can be tolerated if performed at specified times and/or places. The individual is permitted to engage in the target behavior for a specified duration, provided that the behavior does not occur during nonsanctioned times. This procedure involves a form of stimulus isolation in which the behavior comes under the control of a particular stimulus cue presented by the mediator (e.g., time of day, mediator instruction to perform, or completion of an activity). Examples of stimulus control programming have been provided for self-stimulation (Charlop, 1988) and disruptive vocalizations (LaVigna & Donellan, 1986).

CURRICULAR INTERVENTIONS. Curricular approaches to behavior change only recently have come to the forefront (Meyer & Evans, 1986). By curricular interventions, we refer to that body of work and clinical experience that suggests that excess behavior often represents a clear expression of a skill deficit. This deficit may be in the performance of a specific skill (e.g., self-help or leisure-oriented) or may represent the individual's attempt to communicate a need, refuse a demand, or request assistance. If excess behaviors can be shown to have social-communicative intent, then failure to address this social message may lead to, at best, short-term change. As we indicated above, a comprehensive change plan must take into account the functional meaning of the behavior for the individual. When the behavior in question results from a clear skill or communication deficit, then curricular interventions are clearly required.

Curricular interventions can be categorized under the general heading of behavior replacement strategies (Iwata, 1987). In essence, we are attempting to replace the form of the behavior without replacing its function. In order for this approach to be successful, the replacement behavior must (a) fulfill the same function as the target behavior, (b) be as efficient as the target behavior, and (c) obtain reinforcement as reliably as the target behavior.

To the extent that the target behavior obtains reinforcement on a richer schedule or with significantly less effort, replacement will be difficult. For this reason, we suggest intervention across all three domains within a comprehensive framework.

As Figure 1 indicates, our curricular interventions span a number of skill domains. Assessment information obtained on the individual's functioning across these domains dictates whether intervention is appropriate and guides us in deciding what effect, if any, skill training in a given area will have on aberrant behavior. While the current chapter does not permit us to detail all training programs that might be invoked, a sampling of three areas of training should suffice to give the reader an understanding of the curricular domain.

COMMUNICATION TRAINING. A considerable amount of training is devoted to teaching individuals with challenging behaviors alternative means of communicating their intentions. A growing number of researchers (Carr & Durand, 1985a,b; Evans & Meyer, 1985; Horner & Budd, 1985) have found that formal training in asking for help, attention, wants or needs, and choice can dramatically reduce inappropriate behaviors that communicate the same intent. In a recent example, Day, Rea, Schussler, Larsen, and Johnson (1988) employed request training as an alternative, incompatible response to self-injurious behavior (SIB) with two developmentally disabled children. Results indicated decreases in SIB as appropriate requesting increased.

INSTRUCTIONAL CONTROL. Instructional control refers to training in compliance to requests. Our work has confirmed the prior work of Russo, Cataldo, and Cushing (1981) and Parrish, Cataldo, Kolko, Neef, and Egel (1986), who found that compliance often was inversely correlated with aberrant behaviors. Increases in compliance reliably led to decreases in untreated inappropriate behaviors. This has led some researchers to dub compliance a "keystone behavior" (Meyer & Evans, 1986) because of its central importance in creating generalized change. Instruction-following technology has taken many forms, ranging from teaching requisite antecedent behaviors such as eye contact (Hamlet et al., 1984) to the development of systematic differential reinforcement procedures (Engelmann & Colvin, 1983).

In one of the more creative means of teaching generalized instruction following, Mace, Lalli, West, Belifore, Pinter, and Brown (1988) developed a strategy of giving the target individual a series of high probability instructions that were unlikely to lead to noncompliance (e.g., shake hands, give me five). Once compliance was established, a higher risk instruction was given with subsequent increases in compliance for that instruction. The authors postulated that they had established a "behavioral momentum."

SCHEDULE AND RULE FOLLOWING. An important aspect of our curricular interventions involves teaching schedule following across the day. Providing individuals with a written or pictorial schedule has been quite effective in reducing aberrant behavior born of anxiety around unpredictable changes in routines. Particularly for the autistic individuals with whom we have worked, the development of schedule-following skills has been of great help in creating predictability and, incidentally, in enhancing language skills concerning past, present, and future actions. Depending upon the degree of sophistication of the target individual, self-monitoring and self-direction skills also can be taught, thus reducing the commonly observed prompt dependency of this group.

In like manner, teaching individuals who exhibit challenging behaviors to follow posted, stated, or generic rules has proven useful. Viewing rule following as an element in social competence gives it priority as a goal of training. We have found that teaching rule following through correspondence training has merit with some moderately and severely handicapped individuals. As originally formulated (Israel, 1978), it teaches individuals to state their intentions to engage in a particular behavior (the "say" condition) and then follow this with the actual intended behavior (the "do" condition), thus creating a correspondence between the two acts. In our treatment program, we have taught individuals to state the rules that apply in a given situation and their intention to follow those rules. When compliance is forthcoming, we reinforce the individual for doing what they said they were going to do. This has led, in some people, to verbal control over motor behavior; i.e., self-regulation.

CONTINGENCY-BASED INTERVENTIONS. The final component in the Treatment Triad involves contingency management strategies for addressing aberrant behavior and developing reinforcement programs to encourage the absence of excess behavior and the presence of incompatible behaviors. Our approach within this domain follows traditional contingency management procedures, including DRO, DRI, and DRL schedules of reinforcement, and token and other mediated symbolic incentive systems. In terms of ease of implementation, we have found that momentary DRO schedules (Repp, Barton, & Brulle, 1983) work just as well as the more arduous whole interval DRO, with the schedule of contact being easily adjustable to correspond to periods of varying risk.

Generally, we prefer DRI and DRC (Differential Reinforcement of Communicative Behavior) schedules to DRO programs. DRO programs are problematic, in that they merely reinforce the absence of behavior rather than the presence of some specific incompatible response.

A second category of interventions involves the stimulus change of a different type than that described in the section on antecedent interventions. When used as a consequent strategy, stimulus change refers to the provision of a competing stimulus or event contingent upon the aberrant response in an effort to redirect it. To the extent that the individual is functioning within an enriched environment, redirection can be a powerful procedure which can circumvent the need for aversive programs. To be maximally effective, the redirected activity should be one that has a positive valence for the individual or is in some way novel, is physically or functionally incompatible with the target behavior being exhibited, and is provided as early in the escalation sequence as possible.

Considering the subject matter of this volume, we would be remiss without a brief discussion of the use of aversives within the triadic model. As the foregoing discussion implies, the use of aversives is seen as an option of last resort. Aversive consequences should be tried only after all positive avenues have been tried and have failed. Programming negative consequences may be unavoidable, particularly in the case of severely aberrant behaviors such as self-injury, serious aggressive behavior, and life-threatening behaviors such as rumination and pica. If we have done a thorough assessment, designed a treatment protocol that attempts to remove high risk triggering events, provided an enriched environment, and taught functionally equivalent alternatives to the target behavior, then failure to modify these serious aberrant responses would indicate an inability to remove the potency of reinforcement for the behavior excess. In order for our programming to compete in terms of efficiency, reliability, and potency of reinforcement, our experience suggests that we sometimes must decrease the attractiveness of the problematic excess. The use of negative consequence programming is one way to accomplish this end.

If an aversive is contemplated, we and any responsible review team must be convinced that all positive programming efforts have failed, despite consistent efforts on the part of staff. Supporting data must be available for inspection and also as empirical justification of the failure of positive procedures alone to modify the target response. When an aversive is employed, it must be: (a) a procedure that is commonly used with nonhandicapped same-aged peers, (b) conducted in an ecologically engineered environment characterized by extensive skill training programs like those discussed in the curricular section of this chapter, (c) accompanied by a plan to fade out and discontinue its use in favor of a more self-control-oriented program, and (d) approved by all interested parties and reviewed on a regular basis to determine its efficacy.

CONCLUSION

We have presented a multicomponent, *nonaversive* treatment

model that has been found to be successful in the vast majority of serious clinical cases, representing a wide range of severe behavior problems. In spite of its success, we cannot argue, much less prove, that nonaversive procedures will work with all cases. This belief is not universally held. Some behavior analysts like Sidman (1989) and Touchette (1988) feel that nonaversive procedures can be successful with all cases. Other investigators, e.g., and Lovaas (1987) feel there still may be a need for aversives. Just drawing from the reported literature (e.g., Lovaas & Simmons, 1969), there are cases where repeated trials with positive procedures had been tried (for months or years) and failed. Subsequently, aversive techniques successfully suppressed the behavior. Logically, it is impossible to prove that all positive procedures have been tried and have failed. This is due to a potentially infinite number of positive procedures. One will never be able to sample them all. Thus, we practically fall back on the clinical judgment of experts and consumers to make this determination. Mathematically, there is a proportion of individuals with severe behavior problems who can be successfully treated with nonaversive approaches. There is also a proportion of cases that do not benefit from positive approaches and can gain with aversive techniques. Given the advances in nonaversive technology, the former population should increase and the latter decrease over time.

Values and Behavior Treatment

The *aversions* of society toward *aversive technology* should continue to grow. Since the aberrant behavior of severely disabled individuals has little impact on society, more public attention will be drawn to the distasteful nature of the aversive procedures. Individuals who fail to improve with positive programs and who are denied access to an aversive procedure will likely be further cloistered (institutionalized), out of sight (Mulick, 1988), and will have little impact on treatment policy.

Ethicists pondering this issue ought to consider two conflicting sets of values. There is a certain parallel between the issues surrounding capital punishment and victims' rights. When focusing on the odious nature of punishment by execution, one is repelled by the barbaric nature of this form of punishment. Yet, when considering the violation of the victim and appropriate retribution, capital punishment and other extreme aversives may seem palatable (at least they have recently to the majority of the American populace). Similarly, the seemingly abusive nature of aversive procedures must be balanced against the right to receive treatment. Griffith (1983) has presented an eloquent discussion of these often conflicting principles. In citing the *Wyatt v. Stickney* (1972) case, he invokes the *quid pro quo* nature of treatment; i.e., a clear benefit (the cessation of self-injury) must be weighed against a particular cost (the exposure to noxious stimuli). Furthermore, Griffith cites the Eighth and Fourteenth Amendments as the right to protection from harm (self-injury); or as Barrish (1974) has stated, not "applying an effective technology to a person enduring pain and suffering far worse than the small amounts of punishment connected with any techniques," (p. 34) is incorrect. Our point is that values discussion of this issue must display sensitivity to both treatment abuses with aversives and the right to receive particular treatments.

A problem in the consideration of aversive procedures is that it is confounded with quality of treatment issues. That is, one may consider the efficacy of aversive procedure under controlled experimental procedures. Yet, when behavior modification techniques are used in the field by practitioners, there are ample opportunities for abuse. In fact, Durand (1988) has remarked that even among highly trained professionals, he is surprised how many poor practices may be evident. One problem may be "sloppy" practice where contingencies and cues are not delivered properly. More problematic is a violation of the two-phase model. That is, many practitioners rush too quickly into using aversives before an adequate exploration of non-aversives is completed. To prevent this from happening, Durand has advanced an "obstacle" model. Considerable treatment guidelines and judicial safeguards must be put in place in order to prevent the preemptive application of aversives, and the use of aversives (Phase 2) may be entertained only after an exhaustive exploration of positive procedures has been made and proved unsuccessful.

Certification

We feel that more stringent certification procedures are needed to ensure quality control in the application of aversives. In the past, Carr and Lovaas (1983) and Risley (1975) have called for certification procedures. It would be important first to identify a pool of professionals who have considerable experience in using aversives under controlled experimental conditions. In order to become certified in these techniques (parallel to medical board certification), one would have to serve an apprenticeship or internship with an existing certified fellow. Further peer review and inservice activities could be built into this certification process.

In spite of the expanding efficacy of nonaversive technology, we still feel there is a need for a two-phase treatment model. The model needs to be augmented with more regulated and statutory obstacles to ensure treatment quality and to avoid the premature use of aversives. The treatment model is finally sealed with stringent certification requirements for professionals. In summary, we feel that a triadic, two-phase model for the treatment of aberrant behavior should advance the treatment of individuals with serious behavior problems in the most efficacious and humane way.

NOTE

We would like to thank the following persons for providing antecedents and consequences for our efforts on this topic: Enio Cipani, Mark Levine, Luanna Meyer, and Marion Weeks.

REFERENCES

Barrish, I. J. (1974). Ethical issues and answers to behavior modification. *Corrective and Social Psychiatry & Journal of Behavior Technology Methods & Therapy, 20*, 30-37.

Carr, E. G., & Lovaas, O. I. (1983). Contingent electric shock as a treatment for severe behavior problems. In S. Axelrod & J. Apsche (Eds.), *The effects of punishment on human behavior* (pp. 221-246). New York: Academic Press.

Carr, E. G., (1988). Functional equivalence as a mechanism of response generalization. In R. Horner, G. Dunlap, & R. Koegel (Eds.), *Generalization and maintenance: Life-style changes in applied settings.* Baltimore: Paul H. Brookes.

Carr, E. G., & Durand, V. M. (1985a). Reducing behavior problems through functional communication training. *Journal of Applied Behavior Analysis, 18*, 111-126.

Carr, E. G., & Durand, V. M. (1985b). The social-communicative basis of severe behavior problems in children. In S. Reiss & R. Bootzin (Eds.), *Theoretical issues in behavior therapy* (pp. 219-254). New York: Academic Press.

Carr, E. G., Newsom, C. D., & Binkoff, J. A. (1980). Escape as a factor in the aggressive behavior of two retarded children. *Journal of Applied Behavior Analysis, 13*, 101-117.

Charlop, M. (1988). *New technologies for enhancing motivation in autistic children: Reinforcer effectiveness*. NIDRR National Conference on Community Referenced Behavior Management, Santa Barbara, CA.

Day, R. M., Rea, J. A. Schussler, N. G., Larsen, S. E., & Johnson, W. L. (1988). A functionally based approach to the treatment of self-injurious behavior. *Behavior Modification, 12*, 563-589.

Donnellan, A. M., Mirenda, P. L. Mesaros, R. A., & Fassbender, L. L. (1984). Analyzing the communicative functions of aberrant behavior. *Journal of The Association for Persons with Severe Handicaps, 9*, 201-212.

Durand, V. M. (1988). Motivation assessment scale: In M. Hersen & A. Bellack (Eds.), *Dictionary of behavior assessment techniques* (pp. 309-310). Elmsford, NY: Pergamon Press.

Engelmann, S., & Colvin, G. (1983). *Generalized compliance training*. Austin: Pro-Ed.

Evans, I. M., & Meyer, L. H. (1985). *An educative approach to behavior problems: A practical decision model for interventions with severely handicapped learners*. Baltimore: Paul H. Brookes.

Evans, I. M., & Voeltz, L. M. (1982). *The selection of intervention priorities in educational programming of severely handicapped preschool children with multiple behavior problems* (Final report, Grant No. 600-790-1460) Honolulu: University of Hawaii.

Favell, J. E., McGimsey, J. F., & Jones, M. L. (1978). The use of physical restraint in the treatment of self-injury and as positive reinforcement. *Journal of Applied Behavior Analysis, 11*, 225-241.

Favell, J. E., & Reid, D. H. (1988). Generalizing and maintaining improvement in problem behavior. In R. Horner, G. Dunlop, & R. Koegel. (Eds.), *Generalization and maintenance: Lifestyle changes in applied settings*. Baltimore: Paul H. Brookes.

Favell, J. E. (1973). Reduction of stereotypes by reinforcement of toy play. *Mental Retardation, 11*, 21-23.

Gardner, W. I., Cole, C. L., Davidson, D. P., and Orv, C. K. (1986). Reducing aggression in individuals with developmental disabilities: An expanded stimulus control, assessment, and intervention model. *Education and Training of the Mentally Retarded*, 3-12.

Gaylord-Ross, R. (1980). A decision model for the treatment of aberrant behavior in applied settings. In W. Sailor, B. Wilson, & L. Brown (Eds.), *Methods of instruction for severely handicapped students*, Baltimore: Paul H. Brooks.

Griffith, R. G. (1983). The administrative issues: An ethical and legal perspective. In S. Axelrod & J. Apsche (Eds.), *The effects of punishment on human behavio*r, New York: Academic Press.

Hamlet, C. C., Axelrod, S., & Kuerschner, S. (1984). Eye contact as an antecedent to compliant behavior. *Journal of Applied Behavior Analysis, 17*, 553-558.

Heidorn, S. D., & Jensen, C. C. (1984). Generalization and maintenance of the reduction of self-injurious behavior maintained by two types of reinforcement. *Behavior Research and Therapy, 22*, 581-586.

Horner, R. H. (1980). The effects of an environmental "enrichment" program on the behavior of institutionalized profoundly retarded clients. *Journal of Applied Behavior Analysis, 13*, 473-491.

Horner, R. H., & Budd, C. M. (1985). Teaching manual sign language to a nonverbal student: Generalization of sign use and collateral reduction of maladaptive behavior. *Education and Training of the Mentally Retarded, 20*, 39-47.

Israel, A. C. (1978). Some thoughts on correspondence between saying and doing. *Journal of Applied Behavior Analysis, 2*, 271-276.

Iwata, B. A. (1987). Negative reinforcement in applied behavior analysis: An emerging technology. *Journal of Applied Behavior Analysis, 20,* 361-378.

La Vigna, G. W., & Donnellan, A. M. (1986). *Alternatives to punishment: Nonaversive strategies for solving behavior problems*. New York: Irvington Press.

Lovaas, O. I. (1987). Behavioral treatment and normal educational and intellectual functioning in young autistic children. *Journal of Consulting and Clinical Psychology, 55, 3-9.*

Lovaas, O. I., & Simmons, J. A. (1969). Manipulation of self-destruction in three retarded children. *Journal of Applied Behavior Analysis, 2*, 143-157.

Mace, F. C., Lalli, M. L., West, B. J., Belifore, P., Pinter, E., & Brown, D. K. (1988). Behavioral momentum in the treatment of noncompliance. *Journal of Applied Behavior Analysis, 21*, 123-142.

Matson, J. L., & DiLorenzo, T. M. (1984). *Punishment and its alternatives: A new perspective on behavior modification.* New York: Springer.

Meyer, L. H., & Evans, I. M. (1986). Modification of excess behavior: An adaptive and functional approach for educational community contexts. In R. Horner & L. Meyer (Eds.), *Education of learners with severe handicaps* (pp. 315-350). Baltimore: Paul H. Brookes.

Mulick, J. A. (1988). Self-injurious behavior, its treatment, and normalization. *Mental Retardation, 26*, 223-229.

Pace, G. M., Iwata, B. A., Edwards, G. L., & McCosh, K. (1986). Stimulus fading and transfer in the treatment of self-restraint and self-injurious behavior. *Journal of Applied Behavior Analysis, 19,* 381-390.

Parrish, J. M., Cataldo, M. F., Kolko, D. J., Neef, N. A., & Egel, A. L. (1986). Experimental analysis of response covariation among compliant and inappropriate behaviors. *Journal of Applied Behavior Analysis, 19*, 241-254.

Repp, A. C., Barton, L. E., & Brulle, A. R. (1983). A comparison of two procedures for programming the differential reinforcement of other behaviors. *Journal of Applied Behavior Analysis, 16*, 435-445.

Risley, T. R. (1975). Certify procedures not people. In W. S. Wood (Ed.). *Issues in evaluating behavior modification.* Champaign, IL: Research Press.

Russo, D. C., Cataldo, M. F., & Cushing, P. J. (1981). Compliance training and behavioral covariation in the treatment of multiple behavior problems. *Journal of Applied Behavior Analysis, 14*, 209-222.

Schrader, C., & Levine, M. D. (1987). *An ecological and curricular approach to the modification of aberrant behavior.* Paper presented at the California Behavior Analysis Conference.

Schrader, C., & Levine, M. D. (1989). *The treatment triad: A comprehensive approach to behavior management.* Paper presented at the Northern California Association of Behavior Analysis Conference.

Schuler, A. L., & Goetz, L. (1981). The assessment of severe language disorders: Communicative and cognitive considerations. *Analysis and Intervention in Developmental Disabilities, 1,* 333-346.

Sidman, M. (1989). *Coercion and its fallout.* Boston: Authors Cooperative, Inc. Publishers.

Touchette, P. E. (1988). *Punishment/extinction: There is a third way to get rid of problem behavior-counterconditioning.* Paper presented at the Northern California Association of Behavior Analysis Conference.

Touchette, P. E., MacDonald, R. F., & Langer, S. N. (1985). A scatter plot for identifying stimulus control of problem behavior. *Journal of Applied Behavior Analysis, 18,* 343-351.

Weeks, M., & Gaylord-Ross, R. (1981). Task difficulty and aberrant behavior in severely handicapped students. *Journal of Applied Behavior Analysis, 14,* 449-463.

Wyatt v. Stickney, 344 F. Supp. 387 (M. D. Ala. 1972).

Zlutnick, S., Mayville, W. J., & Moffat, S. (1975). Modification of seizure disorders: The interruption of behavior chains. *Journal of Applied Behavior Analysis, 8,* 1-12.

PART V

CHAPTER

27

MODIFYING THE BEHAVIOR OF BEHAVIOR MODIFIERS: ARGUMENTS FOR COUNTERCONTROL AGAINST AVERSIVE PROCEDURES

Dick Sobsey
University of Alberta

In the long run, punishment, unlike reinforcement, works both to the disadvantage of the punished organism and the punishing agency" (Skinner, 1953, p. 183)

As the leading figure in behaviorism, B. F. Skinner (1953) is frequently quoted about the use of punishment by advocates of less intrusive methods of behavioral control to support their arguments against the use of aversive procedures. Skinner's current attitude toward the value of punishment procedures generally appears no more positive than it was in 1953. In his recent work, Skinner (1989) points out that "aversive consequences are responsible for many kinds of problems" and that the "side effects (of punishment) may be severe" (p.78). Perhaps even more important, he suggests that punishment can only be expected to temporarily suppress behavior, and once the aversive consequences are removed, the behavior will continue in the presence of the same discriminative stimuli and the same potential reinforcers much as if the aversive consequence had never been employed. Describing a device he built to slap the paws of rats at each lever press, Skinner reports that "the rats stopped responding, but once free of the slapping, they recovered, and by the end of two 1-hour sessions, the extinction curve was essentially where it would have been if no responses had been slapped" (p. 126).

In spite of these statements and others (e.g., B. F. Skinner Opposes..., 1987), Griffen, Paisey, Stark, and Emerson (1988) point out that Skinner's general opposition to punishment procedures has some exceptions. They quote Skinner from a letter discussing severe self-injury and other extreme forms of excessive behavior:

> If brief and harmless aversive stimuli, made precisely contingent on self-destructive or other excessive behavior, suppress the behavior and leave the children free to develop in other ways, I believe that they can be justified. When taken out of context, such stimuli seem less than humane, but they are not to be distinguished from

> the much more painful stimuli sometimes needed in dentistry and various medical practices. To remain satisfied with punishment without exploring nonpunitive alternative is the real mistake (B. F. Skinner in Griffen, Paisey, Stark, & Emerson, 1988, p. 194).

Skinner's statement presents a concise argument for the use of aversive procedures, and if the assumptions that it contains are accepted as valid, the argument is difficult to refute. The justification in this argument, however, is preceded by a long conditional statement that begins with "if." Therefore, to be justified, in Skinner's estimation, the aversive stimuli must meet four criteria: (a) They must be "brief and harmless." (b) They must be made precisely contingent on self-destructive or other excessive behavior. (c) They must "suppress the behavior." (d) They must "leave the child free to develop in other ways." Skinner also implies a fifth and sixth criterion: (e) They must be used only when less intrusive alternatives are unavailable (implied in his statement regarding nonpunitive alternatives). (f) They must be used only when justified by clear benefit to the client (implied in his description of serious self-injury and requirements for drugs or restraint).

Assuming that these six criteria are met, it is difficult to understand objections raised against the use of aversive procedures, but if contemporary use of aversive procedures fails to meet these essential criteria, its justification is difficult. Although commonly accepted, the underlying assumptions are not well supported by empirical evidence and require careful analysis based on the available evidence.

BRIEF AND HARMLESS PROCEDURES

Brevity

Inappropriate behavior is rarely eliminated quickly through the use of aversive procedures. The failure of brief aversive procedures to eradicate inappropriate behavior is well illustrated in the film, *Randy's up, Randy's down* (Parsons State Hospital and Training School, 1977), which follows a child through his electric shock program to control his self-injurious behavior in a residential facility. On application of the shock program, the subject's inappropriate behavior was dramatically reduced. Equally important, his appropriate behavior was increased. Unfortunately, these improvements were short-lived, and in spite of subsequent exposure to a number of contingent electric shock programs, in the end the subject still was severely self-injurious. Clients like Randy often endure repeated aversive programs, sometimes achieving temporary improvement but without any long-term progress. For example, Stainton (1988) refers to one client on an electric shock program for 12 years and another for two-and-one-half years. To paraphrase Mark Twain's remark on giving up smoking, aversive procedures have cured the self-injurious behavior of a lot of clients, some of them dozens of times over. Therefore, it is not surprising that Hurley and Sovner (1983), when presenting guidelines for the effective use of punishment procedures, suggest that "when a punishment technique is discontinued, the maladaptive behavior may rebound, increasing in frequency to a higher level than before. Thus punishment procedures must somehow be continued almost indefinitely in order to be really effective" (p. 46).

Thus, the implied long-term cure as a result of short-term pain is a myth. People with disabilities are often confronted by a series of aversive programs that continue for years. Rapid reduction in frequency of the inappropriate behavior is common, but long-term elimination is very rare. The dental visit comparison suggested by Skinner implies that a few minutes of pain while having a tooth drilled is merited by the elimination of pain and infection that it produces, but if your dentist is still drilling the same tooth 12 years later, it may be time for a second opinion.

Harmlessness

The low-amperage electric shocks and other aversive stimuli commonly used probably pose little risk to the health of most clients; however, the use of aversive procedures should not be viewed as harmless. A number of problems exist with the use of punishment procedures, which often result in harm to the client, to the staff involved in the program, and to other clients.

HARM THROUGH MISUSE OF AVERSIVE PROCEDURES. Cotter (1967), describes his use of operant conditioning in a Vietnamese Mental Hospital. He describes what most would find to be unethical a program that he set up to encourage hundreds of Vietnamese mental patients to work. Most proponents of the use of aversive procedures with people with mental handicaps would not support his methods. However, the line that separates aversive treatment and abuse is not easily drawn. Cotter (1967) introduces his program description by describing the inspiration that he drew from Lovaas' work using food deprivation with autistic children, and he indicates that he viewed his Vietnamese project as an extension of this work. If qualitative differences exist between these two, they are not clear to Cotter or to many others who model their work after respected advocates of aversive procedures. The danger of misapplication of aversive models by untrained staff, families, and others may be greater than the danger of misapplication by trained professionals. Models of professionals using sophisticated aversive stimuli provide vicarious reinforcement for others to develop and employ their own "aversive techniques" in order to control the behavior of the people who inhabit their environment.

The model of controlling others' behavior through negative reinforcement and punishment procedures also may influence the client treated with aversive procedures as well as other clients who share the environment, to exhibit aggressive behavior. Punishment-induced aggression has been identified as a factor in child abuse and other antisocial behavior (e.g., Berkowitz, 1983; Thyer, 1987). Imitation of aversive control tactics by clients results in more inappropriate behavior which can result in harm to these clients and the people who become the targets of their aggression.

Masking the real problem

All behavior serves some function for the individual who exhibits it. The existence of the extinction phenomenon implies that once stripped of reinforcement value, behavior fades away, perhaps as the result of the response cost of efforts required to perform the behavior or as a result of the competition from other classes of behavior that continue to be functional in securing reinforcement from the environment (cf., Herrnstein, 1961). Although the nature of the reinforcement sought or obtained by self-injurious, aggressive, or disruptive behavior may be unclear to us, the existence of the behavior over time suggests that the behavior is reinforced. Furthermore, the frequency, intensity, and apparent response cost associated with many of these behaviors suggest that the reinforcers obtained, or the punishers escaped or avoided, by this behavior are powerful consequences for the individual. Attempts to suppress behavior through aversive treatment, without considering the reinforcement function that the behavior serves for the individual, may eliminate the little control that people with severe disabilities have over their environment and obscure the problem underlying the behavior. The work of Carr and Durand (1985), Donnellan, La-

Vigna, Zambito, and Thevedt, (1985), among others, suggests that identifying the function of inappropriate behavior and teaching appropriate alternatives to obtain those reinforcers can be an extremely effective, nonintrusive alternative to suppression through aversive procedures.

The suppression of inappropriate behavior through aversive procedures, prior to the identification of the underlying functions, may contribute to learned helplessness in clients by eliminating their last vestige of control over their environments. In studying sexual abuse of people with disabilities (Sobsey & Varnhagen, 1989), we encountered many cases where behavior problems developed in response to abuse. Often this behavior appeared to function to avoid repeated incidents of abuse. Perhaps most frightening, was that we encountered a number of incidents where this inappropriate behavior was treated with intrusive behavior modification procedures and/or psychotropic drugs. The well-meaning parents and professionals who instituted these programs became unknowing accomplices of the abusers, working to suppress the last defense against abuse that was available to their children or clients. Efforts to suppress behavior that result in masking the underlying function of the behavior harm disabled children and adults. When they are eventually confronted with the true nature of the problem and the unintentional harm that they have done to their children and students, these misguided efforts also hurt the well-intentioned individuals who design and implement aversive programs.

PRECISELY CONTINGENT STIMULI

Animal experiments using punishment are conducted in laboratory settings that allow for strict control over environmental conditions and precise contingent application of the aversive stimulus. This degree of experimental control may be impossible outside the laboratory. Repeatedly shocking a rat in a cage may suppress lever presses. In an open environment, the rat may not stick around for the second and third shocks. The obvious and pervasive differences that exist between laboratory and free environments have never been adequately addressed by those in the field of behaviorism. In the laboratory, experimenters wield precise consequences to manipulate subjects' behavior. Outside the laboratory, this paradigm quickly breaks down. The experimenter's behavior is as much a function of the contingencies of the subject, not to mention a plethora of other people and events in the environment, as is the subject's behavior. These differences have never been fully acknowledged or dealt with in the field of behaviorism. Although there is certainly some recognition of these differences, the models presented continue to focus on unidirectional contingencies. The behavior modifier is viewed as controlling the behavior of subjects, but who controls the behavior modifiers? Are they also organisms subject to environmental contingencies, or are they somehow immune to the rules that they rely on to shape others' behavior (cf. Lutzker and Guess, Chapters 32 and 11). Obviously, contingencies are not unidirectional, and even a bidirectional model is simplistic. Both the behavior modifier and the subject are influenced by a rich constellation of environmental events from a multitude of sources. The precision of the application of aversive consequences is limited by competing task demands on trainers, such as differences in training experiences, administrative decisions, the influence of other professionals working with the same clients, staff scheduling concerns, and, from time to time, by advocates and ethical review committees, as well as many other factors. Although some advocates of aversive procedures argue that reducing controls and restrictions on how they implement these procedures would enhance their precision of contingent application, this solution is undesirable. These professionals already exercise great power over the clients they serve. Satisfying this appeal for freedom from restriction on their powers might help to better approximate the laboratory conditions that maximize behavioral control, but it also would further inflate the inequalities between people who are disabled and their caregivers, and reduce the chance for any benefits to generalize to more natural conditions. Ironically, those who see so much value in their control over the behavior of others, even through intrusive means, resist vigorously social control over their own behavior. Skinner (1953) addresses the need for a balance between individuals and society in his discussions of countercontrol. Individuals must exert countercontrol to resist abuse by other individuals and institutions. In familiar terms, "power tends to corrupt, and absolute power corrupts absolutely" (Lord Acton, 1887). However, under the laboratory conditions required for the precise application of an independent variable, counter control is unavailable. If the degree of precision required is ever to be attained, it must be done at cost of the little remaining control that clients exert over their social environments.

Suppress the Behavior

Arguments supporting punishment procedures depend on the belief that aversive consequences will reliably and rapidly suppress inappropriate behavior, ending a threat to the individual or allowing that client to participate in a more normal life. To meet this criterion, there would have to be clear demonstrations of punishment's ability to produce these results. Certainly, there have been experimental demonstrations in the literature of the power of aversive procedures to reduce the frequency of some undesirable behavior, but clear demonstrations of superiority over less intrusive procedures are noticeably lacking for several reasons: selective publication of effective results, data analysis problems (e.g., failure to account for regression in the data),design problems (e.g., lack of phase-sequence control), attempts to compare subjects in noncomparative designs, and unjustified generalization of results of animal studies to human populations.

In their review of 61 studies of aversive procedures with clients with disabilities, Guess, Helmstetter, Turnbull, and Knowlton (1986) point out that "effectiveness cannot be assessed fully because research that shows weak or negative results is neither published nor submitted for review for publication" (p. 25). They also cite a failure of most studies to provide long-term follow-up or generalization data, and they point out that adequate experimental designs were used in only a small proportion of these studies. Therefore, they conclude that the experimental support for the use of such procedures with these clients remains suspect. Similarly, in Riznek's (1987) review of 250 research studies on intervention to reduce self-injurious and aggressive behavior, she concludes that behavioral treatments frequently demonstrate efficacy, but that no advantage has been demonstrated for aversive over nonaversive methods.

At best, experimental support for punishment suggests that for some unknown percentage of clients with disabilities, a reduction, but rarely an elimination, of inappropriate behavior can be produced for some unspecified period of time. Nothing in this implies that less intrusive procedures would fail to produce equal or better results with these same clients. Of course nonaversive procedures do not represent a perfect alternative, but results obtained with these procedures appear to represent an alternative with equal potential effectiveness. For example, Donnellan, LaVigna,

Zambito, and Thevedt (1985), working with 16 clients with developmental disabilities who were referred for severe behavior problems, were able to eliminate or reduce unacceptable behavior of all clients by using only nonaversive procedures in 15 of 16 cases and a mild time-out procedure with the remaining client. In an analysis of 162 studies to decelerate targeted behaviors, published between 1981 and 1985, Lennox, Miltenberger, Spengler, and Erfanian (1988) found that for each class of behavior, less intrusive categories of procedures demonstrated higher mean effectiveness rates than the most intrusive category.

Statistical Regression

One of the problems in attempting to evaluate the relative effects of punishment and reward is statistical regression in the data. Within-subject designs commonly used to evaluate interventions in applied behavior analysis typically compare levels of behavior during treatment and baseline phases. In testing aversive methods of reducing the frequency of inappropriate behavior, researchers typically obtain a reasonably stable measure of inappropriate behavior during baseline and then try an aversive intervention. One common difficulty with this procedure is that in the natural environment levels of inappropriate behavior rarely demonstrate ideal stability. For this reason, researchers often must compromise with data stability. Immediately prior to intervention, inappropriate behavior is typically increasing or decreasing. Most studies on punishment implement aversive procedures when the behavior is increasing for two important reasons: (a) If the behavior were already decreasing, a continued decrease would not provide a powerful demonstration of the intervention; and (b) If the behavior is already decreasing, it is difficult to rationalize ethically the use of the aversive procedure. Texts on single-subject experimental design support the experimental decision to implement interventions that the experimenter hopes will result in decreases during increasing trends, but some present a word of caution. These texts point to the phenomenon of statistical regression as a potential problem that threatens the validity of such research (e. g., Kazdin, 1982). Simply stated, this means if data are variable, during the lowest points, we should expect values to subsequently rise, and during the highest points, we should expect values to fall, with or without intervention (Campbell & Stanley, 1963; Kazdin, 1982). Regression implies that the decision to apply an aversive intervention when behavior is at or near its worst may lead to the perception that the intervention has been effective merely because of the regression phenomenon. The effects of statistical regression on data analysis may be aggravated in comparative designs that reinforce appropriate behavior. Since reinforcement typically is applied when the behavior is already improving, regression will result in behavioral deterioration.

The potential role of the regression phenomenon in producing false results favoring punishment is discussed by Kahneman and Tversky (1973) and by Tversky & Kahneman (1974), and, more importantly, has been empirically verified by Schaffner (1985). Schaffner presented 96 psychology students with simulated performance data and allowed them to select any combination of praise, no comment, mild reprimand, and strong reprimand as intervention. The simulated data remained stable (randomly varied around a mean) in one case and improved (randomly varied around an improving trend) in the second case. Both sets of data were entirely independent of any of the contingencies used. Nevertheless, more than 80% of Schaffner's subjects rated punishment as effective or very effective under both the improvement and no-change conditions, and many more subjects evaluated punishment as more effective than praise, demonstrating the bias toward punishment in specious learning.

Phase Sequence Problems

In order to compare interventions in single-subject research designs, researchers typically must apply these interventions in distinct phases, and the sequence of these phases is of paramount importance. Comparisons that always apply interventions in a fixed sequence are subject to misleading interpretation for many reasons (Kazdin, 1982). As a rule, the last intervention works best in applied behavior analysis since, when an intervention is working well, there is little reason to try a new intervention that has not yet been proven effective or to return to an earlier intervention that has been less effective. Thus, from a researcher's perspective, any controlled comparison of a more-intrusive-to-less-intrusive intervention requires that the more intrusive treatment must demonstrate its superiority when applied before less intrusive alternatives, not just when applied after them.

These comparisons present two kinds of problems. First, if nonaversive procedures already have been shown to be effective, the researcher or clinician has no right to implement apparently unnecessary punishment procedures. Second, if nonaversive procedures have not yet been tested, researchers and clinicians have a responsibility to test them before attempting aversive procedures. This makes sequential-phase comparisons possible only when nonaversive procedures have already failed. In such comparisons, only two results are possible: (a) experimental results favor aversive treatment, or (b) results show both procedures ineffective (such experiments are rarely published and rarely become part of the permanent record of our professional literature). Thus, the results of such experiments are hopelessly biased in favor of aversive procedures, and meaningful direct comparisons of aversive and nonaversive procedures are not available. Therefore, we must rely on less direct evidence.

Weak Support For Aversives

There can be little doubt that aversive procedures have been effective in reducing or decreasing the rate of inappropriate behavior in some individuals, but powerful experimental support for its superiority over nonaversive procedures is lacking. Even in reviews that support the value of punishment, authors present a number of qualifications, limitations, biases, and reservations. Perhaps more importantly, there are many other problems that are not stated.

For example, Gaylord-Ross (1982) presents a review of research and provides some further comparisons of behavioral strategies to reduce inappropriate behavior in clients with severe handicaps. In contrast to his conclusion that aversives are justified, he refers to the support for their use as "evidence from a few single case studies and the logical arguments for greater success of punishment in the most severe cases" (p.198). This statement falls far short of suggesting overwhelming experimental support, but more importantly, it suggests some underlying logic is used, adding greater power to the weak experimental support that is available. This suggests that some researchers and clinicians, believing that punishment is likely to be effective, are more likely to accept weak empirical demonstrations as validating punishment, while exercising more stringent standards in examining alternatives.

Johnson and Baumeister (1981) provide a comprehensive review of the literature on "behavioral techniques for decreasing aberrant behaviors of retarded and autistic persons" (p. 119). They conclude that aversive procedures are "effective for reducing a wide variety of aberrant behaviors" (p. 147), but they also remind us that aversive procedures do not always successfully reduce inappropriate behavior, often fail to generalize across environments (or even beyond a single trainer), may not produce results that are maintained after treatment is withdrawn, and sometimes have undesirable side effects.

FREEDOM TO DEVELOP

Without developing alternatives, we can expect that the suppressive effects of punishment will be temporary and that the inappropriate behavior will return. Skinner's (1989) discussion of rapid, spontaneous recovery of lever pressing after aversive suppression supports this notion. This suggests that a minimal requirement for programs using aversive procedures should be a nonaversive procedure aimed at developing functional alternatives. Foxx, Plaska, and Bittle (1986) address the need to include these positive program components in establishing minimum requirements for using shock as an aversive. This points out the need for basing programs on reinforcing desirable behavior and declaring that "reliance on shock as a primary means of behavior control is unacceptable" (p.7). However, few accounts of aversive programs include mention of these positive components. Many, perhaps most, aversive programs merely suppress behaviors without any attempt to replace them with appropriate functional alternatives. This suppress-and-hope strategy may occasionally work if other environmental events provide opportunities for the development of functional alternatives, but this result is unlikely, especially if the client remains in the same environment that contributed to the unacceptable behavior. If simple functional alternatives had been available to the clients without the benefit of training, it is unlikely that the extremely deviant behavior that has now been suppressed would have developed. Alternatively, if functional alternatives can be taught, aversive suppression of behavior may be unnecessary.

UNAVAILABLE ALTERNATIVES

Of course, even advocates for the use of aversive procedures would not condone their use if less intrusive alternatives were available. Advocates and opponents of aversive procedures disagree about the relative effectiveness of aversives and their alternatives, as well as what constitutes sufficient efforts to evaluate alternatives before aversive procedures are implemented.

Two conceptual problems exist in experimental studies comparing punishment with less intrusive alternatives: (a) ethical bias of results, and (b) lack of examination of environmental factors. Ethical bias of results occurs as a result of the conflict between the research objectivity and ethical responsibility of investigators. Research objectivity requires that comparisons between aversive and nonaversive procedures be made with appropriate subjects and under similar conditions that allow either procedure an equal chance of succeeding. Ethical constraints using the least intrusive alternative, however, only allow the researcher to apply aversive procedures when nonaversives have failed or have a very low probability of success. Therefore, ethical comparison of these techniques cannot be completed from an unbiased perspective. Ethical comparisons can be made only when nonaversive methods have already failed or have little probability of success, which hopelessly biases the results of these comparative studies.

A lack of consideration of environmental factors is the second problem. Comparative reviews typically include DRO, DRI, extinction, time-out, and aversive procedures, but they rarely include procedures related to internal or external setting events. For some readers, the need to consider the function of the aberrant behavior may seem contrary to applied behavior analysis, but this is not the case. The need to consider context has been recognized by leading behaviorists for years (e.g., Keller & Schoenfeld, 1950; Michael, 1982) and still remains an essential (e.g., Hawkins, 1989), though poorly addressed, issue.

In one of the better group comparative studies with results favoring punishment, Gaylord-Ross (1982) compared intrusive and less intrusive interventions. Results favored contingent restraint (a punishment procedure), and Gaylord-Ross ranked the interventions in the following order (from least to most effective): baseline, reinforcement withdrawal, omission training, differential reinforcement of incompatible behavior, and contingent restraint. While the punishment procedure did produce the lowest mean level of self-injurious behavior, several other procedures were also effective. In fact, the punishment procedure was the most effective intervention for only 10 of the 22 subjects, indicating that equal or better results were obtained for the majority of subjects with less intrusive procedures. This finding would be difficult to justify in a model that requires the exhaustion of less intrusive methods before the application of punishment. Even discounting this fact, there is a second procedural problem that raises a serious question about the results of this study. The contingent restraint procedure required the trainer to restrain the arms of the client for 1 minute each time that the self-injurious behavior occurred. To compensate for this procedure, rates of self-injury during this condition were prorated to adjust the length of the observation period. This adjustment, when no self-injury was possible, was an appropriate but inadequate control for the bias introduced. Self-injurious behavior is rarely, if ever, randomly distributed across time. Therefore, self-injurious responses are more likely to occur at times immediately following other self-injurious responses, and the loss of these minutes of data systematically removes the observations most likely to contain the self-injurious behaviors. True equivalence would be obtained by eliminating the data from other conditions that occurred within 1 minute from the first behavior in each episode. Again, a systematic bias favoring punishment is introduced.

In another thorough review of decelerative treatment procedures, Lennox, Miltenberger, Spengler, and Erfanian (1988) found less intrusive procedures to be more effective than more intrusive procedures. In five classes of inappropriate behavior for which published studies were available in each of the three intrusiveness levels identified, the least intrusive level (e.g., antecedent control, satiation, instruction) produced the highest mean percent of effectiveness in three classes, and the second level (e.g., extinction, disapproval, overcorrection) produced the best results in the other two classes. The most intrusive level (e.g., facial screening, mechanical restraint, contingent slapping, taste aversion) was least effective in three of the five categories, with second place finishes in the other two.

Considering the dearth of comparative research, the design problems common in the comparisons that do exist, the mixed results of research on the effectiveness of punishment, and the existing studies suggesting that nonaversive treatments can also wield powerful results, no clear case exists to suggest that aversive methods are more effective than their nonaversive alternatives.

The Mystique Of Intrusiveness

The doctrine that suggests that we begin treatment with the least intrusive method and use more intrusive methods when less intrusive ones fail is an important ethical and legal principle. However, the understanding of this rule has contributed to the superstitious belief in the power of punishment. It should be pointed out that the "least intrusive" rule has legal and judicial foundations; it is not derived from behavioral theory, educational theory, or research. Basically, it implies that "the government that governs least, governs best." Although the state has some right to exercise control for certain purposes, it has a responsibility to exercise this control in a manner that intrudes least on the people it governs. Therefore, although summary execution might be used to control littering, the government has a responsibility to exercise less intrusive means whenever possible. Similarly, while therapists may have a right to control a certain behavior, they have a responsibility to do so in the least intrusive manner. Thus, the alternatives in behavior management are often portrayed as a continuum from least to most intrusive, indicating that the most intrusive is a last resort when all else fails and that each step toward this alternative may be taken only after the previous method fails. This continuum is typically portrayed as unidimensional. Unfortunately, the application of this continuum requires that the last or most intrusive procedure attempted is the only procedure that can be demonstrated as being effective because more intrusive procedures can only be used when less intrusive ones have already failed and cannot be applied when a less intrusive one has already been demonstrated as effective. This creates an illusion that more intrusive methods are also more effective methods, when no such conclusion is justified. Just as we generally find things (if we find them at all) in the last place that we look (because when we have found them we stop looking), we generally succeed in controlling undesirable behavior (if we succeed at all) with the last intervention that we try. In reality, there is every reason to believe that more aversive interventions can be more effective in some cases after nonaversive alternatives fail. Similarly, nonaversive interventions will prove to be more effective in some cases, even after more aversive alternatives fail. Effectiveness is an independent characteristic unrelated to intrusiveness.

This relationship between effectiveness and aversiveness may be confused further by animal experiments that suggest that increasing the intensity of an aversive stimulus increases its power to control behavior. However, these experiments present a very different comparison, a true continuum of amplitude of a single variable (e.g., electric shock), not an artificial continuum of qualitatively different procedures (e.g., aversive and nonaversive alternatives).

Neither empirical data nor underlying concepts provide adequate evidence to demonstrate that one category of intervention is commonly more effective than another. Therefore, a discussion comparing the merits of aversive and nonaversive alternatives cannot be presented as one that compares the merits of harsh but effective procedures against humanistic but weak procedures.

CLEAR BENEFIT TO THE CLIENT

This final criterion cannot be addressed apart from the discussion of the previous criteria because it flows directly from them. If aversive procedures were truly brief and harmless, precisely applied, provided to be effective ways to suppress dangerous behavior, and allowed freedom to develop more adaptive behavior, and nonaversive alternatives were indisputably unavailable, then aversive procedures would be of clear benefit to the client. However, aversive procedures often are used for extended periods, produce harm, are imprecisely applied, fail to reliably eliminate the targeted behavior, and are used in place of nonaversive alternatives that focus on developing appropriate behavior (rather than in conjunction with these alternatives). Therefore, failing on the other criteria, the criterion of clear benefit cannot be met.

There may be, and probably have been, some individuals whose interests are best served by the application of aversive procedures, but there have been many others whose interests have been violated by them. People with intellectual impairment do have a right to safe and effective treatment, but the issue of the right to seek effective treatment becomes incredibly complex when even professionals in the field disagree on the value of the procedures in question and the clients receive the treatment against their will on the basis of consent of a surrogate decision maker. Such procedures should be considered for use only in rare circumstances, and additional countercontrol measures should be in place to minimize their use. Due process procedures are required to protect all members of our society from other forms of punishment. The protection of the law and the right to due process are not conferred as a result of criminal accusations but, rather, are a result of the penalties faced. Consequently, we cannot justify punishing other members of society without a trial simply because we do not accuse them of a crime. If we accept less rigorous procedures for the implementation of aversive procedures for people with disabilities, we provide them with less protection than we would if they were criminals. Currently, many people with disabilities in our society are not being treated like criminals: Criminals have more rights. Equal protection would require us to give people with disabilities the same protection. On the whole, the use of aversive procedures has a poor record, but if there are appropriate circumstances for their use, each case must be individually assessed. If the implementation of aversive procedures can be justified for some individuals, a court order should be required after a hearing to review the potential risks and benefits to the individual.

REFERENCES

Acton, Lord [J. E. E. Dalberg] (1887, April 5), Letter to Mandell Creighton.

Berkowitz, L. (1983). The experience of anger as a parallel process in the display of impulsive, "angry" aggression. In R. G. Geen & E. U. Donnerstein (Eds.), *Aggression: Theoretical and empirical reviews: Vol. 1. Theoretical and methodological issues*. (pp. 103-133). New York: Academic Press.

Campbell, D. T., & Stanley, J. C. (1963). *Experimental and quasi-experimental designs for research*. Chicago: Rand-McNally.

Carr, E. G., & Durand, V. M. (1985). Reducing behavior problems through functional communication training. *Journal of Applied Behavior Analysis, 28*, 111-126.

Cotter, L. H. (1967). Operant conditioning in a Vietnamese mental hospital. *American Journal of Psychiatry, 124*, 23-28.

Donnellan, A. W., LaVigna, G. W., Zambito, J., & Thevedt, J. (1985) A time limited intervention program model to support community placement for persons with severe handicaps. *Journal of the Association for Persons with Severe Handicaps, 10*, 123-131.

Foxx, R. M., Plaska, T. G., & Bittle, R. G. (1986). Guidelines for the use of shock to treat aberrant behavior. In M. Hersen, R. M. Eisler, & P. M. Miller (Eds.), *Progress in behavior modification, Vol. 20* (pp. 1-34). Orlando, FL: Academic Press.

Gaylord-Ross, R. J. (1982). Curricular considerations in treating behavior problems of severely handicapped students. *Advances in Learning and Behavioral Disabilities, 1*, 193- 224.

Griffen, J. C., Paisey, T. J., Stark, M. T., & Emerson, J. H. (1988). B. F. Skinner's position on aversive treatment. *American Journal of Mental Deficiency, 93*, 104-105.

Guess, D., Helmstetter, E., Turnbull, H. R., & Knowlton, S. (1986). *Use of aversive procedures with persons who are disabled: An historical review and critical analysis*, (Monograph #2) Seattle: The Association for Persons with Severe Handicaps.

Hawkins, R. P. (1989). Yes, context matters: Behavior analysis is maturing. *American Journal on Mental Retardation, 93*, 357-360.

Herrnstein, R. J. (1961). Relative and absolute strength of responses as a function of frequency of reinforcement. *Journal of the Experimental Analysis of Behavior, 4*, 267-272.

Hurley, A. D., & Sovner, R. (1983). Behavior modification techniques II: Punishment. *Psychiatric Aspects of Mental Retardation Newsletter, 2(12)*, 45-48.

Johnson, W. L., & Baumeister, A. A. (1981). Behavioral techniques for decreasing aberrant behaviors of retarded and autistic persons. In M. Hersen, R. M. Eisler, & P. M. Miller (Eds.), *Progress in behavior modification, Vol.12* (pp. 119-170). New York: Academic Press.

Kahneman, D., & Tversky, A. (1973). On the psychology of prediction. *Psychological Review, 80*, 237-251.

Kazdin, A. E. (1982). *Single-case research designs: Methods for clinical and applied settings*. New York: Oxford University Press.

Keller, F. S., & Schoenfeld, W. N. (1950). *Principles of psychology*. New York: Appleton-Century-Crofts.

Lennox, D. B., Miltenberger, R. G., Spengler, P., & Erfanian, N. (1988). Decelerative treatment practices with persons who have mental retardation: A review of five years of literature. *American Journal on Mental Retardation, 92*, 492-501.

Michael, J. (1982). Distinguishing between discriminative and motivational functions of stimuli. *Journal of the Experimental Analysis of Behavior, 37,* 149-155.

Parsons State Hospital and Training Center. (1977). *Randy's up, Randy's down*. [film]. Parsons, KS: Producer.

Riznek, L. A. (1987). *Review of the literature related to self-injury and aggressive behaviour among developmentally handicapped persons.* Toronto: Ontario Ministry of Community and Social Services.

Schaffner, P. E. (1985). Specious learning about reward and punishment. *Journal of Personality and Social Psychology, 48*, 1377-1386.

Skinner, B. F. (1953). *Science and human behavior*. New York: Free Press.

B. F. Skinner Opposes Use of Punishment. (1987, November). LINKS, 23 (11).

Skinner, B. F. (1989). *Recent issues in the analysis of behavior*. Columbus, OH: Charles E. Merrill.

Sobsey, D., & Varnhagen, C. (1989). Sexual abuse of people with disabilities. In M. Csapo & L. Gougen (Eds.), *Special education across Canada: Challenges for the 90's*. (pp. 199-218). Vancouver: Centre for Human Development & Research.

Stainton, T. (1988) Aversive conditioning: Necessity or failure? In G. Allan Roeher Institute. *The language of pain: Perspectives on behavior management*. Downsview, Ontario: G. Allan Roeher Institute.

Thyer, B. A. (1987). Punishment-induced aggression: A possible mechanism of child abuse? *Psychological Reports, 60*, 129-130.

Tversky, A., & Kahneman, D. (1974). Judgment under uncertainty. *Science, 185*, 1124-1131.

CHAPTER

28

THE CONTROVERSY OVER AVERSIVES: BASIC OPERANT RESEARCH AND THE SIDE EFFECTS OF PUNISHMENT

Thomas R. Linscheid and Patricia Meinhold
The Ohio State University

The existence of the current volume is ample testimony to the ongoing controversy surrounding the use of "aversive procedures" to treat severe behavior disorders in individuals with mental retardation or developmental disabilities. In reality, the controversy boils down to one of choice versus no-choice regarding the decision to use aversive procedures in an overall comprehensive treatment program. In the "no-choice" situation, parents, legal guardians, clinicians, and human rights committees are prohibited from making certain choices. In the "choice" position, these individuals are allowed to make choices regarding the use of aversive procedures, but only in controlled and supervised situations in which full informed consent is obtained from the client and the client's parents or legal guardians.

In this controversy, the roles of science and ideology in decision making have often been discussed (Guess, Helmstetter, Turnbull, & Knowlton, 1986; Meinhold & Mulick,1990; Mulick, in press). Statements by proponents of a complete ban on the use of treatment procedures employing aversive stimuli (e.g., Guess, et al., 1986) have been based largely on ideological grounds, rather than scientific ones, although behavioral science research is frequently cited in support of such a ban (Mulick, in press). The relationship between science and social values and goals is complex, and technologies that have a significant impact on society need to be examined from the perspective of both scientific and social criteria (see Meinhold & Mulick, 1990, for a detailed discussion of decision making about technologies).

For example, science has provided us with the capability through prenatal diagnosis and abortion to eliminate Down's syndrome if every expectant mother were tested and agreed to an abortion if the fetus is shown to have the condition. Clearly, the scientific or technological accuracy of prenatal screening for Down's syndrome is a critical component of such a decision, but additional factors such as personal ideology, religious beliefs, and society's role in the protection of people with handicaps are just a few of the concerns that are also relevant. This issue is complicated by recent evidence that the capabilities of individuals with Down's syndrome, given appropriate education and training, are higher than once thought (Pueschel, 1978). A socially or ideologically motivated decision to seek or not to seek an abortion of a fetus with Down's syndrome does not change the scientific accuracy of prenatal screening or the scientific evidence about the prognosis for intellectual development in Down's syndrome children. The scientific integrity of the technology is not dependent on its social uses (although the uses of the technology may be limited by scientific evidence).

In this chapter, we will discuss some of the ways that scientific evidence about the effects of aversive stimulation may have been misrepresented or misunderstood in the debate about the use of aversive stimuli in treatment procedures. We will review some of the behavioral research frequently cited in statements of the anti aversive position and present some caveats for how these data should be applied (or should not be applied) to treatment questions. Finally, we will present a selective review of some research on the "side effects" of various behavioral contingencies, with suggestions for ways in which the current experimental literature might be applied to a range of questions about behavioral treatment procedures.

THE APPLICATION OF BEHAVIORAL SCIENCE TO APPLIED ISSUES

The interplay between science and ideology is crucial for the future and progress of mankind, and the two must, by necessity, interplay. In this process, two major errors can occur. The first occurs when scientists assume that science always exists independent of the theology, morals, and ethics of the world in which it resides. We all know that those topics chosen for study, the biases inherent in conducting scientific experiments, and the interpretation of data can influence scientific activity and findings. We cannot say that every scientist functions independently of values, motivations, and past life experiences. However, a defining feature of scientific study is recognition and either control for, or elimination of, social and personal bias in scientific inquiry whenever possible. The *explicit* influence of social motivations belongs in the realm of policy development and individual decisions about the application of scientific evidence, not in the interpretation of scientific data.

Scientific evidence and social values also interact (in inappropriate ways) when scientific evidence is presented or interpreted in the service of ideological positions. This is a misuse of science that is often either overlooked or justified by those with strong ideological positions. Ideologues select only those studies that support their point of view and ignore experiments or lines of research that question their position. The existence of discussion sections in scientific reports suggests that even though studies are conducted in a rigid, scientific manner, interpretation of data is open for debate so that, although a study may not be ignored, results may be reinterpreted in the service of an ideological bias. Finally, certain positions can be supported through the inappropriate and inaccurate application of experimental evidence to an applied question. This problem generally occurs when the purpose of an experimental study and the conditions under which it was conducted are not directly applicable to the question at hand. For example, it can occur when the research employs conditions or paradigms that are poor models of applied situations, or when a highly controlled experimental situation differs from the applied context on important dimensions (e.g., the range or intensity of stimuli employed, the response repertoire of the organism under study, complex social stimuli or responses). Inappropriate applications of experimental evidence also occur when certain elements of experimental and applied situations are similar but others differ, making interpretation difficult and thus requiring extensive qualification of a particular application.

In the controversy regarding the use of aversives, much reference has been made to the behavioral literature and what it may have to tell us regarding the use of both positive and aversive procedures. This literature is characterized by two tracts, basic and applied, as evidenced by the existence of two prominent journals, *Journal of the Experimental Analysis of Behavior* and *Journal of Applied Behavior Analysis*. These two journals represent two lines of research that have evolved from the behavioral approach to psychology. The experimental analysis of behavior is characterized by the investigation of learning phenomenon, generally studied in highly controlled experimental and laboratory settings in which the relationship between environmental events and behavior can be precisely controlled and quantified. In applied behavioral research, the application of behavioral principles to therapeutic behavior change is generally studied in less restrictive laboratory settings, and experimenters often have less control of environmental variables than in the experimental analysis literature. Studies in the *Journal of the Experimental Analysis of Behavior* usually are not conducted to produce therapeutic behavior change, although the goal of most studies in the applied literature is therapeutic behavior change.

Recently, several writers have lamented the separation between basic and applied behavior analysis (Durand, 1987; Redmon & Farris, 1987), and have suggested a return to behavioral roots where possible and a reemphasis on strategies of functional analysis. We concur with this call for, at minimum, a reawakening of our interest and knowledge about basic and applied behavioral research and what that information can contribute to the ongoing controversy surrounding aversive treatment procedures. This is not to suggest that a reexamination of basic operant and respondent animal research will solve the dilemma but, rather, a suggestion that knowledge of basic research will improve our ability to evaluate objectively statements being made by both sides of this controversy which are reportedly based on "the literature."

In this chapter, we will examine basic research on the effects of aversive stimuli as they pertain to elicited aggression and emotional reactions, and response variation and induction.

BASIC RESEARCH ON AVERSIVE STIMULI

Elicited Aggression And Elicited Emotional States

One of the arguments against the use of punishment procedures for treating severe behavior problems is that punishment leads to emotional distress and aggression toward others in the environment. In a recent book by one of the early leaders in the field of animal operant research (Sidman, 1989), an entire chapter is devoted to the phenomenon of aggression elicited by punishment. Sidman describes aggression in animals and man resulting from punishment and aversive stimuli, and uses this phenomenon to explain world terrorism and revenge. Likewise, LaVigna and Donnellan (1986), leading proponents of a strictly nonaversive agenda, state that "the early literature on punishment demonstrated that aggression may be elicited by punishment and that this response to an aversive stimulus or event appears to be unlearned" (p. 178). Other authors, well known for their strong antiaversive position, make numerous statements in reference to the tendency of aversive stimuli to elicit emotional states, aggressive responses or other undesirable behaviors (cf. Meyer & Evans, 1989).

These statements are interesting in light of other published reports describing positive side effects occurring in individuals who have undergone treatment of severe behavior problems using aversive conditioning procedures. Reviews of published studies in which electric shock has been used as a punishing stimulus to decrease rates of self-injurious and aggressive behavior have indicated that positive side effects outnumber negative side effects generally in the range of 5 to 1 (Carr & Lovaas, 1983; Favell et al., 1982). While these reports are often anecdotal, Linscheid, Iwata, Ricketts, Williams, and Griffin (1990) have recently documented an increase in behaviors suggesting a calm, relaxed state during treatment with contingent electrical stimulation applied by an automated electric shock device. Apparently, findings from early animal studies on elicited aggression behavior and observations from human studies on the effects of punishment may not be in agreement (See Axelrod & Apsche, 1983, for a discussion of the effects of punishment on human behavior).

To address these seemingly inconsistent findings, we will review the early research on elicited aggression in order that the reader may judge the applicability of these early studies to the use of operant punishment procedures for severe behavior disorders. Interestingly, studies of elicited aggression were generally undertaken using electric shock and a major focus in the controversy between advocates of aversives and nonaversives has been on the introduction of an automated shock device known as the Self-Injurious Behavior Inhibiting System or SIBIS (Linscheid et al., 1990).

The phenomenon of elicited aggression was first noted 50 years ago by O'Kelly and Steckle (1939). Early reports studied the phenomenon by placing two animals, most commonly rats, in a small chamber and periodically delivering electric shock to the feet of the animals through the floor grid. While the phenomenon was noted much earlier, the first parametric investigation of the effect was reported in 1962 (Ulrich & Azrin, 1962). Ulrich and Azrin defined fighting between the rats as suddenly facing each other in an upright position, with heads thrust forward, and vigorously striking at each other with their mouths wide open. This behavior was measured by a simple frequency count in which a new response was recorded only for those fighting episodes separated by at least one second from the previous episode. Rats known to be docile were studied in pairs in a small chamber from which no escape was possible.

In the first experiment, the effect of the frequency of electric shock on fighting behavior was investigated. Shocks were delivered at frequencies of 0.1, 0.6, 2, 6, 20 and 38 per minute. Three separate pairs of animals were studied. Results indicated a clear positive relationship between the frequency of the shocks and frequency of fighting. More frequent shocks also resulted in a higher percentage of shocks which elicited fighting. When shock frequency was low, the percentage of shocks which resulted in fighting episodes decreased. When only one shock (0.1 per minute) was received during the 10-minute testing session, fighting responses occurred following one-third to two-thirds of the shocks. In contrast, at a frequency of 38 shocks per minute, fighting responses occurred after more than 85% of the shock deliveries.

Shock intensity was also investigated, using a fixed frequency of 20 shocks per minute. Interestingly, while the range of shock intensity was from 0.5 milliampere to 5.0 milliamperes, the highest rate of fighting was elicited at an intensity of 2.0 milliamperes. The authors ascribed the decreased rate of fighting at higher intensities to debilitating effects of the shock. Apparently, high intensity shocks elicited other behaviors, such as running, biting the grid, and jumping to escape.

Ulrich and Azrin investigated two other factors related to fighting behavior. In one experimental manipulation, they allowed rats to escape or avoid the electric foot shock by straddling grids so that their feet were in contact with only either the positive or negative electrical charges of the shock device. The rat's ability to do this was noted in prior research and, indeed, to counteract this phenomenon, shock scramblers are frequently used. These scramblers continually and rapidly reverse the polarity of adjoining grids so that animals are not able to avoid or escape the shock. During sessions in which the scrambler was turned off, allowing escape from or avoidance of the shock, the number of fighting episodes decreased dramatically. By observation, when rats were effectively straddling the bars and avoiding or escaping the shock, no fighting occurred. This is an important and significant finding in light of subsequent research to be reviewed later: the ability to escape or avoid preprogrammed electric shock results in the near total absence of elicited aggression.

The effects of the size of the experimental chamber on fighting responses was also studied. Results clearly indicated that a small, confined area in which the initial studies were done (.25 square feet) resulted in fighting responses to nearly 100% of the shock applications. Increasing the area of the chamber to one square foot reduced the percentage of fighting responses to approximately 60%, and an increase to 2.25 square feet and above reduced the rate of fighting responses to 10% or less. It is clear that the size of the experimental chamber (presumably mediated by the close physical proximity of subjects) affects the rate of fighting responses. Ulrich and Azrin further found that elicited fighting responses occurred in hamsters and rats but failed to occur in mature guinea pigs, and that lower intensities, which failed to elicit fighting in rats, were capable of eliciting the fighting response in hamsters. When a rat and a guinea pig were placed in a cage together, the rat attacked the guinea pig following electric shock, but the guinea pig failed to attack. This result suggests that there may be species differences in the existence of the fighting response and in the intensity needed to elicit the response. The authors also noted that other aversive stimuli, such as intense heat, could elicit the fighting responses, but that loud noise and moderate cold failed to do so. While Ulrich and Azrin (1962) did not find fighting or attack responses to inanimate objects, or even to another recently deceased rat, Azrin, Hutchinson, and Sallery (1964) were able to demonstrate aggressive responses to inanimate objects by monkeys. To study this phenomenon, they strapped monkeys into a small test chamber so that the monkey could not engage in gross physical movement and the electrical stimulation could be consistently applied to a portion of the animal's tail. A bite bar, similar to a section of rubber hose, was mounted directly in front of the animal, and bites (attacks) on the bar were recorded through mechanical and electrical devices.

Hutchinson (1977) describes a paradigm for measuring bite reactions in humans, using EMG feedback without the awareness of the subjects. These procedures with monkeys and humans have allowed the investigation of the effects of aversive stimulation presentation without requiring the physical proximity of another animal of the same species. Hutchinson summarizes the results of a series of studies in which the occurrence of sensory scanning, manual manipulation, and locomotion responses reliably accompany the presentation of noncontingent aversive stimuli when repeatedly delivered in a temporal pattern that is discriminable to the subject. As a time for the aversive stimulation nears, these responses occur at a progressively increasing rate until just before the aversive stimulus, when all reactions cease. Despite the subject's being able to discriminate the impending delivery, of the aversive stimulation, attack reactions occur only after the actual delivery, and the alternative responses (such as sensory scanning, locomotion, and manual manipulation) appear to be prepotent prior to the delivery of the stimulus. When the opportunity to attack was eliminated by removing the bite bar, manual responses and sensory scanning increased. Hutchinson concluded that when allowed, "attack reactions are prepotent over other locomotor manipulative reactions subsequent to aversive stimulation" (p. 420).

Hutchinson notes, however, that this response may be contingent upon an experimental apparatus which does not allow free movement and confines the animal by nature of the small area of the chamber. Also, in the case of humans, subjects were aware that they would be exposed to aversive stimuli, and they were guaranteed beforehand that the intensity would not be intolerable and that they would receive monetary remuneration for their participation. Hutchinson warns strongly that interpretation of these results must be conservative because the testing paradigms were designed to prevent a whole class of behaviors (gross motor movement, fleeing) which are known to occur in humans and animals in response to aversive stimulation in the natural environment. The issue of response alternatives will be discussed in more detail later in this chapter.

Hutchinson's warnings regarding the interpretations of these findings, given the highly structured and controlled nature of the experimentation, are particularly important in light of a series of studies that examined the effects of escape and avoidance responses on elicited aggression. Early studies on elicited aggression used preprogrammed, unavoidable, noncontingent electrical stimulation. The Ulrich and Azrin (1962) study showed that providing opportunities for escape or avoidance when the shock scrambler was turned off resulted in lower rates of fighting behavior. This phenomena was systematically evaluated by Azrin, Hutchinson and Hake (1966) in a series of experiments using both rats and monkeys. The first experiment investigated whether the opportunity to attack would interfere with the acquisition of an escape response. Two groups of rats were used to study this question. The first group (control) was placed in a standard operant chamber in which the lever press response could terminate a 1-second electrical stimulus applied through a floor grid. A lever press between shock deliveries had no effect. While the shock was programmed to last one second, depression of the lever at any time during the shock immediately terminated it (escape response). The control group's acquisition of the escape response was studied while rats were alone in the operant chamber. The second group of rats experienced the same conditions, except that a second or target rat was also in the operant chamber. The target rat was restrained by a harness device in one corner of the chamber opposite the lever, and did not receive the electric shock.

Results indicated that both groups of rats acquired the escape response, but that the group of rats placed in the chamber alone acquired the escape response more rapidly and to a greater extent. Rats that were placed in the chamber with another rat achieved only a 50 percent probability of avoiding or escaping the stimulus, and on trials when the electrical stimulation was not escaped, the rats engaged in attack behavior. The 50 percent probability, however, was based on a group mean. In examining the behavior of individual rats, the authors found that there were some rats that had learned to escape the shock on nearly 100 percent of the trials. In these cases, attack responses dropped proportionally and to zero in some cases. Rats that had not learned the escape response during the initial acquisition phase were provided with escape learning opportunities without the presence of a second rat. Once the escape response was acquired, the second rat was reintroduced. In this situation the escape response dominated the attack response, which was reduced to near zero. There appeared to be some rats that were capable of learning the escape response, even though the opportunity for attack was present and some rats for whom acquisition of the escape response was prevented by the competing attack response. Given the opportunity to learn the escape response, however, animals chose to engage in this response to electric shock when a second animal subsequently was reintroduced.

In a second experiment, Azrin, Hutchinson and Hake (1966) demonstrated that as the requirement for escape increased (i.e., increasing fixed ratio responses required to terminate the shock), the attack responses dominated. From these two experiments, the authors concluded that, despite the presence of another animal in the chamber and the opportunity to attack, some of the animals were able to learn the escape response. The dominant response to the aversive stimulus appeared to be escape rather than attack once the escape response was learned.

In a second set of experiments using monkeys as subjects, electric shocks were programmed to occur every 30 seconds, but could be avoided by a lever press occurring at any time during that 30-second interval. A bite bar mounted in the chamber recorded the amount of elicited aggression. During a baseline phase in which the lever was not available and shocks were delivered at 30-second intervals regardless of the animal's behavior, high rates of biting were observed. Once animals successfully acquired the avoidance response, however, bites occurred only when shocks were delivered (i.e., when the animal failed to press the lever within 30 seconds). The number of bites per session was directly related to the number of shocks received.

Unlike the previous experiments in which rats were subjects and the physical distance between the target rat and the manipulandum prevented both responses from occurring, monkeys in this study could engage in the biting response and the avoidance lever press response simultaneously. The results indicate that animals that have acquired an avoidance response do not show elicited aggression, which was a biting response in this case.

To further demonstrate the finding that decreases in biting were not related to some type of response incompatibility with the lever press response, another experiment was conducted in which the monkeys had to depress the lever and keep it depressed in order to escape electric shocks that were delivered every 1 second at a duration of 1/10 of a second. As long as the monkey held the lever down, no shocks were received, but, when the lever was released, a rapid series of shocks was delivered. Animals in this study quickly learned to depress the lever and hold it down for the entire duration of a session. When animals were successfully escaping the shock by depressing the lever, bites were practically nonexistent. During reversal phases, when depressing the lever failed to prevent the shock pulses from being delivered, bites increased dramatically and lever depression decreased.

Further experiments in this series confirmed the fact that both escape and avoidance responses either decrease dramatically or totally eliminate aggressive responses. Results clearly showed that both escape and avoidance responses are prepotent over attack responses, and that the presence of another animal interferes with the acquisition of escape behavior when the two responses are physically incompatible. Once escape or avoidance is learned, however, animals engage in these behaviors almost exclusively, despite the presence of a target animal or object.

Interestingly, elicited aggressive responses have been described as reflexive in nature, suggesting that they are elicited rather than emitted. In light of the above results, however, there may be a high degree of variability in reflexive responses to noncontingent aversive stimulation, and a fighting response may be prepotent over the flight response only if escape or avoidance is not possible. In support of this, Hake (1969) demonstrated that monkeys would work to change a schedule from unavoidable to avoidable shocks. Hake interpreted this result to mean that animals found the reduction in potential shocks to be rewarding, suggesting that animals prefer situations in which they, by their behavior, are capable, of avoiding shock even though the potential for shock remains the same.

Aggression Elicited By Positive Reinforcement

The studies reviewed to this point have demonstrated the existence of elicited aggression in situations in which escape and avoidance are not possible, and aversive electrical stimulation is programmed noncontingently. Interestingly, elicited aggression also occurs in situations in which only positive reinforcement is programmed. Gentry (1968) showed that pigeons responding to an FR 50 schedule of food reinforcement engaged in attack behavior toward another pigeon. Typically, the pigeons would emit the 50 responses required for food reinforcement, eat the food and then attack a second pigeon that was in the chamber but was physically restrained from engaging in food-reinforced pecking behavior.

Aggression appears to be elicited by extinction as well. Pigeons, conditioned to peck a key for food reward, attacked another live pigeon, or a stuffed model of a pigeon, at the onset of a signaled or unsignaled period of extinction (Azrin, Hutchinson, & Hake, 1967). Hutchinson, Azrin, and Hunt (1968) demonstrated both schedule-induced and extinction-induced aggression in squirrel monkeys. Subjects were tested in an operant chamber in which lever pressing produced food reinforcement on an FR schedule, and a bite bar (rubber hose) was present. Biting occurred at two times: during the postreinforcement pause and early in the ratio response runs. Biting responses increased with transitions to higher ratios and in response to extinction.

Elicited aggression may not be just a phenomena of noncontingent presentation of aversive stimuli, but also may be elicited by the properties of a schedule of positive reinforcement. This seeming negative side effect and other potential negative side effects of positive reinforcement have been discussed further by Balsam and Bondy (1983) who refer to applications with humans. The phenomenon of aggression elicited by extinction is particularly relevant to examining the aggressive or distressed emotional responding noted in some aversive treatment studies with humans. If one can assume that the target behavior (e.g., self-injurious behavior) has been maintained by its consequences (positive or negative reinforcement), then the application of an aversive stimulus intended as a punisher functionally initiates a period of extinction because the behavior fails to produce the reinforcement (as well as producing the contingent aversive stimulus). Whether aggression or emotional distress is elicited by extinction or by the aversive stimulus is unknown. Since it has been shown that avoidance of the aversive stimulus will eliminate the aggressive response (and in these clinical applications, simple response inhibition always functions as an effective avoidance response), it seems likely that the observed aggression or emotional distress may be the result of extinction rather than the aversive stimulus.

To summarize, the phenomena of elicited aggression has been studied primarily in lower animals in situations in which alternative responding has been prevented by physical means and aversive electrical stimulations have been programmed noncontingently. In these situations, attack responses are determined by variables, including physical proximity of the animals, species of the animals, opportunities for escape or avoidance, intensity of the stimulation, and general size of the experimental chamber. There is also evidence that programmed aversive stimulation affects the rate of other manipulative responding, and can lead to increases in repetitive and motor behaviors and environmental vigilance. Given this summary, application of findings from elicited aggression studies on animals to programmed contingent punishment treatment procedures with humans is questionable. Generally, in behavior modification programs utilizing aversive stimuli as contingent punishment, individuals are not confined to small areas in which they are forced into close physical proximity with other individuals, and human subjects nearly always have available to them responses which serve to escape or avoid contingent presentation of the aversive stimulation. In some cases, the avoidance response is simply the absence of the target behavior (e.g., head banging). Given that some correspondence exists between animal studies and human applications, elicited aggression does not appear to be a necessary by-product of contingent aversive stimulation. What responses or response classes, then, can be expected when a given target behavior is suppressed by punishment? Recent research on response distribution may help to answer this question and will be reviewed in the next section.

Multiple Response Analyses And Response Distribution

Historically, behavioral scientists have studied the side effects of both punishment and reinforcement contingencies *directly,* using several different experimental paradigms. For example, the concurrent schedule preparation, in which an animal is presented with two or more response alternatives (e.g., pecking on either of two keys, each of which is associated with a different schedule of reinforcement), has a long history in the experimental analysis of behavior (e.g., Catania, 1962, 1963; Herrnstein, 1961). Concurrent schedule preparations allow for tests of the "competition" between schedules (or between responses associated with alternative schedules) and provide information about how changes in the schedule associated with one response can affect the rate of *other* responses. This is precisely the question that we are often faced with in planning a behavioral intervention. For example, what will happen to the rate of social approach if all social consequences for tantrums are removed?

Over the past decade or so, several models of response distribution have emerged from ethologic studies of the economics of response allocation (for example, studies of foraging), and from related optimality and maximizing accounts of response allocation (e.g., Rachlin & Burkhard, 1978; Staddon, 1980). For example, an optimality account of response distribution might assume that organisms distribute their responses in such a way that the "optimal" relationship between effort and obtained reinforcement (or between related measures such as number of responses and reinforcement rate) is maintained as the organism adjusts to changes in schedule requirements. Mathematical models have been developed describing the changes in response distribution that will be necessary to reach and maintain optimal ratios of responses to reinforcement (e.g., Staddon, 1980).

Although no single result or methodology taken from the experimental study of response allocation can be applied to treatment issues in mental retardation without careful translation, the relevance of this area of study to common clinical situations should be clear. For example, the apparent competition between the sensory consequences that maintain some stereotyped behaviors and SIB (e.g., Rincover & Devany, 1982) and the social or edible consequences scheduled to follow more adaptive skills (e.g., language or social behavior) is familiar to clinicians working with severely disabled clients. How do we induce a client to "choose" adaptive over maladaptive responding? These questions are especially relevant to treatment planning for disorders maintained by multiple sources of reinforcement or by reinforcers, such as self-stimulation, over which the clinician may have little control. We know very little about the limits on scheduled sources of reinforcement; for example, potential limits imposed by the availability of alternative schedules of reinforcement provided by sensory stimulation, escape, or other "unscheduled" events.

The relationship between these kinds of clinical questions and experimental work on processes such as response distribution and choice is complex, but behavioral clinicians should strive to draw appropriate analogies between the two. For example, the success of careful applications of animal experimental work to the treatment of behavior disorders is attested to by the recent application of a response deprivation model to the identification of novel sources of reinforcement and idiosyncratic punishment effects in treating people with mental retardation (e.g., Aeschleman & Williams, 1989; Holburn & Dougher, 1986; Konarski, Johnson, Crowell, & Whitman, 1981). These investigators found that the relative restriction of a response (response deprivation in comparison to the unrestricted, baseline rate of responding) can determine the reinforcing or punishing "value" of a response, regardless of the nature of the response itself. For example, Holburn and Dougher (1986) found that noncontingent placement of the experimenter's hand over one client's mouth could function as either a punisher or as a reinforcer, depending on the rate of hand placements in comparison with the baseline rate of this behavior.

Response deprivation procedures and other modern investigations of response distribution are based on multiple-response analyses, an analytic methodology that only recently has begun to be employed in applied research in mental retardation (see, for example, Schroeder, Kanoy, Mulick, Rojahn, Thios, Stevens, & Hawk, 1982; Vyse & Mulick, 1988). One experimental preparation of this type with particular relevance to questions about the side effects of positive and negative behavioral interventions involves the measurement of multiple responses during baseline, followed by some experimental disruption in this optimal or unrestricted distribution of responding (e.g., Timberlake, 1984; Timberlake & Allison, 1974). Baseline responding can be disrupted experimentally by simply removing the opportunity for the organism to engage in one of the responses (for example, by removing the wheels provided for running) or by application of an aversive event contingent on episodes of the behavior.

Dunham and Grantmyre (1982) studied the species-specific behavior of gerbils in an unrestricted baseline and then imposed a brief electric shock contingent upon one behavior in the repertoire (e.g., eating seeds). They found that when one behavior was suppressed by the punishment contingency, the animals redistributed their other responses (e.g., digging, wheel running, and grooming) in a predictable manner, based on the relative baseline rates of the behaviors and on the sequential ordering of these responses in the ongoing stream of behavior. Notably, in this study, animals redistributed their responding among the available alternatives in the same manner, regardless of whether one response was removed through application of a response contingent shock or whether the food tray or other opportunity for the behavior simply was removed. The authors discuss this result as evidence that perhaps response allocation and response hierarchies have as much relevance to the effects of aversive stimulation as traditional fear conditioning conceptualizations.

Experimental analysts have long debated and researched the processes involved in response suppression under schedules of response contingent aversive stimulation, extinction, and a variety of other contingencies. Early conceptualizations have been extended and, in some cases, challenged by experimental investigations of phenomena, such as "response-specific inhibition" (e.g., Anger, 1983), differential control over interresponse times (e.g., Sizemore & Maxwell, 1985), and the role of negative reinforcement of response omission in punishment procedures (e.g., Arbuckle & Lattal, 1987). Investigations of these and related phenomena demonstrate the breadth of current theory and research in mechanisms of response suppression. An exclusive focus on the historical conditioned emotional response paradigm (e.g., Estes & Skinner, 1941) no longer seems sufficient for understanding the complex effects of therapeutic response suppression procedures.

RESPONSE CLASSES AND FUNCTIONAL ANALYSIS

How might response distribution models and other recent approaches to response suppression influence our thinking about some common treatment debates? Recently, several applied investigators have reemphasized the point that the factors related to abnormal behaviors in mentally retarded people vary across individuals and that careful, individualized assessment is necessary in order to identify the function of the behavior (e.g., Carr, 1977; Iwata, Dorsey, Slifer, Bauman, & Richman, 1982; Romanczyk, in press; Schroeder, Mulick & Rojahn, 1980). The function of a behavior disorder refers to the consequences (e.g., social attention, escape from aversive teaching interactions) that are maintaining the behavior. Authors have suggested, for example, that severe behavior problems in disabled people often serve a range of communicative functions for individuals who lack the language skills to convey their needs in a more adaptive manner (e.g., Carr & Durand, 1985; Donnellan, LaVigna, Zambito, & Thevedt, 1985). It has been suggested that treatment strategies should focus on teaching new skills (especially language skills) that have the same function as the maladaptive response. For example, a student who hits his head in order to induce a teacher to remove task demands may be trained to point to a picture to obtain a break from the task demand (Meyer & Evans, 1989). Advocates of the communication hypothesis have criticized aversive interventions because they may directly suppress responses that have a communicative function, depriving the individual of their only means of communication. This suppression of a client's only means of obtaining desired consequences is expected to lead to distressed emotional states and even aggression.

Reliance on a communication model of maladaptive responding suggests that *response class* membership is the most important determinant of response redistribution during treatment. That is, this perspective assumes that when a response maintained by social reinforcement is reduced, the alternative response most likely to increase is another response maintained by social reinforcement. Although in some cases explicit shaping of a new communication response (using social consequences) may be the most efficient means of establishing a response alternative, in most cases, individuals have a multitude of alternative responses available in their repertoires, many of which are maintained (although at low response strength) by social consequences.

The preceding discussion of the determinants of response distribution in the face of changing contingencies and the interaction between schedules of reinforcement are relevant to the use of alternative response class members to reduce an undesirable form of responding. First, when two competing sources of reward are available for different responses, there will be complex adjustments in the rate of responding on each schedule. Response allocation rules (such as matching and maximizing) suggest that individuals will continue to produce a significant rate of maladaptive responding, despite scheduled, functionally equivalent consequences for an alternative behavior. The degree to which maladaptive responses may continue to be produced will be dependent on the rate at which maladaptive behavior continues to be followed by an effective consequence. As noted in a previous section, this kind of competition between available schedules can have important treatment implications, especially in cases where the therapist or teacher does not have complete control over the schedule of reinforcement for the maladaptive response (e.g., when the behavior provides sensory consequences or when it provides brief episodes of escape from demands).

Finally, the assumption that responses redistribute during treatment on the basis of common response class membership is placed in some doubt by research on the structural and hierarchical distributions of response repertoires. For example, the studies of response reallocation described above (e.g., Dunham & Grantmyre, 1982) suggest that responses may redistribute on the basis of sequential relationships between responses rather than only on the basis of common consequences. For example, Dunham and Grantmyre (1982) found that when food was removed from the environment (making eating unavailable as a response alternative), gerbils redistributed their responding among alternatives such as running, digging, and grooming. These authors explicitly questioned the usefulness of what they termed *functional relevance* of baseline responses in determining redistributions after punishment or simple response restriction manipulations. Apparently, the effects of changes in complex response repertoires are affected by a range of factors, including the pretreatment organization of responding (both functional and structural relationships between responses), as well as schedule interactions.

SUMMARY AND CONCLUSIONS

In this chapter, we examined the use of behavioral studies of aversive stimulation and related experimental work in support of an antiaversive position in the current controversy over the use of aversive stimuli in the treatment of behavior disorders. Many writers in commenting on the current controversy, have cited early behavioral studies of punishment as evidence of undesirable side effects (especially elicited aggression and other evidence of negative emotional reactivity) associated with the use of treatment procedures employing aversive stimuli. We suggested that this use of the behavioral research literature has been unduly influenced by ideological concerns and has not generated a balanced discussion of the experimental evidence for side effects associated with a range of behavioral contingencies. In a brief review of the most often cited literature on punishment effects, we discussed the limited applicability of early punishment paradigms to current questions about the therapeutic use of punishment, especially with respect to the noncontingent application of shock and other features of these experimental procedures. More recent conceptualizations and empirical evidence were discussed as well, and these appeared to have important applications to treatment concerns. In particular, models of response distribution and choice may have direct relevance to clinical situations in which we attempt to induce clients to choose adaptive over maladaptive responding.

The application of basic research in the experimental analysis of behavior has a long and productive history in treatment of people with mental retardation. This research and the concepts associated with basic processes of behavior change can appear deceptively simple. In fact, theories of learning continue to evolve and the experimental analysis of behavior continues to develop methods and concepts with complex relationships to applied questions. We agree with others (e.g., Redmon & Farris, 1987) in calling for applied behavior analysts to examine the experimental literature for paradigms and concepts relevant to current treatment concerns. We would caution, however, that a thoughtful and unbiased assessment of the experimental literature will be required if we are to continue to develop an empirical and objective science of behavior change.

REFERENCES

Aeschleman, S. R., & Willians, M. L. (1989). A test of the response deprivation hypothesis in a multiple-response context. *American Journal of Mental Retardation, 93*, 345-353.

Anger, D. (1983). Reinforcement of inhibition. *Journal of the Experimental Analysis of Behavior, 39*, 213-226.

Arbuckle, J. L., & Lattal, K. A. (1987). A role for negative reinforcement of response omission in punishment? *Journal of the Experimental Analysis of Behavior, 48*, 407-416.

Axelrod, S. & Apsche, J. (Eds.). (1983). *The effects of punishment on human behavior*. New York: Academic Press.

Azrin, N. H., Hutchinson, R. R., & Hake, D. F. (1966). Extinction induced aggression. *Journal of the Experimental Analysis of Behavior, 9*, 191-204.

Azrin, N. H., Hutchinson, R. R., & Hake, D. F. (1967). Attack, avoidance, and escape reactions to aversive shock. *Journal of the Experimental Analysis of Behavior, 10*, 131-148.

Azrin, N. H., Hutchinson, R. R., & Sallery, R. D. (1964). Pain aggression toward inanimate objects. *Journal of the Experimental Analysis of Behavior, 7*, 223-228.

Balsam, P. D., & Bondy, A. S. (1983). The negative side effects of reward. *Journal of Applied Behavior Analysis, 16*, 283-296.

Carr, E. G. (1977). The motivation of self-injurious behavior: A review of some hypotheses. *Psychological Bulletin, 84*, 800-816.

Carr, E. G., & Durand, V. M. (1985). Reducing behavior problems through functional communication training. *Journal of Applied Behavior Analysis, 28*, 111-126.

Carr, E. G., & Lovaas, O. I. (1983). Contingent electric shock as a treatment for severe behavior problems. In S. Axelrod J. Apsche (Eds.), *The effects of punishment on human behavior* (pp. 221-246). New York: Academic Press.

Catania, A. C. (1962). Independence of concurrent responding maintained by interval schedules of reinforcement. *Journal of the Experimental Analysis of Behavior, 5*, 175-184.

Catania, A. C. (1963). Concurrent performances: Reinforcement interaction and response independence. *Journal of the Experimental Analysis of Behavior, 6*, 253-263.

Donnellan, A. W., LaVigna, G. W., Zambito, J., & Thevedt, J. (1985). A time limited intervention program model to support community placement of persons with severe handicaps. *Journal of the Association for Persons with Severe Handicaps, 10*, 123-131.

Dunham, P. J., & Grantmyre, J. (1982). Changes in a multiple-response repertoire during response-contingent punishment and response restriction: Sequential relationships. *Journal of the Experimental Analysis of Behavior, 37*, 123-134.

Durand, V. M. (1987). "Look Homeward Angel:" A call to return to our (functional) roots. *The Behavior Analyst, 10*, 299-302.

Estes, W. K., & Skinner, B. F. (1941). Some quantitative properties of anxiety. *Journal of Experimental Psychology, 29*, 390-400.

Favell, J. E., Azrin, N. H., Baumeister, A. A., Carr, E. G.,Dorsey, M. F., Forehand, R., Foxx, R. M., Lovaas, I. O., Rincover, A., Risley, T. R., Romanczyk, R. G., Russo, D. C., Schroeder, S. R., & Solnick, J. V. (1982). The treatment of self-injurious behavior. *Behavior Therapy, 13*, 529-554.

Gentry, W. D. (1968). Fixed-ratio schedule induced aggression. *Journal of the Experimental Analysis of Behavior, 11*, 813-817.

Guess, D., Helmstetter, H., Turnbull, H. R., & Knowlton, S. (1986). *Use of aversive procedures with persons who are disabled: An historical review and critical analysis*. Seattle, WA: The Association for Persons with Severe Handicaps.

Hake, D. F. (1969). Actual versus potential shock in making shock situations function as negative reinforcers. *Journal of the Experimental Analysis of Behavior, 11*, 385-403.

Herrnstein, R. J. (1961). Relative and absolute strength of response as a function of frequency of reinforcement. *Journal of the Experimental Analysis of Behavior, 4*, 267-272.

Holburn, C. S., & Dougher, M. J. (1986). Effects of response satiation procedures in the treatment of aerophagia. *American Journal of Mental Deficiency, 91*, 72-77.

Hutchinson, R. R. (1977). By-products of aversive control. In W. K. Honig & J. E. R. Staddon (Eds.), *Handbook of operant behavior* (pp. 415-431). Englewood Cliffs, NJ: Prentice-Hall.

Hutchinson, R. R., Azrin, N. H., & Hunt, G. M. (1968). Attack produced by intermittent reinforcement of a concurrent operant response. *Journal of the Experimental Analysis of Behavior, 11*, 489-495.

Iwata B. A., Dorsey, M. F., Slifer, K. J., Bauman, D. E., & Richman, G. S. (1982). Toward a functional analysis of self-injury. *Analysis and Intervention in Developmental Disabilities, 2*, 3-20.

Konarski, E. A., Jr., Johnson, M. R., Crowell. C. R., & Whitman, T. L. (1981). An alternative approach to reinforcment for applied researchers: Response deprivation. *Behavior Therapy, 12*, 653-666.

LaVigna, G. W., & Donnellan, A. W. (1986). *Alternatives to punishment: Solving behavior problems with non-aversive strategies*. New York: Irvington.

Linscheid, T. R., Iwata, B. A., Ricketts, R. W., Williams, D. E., & Griffin, J. C.

(1990). Clinical evaluation of the Self-Injurious Behavior Inhibiting System (SIBIS). *Journal of Applied Behavior Analysis, 23*, 53-78.

Meinhold, P. M., & Mulick, J. A. (in press). Risks, choices, and behavioral treatment. *Behavioral Residential Treatment, 5*, 29-44.

Meyer, L H., & Evans, I. M. (1989). *Non-aversive intervention for behavior problems: A manual for home and community*. Baltimore, MD: Paul H. Brookes.

Mulick, J. A. (in press). The ideology and science of punishment in mental retardation. *American Journal of Mental Retardation*.

O'Kelly, L. E., & Steckle, L. C. (1939). A note on long enduring emotional responses in rats. *Journal of Psychology, 8*, 125-131.

Pueschel, S. F. (1978). *Down syndrome: Growing and learning*. Kansas City, MO: Sheed, Andrews and McMeel,Inc.

Rachlin, H., & Burkhard, B. (1978). The temporal triangle: Response substitution in instrumental conditioning. *Psychological Review, 85*, 22-47.

Redmon, W. K., & Farris, H. E. (1987). Application of basic research to the treatment of children with autistic and severely handicapped behaviors. *Education and Treatment of Children, 10*, 326-337.

Rincover, A., & Devany, J. (1982). The application of sensory extinction procedures to self-injury. *Analysis and Intervention in Developmental Disabilities, 2*, 67-81.

Romanczyk, R. G. (in press). Aversive conditioning as a component of comprehensive treatment: The impact of etiological factors on clinical decision making. In S. Harris and J. Handleman (Eds.), *Life-threatening behavior: Aversive vs. non-aversive interventions*. New Brunswick, NJ: Rutgers University Press.

Schroeder, S. R., Mulick, J. A., & Rojahn, J. (1980). The definition, taxonomy, epidemiology, and ecology of self-injurious behavior. *Journal of Autism and Developmental Disorders, 10*, 417-432.

Schroeder, S. R., Kanoy, R. C., Mulick, J. A., Rojahn, J., Thios, S. J., Stevens, M., & Hawk, B. (1982). Maintenance of programs for self-injurious behavior. In J. H. Hollis & C. E. Meyers (Eds.), *Life-threatening behavior: Analysis and intervention* (pp. 105-160). Washington, DC: American Association on Mental Deficiency.

Sidman, M. (1989). *Coercion and its fall-out*. Boston: Authors Cooperative, Inc.

Sizemore, O. J., & Maxwell, R. R. (1985). Selective punishment of interrresponse times: The roles of shock intensity and scheduling. *Journal of the Experimental Analysis of Behavior, 44*, 355-366.

Staddon, J. E. R. (1980). Optimality analyses of operant behavior and their relation to optimal foraging. In J. E. R. Staddon (Ed.), *Limits to action: The allocation of individual behavior* (pp. 101-141). New York: Academic Press.

Timberlake, W. (1984). A molar equilibrium theory of learned performance. In G. Bower (Ed.), *The psychology of learning and motivation:* Vol. 14. (pp. 1-58). New York: Academic Press.

Timberlake, W., & Allison, J. (1974). Response deprivation: An empirical approach to instrumental performance. *Psychological Review, 81*, 146-164.

Ulrich, R. E., & Azrin, N. H. (1962). Reflexive fighting in response to aversive stimulation. *Journal of the Experimental Analysis of Behavior, 5*, 511-520.

Vyse, S. A., & Mulick, J. A. (1988). Ecobehavioral assessment of a special education classroom: Teacher-student behavioral covariation. *Journal of the Multihandicapped Person, 1,* 201-216.

CHAPTER

29

LABORATORY TO APPLICATION: AN EXPERIMENTAL ANALYSIS OF SEVERE PROBLEM BEHAVIORS

W. Frank Epling and W. David Pierce
The University of Alberta

The science of behavior has been successfully applied to a variety of human problems. Based on this success, we can conclude that operant principles are relevant to an analysis of severe behavior problems. In this chapter, we discuss laboratory-based research that has implications for the analysis and control of self-injurious and aggressive behavior. This research concerns the effects of establishing operations, interaction of schedules of reinforcement, and the matching law for single and concurrent operants.

When people repeatedly hurt themselves, the behavior is labeled self-injurious. When the form of that behavior is changed so that it injures other people, it is often called aggressive. Each of these behaviors becomes a social problem when it occurs frequently and/or is intense. For example, people who lightly scratch themselves a few times each day are not self-injurious. However, individuals who dig at their skin at a high rate are seen as self-injurious. In order to predict and control such behavior, we believe applied researchers should examine basic research for the conditions that affect both the form and frequency of responding.

The form and frequency of responding may covary or occur independently, depending on the contingencies of reinforcement. For example, when high rates of behavior are reinforced, the frequency of responding may change, but the form of the response may remain unaffected. In other cases, when response topography is being shaped, the form may change while the rate remains constant. In still other cases, fewer responses but greater intensity would be required for reinforcement. In this case, rate and topography would covary. Thus, the rate and topography of behavior can depend on the operating contingencies of reinforcement.

Analytically, rate is a more sensitive measure of operant strength than topography, because rate directly indexes the probability that a given behavior will occur (Skinner, 1969, pp. 88-92). On the other hand, the form of a response only indirectly relates to operant strength. Research has shown that response topography may often be a by-product of the conditions controlling operant rate (Antonitis, 1951; Eckerman & Lanson, 1969). In addition, similar forms of a behavior may arise from completely different contingencies of reinforcement. For these reasons, attention only to topography in applied settings may obscure the actual controlling variables. Thus, most of our discussion will concern an analysis of response rate and contingencies of reinforcement.

In addition to direct contingencies such as schedules of reinforcement, there are broader contingencies that are labeled establishing operations. This kind of behavior usually occurs following severe social or sensory deprivation. The behavior appears similar to the stereotyped responses emitted by humans who are diagnosed as autistic or mentally retarded. Because of this correspondence, we feel that these studies should be addressed in this chapter. Our analysis is that social isolation and sensory deprivation are global motivational procedures that may be classified as *establishing operations* (Michael, 1982).

Establishing operations, such as deprivation or satiation, change the functional effectiveness of stimuli and consequences that control behavior. These procedures also change the probability of responses that are related to specific reinforcers. Thus, motivating operations may be considered procedures that increase or decrease the control of behavior by environmental contingencies (both internal and external to the individual).

Unfortunately, little research has been directed at the environmental contingencies that are activated by these establishing operations. Specification of the operating contingencies is important because, as we later demonstrate, behavioral interventions have different effects, depending on the schedules of reinforcement that maintain behavior.

The operating contingencies of reinforcement depend on the structure of the environment. Conceptually, the environment may be analyzed as affecting single or multiple operants. Most applied behavior analysts have emphasized principles derived from the study of the single operant. These principles (e.g., discrimination, successive approximation, conditioned reinforcement) are familiar to applied analysts, and there is no need to review them here. On the other hand, there are unusual interactions between schedules of reinforcement and punishment that may be of interest. We will address such schedule effects and suggest how these effects have applied importance.

Recently, several researchers have pointed to the importance of concurrent operant principles for the analysis of human behavior (Bradshaw & Szabadi, 1988; McDowell, 1982, 1988; Pierce & Epling, 1983). Concurrent schedules of reinforcement show that operant behavior is multiply determined, and that consideration must be given to alternative sources of reinforcement, variables that bias responding, and conditions that affect sensitivity to the operating contingencies. Even the single operant is, in fact, only one of many response alternatives. In this chapter, we will describe the matching law as a basic principle for examining the conditions under which the rate of multiple behaviors can be studied. Additionally, we will discuss the analysis of the single operant from a matching perspective. Finally, principles of choice will be shown to have importance for the modification of severe problem behaviors.

ESTABLISHING OPERATIONS AND RESPONSE TOPOGRAPHY

Monkeys exposed to social isolation exhibit a wide range of bizarre and stereotyped responses. In many instances, these responses resemble the aberrant behavior of humans who are judged to be retarded, autistic, or mentally disturbed. Social isolation may be considered a powerful establishing operation for social species. In monkeys, isolation prevents tactile, auditory, visual, and olfactory stimulation from other animals. Each source of stimulation provides functional events that ordinarily establish and maintain adaptive interaction with the environment.

Cross and Harlow (1965) investigated the behavior of 84 rhesus macaques between 1 and 7 years old that were deprived of social contact. The researchers classified various responses in terms of topography, including aggressive behavior, body rocking, self-clasping, biting of self, hair pulling, self-mutilating acts, and many other repetitive and stereotyped activities. They found that social isolation induced self-injury more in older animals than in younger monkeys. On the other hand, younger animals directed more aggressive actions toward external sources. For example, the young monkeys were likely to make threatening gestures and shake their cages. Both self-directed and externally directed aggression were more frequent when the animals were exposed to an event that signaled handling of the animals (a large black glove was slowly moved across the animal's cage). Apparently, the aberrant behavior was under stimulus control, since its frequency changed as a function of the presence or absence of the handling stimulus. Thus, seemingly innocuous events may set the occasion for self-injury or aggression to others if preceded by an establishing operation (i.e., social deprivation).

In another study, Melzack and Scott (1957) investigated the behavior of Scottish terriers that had been raised in sensory isolation for 7 months. The dogs burned themselves when a lighted match was held in front of them. As soon as the match was presented, the dogs put their noses into the flame and then quickly jerked away. However, the animals rapidly returned to the flame, excitedly hovered around it, and repeatedly burned themselves. Other research by Thompson, Melzack and Scott (1956) found that bizarre behavior, such as tail biting, occurred in dogs following sensory deprivation. Apparently, sensory isolation serves as an establishing operation for stimulus across various perceptual dimensions. One interpretation of the "burning flame" experiment is that visual stimuli became prepotent and controlled approach responses, even when accompanied by contingencies of avoidance.

These studies of severe deprivation do not by themselves account for the emergence of bizarre behavior. Presumably, the establishing operations of such studies alter the discriminative and reinforcing effectiveness of numerous environmental events (both internal and external). These events, as part of the operating contingencies, shape and maintain unusual forms of behavior. In other words, establishing operations indirectly affect the topography of behavior by altering contingencies of reinforcement.

Unfortunately, research on global deprivation operations has not addressed this issue, and we do not know how these events are arranged. There is, however, evidence that the topography of an animal's behavior (i.e., force of bar press) can be shaped by both differential reinforcement (Notterman & Mintz, 1965; Skinner, 1938, pp. 314-322) and schedules of reinforcement. Generally, intermittent reinforcement schedules produce greater response variability than continuous reinforcement (Antonitis, 1951; Eckerman & Lanson, 1969).

Our analysis of the animal research suggests that stereotyped and other unusual behaviors are shaped and maintained by events that become prepotent due to major disruptions in an organism's developmental history. Such disruptions may result from changes in life circumstances or from biological impairment. Individuals who are neurologically impaired may be deprived as much as the person who experiences social isolation. These disruptions (environmental or biological) may be analyzed as *establishing operations that alter the contingencies of reinforcement* controlling behavior. From this perspective, severe problem behaviors may be maintained by some unspecified schedule or reinforcement that in turn is controlled by establishing operations. In the next section, we will show that response-reduction procedures may interact with these schedules of reinforcement.

OPERANT INTERACTIONS AND SCHEDULES OF REINFORCEMENT

Conceptually, we may analyze most behavior as an operant that is controlled by its consequences. This analysis does not directly refer to other sources of reinforcement as variables that affect the target behavior. Instead, the analysis focuses on the discriminative stimulus-response-reinforcement paradigm (SD-R-SR) and the operating contingencies of reinforcement. Typically, the events that precede or follow behavior are manipulated by the environment. Although alternative sources of reinforcement have implications for behavior control, the SD-R-SR model has been successfully applied to a variety of human problems (see *Journal of Applied Behavior Analysis*). Because of this success, we would like to consider the implications of this model for the modification of severe problem behaviors.

One of the most important variables affecting the strength (e.g., rate and intensity) of operant behavior is the schedule of reinforcement (Ferster & Skinner, 1957; Zeiler, 1977). Reinforcement schedules account for many basic properties of behavior, such as persistence, aggression, motivation, and enthusiasm that observers attribute to us.

Imagine that you ask two students to observe a pigeon pecking a key on a multiple schedule of reinforcement. In this experiment, the pigeon is at 80 percent weight and both component schedules are arranged to deliver food at the same rate. A green light signals differential reinforcement of high rate (DRH) and a red light signals differential reinforcement of low rate (DRL). One student observes the bird in the presence of the green light (DRH) and concludes that the pigeon is highly motivated and enthusiastic. The second student observes the bird in the red light (DRL) and infers that the bird is lazy and uninterested in the task. Although both students base their judgment on the pigeon's rate of response, the animal's rate of response is completely controlled by the operating schedules.

In human environments, schedules of reinforcement arise from the structure of the physical environment, internal stimulation of the person, and social interaction. In a discussion of reinforcement history and socialization, Bijou (1970) showed how reinforcement schedules are *established* by the structure of the environment.

> ...The location of an infant's crib may establish a characteristic schedule. If, in a small home, the crib is in the kitchen where the mother is working, social reinforcement from the mother will, after a time, probably be on a small variable interval or ratio schedule. If, on the other hand, the crib is in a distant bedroom down the hall or on the second floor, it is quite likely that the baby's response will be reinforced on a large variable interval or ratio schedule. The responses required for social reinforcement under each set of circumstances would establish a characteristic form and chain of responding (p. 54).

In applied settings, the physical and social arrangement of the environment may set up schedules of reinforcement that establish and maintain problem behaviors. Analysis of schedule effects suggests that most behavior problems are due to contingencies that control rate and intensity of response. When reinforcement or punishment procedures are used to change a target behavior, the effectiveness of these operations will depend on the maintaining schedule of reinforcement. In other words, response elimination procedures interact with the current conditions maintaining behavior (Azrin & Holz, 1966).

One interesting example of this interaction is reported by Morse and Kelleher (1977). Squirrel monkeys responded for food on a variable-interval schedule of reinforcement, in which electric shock was superimposed on a food schedule. Next, the food schedule was eliminated while the shock was continued. Results showed that responding continued, despite the absence of food, and did so in a way that was characteristic of fixed-interval schedule performance reinforced by food. One implication is that the maintaining schedule for an operant can interact with contingencies of punishment and produce unexpected and unwanted effects. These results may be analogous to applied settings in which inappropriate responding is treated aversively, yet is maintained by the individual.

Schedules of avoidance or escape can also interact with punishment procedures. In some instances, such interactions have resulted in the maintenance of self-punitive behavior. Byrd (1969) placed two cats on an avoidance schedule, in which a response delayed shock for 1 minute. If the cats did not respond, shock was delivered every 5 seconds. Eventually, the animals responded at a rate that allowed them to avoid most of the shocks. Next, the cats were shocked every 15 minutes no matter what they did. Then, the avoidance schedule was removed while the noncontingent shocks were continued. Surprisingly, the rate of responding increased for both animals. Finally, the noncontingent shocks were made contingent on responding. In this situation, the cats would not receive shocks unless they produced them. The cats continued to respond and received most of the scheduled shocks. This study and others suggest that attempts to punish avoidance responses occasionally may increase, rather than suppress, the unwanted behavior (Morse, Mead, & Kelleher, 1967; McKearney, 1968; Branch & Dworkin, 1981).

High-rate behavior is usually maintained by schedules of positive or negative reinforcement (schedule-induced behavior may be an exception, see Staddon, 1977). When behavior is a social problem, and attempts are made to reduce its frequency with aversive procedures, laboratory research suggests that complex interactions can occur. Applied analysts have found that self-injurious behavior produces various consequences, including social attention (Lovaas, Freitag, Gold, & Kassorla, 1965), tangible reinforcers (Lovaas & Simmons, 1969) escape from aversive situations (Durand, 1982; Romanczyk, Colletti, & Plotkin, 1980), and sensory stimulation (Lovaas, Newsom, & Hickman, 1987; Rincover & Devany, 1982). These contingencies are delivered on various schedules of reinforcement that may affect the procedures designed to decrease responding. Although specifying the maintaining schedules in applied settings is difficult, this kind of analysis could increase the effectiveness of treatment procedures. Attention to the maintaining schedules of reinforcement also may improve generalizability of interventions, both within and across individuals.

Another way to increase the generality and effectiveness of treatment is to view applied settings as environments that provide alternative sources of reinforcement. Even in the single operant setting, principles of choice and preference are operating. The basic analysis of behavioral choice comes from the work on concurrent schedules of reinforcement. This research is receiving more attention from applied analysts (McDowell, 1982; Myerson & Hale, 1984) and may be useful for the control of severe behavior problems. In the next section, we will discuss the matching law and how it relates to the distribution of maladaptive behavior in applied settings.

BEHAVIORAL CHOICE AND MATCHING LAW

In applied settings, many alternative sources of reinforcement operate to control behavior. These reinforcers compete for behavior and provide a number of response alternatives. Reinforcement is arranged by ward routines, patterns of social interaction, structure of the physical environment, and other external events. Additional reinforcement is provided by daydreaming, thinking, neurochemical changes, and other internal sources of stimulation. Any of these reinforcing consequences can occur sequentially or simultaneously (as in multiple or concurrent schedules of reinforcement), and can affect behavior in ways that may not be obvious.

Matching and Problem Behavior

Behavioral researchers usually account for choice in terms of the matching law (Herrnstein, 1961) which states that relative behavior or time matches the relative rate of reinforcement. Within the matching theory, a source of reinforcement is called an alternative. A person distributes responses in accord with the relative, rather than absolute, rate of reinforcement from an alternative. Thus, if 40 percent of the available reinforcement is arranged by Alternative A, then 40 percent of the individual's time and behavior will be directed at this alternative. A formal statement of this relationship is presented in Equation 1.

$$(1)\ B1/(B1 + B2) = R1(R1 + R2)$$

This equation shows the matching law as an equality of proportions. The B1 and B2 symbols represent the behavior directed at two alternative sources of reinforcement, while R1 and R2 refer to the rate of reinforcement from the two alternatives. Behavior can be measured as time, or as the frequency of responding, allocated to the respective alternatives. The equation shows that the distribution of behavior matches the distribution of reinforcement from the alternatives.

There have been more than 25 years of research on concurrent schedules of reinforcement and the matching law. Much of the research has focused on the behavior of laboratory animals in highly controlled settings (see de Villiers, 1977, for a review). However, the matching law also describes human behavior on concurrent schedules of reinforcement (Bradshaw & Szabadi, 1988; Pierce & Epling, 1983; Takahashi & Iwamoto, 1982). The principle of matching has been extended to human behavior in natural (Conger & Killeen, 1974; McDowell, 1988; Pierce, Epling, & Greer, 1981) as well as clinical settings (McDowell, 1982; Myerson & Hale, 1984). Generally, the evidence suggests that matching theory may have great relevance for the analysis of problem behavior.

Human behavior exists, of course, under a multiplicity of reinforcers, and Equation 1 can be extended to account for reinforcement delivered by many alternatives. This can be seen in Equation 2 which is a generalized statement of the proportion equation. Since,

$$B1(B1+B2+B3...+Bn)=$$
$$R1/(R1+R2+R3...+Rn)$$

Then:

$$(2)\ B1/\Sigma B_i = R1/\Sigma R_i$$

In this case, the behavior distributed to a specific alternative (B1) is expressed as a proportion of the total responses given to all *known* sources of reinforcement (ΣB_i). Also, the relative rate of reinforcement for a given alternative (R1) is written as a proportion of the total amount of reinforcement for specified response alternatives (ΣR_i) in the situation. The proportion equations show that a given target behavior must be analyzed with respect to all simultaneously available sources of reinforcement.

For example, applied analysts have used the differential reinforcement of incompatible behavior (DRI) to modify self-injurious and stereotyped responses (for a review, see Gorman-Smith & Matson, 1985). In this case, reinforcement is explicitly arranged for a specified response other than the inappropriate one. Suppose, for example, that a child emits high rates of head banging and screaming in a 2-hour teaching situation, and that careful observation shows that both responses are maintained by adult attention. A DRI procedure is established, and the child is reinforced with social attention for sitting quietly in a chair and attending to instructional material. Additionally, staff are advised to ignore head banging and screaming. Given the serious nature of the problem behavior, staff are unlikely to ignore all head banging and screaming, so complete extinction will not occur. Thus, the rates of reinforcement for the two target operants are substantially reduced, but they are not eliminated.

From a single operant perspective, the schedules controlling head banging and screaming have become more intermittent, making the behavior harder to eliminate. Also, the DRI procedure is said to work only because "incompatible" behavior comes to high strength. Given the conflicting contingencies, predicting the outcome of the treatment package is difficult. The proportional form of the matching law which considers multiple operants suggests a different analysis of the situation.

Equation 2 can be used to understand the controlling variables in the teaching situation. Head banging is B1, screaming is B2, and attending to instructional material is B3; these responses are maintained by schedules of social reinforcement, R1, R2, and R3, respectively. Assume that head banging and screaming each produce 5 reinforcers per hour (R1=5, R2=5) and attending to instructional material pays off at 30 reinforcers per hour (R3= 30). The proportional rate of reinforcement for head banging (or screaming) is 5/(5+ 5+ 30) or 12.5 percent of the total reinforcement in the situation as shown in Equation 2.

$$\frac{\text{head banging}}{\text{all behavior}} = \frac{\text{reinforcement for HB}}{\text{all reinforcement}} = \frac{5}{(5+5+30)} = \frac{R1}{R1+R2+R3} = 12.5\%$$

Thus, if the child follows the matching law, he would be spending about 8 minutes each hour (5/40 X 60 minutes) engaged in head banging (or screaming).

Prior to implementing the DRI, the attempt to have staff ignore these operants reduces the rates of reinforcement, R1=2/hour and R2=2/hour.

Although these operants are intermittently reinforced, the proportion equation predicts that the child will now spend about 4 minutes head banging and 2 minutes screaming. If the DRI procedure increased reinforcement for attending to instruction (R3) from 30 to 50 reinforcers per hour, the reduction would be more dramatic. According to the matching law, head banging would now occur about 2 minutes per hour and screaming, just over 1 minute each hour.

Notice that B3 does not have to be an incompatible response to produce these effects. According to the matching law, adding another source of attention reduces the relative rate of reinforcement for both target operants. Thus, the researcher could have reinforced "thumb twiddling" and thereby reduced screaming. The most important limitation to these predictions is that additional reinforcement must be substitutable in the economic sense of having the same value (Myerson & Hale, 1984). If additional reinforcement is not substitutable, persons may not match relative rate of behavior to rate of reinforcement. This suggests that applied researchers should pay more attention to the nature of the reinforcers than to the topography of incompatible responses (cf., O'Brien & Repp, in press).

The proportional form of the matching law may also explain occasional instances of symptom substitution. In the example above, the rate of reinforcement for screaming could reduce to zero if staff totally ignored the child. Now suppose reinforcement for head banging and attending to instructional material remained unaffected (this could happen if DRI was not implemented and if head banging was too aversive to ignore). In this case, the proportional rate of reinforcement for head banging would *increase* (due to reduced reinforcement for screaming), and the child would spend relatively more time engaged in this behavior.

Generalized Matching and Reinforcement Schedules.

The matching law can also be expressed as the ratio of behavior to the ratio of reinforcement from two alternatives. Equation 3 shows this equality of ratios and is derived from Equation 1.

$$(3)\ B1/B2 = R1/R2$$

In this equation, B1 and B2 are either time behaving or rate of behavior directed toward two alternative sources of reinforcement, and R1 and R2 are the rates of reinforcement from these alternatives. Research shows that a strict equality of ratios does not always describe behavioral choice. Baum (1974) proposed a more general model that accounted for two kinds of behavioral deviations from matching. Equation 4 is the generalized form of the ratio equation.

$$(4)\ B1/B2 = k(R1/R2)^{a}$$

The values *k* and *a* describe two types of deviation from perfect matching, bias, and sensitivity. When *k* and *a* are both equal to 1.00, Equation 4 is the same as Equation 3 where the behavior ratio matches the reinforcement ratio. A value of *k* that departs from 1.00 reflects preference due to some asymmetry or bias between the alternatives. Response bias is important because people often show a preference for one person over another, despite the fact that both deliver similar rates of reinforcement. People simply respond differently to variations in characteristics such as age, sex, skin color, and reward inequity (Sunahara & Pierce, 1982).

The value of *a* represents the individual's sensitivity to differences between alternative rates of reinforcement. The most common finding is called *undermatching* and occurs when *a* is less than 1.00. To illustrate, deviation from matching could occur if an unsignaled change in rate of reinforcement took place. A person who receives reinforcement from two friends may not notice a gradual shift in rate of reinforcement by one of them. In this case, there is a large change in relative reinforcement and a small change in relative behavior. Another condition that produces undermatching is rapid switching between alternatives. This is prevented when a changeover delay (COD) is programmed so that changing is never reinforced (Pliskoff, 1971).

One issue of practical importance is the effect of punishment on response bias and sensitivity. When human behavior is maintained in two conditions on concurrent VI VI schedules of positive reinforcement, a punishment procedure applied to one alternative may affect the equation. For example, when humans were responding for money on a concurrent schedule, Bradshaw, Szabadi, and Bevan (1979) superimposed a VR schedule of punishment on one alternative. The rate of responding was suppressed on the punished alternative, and this was accompanied by a rate increase on the other schedule. Subjects showed a substantial bias in favor of the nonpunished alternative and considerable undermatching.

Bradshaw and Szabadi (1988) cited dissertation research by De Waard (1980) who also investigated the effects of punishment on human behavior. In this study, VI punishment was superimposed on one alternative of concurrent VI VI schedules of positive reinforcement. This procedure produced bias in favor of the nonpunished alternative with only minor changes in sensitivity. Generally, this research suggests that punishment will shift behavior to a nonpunished alternative, regardless of the schedule of punishment. Also, the amount of behavior directed to the nonpunished alternative will be greater than expected on the basis of the relative rate of reinforcement.

At the applied level, changing the rate of reinforcement for a desired response or punishing an undesirable behavior may produce behavior change that is unexpected in direction or frequency. Such changes can be anticipated if the applied analyst considers various sources of deviation. One strategy is to use schedules that program high rates of reinforcement to overcome response bias. On the other hand, punishment can be used to produce bias toward a socially acceptable alternative. When the issue is sensitivity to the operating contingencies, matching will occur if alternative sources of reinforcement are clearly signaled and indiscriminate switching between alternatives is prevented.

The matching law can be used to predict the most effective schedules of reinforcement in applied settings for those wanting to use reinforcement. Based on derivations of the ratio equation (Equation 4) and supporting research, Myerson and Hale (1984) have shown that VI schedules are the most desirable way of delivering reinforcers when the schedule maintaining the target behavior is unknown. When behavior is maintained by ratio-like contingencies, a richer ratio schedule will shift responding in the desired direction. The problem is that there will be no change in behavior if the intervention schedule is lean relative to the maintaining schedule. Basically, an intervention is either completely successful or a total failure when ratio schedules are programmed. In contrast, interval-like contingencies will always redirect behavior to the desired alternative, although such a schedule may not completely eliminate the problem behavior.

When severe problem behavior is maintained by interval contingencies, VI schedules remain the most desirable form of intervention. Under these conditions, Myerson and Hale used the matching equations to show that treatments based on interval contingencies are more efficient than ratio interventions. They stated that "...if the behavior analyst offers a VI schedule of reinforcement for competing responses two times as rich as the VI schedule for inappropriate behavior, the result will be the same as would be obtained with a VR schedule three times as rich as the schedule for inappropriate behavior" (pp. 373-374). Generally, behavior change will be more predictable and successful if interval schedules are used to reinforce incompatible behavior.

THE QUANTITATIVE LAW OF EFFECT

The matching law (as well as common sense) suggests that multiple sources of environmental control are operating in human settings. Even when the applied analyst focuses on a single target behavior, the control exerted by unknown alternative sources of reinforcement are important. This is seen in Equation 5.

$$(5)\ B1/(B1 + Be) = R1/(R1 + Re)$$

The difference between this equation and Equation 1 is that Be refers to all behavior directed to *unknown* extraneous sources of reinforcement and Re represents these sources. If B1 + Be are equal to k (the total behavioral output), then Equation 5 may be written as:

$$B1/k = R1/(R1 + Re)$$

Solving this expression for the single operant, B1 yields Equation 6.

$$(6)\ B1 = kR1/(R1 + Re)$$

Equation 6 is often called Herrnstein's (1970) quantitative law of effect. This equation states that the rate of responding (B1) in a single operant setting is a hyperbolic function of the scheduled reinforcement (R1) and all extraneous sources of reinforcement (Re). The hyperbolic function means that the rate of responding rises rapidly toward the asymptote k as the rate of reinforcement (R1) increases, holding Re constant.

In recent papers, McDowell (1981, 1982, 1988) has shown that clinically relevant behavior conforms to the quantitative law of effect. He reports that the self-injurious scratching by an 11-year-old boy was described by Equation 6 (McDowell, 1981). The boy's scratching had caused lesions on his scalp, face, back, arms, and legs. An analysis by Carr and McDowell (1980) showed that the self-injurious behavior was reinforced by reprimands from members of his family. Additionally, the behavior was under stimulus control, occurring primarily in the living room while the family watched television. The researchers gathered data on number of reprimands and number of scratches per hour.

When McDowell (1981) fit the boy's data to Herrnstein's hyperbolic equation, he explained 99.67 percent of the variance in this self-mutilating behavior. Importantly, the hyperbolic equation fit human data in an uncontrolled environment where many extraneous factors could operate. McDowell (1988) commented that the evidence is strong support for the relevance of the matching law in natural human settings. The study also suggests another way that applied analysts can discover the reinforcing consequences of problem behavior. Powerful behavioral consequences will control behavior in a manner described by Equation 6.

An important implication of the quantitative law of effect pertains to influence of extraneous sources of reinforcement (Re). Notice in Equation 6 that increases in Re decrease the rate of the target behavior while a reduction in Re has the opposite effect. This suggests that problem behavior can be reduced by increasing extraneous reinforcement. Also, appropriate behavior may be increased by lowering the overall hedonic value of the environment. Problem behavior that cannot be directly manipulated by contingency management may be amenable to control by altering extraneous sources of reinforcement. For example, aggressive behavior is difficult to eliminate with extinction or punishment because these interventions may initially escalate the problem behavior. Simply enriching the environment with toys, music, games, or television may increase Re and reduce aggressive behavior.

Enrichment of the environment has been used to reduce self-injurious behavior. Rincover (1986) reports two studies (Carr, Newsom, & Binkoff, 1976; Solnick, Rincover, & Peterson, 1977) where self-injury resulted in escape from aversive situations. Rather than changing the consequences of escape behavior, the researchers decided to reduce the aversiveness of the setting, thereby reducing the need for the escape behavior. Thus, the learning tasks remained, but the setting was enriched by introducing stories or toys, music, and social interaction between instructional trials (Rincover, 1986). This procedure eliminated self-injurious behavior. According to Equation 6, this outcome is expected because the researchers increased extraneous sources of reinforcement producible only by adaptive behaviors.

CONCLUSION

This chapter has outlined some of the complex relationships that control operant behavior in the laboratory and natural settings. Interactions between maintaining conditions and procedures of behavior change are the rule rather than the exception. In single operant settings, contingencies of reinforcement that maintain behavior interact with response elimination procedures. The topography of behavior that emerges from interactions with the environment depends on establishing operations that precede and alter SD-R-SR relationships. Establishing operations may be global and relatively permanent (e.g., social isolation) or circumscribed and momentary (e.g., deprivation for sleep).

Although the linear analysis of operant behavior (SD-R-SR) has broad utility, many intervention procedures may be analyzed as conditions that determine behavioral choice. The matching law is the fundamental principle of choice, and the mathematical expressions of this law have applied importance. Even when interest is focused on a single target behavior, principles of choice are operative and may determine the success or failure of behavior modification procedures. The most important implication of matching for the control of severe problem behavior is the specification of novel behavior-change strategies.

REFERENCES

Antonitis, J. J. (1951). Response variability in the white rat during conditioning, extinction, and reconditioning. *Journal of Experimental Psychology, 42,* 273-281.

Azrin, N. H., & Holz, W. C. (1966). Punishment. In W. K. Honig (Ed.), *Operant behavior: Areas of research and application* (pp. 380-447). Englewood Cliffs, NJ: Prentice-Hall.

Baum, W. M. (1974). On two types of deviation from the matching law: Bias and undermatching. *Journal of the Experimental Analysis of Behavior, 20,* 137-153.

Bijou, S. W. (1970). Reinforcement history and socialization. In R. A. Hoppe, G. A. Milton, & E. C. Simmel (Eds.), *Early experiences and the processes of socialization* (pp. 43-58). New York: Academic Press.

Bradshaw, C. M., & Szabadi, E. (1988). Quantitative analysis of human operant behavior. In G. Davey & C. Cullen (Eds.), *Human operant conditioning and behavior modification* (pp. 225-259). New York: John Wiley & Sons.

Bradshaw, C. M., Szabadi, E., & Bevan, P. (1979). The effect of punishment on free-operant choice behavior in humans. *Journal of the Experimental Analysis of Behavior, 31*, 71-81.

Branch, M. N., & Dworkin, S. I. (1981). Effects of ratio contingencies on responding maintained by schedules of electric shock presentation (response-produced shock). *Journal of the Experimental Analysis of Behavior, 36,* 191-205.

Byrd, L. D. (1969). Responding in the cat maintained by response-independent electric shock. *Journal of the Experimental Analysis of Behavior, 12*, 1-10.

Carr, E. G., & McDowell, J. J. (1980). Social control of self-injurious behavior of organic etiology. *Behavior Therapy, 11,* 402-409.

Carr, E. G., Newsom, C. D., & Binkoff, J. A. (1976). Stimulus control of self-destructive behavior in a psychotic child. *Journal of Abnormal Child Psychology, 4,* 139-153.

Conger, R., & Killeen, P. (1974). Use of concurrent operants in small group research. *Pacific Sociological Review, 17*, 399-416.

Cross, H. A., & Harlow, H. F. (1965). Prolonged and progressive effects of partial isolation on the behavior of macaque monkeys. *Journal of Experimental Research on Personality, 1*, 39-49.

de Villiers, P. (1977). Choice in concurrent schedules and a quantitative formulation of the law of effect. In W. K. Honig & J. E. R. Staddon (Eds.), *Handbook of operant behavior* (pp. 233-287). Englewood Cliffs, NJ: Prentice-Hall.

De Waard, R. J. (1980). *Matching and failure of response independence by human subjects on concurrent VI VI schedules of reinforcement*, unpublished doctoral dissertation, University of Milwaukee, Wisconsin.

Durand, V. M. (1982). Analysis and intervention of self-injurious behavior. *Journal of The Association for the Severely Handicapped, 7*, 44-53.

Eckerman, D. A., & Lanson, R. N. (1969). Variability of response location for pigeons responding under continuous reinforcement, intermittent reinforcement, and extinction. *Journal of the Experimental Analysis of Behavior, 12*, 73-80.

Ferster, C. G., & Skinner, B. F. (1957). *Schedules of reinforcement*. Englewood Cliffs, NJ: Prentice-Hall.

Gorman-Smith, D., & Matson, J. L. (1985). A review of treatment research for self-injurious and stereotyped responding. *Journal of the Mental Deficiency Research, 29*, 295-308.

Herrnstein, R. J. (1970). On the law of effect. *Journal of the Experimental Analysis of Behavior, 13*, 243-266.

Herrnstein, R. J. (1961). Relative and absolute strength of response as a function of frequency of reinforcement. *Journal of the Experimental Analysis of Behavior, 4*, 267-272.

Lovaas, O. I., Freitag, G., Gold, V. J., & Kassorla, I. C. (1965). A recording method and observations of behaviors of normal and autistic children in free play settings. *Journal of Experimental Child Psychology, 2*, 108-120.

Lovaas, O. I., Newsom, C., & Hickman, C. (1987). Self-stimulatory behavior and perceptual reinforcement. *Journal of Applied Behavior Analysis, 20*, 45-68.

Lovaas, O. I., & Simmons, J. Q. (1969). Manipulation of self-destruction in three retarded children. *Journal of Applied Behavior Analysis, 2*, 143-157.

McDowell, J. J. (1981). On the validity and utility of Herrnstein's hyperbola in applied behavior analysis. In C. M. Bradshaw, E. Szabadi, & C. F. Lowe (Eds.), *Quantification of steady-state operant behavior*. Amsterdam: Elsevier/North Holland Biomedical Press.

McDowell, J. J. (1982). The importance of Herrnstein's mathematical statement of the law of effect for behavior therapy. *American Psychologist, 37*, 771-779.

McDowell, J. J. (1988). Matching theory in natural human environments. *The Behavior Analyst, 11*, 95-109.

McKearney, J. W. (1968). Maintenance of responding under a fixed-interval schedule of electric shock presentation. *Science, 160*, 1249-1251.

Melzack, R. A., & Scott, T. H. (1957). The effects of early experience on the response to pain. *Journal of Comparative and Physiological Psychology, 50*, 155-161.

Michael, J. (1982). Distinguishing between discriminative and motivational functions of stimuli. *Journal of the Experimental Analysis of Behavior, 37*, 149-155.

Morse, W. H., & Kelleher, R. T. (1977). Determinants of reinforcement and punishment. In W. K., Honig & J. E. R. Staddon (Eds.), *Handbook of operant behavior* (pp. 174-200). Englewood Cliffs, NJ: Prentice-Hall.

Morse, W. H., Mead, R. N., & Kelleher, R. T. (1967). Modulation of elicited behavior by a fixed-interval schedule of electric shock presentation. *Science, 157*, 215-217.

Myerson, J., & Hale, S. (1984). Practical implications of the matching law. *Journal of Applied Behavior Analysis, 17*, 367-380.

Notterman, J. M., & Mintz, D. E. (1965). *Dynamics of response*. New York: John Wiley & Sons.

O'Brien, S., & Repp, A. C. (in press). A review of 30 years of research on the use of differential reinforcement to reduce inappropriate responding. *Behavior Modification*.

Pierce, W. D., & Epling, W. F. (1983). Choice, matching, and human behavior: A review of the literature. *The Behavior Analyst, 6*, 57-76.

Pierce, W. D., Epling, W. F., & Greer, S. M. (1981). Human communication and the matching law. In C. M. Bradshaw, E. Szabadi, & C. F. Lowe (Eds.), *Quantification of steady-state operant behavior*. Amsterdam: Elsevier/North Holland Biomedical Press.

Pliskoff, S. S. (1971). Effects of symmetrical and asymmetrical changeover delays on concurrent performances. *Journal of the Experimental Analysis of Behavior, 16*, 249-256.

Rincover, A. (1986). Behavioral research in self-injury and self-stimulation. *Psychiatric Perspectives on Mental Retardation, 9*, 755-766.

Rincover, A., & Devany, J. (1982). The application of sensory extinction procedures to self-injury. *Analysis and Intervention in Developmental Disabilities, 2*, 67-81.

Romanczyk, R. G., Colletti, G., & Plotkin, R. (1980). Punishment of self-injurious behavior: Issues of behavior analysis, generalization, and the right to treatment. *Child Behavior Therapy, 2*, 37-54.

Skinner, B. F. (1969). *Contingencies of reinforcement: A theoretical analysis*. New York: Appleton-Century-Crofts.

Skinner, B. F. (1938). *The behavior of organisms*. New York: Appleton-Century-Crofts.

Solnick, J. V., Rincover, A., & Peterson, C. R. (1977). Determinants of the reinforcing and punishing effects of time-out. *Journal of Applied Behavior Analysis, 8*, 415-424.

Staddon, J. E. R. (1977). Schedule-induced behavior. In W. K. Honig & J. E. R. Staddon (Eds.), *Handbook of operant behavior* (pp. 125-152). Englewood Cliffs, NJ: Prentice-Hall.

Sunahara, D. F., & Pierce, W. D. (1982). The matching law and bias in a social exchange involving choice between alternatives. *Canadian Journal of Sociology, 7*, 145-166.

Takahashi, M., & Iwamoto, T. (1982). Recent developments in the study of choice behavior: 1. Fundamental outcomes and critical issues. *Japanese Psychological Review, 25*, 192-230.

Thompson, W. R., Melzack, R., & Scott, T. H. (1956). Whirling behavior in dogs as related to early experience. *Science, 123*, 939.

Zeiler, M. (1977). Schedules of reinforcement: The controlling variables. In W. K. Honig & J. E. R. Staddon (Eds.), *Handbook of operant behavior (pp. 201-232)*. Englewood Cliffs, NJ: Prentice-Hall, Inc.

CHAPTER

30

ON THE EMPIRICAL BASIS FOR USING AVERSIVE AND NONAVERSIVE THERAPY

David A. Coe and Johnny L. Matson
Louisiana State University

Behavior therapy for individuals with developmental disabilities dates back to the 1960s. At that time, a small but innovative group of individuals pioneered many of the concepts and procedures that are in widespread use today. From this beginning, behavior therapy has gained worldwide recognition as the treatment of choice for modifying the behavior of individuals with autism, mental retardation, and other developmental disorders. This distinction has been made possible by remarkable advances in assessment and treatment procedures in the last three decades. From its inception, the approach has been controversial, dating back to the classic Skinner-Rogers debate on free will. More recently, a debate has arisen over the appropriateness of behavior modification procedures that include aversives. Several parent and professional groups, among them The Association for Persons with Severe Handicaps (TASH) and the Association for Retarded Citizens (ARC), have made public statements opposing these methods. Bills have even been introduced in Massachusetts and other states to regulate or severely restrict their use (Matson & Taras, 1989). Opponents of aversives have presented a variety of defenses for their position. They have argued that aversive procedures currently in use are (a) inhumane and infrequently used with nonhandicapped individuals; (b) typically ineffective, producing only temporary suppression of behavior; (c) frequently associated with negative side effects; (d) highly likely to be misused or abused; or (e) simply not necessary. In contrast, other groups have defended the utility and need for aversive procedures. The Association for Behavior Analysis and Division 33 of the American Psychological Association, for example, have introduced positions defending the use of aversives in conjunction with reinforcement procedures (Matson & Taras, 1989). Proponents of aversives have argued that these techniques are (a) not inhumane and are necessary, given the considerable problems and limitations of many individuals with developmental disabilities; (b) typically more effective than reinforcement procedures alone; (c) rarely associated with negative side effects when properly used and, in fact, commonly associated with positive side effects; and (d) safe with proper supervision and regulation.

This debate has become a very heated and pivotal one, the outcome of which may well determine accepted treatment practices for years. Given the high stakes, the extent of rhetoric and misinformation without substantiating objective data is dismaying. This state of affairs seems to us to be unconscionable, given that most treatment techniques at issue have been in use for the last 20 to 25 years and are some of the best empirically supported approaches. While ethical considerations are important in treatment choice, information on the suitability and effectiveness of treatment should, in our view, enter heavily into the equation. The current article attempts to redress an imbalance in the treatment acceptability debate of recent years by addressing the role of empirical data in treatment evaluation and selection. Our comments specifically address four major topics. First, a definition of aversive procedures for this particular paper is made. Second, consideration of what variables to target in measuring treatment effectiveness is discussed. Third, a survey of what recent literature reviews and analyses tell us concerning the efficacy of aversive and nonaversive treatments is made for behaviors where aversive and nonaversive procedures have both been regularly employed-self-injury, aggression, property destruction and stereotypy. Finally, the status of current data on treatment efficacy is presented, along with suggestions for future investigation.

DEFINITIONS

Given the sporadic and varied descriptions of aversives, a definition of the term merits our initial consideration. In everyday terms, aversives and nonaversives are commonly defined as if aversiveness is an intrinsic property of stimuli and synonymous with discomfort or pain. In this framework, stimuli such as shock, sensory deprivation, and verbal reprimands are viewed as effective because they create sufficient discomfort to discourage further responding. In the behavior analysis framework, which has been the conceptual basis for behavior modification, however, stimuli are defined in terms of effects they exert on behavior. A reinforcer is any stimulus that reliably increases the frequency of a response preceding the reinforcer's presentation or removal. In contrast, a punishing stimulus reliably decreases the frequency of a response that precedes the stimulus' presentation or removal. An aversive, conversely, is any stimulus that reliably increases the frequency of a response that precedes its removal or reliably decreases the frequency of a response that precedes its presentation. [Note that an aversive is not equivalent to punishment because an aversive could be used in either a reinforcement (i.e., negative reinforcement) or punishment context]. Also, a stimulus that is aversive for one person or in one setting may not be so in other cases. This appears to be particularly true for individuals with severe developmental disabilities whose behavior is strengthened and weakened by stimuli in many different ways. Self-injury would appear to be a prime example, where individuals engage in behaviors that would be highly painful for most people. Another classic example, presented in a study by Favell, McGimsey and Jones (1978), demonstrated that restraint, a procedure commonly conceptualized as punishing, could function as a reinforcer. For this reason, in the absence of data measuring effectiveness on emotional and adaptive behaviors, one cannot state that "aversives" for developmentally disabled people operate by virtue of the same mechanisms we view in others; i.e., pain. We are aware that most nonaversive advocates do not make this distinction. Indeed, "aversive," like "punishment," may be a misleading and unfortunate term because of the additional connotations it carries.

For the purposes of this article, however, *aversive* will be any stimulus that reliably decreases the frequency of a response that precedes its presentation or reliably increases the frequency of response that precedes its removal.

Similarly, a nonaversive will be any stimulus that reliably increases the frequency of a response that precedes its presentation or decreases the frequency of a response that precedes its removal. We recognize that "nonaversive" is a misnomer in a sense, because a deprivation state must first exist (e.g., hunger or thirst) before food, drink, or other items prove to be reinforcing. Finally, please note that we are using the term aversive as a short- hand and recognize that it is a misnomer for the treatment literature with developmentally disabled persons. Rather, more accurate descriptors would be the terms aversive and positive reinforcement, since the former method is only rarely used alone in reported studies.

EMPIRICAL EVIDENCE OF TREATMENT EFFICACY: CRITERIA

A behavioral treatment may exert many effects on behavior, both immediate and long-term, positive or negative in nature; it may also impinge upon the original target behavior or other behaviors. Specification of criteria for treatment effectiveness has become a major concern in the developmental disability literature (e.g., Favell et al., 1982). Methodological rigor also has become a priority, with greater emphasis on adequate controls for experimental manipulations along the lines of adequate baseline measures, use of control groups or adequate single case controls (i.e., multiple baseline or reversal design), measures of treatment integrity, as well as reliability assessment. Barlow and Hersen (1984) and Kirk (1982) provide useful coverage of single case and group designs, respectively.

Although an intervention may influence or be influenced by many possible variables, they can be grouped into several major categories, eight of which are treated here: (a) magnitude of effect, (b) speed of effect, (c) durability of effect, (d) generality of effect, (e) side effects, (f) clinical significance, (g) labor intensiveness, and (h) controlling variables. For each, a brief definition and discussion of its relevance to treatment-outcome evaluation is provided.

Magnitude of Effect

An initial consideration should be the extent to which the target behavior is suppressed by treatment. Although magnitude is important, treatment that reduces a behavior to near zero levels, or to a small fraction of its baseline level, is of doubtful significance if the behavior was not that substantial originally. Change may be measured along temporal or severity dimensions, or ideally both. Temporal measures typically involve measures of behavior frequency or duration. Frequency indicates the number of occurrences of the behavior in question per unit time. Duration reflects how long a time a behavior occurs for when it is present. The latter is a useful measure where the behavior occurs over an extended time period (e.g., rumination), or occurs at a high but relatively constant rate. In the latter case, duration may be easier to assess than frequency, while still providing sufficient information. Frequency or duration is the usual dimension by which magnitude of change is assessed. Behaviors, however, may exhibit changes in severity independent of changes in temporal properties. Severity may be a particularly important factor to consider in cases of self-injury or aggression where the behavior may be of low frequency but variable or high intensity. Treatments may reduce frequency but actually increase intensity.

Speed of Effect

Speed of effect refers to the rate at which treatment effects are obtained. In cases of severe and potentially life-threatening behavior problems, speed of behavior change may be a primary consideration when any instance of the behavior may cause injury or death. Two treatments may ultimately lead to equal suppression of behavior, but if one is effective more rapidly, then it should be the treatment of choice if no other differences exist between these treatments.

Durability of Effect

The goal of most behavior management programs is permanent change in behavior. If a client engages in self-injury, for example, we hope that our treatment program produces changes that permanently eliminate this behavior. Although there has been considerable focus on the speed of effect, the durability of effect is often neglected and may be just as important. Follow-up observations of individuals may take weeks, months, or years after treatment implementation to determine how permanent intervention effects are. For example, two interventions may lead to equally immediate effects, but one may retain effectiveness for a longer period.

Generality of Effect

Typically, unless the recipient of treatment continually resides in one setting, treatment effects will need to transfer to other settings. Generality of effects refers to the extent to which treatment results generalize from the setting in which treatment was conducted to other settings. One early criticism leveled against use of shock was that its effects did not generalize to different settings. The same argument, however, could be applied to many reinforcement-based programs. Generality of effect can be evaluated by measuring the same behavior in different settings.

Side Effects

As noted earlier, behavioral interventions may exert effects on behaviors other than those specifically targeted. These side effects may be either positive or negative in nature. For example, a particular intervention may lead to increased participation in programming once a self-injurious or aggressive response has been suppressed, (a positive side effect), or conversely, may lead to increased fear or withdrawal from intervention agents (a negative side effect). Treatment side effects can be identified by simultaneously monitoring a range of collateral behaviors-participation and progress in programming, emotional behavior, and responsiveness to social interaction using direct observations, as well as standardized rating scales such as the Vineland Adaptive Behavior Scales (Sparrow, Balla, & Cicchetti, 1984); the American Association on Mental Deficiency's Adaptive Behavior Scales (Lambert & Windmiller, 1981; Nihira, Foster, Shellhaas & Leland, 1974); the Aberrant Behavior Checklist (Aman, Singh, Stewart, & Field, 1985); and the Psychopathology Instrument for Mentally Retarded Adults (Senatore, Matson, & Kazdin, 1983).

Clinical Significance

Clinical significance represents a combination of the above factors-magnitude of change, rapidity, durability, generality, and side effects. It asks whether treatment makes a substantial difference in the overall functioning of the individual. Clinical significance also encompasses considerations about the importance of a particular response. For example, considerable controversy exists as to the necessity to treat stereotypy (LaGrow & Repp, 1984). While stereotypy may intervene with learning in some cases, it may provide stimulation in an inadequate institutional setting.

Labor Intensiveness

Like it or not, this factor will be a prime consideration in applied settings where staff resources are limited. A particular program may potentially exert great and positive effects on an individual's life, yet require so much time and effort as to be unfeasible. Programs that demand excessive effort may be implemented incorrectly, posing risks to treatment recipients and agents. In order for behavior therapy to continue to have clinical relevance, its techniques must be viable in applied settings.

Controlling Variables

A most important area of research in the developmental disabilities field in recent years has been the study of controlling variables for self-injury and stereotypy. Work by Iwata, Dorsey, Slifer, Bauman, and Richman (1982), Parrish, Iwata, Dorsey, Bunck, and Slifer (1985), as well as Sturmey, Carlsen, Crisp, and Newton (1988), has demonstrated that self-injurious and stereotypic behaviors may be controlled by variables that vary from one case to the next. One individual's self-injurious response, for example, may be precipitated by situations in which increased work demands are made; another's by lack of social or sensory stimulation. Topographically similar responses may be governed, therefore, by a heterogeneous group of variables. Axelrod (1987) has drawn a distinction between structural and functional factors. Structural factors pertain to events that precede or occur simultaneously with the response, such as discriminative stimuli or setting events. Functional factors pertain to factors that follow the target response, that is, its consequences.

Advances in functional and structural analyses indicate that less intrusive treatments for inappropriate behaviors may be possible when the variables exerting control over these behaviors are known. It is, therefore, incumbent upon the researcher or clinician to conduct an assessment of controlling variables to guide and justify treatment implementation, except in cases of extreme emergency. A treatment that may be perfectly adequate for behavior due to one etiology may be ineffective when another etiology is involved or must be implemented with such intensity as to be excessively intrusive.

The eight criteria for treatment evaluation listed herein constitute an agenda for evaluation of treatment effectiveness in empirical terms. Faithfully applied, they take discussion of treatment effects out of the realm of speculation and abstract generalities and provide guidelines for clinicians, researchers, and client guardians. Having outlined and argued for an empirical examination of therapies, however, we feel compelled to justify this approach on the basis of actual data. Recent reviews of the actual evidence for use of aversive and nonaversive therapies are our next topic.

EVIDENCE FOR USE OF AVERSIVE AND NONAVERSIVE THERAPIES

Despite the considerable debate over the relative efficacies of nonaversive and aversive treatments, there have been surprisingly few data-based reviews. Moreover, in the few available reviews, the focus was on magnitude of immediate treatment effects, since few studies report follow-up or generalization results. Many parameters of treatment, such as the relationship of immediacy of treatment delivery on treatment effects and side effects, must be determined indirectly or through a review of the animal literature. Perhaps the biggest impediment to a literature review is the fact that most studies have involved single-case designs that typically address the effectiveness of only one intervention on behavior. Our view is that the animal literature is useful in the discovery of general laws of learning, but that these laws may differ for humans, particularly emotionally troubled humans, those people who are most likely to receive treatment with aversives.

Gorman-Smith and Matson (1985) reviewed treatment literature between 1976 and 1983 for self-injurious and stereotyped behaviors. Magnitude of treatment effect was computed using metaanalysis, comparing the average of each subject's baseline data to the average for the last 5 days of treatment. Mean differences over the control or baseline standard deviation were then used in the calculation. Gorman-Smith and Matson's review was limited by the small number of cases for certain procedures, but some interesting findings were nevertheless obtained. For example, aversives such as physical restraint and overcorrection, as well as combination aversive-nonaversive programs, produced some of the strongest effects. Among the effect sizes obtained were 13.7 for air splint, 8.7 for physical restraint, 7.6 for overcorrection and reinforcement, 6.9 for water mist, and 6.6 for overcorrection. Treatments that proved less effective included differential reinforcement of other behavior (1.0) and facial screening, (0.84). Treatment also proved more effective for stereotypies than self-injury. The authors noted that their findings potentially could have been compromised by a treatment-by-behavior confound. That is, certain treatments might appear more or less effective because they were used to treat more or less intransigent behaviors.

Lundervold and Bourland (1988) reported the results of a more recent literature review covering the years 1980 to 1985, with a focus on self-injury, aggression, and property destruction. This review covered 62 separate interventions. These authors categorized treatment effects using a three-point scale, assigning a value of 0 for 50% or less reduction, from baseline, a value of 1 for 51 to 74% reduction, and a value of 2 for 75 to 100% reduction from baseline. These results are subject to similar reservations noted by Gorman-Smith and Matson (1985); namely, small numbers of studies and possible treatment-by-behavior confounds. Nevertheless, a similar pattern of trends emerged from this separate review; namely, aversive and combination aversive-nonaversive procedures were more effective than nonaversive procedures alone. For example, the highest mean ratings were obtained by facial screening and response interruption, plus differential reinforcement of other behavior or differential reinforcement of incompatible behavior (DRO or DRI) procedures (1.8). DRI procedures were slightly less effective (1.6). Antecedent, reinforcement, and punishment control procedures were more effective than basic antecedent and reinforcement control procedures (1.2 to 1.0). Finally, basic DRO procedures were typically the least effective intervention, obtaining a mean rating of 0.0. We should note that no tests of clinical significance between group means were computed. Also, the tentative nature of present reviews is illustrated by the fact that facial screening was one of the least effective interventions in the Gorman-Smith and Matson survey, but one of the most effective in this latter survey. Despite these misgivings, however, Lundervold and Bourland's review is a thorough one that should serve as a model for future work.

Other reviews have looked at a more restricted range of behaviors. LaGrow and Repp (1984), for example, looked at the relative efficacies of treatments for stereotypies. In this review, each intervention was assigned one of five levels of effectiveness: (1) extremely effective (responding reduced to 5 percent or less of baseline levels); (2) very effective (responding reduced to between 6 and 25% of baseline levels); (3) effective (responding reduced to between 26 and 50% of baseline levels); (4) moderately effective (responding reduced to between 51 and 67% of original rate); and (5) minimally effective (responding reduced to no more than 68% of baseline levels). Here, too, punishment and reinforcement-punishment combinations proved most effective. A mean effectiveness rating of 1 was obtained by (a) electric shock, (b) physical restraint and overcorrection, (c) physical restraint and DRO, and (d) overcorrection and DRI. Basic DRI and DRO procedures obtained mean ratings of 2 and 3, respectively. Once again, however, these differences were not statistically tested.

A fourth review by Starin and Fuqua (1987) compared the effectiveness of interventions in the treatment of rumination. This review noted more positive effects for electric shock, food satiation, noxious taste, and overcorrection procedures. DRO procedures once again appeared to be less effective. Faulty methodological designs, including insufficient baselines and possible sequence effects, appeared to be particularly problematic for this literature.

Greater effectiveness of aversive and combination aversive-nonaversive procedures also has been demonstrated at the single case level in a number of separate studies. Azrin, Belasel, and Wisotzek (1982), for example, reported that a combination of response interruption and DRI was more effective in treatment of self-injury than either DRI, DRO, instructional prompting or, in one case, response interruption alone. Similarly, Slifer, Iwata, and Dorsey (1984) found that a contingent response interruption procedure, in combination with DRO or DRI schedules, reduced eye gouging by a profoundly mentally retarded individual more effectively than DRO alone. These findings have not been confined to self-injury alone. Luiselli, Suskin, and Slocumb (1984) found immobilization time-out and DRO to be more effective than DRO alone in treatment of aggression in a 7-year-old boy with severe to moderate mental retardation. The growing popularity of multiple baseline and alternating treatment designs has made treatment comparisons for individual subjects a relatively easy matter, and more such work is likely in the future.

Apart from immediate magnitude effects, the only other treatment effect that has garnered real interest to date is treatment side effects. The literature here is even more sparse, given the fact that only a handful of studies have reported side effects. Lichstein and Schreibman (1976), in an early review of the effects of electric shock on autistic subjects, noted evidence for both positive and negative side effects. Their finding,s indicated that fear of the shock apparatus appeared to be the most common negative finding, while increases in social behavior and positive emotional behavior were the most common positive findings. This study only covered 13 subjects, however. A more recent review by Matson and Taras (1989) covered 382 studies published between 1967 and 1987. Matson and Taras tabulated positive and negative side effects anecdotally noted in these original studies. A striking preponderance of positive side effects was noted (212 to 16). Moreover, there were rather small differences across treatments with respect to positive side effects. Therefore, treatments that are generally considered more intrusive to individuals, a prime example being electric shock, appear to produce similar rates of positive side effects on the basis of case reports.

DISCUSSION

On the basis of published studies to date, a case for the use of both aversive and nonaversive procedures can be made in the treatment of maladaptive behaviors such as self-injury, aggression, property destruction, and stereotypy. Present findings, however, suggest that aversive procedures and a combination of aversive and nonaversive procedures are more effective than nonaversive procedures alone in suppressing these behaviors. We once again remind the reader that positive procedure and nonaversive procedure are at a fundamental level misnomers, but that they are used here for consistency of terminology used in other chapters. For example, Gentle Teaching involves several aversive components such as time-out and restraint (i.e., the person is kept against his/her will in a restricted area). DRO and other reinforcement procedures also constitute aversive procedures, in that they presuppose a state of deprivation to be effective. In the case of Gentle Teaching, for example, personal interaction is delivered contingent on specific responses. Those studies that do report side effects suggest that more intrusive procedures do not precipitate an inordinate share of negative effects and, in fact, may produce similar rates of positive side effects. Greater use of statistical analyses is needed, however.

One outstanding question with regard to the present literature is its representativeness. The tendency to accept publication of positive findings is especially problematic in an area that primarily depends on single case studies for its data base. The literature is rife with single case studies that report the efficacy of aversive procedures and precious few that demonstrate positive procedures to treat serious behavior problems. Interpretation of relative treatment efficacies is problematic because published findings may contain treatment-behavior confounds. Such a confound might work to the advantage of less intrusive procedures, however. The developmental disability field might benefit from greater emphasis on group studies. Such work could reveal how representative various reports are on controlling variables and treatment efficacy. A prime case in point, for example, involves recent proclamations for exclusive use of nonaversives (LaVigna & Donnellan, 1986; McGee, Menolascino, Hobbs, & Menousek, 1987) which typically have been accompanied by poorly described and inadequately controlled demonstrations of their effectiveness. At this point in time, it is not clear to what extent the claims are legitimate for programs such as Gentle Teaching. Obviously, if such procedures could be demonstrated to be regularly effective, they would be very important indeed. Recent studies, however, suggest that in at least some cases, such methods may be ineffective (Jordan, Singh, & Repp, 1989; Singh & Jones, 1989). Only group studies with random assignment of subjects, however, can pass definitive judgment on the validity and generalizability of various procedures. We envision studies that initially involve functional assessment of controlling variables, with subsequent implementation and evaluation of various treatment procedures via alternating and multiple baseline designs.

Another problem with the present literature is its almost exclusive focus on measuring immediate treatment effects. A number of other criteria for evaluating treatment have been articulated, but have received little recognition to date. For example, Lundervold and Bourland (1988), in their review of more methodologically sound studies, reported that only 13% provided a functional analysis of the target behavior, 18% evaluated maintenance of effects over 6 months, 2% assessed generalization, and 8% collected data on collateral behaviors. While many call for general ethical standards, an argument could be made for general standards in reporting results of studies. Such standards would make it possible to aggregate findings across studies and derive general conclusions. One striking fact about reviews of treatment efficacy, however, is the number of common findings across studies, despite limitations in methodology, small numbers of subjects, and other issues. This suggests to us that an even clearer picture of treatment effectiveness would emerge from a more rigorous and systematic approach to treatment evaluation.

There has been considerable commentary by the nonaversive forces that there are sufficient positive procedures to preclude the need for aversives. At best, this is a *gross* exaggeration of the situation and, at worst, it is academic and professional dishonesty. Given that the health and safety of thousands of people are at stake, this issue is one to be approached in all seriousness. Those who reject data-based decisions have argued that treatment is a moral issue. Of course it is. But there are other factors that must be employed, and these include treatment effectiveness. Decisions on treatment cannot be made by popular beliefs alone. Further, ignoring facts weakens professionalism by ignoring the basic principle of using only techniques with scientific support to treat particular problems.

In light of present findings on functional relationships, it is hard to justify the use of more intrusive procedures without clear indication that a simple manipulation of programming or environment would not suffice. At the same time, recent work (e.g., Iwata et al., 1982) suggests that absolute pronouncements on treatment are just not possible. Acts of stereotypy, self-injury, aggression, and physical destruction are heterogeneous with respect to etiology and treatment. One treatment may suffice in one case and not in another, or may vary for the same person over time. Functional and structural analyses may make such determinations possible in many cases. Unfortunately, there is no empirical basis for us at this point in time to entirely forgo aversives. While further progress may someday make totally nonaversive procedures possible, this is highly unlikely in the next 25 years given the time necessary to conduct the required research. We must move cautiously and steadily toward developing treatments. Data looking at maintenance issues alone dictates that we run studies of several years' duration. Clinicians are ethically bound to offer the best treatments currently available, aversive and nonaversive alike, and must not make individuals with developmental disabilities suffer for ideological whims.

REFERENCES

Aman, M. G., Singh, N. N., Stewart, A. W., & Field, C. J. (1985).The Aberrant Behavior Checklist: A behavior rating scale for the assessment of treatment effects. *American Journal of Mental Deficiency, 89*, 485-491.

Axelrod, S. (1987). Functional and structural analyses of behavior: Approaches leading to reduced use of punishment procedures? *Research in Developmental Disabilities, 8*, 165-178.

Azrin, N. H., Belasel, V. A., & Wisotzek, I. E. (1982). Treatment of self-injury by a reinforcement plus interruption procedure. *Analysis and Intervention in Developmental Disabilities, 2*, 105-113.

Barlow, D. H., & Hersen, M. (1984). *Single case experimental designs* (2nd. ed.). New York: Pergamon.

Favell, J. E., Azrin, N. H., Baumeister, A. A., Carr, E. G., Dorsey, M. F., Forehand, R., Foxx, R. M., Lovaas, O. I., Rincover, A., Risley, T. R., Romanczyk, R. G., Russo, D. C., Schroeder, S. R., & Solnick, J. V. (1982). The treatment of self-injurious behavior. *Behavior Therapy, 13*, 529-554.

Favell, J., McGimsey, J., & Jones, M. (1978). The use of physical restraint in the treatment of self-injury and as positive reinforcement. *Journal of Applied Behavior Analysis, 11*, 225-241.

Gorman-Smith, D. & Matson, J. L. (1985). A review of treatment research for self-injurious and stereotyped responding. *Journal of Mental Deficiency Research, 29*, 295-308.

Iwata, B. A., Dorsey, M. F., Slifer, K. J., Bauman, K. E., & Richman, G. S. (1982). Toward a functional analysis of self-injury. *Analysis and Intervention in Developmental Disabilities, 2,* 3-20.

Jordan, J., Singh, N. N., & Repp, A. C. (1989). An evaluation of gentle teaching and visual screening in the reduction of stereotypy. *Journal of Applied Behavior Analysis, 22,* 9-22.

Kirk, R. E. (1982). *Experimental Design* (2nd ed.). Belmont, CA: Brooks/Cole.

LaGrow, S. J., & Repp, A. C. (1984). Stereotypic responding: A review of intervention research. *American Journal of Mental Deficiency, 88,* 595-609.

Lambert, N. M., & Windmiller, M. (1981). *AAMD Adaptive Behavior Scale - School Edition.* Washington, DC: American Association on Mental Deficiency.

LaVigna, G. W., & Donnellan, A. M. (1986). *Alternatives to punishment: Solving behavior problems with non-aversive strategies.* New York: Irvington.

Lichstein, K. L., & Schreibman, L. (1976). Employing electric shock with autistic children: A review of the side effects. *Journal of Autism and Childhood Schizophrenia, 6,* 163-173.

Luiselli, J. K., Suskin, L., & Slocumb, P. R. (1984). Application of immobilization time-out in management programming with developmentally disabled children. *Child and Family Behavior Therapy, 6,* 1-15.

Lundervold, D., & Bourland, G. (1988). Quantitative analysis of treatment of aggression, self-injury, and property destruction. *Behavior Modification, 12,* 590-617.

Matson, J. L., & Taras, M. E. (1989). A 20 year review of punishment and alternative methods to treat problem behaviors in developmentally disabled persons. *Research in Developmental Disabilities, 10,* 85-104.

McGee, J. J., Menolascino, F. J., Hobbs, D. C., & Menousek, P. E. (1987). *Gentle Teaching.* New York: Human Sciences Press.

Nihira, K., Foster, R., Shellhaas, N., & Leland, H. (1974). *AAMD Adaptive Behavior Scale Manual.* Washington, DC: American Association on Mental Deficiency.

Parrish, J. M., Iwata, B. A., Dorsey, M. F., Bunck, T. J., & Slifer, K. J. (1985). Behavior analysis, program development, and transfer of control in the treatment of self-injury. *Journal of Behavior Therapy and Experimental Psychiatry, 16,* 159-168.

Senatore, V., Matson, J. L., & Kazdin, A. E. (1983). An inventory to assess psychopathology of mentally retarded adults. *American Journal of Mental Deficiency, 89,* 459-466.

Singh, N. N., & Jones, L. J. (1989). *Comparative effects of gentle teaching and visual screening on self-injurious behavior.* Paper presented at the meeting of the American Psychological Association, New Orleans, LA.

Slifer, K. J., Iwata, B. A., & Dorsey, M. F. (1984). Reduction of eye gouging using a response interruption procedure. *Journal of Behavior Therapy and Experimental Psychiatry, 15,* 369-375.

Sparrow, S. S., Balla, D. A., & Cicchetti, D. V. (1984). *Vineland Adaptive Behavior Scales: Survey Form Manual.* Circle Pines, MN: American Guidance Service.

Starin, S. P., & Fuqua, R. W. (1987). Rumination and vomiting in the developmentally disabled: A critical review of the behavioral, medical and psychiatric research. *Research in Developmental Disabilities, 8*, 575-605.

Sturmey, P., Carlsen, A., Crisp, A. G., & Newton, J. T. (1988). A functional analysis of multiple aberrant responses: A refinement and extension of Iwata et al.'s (1982) methodology. *Journal of Mental Deficiency Research, 32*, 31-46.

PART VI

CHAPTER

31

LEAST RESTRICTIVE USE OF REDUCTIVE PROCEDURES: GUIDELINES AND COMPETENCIES

Gina Green

E.K. Shriver Center for Mental Retardation, Inc.

The sociolegal doctrine of the least restrictive alternative (LRA) has had a far-reaching impact on services for individuals with behavior disorders. In its broadest sense, the LRA principle has evolved in statutes and case law over nearly three decades to mean that all citizens should be permitted to live, work, play, learn, and receive services in contexts that are as free as possible of undue constraints on their liberties (Herr, Arons, & Wallace, 1983; Turnbull, 1981). When applied to services for individuals with behavior problems, the LRA doctrine often has been interpreted in absolute terms. For example, it has been invoked to constrain or prohibit the use of some behavior change procedures on the basis of their appearances and their short-term effects, without regard to the larger context in which the methods are used or the probable long-term effects on the individual's overall functioning.

Concerns about actions that cause discomfort or limit options are certainly justified on both moral and empirical grounds. It can be argued, however, that recent movements to prohibit all use of certain behavior change methods have taken these concerns to an extreme, and that such prohibitions restrict the rights of some recipients of services, as well as service providers. This chapter rests on the premise that the many rules (in the form of guidelines, policies, or laws) that govern the use of behavior change procedures are indeed restrictive, but for reasons different than those typically cited. With few exceptions, such rules are limited significantly because they have: (a) focused on procedures that are aversive or restrictive on their face, while paying relatively little attention to procedures that appear benign; (b) failed to specify the skills required for proper implementation of procedures to reduce behaviors, including positive procedures; and (c) stated or implied punishment contingencies for deviations from the rules rather than positive reinforcement for appropriate behavioral programming.

LIMITATIONS OF EXISTING GUIDELINES

Attempts to apply the LRA principle to treatment for consumers with various disabilities, coupled with reactions to well-publicized cases of consumer abuse and neglect, have resulted in volumes of written rules intended to control the behaviors of those who deliver services to these consumers. Rules have ranged in form from general guidelines and treatment-decision models published in journal articles and books (e.g., Favell et al., 1982; Favell & Reid, 1988; Gast & Wolery, 1987; Gaylord-Ross, 1980; Lovaas & Favell, 1987; Matson & Di-Lorenzo, 1984; Repp & Deitz, 1978) to comprehensive state statutes and regulations (e.g., Florida, Minnesota). Many sets of rules have dealt primarily or exclusively with the use of techniques that are patently aversive or restrictive (e.g., Foxx, Plaska, & Bittle, 1986; Lovaas & Favell, 1987; Repp & Deitz, 1978; Romanczyk, Colletti, & Lockshin, 1981; Thomas, 1977). Although most have emphasized the importance of interventions to increase functional alternative behaviors and use of the least restrictive methods to reduce problem behaviors, the majority of rules have stated or implied an assumption that positive procedures do not require the formal scrutiny that is mandated for restrictive treatments.

Procedures that use positive reinforcement, however, are not inherently exempt from misuse and abuse. Indeed, *any* attempt to influence behavior, no matter what label is applied to the method used, might be seen as a violation of personal freedom (Thomas & McGuire, 1988). The correct application of differential reinforcement requires at least as much skill and care as the use of procedures such as nonexclusionary time-out (Favell & Reid, 1988). In addition, maladaptive behaviors sometimes increase as a function of schedules of positive reinforcement (Wieseler, Hanson, Chamberlain, & Thompson, 1988), or of demands for adaptive responses (e.g., Mace, Browder, & Lin, 1987). Many of the so-called "positive" reductive techniques (e.g., differential reinforcement of other behavior to reduce aggression or self-injury) require precise implementation to ensure that dysfunctional behaviors are not reinforced inadvertently.

It appears inevitable that the use of behavioral technology will be regulated by someone, to some extent, at some point. If guidelines and regulations address only procedures that are labeled aversive or restrictive, two outcomes seem likely: (a) the misuse or abuse of arbitrarily defined positive procedures will go undetected; and (b) change agents will avoid using procedures that have been relegated to the aversive/restrictive category, even in those cases where the brief application of such procedures (in combination with actions to increase appropriate behaviors) would be the most effective treatment.

Of the many variables that determine the restrictiveness of any behavioral intervention, none is more important than the competence of the individuals who design and implement interventions. Even interventions that rely exclusively on positive methods can impose severe restrictions on consumers if they are not implemented properly. Several authors have stressed the critical role of the behaviors of change agents, especially when interventions to reduce behaviors are used (e.g., Favell et al., 1982; Favell & Reid, 1988; Foxx et al., 1986; Lovaas & Favell, 1987; Risley, 1975; Thomas, 1977; Thomas & Murphy, 1981). Yet, most guidelines and statutory requirements for using reductive techniques have emphasized procedural safeguards for consumers, only *implying* the skills required to implement those safeguards. Some have addressed change agent competencies, but only in general terms, while a few have specified competencies without relating them directly to procedural guidelines. Additionally, like most formal rules, many of the guidelines, policies, and regulations governing the use of reductive procedures are themselves coercive: they state or imply punishment contingencies as a means of controlling the behavior of change agents (cf. Sidman, 1989). It does not make good behavioral sense to use coercive contingencies to get change agents to behave noncoercively toward consumers.

TOWARD SYNTHESIS AND EXPANSION

This chapter synthesizes guidelines for using procedures to reduce behaviors and the skills required to design and carry out such procedures. Unlike most of the published guidelines and regulations, this discussion includes positive procedures as well as procedures commonly labeled aversive and restrictive. Each guideline is listed and discussed briefly, followed by an enumeration of the behaviors desired for adherence to that guideline. Instead of implying negative consequences for failure to demonstrate competencies, the competencies are stated as behaviors to be reinforced. For example, employers or supervisors could provide reinforcers in the form of praise, time off, pay increases, bonuses, and so forth to change agents when they demonstrate these skills. Competencies of other personnel -- family members, supervisors, administrators, members of Behavior Management and Human Rights Committees -- are not addressed. They are at least as important as the competencies of the primary change agent if behavior change programs are to be implemented in the least restrictive fashion, but space does not permit their inclusion. The competencies described here may be considered minimal, generic skills for a change agent; the lists are not exhaustive. Several competencies apply to more than one guideline, so they are cross-referenced. No strict sequence is implied by the order in which the guidelines and competencies are presented. In practice, activities to implement several of these recommendations are likely to be concurrent.

The guidelines are an amalgamation of commonly accepted best-practices and information from many published sources (Axelrod, 1987; Dunlap, Johnson, & Winterling, 1987; Favell et al., 1982; Favell & Reid, 1988; Florida Department of Health and Rehabilitative Services, 1982; Foxx, Plaska, & Bittle, 1986; Gast & Nelson, 1977; Gast & Wolery, 1987; Gaylord-Ross, 1980; Lovaas & Favell, 1987; May et al., 1976; Naumann, Maus, & Thomas, 1983; Nolley et al., 1980; Repp & Deitz, 1978; Risley, 1975; Romanczyk, Colletti, & Lockshin, 1981). Additional sources especially useful for identifying competencies include Florida Department of Health and Rehabilitative Services, 1982, 1988; Thomas, 1977; Thomas & Murphy, 1981.

GUIDELINES AND RELATED COMPETENCIES

1. Decide if Formal Intervention is Necessary

Whether the referral problem indicates a behavioral excess or a deficit, the first step is to determine if a problem really exists, and, if so, for whom it is a problem. The consumer should be the primary beneficiary of treatment. If a behavior (e.g., a stereotypy such as finger tapping, or failure to comply with every request) annoys others but is not likely to restrict the individual's opportunities to earn reinforcers to any significant degree, then intervention probably is not warranted. Objective measurement is necessary to make such a determination, with particular attention to the context(s) in which the behavior occurs or should occur, the functions it serves, and specific antecedents and consequences. A medical evaluation (including nutritional analysis where indicated) should be obtained if there is any possibility that a physiological condition might contribute to the behavior.

For implementing this guideline, contingencies should be established to reinforce the following behaviors by change agents:

1.1 Read the individual's records and note medical history, medications being taken, present levels of functioning (particularly social, self-help, and communication skills), current treatment protocols, previous interventions, plans for alternative placements, reinforcer preferences, family or guardian involvement in treatment programs, and all other information that is relevant to the referral question.

1.2 If a comprehensive medical evaluation has not been conducted within the past six months, make arrangements for one as soon as possible. Discuss results with the examining physician, psychopharmacological and other medical personnel, and the treatment team to determine whether medical or dietary intervention is indicated instead of, or as an adjunct to, behavioral intervention.

1.3 Interview others in the individual's environment, and record their estimates of the following for target behavior(s), as well as for alternative and collateral behaviors: (a) rate, intensity, and topography; (b) the conditions under which the behavior occurs or fails to occur; (c) events that typically precede and follow occurrences of each behavior; (d) reinforcement history; (e) living and employment options available to the consumer at present and in the future, and skills needed in those environments; and (f) the extent to which the problem restricts options, now and in the foreseeable future.

1.4 Observe the person under as many conditions as possible. Record in objective terms the relevant dimensions of the behaviors (rate, duration, intensity, topography, etc.), and typical antecedents (including setting events) and consequences (see also Competencies 6.9 - 6.11).

1.5 Examine the environments in which the person is expected to function. Determine whether the problem can be modified by changing the physical or social environment (e.g., noise level, physical arrangements, nature or quantity of demands, nature or quantity of social interactions, etc.).

2. Establish the Feasibility of an Intervention

When a determination has been made that the client is likely to benefit from actions intended to change behavior, the change agent should determine whether an intervention can be carried out -- legally, ethically, and practically -- in the present context. At this point, the change agent should consider several possible intervention strategies and evaluate the feasibility of each. Factors to be considered include (a) whether the change agent has the expertise to develop, implement, and monitor each of the alternative interventions; (b) availability and skills of others involved in the intervention, especially the interdisciplinary team; (c) administrative support, including agency commitment to treatment research and evaluation; (d) likelihood and extent of involvement by the consumer and significant others; (e) resource availability (time, materials, expert consultants); (f) agency, state, and federal policies and statutes governing use of the prospective interventions; (g) ethical standards for providing behavioral treatment; (h) provisions for accountability, including Behavior Management and Human Rights Committees and direct, frequent, and competent supervision; and (i) whether the present context will enable training for maintenance and generalization of behavior change, especially opportunities for training in the community.

To ensure that decisions about the feasibility of intervening are congruent with LRA principles, reinforcement should be provided for change agents when they:

2.1 State the professional privileges accorded by a license, certification, registration, or other procedure, by describing the types of intervention activities in which they can and cannot engage.
2.2 Describe the skills needed by others likely to be involved in each intervention.
2.3 Discuss prospective interventions with the appropriate administrator, and obtain a specific commitment for support.
2.4 Discuss prospective interventions with the consumer, legal guardian, advocate, family members, and significant others.
2.5 Estimate the resources necessary to implement each prospective intervention, including all personnel, time commitments for each person, money, materials, transportation, and consultation.
2.6 State the ethical standards for providers of behavioral treatment (e.g., American Psychological Association, Association for the Advancement of Behavior Therapy, other national and state professional organizations) and the ethical issues raised by each of the prospective interventions.
2.7 List agency, state, and federal regulations as they apply to each of the prospective interventions.
2.8 Describe the accountability requirements for each prospective intervention, including (a) the procedures and time required to obtain internal and external reviews; (b) the procedures and time required to obtain informed consent for treatment; (c) the type, quantity, and frequency of data collection; and (d) the nature and frequency of supervision.
2.9 For each prospective intervention, indicate the plan for maintenance and generalization and the extent to which that plan can be met in the present context. In addition, describe opportunities for training in the community, and the resources necessary for such training (see also Competencies 6.22 - 6.24).

3. Document the Absence or Failure of Prior Interventions

Most guidelines and regulations include explicit statements that the failure of prior "less restrictive" interventions must be documented before "more restrictive" procedures can be used. The number and duration of prior interventions, competence with which they were implemented, and acceptable evidence that they failed are usually left unspecified. There are no generic rules for making such assessments, of course; these issues must be determined on a case-by-case basis. Contingencies should be established, however, to promote very careful evaluations of prior treatments before *any* intervention begins. Perhaps the statement made most frequently by change agents faced with a difficult behavior problem is, "We tried reinforcement, and it didn't work." There are so many variations of positive reinforcement procedures and so many complexities and subtleties in the skilled application of reinforcement contingencies that it is very unlikely that all possibilities have been exhausted in any case (Sidman, 1989). When increasing rather than decreasing behaviors is the goal, intrusiveness should be no less an issue. With individuals who are labeled "disabled," the tendency often is to use multicomponent training strategies that require maximum trainer involvement and permit minimal independence; i.e., procedures that are more restrictive or intrusive than might be necessary. Careful review of prior training, coupled with a thorough assessment of the consumer's present skills, can help ensure that the least restrictive strategies are used to teach useful behaviors.

In addressing this guideline, change agents should:

3.1 Review all available client records for information about prior interventions. If possible, talk to the persons involved. Note what was done, when, for how long, by whom, with what results, and how the results were documented.

3.2 Evaluate the evidence about each prior intervention as to whether (a) behaviors were defined clearly and objectively; (b) a clear and complete description of procedures is available; (c) measures of treatment effects were appropriate, valid, and reliable; (d) reported effects are believable (i.e., the intervention was properly evaluated (refer to Competencies 6.3, 6.9 - 6.21).

3.3 Decide whether in fact *all* possible less restrictive alternatives have been tested adequately.

4. Research Proposed Interventions

Whether the primary objective of intervention is to decrease behaviors, increase behaviors, or both, the individual(s) responsible for designing the intervention should search the professional literature early in the planning process. An objective definition of the behavioral problem should direct the review of published research. *All* alternative procedures should be investigated, not just one type of intervention, for at least two reasons. First, focusing the research on one intervention may mean that other, more effective or less restrictive interventions are overlooked. Second, more than one strategy should be planned from the outset so that if the first one tried does not work, little time is lost in implementing a backup plan. In evaluating any published study, the change agent should consider (a) the degree to which the behaviors, consumer, and settings resemble those in the research report; (b) whether the published report includes enough information about treatment procedures that they could be replicated in the present case; (c) whether the contingencies described in the research report can be carried out in the present context, given personnel, time, resources, etc.; and (d) the extent to which the procedures have been shown to produce believable, reliable, and socially acceptable results.

Change agents should demonstrate that they can:

4.1 Describe and discuss current research on the application of validated procedures to decrease and increase behaviors as a result of reading professional journals, attending professional organization conferences, participating in inservice training and continuing education opportunities, and consulting with knowledgeable professionals.

4.2 Identify factors in published studies that influence the validity, reliability, and generality of the findings (especially measurement, research design, procedural integrity, and conclusions).

4.3 Identify at least two intervention strategies that have been demonstrated to be effective with consumers, behaviors, and settings similar to the present case. List the known and potential side effects (positive and negative) of each strategy.

5. Conduct a Functional Analysis

Analysis of the contingencies that control behavioral excesses and deficits is necessary for effective intervention. The first step should be careful observation of the problem behavior in a range of naturalistic conditions (e.g., Touchette, MacDonald, & Langer, 1985), recording antecedent and consequent events that are correlated with occurrences of the behavior. But a valid functional analysis must go beyond naturalistic observation. After potential controlling variables are identified, the consumer should be presented different antecedents and consequences systematically. The goal of this analysis should be to verify the functions that the problem behavior actually serves for the consumer, to identify alternative behaviors that could serve the same function (with an emphasis on communication and social skills), and to identify effective reinforcers for behaviors to be increased (e.g., Green et al., 1988; Mason, McGee, Farmer-Dougan, & Risley, 1989; Pace, Ivancic, Edwards, Iwata, & Page, 1985; Wacker, Berg, Wiggins, Muldoon, & Cavanaugh, 1985). Several excellent examples of functional analyses are described in the literature (e.g., Carr & Durand, 1985; Day, Rea, Schussler, Larsen, & Johnson, 1988; Gaylord-Ross, 1982; Iwata, Dorsey, Slifer, Bauman, & Richman, 1982; Mace & Knight, 1986; Mace, Page, Ivancic, & O'Brien, 1986; Repp, Felce, & Barton, 1988; Slifer, Ivancic, Parrish, Page, & Burgio, 1986).

To conduct functional analyses of behaviors, change agents should:

5.1 Describe and discuss published examples of functional analyses.

5.2 Observe the consumer in a variety of everyday situations, recording occurrences of the problem behavior under different conditions. Attend particularly to (a) times of day, (b) factors in the physical environment (space, noise, temperature, light, play objects, etc.), (c) behaviors of others before and after occurrences of the problem behavior, (d) task demands, and (e) the consumer's communication skills (see also Competencies 6.9 - 6.15).

5.3 Develop or refine definitions of the problem behavior and functional alternative behaviors. Write definitions in unambiguous, observable, measurable terms (see also Competencies 6.3 - 6.4).

5.4 From the naturalistic observations, identify antecedents and consequences that correlate highly with instances of the problem behavior. Systematically introduce and then remove one of those events at a time, recording occurrences of the problem behavior and other behaviors that may be related over several observations. Repeat with each event until the controlling variables have been verified.

5.5 From the naturalistic observations, information obtained from consumer records, and interviews with others who have observed the consumer, identify potential reinforcers for at least one functional response that is an alternative to the problem behavior. Arrange to present each potential reinforcer contingent on several occurrences of the alternative behavior (or an approximation), and record occurrences of the alternative behavior.

6. Develop a Proposal for an Intervention That is Integrated with Other Aspects of the Consumer's Habilitation Program

A proposed intervention plan should be written for review by several parties (discussed later). This guideline has several components, and each is addressed separately with its related competencies.

CONSUMER PARTICIPATION. As early as possible in the planning process, the consumer, along with the family, guardian, and/or advocate, should be involved in decisions about the intervention. The change agent should:

6.1 Discuss with the consumer and the family or guardian in terms that they can understand (a) target behaviors; (b) proposed interventions and alternatives, including the alternative of no treatment; (c) short- and long-term restrictions, costs, risks, and benefits of all alternatives; and (d) short- and long-term treatment goals. Proceed with planning based on the consumer's choices.

INTERDISCIPLINARY TEAM PARTICIPATION. Members of the interdisciplinary team, including the change agent's immediate supervisor, also should be involved early in the planning process. The change agent should:

6.2 Discuss with members of the interdisciplinary team all of the issues listed in 6.1 above, as well as their role in implementing the intervention. Solicit suggestions before proceeding with planning.

BEHAVIORAL DEFINITIONS. The problem behavior and all alternative and collateral behaviors (i.e., those that should and may be affected by the intervention) should be defined clearly, based on the original referral, initial observations, review of literature, functional analysis, and consumer input.

6.3 Write behavioral definitions in unambiguous, objective, measurable terms.

6.4 Ask others (e.g., members of the interdisciplinary team, supervisor) to read the definitions, observe the consumer, and record occurrences and nonoccurrences of the behaviors. Record concurrently but independently, and then compare recordings for consistency. Revise the definitions and repeat this test until a high level of agreement (e.g., 95% of all occurrences and nonoccurrences) is attained with each observer.

CURRENT LEVELS OF BEHAVIORS (BASELINE). Before an intervention is devised, have accurate, objective information about the extent to which the proposed targets of the intervention are occurring.

6.5 State the current (baseline) levels of the behaviors in clear, objective terms. Describe the conditions under which baseline assessment was conducted, for how long, and by whom.

6.6 Graph the baseline data and attach a copy of the graph to the intervention proposal.

RATIONALE. The proposal should include a clear, concise statement of the rationale for the intervention, incorporating all of the information gathered in preceding steps. The behavior(s) to be reduced and functional behavior(s) to be increased should be addressed.

6.7 Write the rationale for the intervention, including (a) the referral question; (b) evidence that intervention is warranted (including the present levels of the behaviors); (c) past interventions and their outcomes; (d) how the proposed intervention is likely to affect overall level of functioning, in the immediate and more distant future, and in the whole range of present and future living and work environments; (e) literature supporting the proposed intervention; (f) data showing that other less restrictive alternatives have been exhausted; and (g) other intervention strategies that could be employed. The rationale should be written in precise but nontechnical terms, understandable to parents or guardians, team members, supervisors, and other reviewers.

MEASUREMENT AND DATA COLLECTION. Accurate and reliable measurement of behaviors over the course of an intervention is critical for evaluating effectiveness, and often differentiates successful from unsuccessful programs

(Risley, 1975). Up-to-the-minute progress data must be readily available to, and easily interpretable by, everyone involved in the intervention. Data should be reviewed frequently. The change agent must be able to:

6.8 Demonstrate skills in observing and recording behaviors reliably, given behavioral definitions, recording procedures, and instruments.

6.9 Define and illustrate standard behavioral assessment methods (event, duration, momentary time sampling, discrete trial, rating scales, task analysis, behavioral codes, and social validity).

6.10 Select an assessment method that is appropriate to the target behaviors, collateral behaviors, and the intervention context, and develop appropriate scoring methods (including selecting and using instrumentation, devising recording forms, and writing clear instructions for data collectors).

6.11 Specify when and how often data will be recorded, including follow-up and generalization assessments.

6.12 Specify how data will be graphed for visual analysis.

6.13 Specify who will record and graph behavior.

6.14 Specify how primary and secondary data collectors will be trained to conduct assessments, including interobserver agreement procedures, contingencies for accurate recording, and means of correcting data collection errors.

EVALUATION. Treatment effectiveness can be judged with confidence only when the course of treatment is evaluated objectively and systematically. The change agent must arrange events and actions over a period of time that, in conjunction with continuous measurement of the target behavior(s), make possible evaluating whether any observed changes in the consumer's behavior(s) are due to those events (i.e., the intervention and removing or changing the intervention) and not to other factors. The change agent should demonstrate that he/she can:

6.15 Describe procedures for evaluating behavior change objectively over time, under conditions with and without planned interventions in place.

6.16 For the presenting target behavior(s), proposed intervention, and treatment context, select appropriate procedures with which to evaluate the effects of the intervention.

6.17 For the evaluation procedure selected, describe clearly each phase or condition, the planned minimal length of each phase, criteria for determining stability of data, and criteria for changing phases.

PROCEDURES. The procedures for carrying out the intervention should be written in clear, specific terms. Contingencies for both increasing deficit behaviors and decreasing problem behaviors should be clear, and the procedures should tell who will review them; everyone who is responsible for implementing the program; exactly *what* will occur, *where, when, how often;* and *who* will be involved. A step-by-step checklist or flow chart may be included.

To address this component, the change agent should:

6.18 Document a history of supervised, "hands on" experience in using validated behavior change techniques, including at least (a) differential reinforcement of alternative behavior, incompatible behavior, other behavior, low rates of responding, high rates of responding; (b) shaping; forward chaining, and backward chaining; (c) use of verbal, gestural, modeling, physical, and time delay prompts; (d) delivery of primary and secondary reinforcers on various reinforcement schedules; (e) teaching simple and conditional discriminations; (f) task analysis; (g) graduated guidance; (h) strategies to promote self-management; (i) extinction; (j) response cost; (k) reprimands; (l) non-exclusionary and exclusionary time-out from positive reinforcement; (m) overcorrection; (n) positive practice; (o) visual screening; (p) contingent restraint; and (q) contingent application of negative stimuli.

6.19 Write a description of how the intervention is to be carried out, including (a) the setting(s), time(s), and person(s) responsible; (b) materials needed; (c) specific instructions and other prompts to be used; (d) consequences for each behavior and the schedule of their delivery; (e) data recording instructions; (f) steps for fading prompts; (g) steps for thinning consequences; (h) decision rules for on-the-spot modifications; and (i) strategies for handling anticipated problems.

6.20 Demonstrate the intervention for others.

GENERALIZATION AND MAINTENANCE. Every intervention should include ways to promote generalization across time and settings. When the initial treatment is highly structured, the behavior change should be firmly established before moving to a less structured approach. From that point, further intervention should take place in a variety of settings, with as many as possible in the community. At a minimum, several relevant persons in other settings (including peers) should be trained to carry out the intervention. Another critical component is selecting target behaviors that are most likely to garner positive reinforcement in the widest range of circumstances.

Positive reinforcers should be provided to change agents when they:

6.21 Document supervised, "hands on" experience in using validated techniques for promoting generalization and maintenance of behavior change, including at least (a) teaching relevant behaviors, (b) modifying antecedents and consequences for maladaptive behaviors, (c) recruiting natural reinforcers, (d) using sufficient stimulus examplars, (e) using sufficient response exemplars, (f) training loosely; (g) using indiscriminable contingencies, (h) reinforcing unprompted generalizations, (i) programming common stimuli, (j) thinning reinforcement, (k) increasing delays between behaviors and consequences, (l) changing from contrived to natural reinforcers, (m) fading change agent involvement, and (n) teaching self-management (see Horner, Dunlap, & Koegel, 1988).

6.22 Write a clear description of procedures for promoting generalization and maintenance, as in Competency 6.19.

6.23 Demonstrate techniques for promoting generalization and maintenance.

SHORT- AND LONG-TERM OBJECTIVES. The short-term (e.g., one month, three months) and long-term (e.g., one year or longer) aims of the intervention should be stated clearly. For each phase of the proposed intervention, criteria for progressing to the next phase should be specified in the description of the procedures. The consumer and the family, guardian, or advocate should be involved in setting goals, as should the interdisciplinary team.

6.24 State the level of the target behaviors, relative to baseline, that should be achieved over relatively short periods of time and over a longer period. Include specific criteria for determining when the intervention should be changed or terminated.

7. Obtain Reviews of the Proposal

Review mechanisms vary across settings and may include opportunities for reviews by supervisors, consumers and their families or guardians, administrators, interdisciplinary team consultants, outside auditors, a Behavior Management Committee, and/or a Human Rights Committee. Many statutes and agency policies now mandate reviews and specify timelines for initial and periodic reviews of the written proposal, as well as actual implementation of the intervention. (Unfortunately, so-called "nonrestrictive" programs are usually exempt from review.) Reviews should be treated as opportunities for differentially reinforcing efforts to deliver quality programming and enhance professional skills. To facilitate the review process, the change agent should:

7.1 Determine dates for review committee meetings. Request initial review of the proposed program at the earliest possible date.
7.2 Distribute copies of the written proposal to relevant reviewers in advance of the scheduled meeting.
7.3 Be prepared to provide supplemental information or answer questions posed by reviewers.
7.4 Explain the proposed intervention in clear, nontechnical terms.
7.5 Negotiate modifications suggested by reviewers, and change the plan accordingly.
7.6 Arrange for periodic internal and external reviews of the written procedures, data, and implementation.
7.7 Write progress reports for reviewers that are clear, concise, and jargon-free.

8. Obtain Informed Consent to Treatment

Once the intervention has been approved, written consent to participate must be obtained from the consumer or legal guardian. Valid consent must be competent, informed, and voluntary (Herr, Arons, & Wallace, 1983). To ensure that these requirements are met, the change agent should:

8.1 Describe for the consumer and/or guardian in terms that make sense to them (a) exactly what the intervention involves; (b) known and potential short- and long-term risks and benefits, including positive and negative side effects; (c) all viable alternative interventions and their risks and benefits, including no treatment; (d) the probability that the intervention will be successful; and (e) costs to the consumer, including money, time, and effort.
8.2 State clearly that consent to participate is voluntary and may be withdrawn at any time without penalty or loss of other services.
8.3 Obtain signatures of the consumer and/or guardian on the consent form.

9. Train Others

Consistent implementation of treatment procedures is essential for effectiveness. Over the course of a comprehensive intervention, many people may be called upon to record data and apply the strategies. Contingencies must be arranged to reinforce accurate and consistent implementation by all involved. Others may need to be trained to help the implementers read and interpret data; e.g., the consumer and family, guardian, or advocate; supervisors and administrators; interdisciplinary team members; auditors; and members of review committees.

Change agents should:

9.1 Provide clear, step-by-step verbal instructions and demonstrations of procedures for individuals who will apply them. Include data recording, graphing, and interobserver reliability procedures as appropriate (refer to Competencies 6.9-6.15, 6.19- 6.24).

9.2 Observe implementation on a regular basis. Reinforce correct applications and provide corrective feedback as needed.

9.3 Provide clear written and verbal explanations of graphed data on the consumer's progress to anyone who has legal access to such data.

10. Monitor and Evaluate the Intervention

Monitoring should be a continuous, ongoing activity. Frequent review of the course of treatment is essential to providing the least restrictive, most effective, socially valid intervention.

The program developer should:

10.1 Review graphed data frequently with staff who are directly involved with the intervention.

10.2 Check interobserver agreement at least weekly, and remediate any problems (e.g., by retraining observers, reinforcing accurate recording, revising behavioral definitions).

10.3 Conduct regular direct observations of implementation by each person responsible for the program.

10.4 Arrange for direct observations of program implementation by the consumer's family or guardian, supervisors, interdisciplinary team members, expert consultants, review committees, and relevant members of the community.

10.5 Revise the intervention based on these evaluations; or

10.6 Terminate the intervention, if either (a) the objectives of the program have been achieved (refer to Competency 6.25); or (b) the intervention is clearly not producing the desired effect; i.e., the data show no clear evidence of progress in the established timelines (see Competencies 6.9 - 6.18 and 6.25).

SUMMARY

A compilation of guidelines for using procedures to change problem behaviors and associated competencies for primary change agents has been presented. The scope of procedures to which these guidelines apply has been expanded beyond the usual list of strategies that are labeled "aversive" or "restrictive" to include all behavior change techniques. Unless the formal rules that are intended to control the use of behavioral procedures are broadened to include positive procedures, the goal of least restrictive treatment for persons with developmental disabilities cannot be realized fully. This implies that the systems in which behavioral interventions occur must provide powerful positive reinforcers for change agent behaviors that, in turn, result in constructive, noncoercive interventions with consumers. Ultimately, the least restrictive treatment should consist of competent behavioral programming that applies the most effective methods to maximize positive outcomes for consumers.

NOTE

Thanks are extended to the editors; to Mary Crowley for assistance in gathering information for this chapter; and to Marty McMorrow for discussions that set the occasion for much that is written here.

REFERENCES

Axelrod, S. (1987). Functional and structural analyses of behavior: Approaches leading to reduced use of punishment procedures? *Research in Developmental Disabilities, 8*, 165-178.

Carr, E.G., & Durand, V.M. (1985). Reducing behavior problems through functional communication training. *Journal of Applied Behavior Analysis, 18*, 111-126.

Day, R.M., Rea, J.A., Schussler, N.G., Larsen, S.E., & Johnson, W.L. (1988). A functionally based approach to the treatment of self-injurious behavior. *Behavior Modification, 12*, 565-589.

Dunlap, G., Johnson, J., Winterling, V., & Morelli, M.A. (1987). The management of disruptive behavior in unsupervised settings: Issues and directions for a behavioral technology. *Education and Treatment of Children, 10*, 367-382.

Favell, J.E., Azrin, N.H., Baumeister, A.A., Carr, E.G., Dorsey, M.F., Forehand, R., Foxx, R.M., Lovaas, O.I., Rincover, A., Risley, T.R., Romanczyk, R.G., Russo, D.C., Schroeder, S.R., & Solnick, J.V. (1982). The treatment of self-injurious behavior. *Behavior Therapy, 13*, 529-554.

Favell, J.E., & Reid, D.H. (1988). Generalizing and maintaining improvement in problem behavior. In R.H. Horner, G. Dunlap, & R.L. Koegel (Eds.), *Generalization and maintenance: Life-style changes in applied settings* (pp. 171-196). Baltimore: Paul H. Brookes.

Florida Department of Health and Rehabilitative Services (1982). *HRS Manual: Behavioral programming and management*. (HRSM 160-4). Tallahassee, FL: Author.

Florida Department of Health and Rehabilitative Services (1988). *Information and registration booklet for the Florida Behavior Analysis Certification Examination*. Tallahassee, FL: Author.

Foxx, R.M., Plaska, T.G., & Bittle, R.G. (1986). Guidelines for the use of contingent electric shock to treat aberrant behavior. *Progress in Behavior Modification, 20*, 1-34.

Gast, D.L., & Nelson, C.M. (1977). Legal and ethical considerations for the use of timeout in special education settings. *The Journal of Special Education, 11*, 457-467.

Gast, D.L., & Wolery, M. (1987). Severe maladaptive behaviors. In M.E. Snell (Ed.), *Systematic instruction of persons with severe handicaps* (3rd ed.). (pp. 300-332). Columbus: Charles E. Merrill.

Gaylord-Ross, R.J. (1980). A decision model for the treatment of aberrant behavior in applied settings. In W. Sailor, B. Wilcox, & L. Brown (Eds.), *Methods of instruction for severely handicapped students*. (pp. 135-158). Baltimore: Paul H. Brookes.

Gaylord-Ross, R.J. (1982). Curricular considerations in treating behavior problems of severely handicapped students. *Advances in Learning and Behavioral Disabilities, 1*, 193-224.

Green, C.W., Reid, D.H., White, L.K., Halford, R.C., Brittain, D.P., & Gardner, S.M. (1988). Identifying reinforcers for persons with profound handicaps: Staff opinion versus systematic assessment of preferences. *Journal of Applied Behavior Analysis, 21*, 31-43.

Herr, S.S., Arons, S., & Wallace, R.E. (1983). *Legal rights and mental health care*. Lexington, MA: Lexington Books.

Horner, R.H., Dunlap, G., & Koegel, R.L. (1988). *Generalization and maintenance: Life-style changes in applied settings*. Baltimore: Paul H. Brookes.

Iwata, B.A., Dorsey, M.F., Slifer, K.J., Bauman, K.E., & Richman, G.S. (1982). Toward a functional analysis of self-injury. *Analysis and Intervention in Developmental Disabilities, 2*, 3-20.

Lovaas, O.I, & Favell, J.E. (1987). Protection for clients undergoing aversive/restrictive interventions. *Education and Treatment of Children, 10*, 311-325.

Mace, F.C., Browder, D.M., & Lin, Y. (1987). Analysis of demand conditions associated with stereotypy. *Journal of Behavior Therapy and Experimental Psychiatry, 18*, 25-31.

Mace, F.C., & Knight, D. (1986). Functional analysis and treatment of severe pica. *Journal of Applied Behavior Analysis, 19*, 411-416.

Mace, F.C., Page, T.J., Ivancic, M.T., & O'Brien, S. (1986). Analysis of environmental determinants of aggression and disruption in mentally retarded children. *Applied Research in Mental Retardation, 7*, 203-221.

Mason, S.A., McGee, G.G., Farmer-Dougan, V., & Risley, T. (1989). A practical strategy for ongoing reinforcer assessment. *Journal of Applied Behavior Analysis, 22*, 171-179.

Matson, J.L., & DiLorenzo, T.M. (1984). *Punishment and its alternatives*. New York: Springer.

May, J.G., Risley, T.R., Twardosz, S., Friedman, P., Bijou, S., & Wexler, O. (1976). Guidelines for the use of behavioral procedures in state programs for retarded persons. (NARC Monograph). Arlington, TX: Mental Retardation Research.

Naumann, C.E., Maus, M., & Thomas, D.R. (1983). An analysis of guidelines for the use of locked room timeout. *Behavioral Engineering, 8*, 77-89.

Nolley, D., Boelkins, D., Kocur, L., Moore, M.K., Goncalves, S., & Lewis, M. (1980). Aversive conditioning within laws and guidelines in a state facility for mentally retarded individuals. *Mental Retardation, 18*, 295-298.

Pace, G.M., Ivancic, M.T., Edwards, G.L., Iwata, B.A., & Page, T.J. (1985). Assessment of stimulus preference and reinforcer value with profoundly retarded individuals. *Journal of Applied Behavior Analysis, 18*, 249-255.

Repp, A.C., & Deitz, D.E.D. (1978). On the selective use of punishment - Suggested guidelines for administrators. *Mental Retardation, 16*, 250-254.

Repp, A.C., Felce, D., & Barton, L.E. (1988). Basing the treatment of stereotypic and self-injurious behaviors on hypotheses of their causes. *Journal of Applied Behavior Analysis, 21*, 281-289.

Risley, T.R. (1975). Certify procedures not people. In W.S. Wood (Ed.), *Issues in evaluating behavior modification: Proceedings of the First Drake Conference on Professional Issues in Behavior Analysis, 1974* (pp. 159-181). Champaign, IL: Research Press.

Romanczyk, R.G., Colletti, G., & Lockshin, S. (1981). *Developing a policy concerning the use of aversive procedures: Ethical, legal, and empirical issues*. Paper presented at the meeting of the Association for Behavior Analysis, Milwaukee.

Sidman, M. (1989). *Coercion and its fallout*. Boston: Authors Cooperative.

Slifer, K.J., Ivancic, M.T., Parrish, J.M., Page, T.J., & Burgio, L.D. (1986). Assessment and treatment of multiple behavior problems exhibited by a profoundly retarded adolescent. *Journal of Behavior Therapy and Experimental Psychiatry, 17*, 203-213.

Thomas, D.R. (1977). *Staff competencies required for implementation of aversive and deprivation procedures.* Paper presented at the meeting of the American Psychological Association, San Francisco.

Thomas, D.R., & McGuire, P.S. (1988). Balancing right to treatment with intrusiveness: The psychotherapist's judgment rule. *Behavioral Residential Treatment, 3*, 211-222.

Thomas, D.R., & Murphy, R.J. (1981). Practitioner competencies needed for implementing behavior management guidelines. *The Behavior Therapist, 4*, 7-10.

Touchette, P.E., MacDonald, R.F., & Langer, S.N. (1985). A scatter plot for identifying stimulus control of problem behavior. *Journal of Applied Behavior Analysis, 18*, 343-351.

Turnbull, H.R. III (Ed.) (1981). *The least restrictive alternative: Principles and practices.* Washington, D.C.: American Association on Mental Deficiency.

Wacker, D.P., Berg, W.K., Wiggins, B., Muldoon, M., & Cavanaugh, J. (1985). Evaluation of reinforcer preferences for profoundly handicapped students. *Journal of Applied Behavior Analysis, 18*, 173-178.

Wieseler, N.A., Hanson, R.H., Chamberlain, T.P., & Thompson, T. (1988). Stereotypic behavior of mentally retarded adults adjunctive to a positive reinforcement schedule. *Research in Developmental Disabilities, 9*, 393-403.

CHAPTER

32

"DAMN IT, BURRIS, I'M NOT A PRODUCT OF WALDEN TWO," OR WHO'S CONTROLLING THE CONTROLLERS

John R. Lutzker
University of Judaism

In the novel, *Walden Two* (Skinner, 1948), Frazier, the founder of the Utopian community, invites the narrator, Burris, to his room, reveals his personal slovenliness, and self-analytically proclaims, "You think I'm conceited, aggressive, tactless, selfish...well, you're perfectly right..., but, ...damn it, Burris, I'm not a product of Walden Two." This revelation by Frazier is the crux of the moral issue of Walden Two; that is, who controls the controllers? Needless to say, there is considerable emotion attached to the aversive/nonaversive argument that has plagued behavior analysts over the past few years. This chapter will put forth a position that the most relevant approach to this issue is a scientific one with one moralistic caveat: the concern that even if there were solid evidence in favor of aversive control, there is little, if any, evidence that those who might apply aversive procedures are under sufficient scrutiny to be allowed to carry out these procedures. The basic tenets of this chapter are (a) There is weak evidence supporting the *effectiveness* of aversive procedures with developmentally disabled persons. (b) The evidence that there is sufficient scrutiny over the mediators of aversive procedures is especially weak. (c) We have not sufficiently explored a broad-based ecobehavioral approach as an alternative to the use of aversives. (d) We know too little about biological and other etiological factors governing behavior so severe that it may warrant consideration of aversive procedures. (e) Issues of civil rights and social validation should be approached as empirically as we view outcome data.

Thus, this chapter takes a negative but qualified view of the consideration of aversive procedures with developmentally disabled individuals.

SCIENTIFIC EVIDENCE

Behavior modification (today more frequently called applied behavior analysis) began to flourish around 1964. At that time, along with behavior therapy, it was truly a radical departure from the practices of psychology and related fields.

Two aspects of its methodology were especially different: the collection of data which was based on the direct observation of operationally defined behavior; and, the use of single-subject research designs to demonstrate that behavior change was a function of the specific procedures utilized, and not some other spurious events. Thus, for many, the applied side of psychology had finally become a science. From this new science, great excitement and hope were generated as clinical change was produced with previously intractable problems, such as autism (Wolf, Risley, & Mees, 1964), schizophrenia (Ayllon & Azrin, 1964), and profound mental retardation (Bijou, 1963). Science and methodology became the hallmarks of behavior modification and remain so for behavior analysis today. In their seminal article in the first issue of the *Journal of Applied Behavior Analysis*, Baer, Wolf, and Risley (1968) dissected the label "applied behavior analysis." In particular, they noted that "applied" means socially and clinically significant; that is, the target behavior should be relevant, and the outcome should be dramatic. Further, generalization should occur across situations, behaviors, and, most importantly for this discussion, *time*. That is, treatment effects must be *durable*. This is where the issue of the use of aversive procedures breaks down.

Behavior analysis is a field priding itself on a scientific foundation; yet, the argument over the use of aversive procedures with developmentally disabled persons has remained largely an emotional one, although it also has dealt with policy. Recently, Schroeder and Schroeder (1989) asked some poignant questions regarding the scientific base of the aversive/nonaversive controversy. Among the 20 science, philosophy and ethics, and advocacy questions they generated, one was, "Do we know and agree upon the criteria for successful treatment?" One would think that if practitioners and researchers in our field were to use and recommend extraordinary procedures that involve painful or unpleasant stimulation to individuals who cannot advocate for themselves, the answer to this question would be well established. Unfortunately, it has barely been addressed. Years ago, the Association for Behavior Analysis (ABA) and the Association for the Advancement of Behavior Therapy (AABT) should have commissioned "blue ribbon" panels to address this issue and to generate policies for the organizations. Such policies could have served as guidelines for states in forming statewide policies in the delivery of services to developmentally disabled persons. In 1982, the AABT did publish an article on standards of care which addressed the treatment of self-injurious behavior (Favell, Azrin, Baumeister, Carr, Dorsey, Forehand, Foxx, Lovaas, Rincover, Risley, Romanczyk, Russo, Schroeder, & Solnick, 1982); however, this document apparently has not been used to help legislators form policies, nor has it been widely cited during the aversive/nonaversive debate.

Another important question asked by Schroeder and Schroeder (1989) was, "Do we know and can we list what stimuli are punishing, aversive, painful, or repulsive to our clients?" Again, the answer to this question represents much more speculation than science. On the surface, speculation might seem the only mode for addressing this issue. Subjectively, we can ask questions such as, "Would I want to receive electric shock to my forearm? Would I want water mist in my face? Would I want my face covered by a terry cloth bib?" Or, we could ask," Would I want my own children to experience these procedures?" Of interest, however, is the point that to a degree these questions can be addressed empirically. For example, Martin (1977) wanted to know which of three kinds of feedback chronically ill children preferred and which caused them to perform at the highest rate when working on simple tasks. The forms of feedback were ignoring, reprimanding, or praising. During each experimental session, children received all three forms of feedback. Curiously, they worked hardest whenever they were reprimanded; however, in a probe following each session, they never chose to play the game or perform the task on which they had been reprimanded in the prior session. This seems a clear statement of preference by the children. Similarly, Redd, Morris, and Martin (1975) utilized different adults to deliver these consequences to children for performing a singular task. Each session, a different adult either praised, reprimanded, or ignored the child. Once again, when given a choice of which adult with whom to play after a session, children never chose the adult who had reprimanded them during the prior session. These results represent the kinds of side effects often mentioned in textbook discussions of punishment; yet, such effects have seldom been assessed in any applied research with humans.

Schroeder and Schroeder (1989) also ask; "Is the frequency of publication about a behavior intervention procedure closely related to the effectiveness of that procedure?" The likely answer is that frequency may be related more to its current novelty, current controversy, or acceptability than to its efficacy. Thus, unfortunately, for a field that puts so much stock in science, few answers to pertinent scientific questions have been addressed regarding the aversive/nonaversive debate. Further, the most relevant question has never been addressed; that is, do we have good evidence that aversive procedures produce clear-cut, long-term behavior change? The answer is an unequivocal "no." There has not been a large N study with long-term follow-up on a singular procedure such as shock or water mist, nor has there been one with aversive procedures as a category. Neither have any studies compared significant numbers of cases wherein aversive procedures were and were not used in treating similar sets of serious behaviors. Also, follow-up periods have been remarkably short in small N studies. For example, Dixon, Helsel, Rojahn, Cipollone, and Lubetsky (1989) examined the use of visual screening and aromatic ammonia with a developmentally disabled child who manifested high levels of aggressive, destructive, and loud screeching behaviors. Only two follow-up data points were presented after over 60 baseline and treatment sessions. The authors would have been prudent in a case such as this to follow up 3, 6, 9, and 12 months later, particularly because there are so few published articles dealing with these two procedures individually, let alone in combination with each other. Thus, the point is that we have a serious emotional controversy raging in the absence of any respectable evidence in large numbers that aversive procedures produce durable behavior change. No drug or experimental procedure would ever be allowed by the FDA with such a similar paucity of data.

WHAT IF AVERSIVES WERE EFFECTIVE?

One of the four advocacy questions asked by Schroeder and Schroeder (1989) is; "Do we know that there are some procedures that are not used abusively and others that frequently are used abusively?" Again, the answer to this question is an unequivocal "no." Although some research has addressed the acceptability of a variety of treatment procedures rated by parents, teachers, professionals, and paraprofessionals, there have been no attempts to examine the abusive "risk factors" various treatment procedures hold, nor do we have any true sense of whether or not any given procedures are used abusively in homes, schools, or institutions. Certainly, there is an occasional exposé concerning abuse in a care home, foster home, or institution; however, formal large-scale evaluations have not been attempted.

One might suggest that current child abuse laws and institutional regulations eliminate the concern over abuse of procedures, but this presumption is hardly the case. While regulations, laws, and human rights and human subjects research committees have, hopefully, reduced risk, there is no assurance that major abuse does not still occur. In fact, this issue becomes a definitional one and remains an integral part of the whole aversive/nonaversive controversy. What is abusive? Is the use of currently *approved* procedures, even under careful scrutiny, abusive nonetheless? Are facial screening, shock, water mist, a variety of overcorrection procedures, seclusion time-out, aromatic ammonia, pinching, and so on "inherently immoral" (another term embedded in a question asked by Schroeder & Schroeder, 1989)? In discussing the right to effective behavior treatment, Van Houten et al. (1988) have suggested that individuals have a right to basic dignity. Most of these aversive procedures would seem to deny this right. Despite having developed facial screening (Lutzker, 1978), a procedure that I have not recommended in over 10 years, I was always struck by how undignified, in fact, outright ugly, this procedure is. Beyond the definitional and philosophic issue of morality is the issue of proper scrutiny. Perhaps the setting that creates the most risk is a child's natural home. Once aversive procedures are introduced in the home, what safeguards exist to prevent parents, siblings, babysitters, or housekeepers from abusing a child with any aversive procedure? A parent might reason that if it "works" with self-injury, it could be used for noncompliant, "sassy" verbal behavior, or merely when the parent is frustrated and angry at the child, regardless of that child's behavior. This problem extends, of course, to all other settings, such as foster care and residential settings. The more public the setting, presumably the less likelihood of blatant abuse, but the potential exists, nevertheless. The surest prevention of abuse of aversive procedures is not to equip parents, teachers, and care providers with these techniques in the first place.

In proposing a code of ethics for behavior analysis, Bailey (1988) has said, "The behavior analyst will not recommend the use of procedures which the staff are not competent to carry out, or where insufficient supervision and proper controls exist to assure that behavioral procedures are properly instituted." He further suggests: "The behavior analyst recognizes the potential for abuse of aversive procedures...as well as the negative side effects associated with each.... The behavior analyst...should recommend and support the use of such a procedure only when the necessary controls and protections are in place to prevent abuse." We have poor evidence at best that good quality training and proper safeguards are in place in *most* settings.

Finally, the lack of scientific evidence on the efficacy of aversive procedures and the failure of behavior analysts to have thoroughly and thoughtfully addressed these issues calls into question why we, as professionals, should be trusted as the experts who might advise mediators of treatment, or chair committees to oversee the use of aversive procedures, or advise human subjects committees. How do we know that our professional judgment is so prudent, accurate, or ethical (Griffith & Spreat, in press)? Indeed, none of us is a product of Walden Two, and our desire to develop effective procedures may adversely bias these other ethical/moral/philosophical concerns. As Iwata (1988) has suggested, the public should guide these issues. We are not in a proper position to do so.

BIOLOGICAL AND ECOLOGICAL ALTERNATIVES

Behavior analysts have been slow to recognize the role of biological factors in the etiology and partial maintenance of some behaviors (Lutzker, 1989). Obviously, the most severe forms of self-injurious behavior and probably other kinds of impulsive, stereotypic, and hyperactive behavior are governed, at least in part, by poorly understood biological factors (Gardner, in press).

Thus, using aversive procedures for behaviors that may be only partly controlled by environmental factors produces a scientific, practical, and ethical dilemma. The scientific/practical problem is that antecedent and consequent events will have only modest impact on behavior that is only partly controlled by those factors. The ethical problem is that using our singular, narrow strategies to treat behavior that may not be very treatable with them is inappropriate. Behavior analysts may play a key role in providing observational and research design strategies to evaluate drugs that are developed to treat severe SIB. Furthermore, these strategies will continue to be useful in providing more functional assessments regarding the role of environmental/ecological factors in maintaining serious behavior disorders.

In the mid-70s, a lively discussion began among behavior analysts and ecological psychologists (Rogers-Warren & Warren, 1977) concerning the need for each field to recognize and to utilize some of the attributes of the other. Out of these discussions came the term, "ecobehavioral," which means that behavior should be assessed and treated within its ecological context. For example, we have suggested that whenever problem behavior displayed by a child becomes a target for treatment, regardless of how simple that behavior seems, for durable treatment effects, it should be examined and treated from an ecobehavioral perspective (Lutzker, Touchette, & Campbell, 1988). Thus, in the case of a self-injurious child being treated ecobehaviorally in the home, several assessments would be made. For example, in addition to examining potential situational antecedents and consequences to SIB, ecobehavioral therapists might also assess the mother's level of stress. If it were found to be high, some stress-reduction procedures would help her to be able to handle the strain of whatever treatment program that she might be asked to help implement with her child. Additionally, the child and significant others would be observed in their interactions in all settings in which the child functions. SIB might even be viewed as a communication deficit.

An example of the ecobehavioral approach in treating families with developmentally disabled children is Project Ecosystems (Lutzker, Campbell, Newman, & Harrold, 1989). Rather than focusing narrowly on the target behavior of the child with severe behavioral excesses or deficits, and who thus may be in danger of placement into a more restrictive setting, this ecobehavioral approach would assess mother-child interactions and, child-sibling interactions, would observe at the child's school, would perhaps have the mother complete a depression inventory, would examine family activity patterns, and would plan treatment accordingly. Similarly, in treating any severe behavioral excess, an ecobehavioral approach should be explored. This approach would seem to be an essential element of a right to *effective* treatment (Van Houten, et al., 1988). To date, although this approach appears in the literature with somewhat more frequency than in the past, the mode unfortunately remains a more narrow focus on the target behavior. The logic of learning theory on which principles of behavior change have been founded, along with principles of generalization, would suggest that ecobehavioral approaches would provide a higher probability of *durable* success than would a narrow focus. Aversive procedures have never been used on children served by Project Ecosystems; they are irrelevant.

SOCIAL VALIDATION

Social validation takes several forms, including formal queries from consumers on the appropriateness of our goals, procedures, and outcomes. Also, these queries have been asked of experts, parents, teachers, care providers, and, when possible and relevant, recipients of our services. For example, a recent poll of 144 direct care staff showed "widespread rejection of aversive reductive procedures" (Tarnowski, Rasnake, Mulick, & Kelly, 1989). But, most social validation research has been with a low N and has not addressed the serious issue of aversive procedures at a moral/practical level. The most important groups to ask if treatment goals are relevant and if aversive procedures should be considered are parents, politicans, community leaders, advocacy groups, and theologians. They represent persons who should be more aware, more educated, and more involved in guiding behavior analysis in its continued growth, and, hopefully, its repproachement with the rest of psychology and other related disciplines (Bernstein, 1989).

CONCLUSIONS

Behavior analysis is a field with strong roots in science; yet the data are not evident or in sufficient quantity to justify the use of aversive procedures with severely impaired individuals. There are no large-scale demonstrations that aversive procedures are effective over time. There are very few individual studies that have examined side effects of aversive procedures. Similarly, few studies have examined the ecological context of serious behavior problems. Also, biology may play a mitigating role against trying to punish certain behaviors. Social validation of treatment goals and procedures has not been accomplished at the public level. Finally, even if many of these issues are addressed, we should be seriously concerned with preventing abuse of aversive procedures. There simply are not sufficient safeguards to suggest that the mediators of aversive procedures would apply them in a conscientious, ethical manner. No one is a product of Walden Two.

NOTE

Appreciation is extended to Fran Zimmermann for her help in preparing this manuscript.

REFERENCES

Ayllon, T., & Azrin, N.H. (1964). Reinforcement and instruction with mental patients. *Journal of the Experimental Analysis of Behavior, 7*, 327-331.

Baer, D.M., Wolf, M.M., & Risley, T.R. (1968). Some current dimensions of applied behavior analysis. *Journal of Applied Behavior Analysis, 1*, 91-98.

Bailey, J.S. (1988). *The behavior analyst's code of ethics: A modest proposal*. Paper presented at the 14th Annual Meeting of the Association for Behavior Analysis, Philadelphia, PA.

Bernstein, G.S. (1989). Social validity and the debate over the use of aversive/intrusive procedures. *The Behavior Therapist, 12*, 123-125.

Bijou, S.W. (1963). Theory and research in mental (developmental) retardation. *Psychological Record, 13*, 95-110.

Dixon, M.J., Helsel, W.J., Rojahn, J., Cipollone, R., & Lubetsky, M.J.(1989). Aversive conditioning of visual screening with aromatic ammonia for treating aggressive and disruptive behavior in a developmentally disabled child. *Behavior Modification, 13*, 91-107.

Favell, J.E., Azrin, N.H., Baumeister, A.A., Carr, E.G., Dorsey, M.F., Forehand, R., Foxx, R.M., Lovaas, O.I., Rincover, A. R., Risley, T.R., Romanczyk, R.G., Russo, D.C., Schroeder, S.R., & Solnick, J.V. (1982). The treatment of self-injurious behavior. *Behavior Therapy, 13*, 529-554.

Gardner, W.I. (in press). But in the meantime: A client perspective of the debate over the use of aversive/intrusive therapy procedures. *The Behavior Therapist*.

Griffith, R.G., & Spreat, S. (in press). Aversive behavior modification procedures and the use of professional judgment. *The Behavior Therapist.*

Iwata, B.A. (1988). The development and adoption of controversial default technologies. *The Behavior Analyst, 11*, 149-157.

Lutzker, J.R. (1978). Reducing self-injurious behavior in three classrooms by facial screening. *American Journal of Mental Deficiency, 82*, 510-513.

Lutzker, J.R. (1989). *The failure of behavior analysis: Where are Dick Nixon and Hank K. when we need them?* Paper presented at the Eighth Annual Conference of the Northern California Association for Behavior Analysis, Millbrae, CA.

Lutzker, J.R., Campbell, R.V., Newman, M.R., & Harrold, M. (1989). Ecobehavioral interventions for abusive, neglectful, and high-risk families. In G.H.S. Singer and L.K. Irvin (Eds.), *Support for Caregiving Families* (pp. 313-326). Baltimore: Paul H. Brookes.

Lutzker, J.R., Touchette, P.E., & Campbell, R.V. (1988). Parental positive reinforcement might make a difference: A rejoinder to Forehand. *Child and Family Behavior Therapy, 10*, 25-33.

Martin, J.A. (1977). Effects of positive and negative adult-child interactions on children's task performance and task preferences. *Journal of Experimental Child Psychology, 23*, 493-502.

Redd, W.H., Morris, E.K., & Martin, J.A. (1975). Effects of positive and negative adult-child interactions on children's social preference. *Journal of Experimental Child Psychology, 19*, 153-164.

Rogers-Warren, A. & Warren, S. (1979). *Ecological perspectives in behavior analysis*. Baltimore: University Park Press.

Schroeder, S.R., & Schroeder, L.S. (1989). The role of the AAMR in the aversives controversy. *Mental Retardation, 27*, iii-v.

Skinner, B.F. (1948). *Walden Two*. New York: Macmillan.

Tarnowski, K.J., Rasnake, L.K., Mulick, J.A., & Kelly, P.A. (1989). Acceptability of interventions for self-injurious behavior. *American Journal of Mental Retardation, 93*, 575-580.

Van Houten, R., Axelrod, S., Bailey, J.S., Favell, J.E., Foxx, R.M., Iwata, B.A., & Lovaas, O.I. (1988). The right to effective behavioral treatment. *The Behavior Analyst, 11*, 111-114.

Wolf, M.M., Risley, T.R., & Mees, H. (1964). Application of operant conditioning procedures to the behavior problems of an autistic child. *Behaviour Research and Therapy, 1*, 305-312.

CHAPTER

33

TREATMENT ACCEPTABILITY: CONSUMER, THERAPIST, AND SOCIETY

Shirley O'Brien and Kathryn G. Karsh
Educational Research and Services Center

They are asking participants in a behavioral treatment program how much they like it. Why, of course they should like it. After all, we are doing it to them for their own good, aren't we? And even if they say they don't like it, we know what is best for them. Clearly, if the procedure is effective, it is just not important whether anyone says they like it or not. (Wolf, 1978, p. 206).

Treatment acceptability has been described as, "judgments by laypersons, clients, and others of whether treatment procedures are appropriate, fair, and reasonable for the problem or client" (Kazdin, 1981, p. 493). Thus, acceptability is defined as the evaluation of treatment procedures by potential consumers, without regard for knowledge or experience. Acceptability ratings are derived from consumer judgments as to whether or not they, the consumers, think they will like treatment. As Kazdin (1980a) notes, "Judgments of acceptability are likely to embrace evaluation of whether treatment is appropriate for the problem, whether treatment is fair, reasonable, and intrusive, and whether treatment meets with conventional notions about what the treatment should be" (p. 259).

Concerns about treatment acceptability increase when the consumer is either a child and/or developmentally disabled, or as a function of the individual's age, intellectual capabilities, or legal status. Often, significant others (e.g., parents, judges) for children or those with developmental disabilities must evaluate the acceptability of a proposed treatment. This evaluation is conducted at a pretreatment level with acceptability dependent on (a) previous demonstration of the effectiveness of the procedure, (b) understanding of behavioral principles, and (c) effort required by others for implementation of treatment. Compelling reasons to evaluate treatment acceptability and identify procedures that are desirable and effective, resulting in decreased attrition and increased compliance by the consumer, arise from legal and ethical concerns and a need to increase behavioral treatment compliance.

FACTORS INFLUENCING ACCEPTABILITY

Witt and Elliot (1985) suggested that three components influence acceptability. These include (a) treatment use, (b) treatment compliance, and (c) treatment effectiveness. Reimers, Wacker, and Koeppl (1987) expanded this model to include "understanding" as a fourth element. However, neither of these two models encompasses all of the variables influencing acceptability. Acceptability should be perceived as an ongoing evaluative process, with remediation or training provided when the consumer has poor understanding, there is low compliance, or there is low treatment effectiveness. For example, for a treatment to be judged acceptable, the consumer must have an understanding of the implemented procedures. Early acceptability studies (e.g., Kazdin, 1980a, 1980b) used only pretreatment evaluation, thus limiting understanding. Additionally, acceptability influences compliance, which impacts directly on treatment effectiveness. That is, an individual's ratings of a treatment's appropriateness (e.g., the prescribed procedures are deemed unacceptable) might affect his/her compliance with implementing the precribed techniques. These factors of understanding, compliance, use, and effectiveness are central to treatment acceptability and, therefore, are discussed individually below.

Treatment Understanding

Consumer education has been found to increase the acceptability of treatment procedures (Kazdin, 1980b; Mudford, 1987; Singh & Katz, 1985). Studies evaluating consumer understanding have shown that acceptability can be increased by (a) modifying an unacceptable procedure (Kazdin, 1980b), (b) using course lectures describing treatment rationales (Singh & Katz, 1985), or (c) "advertising" a treatment package (Mudford, 1987).

Treatment Compliance and Use

Treatment compliance refers to whether the procedure is implemented as intended. This factor may well be influenced by pretreatment acceptability. In fact, an inverse relationship appears to exist between treatment compliance and its complexity. The greater the complexity of the treatment program, the more likely it is that treatment compliance will not be maintained. As such, complex treatment interventions may require alterations in the prescribed procedures in order to achieve acceptable and effective implementation. Similarly, people who find a proposed treatment unacceptable may be less likely to comply with the proposed procedures than if they perceive treatment as highly acceptable. However, there is also the consideration that a treatment initially may be deemed as highly acceptable, but will be ineffective, resulting in lower compliance during treatment or maintenance. Psychologists often provide consultative services to teachers and parents from whom compliance is a precursor to effectiveness. For a treatment to be highly effective, there has to be high compliance with the prescribed protocol. Low compliance cannot result in high effectiveness.

Treatment Effectiveness

Consideration must be given to treatment effectiveness because, "its practical importance, specifically its power in altering behavior enough to be socially important, is the essential criterion" (Baer, Wolf, & Risley, 1968, p. 96). In the initial development of any treatment protocol, concern focuses on whether the new treatment procedure is more effective than other existing methods. Behavioral technology has advanced over the last 20 years so that therapists frequently have more than one alternative available for treating a particular behavior problem. When the therapist or consumer is presented with two treatments that are equally acceptable, with these two treatments being aversive and nonaversive, both aversive, or both nonaversive, how does one determine which treatment will be implemented? Evaluation of a treatment's effectiveness may provide the needed answer. For example, results may show that while both treatments are equally acceptable, one is more effective, producing greater maintenance of behavior change. The components that establish a treatment's effectiveness are multidimensional. Therefore, an ineffective treatment may result from variables such as the schedule of punishment, satiation, the reinforcer's strength, or treatment compliance.

The interrelationship of effectiveness to the acceptability of treatment may be evaluated either before or after treatment. Low or high pretreatment acceptability may result in either low or high compliance. While low compliance produces low effectiveness, high compliance may result in low or high effectiveness. In contrast, posttreatment acceptability is based on a treatment's effectiveness. A treatment that was initially considered to be unacceptable, but was then highly effective, will probably be viewed as acceptable. Thus, a treatment, may be considered either acceptable or unacceptable prior to treatment, but this view may change based on the effectiveness of treatment.

CONSIDERATIONS FOR AN ACCEPTABILITY MODEL

The groundwork for treatment acceptability derives from Wolf's (1978) seminal paper on social validity, which identified three questions to consider in treatment selection and evaluation:

1. The social significance of the *goals*. Are specific behavioral goals really what society wants?
2. The social appropriateness of the *procedures*. Do the ends justify the means? That is, do the participants, caregivers, and other consumers consider the treatment procedures acceptable?
3. The social importance of the *effects*. Are consumers satisfied with the results? All the results, including any unpredicted ones?

Social validity refers to consumer evaluations of treatment and, therefore, is feedback provided by the consumer *after* the implementation of treatment. These three "judgments of social validity" are proposed to guide an individual in evaluating the social importance of an intervention. The goals for treatment identify where the effort is directed. The social appropriateness of treatment goals have been evaluated using social comparisons and subjective evaluations (Kazdin & Matson, 1981). The social appropriateness of the procedures requires individuals to rate the acceptability of the focus of the intervention. Typically, this has been the rating of several different treatment alternatives. Finally, the social importance of the effects evaluates satisfaction with the outcome, maintenance, and generalization of treatment. These three judgments occur pretreatment and posttreatment to provide an ongoing evaluative process. Unfortunately, no research has evaluated both pretreatment and posttreatment acceptability in either an analogue or naturalistic situation. Judgments of the acceptability of the *goals, procedures,* and *effects* of any procedure may be made by the *consumer* (e.g., the child, or the parent), the *therapist* (e.g., the clinician, teacher, or parent), or *society*. This tripartite model for therapeutic evaluation was proposed by Strupp and Hadley (1977). Bernstein (1989) has taken Wolf's (1978) three levels of social validation (i.e., goals, procedures, and effects) and combined them with Strupp and Hadleys' (1977) three perspectives (i.e., consumer, therapist, and society) for evaluating treatment. The result is a 3 by 3 matrix. We have used this matrix as a guide for identifying and specifying the theoretical and research-based findings on acceptability. Acceptability is not a unitary concept, but multidimensional. Table 1 provide a listing of the variables which appear to influence acceptability.

TABLE1: Variables Influencing Acceptability

	CONSUMER	THERAPIST	SOCIETY
Were the Goals Acceptable?	– Treatments which improved the quality of life were more acceptable.	– Implementation of procedures which were desirable increased ratings. – Implementaion of procedures which were effective increased ratings. – Implementation of least restrictive procedures increased ratings. – Implementation of least intrusive procedures increased ratings.	– Treatments producing reductions in maladaptive behavior to an acceptable community level received higher ratings. – Treatments producing increased participation in the community were more acceptable.
Were the Procedures Acceptable?	– Reason or rationale given by the therapist increased rating. – Interventions were rated more acceptable for older children. – Reinforcement was more acceptable than punishment. – Understanding of behavioral principles increased acceptability. – Interventions to increase behavior were more acceptable than those to decrease behavior. – Type of educator and type of child disability did not affect acceptability ratings. – Treatments producing marked effects were more acceptable than treatments producing weaker effects. – More experienced staff viewed a treatment as less acceptable than less exerienced staff. – The acceptability rating of a treatment was higher for more severe behavior problems. – Children rated treatments as less acceptable than parents did. – Differential reinforcement procedures were rated as most acceptable.	– What treatment was called, reason given, and how the treatment was described influenced the rating. – Less complex and time-consuming interventions were more acceptable. – The client's previous history with a procedure affected the rating.	– Procedures that incuded the least restrictive alternative, review of a treatment plan by a Peer Review Committee and Human Rights Committee, and compliance with Federal and State laws were more acceptable. – Treatments that demonstrated effectiveness by scientific method were rated as more acceptable. – The establishment of procedural safeguards, including consent for treatment, increased acceptability.

Table 1: Variables Influencing Acceptability continued

	CONSUMER	THERAPIST	SOCIETY
Were the Effects-Acceptable?	– More effective treatments were rated as more acceptable. – Adverse side effects lowered acceptability ratings. – Financial status of the client and financial and emotional costs of the treatment affected rating. – Post-treatment acceptability ratings were influenced by treatment effectiveness.	– A significant reduction in the maaldaptive behavior increased acceptability. – The degree and speed of suppression of the maladaptivebehavior influenced the rating. – The occurrence of temporal, stimulus, or response generalization increased acceptability.	– Treatmentsproducing increasednormalization were more acceptable. – Presence of positive or negative side effects to others influenced the rating. – Rigorous evaluation of the effects increased acceptability. – Ratings varied as a function of who evaluated thetreatment.

In order to conceptualize Table 1, an understanding of the research literature on treatment acceptability is necessary. A review of this literature is presented below. For this chapter, only those articles that used subjects or case descriptions associated with individuals with developmental disabilities were reviewed.

Research On Acceptability

The acceptability research on individuals with developmental disabilities comes from two perspectives, psychology and education. Within each perspective, the focus of research is very similar. Table 2 provides an evaluative review of these articles.

The initial acceptability research was conducted by Kazdin (1978, 1980a, 1980b, 1981) who used undergraduate college students to rate the acceptability of treatment procedures when presented with one of two case vignettes. In all studies, one case described a child with normal development, while the second described a child functioning at the educable or trainable level of mental retardation, with hyperactive, noncompliant or aggressive behaviors. The dependent variables were subjective evaluations of treatment acceptability and included the Treatment Evaluation Inventory (TEI) (Kazdin, 1980a, 1980b), and the Semantic Differential (Osgood, Succi, & Tannenbaum, 1957). The TEI consists of 15 questions and uses a 7-point Likert-type scale for each question. The Semantic Differential comprises a list of 15 bipolar adjectives which assess the evaluative (good-bad), potency (strong-weak) and activity (fast-slow) aspects of treatment. Kazdin's initial studies found that undergraduate students rated (a) differential reinforcement of incompatible behaviors as more acceptable than other treatments, (b) positive treatments as generally more acceptable than negative treatment procedures, (c) case severity as a factor when rating acceptability, (d) nonexclusionary time-out as more acceptable than exclusionary time-out, and (e) aversive side effects as reducing the acceptability of treatment. Kazdin then extended this line of analogue research to include evaluations by parents, children, and staff members (Kazdin, 1984; Kazdin, French, & Sherick, 1981). These studies found (a) treatments described as producing marked effects were rated higher than those producing weaker effects, (b) children viewed medication as the most acceptable form of treatment, and (c) children's acceptability ratings of behavioral treatments were less than those of their parents.

Table 2: Treatment Acceptability Research

Author and Year	Number of Subjects	Subjects	Population Evaluated	Dependent Variable	Independent Variable	Results
Epstein et al. (1986)	89	Regular and special educators	1st grade boy with hyperactive behaviors	TEI	1. Special education 2. Affective education 3. Counseling 4. Behavior modification 5. Medication	- Order of acceptability was special education, counseling, affective education, behavior modification, and medication.
Kazdin (1980a) (Exp. 1)	88	College students	5-yr.-old normal female, w/oppositional behaviors 10-yr.-old male, EMH, w/disruptive behaviors	TEI SD	1. DRI 2. Time-out 3. Medication 4. Shock	- DRI was most acceptable procedure.
Kazdin (1980a) (Exp. 2)	94	College students	5-yr.-old normal female, w/oppositional behaviors 10-yr.-old male, EMH, w/disruptive behaviors	TEI SD	1. DRI 2. Time-out 3. Medication 4. Shock	- All treatments rated as more acceptable with more severe cases.
Kazdin (1980b) (Exp. 1)	144	College students	8-yr.-old normal female, w/disruptive behaviors 10-yr.-old male, EMH, w/disruptive behaviors	TEI SD	1. Isolation 2. Contingent observation 3. Ignoring 4. DRI	- DRI and nonexclusionary time-out were more acceptable than isolation.
Kazdin (1980b) (Exp. 2)	104	College students	8-yr.-old normal female, w/disruptive behaviors 10-yr.-old male, EMH, w/disruptive behaviors	TEI	1. Isolation 2. Isolation as part of contingency contract 3. Ignoring 4. DRI	- Isolation was more acceptable as part of contingency contract or as backup for other forms of time-out.
Kazdin (1981) (Exp. 1)	112	College students	8-yr.-old normal female, w/aggression and conduct disorder 10-yr.-old male, TMH, w/hyperactive behaviors	TEI SD	1. DRI 2. Time-out 3. Positive practice 4. Medication	- DRI was rated as the most acceptable treatment followed by positive practice, time-out, and medication.

Table 2: Treatment Acceptability Research continued

Author and Year	Number of Subjects	Subjects	Population Evaluated	Dependent Variable	Independent Variable	Results
Kazdin (1981) (Exp. 2)	112	College students	8-y.-old female w/aggression & conduct disorder 10-yr.-old male, TMH, w/hyperactive behaviors	TEI SD	1. DRI 2. Time-out 3. Positive practice 4. Medication	- Presence of adverse side effects reduced acceptability of all treatments.
Kazdin (1984)	40 parents 40 children inpatients	Parents of inpatients 5-to 13-yr.-old inpatients	8-yr.-old female w/aggression & conduct disorder 10-yr.-old male, TMH, w/hyperactive behaviors	SD	TEI 2. Locked seclusion 3. Medication	1. Time-out- Children viewed medication as most acceptable treatment. - Treatments producing marked effects were rated higher than those producing weaker effects.
Kazdin et al. (1981)	32 children inpatients 32 parents 32 staff	7-to 13-yr.-old inpatients Parents or staff of inpatients	8-yr.-old female, w/aggression & conduct disorder 10-yr.-old male TMH, w/hyperactive behaviors	TEI SD	1. DRI 2. Time-out 3. Positive practice 4. Medication	- DRI was most acceptable. - Children rated treatments as less acceptable than parents.
Irvin & Lundervold (1988)	58	Special educators	Nondescribed	An adapted-magnitude estimation scaling	18 different interventions	- Ratings of restrictiveness and acceptability were negatively correlated.
Martens et al. (1985)	54	Regular and special educators	10-yr.-old normal male w/daydreaming behaviors 10-yr.-old normal male w/destructive behaviors	IRP SD	1. Mode of case presentation (videotape or written) 2. Behavior problem severity 3. Effort, time, and skill required by intervention	- Interventions requiring moderate amounts of time were more acceptable. - Acceptability ratings increased with problem severity. - No effect was found for modality of case presentation.

Table 2: Treatment Acceptability Research continued

Author and Year	Number of Subjects	Subjects	Population Evaluated	Dependent Variable	Independent Variable	Results
Mudford (1987)	20 nurses 20 staff	Adults	Individual with profound retardation & stereotypy (No sex or age given)	TEI SD	1. DRI 2. Visual screening (VS) 3. Combined (DRI + VS)	- DRI was most acceptable to nurses. - DRI or DRI + VS was most acceptable to staff. - Acceptability ratings were increased when punishment also included reinforcement.
Pickering & Morgan (1985)	119	Parents of normal, autistic, and MR children	10-yr.-old male w/ severe retardation and self-injurious behavior	TEI SD	1. DRO 2. Time-out 3. Overcorrection 4. Shock	- All parents agreed on DRO as most acceptable, followed by time-out and overcorrection. Shock was unacceptable.
Singh & Katz (1985)	96	College students	8-yr.-old, normal child with aggression 16-yr.-old, TMH w/ hyperactive behavior	TEI SD	1. DRI 2. Time-out 3. Positive practice 4. Humanistic parenting	- Before lecture, DRI was rated most acceptable. - After lecture, all treatments were rated equally acceptable.
Singh et al. (1987)	96	Mothers of MR children	8-yr.-old, TMH with aggression 16-yr.-old TMH w/ hyperactive behavior	TEI SD	1. DRI 2. Time-out 3. Positive practice 4. Medication	- DRI was most acceptable procedure.
Tarnowski et al. (1989)	144	Direct care staff	Severely retarded child w/head banging Severely retarded adult with head banging	IRP	1. Child or adult 2. Work setting 3. Type of intervention 4. Behavior problem severity	- Accelerative interventions were more acceptable than reductive. - Stimulus control was most acceptable treatment.

Table 2: Treatment Acceptability Research continued

Author and Year	Number of Subjects	Subjects	Population Evaluated	Dependent Variable	Independent Variable	Results
Witt et al. (1984)	180	Preservice and student teachers	Individuals with 3 levels of behavior (daydreaming, obscene language, property destruction) (No age or sex given)	IRP	1. Behavior problem severity 2. Type of intervention 3. Teacher time required	- Acceptability ratings were higher for positive treatments than for reductivetreatments. - Less complex and time-consuming interventions were rated as more acceptable.
Witt et al. (1984)	180	Regular and special educators	Severity of behavior problem varied	IRP	1. Behavior problem severity 2. Type of intervention 3. Teacher time required	- Interventions were rated as more acceptable when problem was severe. - More experienced teachers rated treatments as less acceptable.

We should note that all of Kazdin's studies have been analogue measures. Therefore, these studies may lack ecological validity; having college students rate the acceptability of treatments cannot be equated with ratings by experts in the field of mental retardation or by those who care for these individuals. Additionally, all acceptability ratings were obtained prior to treatment intervention. Therefore, these ratings cannot be used to determine consumer acceptability of treatment compliance or effectiveness.

Extending Kazdin's research, Pickering and Morgan (1985) had parents of normal, autistic, and handicapped individuals read a case vignette of a 10-year-old male with severe mental retardation and self-injurious behavior. All parents then rated the acceptability of several alternative treatments using the TEI and the Semantic Differential measures. Differential reinforcement of other behaviors (DRO) was found to be the most acceptable treatment, followed by time-out, and overcorrection. Shock was rated as an unacceptable form of treatment. Singh, Watson, and Winton (1987) used these same dependent measures, the TEI and Semantic Differential, and had mothers with mentally retarded children evaluate differential reinforcement of incompatible behaviors (DRI), positive practice, time-out, and drug therapy as treatment procedures. The authors provided case descriptions of two children, both described as trainably mentally retarded, one with severe aggression and the other with hyperactive behaviors. DRI was rated as the most acceptable treatment. Extending the work of Singh et al. (1987), Mudford (1987) had nurses and staff who worked with individuals with mental retardation read a case description of a profoundly retarded individual (no age or sex information was provided) with stereotypy. Using the TEI and the Semantic Differential, the nurses and staff evaluated the treatments of DRI, visual screening (VS), and DRI with VS. DRI was found to be the most acceptable form of treatment, with the acceptability rating increasing for punishment (VS) when it included a reinforcement component (DRI). Singh and Katz (1985) used the TEI and Semantic Differential to evaluate undergraduate students' acceptability of four treatment procedures: (1) humanistic parenting, (2) DRI, (3) positive practice, and (4) time-out. The case descriptions were adapted from Kazdin's vignettes, and included a normal child who exhibited severe aggression and an adolescent with trainable mental retardation and hyperactivity. The unique component of this study was the preevaluation to postevaluation of acceptability ratings after a lecture on the proposed treatment alternatives. Initially, DRI was rated as the most effective. After the lecture, all treatments were rated as equally effective.

Kazdin's acceptability research has been extended to educational environments. The dependent variables for these studies have included the TEI and the Intervention Rating Profile (IRP; Witt & Martens, 1983). The IRP is a 20-item rating scale which evaluates teacher acceptability ratings for classroom interventions. The independent variables evaluated by the IRP include intervention complexity, behavior problem severity, jargon of treatment description, teacher experience, need for intervention, teacher knowledge of procedures, and outcome information.

An initial study by Witt and Martens (1983) found that preservice teachers rated five factors as affecting acceptability of classroom intervention: (1) suitability of intervention for mainstreamed classroom, (2) risk of intervention to the child, (3) teacher time, (4) negative side effects on other children, and (5) the skill of the teacher. In a follow-up study by these authors, (Witt, Martens, & Elliot, 1984) teacher time, behavior problem severity, and type of intervention were each identified by preservice teachers as salient factors in assessing treatment acceptability. Treatment procedures that were less time-consuming were rated as more acceptable. This finding is understandable when it is recognized that a teacher has a classroom full of students and cannot devote the day to behavioral programming. However, these preservice teachers did indicate a willingness to increase the time commitment proportionally to the severity of the behavior problem.

Epstein, Matson, Repp, and Helsel (1986) conducted two experiments to evaluate the acceptability of treatment alternatives based on teacher status (regular or special educator) and disability (mental retardation or learning disability). The teachers rated the acceptability of treatment alternatives as special education programming, followed by counseling, affective education, behavior modification, and medication.

In another study evaluating specific types of treatments, Irvin and Lundervold (1988) evaluated the acceptability, restrictiveness, intrusiveness, and efficacy of 18 treatments as rated by 58 special educators. Differential reinforcement, followed by simple correction, extinction, social disapproval, and contingent observation were rated as the most acceptable treatments. It should be noted that there was low variability across the treatments, possibly suggesting confusion as to the efficacy of these 18 treatment techniques. Taken at face value, these efficacy and acceptability ratings suggest that caution is warranted in allowing teachers to choose between two interventions.

Tarnowski, Rasnake, Mulick, and Kelly (1989) used the IRP to evaluate 144 direct care staffs' acceptability of 6 behavioral interventions. Stimulus control, followed by DRI, DRO, overcorrection, physical restraint, and shock were rated by the staff as most to least acceptable. This finding of differential reinforcement as one of the most acceptable and shock as the least acceptable treatment is consistent with previous research findings (e.g., Irvin & Lundervold, 1988; Pickering & Morgan, 1985).

COMMENTS

The majority of acceptability research has been conducted with individuals ranging from normal functioning to moderate levels of mental retardation. These findings should not be generalized to those individuals with severe and profound retardation, the very people with whom more restrictive procedures are used (see Chapter 12 by Paisey, Whitney, and Hislop). Little acceptability research has been conducted with individuals with severe and profound retardation, who are frequently the focus of intensive behavioral interventions and present with more severe behavior problems. More research is needed on the factors influencing treatment acceptability for individuals with developmental disabilities. Unfortunately, with this population, we do not know if acceptability is affected by (a) past exposure to treatment, (b) level of retardation, (c) severity of the problem, (d) who is providing the consent, (e) evaluation in naturalistic settings, (f) objective (vs. subjective) evaluations, (g) use of multiple treatment components, and (h) consumer participation in treatment selection.

The severity of the presenting behavior problems frequently increases proportionately with the level of mental retardation. Tarnowski et al. (1989) also suggested that the severity of the problem may be an important variable in the acceptability of a treatment. However, the majority of the acceptability studies have evaluated the appropriateness of a single treatment procedure for mild to moderate behavior problems (e.g, noncompliance and hyperactivity). Acceptability may also vary as a function of treatment implementation. When one treatment is found to be ineffective with severe behavior problems, an alternative treatment is usually tried. A once less acceptable treatment may become more acceptable due to the lack of effectiveness of a previously acceptable, now unacceptable, treatment alternative. Ultimately, in some instances we may find ourselves in a dilemma between selecting a less acceptable treatment or no treatment.

Individuals with mental retardation and behavior problems frequently demonstrate maladaptive behaviors across settings. Thus, numerous individuals across settings (e.g., parents at home, teachers, aides, and therapists) may be required to implement the treatment protocol. Must the proposed treatment be acceptable to all individuals for treatment to be effective? Research has not addressed this issue.

Based on the information presented in this chapter, we can conclude that the acceptability research on treatment procedures for individuals with developmental disabilities is rudimentary. We have identified three primary components that influence acceptability: (1) treatment understanding, (2) treatment compliance and use, and (3) treatment effectiveness. Yet, very little is known about the function of each of these components in determining the acceptability of treatments for persons with severe handicaps.

Future research needs to address the function of actual treatment implementation in naturalistic settings in order to determine which variables in the implementation process may affect acceptability. We often assume that those treatments that are effective are also acceptable. This may be the case, as well as a reciprocal relationship where acceptable treatments increase effectiveness (Reimers et al., 1987).

Acceptability may be a function, however, of many factors as yet unidentified. Acceptability may be influenced by institutional policies and practices, issues of practicality, previous staff experiences, and/or parent training and experiences. Acceptability may be directly related to attitudes toward persons with developmental disabilities and what is perceived to be "good" for those individuals (see Chapter 6 by Hayes and McCurry).

Treatment programs will continue to be selected and implemented. When professionals select treatments, decision to be considered will include (a) severity and duration of the behavior problem, (b) complexity of the intervention, (c) the type of treatment procedure, (d) the restrictiveness of the treatment procedure, and (e) the consumer's knowledge of behavioral principles. In order to assist in the decision making, much of the acceptability research has sought to take a "majority" approach to the study of acceptability (Garfield, 1983). This attempt has been directed toward identifying the treatments preferred by the majority of the consumers. Another approach is to identify those variables that influence the consumer's acceptability rating of an intervention. This argues for research which occurs in naturalistic settings, includes treatment implementation, and examines consumer variables (e.g., ease of implementation, length of treatment, success of treatment).

If we can bring consumer variables into the methodology of individual treatment selection, then we should be closer to treatment decisions that are based on scientific knowledge and not tradition. To this end, we may identify a causal link between treatment acceptability and treatment effectiveness which will greatly benefit both consumers and therapists.

REFERENCES

Baer, D. M., Wolf, M. M., & Risley, T. R. (1968). Some current dimensions of applied behavior analysis. *Journal of Applied Behavior Analysis, 1*, 91-97.

Bernstein, G. S. (1989). Social validity and the report of the ABA task force on right to effective treatment. *The Behavior Analyst, 12*, 197.

Epstein, M. H., Matson, J. L., Repp, A. C., & Helsel, W. J. (1986). Acceptability of treatment alternatives as a function of teacher status and student level. *School Psychology Review, 15*, 84-90.

Garfield, S. (1983). Some comments on consumer satisfaction in behavior therapy. *Behavior Therapy, 14*, 237-241.

Irvin, L. K., & Lundervold, D. A. (1988). Social validation of decelerative (punishment) procedures by special educators of severely handicapped students. *Research in Developmental Disabilities, 9*, 331-350.

Kazdin, A. E. (1980a). Acceptability of alternative treatments for deviant child behavior. *Journal of Applied Behavior Analysis, 13*, 259-273.

Kazdin, A. E. (1980b). Acceptability of time-out from reinforcement procedures for disruptive child behavior. *Behavior Therapy, 11*, 329-344.

Kazdin, A. E. (1981). Acceptability of child treatment techniques: The influence of treatment efficacy and adverse side effects. *Behavior Therapy, 12*, 493-506.

Kazdin, A. E. (1984). Acceptability of aversive procedures and medication as treatment alternatives of deviant child behavior. *Journal of Abnormal Child Psychology, 12*, 289-302.

Kazdin, A. E., French, N. H., & Sherick, R. B. (1981). Acceptability of alternative treatments for children: Evaluations by inpatient children, parents, and staff. *Journal of Consulting and Clinical Psychology, 49*, 900-907.

Kazdin, A. E., & Matson, J. L. (1981). Social validation in mental retardation. *Applied Research in Mental Retardation, 2*, 39-53.

Martens, B. K., Witt, J. C., Elliott, S. N., & Darveaux, D. X. (1985). Teacher judgments concerning the acceptability of school-based interventions. *Professional Psychology: Research and Practice, 16*, 191-198.

Mudford, O. C. (1987). Acceptability of a visual screening procedure for reducing stereotypy in mentally retarded children: Evaluation by New Zealand institutional staff. *Behavior Change, 4*, 4-13.

Osgood, C. E., Succi, G. J., & Tannenbaum, P. H. (1957). *Measurement of meaning.* Urbana: University of Illinois Press.

Pickering, D., & Morgan, S. B. (1985). Parental ratings of treatments of self-injurious behavior. *Journal of Autism and Developmental Disorders, 15*, 303-314.

Reimers, T., Wacker, D., & Koeppl, G. (1987). Acceptability of behavioral interventions: A review of the literature. *School Psychology Review, 16*, 212-227.

Singh, N. H., & Katz, R. C. (1985). On the modification of acceptability ratings for alternative child treatment. *Behavior Modification, 9*, 375-386.

Singh, N. N., Watson, J. E., & Winton, A. S. (1987). Parents' acceptability ratings of alternative treatments for use with mentally retarded children. *Behavior Modification, 11*, 17-26.

Strupp, H. H., & Hadley, S. W. (1977). A tripartite model of mental health and therapeutic outcome. *American Psychologist, 32*, 187-196.

Tarnowksi, K. J., Rasnake, L. K., Mulick, J. A., & Kelly, P. A. (1989). Acceptability of behavioral interventions for self-injurious behavior. *American Journal on Mental Retardation, 93*, 575-580.

Witt, J. C., & Elliot, S. N. (1985). Acceptability of classroom management strategies. In T. R. Kratochwill (Ed.), *Ad-*

vances in School Psychology (Vol. 4, pp. 251-288). Hillsdale, NJ: Lawrence Erlbaum.

Witt, J. C., Elliott, S. N., & Martens, B. K. (1984). Acceptability of behavioral interventions used in classrooms: The influence of amount of teacher time, severity of behavior problem, and type of intervention. *Behavioral Disorders, 9*, 95-104.

Witt, J. C., & Martens, B. K. (1983). Assessing the acceptability of behavioral interventions. *Psychology in the Schools, 20*, 510-517.

Witt, J. C., Martens, B. K., & Elliot, S. N. (1984). Factors affecting teachers' judgments of the acceptability of behavioral interventions: Time involvement, behavior problem severity and the type of intervention. *Behavior Therapy, 15*, 204-209.

Wolf, M. M. (1978). Social validity: The case for subjective measurement of how applied behavior analysis is finding its heart. *Journal of Applied Behavior Analysis, 11*, 203-214.

Author Index

Ackerman, A., 289, 292-295
Ackron, G. S., 116
Acton, Lord, 425, 431
Adamson, L. B., 337, 341
Aeschleman, S. R., 444, 447
Ager, A., 191, 194, 336
Ainsworth, M. D. S., 211, 213, 238, 252
Alberto, P. A., 3, 7
Albin, R. W., 141, 273, 275, 284-285, 362, 377, 378
Alfieri, P. A., 181, 195
Allen, W. B., 51, 53
Allen, G. E., 135, 142
Allison, J., 444, 449
Allyon, T. 316, 325, 496, 500
Alpert, M.316, 325
Altman, K.341, 343
Altmeyer, B. K., 189, 194, 331, 344
Alwell, M. , 276, 284
Aman, M. G., 468, 473
Amnesty International Publications, 159, 170
Anderson, J. 141, 273, 284, 377
Anderson, L., 316, 325
Anderson, S. R., 277, 282
Angell, M. J., 222, 229
Anger, D., 445, 447
Antonitis, J. J., 451, 453, 461
Apsche, J., 175, 193, 228, 295-296, 304, 325, 438, 447
Arbuckle, J. L., 445, 491
Arons, S., 479, 489, 491
Association for Persons with Severe Handicaps, 53, 71, 140, 166, 170,
Atkinson, C., 115
Ault, M. H., 306, 325
Austen, S., 135, 142
Avery, D. L., 277, 282
Axelrod, S., 17, 18, 22, 23, 29, 57, 59, 62, 64, 67-69, 71-72, 117, 134, 140, 142, 175, 179, 180, 193, 197, 262, 263, 266, 268, 270, 288, 289, 295, 296, 304, 325, 385, 401, 410, 415, 438, 447, 469, 473, 481, 491, 501
Azrin, N. H., 43, 46, 53, 55, 61, 62, 64, 65, 70, 74, 84, 92, 93, 98, 119, 126, 135, 141, 253, 258, 260, 268, 291, 296, 387, 395, 400, 439, 441, 442, 447, 447-449, 454, 461, 471, 473, 491, 496, 500

Backus, L., 117, 175, 197, 270
Baer, D. M., 17, 28, 34, 35, 39, 41, 44, 45, 47, 52, 53, 61, 70, 71, 111, 117, 124, 127, 129, 140, 245, 251, 252, 254, 262, 270, 301, 304, 308, 317, 319, 325, 329, 334, 342, 356, 359, 363, 364, 374, 378, 496, 500, 504, 514
Bachman, J. A., 302, 325, 363, 374
Bailey, D. B., 3, 7, 133, 143
Bailey, J. S., 18, 25, 29, 57, 64, 72, 117, 126, 142, 175, 197, 262, 268, 270, 316, 317, 320, 321, 325, 381, 382, 384, 385, 386, 392, 393, 397, 400, 401, 498, 500, 501,
Bakan, D., 252
Bakeman, R., 337, 341, 342
Baker, B. L., 293, 296
Ball, P. M., 181, 197
Balla, D. A., 468, 474
Balow, E. A., 332, 344
Balsam, P., 61, 70, 138, 140, 165, 170, 262, 268, 442, 447
Bandura, A., 363, 374
Barber, P., 117, 175, 197, 270
Barlow, D. H., 217, 220, 228, 262, 267, 467, 473
Barmann, B. C., 341, 342
Barnard, J. D., 341, 343
Barnish, I. J., 413, 414
Baroff, G. S., 318, 329
Baron, G., 277, 284
Barrera, F. J., 20-22, 25, 199, 209, 211, 213, 214
Barrett, P., 218, 229
Barrett, R. P., 323, 325, 328, 363, 374
Barron, J., 329, 363, 378
Barton, E. S., 317, 325
Barton, L. E., 24, 29, 76, 85, 138, 139, 140, 142, 178, 191, 196, 263, 270, 319, 328, 331, 340, 342, 345, 362, 382, 378, 388, 400, 412, 416, 485, 492, 493
Bateson, G., 238, 252
Baum, W. M., 115, 458, 461
Bauman, D. E., 445, 448
Bauman, K. E., 24, 28, 75, 84, 138, 141, 177, 195, 263, 269, 309, 327, 344, 350, 358, 363, 377, 382, 388, 400, 469, 474, 485, 492
Baumeister, A. A., 55, 87, 100, 141, 147, 154, 161, 170, 171, 195, 227, 228, 237, 253, 268, 296, 303, 314, 315, 325, 326, 327, 339, 341, 342, 363, 364, 370, 375, 388, 392, 400, 427, 432, 448, 473, 491, 496, 500
Beale, I. L., 218, 299
Beasty, A., 94, 100
Beavin, J. H., 238, 254
Bechtel, D. R., 44, 55, 182, 194
Becker, W. C., 245, 252
Becker, J., 62, 72
Belasel, V. A., 471, 372
Belifore, P., 80, 85, 320, 327, 411, 416
Bell, S. M., 238, 252
Bell, L. K., 368, 378
Bellack, A. S., 93, 98
Bellamy, G. T., 150, 154
Benson, H. A., 368, 377
Bentall, R. P., 94, 100

Berg, W. K., 21, 24, 29, 79, 85, 263, 270, 309, 329, 341, 346, 349, 350, 359, 367, 379, 485
Berkman, K. A., 43, 44, 53, 262, 268, 273, 282
Berkowitz, A. J., 6, 7
Berkowitz, L., 423, 431
Berkson, G., 314, 315, 322, 325, 326, 339, 342
Berotti, D., 371, 378
Berry, M. F., 53
Bernstein, G. S., 290, 293, 296, 500, 505, 514
Besalel, V. A., 258, 260
Bessman, C. A., 307, 326
Bettelheim, B., 291, 296
Bevan, P., 458, 460
Biglan, A., 88, 98
Bijou, S. W., 306, 307, 325, 334, 342, 363, 377, 461, 492, 496, 500
Biklen, D., 332, 342
Billingsley, F. F., 116, 138, 139, 140, 141, 278, 284, 367, 375, 377
Binkoff, J. A., 76, 84, 177, 193, 194, 237, 252, 275, 283, 309, 326, 340, 342, 363, 367, 375, 376, 409, 415, 460, 461
Bird, F., 180, 193, 275, 282, 371, 375
Birnbrauer, J. S., 22, 109, 115, 231, 266, 268, 363, 379
Bittle, R. G., 44, 55, 182, 194, 213, 365, 377, 431, 480, 481, 491
Blake, A., 67, 70
Blake, M., 264, 265, 268
Blatt, B., 48, 53
Blew, P. A., 341, 344, 370, 377
Blunden, R., 191, 194, 336
Boe, R. B., 364, 370, 375
Boelkins, D., 492
Boff, C., 252
Boff, L., 252
Bondy, A., 61, 70, 138, 140, 165, 170, 262, 268, 442, 447
Bornstein, M. H., 342
Borthwick, S. A., 331, 342
Bostow, D. E., 126, 317, 325
Bourland, G., 363, 378, 470, 472, 474
Bowlby, J., 211, 213
Boyce, D. A., 341, 345
Braaten, S., 137, 139, 143
Bradshaw, C. M., 452, 456, 458, 459, 461
Branch, M. N., 455, 461
Branston, M. B., 219
Brayfield, F. M., 255, 260
Bricker, W., 153, 154, 363, 378
Bristow, A., 62, 72
Brittain, D. P., 21, 28, 306, 327, 491
Browder, D. M., 76, 85, 319, 327, 480, 492
Brown, L., 219, 228
Brown v. Board of Education, 154
Brown, D. K., 80, 85, 320, 327, 411, 416
Brownlee, J. R., 337, 342
Brownstein, A. J., 96, 99
Bruel, H. H., 52, 53
Bruininks, R. H., 63, 70, 331, 332, 342, 344
Brulle, A. R., 139, 140, 412, 416
Bruner, J., 342
Bruwier, D., 65, 70
Buber, M., 252
Buckley, E. G., 53
Budd, C. M., 275, 284, 367, 377, 411, 416
Bunck, T. J., 176, 196, 321, 328, 469, 474
Burgio, L. D., 485, 492
Burke, M., 116
Burkhard, B., 443, 449
Busch, L., 182, 194
Butterfield, E. C., 22, 255, 260
Byrd, L. D., 455, 461

Campbell, H. J., 331, 343
Campbell, J., 50, 53
Campbell, D. T., 426, 431
Campbell, R. V., 499, 501
Canipe, V. S., 340, 344
Cannon, P. R., 181
Caputo, J. N., 258, 260
Carlsen, A., 177, 197, 309, 329, 469, 474
Carlson, J. I., 36, 53, 274, 283, 365, 371, 376, 378
Carlson, J. S., 332, 342
Carr, E. G., 22, 24, 25, 36, 37, 42, 45, 48, 53, 65, 70, 76, 78, 84, 119, 125, 126, 138, 141, 177, 178, 179, 180, 181, 186, 193, 194, 237, 252, 253, 263, 266, 268, 273, 274, 275, 282, 283, 284, 287, 288, 291, 294, 296, 302, 309, 310, 312, 314, 318, 319, 323, 325, 326, 332, 338, 339, 340, 342, 343, 350, 355, 358, 361, 363, 364, 365, 367, 368, 371, 375, 376, 377, 378, 382, 388, 390, 400, 404, 406, 409, 411, 414, 415, 423, 431, 438, 445, 447, 448, 460, 461, 473, 485, 491, 496, 500
Carrigan, P., 94, 100
Carroll, M., 323, 326
Casey, K., 226, 228
Casto, G., 277, 283
Cataldo, M. F., 33, 34, 35, 36, 40, 41, 45, 46, 48, 49, 50, 54, 79, 80, 85, 104, 115, 170, 178, 196, 281, 283, 302, 307, 309, 314, 315, 323, 326, 327, 332, 343, 357, 358, 363, 365, 376, 411, 416
Catania, A. C., 94, 98, 100, 443, 447
Cavanaugh, J., 21, 29, 484, 493
Certo, N., 219, 228
Chamberlain, T. P., 480, 493
Chan, S. T. S., 53
Charlop, M., 357, 258, 410, 415
Chesnick, M., 277, 284
Chomsky, N., 252, 253
Christian, H. G., 56
Christian, W. P, 277, 282
Cicchetti, D. V., 468, 474
Cigrand, K. K., 79, 85, 263, 270, 309, 329, 341, 346, 350, 351, 359
Cipani, E., 56
Cipplone, R., 497, 500
Clark, H., 56
Clark, M., 36, 43, 54, 158, 170
Cobben, A., 65, 70
Coe, D. A., 19, 27, 465
Cohen, M. N., 332, 343

Colavecchia, B., 264, 271
Cole, C. L., 405, 415
Colletti, G., 455, 463, 480, 481, 492
Colvin, G., 411, 415
Commonwealth of Massachusetts, Office for Children, Division of Administrative Law Appeals, 154
Con, A. A., 55
Conger, R., 456, 461
Conrin, J., 44, 56, 320, 328
Consensus Development Panel on Destructive Behaviors in Persons with Developmental Disabilities, 301, 302, 326
Cook, J. W., 161, 170, 351, 359
Cook, R., 321, 329
Cooper, L. J., 79, 85, 263, 270, 309, 329, 341, 346, 350, 359
Corbett, J. A., 331, 343, 345
Cordisco, L., 218, 229, 323, 328
Corte, H. E., 43, 54, 320, 326
Costanzo, P. R., 212, 213
Cotter, L. H., 423, 431
Covert, A., 125, 126, 288, 196, 331, 344
Cowdery, G., 309, 327, 358
Cresson, O., 94, 100
Crimmins, D. B., 18, 24, 28, 76, 77, 78, 84, 137, 141, 305, 306, 310, 326, 340, 343, 362, 363, 376, 378
Crisp, A. G., 177, 197, 309, 329, 469, 474
Cromwell, R. L., 255, 257, 260
Cronin, K. A., 245, 253
Cross, H. A., 452, 462
Crowley, R., 116
Crowell, C. R., 444, 448
Cunningham, S., 94, 100
Curcio, C., 182, 196
Curry, J. M., 255, 260
Cushing, P. J., 79, 85, 411, 416
Cutler, A., 323, 329
Cuvo, A. J., 245, 253

D'Amato, M. R., 94, 98
Dalrymple, S. D., 36, 56
Dancis, J., 316, 325
Danielson, L. C., 150, 154
Darveaux, D. X., 515
Datta, P. C., 329, 363, 378
Davenport, R. K., 315, 322, 326
Davidson, D. P., 405, 415
Davidson, P. W., 323, 326
Davis, P., 321, 326
Dawson, M. J., 43, 56, 124, 218, 229, 230
Day, R. M., 309, 313, 316, 317, 318, 326, 411, 415, 485, 491
Dayan, M., 189, 194
De Waard, R. J., 462
de Villiers, P., 456, 462
Deitz, D. E. D., 25, 29, 46, 54, 137, 142, 265, 270, 332, 334, 340, 345, 346, 480, 481, 492
Deitz, S. M., 46, 54, 124, 126, 270, 332, 345, 363, 364, 376
deKock, U., 191, 194, 196, 336, 343
Demchak, M. A., 363, 376
Demetral, G. D., 218, 228
Destro, R. A., 53
Devaney, J. M., 94, 95, 98, 316, 321, 329
Devany, J. M., 96, 99, 237, 254, 263, 266, 270, 363, 378, 444, 449, 455, 463
Dickerson, R., 40, 56, 188, 189
DiLorenzo, T. M., 74, 85, 93, 100, 175, 180, 190, 304, 328, 416, 480, 492
DiPietro, E. K., 277, 282
Dixon, M. H., 94, 98
Dixon, M. J., 182, 196, 497, 500
Doke, L. A., 387, 400
Dollman, C., 280, 283
Dominque, D., 277, 284
Donnellan, A. M., 17, 18, 22, 33, 35, 36, 37, 39, 40, 41, 42, 43, 44, 45, 48, 52, 54, 55, 57, 66, 67, 68, 70, 71, 78, 84, 124, 126, 133, 137, 138, 141, 142, 175, 177, 178, 180, 194, 195, 237, 253, 261, 263, 266, 267, 269, 273, 275, 283, 284, 287, 288, 290, 296, 406, 409, 410, 415, 416, 423, 425, 431, 437, 445, 448, 472, 474
Dores, P. A., 180, 193, 275, 282, 371, 375
Dorsey, M. F., 28, 40, 55, 56, 75, 84, 138, 141, 177, 188, 195, 196, 197, 253, 263, 268, 269, 296, 309, 321, 326, 327, 328, 344, 350, 358, 363, 377, 382, 387, 388, 400, 445, 448, 469, 471, 473, 474, 485, 491, 492, 496, 500
Dougher, M. J., 258, 260, 444, 448
Drabman, R. S., 332, 344
Drum, C., 44, 56, 320, 328
Duncan, D., 218, 229, 323, 328
Dunham, P. J., 444, 446, 448
Dunlap, G., 20, 23, 25, 125, 126, 141, 151, 154, 273, 275, 277, 280, 283, 284, 285, 286, 288, 339, 340, 343, 347, 364, 368, 376, 377, 379, 481, 488, 491
Dura, J. R., 323, 326, 364, 376
Durand, V. M., 6, 7, 18, 24, 28, 76, 77, 78, 84, 125, 126, 137, 138, 141, 178, 179, 180, 193, 194, 237, 252, 253, 263, 266, 268, 273, 275, 282, 283, 288, 296, 305, 306, 309, 310, 314, 318, 326, 339, 340, 343, 350, 358, 362, 363, 367, 368, 371, 375, 376, 382, 388, 390, 400, 404, 405, 407, 411, 413, 414, 415, 423, 431, 437, 445, 447, 448, 455, 462, 485, 491
Dworkin, S. I., 455, 461
Dyer, K., 262, 270, 273, 275, 283, 285, 341, 344, 368, 370, 376, 377, 378

Eason, L. J., 276, 283, 341, 343
Eckerman, D. A., 451, 453, 462
Eddy, M., 367, 375
Edelson, S. M., 363, 376
Edgar, E., 164, 170
Edwards, G. L., 21, 29, 81, 85, 485, 492
Edwards, R. L., 277, 282
Egel, A. L., 80, 85, 178, 196, 320, 326, 409, 411, 416
Eichlinger, J., 166, 171
Elliott, S. N., 43, 54, 57, 356, 357, 358, 359, 503, 512, 515-516

Elmore, B., 327, 254
Emerson, J. H., 189, 194, 421, 422, 432
Engelmann, S., 252, 411, 415
Epling, W. F., 27, 451, 452, 456, 463
Epstein, M. H., 508, 513, 515
Epstein, L. H., 387, 400
Epstein, Y. M., 370, 376
Erfanian, N., 36, 56, 158, 171, 175, 195, 237, 253, 262, 269, 426, 429, 432,
Estes, W. K., 455, 458
Etzel, B., 166, 170
Evans, I. M., 133, 137, 138, 139, 141, 175, 194, 273, 283, 285, 332, 340, 343, 345, 371, 376, 408, 409, 410, 411, 415, 416, 437, 445, 449
Evans, T. P., 341, 345
Eyman, R. K., 331, 332, 342, 343
Ezorsky, G., 91, 92, 98

Farmer-Dougan, V., 21, 28, 484, 492
Farris, H. E., 437, 449
Fassbender, L. L., 36, 54, 78, 84, 137, 138, 141, 177, 194, 237, 253, 275, 283, 288, 296, 406, 415
Faust, M., 315, 328
Favell, J. E., 18, 29, 34, 37, 43, 44, 51, 55, 56, 57, 61, 64, 71, 72, 115, 117, 137, 138, 139, 141, 142, 175, 178, 181, 194, 196, 197, 211, 214, 237, 251, 253, 262, 265, 266, 267, 268, 269, 270, 276, 283, 287, 288, 289, 280, 292, 293, 296, 297, 316, 322, 326, 363, 376, 385, 401, 403, 407, 415, 438, 448, 466, 467, 473, 480, 481, 491, 496, 500, 501
Faw, D. G., 213
Faw, G. D., 365, 377
Federal Habilitation Facilities Guidelines, 397
Fehrenbach, P. A., 237, 253
Feinstein, C., 323, 325, 363, 374
Felce, D., 24, 25, 29, 76, 85, 138, 142, 178, 191, 194, 196, 263, 270, 319, 328, 336, 343, 345, 346, 362, 378, 382, 388, 400, 485, 492
Feldman, M., 23, 261, 268
Fenske, E. C., 277, 284
Fenton, L. R., 341, 344, 357, 358, 370, 377
Ferster, C. B., 93, 101, 123, 126
Ferster, C. G., 454, 462
Fiedler, C., 117, 175, 197, 207
Field, C. J., 468, 473
Fielding, L., 52, 53
Fiello, R. A., 80, 85
Finney, J., 161, 170
Firestone, P. B., 125, 126
Florida Department of Health and Rehabilitative Services, 481, 491
Forehand, R., 55, 113, 116, 141, 161, 171, 268, 296, 315, 326, 448, 473, 491, 496, 500
Foster, R., 468, 474
Fox, J. J., 334, 346, 371, 379
Foxx, C. M., 180, 182, 194, 203, 211, 213
Foxx, R. M., 18, 29, 41, 43, 44, 55, 57, 64, 72, 117, 122, 126, 135, 141, 142, 175, 180, 182, 191, 194, 197, 213, 266, 268, 269, 270, 296, 363, 365, 377, 378, 385, 387, 395, 400, 401, 431, 448, 473, 480, 481, 491, 496, 500, 501
Frankel, F., 43, 56, 339, 343, 363. 377
Freagon, S., 20, 145
Freeman, B. J., 339, 343
Freitag, G., 177, 195, 288, 296, 311, 327, 363, 378, 455, 462
French, N. H., 135, 142, 507, 515
Frentz, C., 60, 70
Friedman, M., 53
Friedman, P. R., 159, 170, 492
Friman, P., 161, 170, 341, 343
Fulcher, G., 226, 228
Fuqua, R. W., 181, 197, 471, 474

Gallop, H. R., 312, 328
Galvin, G., 43, 54, 357, 358
Gamache, T. B., 178, 195
Gambrill, E. D., 305, 327,
Garcia, E., 120, 127, 317, 325
Gardner, S. M., 21, 28, 306, 327, 491
Gardner, W. I., 6, 7, 87, 100, 405, 415, 498, 501
Garfield, S., 514, 515
Gast, D. L., 19, 129, 480, 481, 491
Gates, J. J., 386, 400
Gaylord-Ross, R. J., 25, 137, 141, 177, 180, 194, 197, 314, 315, 319, 330, 339, 340, 344, 346, 363, 368, 379, 390, 400, 403, 404, 409, 415, 417, 427, 429, 432, 480, 4811, 485, 491
Gent, P. J., 151, 154
Gentry, W. D., 442, 448
George, M. J., 147, 154
Gedye, A., 282, 284
Ginsberg, H. J., 370, 377
Gleason, D. J., 82, 84
Gleick, J., 47, 55
Glenn, S., 88, 99
Goetz, L., 276, 284, 406, 417
Gold, M. W., 245, 253
Gold, V. J., 177, 195, 288, 296, 311, 327, 363, 378, 455, 462
Goncalves, S., 492
Gonzalez, L., 237
Gordon, W. C., 363, 378
Goren, E. R., 43, 56
Gorman-Smith, D., 237, 253, 262, 269, 457, 462, 470, 473
Gottlieb, J., 340, 345
Gottman, J. M., 337, 342
Grantmyre, J., 444, 446, 448
Green, C. W., 21, 27, 28, 219, 229, 306, 327, 340, 344, 485, 491
Green, G., 479
Greenspoon, J., 202, 213
Greenwood, C. R., 3, 7
Greer, S. M., 456, 463
Gregory, P. R., 43, 56
Griffen, H. C., 63, 71
Griffin, J. C., 182, 189, 194, 195, 331, 341, 421, 422, 432, 438, 448

Griffith, R. G., 93, 99, 289, 293, 296, 413, 415, 498, 501
Groden, G., 277, 284, 362, 377
Groden, J., 277, 284
Grossman, H. J., 218, 219, 228
Grossman, J. A., 312, 330
Gruenewald, L., 219, 228
Guess, D., 18, 20, 27, 35, 37, 40, 41, 43, 45, 46, 49, 53, 55, 75, 84, 117, 137, 141, 157, 164, 168, 170, 175, 190, 194, 197, 237, 253, 258, 260, 261, 266, 269, 270, 315, 317, 319, 325, 327, 329, 364, 365, 368, 377, 378, 424, 425, 432, 435, 448

Hackenberg, T., 363, 379
Hadley, S. W., 505, 515
Hake, D. F., 43, 53, 64, 70, 93, 98, 180, 197, 313, 330, 441, 442, 447, 448
Halderman v. Pennhurst, 154
Hale, S., 455, 456, 457, 459, 463
Halford, R. C., 21, 28, 306, 327, 491
Hall, J. C., 63, 71
Hall, R. V., 124, 126
Halle, J. W., 363, 376
Hamlet, C. C., 410, 411, 415
Hammer, D., 323, 326, 364, 376
Hamre-Nietupski, S., 219, 228
Hansen, C., 160, 170
Hanson, R. H., 480, 493
Hare, R., 108, 115
Haring, N., 160, 170
Harlow, H. F., 452, 462
Harman, M. L., 25, 29, 178, 196, 336, 345, 346
Harmatz, M. G., 317, 327
Harris, J., 170, 282, 283, 302, 314, 315, 323, 326, 363, 376
Harris, J. C., 226, 228
Harris, M., 88, 99
Harris, S. L., 321, 327
Harrold, M., 499, 501
Hartmann, D. P., 109, 115, 117
Harzem, P., 94, 100, 124, 126
Hauber, F. A., 63, 70
Hawk, B., 117, 444, 449
Hawkins, R. P., 363, 377, 429, 432
Hays, B., 367, 379
Hayes, L. J., 18, 26, 28, 87, 94, 95, 96, 99, 514
Hayes, S. C., 88, 93, 94, 95, 96, 98, 99, 101, 220, 228, 363, 377
Haywood, H. C., 93, 99
Heal, L. W., 63, 70
Hearst, E., 182, 194
Heidorn, S. D., 316, 319, 320, 327, 409, 415
Helmstetter, E., 40, 55, 75, 84, 117, 137, 141, 157, 164, 170, 175, 194, 197, 237, 253, 258, 260, 261, 269, 270, 365, 377, 425, 432, 435, 448
Helsel, W. J., 497, 500, 513, 515
Henry, G. W., 6, 7
Herbert-Jackson, E., 317, 328
Herr, S. S., 479, 489, 491
Herrnstein, R. J., 27, 28, 115, 120, 122, 126, 432, 443, 448, 456, 460, 462
Hersen, M., 93, 98, 217, 228, 262, 269, 467, 473
Heshusius, L., 164, 171
Hickman, C., 116, 177, 195, 226, 228, 237, 253, 314, 327, 388, 400, 455, 462
Hill, B. K., 63, 70, 331, 332, 344
Hilton, J., 135, 142
Hineline, P. N., 120, 126, 327
Hinerman, P., 161, 171
Hislop, P. M., 20, 175, 179, 186, 196, 332, 513
Hively, W., 212, 213
Hobbs, D. C., 175, 195, 199, 214, 215, 229, 238, 261, 270, 273, 285, 472, 474
Hock, M. L., 80, 85, 320, 327
Hoehler, F. K., 329, 363, 378
Hoekema, D. A., 91, 99
Holburn, C. S., 258, 260, 444, 448
Hole, W. T., 323, 325, 363, 374
Hollis, J. H., 53, 340, 344
Holman, J., 110, 112, 115
Holz, W. C., 61, 62, 64, 70, 74, 84, 92, 93, 98, 119, 126, 291, 296, 454, 461
Honig, W. K., 55, 296
Hope, M. L., 370, 377
Horner, R. H., 80, 85, 111, 115, 116, 137, 138, 139, 141, 273, 274, 275, 278, 284, 285, 315, 316, 321, 327, 340, 341, 344, 362, 363, 367, 377, 378, 408, 411, 416, 481
Houts, A. C., 33, 46, 47, 49, 50, 52, 55, 73, 85
Hoyson, M., 278, 286
Hughes, S., 94, 100
Hung, D. W., 237, 253
Hunt, F. M., 312, 328
Hunt, G. M., 442, 448
Hunt, P., 276, 284
Hurley, A. D., 422, 432
Hutchinson, R. R., 34, 36, 43, 46, 55, 93, 98, 99, 439, 441, 442, 447, 448
Hyman, S. L., 178, 195

Iano, R., 168, 171
Insalaco, C., 161, 171
Irvin, L. K., 135, 141, 266, 269, 509, 513, 515
Israel, A. C., 411, 416
Ivancic, M. T., 21, 29, 309, 328, 485, 492
Iwamoto, T., 456, 463
Iwata, B. A., 18, 21, 24, 28, 29, 34, 35, 41, 46, 49, 55, 57, 64, 68, 70, 72, 75, 77, 81, 83, 84, 85, 117, 138, 141, 142, 175, 177, 178, 180, 181, 182, 186, 191, 195, 196, 197, 237, 253, 258, 260, 263, 266, 269, 270, 301, 302, 309, 313, 315, 318, 319, 320, 321, 322, 323, 326, 327, 328, 338, 339, 344, 350, 352, 357, 358, 363, 377, 382, 385, 387, 388, 400, 401, 409, 410, 416, 438, 445, 448, 469, 471, 473, 474, 485, 492, 498, 501

Jackson, G. M., 111, 116
Jackson, D., 124, 126, 254
Jacobsen, J. W., 6, 7, 331, 344
Jamieson, B., 278, 286
Jamner, J. P., 258, 260
Jenkins, J., 62, 72

Jensen, C. C., 316, 319, 320, 327, 409, 415
Jenson, W., 161, 171
Johnson, C. R., 116
Johnson, L. F., 20, 23, 25, 151, 154, 273, 288
Johnson, M. R., 444, 448
Johnson, S., 130, 143
Johnson, W. L., 237, 253, 309, 326, 411, 427, 432, 485
Johnston, J., 43, 56, 62, 70, 109, 116, 320, 328, 481, 491
Jones, J. R., 180, 194, 213
Jones, L. J., 21, 22, 211, 212, 214, 215, 217, 218, 219, 220, 224, 229, 472m 474
Jones, M. L., 34, 43, 55, 181, 194, 267, 269, 415, 466, 473
Jordan, J., 67, 70, 211, 212, 213, 217, 218, 220, 224, 226, 228, 267, 269, 323, 327, 472, 474
Joyce, M., 52, 53
Justine, R. S., 332, 343

Kahneman, D., 426, 432, 433
Kalsher, M., 309, 327, 358
Kanfer, F. H., 363, 377
Kanner, L., 291, 296
Kanoy, R. C., 117, 444, 449
Kantor, J. R., 88, 89, 99, 334, 344
Kaplan, F., 48, 53
Karsh, K. G., 24, 25, 28, 29, 178, 196, 331, 336, 340, 341, 344, 345, 346
Kasari, C., 339, 342
Kassorla, I. C., 177, 195, 288, 296, 311, 327, 363, 378, 455, 462
Katz, R. C., 117, 135, 142, 357, 359, 504, 510, 515
Kaufman, M. E., 339, 344
Kazdin, A. E., 3, 7, 43, 55, 93, 99, 109, 110, 116, 117, 135, 136, 142, 220, 228, 244, 246, 253, 267, 269, 289, 297, 357, 359, 426, 427, 432, 468, 474, 503, 504, 505, 507-509, 512, 515
Kedesdy, J. H., 103, 116, 323, 329
Kelleher, R. T., 36, 56, 454, 455, 463
Keller, F. S., 429, 432
Keller, M., 268
Kelley, B., 212, 213
Kelley, M. L., 60, 70
Kelly, J., 332, 339, 342, 344
Kelly, P. A., 74, 85, 135, 142, 188, 197, 500, 501, 513, 515
Kemp, D. C., 367, 371, 375, 378
Kendall, K. A., 21, 215
Kendall, S. B., 94, 99
Kennell, J. H., 211, 213
Kern, L., 273, 275, 284, 341, 344, 370, 377
Keyes, J. B., 189, 194
Kiely, D., 180, 194, 213
Killeen, P., 456, 461
Kilman, B. A., 48, 54
Kimber, C., 386, 400
Kimble, G. A., 93, 99
Kinder, M. I., 288, 296
Kircher, A., 161, 171
Kirk, R. E., 467, 474
Kishi, G., 371, 376
Kistner, J. A., 363, 378
Klaus, M. H., 211, 213
Kleene, B. M., 323, 326
Klein, N. K., 245, 254
Knight, D., 182, 195, 309, 328, 485, 492
Knoll, J., 160, 172
Knowlton, S., 40, 55, 75, 84, 137, 141, 157, 175, 194, 237, 253, 258, 260, 261, 269, 365, 377, 425, 432, 435, 448
Kocur, L., 492
Koegel, R. K., 273, 276, 279, 282, 284
Koegel, R. L., 116, 125, 126, 144, 273, 276, 282, 284, 288, 296, 331, 340, 341, 343, 344, 368, 370, 377, 378, 488, 491, 503
Koeppl, G., 356, 359, 515
Kohlenberg, B. S., 96, 99
Kohr, M., 73, 85
Kolko, D. J., 80, 85, 178, 196, 411, 416
Kologinsky, E., 367, 375
Konarski, E. A., 258, 260, 332, 346, 444, 448
Kop, P. F. M., 94, 99
Kramer, H., 51, 55
Kramme, K. W., 125, 126
Krantz, P. J., 277, 284
Krashen, S., 277, 284
Krasner, L., 33, 46, 47, 49, 50, 52, 55, 363, 379
Kratochwill, T. R., 80, 85
Kuerschner, S., 410, 415
Kuhn, T., 164, 168, 171

Labadie, B. D., 211, 213
LaGrow, J., 67, 70, 181, 195, 237, 253, 332, 344, 468, 470, 474
Lakatos, I., 210, 213
Lakin, K. C., 63, 70, 137, 143, 342
Lalli, J. S., 80, 85, 320, 327, 411, 416
Lambert, N. M., 468, 474
Lambert, J. L., 65, 70
Langer, S. N., 18, 24, 29, 43, 57, 77, 85, 137, 142, 177, 197, 263, 270, 275, 286, 307, 329, 364, 369, 379, 388, 401, 405, 484, 493
Lanson, R. N., 451, 453, 462
Lanzi, F., 6, 7, 64, 65, 71
Larsen, S. E., 309, 326, 411, 485, 491
Laties, V. G., 94, 99
Lattal, K. A., 445, 457
LaVigna, G. W., 17, 18, 23, 33, 35, 36, 37, 39, 41, 42, 43, 44, 45, 49, 52, 54, 55, 57, 66, 67, 68, 70, 71, 124, 126, 133, 138, 141, 142, 175, 180, 195, 261, 263, 265, 266, 267, 269, 273, 284, 287, 288, 290, 296, 409, 410, 416, 423, 425, 431, 437, 438, 445, 448, 472, 474
Lawler, J., 363, 379
Lazar, R., 94, 100
Leaf, R. B., 292, 297
Leander, J. D., 94, 99
LeBlanc, J. M., 364, 378
Leitenberg, H., 124, 127
Leland, H., 468, 474
Lenneberg, E. H., 277, 284

Lennox, D. B., 36, 56, 158, 171, 175, 195, 237, 244, 251, 253, 262, 269, 426, 429, 432
Levin, L., 371, 378
Levine, M. D., 405, 409, 416
Levitt, H., 339, 344
Lewis, M. H., 117, 177, 179, 195, 227, 228, 388, 392, 400, 492
Lichstein, K., 211, 213, 287, 294, 296, 471, 474
Linn, Y., 76, 85, 480, 492
Lindquist, J. C., 367, 375
Linschied, T. R., 26, 27, 182, 188, 195, 196, 251, 253, 435, 438, 448
Lipinski, D., 40, 56, 64, 71, 188, 197
Lipkens, R., 94, 99
Lipner, C., 177, 194, 344
Lipovenko, D., 213
Lippman, L. G., 94, 99
Lipton, M. A., 117
Littman, R. A., 363, 378
Litrownik, A., 331, 345
Livesay, J., 41, 43, 55, 266, 269
Lloyd, J. W., 1
Locke, B. J., 43, 54, 320, 326
Lockshin, S., 480, 481, 492
Long, J. S., 116
Loo, C. M., 370, 378
Lord Acton, 425
Loukas, E., 94, 98
Lovaas, O. I., 18, 29, 37, 44, 55, 56, 57, 64, 65, 70, 72, 111, 116, 117, 119, 126, 137, 141, 142, 175, 177, 179, 182, 195, 197, 226, 228, 237, 251, 253, 254, 267, 268, 269, 271, 278, 285, 287, 288, 289, 291, 292, 293, 294, 296, 297, 308, 311, 312, 314, 416, 326, 327, 331, 345, 363, 376, 378, 385, 387, 388, 400, 401, 403, 413, 414, 416, 424, 447, 448, 455, 462, 473, 480, 481, 491, 492, 496, 500, 501
Love, S. R., 213, 262, 269
Lovett, H., 175, 195
Lowe, C. F., 94, 95, 100
Lubetsky, M. J., 497, 500
Luce, S., 262, 270, 275, 285
Ludewig, D., 336, 344
Luiselli, J. K., 18, 73, 82, 83, 84, 85, 180, 341, 345, 471, 474
Lund, D., 124, 126
Lundervold, D. A., 135, 141, 266, 269, 363, 378, 470, 472, 474, 509, 513, 515
Lutifiyya, Z., 160, 172
Lutzker, J. R., 27, 28, 218, 228, 424, 495, 498, 499, 501
Lyn, Y., 319, 327
Lynch, V., 137, 142

MacDonald, R. F., 18, 24, 29, 43, 57, 77, 85, 137, 142, 177, 197, 263, 270, 275, 286, 307, 329, 364, 369, 379, 388, 401, 405, 417, 484, 493
Mace, F. C., 76, 80, 85, 179, 182, 195, 309, 316, 317, 319, 320, 322, 327, 328, 411, 416, 480, 485, 492
MacKenzie-Keating, S. E., 264, 271
MacLean, W., 117
MacLean, W. E., 337, 342, 364, 370, 375
Madle, R. A., 312, 328
Mailman, R. B., 177, 195, 227, 228, 229, 388, 392, 400
Malott, R. W., 94, 100
Mann, R., 331, 345
Manning, P. J., 124, 222
Marshburn, E., 218, 229
Martens, B., 357, 359, 509, 512, 515, 516
Martin, M., 196, 191
Martin, G., 161, 171, 263, 269
Martin, G. L., 93, 100
Martin, J. A., 496, 497, 501
Martin, P. L., 363, 378
Martin, R., 38, 41, 56
Mason, M., 189, 194, 331, 344
Mason, S. A., 21, 28, 309, 318, 322, 323, 328, 485, 492
Mason, W. A., 314, 315, 322, 325
Masserman, J. H., 64, 71
Massey, P., 161, 171
Masters, L. F., 385, 400
Mastropieri, M. A., 277, 283
Matson, J. L., 19, 27, 61, 62, 71, 74, 85, 93, 100, 116, 175, 180, 195, 211, 214, 237, 253, 261, 262, 265, 267, 269, 270, 287, 289, 297, 303, 416, 457, 462, 465, 468, 470, 471, 473, 474, 480, 492, 505, 513, 515
Matthews, B. A., 94, 98, 100
Matthjis, W., 94, 99
Maus, M., 481, 492
Maxwell, R. R., 445, 449
May, J. G., 481, 492
Mayer, G. R., 93, 100, 119, 124, 127, 263, 270, 305, 329, 379
Mayville, W. J., 410, 417
McAfee, J. K., 339, 345, 364, 370, 378
McCarn, J. E., 219, 229
McClannahan, L. E., 277, 284
McConnachie, G., 371, 378
McCosh, K. C., 81, 85, 409, 416
McCoy, D. E., 364, 378
McCurry, C., 18, 26, 28, 87, 514
McDowell, J. J., 122, 126, 237, 252, 363, 375, 452, 455, 456, 460, 461, 462
McEachin, J. J., 292, 297
McEvoy, M. A., 278, 285
McFalk, J., 6, 7
McGee, J., 22, 28, 67, 71, 171, 175, 195, 199, 201, 202, 204, 209, 210, 211, 214, 215, 216, 217, 219, 221, 226, 227, 228, 229, 237, 238, 244, 245, 250, 254, 261, 262, 266, 270, 273, 285, 323, 328, 472, 474
McGee, G. G., 21, 28, 163, 273, 285, 485, 492
McGimsey, J. F., 34, 55, 181, 194, 267, 269, 276, 283, 322, 326, 363, 376, 415, 466
McGonigle, J. J., 182, 196, 218, 221, 229, 323, 328
McGuigan, C., 137, 142
McGuire, P. S., 480, 493
McKearney, J. W., 445, 462
McMahon, R. J., 113, 116
McMorrow, M. J., 44, 45, 182, 194
McSween, T., 387, 400

Mead, R. N., 36, 56, 455, 463
Measel, C. J., 181, 195
Mees, H., 496, 501
Meinhold, P. M., 26, 27, 435, 449
Melzack, R. A., 453, 462, 463
Menolascino, F. J., 67, 71, 175, 195, 199, 214, 215, 217, 219, 226, 227, 228, 229, 238, 261, 270, 273, 285, 472, 474
Menousek, P. E., 175, 195, 199, 214, 215, 238, 261, 270, 273, 285, 472, 474
Mesaros, R. A., 78, 84, 137, 141, 176, 194, 253, 275, 283, 406, 415
Mesibov, G. B., 54
Meyer, L. H., 43, 44, 53, 133, 137, 138, 139, 141, 166, 171, 194, 237, 262, 268, 273, 282, 283, 285, 332, 340, 343, 345, 371, 376, 408, 410, 411, 415, 416, 437, 445, 449
Meyer, M. M., 94, 99
Meyers, C. E., 53, 331, 342
Meyerson, L., 316, 320, 321, 325
Meyerson, J., 96, 99
Meyher, L. H., 175
Michael, J., 28, 53, 311, 316, 325, 328, 429, 432, 452, 462
Miles, E., 341, 345
Millichamp, C. J., 221, 229
Miltenberger, R. G., 36, 56, 73, 85, 158, 171, 175, 195, 237, 253, 262, 269, 426, 429, 432
Mintz, D. E., 453, 463
Mirenda, P. L., 78, 84, 137, 141, 177, 194, 237, 253, 275, 283, 406, 415
Moffat, S., 410, 417
Moniz, D., 180, 193, 275, 282, 371, 375
Moore, C., 268
Moore, J., 178, 180, 196, 214, 217, 229
Moore, M. K., 492
Morelli, M. A., 280, 283, 491
Morgan, R. L., 112, 116, 188, 196
Morgan, S. B., 73, 85, 510, 512-513, 515
Mori, A. A., 385, 400
Morris, E. K., 497, 501
Morse, W. H., 36, 56, 454, 455, 463
Moseley, A., 315, 321, 328
Mudford, O. C., 67, 68, 71, 262, 270, 510, 512, 515
Muldoon, M., 21, 29, 485, 493
Mulhauser, M. B., 151, 154
Mulhorn, T., 314, 328
Mulick, J. A., 74, 85, 103, 113, 116, 117, 124, 127, 135, 142, 163, 171, 177, 179, 188, 196, 197, 258, 260, 323, 326, 363, 364, 376, 378, 379, 413, 416, 435, 444, 445, 449, 450, 500, 501, 513, 515
Munn, F., 268
Munson, R., 138, 140
Murphy, G. H., 331, 345
Murphy, R. J., 480, 481, 493
Myerson, J., 455, 456, 457, 459, 463

Nass, R., 40, 56, 188, 197
National Institute of Health (NIH), 56, 331, 345
Nau, P. A., 264, 271
Naumann, C. E., 481, 492
Neef, N. A., 80, 85, 178, 196, 411, 416
Neel, R. S., 367, 375
Negri-Shoutlz, N., 36, 39, 41, 42, 52, 54, 138, 141, 288, 290, 296
Neisworth, J. T., 161, 171, 312, 328
Nelson, C. M., 481, 491
Nelson, R. O., 94, 95, 98
Neuman, P., 68, 71
Neuringer, C., 28, 53
Newman, M. R., 499, 501
Newsom, C. D., 61, 71, 76, 84, 111, 116, 177, 178, 180, 193, 194, 195, 196, 211, 214, 226, 228, 237, 252, 253, 266, 270, 275, 276, 283, 287, 290, 297, 309, 314, 326, 327, 340, 341, 342, 343, 363, 375, 376, 388, 400, 409, 415, 455, 460, 461, 462
Newton, J. T., 177, 194, 309, 329, 469, 474
Nielsen, G., 130, 143
Nietzel, M. T., 161, 171
Nihira, K., 468, 474
Nolley, D., 481, 492
Northup, J., 24, 349, 351, 359, 367, 379
Norton, G. R., 135, 142
Notterman, J. M., 453, 463
Novak, C. G., 79, 85

O'Brien, J., 52, 56
O'Brien, S., 17, 24, 26, 28, 309, 328, 332, 345, 458, 463, 485, 492
O'Connor, G., 147, 154, 332, 343
O'Donnell, J. M., 252, 254
O'Kelly, L. E., 449
O'Leary, S. G., 62, 71
O'Neill, R. E., 141, 273, 275, 284, 285, 286, 339, 347, 362, 364, 368, 377, 378, 379
Odom, S. L., 278, 285
Oldenquist, A., 18, 45, 56, 103, 332, 346
Olinger, E., 24, 29,. 180, 196, 226, 229, 332, 338, 346
Oliver, C., 331, 345
Olley, J. G., 277, 285, 292, 297
Olson, D. R., 24, 29, 180, 196, 226, 229, 332, 338, 346
Ong, P., 387, 400
Orloff, E. R., 36, 56
Orv, C. K., 405, 415
Osgood, C. E., 507, 515

Pace, G. M., 21, 29, 81, 85, 178, 195, 309, 327, 358, 409, 416, 485, 492
Pacitti, W. A., 124, 127
Packard, D., 321, 329
Page, T. J., 21, 29, 309, 328, 485, 492
Paisey, T. J., 20, 21, 175, 178, 179, 180, 181, 182, 186, 189, 194, 196, 212, 214, 217, 229, 332, 339, 421, 422, 432, 513
Palumbo, L. W., 24, 361
Pardo, R., 339, 343
Park, H., 390, 400
Park-Lee, S., 166, 171
Park-Yu, N., 68, 71
Parker, L. H., 307, 326

Parrish, J. M., 73, 80, 85, 177, 178, 180, 196, 321, 328, 357, 358, 411, 416, 468, 474, 485, 492
Parrott, L. J., 95, 96, 100
Parson, M. B., 219, 229
Parsons State Hospital and Training Center, 432
Patterson, G. R., 294, 297, 363, 378
Pear J. J., 93, 100, 161, 171, 263, 269, 340, 346
Pearson, J., 307, 326
Pennypacker, H. S., 109, 116
Peoples, A., 321, 329
Peters, W., 52, 53
Petersen, P. B., 161, 171
Peterson, C. R., 62, 71, 115, 123, 127, 181, 197, 303, 329, 460, 462
Peterson, L., 288, 297
Peterson, R. F., 43, 54, 288, 297, 306, 325, 357, 358, 363, 377
Pfifner, L. J., 62, 71
Phillips, J. F., 219, 229
Physicians' Desk Reference, 390
Pickering, D., 73, 85, 510, 512-513, 515
Pierce, W. D., 27, 451, 452, 456, 458, 463
Pinter, E., 80, 85, 320, 327, 411, 416
Plaska, T. G., 431, 480, 481, 491
Plienis, A. J., 277, 280, 283, 285
Pliskoff, S. S., 458, 463
Plotkin, R., 455, 463
Plummer, S., 363, 378
Poling, A., 120, 127, 318, 328
Polman, V. A., 370, 377
Popkewitz, T. S., 46, 48, 49, 56
Popper, K. R., 165, 171, 210, 214
Porterfield, J. K., 317, 328
Premack, D., 258, 260
Prizant, B. M., 277, 285
Pueschel, S. F., 435, 449
Pumpian, I., 219, 228
Pyles, D. A. M., 25, 381, 382, 384, 385, 386, 392, 393, 397, 400, 401

Rachlin, H., 443, 449
Racino, J., 160, 172
Ramirez, B. C., 53
Rasmussen, W. A., 317, 327
Rasnake, L. K., 74, 85, 135, 142, 188, 197, 500, 501, 513, 515
Rast, J., 43, 56, 316, 320, 321, 328
Rauzin, R., 94, 100
Rawls, J., 108, 116
Rawson, R. A., 124, 127
Rea, J. A., 309, 326, 411, 415, 485, 491
Reardon, D. M., 315, 328
Redd, W. H., 497, 501
Redmon, W. K., 437, 449
Reed, G., 289, 295
Reese, E., 305, 328
Reichler, R. J., 291, 297
Reid, J. E., 307, 326
Reid, D. H., 21, 28, 115, 137, 141, 219, 229, 306, 321, 326, 327, 340, 344, 407, 415, 480, 481, 491
Reimers, T., 134, 135, 142, 349, 356, 357, 358, 359, 367, 379, 503, 514
Repp, A. C., 17, 19, 24, 25, 26, 27, 28, 29, 46, 54, 67, 70, 76, 85, 124, 137, 138, 139, 140, 142, 178, 180, 181, 191, 194, 195, 196, 213, 217, 226, 228, 229, 237, 253, 263, 265, 267, 269, 270, 319, 322, 323, 327, 328, 331, 332, 334, 336, 338, 339, 340, 341, 342, 343, 344, 345, 346, 362, 378, 382, 388, 401, 412, 416, 458, 463, 468, 470, 472, 474, 480, 481, 485, 492, 513, 515
Reynolds, G. S., 11, 116, 119, 127, 263
Reynolds, W. B., 6, 7
Rhodes, W. C., 44, 56
Richardson, J. S., 323, 328
Richman, G. S., 24, 28, 75, 84, 138, 141, 177, 195, 263, 269, 309, 327, 344, 363, 377, 382, 388, 400, 445, 448, 469, 474, 485, 492
Richmond, G., 264, 270, 350, 358
Rickert, V., 73, 85
Ricketts, R. W., 182, 189, 194, 195, 438, 448
Rimmer, B., 24, 387, 400
Rincover, A., 55, 61, 62, 71, 123, 127, 141, 178, 181, 196, 197, 210, 214, 237, 253, 254, 263, 266, 268, 270, 287, 290, 296, 297, 303, 316, 321, 328, 329, 363, 377, 378, 444, 448, 449, 455, 460, 463, 473, 491, 492, 496, 500
Risley, T., 116, 485, 492
Risley, T. R., 21, 28, 55, 110, 141, 252, 253, 268, 296, 301, 317, 325, 328, 363, 374, 414, 416, 448, 473, 480, 481, 487, 491, 492, 496, 500, 501, 504, 514
Ritvo, E., 339, 343
Riznek, L. A., 425, 432
Robbins, F. R., 20, 23, 25, 151, 154, 273, 277, 280, 283, 285, 288
Robinson, J., 180, 193, 275, 282, 371, 375
Robinson, S., 24, 36, 53, 274, 283, 332, 361, 365, 376
Rochin, B. R., 292, 297
Rockowitz, R. J., 323, 326
Rodrique, J. R., 73, 85
Rogers, M. C., 307, 326
Rogers-Warren, A., 112, 116, 499, 501
Rojahn, J., 18, 45, 56, 103, 113, 117, 177, 179, 182, 196, 197, 218, 229, 332, 346, 363, 364, 378, 379, 444, 445, 449, 497, 500
Rolider, A., 19, 119, 319, 329
Rollings, J. P., 363, 375
Romanczyk, R. G., 43, 55, 56, 141, 161, 171, 253, 268, 296, 332, 346, 363, 378, 445, 455, 463, 488, 449, 473, 480, 481, 491, 492, 496, 500
Ronker et al. v. Walter et al., 54
Roos, T. L., 92, 100
Rose, T., 3, 7
Rosenfarb, I., 94, 99
Rosenthal, S. L., 277, 285
Rosenthal, T. L., 191, 196, 292, 297
Rowan, V. C., 340, 346
Rubinstein, B. D., 288, 296
Rusch, F. R., 3, 7
Rusch, R. G., 63, 71, 109, 117

Russo, D. C., 55, 79, 80, 85, 141, 253, 296, 411, 416, 448, 473, 491, 496, 500
Rutherford, G., 315, 319, 327, 329, 364, 378
Rutter, M., 27, 285, 287, 297
Ryan, C., 120, 127, 318, 328

Sackett, G. P., 337, 346
Sailor, W., 141,, 273, 284, 319, 329, 364, 377, 378
Sajwaj. T. E., 111, 116, 387, 400
Sallery, R. D., 437, 447
Salmon, D. P., 94, 98
Sameoto, D., 264, 271
Sandman, C. A., 323, 329, 363, 378
Santarcangelo, S., 262, 264, 270, 275, 285
Sarason, S., 160, 171
Saslow, G., 363, 377
Sasso, G., 24, 349, 351, 359, 367, 379
Saxby, H., 191, 194, 336, 343
Schaal, D., 363, 379
Schaeffer, B., 254, 288, 296
Schaffner, P. E., 426, 432
Schell, R. M., 276, 283,322, 326, 363, 376
Schepis, M. M., 219, 229
Schoenfeld, W. N., 429, 432
Schopler, E., 291, 297
Schopler, I. E., 54
Schrader, C., 25, 237, 254, 403, 405, 409, 416
Schreibman, L., 211, 213, 279, 284, 287, 294, 296, 312, 326, 471, 474
Schroeder, C. S., 6, 7, 117, 363, 379
Schroeder, L. S., 496, 497, 498, 501
Schroeder, S. R., 6, 7, 18, 19, 29, 45, 55, 56, 103, 117, 141, 177, 179, 197, 253, 268, 296, 310, 329, 332, 338, 346, 363, 364, 378, 379, 444, 445, 448, 449, 473, 491, 496, 497, 498, 500, 501
Schuler, A. L., 44,, 54, 406, 417
Schussler, N. G., 309, 326, 411, 415, 485, 491
Schwied, E., 363, 377
Scott, T. H., 453, 462, 463
Senatore, V., 468, 474
Setting the Stage, 67
Shapiro, S. T., 122, 126
Shaull, J., 237, 254
Shaver, J., 56
Shelby, J., 96, 99
Shellhaas, N., 468, 474
Sherick, R. B., 135, 142, 507, 515
Shevin, M., 245, 254
Shimmoff, E., 94, 98, 100
Shoemaker, S., 137, 142
Sidman, M., 33, 38, 56, 94, 100, 109, 117, 297, 413,, 417, 437, 449, 480, 492,
Siegel-Causey, E., 368, 377
Sigford, B. B., 342
Simeonnson, R. J., 277, 285, 292, 297
Simmons, J. A., 403, 413, 416
Simmons, J. Q., 43, 56, 116, 177, 195, 254, 288, 308, 311, 316, 327, 363, 377, 378, 387, 400, 455, 462
Singer, G. H. S., 80, 85, 273, 275, 285
Singer, J., 80, 85, 273, 285
Singh, N. N., 21, 24, 29, 43, 56, 67, 70, 83, 85, 113, 117, 124, 135, 142, 180, 181, 196, 197, 211, 212, 213, 214, 215, 217, 218, 219, 220, 221 , 222, 224, 226, 228, 229, 267, 269, 288, 297, 323, 327, 332, 338, 340, 346, 357, 359, 468, 472, 473, 474, 504, 510, 512, 515
Sitkei, G. F., 147, 154
Sizemore, O. J., 445, 449
Skinner, B. F., 25, 66, 71, 93, 95, 100, 112, 117, 123, 126, 158, 171, 202, 214, 251, 254, 303, 318, 329, 346, 362, 379, 382, 401, 421, 422, 425, 428, 432, 445, 448, 451, 453, 454, 462, 463, 495, 501
Skrtic, T., 164, 165, 168, 171, 172
Slifer, K. J., 24, 28, 75, 84, 138, 141, 177, 195, 196, 263, 269, 309, 321, 327, 328, 344, 350, 358, 363, 377, 382, 388, 400, 445, 448, 469, 471, 473, 474, 485, 492
Slocumb, P. R., 471, 474
Sluzki, C. E., 238, 254
Smith, D. W., 262, 264, 271
Smith, M. D., 180, 197
Smith, N. F., 124, 127
Smith, R. M., 161, 171
Smith, T., 23, 287, 289, 293, 295, 297
Smoley, S. R., 302, 329
Snell, M. E., 133, 142
Sobsey, D., 25, 26, 87, 100, 421, 424, 432
Solnick, J. V., 55, 62, 71, 115, 123, 127, 141, 181, 197, 253, 268, 296, 303, 329, 363, 377, 448, 460, 463, 473, 496, 500
Sorrell, S., 387, 400
Sovner, R., 422, 432
Sparrow, S. S., 468, 474
Spengler, P., 36, 56, 158, 171, 175, 195, 237, 253, 262, 269, 426, 429, 432
Spradlin, J. E., 94, 98
Sprague, J. R., 275, 285, 362, 378
Sprague, R. L., 332, 343
Spranger, J., 51, 55
Spreat, S., 6, 7, 40, 41, 56, 64, 65, 71, 188, 189, 197, 498, 501
Sroufe, L. A., 238
St. Maurice, H., 46, 48, 49, 56
Staddon, J. E. R., 55, 443, 449, 445, 463
Stainton, T., 422, 433
Stanley, J. C., 426, 431
Starin, S. P., 181, 197, 471, 474
Stark, J., 226, 228
Stark, M. T., 189, 194, 331, 344, 421, 422, 432
Steckle, L. C., 449
Steege, M., 24, 78, 85, 263, 270, 309, 313, 315, 318, 319, 320, 322, 329, 341, 346, 349, 350, 351, 359, 367, 379
Stephens, M., 117
Stevens, M., 444, 449
Stewart, J., 339, 342
Stewart, A. W., 468, 473
Stokes, T. F., 61, 71, 111, 117, 124, 127, 245, 254, 262, 270, 356, 359
Stone, J., 212, 213

Storey, K., 275, 285, 362, 378
Strain, P. S., 278, 286
Stretch, R., 36, 56
Strisik, P, 337, 341
Strupp, H. H., 505, 515
Sturmey, P., 177, 181, 197, 309, 329, 469, 474
Sugai, G. M., 3, 7, 133, 143
Sulkes, S., 323, 329
Sulzer-Azaroff, B., 61, 71, 93, 100, 119, 124, 127, 263, 270, 305, 329, 363, 379
Summers, J. A., 117, 175, 197, 270
Sunahara, D. F., 458, 463
Suskin, L., 471, 474
Succi, G. J., 507, 515
Swanson, J. M., 329, 363, 378
Szabadi, E., 452, 456, 458, 459, 461
Szymanski, L., 323, 329

Tailby, W., 94, 100
Takahashi, M., 456, 463
Tannenbaum, P. H., 507, 515
Taplac, N., 392, 400
Taras, M. E., 61, 62, 71, 75, 85, 175, 195, 211, 214, 262, 267, 270, 287, 289, 296, 465, 471, 474
Tarjan, G., 332, 343
Tarnowski, K. J., 73, 85, 135, 142, 188, 197, 500, 501, 510, 513, 515
Tarpley, H. D., 310, 329
Tate, B. G., 318, 329
Taubman, M. T., 363, 376
Taylor, J. C., 36, 53, 274, 283, 332, 342, 365, 376
Taylor, S., 153, 155, 160, 172
Teodoro, G. M., 20, 21, 22, 25, 199, 209, 211, 213, 214
Thelen, M. A., 237, 253
The Association for Retarded Citizens, 53
Thevedt, J., 424, 426, 431, 445, 448
Thvedt, J., 44, 54
Thios, S. J., 117, 444, 449
Thomas, D. R., 252, 480, 481, 492, 493
Thomas, E. J., 217, 230
Thomas, M., 336, 343
Thompson, T., 87, 93, 100, 363, 379, 480, 493
Thompson, W. R., 453, 463
Thyer, B. A., 423, 433
Tilley, K. L., 94, 99
Timberlake, W., 444, 449
Tinbergen, E. A., 291, 297
Tinbergen, N., 291, 297
Tomie, A., 94, 98
Touchette, P. E., 18, 24, 29, 37, 43, 46, 57, 77, 82, 85, 137, 142, 177, 179, 197, 263, 270, 275, 286, 307, 329, 364, 369, 379, 388, 401, 405, 408, 409, 413, 417, 483, 493, 499, 501
Troutman, A. C., 3, 7
Turnbull, H. R., 40, 55, 75, 84, 103, 117, 137, 141, 150, 155, 157, 164, 170, 175, 194, 197, 237, 253, 258, 260, 261, 266, 269, 270, 365, 377, 425, 432, 435, 448, 479, 493
Tversky, A., 426, 432
Twardosz, S., 116, 492

Uhl, C. N., 120, 127
Ullmann, L. P., 363, 379
Ulman, J. D., 61, 71
Ulrich, R. E., 43, 57, 439, 449
Underwood, B., 191, 196
Unger, R. M., 252, 254
U.S. Department of Education, 331, 346
U.S. Department of Health and Human Services, 301, 330

Van Acker, R., 25, 29, 178, 196, 336, 345, 346
Van Houten, R., 18, 19, 29, 33, 35, 52, 57, 62, 64, 71, 72, 117, 119, 122, 123, 124, 127, 137, 142, 175, 197, 261, 264, 265, 270, 271, 288, 297, 317, 329, 385, 401, 498, 499, 501
Varnhagen, C., 424, 432
Voeltz, L. M., 409, 415
Vollmer, T. R., 24, 301
Vukelich, R., 180, 197, 313, 330
Vyse, S. A., 441, 450

Wacker, D., 21, 24, 29, 79, 85, 134, 135, 142, 263, 270, 309, 329, 341, 346, 349, 350, 351, 356, 357, 359, 367, 379, 485, 493, 503, 515
Wahler, R. G., 79, 85, 237, 254, 334, 346, 363, 371, 379
Wainczak, S., 179, 186, 196
Walker, G., 161, 171
Wallace, R. E., 479, 489, 491
Warren, S., 112, 116, 499, 501
Waters, E., 238
Watkins, K. M., 332, 346
Watson, J. E., 288, 297, 512, 515
Watzlawick, P., 238, 254
Way, P. J., 340, 344
Weeks, M., 177, 180, 194, 197, 314, 315, 319, 330, 339, 340, 344, 346, 364, 368, 379, 409, 417
Weiner, H., 94, 100, 101
Weisler, N., 52, 53
Weiss, B., 94, 99
Weiss, R., 6, 7
Welch, M. G., 291, 297
Wells, M. E., 262, 264, 271
Wenzel, A. M., 363, 378
Wesolowski, M. D., 65, 70
West, B. J., 80, 85, 320, 327, 411, 416
Wetherby, A. M., 277, 285, 286
Wexler, O., 492
White, D. M., 109, 117
White, G., 130, 143
White, L. K., 21, 28, 306, 327, 491
White, M. J., 276, 283, 341, 343
White, O. R., 120, 127, 138, 140
Whitman, T. L., 444, 448
Whitney, R. B., 20, 175, 178, 179, 180, 181, 182, 186, 196, 214, 217, 229, 333, 513
Wieseler, N. A., 480, 493
Wiggins, B., 21, 29, 485, 493
Willems, E. P., 334, 346
Williams, C., 329, 363
Williams, D. E., 182, 189, 194, 195, 331, 344, 438, 448

Williams, M. L., 444, 447
Williams, T., 363, 378, 379
Willis, K. D., 178, 195
Willis, T. J., 33, 37, 39, 52, 55, 57
Wilson, G. T., 267, 269
Wilson-Morris, M., 94, 100
Wincze, J. P., 199, 127
Windmiller, M., 468, 474
Winterling, V., 273, 275, 283, 286, 339, 340, 347, 364, 368, 376, 379, 481, 492
Winton, A. S. W., 181, 197, 218, 226, 229, 288, 297, 512, 515
Wisotzek, I. E., 471, 473
Witt, J. C., 43, 54, 57, 356, 357, 358, 359, 503, 511, 512, 515, 516
Wolchik, S., 321, 327
Wolery, M., 3, 7, 19, 129, 133, 137, 138, 143, 480, 481, 491
Wolf, M. M., 43, 54, 110, 117, 133, 134, 135, 143, 252, 301, 320, 325, 326, 341, 363, 374, 379, 496, 500, 501, 504, 514, 516
Wolfensberger, W., 103, 118
Wood, F. H., 137, 139, 143
Woodward, P., 44, 54
Wulfert, E., 94, 101
Wyatt v. Stickney, 413, 417
Wylie, A. M., 312, 330

Yanson, M. S., 370, 377
Young, J. A., 119, 127
Youngberg v. Romeo, 97, 101

Zabel, R. H., 93, 101
Zalenski, S., 277, 284
Zaleski, W. A., 323, 328
Zambito, J., 44, 54, 424, 426, 431, 445, 448
Zarcone, J. R., 24, 301
Zeglob, L. E., 62, 72
Zeiler, M. D., 120, 127, 454, 463
Zeph, L., 166, 172
Zettle, R. D., 94, 99
Zilboorg, G., 6, 7
Zimmerman, E. M., 124, 127
Zimmerman, J., 94, 101, 124, 127
Zlutnick, S., 410, 417
Zukotynski, G., 189, 194

Subject Index

Abuse, 424, 498
Academic community, 164
Acceptability, 135, 503
Acceptability ratings, 503, 508, 512, 514
Acceptability research, 507, 512, 513
Acceptability of treatment procedures, 507
Accountability, 483
Active and passive behavior management, 384
Adhominem rhetoric, 103
Advocates, 466
Agencies, 151
Aggression, 177-178, 190, 184-187, 189, 237, 349, 437
Alternatives, 148
Alternative and collateral behaviors, 482
ALT-R, 36, 39
American Association on Mental Retardation, 6, 9, 39, 261
American Psychological Association, 6, 11, 465, 483
Amnesty International, 159
An alternative to the least restrictive model, 386
Analogue Assessments, 18, 24, 184, 350, 353, 355
Antecedents, 2, 404
Arousal reduction, 78
Arousal theory, 338
Assessment, 138
Assessment-derived intervention, 83
Association for the Advancement of Behavior Therapy (AABT), 27, 483, 496
Association for Behavior Analysis (ABA) 6, 8, 27, 66, 51, 465, 496
Association for Persons with Severe Handicaps, 6, 10, 33, 66, 137, 151, 160, 167, 261, 465
Association for Retarded Citizens, 465
Attachment, 211
Attention, 177-178, 180, 184-187, 189-190
Attention-motivated, 192
Attention seeking/communication attempt, 390
Autism, 274-275, 279
Autistic children, 287-288, 291-292
Automatic reinforcement, 303, 309, 311, 312, 314, 316
Avoidance, 455

B3, 202
Banshee, 1
Behavioral definitions, 486
Behavioral modification, 443
Behavioral paradigm, 165
Behavioral problem severity, 512
Behavioral psychology, 252
Behavioral treatment, 287, 291
Best-practice, 399
Biological and other etiological factors, 495
Bonded relationships, 245
Bonding, 201, 210, 211, 216, 217, 215, 220, 222, 224, 226, 227
Brown vs. Board of Education, 151

Caregiver Interactional Observation System (CIOS), 240
Certification procedure, 414
Challenging behavior, 145
Change agent competencies, 480
Checklists, 392
Choice, 455, 458, 461
Chronic behavior problems, 395
Civil rights, 495
Client Protection Procedure, 399
Clinical and research ethics, 258
Clinical significance, 112, 468
Clinically ethical, 256
Code of ethics, 498
Cold Fusion, 212
Collateral, 217
Communication, 179, 186
Communication hypothesis, 338, 445
Communication theory, 26
Communication training, 372, 410
Communicative, 176, 178, 183, 187
Communicative function, 137
Community acceptance, 112
Companionship, 250
Compliance training, 79
Computer-based data collection system (PCS), 336
Concurrent schedule, 124, 452, 455, 458
Conditional probabilities, 307, 308, 337
Conditioning theory, 338
Consequences, 2, 334
Consumer evaluations, 505
Consumer satisfaction, 112
Consumer understanding, 504
Consumer variables, 514
Consumers, 503
Contingencies of reinforcement, 231-232
Contingency, 3
Contingency management strategies, 411
Contingent electric shock, 251, 422
Contingent reduction in reinforcement density (CRRD), 122
Contingent reinforcement postponement(CRP), 122, 125
Continuum, 41
Continuum of effectiveness, 42
Council for Children with Behavioral Disorders, 6, 13

Counter control, 425
Covariation, 110, 111
Crisis intervention, 264
Crisis management, 361, 366, 369, 374
Critieria for success, 110
Cultural acts, 88
Cultural behaviors, 88, 89
Curricular interventions, 410
Cycles, 392

Data-based approach for determining causes, 392
Decision making, 435
Decision model, 137
Degree and rapidity of suppression, 110
Demand, 177-178, 180-181, 183-184, 186, 190
Deprivation, 312
Descriptive analysis, 305, 307
Deterrence, 91
Developmentally handicapped individuals, 123
Dietary changes, 391
Differential reinforcement of alternative behaviors (DRA), 26, 186, 288, 289, 294, 295, 301, 303, 312, 315, 317, 318, 320, 353
Differential reinforcement for compliance (DRC), 393, 412
Different communication of communication, 355
Differential reinforcement of incompatible behavior (DRI), 19, 26, 36, 37, 39, 112, 113, 119, 121, 124, 125, 186, 303, 312, 315, 318, 332, 341, 367, 374, 412, 428, 456, 457, 458, 470, 471
Differential reinforcement of low rate of responding (DRL), 39, 119, 123, 124, 186, 412, 454
Differential reinforcement of other behavior (DRO), 19, 36, 39, 42, 52, 80, 112, 119, 120, 121, 122, 123, 125, 163, 183, 184, 185, 186, 301, 303, 314, 315, 318, 320, 321, 332, 341, 363, 365, 367, 370, 372, 373, 374, 388, 412, 428, 470, 471, 472
Dignity, 105, 106
Discriminative stimulus, 311
Domination, 251
DRH, 454
DRI + I, 218
Durability of effect, 468
Durability of suppression, 110

Early intervention, 273-274, 276-277, 279, 281-282
Early interventionists, 278
Ecobehavioral, 22, 499
Ecobehavioral approach, 495
Effective, 35, 37-39, 43, 51-53
Effectiveness, 41, 43, 44, 51, 135
Effective treatment, 51, 106
Effects, 133-134, 137, 140
Efficiency, 132
Electric shock, 35-36, 42, 52, 438
Element treatment, 43
Emotional distress, 437
Environmental enrichment, 408
Environmentally dependent behaviors, 24, 333-334
Environmentally independent behaviors, 24, 333-334
Epson HX-20, 336
Escape, 2, 177, 180-181, 183-184, 189-190, 291, 318, 319, 320, 352, 354, 355, 389, 439, 440, 441, 442, 455
Escape DRA, 320
Escape DRO, 320
Escape extinction, 76
Establishing operation, 311-312, 314-315, 452 453, 461
Ethical behavior, 257
Evaluation, 487
Evaluative responses, 90
Event-based lag analyses, 337
Event-lag analysis, 178
Evidence supporting the effectiveness of aversive procedures with developmentally disabled persons, 495
Explosive outbursts, 2
Extinction, 3, 65, 78, 311, 313, 315, 317, 319, 321, 322, 324, 390, 428, 442

Facial screening, 3
Food deprivation, 423
Form and frequency of responding, 451
Freedom from harm position, 262
Function of behavior, 383, 386, 404, 444
Function versus topography of behavior, 381
Functional analysis, 3, 21, 24, 25, 41, 76, 138, 176, 178, 180, 181, 182, 183, 184, 186, 187, 188, 189, 190, 191, 192, 193, 200, 263, 267, 2735, 277, 288, 301, 303, 304, 305, 308, 309, 310, 315, 316, 322, 324, 333, 340, 350, 355, 358, 363, 367, 369, 371, 372, 383, 404-484, 485
Functional assessment, 75
Functional behaviors, 123-124
Functional categories of behavior, 388
Functional communication, 275
Functional communication training, 78
Functional equivalence, 18, 23, 24, 77, 78, 79, 178, 182, 237, 339, 446
Functional treatment, 372, 373, 374
Functionally equivalent behaviors, 407
Functionally equivalent response, 367

Generalization, 61, 97, 110, 111, 138, 139, 167, 175, 182, 184, 187-188, 192, 226, 262, 267, 468, 472, 488
Gentle Teaching, 4, 21, 22, 199, 201, 202, 203, 204, 205, 209, 210, 211, 212, 215, 216, 217, 219, 220, 221, 222, 224, 226, 227, 238, 239, 244, 246, 250, 251, 252, 472
Goals, 133-134, 137, 140

Habilitation, 2
Head banging, 1, 220
Hidden punishment, 264
Hierarchies, 65
Homeostasis, 338

Human experimentation committees, 255-258
Human rights and human subjects, 497
Human Rights Committee (HRC), 8, 63, 64, 481, 482, 489
Human valuing, 211
Hypothesis-driven treatment, 333, 338, 339, 362, 363

Ideology, 435-436
Ignore, 216
Ignore-redirect-reward, 215
Ignore-redirect-reward paradigm, 202
Illness/pain/discomfort/deprivation, 391
Immediate treatment versus understanding behavior, 382
Indirect assessments, 24
Indirect methods of assessment, 305
Individual differences, 388
Indoctrination, 165
Informed consent, 139, 255, 258, 259, 260, 293, 489
Institutional and other segregated settings, 159
Instructional control, 411
Integration, 150
Interactions, 238
Interdependence, 245
Interrupt, 216
Intervention complexity, 512
Intervention plan, 485
Intervention Rating Profile (IRP), 512, 513

Journal of Applied Behavior Analysis, 57
Judges, 135

Least Restrictive Alternative, 17, 479
Least restrictive/intrusive intervention, 265
Least Restrictive Model, 385
Limiting conditions of the research, 385
Local Human Rights Committees, 5
Long-term behavior change, 497

Magnitude of Effect, 467
Maintain, 191, 193, 235
Maintaining conditions, 349
Maintenance, 61, 110, 111, 138, 139, 167, 175, 183, 184, 185, 187-188, 190, 232, 233, 371, 488
Maladaptive behavior, 2
Matching law, 27, 122, 452, 455, 456, 457, 458, 459, 461
Masking, 424
Measurement and data collection, 486
Measuring the reliability with which treatment are implemented, 138
Medication side effects, 390
Minimize damage to client or others, 398
Minimizes physical damage, 256
Minimizes the effects of the behavior, 397
Misapplication, 423
Moral, 87, 106, 107
Motivation Assessment Scale, 76, 305, 306, 407
Motivational factors, 137
Mouthing, 220
MS-DOS portable computers, 336
Multi-element, 42
Multi-element treatment, 39, 44

National Institutes of Health Consensus Conference, 6, 37, 45, 48, 131, 132, 137, 139, 237, 287, 288, 293, 362
National Institute of Mental Health, 256
Natural contingencies, 234
Naturalistic assessments, 24
Naturalistic observation, 306
Needed research, 267
Negative reinforcement, 11, 60, 78, 120, 130, 177, 179, 181, 186, 190, 192, 302, 303, 308, 309, 310, 311, 312, 313, 314, 316, 320, 324, 335, 338, 339, 341, 353, 466
Neo-Kantian and Utilitarian Arguments, 108
Non-exclusionary time-out, 122
Nonfunctional treatment, 372, 373, 374
Nonparticipation, 251
Nonprogrammatic and unrecognized use of intrusive procedures, 263
Normalized, 60

Objectives, 488
One-on-one teaching, 125
On task, 220
Operant analysis, 177, 186, 188, 191-192
Operant assessment, 184
Outclinic assessment, 349
Outcome requirements, 43
Outcomes, 43
Overcorrection, 3, 65, 75, 112, 113, 135, 161, 181, 216, 224, 239, 244, 245, 251, 288, 290, 395, 470, 488

Paradigm, 164
Parents, 147
Peer review, 139
Peer Review Committee (PRC), 8, 63
Person rewards, 201
Personnel trainers, 168
Person's Interactional Observation System (PIOS), 241
Physiological causes, 392
Placements, 148
Positive reinforcement, 302, 309, 311, 312, 315, 316, 324, 335, 338, 339, 341, 442
Positive reinforcement hypothesis, 340
Positive side effects, 437, 471
Posttreatment acceptability, 505
Predictor variables, 266
Preference, 455
Preschool Training Project (PTP), 279
Pretreatment acceptability, 504, 505
Prevent 281
Preventing, 274, 273, 276
Prevention, 273-274, 281
Preventive, 274
Procedural decay, 160, 161

Procedures, 133-134, 137, 140, 487
Project Ecosystems, 499
Protecting, 240
Psychotropic medication, 2, 391
Punishment, 2, 3, 5, 125, 216, 240, 455, 458-460
Punishment-induced aggression, 423
Pyramid model, 162

Quantitative law of effect, 460

Reciprocation, 241
Reciprocity approach, 105
Reciprocity eliciting, 240
Redirect, 216
Reinforcement, 3, 190-191
Reinforcement-based treatments, 367
Reinforcement density, 120, 125
Reinforcement history, 390
Reinforcer density, 121
Reinforcer-reinforcer interval, 125
Research ethics, 256
Response alternatives, 440
Response allocation, 443, 444, 446, 456, 457, 458, 459, 460
Response bias, 458-459
Response class, 445
Response cost, 3, 390, 393
Response deprivation, 444
Response efficiency, 368
Response-reinforcer interval, 125
Responsibility, 233
Responsive behaviors, 201
Restraint, 3, 24, 264, 274, 466, 470
Retribution, 91
Review, 489
Reward-to-demand ratio, 208
Right to efffective treatment, 106, 261, 265, 266, 267, 499
Risk, 182, 184, 188-190, 192-193
Risk factors, 497
Risk profile, 405
Rule governed behavior, 123

Scatter plot, 18, 307, 405
Schedule and rule following, 411
Schedules of reinforcement, 311, 407, 442, 452, 453, 455, 459
Science, 59
Screaming, 220
Scrutiny over the mediators of aversive procedures, 495
Self-injurious behavior (SIB), 109, 169, 176, 177, 178, 179, 180-192, 199, 200, 201, 202, 204, 205, 208, 211, 218, 219, 221, 224, 227, 237, 246, 250, 255, 257, 258, 259, 261, 264, 266, 280, 292, 301, 302, 305, 307, 308, 309, 311, 313, 315, 316, 317, 319, 322, 323, 324, 333, 349, 350, 351, 352, 353, 355, 357, 362, 363, 365, 367, 369, 370, 373, 390, 403, 411, 412, 413, 422, 429, 438, 451, 453, 457, 466, 468, 469, 470, 480, 496, 499
Self-Injurious Behavior Inhibiting System (SIBIS), 438
Self-stimulation, 111, 177
Self-stimulatory, 124, 177-178, 180, 184-185, 189-192, 237, 388
Sensory extinction, 321
Sensory stimulation, 76, 78
Setting events, 334, 369
Semantic Differential, 507, 512
Seven functional categories of behavior, 388
Severe punishment, 145
Shock, 35, 38, 41, 48, 51, 63, 65, 108, 161, 239, 244, 255, 256, 288, 363, 365, 372, 374, 381, 386, 403, 422, 430, 438, 439, 440, 441, 444, 446, 455, 471
SIBIS, 68, 186
SIB trauma unit, 200
Side effect, 61, 75, 93, 111, 138, 139, 163, 168, 181, 262, 265, 289, 293, 442, 446, 469, 472, 497
Sidman's avoidance, 120-121
Skill development, 273-276, 281-282
Skills acquisition, 332
Skills acquisition training, 341, 395
Social, 183
Social comparisons, 505
Social importance, 505
Social reinforcement, 177, 184
Social validity, 19, 20, 50, 77, 110, 112, 130, 133, 134, 135, 136, 137, 139-140, 505
Social validity judges, 140
Social values, 436
Specious learning, 427
Speed of effect, 467
Spread effect, 160, 161, 167
Spontaneous recovery, 428
Statistical regression, 426
Stereotypic, 177-179, 181, 187
Stereotypies, 180, 470
Stereotypy, 76, 217, 218, 303, 315, 321, 384, 444, 453, 466, 469, 498
Stimulation, 338, 339, 341
Stimulus-based interventions, 332
Stimulus based treatment, 370, 371, 373
Stimulus-based treatments, 368
Stimulus control, 81, 83, 187, 192, 261, 410
Stimulus equivalence, 94, 96
Stimulus feeding, 409
Structural analysis, 178, 186
Subjective evaluations, 507

Tantrum, 177-178, 180, 184, 186, 187
Target behavior(s), 482
Task demands, 2
Task rewards, 201
Task training, 217, 220-221
Taxonomy, 333, 337-338, 341
The Association for Persons with Severe Handicaps (TASH), 166
Time-based lag analyses, 337
Time-out, 3, 64, 65, 112, 113, 123, 130, 146, 180, 181, 216, 234, 239, 244, 245, 251, 266, 288, 290, 303, 317, 318, 352, 355, 386, 426, 428, 480, 488

Treatment acceptability, 356, 503
Treatment compliance, 504, 514
Treatment effectiveness, 503, 504, 514
Treatment Evaluation Inventory (TEI), 507
Treatment selection, 505, 514
Treatment understanding, 504
Treatment use, 503
Triadic Treatment Model, 404
Two-phase treatment model, 403

Undermatching, 458
Utilitarian ethics, 259
Utilitarian view of ethics, 259
Utilitarianism, 105, 258

Value, 38, 46, 47, 49, 50, 51, 52, 53, 145, 150, 251, 413
Value giving, 240
Verbal behavior, 94
Verbal mediator, 123
Violent, 2
Visual screening, 3, 217, 219, 220, 221, 222, 224, 226, 227, 244

Walden Two, 495
Workability, 92